100 Fastest-Growing CAREERS

Your Complete Guidebook to Major Jobs with the Most Growth and Openings

ELEVENTH EDITION

Michael Farr

JIST Works
America's Career Publisher®

100 Fastest-Growing Careers, Eleventh Edition
Your Complete Guidebook to Major Jobs with the Most Growth and Openings

© 2010 by JIST Publishing

Published by JIST Works, an imprint of JIST Publishing
7321 Shadeland Station, Suite 200
Indianapolis, IN 46256
Phone: 1-800-648-JIST   Fax: 1-800-JIST-FAX
E-mail: info@jist.com   Web site: www.jist.com

Some books by Michael Farr:
Best Jobs for the 21st Century
Overnight Career Choice
Next-Day Job Interview
Same-Day Resume
The Quick Resume & Cover Letter Book
The Very Quick Job Search

JIST's Top Careers™ Series:
Top 300 Careers
Top 100 Health-Care Careers
Top 100 Careers Without a Four-Year Degree
Top 100 Careers for College Graduates

Visit www.jist.com for information on JIST, tables of contents, sample pages, and ordering information on our many products.
Quantity discounts are available for JIST products. Please call 800-648-JIST or visit www.jist.com for a free catalog and more information.

Acquisitions Editor: Susan Pines
Development Editor: Stephanie Koutek
Database Work: Laurence Shatkin
Cover Illustration: Alex Nikada, iStockphoto
Cover Layout: Alan Evans
Interior Design: Marie Kristine Parial-Leonardo
Interior Layout: Toi Davis
Proofreaders: Paula Lowell, Jeanne Clark

Printed in the United States of America

12 11 10   9 8 7 6 5 4 3 2 1

ISBN 978-1-59357-783-4

Relax. You Don't Have to Read This Whole Book!

You don't need to read this entire book. I've organized it into easy-to-use sections so you can get just the information you want. You will find everything you need to

★ Learn about the 100 fastest-growing jobs, including their daily tasks, pay, outlook, and required education and skills.

★ Match your personal skills to the jobs.

★ Take seven steps to land a good job in less time.

To get started, simply scan the table of contents to learn more about these sections and to see a list of the jobs described in this book. Really, this book is easy to use, and I hope it helps you.

Who Should Use This Book?

This is more than a book of job descriptions. I've spent quite a bit of time thinking about how to make its contents useful for a variety of situations, including

★ **Exploring career options.** The job descriptions in Part II give a wealth of information on many of the most desirable jobs in the labor market. The assessment in Part I can help you focus your career options.

★ **Considering more education or training.** The information helps you avoid costly mistakes in choosing a career or deciding on additional training or education—and it increases your chances of planning a bright future.

★ **Job seeking.** This book helps you identify new job targets, prepare for interviews, and write targeted resumes. The advice in Part III has been proven to cut job search time in half.

★ **Career planning.** The job descriptions help you explore your options, and Parts III and IV provide career planning advice and other useful information.

Source of Information

The job descriptions come from the good people at the U.S. Department of Labor, as published in the most recent edition of the *Occupational Outlook Handbook*. The *OOH* is the best source of career information available, and the descriptions include the most current, accurate data on jobs. Thank you to all the people at the Department of Labor who gather, compile, analyze, and make sense of this information. It's good stuff, and I hope you can make good use of it.

Mike Farr

Mike Farr

Contents

Summary of Major Sections

Introduction. Provides an explanation of the job descriptions, how best to use the book, and other details. *Begins on page 1.*

Part I: Using the Job-Match Grid to Choose a Career. Match your skills and preferences to the jobs in this book. *Begins on page 15.*

Part II: Descriptions of the 100 Fastest-Growing Careers. Presents thorough descriptions of the 100 fastest-growing jobs. Education and training requirements for these jobs vary from on-the-job training to a four-year college degree or more. Each description gives information on the nature of the work, work environment, employment, training, other qualifications, advancement, job outlook, earnings, related occupations, and sources of additional information. The jobs are presented in alphabetical order. The page numbers where specific descriptions begin are listed in the detailed contents. *Begins on page 31.*

Part III: Quick Job Search—Seven Steps to Getting a Good Job in Less Time. This relatively brief but important section offers results-oriented career planning and job search techniques. It includes tips on identifying your key skills, defining your ideal job, using effective job search methods, writing resumes, organizing your time, improving your interviewing skills, and following up on leads. The last part of this section features professionally written and designed resumes for some of the fastest-growing jobs. *Begins on page 301.*

Part IV: Important Trends in Jobs and Industries. This section includes information on labor market trends. The material is worth your time. *Begins on page 382.*

Detailed Contents

Introduction

This book is about improving your life, not just about selecting and getting a fast-growing job. The career you choose will have an enormous impact on how you live.

A huge amount of information is available on occupations, but most people don't know where to find accurate, reliable facts to help them make good career decisions—or they don't take the time to look. Important choices such as what to do with your career or whether to get additional training or education deserve your time.

If you are considering more training or education, this book will help with solid information. The education and training needed for the jobs described in this book vary enormously. You will notice that many of the better-paying jobs may require more training or education than you now have. Some require brief training or on-the-job experience. Many better-paying jobs, however, call for technical training lasting from a few months to a few years. Others require a four-year college degree or more. But some jobs, such as certain sales and management occupations, have high pay but do not always involve advanced education. This book is designed to give you facts to help you explore your options.

A certain type of work or workplace may interest you as much as a certain type of job. If your interests and values lead you to work in health care, for example, you can choose from a variety of work environments and a variety of industries. This book includes details to help you weigh your options.

The time you spend in career planning can pay off in higher earnings, but being satisfied with your work—and your life—is often more important than the amount you earn. For this reason, I suggest that you begin to explore alternatives by following your interests and finding a career path that allows you to use your skills and talents. This book can help you find the work that suits you best and that offers a promising future.

The 100 Fastest-Growing Careers List

I think it's important for you to understand how I developed the list of the fastest-growing careers for this book. I used the most recent data from the U.S. Department of Labor, which provides growth projections through 2018 for 288 major jobs that encompass 90 percent of the workforce. I started by sorting all of those jobs based on their percent of projected growth through 2018, from highest to lowest. I then sorted the jobs based on the projected number of annual new job openings, also from highest to lowest. For these 288 jobs, the average (mean) growth rate is 10.6 percent, and the average number of openings annually is 15,692.

From these two lists I created a third list based on the relative position of each job on the first two lists. I did this by adding the score for each job's position on the lists. For example, a job with a high percentage of growth and a high number of new job openings appears toward the top.

Perhaps you're wondering why I use figures for both job growth and number of openings. Aren't these two ways of saying the same thing? Actually, both are important. A job may have a fast growth rate overall, but it may be a relatively small occupation with not many people employed in it. So jobs with both a high rate of growth *and* many openings offer the best opportunity.

The 100 jobs with the most favorable combined scores for projected percent increase and annual number of job openings through 2018 appear in the following table. As you can see, the list includes a variety of jobs at all levels of education, training, and interest.

Notice that four of the top 10 fastest-growing jobs are in the health-care area, the most rapidly growing field of all. Another point to notice is that most of the fastest-growing jobs require training or education beyond high school. While job opportunities at all levels of education and training are listed in the table, many better-paying jobs require postsecondary education or training. If you want more information on important labor market trends, consider reading the excellent and brief review of labor market trends in Part IV.

Note that you can find a complete description for each job listed below in Part II. You will also find these jobs listed in the table of contents along with the page number where each job description begins.

The 100 Fastest-Growing Careers

		Percent Growth Through 2018	Annual Job Openings
1.	Home Health Aides and Personal and Home Care Aides	48	103,050
2.	Computer Network, Systems, and Database Administrators	30	46,080
3.	Registered Nurses	22	103,900
4.	Medical Assistants	34	21,780
5.	Accountants and Auditors	22	49,750
6.	Dental Assistants	36	16,100
7.	Human Resources, Training, and Labor Relations Managers and Specialists	22	42,730
8.	Management Analysts	24	30,650
9.	Computer Software Engineers and Computer Programmers	21	45,210
10.	Pharmacy Technicians and Aides	25	18,810
11.	Customer Service Representatives	18	110,840
12.	Licensed Practical and Licensed Vocational Nurses	21	39,130
13.	Physicians and Surgeons	22	26,050
14.	Market and Survey Researchers	28	15,070
15.	Construction Laborers	20	33,940
16.	Heating, Air-Conditioning, and Refrigeration Mechanics and Installers	28	13,620
17.	Barbers, Cosmetologists, and Other Personal Appearance Workers	20	28,580
18.	Teachers—Self-Enrichment Education	32	12,030
19.	Fitness Workers	29	12,380
20.	Nursing and Psychiatric Aides	18	43,210
21.	Dental Hygienists	36	9,840
22.	Computer Systems Analysts	20	22,280
23.	Social and Human Service Assistants	23	15,390
24.	Grounds Maintenance Workers	18	44,950
25.	Public Relations Specialists	24	13,130
26.	Paralegals and Legal Assistants	28	10,400
27.	Cost Estimators	25	10,360
28.	Personal Financial Advisors	30	8,530
29.	Athletes, Coaches, Umpires, and Related Workers	23	10,900

	Percent Growth Through 2018	Annual Job Openings
30. Counselors	18	25,130
31. Physical Therapists	30	7,860
32. Teachers—Postsecondary	15	55,290
33. Teachers—Preschool, Except Special Education	19	17,830
34. Teachers—Kindergarten, Elementary, Middle, and Secondary	13	132,300
35. Receptionists and Information Clerks	15	48,020
36. Medical Scientists	40	6,620
37. Bill and Account Collectors	19	15,690
38. Social Workers	16	26,460
39. Teachers—Special Education	17	20,450
40. Fire Fighters	17	18,530
41. Physical Therapist Assistants and Aides	35	5,390
42. Security Guards and Gaming Surveillance Officers	14	37,690
43. Animal Care and Service Workers	21	9,260
44. Office Clerks, General	12	77,090
45. Plumbers, Pipelayers, Pipefitters, and Steamfitters	16	19,830
46. Veterinary Technologists and Technicians	36	4,850
47. Construction Managers	17	13,770
48. Financial Analysts	20	9,520
49. Secretaries and Administrative Assistants	11	105,750
50. Food and Beverage Serving and Related Workers	10	391,590
51. Billing and Posting Clerks and Machine Operators	15	16,760
52. Desktop Publishers	15	16,760
53. Computer Support Specialists	14	23,460
54. Carpenters	13	32,540
55. Physician Assistants	39	4,280
56. Engineers	11	53,170
57. Instructional Coordinators	23	6,060
58. Environmental Scientists and Specialists	28	4,840
59. Child Care Workers	11	52,310
60. Lawyers	13	24,040
61. Office and Administrative Support Worker Supervisors and Managers	11	48,900
62. Medical Records and Health Information Technicians	20	7,030
63. Advertising, Marketing, Promotions, Public Relations, and Sales Managers	13	21,740
64. Pharmacists	17	10,580
65. Real Estate Brokers and Sales Agents	14	15,910
66. Truck Drivers and Driver/Sales Workers	9	86,250
67. Electricians	12	25,090
68. Occupational Therapists	26	4,580
69. Retail Salespersons	8	162,690
70. Surgical Technologists	25	4,630
71. Bookkeeping, Accounting, and Auditing Clerks	10	46,040
72. Computer and Information Systems Managers	17	9,710
73. Maintenance and Repair Workers, General	11	35,750
74. Medical and Health Services Managers	16	9,940
75. Teacher Assistants	10	41,270

(continued)

(continued)

The 100 Fastest-Growing Careers

	Percent Growth Through 2018	Annual Job Openings
76. Biological Scientists	21	4,860
77. Veterinarians	33	3,020
78. Cargo and Freight Agents	24	4,030
79. Interviewers, Except Eligibility and Loan	16	9,210
80. Police and Detectives	10	32,390
81. Recreation Workers	15	10,720
82. Surveyors, Cartographers, Photogrammetrists, and Surveying and Mapping Technicians	19	5,910
83. Clinical Laboratory Technologists and Technicians	14	10,790
84. Sales Representatives, Wholesale and Manufacturing	7	60,020
85. Hotel, Motel, and Resort Desk Clerks	14	10,950
86. Radiologic Technologists and Technicians	17	6,800
87. Insurance Sales Agents	12	15,260
88. Graphic Designers	13	12,480
89. Stock Clerks and Order Fillers	7	56,260
90. Construction Equipment Operators	12	13,640
91. Water and Liquid Waste Treatment Plant and System Operators	20	4,690
92. Taxi Drivers and Chauffeurs	16	7,730
93. Respiratory Therapists	21	4,140
94. Cooks and Food Preparation Workers	6	73,520
95. Correctional Officers	9	16,920
96. Operations Research Analysts	22	3,220
97. Medical Equipment Repairers	27	2,320
98. Science Technicians	12	12,380
99. Dentists	16	6,150
100. Probation Officers and Correctional Treatment Specialists	19	4,180

Some Advice for Reviewing the Fastest-Growing Careers

Major changes are occurring in our labor market, and Part IV describes these changes. Rapidly growing jobs will often be more attractive career options than jobs that are not growing quickly. Rapidly growing jobs often offer better-than-average opportunities for employment and job security. For this reason, you should pay attention to jobs that are projected to grow rapidly.

But there most likely will be openings for new people in slower-growing or declining jobs. Some slower-growing jobs employ large numbers of people and will create many openings due to retirement, people leaving the field, and other reasons. Considering jobs that are generating large numbers of openings but that may not have high percentage growth rates will give you more options to consider. Information on all major occupational and industry groups is provided in Part IV, including those that are growing more slowly than average or even declining.

Keep in Mind That Your Situation Is Probably Not "Average"

Although the employment growth and earnings trends for many occupations and industries are quite positive, the averages in this book will not be true for many individuals. Earnings and job opportunities vary enormously in different parts of the country, in different occupations, and in different industries. My point is that your situation is probably not average. But this book's solid information is a great place to start. Good information will give you a strong foundation for good decisions.

Four Important Labor Market Trends That Will Affect Your Career

Our economy has changed over the past years, with profound effects on how we work and live. Here are four trends that you must consider in making your career plans.

1. Education Pays

I'm sure you won't be surprised to learn that people with higher levels of education and training have higher average earnings. The data that follows comes from the U.S. Department of Labor. I've selected data to show you the median earnings for people with various levels of education. (The median is the point where half earn more and half earn less.) Based on this information, I computed the earnings advantage of people at various education levels over those who did not graduate from high school. I've also included information showing the average percentage of people at that educational level who are unemployed.

Earnings for Year-Round, Full-Time Workers Age 25 and Over, by Educational Attainment

Level of Education	Median Annual Earnings	Premium Over High School Dropouts	Unemployment Rate
Professional degree	$79,600	$56,000	1.7
Doctoral degree	$81,200	$57,600	2.0
Master's degree	$64,100	$40,500	2.4
Bachelor's degree	$52,600	$29,000	2.8
Associate degree	$39,400	$15,800	3.7
Some college, no degree	$36,300	$12,700	5.1
High school diploma/GED	$32,100	$8,500	5.7
High school dropout	$23,600		9.0

Source: Bureau of Labor Statistics

As you can see in the table, the earnings difference between a college graduate and someone with a high school education is $20,500 a year—enough to buy a nice car, make a down payment on a house, or even take a few months' vacation for two to Europe. As you see, over a lifetime, this earnings difference will make an enormous difference in lifestyle.

The table makes it very clear that those with more training and education earn more than those with less and experience lower levels of unemployment. Jobs that require education and training beyond high school are projected to grow significantly faster than jobs that do not. People with higher levels of education and training are less likely to be unemployed and, when they are, they tend to remain unemployed for shorter periods of time. There are always exceptions, but it is quite clear that a college education results in higher earnings and lower rates of unemployment.

2. Knowledge of Computer and Other Technologies Is Increasingly Important

As you look over the jobs in this book, you may notice that many require computer or technical skills. Even jobs that do not appear to be technical often call for computer literacy. Managers, for example, are often expected to understand and use spreadsheet, word-processing, and database software.

In most fields, people without job-related technical and computer skills will have a more difficult time finding good opportunities because they are often competing with those who have these skills. Employers tend to hire people with the skills they need, and people without these abilities won't get the best jobs. So, no matter what your age, consider upgrading your job-related computer and technology skills if you need to—and plan to stay up to date.

3. Ongoing Education and Training Are Essential

School and work once were separate activities, and most people did not go back to school after they began working. But with rapid changes in technology, most people are now required to learn throughout their work lives. Jobs are constantly upgraded, and today's jobs often cannot be handled by people who have only the knowledge and skills that were adequate for workers a few years ago.

To remain competitive, you will need to constantly upgrade your technology and other job-related skills. This may include taking formal courses, reading work-related materials and Web sites, signing up for on-the-job training, or participating in other forms of education. Upgrading your work skills on an ongoing basis is no longer optional for most jobs.

4. Good Career Planning Is More Important Than Ever

Most people spend more time watching TV in a week than they spend on career planning during an entire year. Yet most people will change their jobs many times and make major career changes five to seven times. For this reason, it is important to spend time considering your career options and preparing to advance.

While you probably picked up this book for its information on jobs, it also provides a great deal of information on career planning. For example, Part I offers an assessment to match your skills to the fastest-growing jobs. Part III gives good career and job search advice. Part IV has useful information on labor market trends. I urge you to read these and related materials because career-planning and job-seeking skills are the keys to surviving in this economy.

Tips on Using This Book

This book is based on information from a variety of government sources and includes the most up-to-date and accurate data available. The job descriptions are well written and pack a lot of information into a brief format. *100 Fastest-Growing Careers* can be used in many ways, and this discussion provides tips for the following individuals:

* ★ Students and others exploring career, education, or training alternatives

* ★ Job seekers

* ★ Employers and business people

* ★ Counselors, instructors, career specialists, librarians, and other professionals

Tips for People Exploring Career, Education, or Training Alternatives

100 Fastest-Growing Careers is an excellent resource for anyone exploring career, education, or training alternatives. Many people do not have a good idea of what they want to do in their careers. Others may be considering additional training or education but may not know what sort of training they should get. If you are one of these people, this book can help in several ways.

Review the list of jobs. Trust yourself. Research studies indicate that most people have a good sense of their interests. Your interests can be used to guide you to career options you should consider in more detail.

Begin by looking over the occupations listed in the table of contents. Look at all the jobs, because you may identify previously overlooked possibilities. If other people will be using this book, please don't mark in it. Instead, on a separate sheet of paper, list the jobs that interest you. Or make a photocopy of the table of contents and use it to mark the jobs that interest you.

Next, look up and carefully read the descriptions of the jobs that most interest you in Part II. A quick review will often eliminate one or more of these jobs based on pay, working conditions, education required, or other considerations. After you have identified the three or four jobs that seem most interesting, research each one more thoroughly before making any important decisions.

Match your skills to the jobs in this book using the Job-Match Grid. Another way to identify possible job options is to answer questions about your skills and job preferences in Part I, "Using the Job-Match Grid to Choose a Career." This section will help you focus your job options and concentrate your research on a handful of job descriptions.

Study the jobs and their training and education requirements. Too many people decide to obtain additional training or education without knowing much about the jobs the training will lead to. Reviewing the descriptions in this book is one way to learn more about an occupation before you enroll in an education or training program. If you are currently a student, the job descriptions in this book can help you decide on a major course of study or learn more about the jobs for which your studies are preparing you.

Do not be too quick to eliminate a job that interests you. If a job requires more education or training than you currently have, you can obtain this training in many ways.

Don't abandon your past experience and education too quickly. If you have significant work experience, training, or education, do not abandon it too quickly. Many people have changed careers after carefully considering what they wanted to do and found that the skills they already had could still be used.

100 Fastest-Growing Careers can help you explore career options in several ways. First, on a separate sheet of paper, list the skills needed in the jobs you have held in the past. Then, using the descriptions in this book as a reference, do the same for jobs that interest you now. By comparing the lists, you will be able to identify skills you used in previous jobs that you could also use in jobs that interest you for the future. These "transferable" skills form the basis for moving to a new career.

You can also identify skills you have developed or used in nonwork activities, such as hobbies, family responsibilities, volunteer work, school, the military, and extracurricular involvements.

If you want to stay with your current employer, the job descriptions can also help. For example, you may identify jobs within your organization that offer more rewarding work, higher pay, or other advantages over your present job. Read the descriptions related to these jobs, because you may be able to transfer into another job rather than leave the organization.

Tips for Job Seekers

You can use the job descriptions in this book to give you an edge in finding job openings and in getting job offers— even when you are competing with people who have better credentials. Here are some ways *100 Fastest-Growing Careers* can help you in the job search.

Identify related job targets. You may be limiting your job search to a small number of jobs for which you feel qualified, but by doing so you eliminate many jobs you could do and enjoy. Your search for a new job should be broadened to include more possibilities.

Go through the entire list of jobs in the table of contents and check any that require skills similar to those you have. Look at all the jobs, since doing so sometimes helps you identify targets you would otherwise overlook.

You may wish to answer questions about your skills and job preferences in Part I, "Using the Job-Match Grid to Choose a Career." Your results can help you identify career options that may suit you.

Many people are not aware of the many specialized jobs related to their training or experience. The descriptions in *100 Fastest-Growing Careers* are for major job titles, but a variety of more-specialized jobs may require similar skills. Reference books that list more-specialized job titles include the *Enhanced Occupational Outlook Handbook* and the *O*NET Dictionary of Occupational Titles*. Both are published by JIST.

The descriptions can also point out jobs that interest you but that have higher responsibility or compensation levels. While you may not consider yourself qualified for such jobs now, you should think about seeking jobs that are above your previous levels but within your ability to handle.

Prepare for interviews. This book's job descriptions are an essential source of information to help you prepare for interviews. If you carefully review the description of a job before an interview, you will be much better prepared to emphasize your key skills.

Negotiate pay. The job descriptions in this book will help you know what pay range to expect. Note that local pay and other details can differ substantially from the national averages in the descriptions.

Tips for Employers and Business People

Employers, human resource professionals, and other business users can use this book's information to write job descriptions, study pay ranges, and set criteria for new employees. The information can also help you conduct more-effective interviews by providing a list of key skills needed by new hires. You and your employees can consult the job descriptions when planning lateral moves and promotions.

Tips for Counselors, Instructors, Career Specialists, Librarians, and Other Professionals

Counselors, instructors, librarians, and other professionals will find this book helpful to clients and students who are exploring career options or job targets. You can help clients and job seekers by encouraging them to review the table of contents to find jobs of interest. You may wish to familiarize them with the structure of the job descriptions so that they can find the information they need easily.

My best suggestion to professionals is to get this book off the shelf and into the hands of the people who need it. Leave it on a table or desk and show people how the information can help them. Wear this book out. Its real value is as a tool used often and well.

Information on the Major Parts of This Book

This book is designed for easy use. The table of contents provides brief comments on each part, and that may be all you need to understand its contents. Here are some additional details for getting the most out of *100 Fastest-Growing Careers*.

Part I: Using the Job-Match Grid to Choose a Career

Part I features an assessment with checklists and questions to match your skills and preferences to the jobs in this book. The seven skills covered in the assessment include artistic, communication, interpersonal, managerial, mathematics, mechanical, and science. The five job characteristics covered in the assessment are economically sensitive, geographically concentrated, hazardous conditions, outdoor work, and physically demanding.

Part II: Descriptions of the 100 Fastest-Growing Careers

Part II is the main section of the book and probably the reason you picked it up. It contains well-written descriptions for the 100 fastest-growing jobs in alphabetical order. The content for these job descriptions comes from the U.S. Department of Labor and is considered by many to be the most accurate and up-to-date available. The jobs provide an enormous variety at many levels of earnings and interest.

To explore career options, do the assessment in Part I or go to the table of contents and identify those jobs that seem interesting. If you are interested in medical jobs, for example, you can quickly spot those that you want to learn more about. You may also see other jobs that look interesting, and you should consider these as well. Your next step would be to read the descriptions for the jobs that interest you and, based on what you learn, identify those that *most* interest you.

Each occupational description follows a standard format, making it easy for you to compare jobs. The following overview describes the information found in each description and offers tips on how to interpret it.

Job Title

This is the title used for the job in the *Occupational Outlook Handbook,* published by the U.S. Department of Labor.

O*NET Codes

The numbers in parentheses that appear just below the title of every job description are from the Occupational Information Network (O*NET)—a system used by state employment service offices to classify applicants and job openings, and by some career information centers and libraries to file occupational information.

O*NET codes are based on the Standard Occupational Classification (SOC) system. You can access O*NET on the Internet at http://www.online.onetcenter.org. The *O*NET Dictionary of Occupational Titles* offers the information in a reader-friendly book and is published by JIST.

Significant Points

This section highlights key occupational characteristics discussed in the job description.

Nature of the Work

This section discusses what workers do on the job, what tools and equipment they use, and how closely they are supervised. Individual job duties may vary by industry or employer. For instance, workers in larger firms tend to be more specialized, whereas those in smaller firms often have a wider variety of duties. Most occupations have

several levels of skills and responsibilities through which workers may progress. Beginners may start as trainees, performing routine tasks under close supervision. Experienced workers usually undertake more difficult tasks and are expected to perform with less supervision.

Some job descriptions mention common alternative job titles or occupational specialties. For example, the job description on accountants and auditors discusses a few specialties, such as public accountants, management accountants, and internal auditors.

Information in this section may be updated from earlier editions for several reasons. One is the emergence of occupational specialties. Information also may be updated due to changing technology that affects the way in which a job is performed. Or job duties may be affected by modifications to business practices, such as restructuring or changes in response to government regulations. An example is paralegals and legal assistants, who are increasingly being utilized by law firms in order to lower costs and increase the efficiency and quality of legal services.

Many sources are consulted in researching the nature of the work section or any other section of a job description. Usual sources include articles in newspapers, magazines, and professional journals. Useful information also appears on the Web sites of professional associations, unions, and trade groups. Information found on the Internet or in periodicals is verified through interviews with individuals employed in the occupation; professional associations; unions; and others with occupational knowledge, such as university professors and counselors in career centers.

The Work Environment subsection identifies the typical hours worked, the workplace environment, physical activities, susceptibility to injury, special equipment, and the extent of travel required. In many occupations, people work regular business hours—40 hours a week, Monday through Friday—but many do not. The work setting can range from a hospital to a mall to an outdoor site. Truck drivers might be susceptible to injury, while paramedics have high job-related stress. Some workers may wear protective clothing or equipment, do physically demanding work, or travel frequently.

Information on various worker characteristics, such as the average number of hours worked per week, is obtained from the Current Population Survey (CPS)—a survey of households conducted by the U.S. Census Bureau for the Bureau of Labor Statistics.

Training, Other Qualifications, and Advancement

After knowing what a job is all about, it is important to understand how to prepare for it. This section describes the most significant sources of education and training, including the education or training preferred by employers, the typical length of training, and the possibilities for advancement. Job skills sometimes are acquired through high school, informal on-the-job training, formal training (including apprenticeships), the U.S. Armed Forces, home study, hobbies, or previous work experience. For example, sales experience is particularly important for many sales jobs. Many professional jobs, on the other hand, require formal postsecondary education—postsecondary vocational or technical training, or college, postgraduate, or professional education.

In addition to training requirements, this book mentions desirable skills, aptitudes, and personal characteristics. For some entry-level jobs, personal characteristics are more important than formal training. Employers generally seek people who read, write, and speak well; compute accurately; think logically; learn quickly; get along with others; and demonstrate dependability.

Some occupations require certification or licensing for entry, advancement, or independent practice. Certification or licensing usually requires completing courses and passing examinations. Some occupations have numerous professional credentials granted by different organizations. In this case, the most widely recognized organizations are listed in this book.

Many occupations increasingly are requiring workers to participate in continuing education or training in relevant skills, either to keep up with the changes in their occupation or to improve their advancement opportunities.

Some job descriptions list the number of training programs. For example, the job description on pharmacists indicates the number of colleges of pharmacy accredited by the American Council on Pharmaceutical Education. The minimum requirements for federal government employment cited in some job descriptions are based on standards set by the U.S. Office of Personnel Management.

The training section may focus on changes in educational, certification, or licensing requirements, such as an increase in the number of hours of required training or in the number of states requiring a license.

Employment

This section reports the number of jobs that the occupation provides, the key industries in which those jobs were found, and the number or proportion of self-employed workers in the occupation, if significant. When significant, the geographic distribution of jobs and the proportion of part-time workers (those working less than 35 hours a week) are mentioned.

Job Outlook

In planning for the future, you need to consider potential job opportunities. This section describes the factors that will result in employment growth or decline.

Employment change. This subsection reflects the occupational projections in the National Employment Matrix. Each occupation is assigned a descriptive phrase based on its projected percent change in employment over the 2008–2018 period. This phrase describes the occupation's projected employment change relative to the projected average employment change for all occupations combined.

Many factors are examined in projecting the employment change for each occupation. One such factor is changes in technology. New technology can either create new job opportunities or eliminate jobs by making workers obsolete. Another factor that influences employment trends is demographic change. By affecting the services demanded, demographic change can influence occupational growth or decline.

Another factor affecting job growth or decline is changes in business practices, such as restructuring businesses or outsourcing (contracting out) work. Corporate restructuring has made many organizations "flatter," resulting in fewer middle management positions. Also, in the past few years, jobs in some occupations have been "off-shored"—moved to low-wage foreign countries. The substitution of one product or service for another can also affect employment projections. Competition from foreign trade usually has a negative effect on employment. Often, foreign manufacturers can produce goods more cheaply than they can be produced in the United States, and the cost savings can be passed on in the form of lower prices with which U.S. manufacturers cannot compete. Another factor is job growth or decline in key industries. If an occupation is concentrated in an industry that is growing rapidly, it is likely that that occupation will grow rapidly as well.

Job prospects. In some cases, this book mentions that an occupation is likely to provide numerous or relatively few job openings. This information reflects the projected change in employment, as well as replacement needs. Large occupations in which workers frequently enter and leave generally provide the most job openings—reflecting the need to replace workers who transfer to other occupations or who stop working.

Key Phrases Used in the Job Descriptions

The following tables explain how to interpret the key phrases used to describe projected changes in employment. They also explain the terms used to describe the relationship between the number of job openings and the number of job seekers. The description of this relationship in a particular occupation reflects the knowledge and judgment of economists in the BLS Office of Occupational Statistics and Employment Projections.

Changing Employment Between 2008 and 2018

If the statement reads	Employment is projected to
Grow much faster than average	Increase 20 percent or more
Grow faster than average	Increase 14 to 19 percent
Grow about as fast as average	Increase 7 to 13 percent
Grow more slowly than average	Increase 3 to 6 percent
Little or no change	Decrease 2 percent to increase 2 percent
Decline slowly or moderately	Decrease 3 to 9 percent
Decline rapidly	Decrease 10 percent or more

Opportunities and Competition for Jobs

If the statement reads	Job openings compared to job seekers may be
Very good to excellent opportunities	More numerous
Good or favorable opportunities	In rough balance
May face, or can expect, keen competition	Fewer

Projections Data

The employment projections table lists employment statistics from the National Employment Matrix. It includes 2008 employment, projected 2018 employment, and the 2008–2018 change in employment in both numerical and percentage terms. Numbers below 10,000 are rounded to the nearest hundred, numbers above 10,000 are rounded to the nearest thousand, and percentages are rounded to the nearest whole number. Numerical and percentage changes are calculated using non-rounded 2008 and 2018 employment figures and then are rounded for presentation in the employment projections table.

Earnings

This section discusses typical earnings and how workers are compensated—by annual salaries, hourly wages, commissions, piece rates, tips, or bonuses. Within every occupation, earnings vary by experience, responsibility, performance, tenure, and geographic area. Almost every job description contains earnings data for wage and salary workers. Information on earnings in the major industries in which the occupation is employed may be given as well.

In addition to presenting earnings data from Bureau of Labor Statistics sources, some job descriptions contain additional earnings data from non-BLS sources. Starting and average salaries of federal workers are based on 2009 data from the U.S. Office of Personnel Management. The National Association of Colleges and Employers supplies information on average salary offers in 2009 for students graduating with a bachelor's, master's, or Ph.D. degree in certain fields. A few job descriptions contain additional earnings information from other sources, such as unions, professional associations, and private companies.

Benefits account for a significant portion of total compensation costs to employers. Benefits such as paid vacation, health insurance, and sick leave may not be mentioned, because they are so widespread. In some job descriptions, the absence of these traditional benefits is pointed out. Although not as common as traditional benefits, flexible hours and profit-sharing plans may be offered to attract and retain highly qualified workers. Less common benefits also include childcare, tuition for dependents, housing assistance, summers off, and free or discounted merchandise or services. For certain occupations, the percentage of workers affiliated with a union is listed.

Related Occupations

Occupations involving similar duties, skills, interests, education, and training are listed.

Sources of Additional Information

No single publication can describe all aspects of an occupation. Thus, this book lists the mailing addresses of associations, government agencies, unions, and other organizations that can provide occupational information. In some cases, toll-free telephone numbers and Internet addresses also are listed. Free or relatively inexpensive publications offering more information may be mentioned; some of these publications also may be available in libraries, in school career centers, in guidance offices, or on the Internet.

Part III: Quick Job Search—Seven Steps to Getting a Good Job in Less Time

For more than 25 years, I've been helping people find better jobs in less time. If you have ever experienced unemployment, you know that it is not pleasant. Unemployment is something most people want to get over quickly—in fact, the quicker the better. Part III will give you some techniques to help.

I know that most of you who read this book want to improve yourselves. You want to consider career and training options that lead to a better job and life in whatever way you define this—better pay, more flexibility, more-enjoyable or more-meaningful work, proving to your mom that you really can do anything you set your mind to, and other reasons. That is why I include advice on career planning and job search in Part III. It includes the basics that are most important in planning your career and in reducing the time it takes to get a job. I hope it will make you think about what is important to you in the long run.

Part III showcases professionally written resumes for some of America's fastest-growing jobs. Use these as examples when creating your own resume. I know you will resist completing the activities in Part III, but consider this: It is often not the best person who gets the job, but the best job seeker. People who do their career planning and job search homework often get jobs over those with better credentials because they have these distinct advantages:

1. **They get more interviews,** including many for jobs that will never be advertised.

2. **They do better in interviews.**

People who understand what they want and what they have to offer employers present their skills more convincingly and are much better at answering problem questions. And, because they have learned more about job search techniques, they are likely to get more interviews with employers who need the skills they have.

Doing better in interviews often makes the difference between getting a job offer and sitting at home. And spending time planning your career can make an enormous difference to your happiness and lifestyle over time. So please consider reading Part III and completing its activities. I suggest you schedule a time right now to at least read it. An hour or so spent there can help you do just enough better in your career planning, job seeking, and interviewing to make the difference.

Part IV: Important Trends in Jobs and Industries

This part is made up of a very good article and charts on labor market trends. This article comes directly from U.S. Department of Labor sources and is interesting, well written, and short. The article and charts will give you a good idea of factors that will impact your career in the years to come.

Other Major Career Information Sources

The information in this book will be very useful, but you may want or need additional facts and guidance. Keep in mind that the job descriptions here cover major jobs and not the many more-specialized jobs that are often related to them. Each job description in this book provides some sources of information related to that job, but here are additional resources to consider. All are available through JIST Publishing.

Occupational Outlook Handbook (or the *OOH*): Updated every two years by the U.S. Department of Labor, this book provides descriptions of more than 300 major jobs covering about 90 percent of the workforce. The *OOH* is the source of the job descriptions used in this book.

Enhanced Occupational Outlook Handbook: This resource includes all descriptions in the *OOH* plus descriptions of more than 5,800 more-specialized jobs that are related to them.

O*NET Dictionary of Occupational Titles: This book is the only printed source of the jobs described in the U.S. Department of Labor's Occupational Information Network (O*NET) database.

New Guide for Occupational Exploration: This important reference features an intuitive system based on extensive research to organize more than 900 jobs into 16 major interest areas and 117 more-specific work groups. The interest areas are based on U.S. Department of Education career clusters to closely link interests, learning, and occupations.

Best Jobs for the 21st Century: This best-selling book includes descriptions for the 500 jobs with the best combination of earnings, growth, and number of openings. Useful lists make jobs easy to explore (examples: highest-paying jobs by level of education or training; best jobs overall; and best jobs for different ages, personality types, interests, and more). Other books in the series include *200 Best Jobs for College Graduates, 300 Best Jobs Without a Four-Year Degree, 50 Best Jobs for Your Personality, 200 Best Jobs Through Apprenticeships, 40 Best Fields for Your Career, 225 Best Jobs for Baby Boomers, 250 Best-Paying Jobs, 10 Best College Majors for Your Personality, 150 Best Jobs for a Better World, 150 Best Jobs for Your Skills, 150 Best Jobs Through Military Training, 150 Best Low-Stress Jobs, 200 Best Jobs for Introverts, 200 Best Jobs for Renewing America,* and *150 Best Recession-Proof Jobs.*

Exploring Careers—A Young Person's Guide to 1,000 Jobs: For youth in grades 7–12 exploring career and education opportunities, this book covers 1,000 job options in an interesting and useful format. Featured are profiles of real people at work, "skill samplers" that help youths better understand whether they have the skills required for certain jobs, and brief descriptions of jobs in logical groups.

Young Person's Occupational Outlook Handbook: This popular resource offers age-appropriate descriptions for each job in the *Occupational Outlook Handbook.* Very easy to use and understand, for grades 4 on.

Using the Job-Match Grid to Choose a Career

By the Editors at JIST

This book describes so many occupations—how can you choose the best job for you? This section is your answer! It can help you to identify the jobs where your abilities will be valued, and you can rule out jobs that have certain characteristics you would rather avoid. You will respond to a series of statements and use the Job-Match Grid to match your skills and preferences to the most appropriate jobs in this book.

So grab a pencil and get ready to mark up the following sections. Or, if someone else will be using this book, find a sheet of paper and get ready to take notes.

Thinking About Your Skills

Everybody knows that skills are important for getting and keeping a job. Employers expect you to list relevant skills on your resume. They ask about your skills in interviews. And they expect you to develop skills on the job so that you will remain productive as new technologies and new work situations emerge.

But maybe you haven't thought about how closely skills are related to job satisfaction. For example, let's say you have enough communication skills to hold a certain job where these skills are used heavily, but you wouldn't really *enjoy* using them. In that case, this job probably would be a bad choice for you. You need to identify a job that will use the skills that you *do* enjoy using.

That's why you need to take a few minutes to think about your skills: the ones you're good at and the ones you like using. The checklists that follow can help you do this. On each of the seven skills checklists that follow, use numbers to indicate how much you agree with each statement:

3 = I strongly agree

2 = I agree

1 = There's some truth to this

0 = This doesn't apply to me

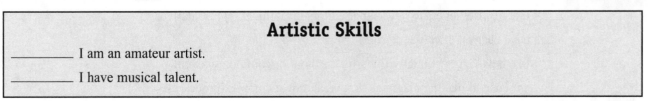

Artistic Skills

_____ I am an amateur artist.

_____ I have musical talent.

(continued)

(continued)

_____ I enjoy planning home makeovers.

_____ I am good at performing onstage.

_____ I enjoy taking photos or shooting videos.

_____ I am good at writing stories, poems, articles, or essays.

_____ I have enjoyed taking ballet or other dance lessons.

_____ I like to cook and plan meals.

_____ I can sketch a good likeness of something or somebody.

_____ Playing music or singing is a hobby of mine.

_____ I have a good sense of visual style.

_____ I have participated in amateur theater.

_____ I like to express myself through writing.

_____ I can prepare tasty meals better than most people.

_____ I have a flair for creating attractive designs.

_____ I learn new dance steps or routines easily.

_____ **Total for Artistic Skills**

A note for those determined to work in the arts: Before you move on to the next skill, take a moment to decide whether working in some form of art is essential to you. Some people have exceptional talent and interest in a certain art form and are unhappy unless they are working in that art form—or until they have given their best shot at trying to break into it. If you are that kind of person, the total score shown above doesn't really matter. In fact, you may have given a 3 to just *one* of the statements in this section, but if you care passionately about your art form, you should toss out ordinary arithmetic and change the total to 100.

Communication Skills

_____ I am good at explaining complicated things to people.

_____ I like to take notes and write up minutes for meetings.

_____ I have a flair for public speaking.

_____ I am good at writing directions for using a computer or machine.

_____ I enjoy investigating facts and showing other people what they indicate.

_____ People consider me a good listener.

_____ I like to write letters to newspaper editors or political representatives.

_____ I have been an effective debater.

_____ I like developing publicity fliers for a school or community event.

_____ I am good at making diagrams that break down complex processes.

_____ I like teaching people how to drive a car or play a sport.

_____ I have been successful as the secretary of a club.

_____ I enjoy speaking at group meetings or worship services.

_____ I have a knack for choosing the most effective word.

_____ I enjoy tutoring young people.

_____ Technical manuals are not hard for me to understand.

_____ **Total for Communication Skills**

Interpersonal Skills

_____ I am able to make people feel that I understand their point of view.

_____ I enjoy working collaboratively.

_____ I often can make suggestions to people without sounding critical of them.

_____ I enjoy soliciting clothes, food, and other supplies for needy people.

_____ I am good at "reading" people to tell what's on their minds.

_____ I have a lot of patience with people who are doing something for the first time.

_____ People consider me outgoing.

_____ I enjoy taking care of sick relatives, friends, or neighbors.

_____ I am good at working out conflicts between friends or family members.

_____ I enjoy serving as a host or hostess for houseguests.

_____ People consider me a team player.

_____ I enjoy meeting new people and finding common interests.

_____ I am good at fundraising for school groups, teams, or community organizations.

_____ I like to train or care for animals.

_____ I often know what to say to defuse a tense situation.

_____ I have enjoyed being an officer or advisor for a youth group.

_____ **Total for Interpersonal Skills**

Managerial Skills

_____ I am good at inspiring people to work together toward a goal.

_____ I tend to use time wisely and not procrastinate.

_____ I usually know when I have enough information to make a decision.

_____ I enjoy planning and arranging programs for school or a community organization.

_____ I am not reluctant to take responsibility when things turn out wrong.

_____ I have enjoyed being a leader of a scout troop or other such group.

_____ I often can figure out what motivates somebody.

_____ People trust me to speak on their behalf and represent them fairly.

_____ I like to help organize things at home, such as shopping lists and budgets.

(continued)

(continued)

_____ I have been successful at recruiting members for a club or other organization.

_____ I have enjoyed helping run a school or community fair or carnival.

_____ People find me persuasive.

_____ I enjoy buying large quantities of food or other products for an organization.

_____ I have a knack for identifying abilities in other people.

_____ I am able to get past details and look at the big picture.

_____ I am good at delegating authority rather than trying to do everything myself.

_____ **Total for Managerial Skills**

Mathematics Skills

_____ I have always done well in math classes.

_____ I enjoy balancing checkbooks for family members.

_____ I can make mental calculations quickly.

_____ I enjoy calculating sports statistics or keeping score.

_____ Preparing family income tax returns is not hard for me.

_____ I like to tutor young people in math.

_____ I have taken or plan to take courses in statistics or calculus.

_____ I enjoy budgeting the family expenditures.

_____ **Subtotal for Mathematics Skills**

x 2   **Multiply by 2**

_____ **Total for Mathematics Skills**

Mechanical Skills

_____ I have a good sense of how mechanical devices work.

_____ I like to tinker with my car or motorcycle.

_____ I can understand diagrams of machinery or electrical wiring.

_____ I enjoy installing and repairing home stereo or computer equipment.

_____ I like looking at the merchandise in a building-supply warehouse store.

_____ I can sometimes fix household appliances when they break down.

_____ I have enjoyed building model airplanes, automobiles, or boats.

_____ I can do minor plumbing and electrical installations in the home.

_____ **Subtotal for Mechanical Skills**

x 2   **Multiply by 2**

_____ **Total for Mechanical Skills**

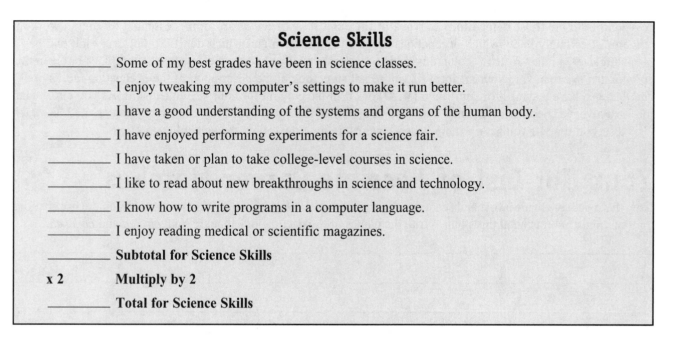

Science Skills

_____ Some of my best grades have been in science classes.

_____ I enjoy tweaking my computer's settings to make it run better.

_____ I have a good understanding of the systems and organs of the human body.

_____ I have enjoyed performing experiments for a science fair.

_____ I have taken or plan to take college-level courses in science.

_____ I like to read about new breakthroughs in science and technology.

_____ I know how to write programs in a computer language.

_____ I enjoy reading medical or scientific magazines.

_____ **Subtotal for Science Skills**

x 2 **Multiply by 2**

_____ **Total for Science Skills**

Finding Your Skills on the Job-Match Grid

Okay, you've made a lot of progress so far. Now it's time to review what you've said about skills so you can use these insights to sort through the jobs listed on the Job-Match Grid.

Look at your totals for the seven skills listed previously. Enter your totals in the left column on this scorecard:

Total	Skill	Rank
_____	Artistic	_____
_____	Communication	_____
_____	Interpersonal	_____
_____	Managerial	_____
_____	Mathematics	_____
_____	Mechanical	_____
_____	Science	_____

Next, enter the rank of each skill in the right column—that is, the highest-scored skill gets ranked 1, the next-highest 2, and so forth. **Important:** Keep in mind that *the numbers in the Total column are only a rough guideline.* If you feel that a skill should be ranked higher or lower than its numerical total would suggest, *go by your impressions rather than just by the numbers.*

Now turn to the Job-Match Grid and find the columns for your #1-ranked and #2-ranked skills. Move down through the grid, going from page to page, and notice what symbols appear in those columns. If a row of the grid has a black circle (●) in *both* columns, circle the occupation name—or, if someone else will be using this book, jot down the name on a piece of paper. These occupations use a high level of both skills, or the skills are essential to these jobs.

Go through the Job-Match Grid a second time, looking at the column for your #3-ranked skill. If a *job you have already circled* has a black circle (●) or a bull's-eye (◉) in the column for your #3-ranked skill, put a check mark next to the occupation name. If none of your selected jobs has a black circle or a bull's-eye in this column, look for a white circle (○) and mark these jobs with check marks.

A second note for those determined to work in the arts: If a *particular* art form is essential for you to work in, you almost certainly know which occupations involve that art form and which don't. So not every job that has a black circle (●) in the "Artistic" column is going to interest you. Circle only the jobs that have a black circle in this column that *are* related to your art form (if you're not sure, look at the description of the occupation in this book) and that also have a symbol of some kind (●, ◑, or ○) in the column for your #2-ranked skill. As you circle each job, also give it a check mark, because there will be so few of them that you won't need to go through the Job-Match Grid a second time. If you have a more general interest in the arts, follow the general instructions.

Your Hot List of Possible Career Matches

Now that you have made a first and second cut of the jobs on the Job-Match Grid, you can focus on the occupations that look most promising at this point. Write the names of the occupations that are both *circled* and *checked:*

_____   _____

_____   _____

_____   _____

_____   _____

_____   _____

_____   _____

This is your Hot List of occupations that you are going to explore in detail *if* they are not eliminated by certain important job-related factors that you'll consider next.

Thinking About Other Job-Related Factors

Next, you need to consider four other job-related factors:

★ Economic sensitivity   ★ Physically demanding work

★ Outdoor work   ★ Hazardous conditions

Economic Sensitivity

You've read about how our nation's economy has gone up and down over the years. When the economy is on an upswing, there are more job openings, but when it veers downward toward recession, jobs are harder to find.

Are you aware that these trends affect some occupations more than others? For example, during an economic upswing, people do more vacation traveling and businesses send more workers on business trips. This keeps travel agencies very busy, so they need to hire more travel agents. When the economy is going down, people cut back on their vacation travel, businesses tell their workers to use teleconferencing instead of business trips, and travel agents are not in demand. Some may be laid off, and people who want to enter this field may find very few openings. By contrast, most jobs in the health-care field are not sensitive to the economy, and automotive mechanics are just as busy as ever during economic slowdowns because people want to keep their old cars running.

So this issue of economic sensitivity (and its opposite, job security) is one that may affect which occupation you choose. Some people want to avoid economically sensitive occupations because they don't want to risk losing their job (or having difficulty finding a job) during times of recession. Other people are willing to risk being in an economically sensitive occupation because they want to profit from the periods when both the economy and the occupation are booming.

> How important is it to you to be in an occupation that *doesn't* go through periods of boom and bust along with the nation's economy? Check one:
>
> _____ It doesn't matter to me.
>
> _____ It's not important, but I'd consider it.
>
> _____ It's somewhat important to me.
>
> _____ It's very important to me.

If you answered "It doesn't matter to me," skip to the next section, "Outdoor Work." Otherwise, turn back to the Job-Match Grid and find the column for "Economically Sensitive."

If you answered "It's not important, but I'd consider it," see whether any of the jobs on your Hot List have a black circle (●) in this column. If so, cross them off and write an "E" next to them.

If you answered "It's somewhat important to me," see whether any of the jobs on your Hot List have a black circle (●) or a bull's-eye (◉) in this column. If so, cross them off and write an "E" next to them.

If you answered "It's very important to me," see whether any of the jobs on your Hot List have *any* symbol (●, ◉, or ○) in this column. If so, cross them off and write an "E" next to them.

Outdoor Work

Some people prefer to work indoors in a climate-controlled setting, such as an office, a classroom, a factory floor, a laboratory, or a hospital room. Other people would rather work primarily in an outdoor setting, such as a forest, an athletic field, or a city street. And some would enjoy a job that alternates between indoor and outdoor activities.

> What is *your* preference for working indoors or outdoors? Check one:
>
> _____ It's very important to me to work **indoors.**
>
> _____ I'd prefer to work mostly **indoors.**
>
> _____ Either indoors or outdoors is okay with me.
>
> _____ I'd prefer to work mostly **outdoors.**
>
> _____ It's very important to me to work **outdoors.**

If you answered "Either indoors or outdoors is okay with me," skip to the next section, "Physically Demanding Work." Otherwise, turn to the Job-Match Grid and find the column for "Outdoor Work."

If you answered "It's very important to me to work **indoors,**" see whether any of the jobs on your Hot List have *any* symbol (●, ◉, or ○) in this column. If so, cross them off and write an "O" next to them.

If you answered "I'd prefer to work mostly **indoors,**" see whether any of the jobs on your Hot List have a black circle (●) in this column. If so, cross them off and write an "O" next to them.

If you answered "I'd prefer to work mostly **outdoors,**" see whether any of the jobs on your Hot List have *no* symbol—just a blank—in this column. If so, cross them off and write an "O" next to them. All the jobs remaining on your Hot List should have some kind of symbol (●, ◉, or ○) in this column.

If you answered "It's very important to me to work **outdoors,**" see whether any of the jobs on your Hot List have either *no* symbol or just a white circle (○) in this column. If so, cross them off and write an "O" next to them. All the jobs remaining on your Hot List should have either a black circle (●) or a bull's-eye (◉) in this column.

Physically Demanding Work

Jobs vary by how much muscle power they require you to use. Some jobs require a lot of lifting heavy loads, standing for long times, climbing, or stooping. On other jobs, the heaviest thing you lift is a notebook or telephone handset, and most of the time you are sitting. Still other jobs require only a moderate amount of physical exertion.

> What is *your* preference for the physical demands of work? Check one:
>
> _____ I don't care whether my work requires heavy or light physical exertion.
>
> _____ I want my work to require only light physical exertion.
>
> _____ I want my work to require no more than occasional moderate physical exertion.
>
> _____ I want my work to require moderate physical exertion, with occasional heavy exertion.
>
> _____ I want my work to require a lot of heavy physical exertion.

If you answered "I don't care whether my work requires heavy or light physical exertion," skip to the next section, "Hazardous Conditions." Otherwise, turn to the Job-Match Grid and find the column for "Physically Demanding Work."

If you answered "I want my work to require only light physical exertion," see whether any of the jobs on your Hot List have *any* symbol (●, ◉, or ○) in this column. If so, cross them off and write a "P" next to them.

If you answered "I want my work to require no more than occasional moderate physical exertion," see whether any of the jobs on your Hot List have either a black circle (●) or a bull's-eye (◉) in this column. If so, cross them off and write a "P" next to them.

If you answered "I want my work to require moderate physical exertion, with occasional heavy exertion," see whether any of the jobs on your Hot List have either a black circle (●), a white circle (○), or *no* symbol in this column. If so, cross them off and write a "P" next to them. All the jobs remaining on your Hot List should have a bull's-eye (◉) in this column.

If you answered "I want my work to require a lot of heavy physical exertion," see whether any of the jobs on your Hot List have either *no* symbol or just a white circle (○) or a bull's-eye (◉) in this column. If so, cross them off and write a "P" next to them. All the jobs remaining on your Hot List should have a black circle (●) in this column.

Hazardous Conditions

Every day about 9,000 Americans sustain a disabling injury on the job. Many workers have jobs that require them to deal with hazardous conditions, such as heat, noise, radiation, germs, toxins, or dangerous machinery. These workers need to wear protective clothing or follow safety procedures to avoid injury.

> What is *your* preference regarding hazardous conditions on the job? Check one:
>
> _____ I want hazardous workplace conditions to be very unlikely.
>
> _____ I want hazardous conditions to be unlikely or minor.
>
> _____ I am willing to accept some major workplace hazards.

If you answered "I am willing to accept some major workplace hazards," skip to the section "Geographically Concentrated Jobs." Otherwise, turn to the Job-Match Grid and find the column for "Hazardous Conditions."

If you answered "I want hazardous workplace conditions to be very unlikely," see whether any of the jobs on your Hot List have *any* symbol (●, ◐, or ○) in this column. If so, cross them off and write an "H" next to them.

If you answered "I want hazardous conditions to be unlikely or minor," see whether any of the jobs on your Hot List have a black circle (●) in this column. If so, cross them off and write an "H" next to them.

If Every Job on Your Hot List Is Now Crossed Off

It's possible that you have crossed off *all* the occupations on your Hot List. If so, consider these two options:

★ You may want to relax some of your requirements. Maybe you were too hasty in crossing off some of the jobs. Take another look at the four job-related factors and decide whether you could accept work that doesn't meet the requirements you set previously—for example, work that is not as much indoors or outdoors as you specified. If you change your mind now, you can tell by the letters in the margin which jobs you crossed off for which reasons.

★ You may want to add to your Hot List by considering additional skills. So far you have considered only occupations that involve your top three skills. You may want to add jobs that have a black circle (●) or a bull's-eye (◐) in the column for your #4-ranked skill and possibly for your #5-ranked skill. If you do add any jobs, be sure to repeat your review of the four job-related factors.

Evaluating Occupations Described in This Book

You are now ready to make the jump from the checklists to the detailed information about jobs in this book. The first detailed issue you need to consider is whether you will be able to find work in your area or have to relocate.

Geographically Concentrated Jobs

Turn to the Job-Match Grid one more time and find the column for "Geographically Concentrated." Look at all the occupations on your Hot List that haven't been crossed off. If there is a symbol in this column, especially a bull's-eye (◐) or a black circle (●), it means that employment for this occupation tends to be concentrated in certain geographic areas. For example, most acting jobs are found in big cities because that's where you'll find most theaters, TV studios, and movie studios. Most water transportation jobs are found on the coasts and beside major lakes and rivers.

If a symbol shows that a Hot List occupation *is* geographically concentrated, the location of the jobs may be obvious, as in the examples of acting and water transportation. If it's not clear to you where the jobs may be found, find the occupation in "The Job Descriptions" section and look for the facts under the heading "Employment" in the description. Once you understand where most of the jobs are, you have to make some decisions:

★ **Are most of the job openings in a geographic location where I am now or would enjoy living?**
If you answered "yes" to this question, repeat this exercise for all the other occupations still on your Hot List. Then jump to the next heading, "Nature of the Work." If you answered "no," proceed to the next bulleted question.

★ **If most of the job openings are in a distant place where I don't want to relocate, am I willing to take a chance and hope to be one of the few workers who get hired in an *uncommon* location?**
If you answered "yes," take a good look at the Job Outlook information in the job description. If the outlook for the occupation is very good and if you expect to have some of the advantages mentioned

there (such as the right degree, in some cases), taking a chance on being hired in an unusual location may be a reasonable decision. On the other hand, if the outlook is only so-so or not good and if you have no special qualifications, you probably are setting yourself up for disappointment. You should seriously consider changing your mind about this decision. At least speak to people in your area who are knowledgeable about the occupation to determine whether you have any chance of success. If you answered "no"—you are not willing to take a chance—cross off this occupation and write a "G" next to it. (If you now have no jobs left on your Hot List, see the previous section titled "If Every Job on Your Hot List Is Now Crossed Off.")

Nature of the Work

When you read the job description for an occupation on your Hot List, you will see that the "Nature of the Work" section discusses what workers do on the job, what tools and equipment they use, and how closely they are supervised. Keep in mind that this is an overview of a diverse collection of workers, and in fact few workers perform the full set of tasks itemized here. In fact, in many cases the work force covered by the job description is so diverse that it actually divides into several occupational specialties, which are italicized.

Here are some things to think about as you read this section:

★ Note the kinds of problems, materials, and tools you will encounter on the job. Are these are a good match for your interests?

★ Also note the work activities mentioned here. Do you think they will be rewarding? Are there many that stand out as unpleasant or boring?

The Work Environment section identifies the typical hours worked, the workplace environment (both physical and psychological), physical activities and susceptibility to injury, special equipment, and the extent of travel required. If conditions vary between the occupational specialties, that is mentioned here. Here are some things to look for in the Work Environment section:

★ If you have a disability, note the physical requirements that are mentioned here and consider whether you can meet these requirements with or without suitable accommodations.

★ If you're bothered by conditions such as heights, stress, or a cramped workspace, see whether this section mentions any conditions that would discourage you.

★ Note what this section says about the work schedule and the need for travel, if any. This information may be good to know if you have pressing family responsibilities or, on the other hand, a desire for unusual hours or travel.

★ If you find a working condition that bothers you, be sure to check the wording to see whether it *always* applies to the occupation or whether it only *may* apply. Even if it seems to be a condition that you cannot avoid, find out for sure by talking to people in the occupation or educators who teach related courses. Maybe you can carve out a niche that avoids the unappealing working condition.

Training, Other Qualifications, and Advancement

In the "Training, Other Qualifications, and Advancement" section, you can see how to prepare for the occupation and how to advance in it. It identifies the significant entry routes—those that are most popular and that are preferred by employers. It mentions any licensure or certification that may be necessary for entry or advancement. It also identifies the particular skills, aptitudes, and work habits that employers value. Look for these topics in this section:

★ Compare the entry requirements to your background and to the educational and training opportunities that are available to you. Be sure to consider nontraditional and informal entry routes, if any are possible, as well as the formal routes. Ask yourself, Am I willing to get the additional education or training that will be necessary? Do I have the time, money, ability, interest, and commitment?

★ Maybe you're already partway down the road to job entry. In general, you should try to use your previous education, training, and work experience rather than abandon it. Look for specifics that are already on your resume—educational accomplishments, skills, work habits—that will meet employers' expectations. If you have some of these qualifications already, this occupation may be a better career choice than some others.

Employment

The "Employment" section in the job description reports how many jobs the occupation currently provides, the industries that provide the most jobs, and the number or proportion of self-employed or part-time workers in the occupation, if significant. In this section, you'll want to pay attention to these facts:

★ Note the industries that provide most of the employment for the occupation. This knowledge can help you identify contacts who can tell you more about the work, and later it can help in your job hunting.

★ If you're interested in self-employment or part-time work, see whether these work arrangements are mentioned here.

Job Outlook

The "Job Outlook" section describes the economic forces that will affect future employment in the occupation. Here are some things to look for in this section:

★ The information here can help you identify occupations with a good job outlook so that you will have a better-than-average chance of finding work. Be alert for any mention of an advantage that you may have over other job seekers (for example, a college degree) or any other factor that might make your chances better or worse.

★ If you are highly motivated and highly qualified for a particular occupation, don't be discouraged by a bad employment outlook. Job openings occur even in shrinking or overcrowded occupations, and with exceptional talent or good personal connections, you may go on to great success.

★ These projections are the most definitive ones available, but they are not foolproof and apply only to a 10-year time span. No matter what occupation you choose, you will need to adapt to changes.

Projections Data

This section of the job description shows a table with projected figures for employment growth. Here are some things to think about when you read this table:

★ Notice that the columns headed "Change 2008–2018" show both the number of workers (gained or lost) and a percentage figure. You need to consider both figures. For example, an occupation with a very small workforce will not create many job openings even though it may be growing fast.

★ For many occupations, this table features two or more rows showing the projections data for various career specializations. By comparing the figures on different rows, you may identify which specializations are expected to grow fastest and create the most job openings.

Earnings

The "Earnings" section discusses the wages for the occupation. Here are some things to keep in mind:

★ The wage figures are national averages. Actual wages in your geographic region may be considerably higher or lower. Also, an average figure means that half of the workers earn more and half earn less, and the actual salary any one worker earns can vary greatly from that average.

★ Remember to consider *all* the pluses and minuses of the job. Not every day of the work week is pay-day, so make your choice based on the whole occupation, not just the paycheck.

Related Occupations

The "Related Occupations" section identifies occupations that are similar to the one featured in the job description in terms of tasks, interests, skills, education, or training. You may find this section interesting for these reasons:

★ If you're interested in an occupation but not strongly committed to pursuing it, this section may suggest another occupation with similar rewards that may turn out to be a better fit. Try to research these related occupations, but keep in mind that they may not all be included in this book.

★ You may want to choose one of these occupations as your Plan B goal if your original goal should not work out. In that case, it helps to identify an occupation that involves similar kinds of problems and work settings but requires *less* education or training.

Sources of Additional Information

This section in each job description lists several sources and resources you can turn to for more information about the occupation. Try to consult at least some of these sources. This book should be only the beginning of your career decision-making process. You need more detailed information from several viewpoints to make an informed decision.

Don't rely entirely on the Web sites listed here. You especially need to talk to and observe individual workers to learn what their workdays are like, what the workers enjoy and dislike about the job, how they got hired, and what effects the job has had on other aspects of their lives. Maybe you can make contact with local workers through the local chapter of an organization listed here.

Narrowing Down Your Choices

The information in the job descriptions should help you cross more jobs off your Hot List. And what you learn by turning to other resources should help you narrow down your Hot List jobs to a few promising choices and maybe one best bet. Here are some final considerations: Have I talked to people who are actually doing this work? Am I fully aware of the pluses and minuses of this job? If there are aspects of the job that I don't like, how do I expect to avoid them or overcome them? If the odds of finding a job opening are not good, why do I expect to beat the odds? What is my Plan B goal if I lose interest in my original goal or don't succeed at it?

The Job-Match Grid

The grid on the following pages provides information about the personal skills and job characteristics for occupations covered in this book. Use the directions and questions that start at the beginning of this section to help you get the most from this grid.

The following is what the symbols on the grid represent. If a job has no symbol in a column, it means that the skill or job characteristic is not important or relevant to the job.

Personal Skills

- ● Essential or high-skill level
- ◉ Somewhat essential or moderate-skill level
- ○ Basic-skill level

Job Characteristics

- ● Highly likely
- ◉ Somewhat likely
- ○ A little likely

Job-Match Grid

	Personal Skills							Job Characteristics				
	Artistic	Communication	Interpersonal	Managerial	Mathematics	Mechanical	Science	Economically Sensitive	Outdoor Work	Physically Demanding	Hazardous Conditions	Geographically Concentrated
Accountants and Auditors		◉	◉	◉	●			○	○			
Advertising, Marketing, Promotions, Public Relations, and Sales Managers	◉	◉	●	●	○				◉		○	
Animal Care and Service Workers		○	○	◉	○	◉	◉	◉	●	◉	○	
Athletes, Coaches, Umpires, and Related Workers	◉	◉	●	●	○	◉	◉		◉	●	○	
Barbers, Cosmetologists, and Other Personal Appearance Workers	●		○	◉		○	●	◉		○	●	
Bill and Account Collectors		◉	◉	●	◉	◉	○	◉				
Billing and Posting Clerks and Machine Operators		◉			○	○		○	○		○	
Biological Scientists	◉	●	◉	●	●	○	●	○	◉	○	●	
Bookkeeping, Accounting, and Auditing Clerks		○	○	◉	◉	○	○	○				
Cargo and Freight Agents		○	◉		○			●	○	○	○	◉
Carpenters	◉	○	○	●	●	●	◉	●	●	●	◉	
Child Care Workers	●	○	◉	○		○	○		◉	◉	○	
Clinical Laboratory Technologists and Technicians	◉	◉	○	○	◉	●	●			◉	●	
Computer and Information Systems Managers	○	○	○	●		◉		●	○		○	
Computer Network, Systems, and Database Administrators	◉	◉	◉	●	◉	●	◉	○	○		○	
Computer Software Engineers and Computer Programmers	◉	●	◉	○	●	●	●	○				
Computer Support Specialists	○	○	○			◉		○	○	○	○	
Computer Systems Analysts	◉	◉	◉	◉	●	●	◉	○				
Construction Equipment Operators				◉	◉	●	◉	●	●	◉	◉	
Construction Laborers					○	◉	○	●	●	●	●	
Construction Managers	○	○	◉	●	●			●	●	○	◉	
Cooks and Food Preparation Workers	○			○		◉	○	●	○	◉	○	
Correctional Officers			◉						◉	●	◉	
Cost Estimators		○	○	◉	◉			◉	○			
Counselors	◉	●	●	◉			◉		○	○		

(continued)

Personal Skills: ●—Essential or high-skill level; ◉—Somewhat essential or moderate-skill level; ○—Basic-skill level
Job Characteristics: ●—Highly likely; ◉—Somewhat likely; ○—A little likely

(continued)

	Personal Skills							Job Characteristics				
	Artistic	Communication	Interpersonal	Managerial	Mathematics	Mechanical	Science	Economically Sensitive	Outdoor Work	Physically Demanding Work	Hazardous Conditions	Geographically Concentrated
Customer Service Representatives	○	◐	◐	○	○	◐		○				
Dental Assistants	○	◐	◐	◐		●	◐			◐	●	
Dental Hygienists		●	◐			◐	●			◐	●	
Dentists	●	●	●	●	◐	●	●			◐	●	
Desktop Publishers		◐			○	○		○	○		○	
Electricians	○		○	◐	◐	●		●	●	●	●	
Engineers	◐	●	●	●	●	◐	●	◐	◐	○	◐	◐
Environmental Scientists and Specialists	◐	●	○	◐	●		●	○	◐		◐	
Financial Analysts	◐	◐	◐	●	●	○	◐	●	◐			
Fire Fighters		◐	●	●	◐	●	●			●	●	●
Fitness Workers	◐	○	◐	○		◐	●	◐	○	●		
Food and Beverage Serving and Related Workers	◐					○		●	○	◐	○	
Graphic Designers	●							○	○		○	○
Grounds Maintenance Workers	◐			○		●	○	○	●	●	●	
Heating, Air-Conditioning, and Refrigeration Mechanics and Installers	○	◐	◐	◐	●	●	●	◐	●	●	●	
Home Health Aides and Personal and Home Care Aides	◐	○	◐			○	○			◐	●	
Hotel, Motel, and Resort Desk Clerks	○	○	○		○	○	○	●	○	○	○	
Human Resources, Training, and Labor Relations Managers and Specialists	◐	◐	◐	◐	○			○	○		○	
Instructional Coordinators	●	●	●	●	◐	○	◐		◐			
Insurance Sales Agents	○	●	●	●	●	○		◐	◐			
Interviewers, Except Eligibility and Loan	○	○	○					○			○	
Lawyers	●	●	●	●	◐		◐	○	◐			
Licensed Practical and Licensed Vocational Nurses	○		○				○			●	◐	
Maintenance and Repair Workers, General	○		○	○	○	●	◐			●	●	
Management Analysts	○	◐	◐	◐	◐	●	◐	○	○		◐	
Market and Survey Researchers	◐	●	●	◐	○		◐	◐	○			
Medical and Health Services Managers	○	○	◐	●	○				○	○	◐	
Medical Assistants	○	○	○							◐	◐	
Medical Equipment Repairers	○	◐	◐	◐	●	●	●		◐	◐	●	
Medical Records and Health Information Technicians										◐	○	
Medical Scientists	●	●	●	●	●	◐	●	○			◐	
Nursing and Psychiatric Aides	○									●	◐	
Occupational Therapists	◐	○	○	○			○			◐	◐	○
Office and Administrative Support Worker Supervisors and Managers	○	◐	●	●	◐	○	○	○	○		○	

Personal Skills: ●—Essential or high-skill level; ◐—Somewhat essential or moderate-skill level; ○—Basic-skill level
Job Characteristics: ●—Highly likely; ◐—Somewhat likely; ○—A little likely

	Personal Skills							Job Characteristics				
	Artistic	Communication	Interpersonal	Managerial	Mathematics	Mechanical	Science	Economically Sensitive	Outdoor Work	Physically Demanding Work	Hazardous Conditions	Geographically Concentrated
Office Clerks, General		○			○			◐		○		
Operations Research Analysts	◐	●	◐	●	●	○	●	○	○			
Paralegals and Legal Assistants	○	◐		○	○			○	○			
Personal Financial Advisors	○	●	◐	●	●		○	○	○			
Pharmacists	○	●	◐	○	●	○	●			◐	◐	
Pharmacy Technicians and Aides		◐			◐	○	◐			◐	◐	
Physical Therapist Assistants and Aides	○		○							●	○	
Physical Therapists	◐	○	○	○			○		○	●	○	
Physician Assistants	○	◐	◐		○		○			◐	◐	
Physicians and Surgeons	◐	●	●	●	◐	●	●				○	◐
Plumbers, Pipelayers, Pipefitters, and Steamfitters	○		○	○	○	●	○	○	●	●	●	
Police and Detectives		◐	●	○	○	○	○		●	●	●	
Probation Officers and Correctional Treatment Specialists	◐	●	●	◐	◐	○	◐		●	○	○	
Public Relations Specialists	●	●	●	◐					◐			◐
Radiologic Technologists and Technicians	○	◐	○		○	○	◐			●	◐	
Real Estate Brokers and Sales Agents	○	◐	●	◐	●		○	●	●	○	○	
Receptionists and Information Clerks		◐	○	○	○	○	○	○		○		
Recreation Workers	●	●	●	●	○	○	◐	◐	●	●	◐	
Registered Nurses	◐	○	◐	◐	○		◐			●	●	
Respiratory Therapists	○	◐	○	○	●	◐	●			◐	◐	
Retail Salespersons	○	○			○			◐	◐	◐	○	
Sales Representatives, Wholesale and Manufacturing		◐	●	●	◐	○	◐	●	●	○	○	
Science Technicians	○	◐	○	◐	●	●	●	◐	◐	◐	●	
Secretaries and Administrative Assistants		◐	○	○	○			○	○		○	
Security Guards and Gaming Surveillance Officers	○							○	●	●	◐	
Social and Human Service Assistants	○	○	◐	○						◐	◐	
Social Workers	◐	●	●	○			○			◐	○	○
Stock Clerks and Order Fillers					○	○		○	◐	◐	○	
Surgical Technologists			○	○		◐	○			◐	●	
Surveyors, Cartographers, Photogrammetrists, and Surveying and Mapping Technicians	◐	○		○	◐	◐	○	◐	●	◐	○	
Taxi Drivers and Chauffeurs						◐		◐	●	◐	◐	◐
Teacher Assistants	◐	◐	◐		◐		◐		○	○		
Teachers—Kindergarten, Elementary, Middle, and Secondary	●	●	●	◐	◐	○	◐		○	◐	○	
Teachers—Postsecondary	◐	●	●	●	●	○	●		○	○	○	
Teachers—Preschool, Except Special Education	●	○	◐	○		○	◐			◐	◐	
Teachers—Self-Enrichment Education	●	◐	◐	○		○	○			○	◐	

(continued)

Personal Skills: ●—Essential or high-skill level; ◐—Somewhat essential or moderate-skill level; ○—Basic-skill level
Job Characteristics: ●—Highly likely; ◐—Somewhat likely; ○—A little likely

(continued)

	Personal Skills							Job Characteristics				
	Artistic	Communication	Interpersonal	Managerial	Mathematics	Mechanical	Science	Economically Sensitive	Outdoor Work	Physically Demanding Work	Hazardous Conditions	Geographically Concentrated
Teachers—Special Education	●	●	●	○	○		○		○	○		
Truck Drivers and Driver/Sales Workers			○		○	●	○	●	●	●	○	
Veterinarians	○	●	●	●	●	●	●		○	○	●	
Veterinary Technologists and Technicians	○	○	○	○	●	○	●	○	○	●	●	
Water and Liquid Waste Treatment Plant and System Operators	○	○		○	●	●	●		●	●	●	

Descriptions of the 100 Fastest-Growing Careers

This is the book's main section. It contains helpful descriptions of the 100 major occupations that have the most-favorable combined scores for projected percent increase and number of job openings through 2018. To learn a job's ranking, see the introduction.

The jobs are arranged in alphabetical order. Refer to the table of contents for a list of the jobs and the page numbers where their descriptions begin. Review the table of contents to discover occupations that interest you, and then find out more about them in this section. If you are interested in medical careers, for example, you can go through the list and quickly pinpoint those you want to learn more about. Or use the assessment in Part I to identify several possible career matches.

While the job descriptions in this part are easy to understand, the introduction provides additional information for interpreting them. Keep in mind that the descriptions present information that is average for the country. Conditions in your area and with specific employers may be quite different.

Also, you may come across jobs that sound interesting but require more education and training than you have or are considering. Don't eliminate them too soon. There are many ways to obtain education and training, and most people change careers many times. You probably have more skills than you realize that can transfer to new jobs. People often have more opportunities than barriers. Use the descriptions to learn more about possible jobs and look into the suggested resources to help you take the next step.

Accountants and Auditors

O*NET 13-2011.00, 13-2011.01, and 13-2011.02)

Significant Points

■ Most jobs require at least a bachelor's degree in accounting or a related field.

■ Job opportunities should be favorable; those who have earned professional recognition through certification or licensure, especially a CPA, should enjoy the best prospects.

■ Much-faster-than-average employment growth will result from an increase in the number of businesses, changing financial laws and regulations, and greater scrutiny of company finances.

Nature of the Work

Accountants and auditors help to ensure that firms are run efficiently, public records kept accurately, and taxes paid properly and on time. They analyze and communicate financial information for various entities such as companies; individual clients; and federal, state, and local governments. Beyond carrying out the fundamental tasks of the occupation—providing information to clients by preparing, analyzing, and verifying financial documents—many accountants also offer budget analysis, financial and investment planning, information technology consulting, and limited legal services.

Specific job duties vary widely among the four major fields of accounting and auditing: *public accounting, management accounting, government accounting,* and *internal auditing.*

Public accountants perform a broad range of accounting, auditing, tax, and consulting activities for their clients, which may be corporations, governments, nonprofit organizations, or individuals. For example, some public accountants concentrate on tax matters, such as advising companies about the tax advantages and disadvantages of certain business decisions and preparing individual income tax returns. Others offer advice in areas such as compensation or employee health-care benefits, the design of accounting and data processing systems, and the selection of controls to safeguard assets. Still others audit clients' financial statements and inform investors and authorities that the statements have been correctly prepared and reported. These accountants are also referred to as *external auditors.* Public accountants, many of whom are *Certified Public Accountants* (CPAs), generally have their own businesses or work for public accounting firms.

Some public accountants specialize in forensic accounting—investigating and interpreting white-collar crimes such as securities fraud and embezzlement, bankruptcies and contract disputes, and other complex and possibly criminal financial transactions, including money laundering by organized criminals. *Forensic accountants* combine their knowledge of accounting and finance with law and investigative techniques to determine whether an activity is illegal. Many forensic accountants work closely with law enforcement personnel and lawyers during investigations and often appear as expert witnesses during trials.

Management accountants—also called *cost, managerial, industrial, corporate, or private accountants*—record and analyze the financial information of the companies for which they work. Among their other responsibilities are budgeting, performance evaluation, cost management, and asset management. Usually, management accountants are part of executive teams involved in strategic planning or the development of new products. They analyze and interpret the financial information that corporate executives need to make sound business decisions. They also prepare financial reports for other groups, including stockholders, creditors, regulatory agencies, and tax authorities. Within accounting departments, management accountants may work in various areas, including financial analysis, planning and budgeting, and cost accounting.

Government accountants and auditors work in the public sector, maintaining and examining the records of government agencies and auditing private businesses and individuals whose activities are subject to government regulations or taxation. Accountants employed by federal, state, and local governments ensure that revenues are received and expenditures are made in accordance with laws and regulations. Those employed by the federal government may work as Internal Revenue Service agents or in financial management, financial institution examination, or budget analysis and administration.

Internal auditors verify the effectiveness of their organization's internal controls and check for mismanagement, waste, or fraud. They examine and evaluate their firms' financial and information systems, management procedures, and internal controls to ensure that records are accurate and controls are adequate. They also review company operations, evaluating their efficiency, effectiveness, and compliance with corporate policies and government regulations. Because computer systems commonly automate transactions and make information readily available, internal auditors may also help management evaluate the effectiveness of their controls based on real-time data rather than personal observation. They may recommend and review controls for their organization's computer systems to ensure their reliability and integrity of the data. Internal auditors may also have specialty titles, such as *information technology auditors, environmental auditors,* and *compliance auditors.*

Technology is rapidly changing the nature of the work of most accountants and auditors. With the aid of special software packages, accountants summarize transactions in the standard formats of financial records and organize data in special formats employed in financial analysis. These accounting packages greatly reduce the tedious work associated with data management and recordkeeping. Computers enable accountants and auditors to be more mobile and to use their clients' computer systems to extract information from databases and the Internet. As a result, a growing number of accountants and auditors with extensive computer skills specialize in correcting problems with software or in developing software to meet unique data management and analytical needs. Accountants also are beginning to perform more technical duties, such as implementing, controlling, and auditing computer systems and networks and developing technology plans.

Work environment. Most accountants and auditors work in a typical office setting. Some may be able to do part of their work at home. Accountants and auditors employed by public accounting firms, government agencies, and organizations with multiple locations may travel frequently to perform audits at branches, clients' places of business, or government facilities.

Almost half of all accountants and auditors worked a standard 40-hour week in 2008, but many work longer hours, particularly if they are self-employed and have numerous clients. Tax specialists often work long hours during the tax season.

Training, Other Qualifications, and Advancement

Most accountants and auditors need at least a bachelor's degree in accounting or a related field. Many accountants and auditors choose to obtain certification to help advance their careers, such as becoming a Certified Public Accountant (CPA).

Education and training. Most accountant and auditor positions require at least a bachelor's degree in accounting or a related field. Some employers prefer applicants with a master's degree in accounting or with a master's degree in business administration with a concentration in accounting. Some universities and colleges are now offering programs to prepare students to work in growing specialty professions such as internal auditing. Many professional associations offer continuing professional education courses, conferences, and seminars.

Some graduates of junior colleges or business or correspondence schools, as well as bookkeepers and accounting clerks who meet the education and experience requirements set by their employers, can obtain junior accounting positions and advance to accountant positions by demonstrating their accounting skills on the job.

Most beginning accountants and auditors work under supervision or closely with an experienced accountant or auditor before gaining more independence and responsibility.

Licensure and certification. Any accountant filing a report with the Securities and Exchange Commission (SEC) is required by law to be a Certified Public Accountant (CPA). This may include senior-level accountants working for or on behalf of public companies that are registered with the SEC. CPAs are licensed by their State Board of Accountancy. Any accountant who passes a national exam and meets the other requirements of the state where they practice can become a CPA. The vast majority of states require CPA candidates to be college graduates, but a few states will substitute a number of years of public accounting experience for a college degree.

As of 2009, 46 states and the District of Columbia required CPA candidates to complete 150 semester hours of college coursework—an additional 30 hours beyond the usual four-year bachelor's degree. California, Colorado, New Hampshire, and Vermont are the only states that do not require 150 semester hours for certification. Many schools offer a five-year combined bachelor's and master's degree to meet the 150-semester-hour requirement, but a master's degree is not required. Prospective accounting majors should carefully research accounting curricula and the requirements of any states in which they hope to become licensed.

All states use the four-part Uniform CPA Examination prepared by the American Institute of Certified Public Accountants (AICPA). The CPA examination is rigorous, and less than one-half of those who take it each year pass every part on the first try. Candidates are not required to pass all four parts at once, but most states require candidates to pass all four sections within 18 months of passing their first section. The CPA exam is now computerized and is offered two months out of every quarter at various testing centers throughout the United States. Most states also require applicants for a CPA license to have some accounting experience; however, requirements vary by state or jurisdiction.

Nearly all states require CPAs and other public accountants to complete a certain number of hours of continuing professional education before their licenses can be renewed. The professional associations representing accountants sponsor numerous courses, seminars, group study programs, and other forms of continuing education.

Other qualifications. Previous experience in accounting or auditing can help an applicant get a job. Many colleges offer students the opportunity to gain experience through summer or part-time internship programs conducted by public accounting or business firms. In addition, as many business processes are now automated, practical knowledge of computers and their applications is a great asset for jobseekers in the accounting and auditing fields.

People planning a career in accounting and auditing should have an aptitude for mathematics and be able to analyze, compare, and interpret facts and figures quickly. They must be able to clearly communicate the results of their work to clients and managers both verbally and in writing. Accountants and auditors must be good at working with people, business systems, and computers. At a minimum, accountants and auditors should be familiar with basic accounting and computer software packages. Because financial decisions are made on the basis of their statements and services, accountants and auditors should have high standards of integrity.

Certification and advancement. Professional recognition through certification or other designation provides a distinct advantage in the job market. Certification can attest to professional competence in a specialized field of accounting and auditing. Accountants and auditors can seek credentials from a wide variety of professional societies.

The Institute of Management Accountants confers the Certified Management Accountant (CMA) designation upon applicants who complete a bachelor's degree or who attain a minimum score or higher on specified graduate school entrance exams. Applicants must have worked at least two years in management accounting, pass a four-part examination, agree to meet continuing education requirements, and comply with standards of professional conduct. The exam covers areas such as financial statement analysis, working-capital policy, capital structure, valuation issues, and risk management.

The Institute of Internal Auditors offers the Certified Internal Auditor (CIA) designation to graduates from accredited colleges and universities who have worked for two years as internal auditors and have passed a four-part examination. The IIA also offers the designations of Certified in Control Self-Assessment (CCSA), Certified Government Auditing Professional (CGAP), and Certified Financial Services Auditor (CFSA) to those who pass the exams and meet educational and experience requirements.

ISACA confers the Certified Information Systems Auditor (CISA) designation upon candidates who pass an examination and have five years of experience auditing information systems. Information systems experience, financial or operational auditing experience, or related college credit hours can be substituted for up to two years of information systems auditing, control, or security experience.

For those accountants with their CPA, the AICPA offers the option to receive any or all of the Accredited in Business Valuation (ABV), Certified Information Technology Professional (CITP), or Personal Financial Specialist (PFS) designations. CPAs with these designations demonstrate a level of expertise in these areas in which accountants practice ever more frequently. The business valuation designation requires a written exam and the completion of a minimum of 10 business valuation projects that demonstrate a candidate's experience and competence. The technology designation requires the achievement of a set number of points awarded for business technology experience and education. Candidates for the personal financial specialist designation also must achieve a certain level of points based on experience and education, pass a written exam, and submit references.

Many senior corporation executives have a background in accounting, internal auditing, or finance. Beginning public accountants often advance to positions with more responsibility in one or two years and to senior positions within another few years. Those who excel may become supervisors, managers, or partners; open their own public accounting firm; or transfer to executive positions in management accounting or internal auditing in private firms.

Management accountants often start as cost accountants, junior internal auditors, or trainees for other accounting positions. As they rise through the organization, they may advance to accounting manager, chief cost accountant, budget director, or manager of internal auditing. Some become controllers, treasurers, financial vice presidents, chief financial officers, or corporation presidents.

Public accountants, management accountants, and internal auditors usually have much occupational mobility. Practitioners often shift into management accounting or internal auditing from public accounting or between internal auditing and management accounting. It is less common for accountants and auditors to move from either management accounting or internal auditing into public accounting. Additionally, because they learn about and review the internal controls of various business units within a company, internal auditors often gain the experience needed to become upper-level managers.

Employment

Accountants and auditors held about 1.3 million jobs in 2008. They worked throughout private industry and government, but 24 percent of accountants and auditors worked for accounting, tax preparation, bookkeeping, and payroll services firms. Approximately 8 percent of accountants and auditors were self-employed.

Most accountants and auditors work in urban areas, where public accounting firms and central or regional offices of businesses are concentrated.

Some individuals with backgrounds in accounting and auditing are full-time college and university faculty; others teach part time while working as self-employed accountants or as accountants for private industry or in government. (See teachers—postsecondary elsewhere in this book.)

Job Outlook

Accountants and auditors are expected to experience much-faster-than-average employment growth from 2008–2018. Job opportunities should be favorable; accountants and auditors who have a professional certification, especially CPAs, should have the best prospects.

Employment change. Employment of accountants and auditors is expected to grow by 22 percent between 2008 and 2018, which is much faster than the average for all occupations. This occupation will have a very large number of new jobs arise—about 279,400 over the projections decade. An increase in the number of businesses, changing financial laws and corporate governance regulations, and increased accountability for protecting an organization's stakeholders will drive job growth.

As the economy grows, the number of business establishments will increase, requiring more accountants and auditors to set up books, prepare taxes, and provide management advice. As these businesses grow, the volume and complexity of information reviewed by accountants and auditors regarding costs, expenditures, taxes, and internal controls will expand as well. The continued globalization of business also will lead to more demand for accounting expertise and services related to international trade and accounting rules and international mergers and acquisitions. Additionally, there is a growing movement towards International Financial Reporting Standards (IFRS), which uses a judgment-based system to determine the fair market value of assets and liabilities. This movement should increase demand for accountants and auditors because of their specialized expertise.

An increased need for accountants and auditors also will arise from a greater emphasis on accountability, transparency, and controls in financial reporting. Increased scrutiny of company finances and accounting procedures will create opportunities for accountants and auditors, particularly CPAs, to audit financial records more thoroughly and completely. Management accountants and internal auditors increasingly will be needed to discover and eliminate fraud before audits and ensure that important processes and procedures are documented accurately and thoroughly. Forensic accountants also will be needed to detect illegal financial activity by individuals, companies, and organized crime rings.

Job prospects. Job opportunities should be favorable. Accountants and auditors who have earned professional recognition through certification or other designation, especially a CPA, should have the best job prospects. Applicants with a master's degree in accounting or a master's degree in business administration with a concentration in accounting also may have an advantage.

Individuals who are proficient in accounting and auditing computer software and information systems or have expertise in specialized areas—such as international business, international financial reporting standards, or current legislation—may have an advantage in getting some accounting and auditing jobs. In addition, employers increasingly seek applicants with strong interpersonal and communication skills. Many accountants work on teams with others who have different backgrounds, so they must be able to communicate accounting and financial information clearly and concisely. Regardless of qualifications, however, competition will remain keen for the most prestigious jobs in major accounting and business firms.

Projections Data from the National Employment Matrix

Occupational title	SOC Code	Employment, 2008	Projected employment, 2018	Change, 2008–2018	
				Number	Percent
Accountants and auditors 13-20	13-20	1,290,600	1,570,000	279,400	22

NOTE: Data in this table are rounded.

In addition to openings from job growth, the need to replace accountants and auditors who retire or transfer to other occupations will produce numerous job openings in this large occupation.

Earnings

Median annual wages of wage and salary accountants and auditors were $59,430 in May 2008. The middle half of the occupation earned between $45,900 and $78,210. The bottom 10 percent earned less than $36,720, and the top 10 percent earned more than $102,380. Median annual wages in the industries employing the largest numbers of accountants and auditors were as follows:

Accounting, tax preparation, bookkeeping, and payroll services	$61,480
Management of companies and enterprises	59,820
Insurance carriers	59,550
Local government	53,660
State government	51,250

According to a salary survey conducted by the National Association of Colleges and Employers, bachelor's degree candidates in accounting received starting offers averaging $48,993 a year in July 2009; master's degree candidates in accounting were offered $49,786 initially.

Wage and salary accountants and auditors usually receive standard benefits, including health and medical insurance, life insurance, a 401(k) plan, and paid annual leave. High-level senior accountants may receive additional benefits, such as the use of a company car and an expense account.

Related Occupations

Accountants and auditors design internal control systems and analyze financial data. Others for whom training in accounting is valuable include bookkeeping, accounting, and auditing clerks; budget analysts; cost estimators; financial analysts; loan officers; personal financial advisors; and tax examiners, collectors, and revenue agents.

Some accountants have assumed the role of management analysts and are involved in the design, implementation, and maintenance of accounting software systems. Others who perform similar work include computer network, systems, and database administrators; computer software engineers; and computer programmers.

Sources of Additional Information

Information on accredited accounting programs can be obtained from

▸ AACSB International—Association to Advance Collegiate Schools of Business, 777 S. Harbour Island Blvd., Suite 750, Tampa, FL 33602. Internet: www.aacsb.edu/accreditation/AccreditedMembers.asp

Information about careers in certified public accounting and CPA standards and examinations may be obtained from

▸ American Institute of Certified Public Accountants, 1211 Avenue of the Americas, New York, NY 10036. Internet: www.aicpa.org

▸ AICPA Examinations Team, Parkway Corporate Center, 1230 Parkway Ave., Suite 311, Ewing, NJ 08628-3018. Internet: www.cpa-exam. org

Information on CPA licensure requirements by state may be obtained from

▸ National Association of State Boards of Accountancy, 150 Fourth Ave. N., Suite 700, Nashville, TN 37219-2417. Internet: www. nasba.org

Information on careers in management accounting and the CMA designation may be obtained from

▸ Institute of Management Accountants, 10 Paragon Dr., Montvale, NJ 07645-1718. Internet: www.imanet.org

Information on careers in internal auditing and the CIA designation may be obtained from

▸ The Institute of Internal Auditors, 247 Maitland Ave., Altamonte Springs, FL 32701-4201. Internet: www.theiia.org

Information on careers in information systems auditing and the CISA designation may be obtained from

▸ ISACA, 3701 Algonquin Rd., Suite 1010, Rolling Meadows, IL 60008. Internet: www.isaca.org

Advertising, Marketing, Promotions, Public Relations, and Sales Managers

(O*NET 11-2011.00, 11-2011.01, 11-2021.00, 11-2022.00, and 11-2031.00)

Significant Points

■ Keen competition is expected for these highly coveted jobs.

■ College graduates with related experience, a high level of creativity, and strong communication and computer skills should have the best job opportunities.

■ High earnings; substantial travel; and long hours, including evenings and weekends, are common.

■ Because of the importance and high visibility of their jobs, these managers often are prime candidates for advancement to the highest ranks.

Nature of the Work

Advertising, marketing, promotions, public relations, and sales managers coordinate their companies' market research, marketing strategy, sales, advertising, promotion, pricing, product development, and public relations activities. In small firms, the owner or chief executive officer might assume all advertising, promotions, marketing, sales, and public relations responsibilities. In large firms, which may offer numerous products and services nationally or even worldwide, an executive vice president directs overall advertising, marketing, promotions, sales, and public relations policies.

Advertising managers. Advertising managers direct a firm's or group's advertising and promotional campaign. They can be found in advertising agencies that put together advertising campaigns for clients, in media firms that sell advertising space or time, and in companies that advertise heavily. They work with sales staff and others to generate ideas for the campaign, oversee a creative staff that develops the advertising, and work with the finance department to prepare a budget and cost estimates for the campaign. Often, these managers serve as liaisons between the firm requiring the advertising and an advertising or promotion agency that actually develops and places the ads. In larger firms with an extensive advertising department, different advertising managers may oversee in-house accounts and creative and media services departments. The *account executive* manages account services departments in companies and assesses the need for advertising. In advertising agencies, account executives maintain the accounts of clients whereas the creative services department develops the subject matter and presentation of advertising. The *creative director* oversees the copy chief, art director, and associated staff. The *media director* oversees planning groups that select the communication medium—for example, radio, television, newspapers, magazines, the Internet, or outdoor signs—that will disseminate the advertising.

Marketing managers. Marketing managers work with advertising and promotion managers to promote the firm's or organization's products and services. With the help of lower-level managers, including *product development managers* and *market research managers,* marketing managers estimate the demand for products and services offered by the firm and its competitors and identify potential markets for the firm's products. Marketing managers also develop pricing strategies to help firms maximize profits and market share while ensuring that the firms' customers are satisfied. In collaboration with sales, product development, and other managers, they monitor trends that indicate the need for new products and services and they oversee product development.

Promotions managers. Promotions managers direct promotions programs that combine advertising with purchasing incentives to increase sales. Often, the programs are executed through the use of direct mail, inserts in newspapers, Internet advertisements, in-store displays, product endorsements, or other special events. Purchasing incentives may include discounts, samples, gifts, rebates, coupons, sweepstakes, and contests.

Public relations managers. Public relations managers plan and direct public relations programs designed to create and maintain a favorable public image for the employer or client. For example, they might write press releases or sponsor corporate events to help maintain and improve the image and identity of the company or client. They also help to clarify the organization's point of view to their main constituency. They observe social, economic, and political trends that might ultimately affect the firm, and they make recommendations to enhance the firm's image on the basis of those trends. Public relations managers often specialize in a specific area, such as crisis management, or in a specific industry, such as health care.

In large organizations, public relations managers may supervise a staff of public relations specialists. (See the description for public relations specialists.) They also work with advertising and marketing staffs to make sure that the advertising campaigns are compatible with the image the company or client is trying to portray. In addition, public relations managers may handle internal company communications, such as company newsletters, and may help financial managers produce company reports. They may assist company executives in drafting speeches, arranging interviews, and maintaining other forms of public contact; oversee company archives; and respond to requests for information. Some of these managers handle special events as well, such as the sponsorship of races, parties introducing new products, or other activities that the firm supports in order to gain public attention through the press without advertising directly.

Sales managers. Sales managers direct the distribution of the product or service to the customer. They assign sales territories, set sales goals, and establish training programs for the organization's sales representatives. (See the description of sales representatives, wholesale and manufacturing.) Sales managers advise the sales representatives on ways to improve their sales performance. In large multiproduct firms, they oversee regional and local sales managers and their staffs. Sales managers maintain contact with dealers and distributors and analyze sales statistics gathered by their staffs to determine sales potential and inventory requirements and to monitor customers' preferences. Such information is vital in the development of products and the maximization of profits.

Work environment. Advertising, marketing, promotions, public relations, and sales managers work in offices close to those of top managers. Working under pressure is unavoidable when schedules change and problems arise, but deadlines and goals still must be met.

Substantial travel may be required in order to meet with customers and consult with others in the industry. Sales managers travel to national, regional, and local offices and to the offices of various dealers and distributors. Advertising and promotions managers may travel to meet with clients or representatives of communications media. At times, public relations managers travel to meet with special-interest groups or government officials. Job transfers between headquarters and regional offices are common, particularly among sales managers.

Long hours, including evenings and weekends, are common. In 2008, more than 80 percent of advertising, marketing, promotions, public relations, and sales managers worked 40 hours or more a week.

Training, Other Qualifications, and Advancement

A wide range of educational backgrounds is suitable for entry into advertising, marketing, promotions, public relations, and sales manager jobs, but many employers prefer college graduates with experience in related occupations.

Education and training. For marketing, sales, and promotions management positions, employers often prefer a bachelor's or master's degree in business administration with an emphasis on marketing. Courses in business law, management, economics, accounting, finance, mathematics, and statistics are advantageous. In addition, the completion of an internship while the candidate is in school is highly recommended. In highly technical industries, such as computer and electronics manufacturing, a bachelor's degree in engineering or science, combined with a master's degree in business administration, is preferred.

For advertising management positions, some employers prefer a bachelor's degree in advertising or journalism. A relevant course of study might include classes in marketing, consumer behavior, market research, sales, communication methods and technology, visual arts, art history, and photography.

For public relations management positions, some employers prefer a bachelor's or master's degree in public relations or journalism. The applicant's curriculum should include courses in advertising, business administration, public affairs, public speaking, political science, and creative and technical writing.

Most advertising, marketing, promotions, public relations, and sales management positions are filled through promotions of experienced staff or related professional personnel. For example, many managers are former sales representatives; purchasing agents; buyers; or product, advertising, promotions, or public relations specialists. In small firms, in which the number of positions is limited, advancement to a management position usually comes slowly. In large firms, promotion may occur more quickly.

Other qualifications. Computer skills are necessary for recordkeeping and data management, and the ability to work in an Internet environment is becoming increasingly vital as more marketing, product promotion, and advertising is done through the Internet. Also, the ability to communicate in a foreign language may open up employment opportunities in many rapidly growing areas around the country, especially cities with large Spanish-speaking populations.

Persons interested in becoming advertising, marketing, promotions, public relations, and sales managers should be mature, creative, highly motivated, resistant to stress, flexible, and decisive. The ability to communicate persuasively, both orally and in writing, with other managers, staff, and the public is vital. These managers also need tact, good judgment, and exceptional ability to establish and maintain effective personal relationships with supervisory and professional staff members and client firms.

Certification and advancement. Some associations offer certification programs for these managers. Certification—an indication of competence and achievement—is particularly important in a competitive job market. Although relatively few advertising, marketing, promotions, public relations, and sales managers currently are certified, the number of managers who seek certification is expected to grow. Today, there are numerous management certification programs based on education and job performance. In addition, the Public Relations Society of America offers a certification program

for public relations practitioners that is based on years of experience and performance on an examination.

Although experience, ability, and leadership are emphasized for promotion, advancement can be accelerated by participation in management training programs conducted by larger firms. Many firms also provide their employees with continuing education opportunities— either in-house or at local colleges and universities—and encourage employee participation in seminars and conferences, often held by professional societies. In collaboration with colleges and universities, numerous marketing and related associations sponsor national or local management training programs. Course subjects include brand and product management; international marketing; sales management evaluation; telemarketing and direct sales; interactive marketing; product promotion; marketing communication; market research; organizational communication; and data-processing systems, procedures, and management. Many firms pay all or part of the cost for employees who complete courses.

Because of the importance and high visibility of their jobs, advertising, marketing, promotions, public relations, and sales managers often are prime candidates for advancement to the highest ranks. Well-trained, experienced, and successful managers may be promoted to higher positions in their own or another firm; some become top executives. Managers with extensive experience and sufficient capital may open their own businesses.

Employment

Advertising, marketing, promotions, public relations, and sales managers held about 623,800 jobs in 2008. The following tabulation shows the distribution of jobs by occupational specialty:

Sales managers	346,900
Marketing managers	175,600
Public relations managers	56,700
Advertising and promotions managers	44,600

These managers were found in virtually every industry. Sales managers held about 56 percent of the jobs; about 62 percent of sales managers were employed in the wholesale trade, retail trade, manufacturing, and finance and insurance industries. Marketing managers held approximately 28 percent of the jobs; the professional, scientific, and technical services and finance and insurance industries employed around 32 percent of marketing managers. About 27 percent of advertising and promotions managers worked in the professional, scientific, and technical services industries and wholesale trade. Around 48 percent of public relations managers were employed in service-providing industries, such as professional, scientific, and technical services; public and private educational services; finance and insurance; and health care and social assistance.

Job Outlook

Employment is projected to grow about as fast as average. As with most managerial jobs, keen competition is expected for these highly coveted positions.

Employment change. Overall employment of advertising, marketing, promotions, public relations, and sales managers is expected to increase by 13 percent through 2018. Job growth will be spurred by competition for a growing number of goods and services, both

Projections Data from the National Employment Matrix

Occupational title	SOC Code	Employment, 2008	Projected employment, 2018	Change, 2008–2018	
				Number	Percent
Advertising, marketing, promotions, public relations, and sales managers	11-2000	623,800	704,100	80,300	13
Advertising and promotions managers	11-2011	44,600	43,900	–800	–2
Marketing and sales managers	11-2020	522,400	596,200	73,700	14
Marketing managers	11-2021	175,600	197,500	21,900	12
Sales managers	11-2022	346,900	398,700	51,800	15
Public relations managers	11-2031	56,700	64,100	7,300	13

NOTE: Data in this table are rounded.

foreign and domestic, and the need to make one's product or service stand out in the crowd. In addition, as the influence of traditional advertising in newspapers, radio, and network television wanes, marketing professionals are being asked to develop new and different ways to advertise and promote products and services to better reach potential customers.

Sales and marketing managers and their departments constitute some of the most important personnel in an organization and are less subject to downsizing or outsourcing than are other types of managers, except in the case of companies that are consolidating. Employment of these managers, therefore, will vary primarily on the basis of the growth or contraction in the industries that employ them. For example, if, as is expected, the number of automobile dealers declines over the next decade, these major employers of sales managers will need fewer of them. Employment of marketing managers will grow about as fast as average at 12 percent between 2008 and 2018, and that of sales managers will grow faster than average at 15 percent over the same period.

Advertising and promotions managers are expected to experience little or no change in employment from 2008 to 2018. Despite large declines in the number of advertising managers in recent years, due mainly to the sharp reduction in the number of advertising agencies and newspaper and periodical publishers, which employ the greatest numbers of these managers, advertising and promotions managers are not expected to experience similar declines in the future. Because advertising is the primary source of revenue for most media, advertising departments are less affected in a downturn. An expected increase in the number of television and radio stations and a sharp increase in the amount of advertising in digital media, such as the Internet and wireless devices, will generate a need for advertising managers to oversee new and innovative advertising programs. A number of these advertising managers will be self-employed.

Public relations managers are expected to see an increase in employment of 13 percent between 2008 and 2018, which is about as fast as average for all occupations, as organizations increasingly emphasize community outreach and customer relations as a way to enhance their reputation and visibility. Especially among the growing number of nonprofit organizations, such as education services, business and professional associations, and hospitals, where many of these workers are employed, public relations managers will be charged with promoting the mission of the organization and encouraging membership or use of the organization's services.

Job prospects. Most job openings for this occupation will be due to the need to replace workers who leave the occupation or retire. However, advertising, marketing, promotions, public relations, and sales manager jobs are highly coveted and are often sought by other managers or highly experienced professionals, resulting in keen competition. College graduates with related experience, a high level of creativity, and strong communication and computer skills should have the best job opportunities. In particular, employers will seek those who have the skills to conduct new types of advertising, marketing, promotions, public relations, and sales campaigns involving new media, particularly the Internet.

Earnings

Median annual wages in May 2008 were $80,220 for advertising and promotions managers, $108,580 for marketing managers, $97,260 for sales managers, and $89,430 for public relations managers.

Median annual wages of advertising and promotions managers in May 2008 in the advertising, public relations, and related services industry were $105,960.

Median annual wages in the industries employing the largest numbers of marketing managers were as follows:

Computer systems design and related services $127,870
Management of companies and enterprises 115,650
Management, scientific, and technical
    consulting services 111,130
Insurance carriers 103,210
Depository credit intermediation 98,510

Median annual wages in the industries employing the largest numbers of sales managers were as follows:

Professional and commercial equipment and
    supplies merchant wholesalers $125,130
Wholesale, electronic markets, and agents
    and brokers 114,670
Automobile dealers 107,500
Management of companies and enterprises 106,980
Department stores 54,560

Wages vary substantially, depending upon the employee's level of managerial responsibility, length of service, and education; the size and location of the firm; and the industry in which the firm operates. For example, manufacturing firms usually pay these managers higher salaries than nonmanufacturing firms. For sales managers, the size of their sales territory is another important determinant of salary. Many managers earn bonuses equal to 10 percent or more of their salaries.

According to a survey by the National Association of Colleges and Employers, starting salaries for marketing majors graduating in 2009 averaged $43,325.

Related Occupations

Advertising, marketing, promotions, public relations, and sales managers direct the sale of products and services offered by their firms and communicate information about their firm's activities. Other workers involved with advertising, marketing, promotions, public relations, and sales include actors, producers, and directors; advertising sales agents; artists and related workers; authors, writers, and editors; demonstrators and product promoters; market and survey researchers; models; public relations specialists; and sales representatives, wholesale and manufacturing.

Sources of Additional Information

For information about careers in advertising management, contact

▸ American Association of Advertising Agencies, 405 Lexington Ave., 18th Floor, New York, NY 10174-1801. Internet: www.aaaa.org

Information about careers and professional certification in public relations management is available from

▸ Public Relations Society of America, 33 Maiden Ln., 11th Floor, New York, NY 10038-5150. Internet: www.prsa.org

Animal Care and Service Workers

(O*NET 39-2011.00 and 39-2021.00)

Significant Points

■ Animal lovers get satisfaction in this occupation, but the work can be unpleasant, physically and emotionally demanding, and sometimes dangerous.

■ Most workers are trained on the job, but employers generally prefer to hire people who have experience with animals; some jobs require formal education.

■ Most positions will present excellent employment opportunities; however, keen competition is expected for jobs as zookeepers and marine mammal trainers.

■ Earnings are relatively low.

Nature of the Work

Many people like animals. But, as pet owners will admit, taking care of them is hard work. *Animal care and service workers*—who include *animal caretakers* and *animal trainers*—train, feed, water, groom, bathe, and exercise animals and clean, disinfect, and repair their cages. They also play with the animals, provide companionship, and observe behavioral changes that could indicate illness or injury. Boarding kennels, pet stores, animal shelters, rescue leagues, veterinary hospitals and clinics, stables, laboratories, aquariums and natural aquatic habitats, and zoological parks all house animals and employ animal care and service workers. Job titles and duties vary by employment setting.

Kennel attendants care for pets while their owners are working or traveling out of town. Beginning attendants perform basic tasks, such as cleaning both the cages and the dog runs, filling food and water dishes, and exercising animals. Experienced attendants may provide basic animal health-care, as well as bathe animals, trim nails, and attend to other grooming needs. Attendants who work in kennels also may sell pet food and supplies, assist in obedience training, or prepare animals for shipping.

Groomers are animal caretakers who specialize in maintaining a pet's appearance. Most groom dogs and a few groom cats. Some groomers work in kennels, veterinary clinics, animal shelters, or pet supply stores. Others operate their own grooming business, typically at a salon or, increasingly, by making house calls. Such mobile services are growing rapidly because they offer convenience for pet owners, flexibility of schedules for groomers, and minimal trauma for pets resulting from their being in unfamiliar surroundings. Groomers clean and sanitize equipment to prevent the spread of disease, as well as maintaining a clean and safe environment for the animals. Groomers also schedule appointments, discuss pets' grooming needs with clients, and collect general information on the pets' health and behavior. Groomers sometimes are the first to notice a medical problem, such as an ear or skin infection, that requires veterinary care.

Grooming the pet involves several steps: an initial brush-out is followed by a clipping of hair with combs and grooming shears; the groomer then cuts the animal's nails, cleans the ears, bathes and blow-dries the animal, and ends with a final trim and styling.

Animal caretakers in animal shelters work mainly with cats and dogs and perform a variety of duties typically determined by the worker's experience. In addition to attending to the basic needs of the animals, caretakers at shelters keep records of the animals, including information about any tests or treatments performed on them. Experienced caretakers may vaccinate newly admitted animals under the direction of a veterinarian or veterinary technician and euthanize (painlessly put to death) seriously ill, severely injured, or unwanted animals. Animal caretakers in animal shelters also interact with the public, answering telephone inquiries, screening applicants who wish to adopt an animal, or educating visitors on neutering and other animal health issues.

Pet sitters look after one or more animals when their owner is away. They do this by traveling to the pet owner's home to carry out the daily routine. Most pet sitters feed, walk, and play with the animal, but some more experienced sitters also may be required to bathe, train, or groom them. Most watch over dogs and a few take care of cats. By not removing the pet from its normal surroundings, trauma is reduced and the animal can maintain its normal diet and exercise regimen.

Grooms, or caretakers, care for horses in stables. They saddle and unsaddle horses, give them rubdowns, and walk them to cool them off after a ride. They also feed, groom, and exercise the horses; clean out stalls and replenish bedding; polish saddles; clean and organize the tack (harness, saddle, and bridle) room; and store supplies and feed. Experienced grooms may help train horses.

In zoos, animal care and service workers, called *keepers*, prepare the diets and clean the enclosures of animals and sometimes assist in raising them when they are very young. They watch for any signs of illness or injury, monitor eating patterns or any changes in behavior and record their observations. Keepers also may answer questions and ensure that the visiting public behaves responsibly toward the exhibited animals. Depending on the zoo, keepers may be assigned to work with a broad group of animals, such as mammals, birds, or reptiles, or they may work with a limited collection of animals such as primates, large cats, or small mammals.

Animal trainers train animals for riding, security, performance, obedience, or assisting people with disabilities. Animal trainers do this by accustoming the animal to the human voice and human contact and teaching the animal to respond to commands. The three most commonly trained animals are dogs, horses, and marine mammals, including dolphins and sea lions. Trainers use several techniques to help them train animals. One technique, known as a bridge, is a stimulus that a trainer uses to communicate the precise moment an animal does something correctly. When the animal responds correctly, the trainer gives positive reinforcement in a variety of ways: offering food, toys, play, and rubdowns or speaking the word "good." Animal training takes place in small steps and often takes months and even years of repetition. During the teaching process, trainers provide animals with mental stimulation, physical exercise, and husbandry. A relatively new form of training teaches animals to cooperate with workers giving medical care: animals learn "veterinary" behaviors, such as allowing for the collection of blood samples; physical, X-ray, ultrasonic, and dental exams; physical therapy; and the administration of medicines and replacement fluids.

Training also can be a good tool for facilitating the relocation of animals from one habitat to another, easing, for example, the process of loading horses onto trailers. Trainers often work in competitions or shows, such as circuses, marine parks, and aquariums; many others work in animal shelters, dog kennels and salons, or horse farms. Trainers in shows work to display the talent and ability of an animal, such as a dolphin, through interactive programs to educate and entertain the public.

In addition to their hands-on work with the animals, trainers often oversee other aspects of animals' care, such as preparing their diet and providing a safe and clean environment and habitat.

Work environment. People who love animals get satisfaction from working with and helping them. However, some of the work may be unpleasant, physically or emotionally demanding, and, sometimes, dangerous. Data from the U.S. Bureau of Labor Statistics show that full-time animal care and service workers experienced a work-related injury and illness rate that was higher than the national average. Most animal care and service workers have to clean animal cages and lift, hold, or restrain animals, risking exposure to bites or scratches. Their work often involves kneeling, crawling, repeated bending, and, occasionally, lifting heavy supplies such as bales of hay or bags of feed. Animal caretakers must take precautions when treating animals with germicides or insecticides. They may work outdoors in all kinds of weather, and the work setting can be noisy. Caretakers of show and sports animals travel to competitions.

Animal care and service workers who witness abused animals or who assist in euthanizing unwanted, aged, or hopelessly injured animals may experience emotional distress. Those working for private humane societies and municipal animal shelters often deal with the public, some of whom may be hostile. Such workers must maintain a calm and professional demeanor while helping to enforce the laws regarding animal care.

Animal care and service workers often work irregular hours. Most animals are fed every day, so caretakers often work weekend and holiday shifts. In some animal hospitals, research facilities, and animal shelters, an attendant is on duty 24 hours a day, which means night shifts.

Training, Other Qualifications, and Advancement

On-the-job training is the most common way animal care and service workers learn their work; however, employers generally prefer to hire people who have experience with animals. Some jobs require formal education.

Education and training. Animal trainers often need a high school diploma or GED equivalent. Some animal training jobs may require a bachelor's degree and additional skills. For example, marine mammal trainers usually need a bachelor's degree in biology, marine biology, animal science, psychology, or a related field. An animal health technician degree also may qualify trainers for some jobs.

Most equine trainers learn their trade by working as a groom at a stable. Some study at an accredited private training school.

Many dog trainers attend workshops and courses at community colleges and vocational schools. Topics include basic study of canines, learning theory of animals, teaching obedience cues, problem solving methods, and safety. Many such schools also offer business training.

Pet sitters are not required to have any specific training, but knowledge of and some form of previous experience with animals often are recommended.

Many zoos require their caretakers to have a bachelor's degree in biology, animal science, or a related field. Most require experience with animals, preferably as a volunteer or paid keeper in a zoo.

Pet groomers typically learn their trade by completing an informal apprenticeship, usually lasting 6 to 10 weeks, under the guidance of an experienced groomer. Prospective groomers also may attend one of the 50 state-licensed grooming schools throughout the country, with programs varying in length from 2 to 18 weeks. Beginning groomers often start by taking on one duty, such as bathing and drying the pet. They eventually assume responsibility for the entire grooming process, from the initial brush-out to the final clipping.

Animal caretakers in animal shelters are not required to have any specialized training, but training programs and workshops are available through the Humane Society of the United States, the American Humane Association, and the National Animal Control Association. Workshop topics include investigations of cruelty, appropriate methods of euthanasia for shelter animals, proper guidelines for capturing animals, techniques for preventing problems with wildlife, and dealing with the public.

Beginning animal caretakers in kennels learn on the job and usually start by cleaning cages and feeding animals.

Certification and other qualifications. Certifications are available in many animal service occupations. For dog trainers, certification by a professional association or one of the hundreds of private vocational or state-approved trade schools can be advantageous. The National Dog Groomers Association of America offers certification for master status as a groomer. To earn certification, applicants must demonstrate their practical skills and pass two exams. The National Association of Professional Pet Sitters offers a two-stage, home-study certification program for those who wish to become pet care professionals. Topics include business management, animal care, and animal health issues, and applicants must pass a written exam to earn certification. The Pet Care Services Association offers a three-stage, home-study program for individuals interested in pet care. Levels I and II focus on basic principles of animal care and customer service, while Level III spotlights management and professional aspects of the pet care business. Those who complete the third stage and pass oral and written examinations become Certified Kennel Operators (CKO).

All animal care and service workers need patience, sensitivity, and problem-solving ability. Those who work in shelters also need tact and communication skills, because they often deal with individuals who abandon their pets. The ability to handle emotional people is vital for workers at shelters.

Animal trainers especially need problem-solving skills and experience in animal obedience. Successful marine mammal trainers also should have good-public speaking skills, because presentations are a large part of the job. Usually four to five trainers work with a group of animals at one time; therefore, trainers should be able to work as part of a team. Marine mammal trainers must also be good swimmers; certification in SCUBA is a plus.

Most horse-training jobs have minimum weight requirements for candidates.

Advancement. With experience and additional training, caretakers in animal shelters may become adoption coordinators, animal control officers, emergency rescue drivers, assistant shelter managers, or shelter directors. Pet groomers who work in large retail establishments or kennels may, with experience, move into supervisory or managerial positions. Experienced groomers often choose to open their own salons or mobile grooming business. Advancement for kennel caretakers takes the form of promotion to kennel supervisor, assistant manager, and manager; those with enough capital and experience may open up their own kennels. Zookeepers may advance to senior keeper, assistant head keeper, head keeper, and assistant curator, but very few openings occur, especially for the higher level positions.

Employment

Animal care and service workers held 220,400 jobs in 2008. Nearly 4 out of 5 worked as nonfarm animal caretakers; the remainder worked as animal trainers. Nonfarm animal caretakers often worked in boarding kennels, animal shelters, rescue leagues, stables, grooming shops, pet stores, animal hospitals, and veterinary offices. A significant number of caretakers worked for animal humane societies, racing stables, dog and horse racetrack operators, zoos, theme parks, circuses, and other amusement and recreation services.

Employment of animal trainers is concentrated in animal services that specialize in training and in commercial sports, where racehorses and dogs are trained. About 54 percent of animal trainers were self-employed.

Job Outlook

Because many workers leave this occupation each year, there will be excellent job opportunities for most positions. Much-faster-than-average employment growth also will add to job openings. However, keen competition is expected for jobs as zookeepers and marine mammal trainers.

Employment change. Employment of animal care and service workers is expected to grow 21 percent over the 2008–2018 decade, much faster than the average for all occupations. The companion pet population, which drives employment of animal caretakers in kennels, grooming shops, animal shelters, and veterinary clinics and hospitals, is anticipated to increase. Pet owners—including a large number of baby boomers, whose disposable income is expected to increase as they age—are expected to increasingly purchase grooming services, daily and overnight boarding services, training services, and veterinary services, resulting in more jobs for animal care and service workers. As more pet owners consider their pets part of the family, demand for luxury animal services and the willingness to spend greater amounts of money on pets should continue to grow. Demand for marine mammal trainers, on the other hand, should grow slowly.

Demand for animal care and service workers in animal shelters is expected to grow as communities increasingly recognize the connection between animal abuse and abuse toward humans and continue to commit private funds to animal shelters, many of which are working hand in hand with social service agencies and law enforcement teams.

Job prospects. Due to employment growth and the need to replace workers who leave the occupation, job opportunities for most positions should be excellent. The need to replace pet sitters, dog walkers, kennel attendants, and animal control and shelter workers leaving the field will create the overwhelming majority of job openings. Many animal caretaker jobs require little or no training and have flexible work schedules, making them suitable for people seeking a first job or for temporary or part-time work. Prospective groomers also will face excellent opportunities as the companion dog population is expected to grow and services such as mobile grooming continue to grow in popularity. The outlook for caretakers in zoos and aquariums, however, is not favorable, due to slow job growth and keen competition for the few positions.

Prospective mammal trainers also will face keen competition as the number of applicants greatly exceeds the number of available positions. Prospective horse trainers should anticipate an equally challenging labor market because the number of entry-level positions is limited. Dog trainers, however, should experience conditions that are more favorable, driven by their owners' desire to instill obedience in their pet. Opportunities for dog trainers should be best in large metropolitan areas.

Projections Data from the National Employment Matrix

Occupational title	SOC Code	Employment, 2008	Projected employment, 2018	Change, 2008–2018	
				Number	Percent
Animal care and service workers 39-2000		220,400	265,900	45,500	21
Animal trainers..39-2011		47,100	56,700	9,600	20
Nonfarm animal caretakers 39-2021		173,300	209,100	35,900	21

NOTE: Data in this table are rounded.

Job opportunities for animal care and service workers may vary from year to year because the strength of the economy affects demand for these workers. Pet owners tend to spend more on animal services when the economy is strong.

Earnings

Wages are relatively low. Median annual wages of nonfarm animal caretakers were $19,360 in May 2008. The middle 50 percent earned between $16,720 and $24,300. The bottom 10 percent earned less than $15,140, and the top 10 percent earned more than $31,590. Median annual wages in the industries employing the largest numbers of nonfarm animal caretakers in May 2008 were as follows:

Spectator sports...$20,520
Other personal services 19,530
Social advocacy organizations 18,640
Veterinary services... 18,380
Other miscellaneous store retailers....................... 18,320

Median annual wages of animal trainers were $27,270 in May 2008. The middle 50 percent earned between $19,880 and $38,280. The lowest 10 percent earned less than $16,700, and the top 10 percent earned more than $51,400.

Related Occupations

Others who work extensively with animals include agricultural workers, other; animal control workers; biological scientists; farmers, ranchers, and agricultural managers; veterinarians; veterinary assistants and laboratory animal caretakers; and veterinary technologists and technicians.

Sources of Additional Information

For career information and information on training, certification, and earnings of a related occupation—animal control officers—contact

▸ National Animal Control Association, P.O. Box 480851, Kansas City, MO 64148-0851. Internet: www.nacanet.org

For information on becoming an advanced pet care technician at a kennel, contact

▸ Pet Care Services Association, 2760 N. Academy Blvd., Suite 120, Colorado Springs, CO 80917. Internet: www.petcareservices.org

For general information on pet grooming careers, including workshops and certification information, contact

▸ National Dog Groomers Association of America, P.O. Box 101, Clark, PA 16113. Internet: www.nationaldoggroomers.com

For information on pet sitting, including certification information, contact

▸ National Association of Professional Pet Sitters, 15000 Commerce Parkway, Suite C, Mount Laurel, NJ 08054. Internet: www.petsitters.org

Athletes, Coaches, Umpires, and Related Workers

(O*NET 27-2021.00, 27-2022.00, and 27-2023.00)

Significant Points

■ These jobs require immense overall knowledge of the game, usually acquired through years of experience at lower levels.

■ Career-ending injuries are always a risk for athletes.

■ Job opportunities will be best for part-time coaches, sports instructors, umpires, referees, and sports officials in high schools, sports clubs, and other settings.

■ Aspiring professional athletes will continue to face extremely keen competition.

Nature of the Work

Few people who dream of becoming paid professional *athletes*, *coaches*, or *sports officials* beat the odds and make a full-time living from professional athletics. Professional athletes often have short careers with little job security. Even though the chances of employment as a professional athlete are slim, there are many opportunities for at least a part-time job as a coach, instructor, referee, or umpire in amateur athletics or in high school, college, or university sports.

Athletes and *sports competitors* compete in organized, officiated sports events to entertain spectators. When playing a game, athletes are required to understand the strategies of their game while obeying the rules and regulations of the sport. The events in which they compete include both team sports, such as baseball, basketball, football, hockey, and soccer, and individual sports, such as golf, tennis, and bowling. The level of play varies from unpaid high school athletics to professional sports, in which the best from around the world compete in events broadcast on international television.

Being an athlete involves more than competing in athletic events. Athletes spend many hours each day practicing skills and improving teamwork under the guidance of a coach or a sports instructor. They view videotapes to critique their own performances and techniques and to learn their opponents' tendencies and weaknesses to gain a competitive advantage. Some athletes work regularly with strength trainers to gain muscle and stamina and to prevent injury. Many athletes push their bodies to the limit during both practice and play, so career-ending injury always is a risk; even minor injuries may put a player at risk of replacement. Because competition at all levels is extremely intense and job security is always precarious, many athletes train year round to maintain excellent form and technique and peak physical condition. Very little downtime from the sport exists at the professional level. Some athletes must conform to regimented diets to supplement any physical training program.

Coaches organize amateur and professional athletes and teach them the fundamental skills of individual and team sports. (In individual sports, *instructors* sometimes may fill this role.) Coaches train athletes for competition by holding practice sessions to perform drills that improve the athletes' form, technique, skills, and stamina. Along with refining athletes' individual skills, coaches are responsible for instilling good sportsmanship, a competitive spirit, and teamwork and for managing their teams during both practice sessions and competitions. Before competition, coaches evaluate or scout the opposing team to determine game strategies and practice specific plays. During competition, coaches may call specific plays intended to surprise or overpower the opponent, and they may substitute players for optimum team chemistry and success. Coaches' additional tasks may include selecting, storing, issuing, and taking inventory of equipment, materials, and supplies.

Many coaches in high schools are primarily teachers of academic subjects who supplement their income by coaching part time. (For more information on high school teachers, see the description of teachers—kindergarten, elementary, middle, and secondary.) College coaches consider coaching a full-time discipline and may be away from home frequently as they travel to competitions and to scout and recruit prospective players.

Sports instructors teach professional and nonprofessional athletes individually. They organize, instruct, train, and lead athletes in indoor and outdoor sports such as bowling, tennis, golf, and swimming. Because activities are as diverse as weight lifting, gymnastics, scuba diving, and karate, instructors tend to specialize in one or a few activities. Like coaches, sports instructors also may hold daily practice sessions and be responsible for any needed equipment and supplies. Using their knowledge of their sport and of physiology, they determine the type and level of difficulty of exercises, prescribe specific drills, and correct athletes' techniques. Some instructors also teach and demonstrate the use of training apparatus, such as trampolines or weights, for correcting athletes' weaknesses and enhancing their conditioning. Like coaches, sports instructors evaluate the athlete and the athlete's opponents to devise a competitive game strategy.

Coaches and sports instructors sometimes differ in their approaches to athletes because of the focus of their work. For example, while coaches manage the team during a game to optimize its chance for victory, sports instructors—such as those who work for professional tennis players—often are not permitted to instruct their athletes during competition. Sports instructors spend more of their time with athletes working one-on-one, which permits them to design customized training programs for each individual. Motivating athletes to play hard challenges most coaches and sports instructors but is vital for the athlete's success. Many coaches and instructors derive great satisfaction working with children or young adults, helping them to learn new physical and social skills, improve their physical condition, and achieve success in their sport.

Umpires, referees, and *other sports officials* officiate at competitive athletic and sporting events. They observe the play and impose penalties for infractions as established by the rules and regulations of the various sports. Umpires, referees, and sports officials anticipate play and position themselves to best see the action, assess the situation, and determine any violations. Some sports officials, such as boxing referees, may work independently, while others such as umpires work in groups. Regardless of the sport, the job is highly stressful because officials are often required to make a decision in a split second, sometimes resulting in strong disagreement among competitors, coaches, and spectators.

Professional *scouts* evaluate the skills of both amateur and professional athletes to determine talent and potential. As a sports intelligence agent, the scout's primary duty is to seek out top athletic candidates for the team he or she represents. At the professional level, scouts typically work for scouting organizations or as freelance scouts. In locating new talent, scouts perform their work in secrecy so as not to "tip off" their opponents about their interest in certain players. At the college level, the head scout often is an assistant coach, although freelance scouts may aid colleges by reporting to coaches about exceptional players. Scouts at this level seek talented high school athletes by reading newspapers, contacting high school coaches and alumni, attending high school games, and studying videotapes of prospects' performances. They also evaluate potential players' background and personal characteristics, such as motivation and discipline, by talking to the players' coaches, parents, and teachers.

Work environment. Irregular work hours are common for athletes, coaches, umpires, referees, and other sports officials. They often work Saturdays, Sundays, evenings, and holidays. Athletes and full-time coaches usually work more than 40 hours a week for several months during the sports season, if not most of the year. High school coaches in educational institutions often coach more than one sport.

Athletes, coaches, and sports officials who participate in competitions that are held outdoors may be exposed to all weather conditions of the season. Athletes, coaches, and some sports officials frequently travel to sporting events. Scouts also travel extensively in locating talent. Athletes, coaches, and sports officials regularly encounter verbal abuse. Officials also face possible physical assault and, increasingly, lawsuits from injured athletes based on their officiating decisions.

Athletes and sports competitors had one of the highest rates of nonfatal on-the-job injuries. Coaches and sports officials also face the risk of injury, but the risk is not as great as that faced by athletes and sports competitors.

Training, Other Qualifications, and Advancement

Education and training requirements for athletes, coaches, umpires, and related workers vary greatly by the level and type of sport. Regardless of the sport or occupation, these jobs require immense overall knowledge of the game, usually acquired through years of experience at lower levels.

Education and training. Most athletes, coaches, umpires, and related workers get their training from having played in the sport at some level. All of these sports-related workers need to have an extensive knowledge of the way the sport is played, its rules and regulations, and strategies, which is often acquired by playing the sport in school or recreation center, but also with the help of instructors or coaches, or in a camp that teaches the fundamentals of the sport.

Athletes get their training in several ways. For most team sports, athletes gain experience by competing in high school and collegiate athletics or on club teams. Although a high school or college degree may not be required to enter the sport, most athletes who get their training this way are often required to maintain specific academic standards to remain eligible to play, which often results in earning a degree. Other athletes, in gymnastics or tennis for example, learn their sport by taking private or group lessons.

Although there may not be a specific education requirement, head coaches at public secondary schools and sports instructors at all levels usually must have a bachelor's degree. For high school coaching and sports instructor jobs, schools usually prefer, and may have to hire teachers willing to take on these part time jobs. If no suitable teacher is found, schools hire someone from outside. College coaches also usually are required to have a bachelor's degree. Degree programs specifically related to coaching include exercise and sports science, physiology, kinesiology, nutrition and fitness, physical education, and sports medicine. Some entry-level positions for coaches or instructors require only experience derived as a participant in the sport or activity.

Each sport has specific requirements for umpires, referees, and other sports officials; some require these officials to pass a test of their knowledge of the sport. Umpires, referees, and other sports officials often begin their careers and gain needed experience by volunteering for intramural, community, and recreational league competitions. They are often required to attend some form of training course or academy.

Scouting jobs often requires experience playing a sport at the college or professional level that makes it possible to spot young players who possess athletic ability and skills. Most beginning scouting jobs are as part-time talent spotters in a particular area or region.

Licensure and certification. The need for athletes, coaches, umpires, and related workers to be licensed or certified to practice varies by sport and by locality. For example, in drag racing, drivers need to graduate from approved schools in order to be licensed to compete in the various drag racing series. The governing body of the sport may revoke licenses and suspend players who do not meet the required performance, education, or training. In addition, athletes may have their licenses or certification suspended for inappropriate activity.

Most public high school coaches need to meet state requirements for certification to become a head coach. Certification, however, may not be required for coaching and sports instructor jobs in private schools. College coaches may be required to be certified. For those interested in becoming scuba, tennis, golf, karate, or other kind of instructor, certification is highly desirable and may be required. There are many certifying organizations specific to the various sports, and their requirements vary. Coaches' certification often requires that one must be at least 18 years old and certified

in cardiopulmonary resuscitation (CPR). Participation in a clinic, camp, or school also usually is required for certification. Part-time workers and those in smaller facilities are less likely to need formal education or training and may not need certification.

To officiate at high school athletic events, umpires, referees, and other officials must register with the state agency that oversees high school athletics and pass an exam on the rules of the particular game. For college refereeing, candidates must be certified by an officiating school and be evaluated during a probationary period. Some larger college sports conferences require officials to have certification and other qualifications, such as residence in or near the conference boundaries, along with several years of experience officiating at high school, community college, or other college conference games.

Other qualifications. Athletes, coaches, umpires, and related workers often direct teams or compete on them. Thus these workers must relate well to others and possess good communication and leadership skills. They may need to pass a background check and applicable drug tests. Athletes who seek to compete professionally must have extraordinary talent, desire, and dedication to training. Coaches must be resourceful and flexible to successfully instruct and motivate individuals and groups of athletes. Officials need good vision, reflexes, and the ability to make decisions quickly.

Advancement. For most athletes, turning professional is the biggest advancement. They often begin to compete immediately, although some may spend more time "on the bench", as a reserve, to gain experience. In some sports, such as baseball, athletes may begin their professional career on a minor league team before moving up to the major leagues. Professional athletes generally advance in their sport by winning and achieving accolades and earning a higher salary.

Many coaches begin their careers as assistant coaches to gain the knowledge and experience needed to become a head coach. Head coaches at large schools and colleges that strive to compete at the highest levels of a sport require substantial experience as a head coach at another school or as an assistant coach. To reach the ranks of professional coaching, a person usually needs years of coaching experience and a winning record in the lower ranks or experience as an athlete in that sport.

Standards for umpires and other officials become more stringent as the level of competition advances. A local or state academy may be required to referee a school baseball game. Those seeking to officiate at minor or major league games must attend a professional umpire training school. To advance to umpiring in Major League Baseball, umpires usually need 7 to 10 years of experience in various minor leagues before being considered for major league jobs.

Finding talented players is essential for scouts to advance. Hard work and a record of success often lead to full-time jobs and responsibility for scouting in more areas. Some scouts advance to scouting director jobs or various administrative positions in sports.

Employment

Athletes, coaches, umpires, and related workers held about 258,100 jobs in 2008. Coaches and scouts held 225,700 jobs; athletes and sports competitors, 16,500; and umpires, referees, and other sports officials, 15,900. About half of all athletes, coaches, umpires, and

Projections Data from the National Employment Matrix

Occupational title	SOC Code	Employment, 2008	Projected employment, 2018	Change, 2008–2018	
				Number	Percent
Athletes, coaches, umpires, and related workers 27-2020		258,100	317,700	59,600	23
Athletes and sports competitors 27-2021		16,500	18,400	1,900	12
Coaches and scouts 27-2022		225,700	281,700	56,000	25
Umpires, referees, and other sports officials 27-2023		15,900	17,600	1,700	10

related workers worked part time or maintained variable schedules. Many sports officials and coaches receive such small and irregular payments for their services—occasional officiating at club games, for example—that they may not consider themselves employed in these occupations, even part time.

Among those employed in wage and salary jobs, 52 percent held jobs in public and private educational services. About 13 percent worked in amusement, gambling, and recreation industries, including golf and tennis clubs, gymnasiums, health clubs, judo and karate schools, riding stables, swim clubs, and other sports and recreation facilities. Another 6 percent worked in the spectator sports industry.

About 16 percent of workers in this occupation were self-employed, earning prize money or fees for lessons, scouting, or officiating assignments. Many other coaches and sports officials, although technically not self-employed, have such irregular or tenuous working arrangements that their working conditions resemble those of self-employment.

Job Outlook

Employment of athletes, coaches, umpires, and related workers is expected to grow much faster than the average for all occupations through 2018. Very keen competition is expected for jobs at the highest levels of sports with progressively more favorable opportunities in lower levels of competition.

Employment change. Employment of athletes, coaches, umpires, and related workers is expected to increase by 23 percent from 2008 to 2018, which is much faster than the average for all occupations. A larger population overall that will continue to participate in organized sports for entertainment, recreation, and physical conditioning will boost demand for these workers, particularly for coaches, umpires, sports instructors, and other related workers. Job growth also will be driven by the increasing number of retirees who are expected to participate more in leisure activities such as golf and tennis, which require instruction. Additionally, the demand for private sports instruction is expected to grow among young athletes as parents try to help their children reach their full potential. Future expansion of new professional teams and leagues may create additional openings for all of these workers.

Additional coaches and instructors are expected to be needed as school and college athletic programs expand. Population growth is expected to cause the construction of additional schools, but funding for athletic programs often is cut first when budgets become tight. Still, the popularity of team sports often enables shortfalls to be offset with the assistance from fundraisers, booster clubs, and parents. In colleges, most of the expansion is expected to be in women's sports.

Job prospects. Persons who are state-certified to teach academic subjects are likely to have the best prospects for obtaining coaching and instructor jobs in schools. The need to replace the many high school coaches will provide most coaching opportunities.

Competition for professional athlete jobs will continue to be extremely keen. In major sports, such as basketball and football, only about 1 in 5,000 high school athletes becomes professional in these sports. The expansion of nontraditional sports may create some additional opportunities. Because most professional athletes' careers last only a few years due to debilitating injuries and age, annual replacement needs for these jobs is high, creating some job opportunities. However, the talented young men and women who dream of becoming sports superstars greatly outnumber the number of openings.

Opportunities should be best for persons seeking part-time umpire, referee, and other sports official jobs at the high school level. Coaches in girls' and women's sports may have better opportunities and face less competition for positions. Competition is expected for higher paying jobs at the college level and will be even greater for jobs in professional sports. Competition should be keen for paying jobs as scouts, particularly for professional teams, because the number of available positions is limited.

Earnings

Median annual wages of athletes and sports competitors were $40,480 in May 2008. The middle 50 percent earned between $21,760 and $93,710. The highest paid professional athletes earn much more.

Median annual wages of umpires and related workers were $23,730 in May 2008. The middle 50 percent earned between $17,410 and $33,150. The lowest-paid 10 percent earned less than $15,450, and the highest-paid 10 percent earned more than $48,310.

In May 2008, median annual wages of coaches and scouts were $28,340. The middle 50 percent earned between $18,220 and $43,440. The lowest-paid 10 percent earned less than $15,530, and the highest-paid 10 percent earned more than $62,660. However, the highest-paid professional coaches earn much more. Median annual wages in the industries employing the largest numbers of coaches and scouts in May 2008 are shown below:

Colleges, universities, and professional schools $39,550
Other amusement and recreation industries.......... 28,720
Other schools and instruction 25,740
Elementary and secondary schools 22,390

Wages vary by level of education, certification, and geographic region. Some instructors and coaches are paid a salary, while others may be paid by the hour, per session, or based on the number of participants.

Related Occupations

Other occupations involved with athletes or sports include dietitians and nutritionists; fitness workers; physical therapists; recreation workers; and recreational therapists.

Other workers who teach and motivate students include teachers—kindergarten, elementary, middle, and secondary.

Sources of Additional Information

For information about sports officiating for team and individual sports, contact

▸ National Association of Sports Officials, 2017 Lathrop Ave., Racine, WI 53405. Internet: www.naso.org

For additional information related to individual sports, refer to the organization that represents the sport.

Barbers, Cosmetologists, and Other Personal Appearance Workers

(O*NET 39-5011.00, 39-5012.00, 39-5092.00, 39-5093.00, and 39-5094.00)

Significant Points

■ Employment is expected to grow much faster than the average for all occupations.

■ A state license is required for barbers, cosmetologists, and most other personal appearance workers, although qualifications vary by state.

■ About 44 percent of workers are self-employed; many also work flexible schedules.

Nature of the Work

Barbers and *cosmetologists* focus on providing hair care services to enhance the appearance of customers. Other personal appearance workers, such as *manicurists and pedicurists*, *shampooers*, and *skin care specialists*, provide specialized beauty services that help clients look and feel their best.

Barbers cut, trim, shampoo, and style hair mostly for male clients. They also may fit hairpieces and offer scalp treatments and facial shaving. In many states, barbers are licensed to color, bleach, and highlight hair, and to offer permanent-wave services. Barbers also may provide skin care and nail treatments.

Hairdressers, hairstylists, and cosmetologists offer a wide range of beauty services, such as shampooing, cutting, coloring, and styling of hair. They may advise clients on how to care for their hair at home. In addition, cosmetologists may be trained to give manicures,

pedicures, and scalp and facial treatments; provide makeup analysis; and clean and style wigs and hairpieces.

A number of workers offer specialized services. Manicurists and pedicurists, called *nail technicians* in some states, work exclusively on nails and provide manicures, pedicures, polishing, and nail extensions to clients. Another group of specialists is skin care specialists, or *estheticians*, who cleanse and beautify the skin by giving facials, full-body treatments, and head and neck massages, as well as apply makeup. They also may remove hair through waxing or, if properly trained, with laser treatments. Finally, in larger salons, shampooers specialize in shampooing and conditioning hair.

In addition to working with clients, personal appearance workers may keep records of hair color or skin care regimens used by their regular clients. A growing number actively sell hair, skin, and nail care products. Barbers, cosmetologists, and other personal appearance workers who operate their own salons have managerial duties that may include hiring, supervising, and firing workers, as well as keeping business and inventory records, ordering supplies, and arranging for advertising.

Work environment. Many full-time barbers, cosmetologists, and other personal appearance workers put in a 40-hour week, but longer hours are common, especially among self-employed workers. Work schedules may include evenings and weekends, the times when beauty salons and barbershops are busiest. Many workers, especially those who are self-employed, determine their own schedules. In 2008, about 29 percent of barbers, hairstylists and cosmetologists worked part time, and 14 percent had variable schedules.

Barbers, cosmetologists, and other personal appearance workers usually work in clean, pleasant surroundings with good lighting and ventilation. Most work in a salon or barbershop, although some may work in a spa, hotel, or resort. Good health and stamina are important, because these workers are on their feet for most of their shift. Prolonged exposure to some hair and nail chemicals may cause irritation, so protective clothing, such as plastic gloves or aprons, may be worn.

Training, Other Qualifications, and Advancement

All states require barbers, cosmetologists, and other personal appearance workers to be licensed, with the exceptions of shampooers. To qualify for a license, most job seekers are required to graduate from a state-licensed barber or cosmetology school.

Education and training. A high school diploma or GED is required for some personal appearance workers in some states. In addition, most states require that barbers and cosmetologists complete a program in a state-licensed barber or cosmetology school. Programs in hairstyling, skin care, and other personal appearance services can be found in both high schools and in public or private postsecondary vocational schools.

Full-time programs in barbering and cosmetology usually last 9 months or more and may lead to an associate degree, but training for manicurists and pedicurists and skin care specialists requires significantly less time. Shampooers generally do not need formal training. Most professionals take advanced courses in hairstyling or other personal appearance services to keep up with the latest trends. They also may take courses in sales and marketing.

Licensure. All states require barbers, cosmetologists, and other personal appearance workers to be licensed, with the exception of shampooers. Qualifications for a license vary by state, but generally a person must have a high school diploma or GED, be at least 16 years old, and have graduated from a state-licensed barber or cosmetology school. After graduating from a state approved training program, students take a state licensing examination. The exam consists of a written test and, in some cases, a practical test of styling skills or an oral examination. In many states, cosmetology training may be credited toward a barbering license, and vice versa, and a few states combine the two licenses. Most states require separate licensing examinations for manicurists, pedicurists, and skin care specialists. A fee is usually required upon application for a license, and periodic license renewals may be necessary.

Some states have reciprocity agreements that allow licensed barbers and cosmetologists to obtain a license in another state without additional formal training, but such agreements are uncommon. Consequently, persons who wish to work in a particular state should review the laws of that state before entering a training program.

Other qualifications. Successful personal appearance workers should have an understanding of fashion, art, and technical design. They also must keep a neat personal appearance and a clean work area. Interpersonal skills, image, and attitude play an important role in career success. As client retention and retail sales become an increasingly important part of salons' revenue, the ability to be an effective salesperson becomes ever more vital for salon workers. Some cosmetology schools consider "people skills" to be such an integral part of the job that they require coursework in that area. Business skills are important for those who plan to operate their own salons.

Advancement. Advancement usually takes the form of higher earnings, as barbers and cosmetologists gain experience and build a steady clientele. Some barbers and cosmetologists manage salons, lease booth space in salons, or open their own salons after several years of experience. Others teach in barber or cosmetology schools or provide training through vocational schools. Still others advance to other related occupations, such as sales representatives for companies that sell salon-related products, image or fashion consultants, or examiners for state licensing boards.

Employment

Barbers, cosmetologists, and other personal appearance workers held about 821,900 jobs in 2008. Of these, barbers and cosmetologists held 684,200 jobs, manicurists and pedicurists 76,000, skin care specialists 38,800, and shampooers 22,900.

Most of these workers are employed in personal care services establishments, such as beauty salons, barber shops, nail salons, day and resort spas. Others were employed in nursing and other residential care homes. Nearly every town has a barbershop or beauty salon, but employment in this occupation is concentrated in the most populous cities and states.

About 44 percent of all barbers, cosmetologists, and other personal appearance workers are self-employed. Many of these workers own their own salon, but a growing number of the self-employed lease booth space or a chair from the salon's owner. In this case, workers provide their own supplies, and are responsible for paying their own taxes and benefits. They may pay a monthly or weekly fee to the salon owner, who is responsible for utilities and maintenance of the building.

Job Outlook

Overall employment of barbers, cosmetologists, and other personal appearance workers is projected to grow much faster than the average for all occupations. Opportunities for entry-level workers should be favorable, while job candidates at high-end establishments will face keen competition.

Employment change. Personal appearance workers will grow by 20 percent from 2008 to 2018, which is much faster than the average for all occupations.

Employment trends are expected to vary among the different occupational specialties. Employment of hairdressers, hairstylists, and cosmetologists will increase by about 20 percent, much faster than average, while the number of barbers will increase by 12 percent, about as fast as average. This growth will primarily come from an increasing population, which will lead to greater demand for basic hair services. Additionally, the demand for hair coloring and other advanced hair treatments has increased in recent years, particularly among baby boomers and young people. This trend is expected to continue, leading to a favorable outlook for hairdressers, hairstylists, and cosmetologists.

Continued growth in the number full-service spas and nail salons will also generate numerous job openings for manicurists, pedicurists, and skin care specialists. Estheticians and other skin care specialists will see large gains in employment, and are expected to grow almost 38 percent, much faster than average, primarily due to the popularity of skin treatments for relaxation and medical well-being. Manicurists and pedicurists meanwhile will grow by 19 percent, faster than average.

Job prospects. Job opportunities generally should be good, particularly for licensed personal appearance workers seeking entry-level positions. A large number of job openings will come about from the need to replace workers who transfer to other occupations, retire, or leave the labor force for other reasons. However, workers can expect keen competition for jobs and clients at higher paying salons, as these positions are relatively few and require applicants to compete with a large pool of licensed and experienced cosmetologists. Opportunities will generally be best for those with previous experience and for those licensed to provide a broad range of services.

Earnings

Median hourly wages in May 2008 for hairdressers, hairstylists, and cosmetologists, including tips and commission, were $11.13. The middle 50 percent earned between $8.57 and $15.03. The lowest 10 percent earned less than $7.47, and the highest 10 percent earned more than $20.41.

Median hourly wages in May 2008 for barbers, including tips, were $11.56. The middle 50 percent earned between $8.93 and $14.69. The lowest 10 percent earned less than $7.56, and the highest 10 percent earned more than $19.51.

Projections Data from the National Employment Matrix

Occupational title	SOC Code	Employment, 2008	Projected employment, 2018	Change, 2008–2018	
				Number	Percent
Barbers, cosmetologists, and other personal appearance workers	—	821,900	987,400	165,500	20
Barbers and cosmetologists	39-5010	684,200	817,400	133,200	19
Barbers	39-5011	53,500	59,700	6,200	12
Hairdressers, hairstylists, and cosmetologists	39-5012	630,700	757,700	127,000	20
Manicurists and pedicurists	39-5092	76,000	90,200	14,300	19
Shampooers	39-5093	22,900	26,300	3,400	15
Skin care specialists	39-5094	38,800	53,500	14,700	38

NOTE: Data in this table are rounded.

Among skin care specialists, median hourly wages, including tips, were $13.81, for manicurists and pedicurists $9.46, and for shampooers $8.32.

While earnings for entry-level workers usually are low, earnings can be considerably higher for those with experience. A number of factors, such as the size and location of the salon, determine the total income of personal appearance workers. They may receive commissions based on the price of the service, or a salary based on the number of hours worked, and many receive commissions on the products they sell. In addition, some salons pay bonuses to employees who bring in new business. For many personal appearance workers, the ability to attract and hold regular clients is a key factor in determining earnings.

Although some salons offer paid vacations and medical benefits, many self-employed and part-time workers in this occupation do not enjoy such benefits. Some personal appearance workers receive free trail products from manufacturers in the hope that they will recommend the products to clients.

Related Occupations

Fitness workers; makeup artists, theatrical and performance; and massage therapists.

Sources of Additional Information

For details on state licensing requirements and approved barber or cosmetology schools, contact your state boards of barber or cosmetology examiners.

State licensing board requirements and a list of licensed training schools for cosmetologists may be obtained from

▸ National Accrediting Commission of Cosmetology Arts and Sciences, 4401 Ford Ave., Suite 1300, Alexandria, VA 22302. Internet: www.naccas.org

Information about a career in cosmetology is available from

▸ National Cosmetology Association, 401 N. Michigan Ave., Chicago, IL 60611. Internet: www.ncacares.org

For information on a career as a barber, contact

▸ National Association of Barber Boards of America, 2703 Pine St., Arkadelphia, AR 71923. Internet: www.nationalbarberboards.com

Bill and Account Collectors

(O*NET 43-3011.00)

Significant Points

■ Employment of bill and account collectors is projected to grow by about 19 percent over the 2008–2018 decade, which is faster than average for all occupations.

■ Most jobs in this occupation require only a high school diploma, though many employers prefer workers with some customer service experience.

■ Job prospects should be favorable, especially for those with related work experience.

Nature of the Work

Bill and account collectors, often called *collectors*, attempt to collect payment on overdue bills. Some are employed by third-party collection agencies, while others—known as *in-house collectors*—work directly for the original creditors, such as mortgage and credit card companies, health-care providers, and utilities.

The duties of bill and account collectors are similar across the many different organizations in which they work. First, collectors are called upon to locate and notify consumers or businesses with delinquent accounts, usually over the telephone, but sometimes by letter. When debtors move without leaving a forwarding address, collectors may check with the post office, telephone companies, credit bureaus, or former neighbors to obtain the new address. This is called "skip tracing." Computer systems assist in tracing by automatically tracking when individuals or companies change their addresses or contact information on any of their open accounts.

Once collectors find debtors, they inform them of the overdue accounts and solicit payment. If necessary, they review terms of sale, or credit contracts. Good collectors use their listening skills to attempt to learn the cause of delinquencies. They generally have the authority to offer repayment plans or other assistance to make it easier for debtors to pay their bills. In many cases, they are able to find payment solutions that will allow the debtor to pay off their accounts. They may also offer simple advice or refer customers to debt counselors.

If a consumer agrees to pay, the collector records this commitment and checks later to verify that the payment was made. If a consumer fails to pay, the collector prepares a statement indicating the consumer's delinquency for the credit department of the establishment. In more extreme cases, collectors may initiate repossession proceedings, disconnect service, or hand the account over to an attorney for legal action. Most collectors handle other administrative functions for the accounts assigned to them, including recording changes of address and purging the records of the deceased.

Because people are very sensitive about their financial problems, collectors must be careful to follow applicable federal and state laws that govern their work. The Federal Trade Commission requires that a collector positively identify the delinquent account holder before announcing that the purpose of the call is to collect a debt. The collector must then issue a statement—often called a "mini-Miranda"—that lets the customer know that he or she is a collector. Collectors also face many state laws that govern how they must proceed in doing their work. Most companies use electronic systems to help collectors remember all laws and regulations governing each call.

Collectors use computers and a variety of automated systems in their jobs. Companies keep records of their accounts using computers, and collectors can keep track of previous collection attempts and other information in computerized notes. Using this information puts them at an advantage when trying to negotiate with consumers. As with most call center workers, they use headsets instead of regular telephones. Many also use automatic dialing, which allows collectors to make calls quickly and efficiently, without the chance of dialing incorrectly.

Work environment. In-house bill and account collectors typically are employed in an office environment, and those who work for third-party collection agencies may work in a call-center environment. Workers spend most of their time on the phone tracking down and contacting people with debts. The work can be stressful, as many consumers are confrontational when pressed about their debts. Successful collectors must face regular rejection and still be ready to make the next call in a polite and positive voice. Fortunately, some consumers appreciate assistance in resolving their outstanding debts, and can be quite grateful.

As in most jobs where workers spend most of their time on the phone, collectors usually have goals they are expected to meet. Typically these include calls per hour and success rate goals. Additionally, because most workers are offered incentives for collecting, they may rely on a certain level of success to meet their own budgetary needs.

Bill and account collectors sometimes must work evenings and weekends. While some collectors work part-time, the majority work 40 hours per week. Flexible work schedules are common.

Training, Other Qualifications, and Advancement

Most employers require collectors to have at a least a high school diploma and prefer applicants with postsecondary education or customer service experience. Employers provide on-the-job training to new employees.

Education and training. Most bill and account collectors are required to have at least a high school diploma. However, employers prefer workers who have completed some college or who have experience in other occupations that involve contact with the public. Previous experience working in a call center is especially helpful.

Once hired, workers receive on-the-job training. New employees learn company procedures under the guidance of a supervisor or other senior worker. Some formal classroom training may also be necessary, such as training in specific computer software. Additional training topics usually include telephone techniques and negotiation skills. Workers also learn the laws governing the collection of debt as mandated by the Fair Debt Collection Practices Act and various state laws.

Other qualifications. Workers should have good communication and people skills because they need to speak to consumers daily, some of whom may be in stressful financial situations. They should be comfortable talking on the telephone with people they have never met. They must be mature and able to handle rejection. Computer literacy and experience with advanced telecommunications equipment is also useful.

Advancement. As collectors gain experience, their success rates generally go up, leading them to earn more money in commissions. Successful collectors are usually given larger accounts with higher earning opportunities. Some become team leaders or supervisors. Workers who acquire additional skills, experience, and training improve their advancement opportunities.

Employment

Bill and account collectors held about 411,000 jobs in 2008. About one quarter of collectors worked in business support services. Another 19 percent worked in finance and insurance, and 18 percent worked for health-care and social assistance providers.

Job Outlook

Employment of bill and account collectors is expected to grow faster than the average for all occupations. Job prospects are expected to be favorable, especially for those with related work experience.

Employment change. Employment of bill and account collectors is projected to grow by about 19 percent over the 2008–2018 decade, which is faster than average for all occupations. New jobs should be created in key industries such as health-care and financial services, which often have delinquent accounts. In-house bill collectors will take on some of these collections, while others will be sold to third-party collection agencies. In both cases, bill and account collectors will be responsible for recovering these debts, causing the occupation to grow.

Job growth will be tempered somewhat by continued outsourcing of collections work to offshore call centers. In recent years, many companies have chosen to use these call centers for some of their debt recovery efforts. Nevertheless, creditors will continue to hire collectors in the United States, as domestic workers tend to have greater success in negotiating with clients.

The occupation should see large growth in the health-care industry. The rapid growth projected in this industry, in combination with increasing prices, should result in many collections opportunities.

Projections Data from the National Employment Matrix

Occupational title	SOC Code	Employment, 2008	Projected employment, 2018	Change, 2008–2018	
				Number	Percent
Bill and account collectors........................ 43-3011	43-3011	411,000	490,500	79,500	19

NOTE: Data in this table are rounded.

This will affect both collectors who work in the health-care industry itself and those who work for collections agencies that accept accounts from health-care providers.

Job prospects. Opportunities for job seekers who are looking for bill and account collector jobs should be favorable due to continued job growth and the need to replace workers who leave the occupation. Those who have experience in a related occupation should have the best prospects. Companies prefer to hire workers who have worked in a call center before, or in another job that requires regular phone-based negotiations.

Unlike most occupations, the number of collections jobs tends to remain stable and even grow during economic downturns. When the economy suffers, individuals and businesses struggle to meet their financial obligations. While this increases the number of debts that must be collected, it also means that fewer people are able to pay their outstanding debt. Companies decide how many collectors to hire based on expected success rates. As a result, the number of collectors does not necessarily increase proportionally to the number of delinquent accounts. Nevertheless, the number of collections jobs tends to remain stable during downturns, although prospective employees may face increased competition for these jobs.

Earnings

Median hourly wages of bill and account collectors were $14.73 in May 2008. The middle 50 percent earned between $12.14 and $18.12. The lowest 10 percent earned less than $10.17, and the highest 10 percent earned more than $22.07. Most bill and account collectors earn commissions based on the amount of debt they recover.

Related Occupations

Bill and account collectors review and collect information on accounts. Other occupations with similar responsibilities include credit authorizers, checkers, and clerks; interviewers, except eligibility and loan; and loan officers.

Collectors spend most of their time on the telephone, speaking with customers. Other jobs that require regular telephone interaction include customer service representatives; and sales representatives, wholesale and manufacturing.

Sources of Additional Information

Career information on bill and account collectors is available from

▸ ACA International, The Association of Credit and Collection Professionals, P.O. Box 390106, Minneapolis, MN 55439. Internet: www.acainternational.org

Billing and Posting Clerks and Machine Operators

(O*NET 43-3021.00, 43-3021.01, 43-3021.02, and 43-3021.03)

Nature of the Work

Billing and posting clerks and machine operators—commonly called *billing clerks*—calculate charges, develop bills, and prepare them to be mailed to customers.

Training, Other Qualifications, and Advancement

Many billing clerks are hired at entry level. They generally need at least a high school diploma and basic software skills.

Job Outlook

Current and Projected Employment

2008 Employment	528,800
2018 Employment	609,600
Employment Change	80,800
Growth Rate	15%

Employment change. Employment is expected to grow faster than average. Automated and electronic billing processes have streamlined billing departments, but job growth is expected due to an increasing number of transactions, especially in the rapidly growing health-care industry.

Job prospects. Prospects should be good. Many job openings will occur as workers transfer to other occupations or leave the labor force.

Earnings

Median annual wages for billing and posting clerks and machine operators were $30,950 in May 2008.

For current wage data, visit the Occupational Employment Statistics program's Occupational Profile for billing and posting clerks and machine operators.

Related Occupations

Bookkeeping, accounting, and auditing clerks; order clerks; and payroll and timekeeping clerks.

Sources of Additional Information

Information on employment opportunities for billing clerks is available from state job banks.

Biological Scientists

(O*NET 19-1021.00, 19-1022.00, 19-1023.00, 19-1029.00, 19-1029.01, 19-1029.02, and 19-1029.03)

Significant Points

- Biotechnological research and development should continue to drive much faster than average employment growth.
- A Ph.D. is usually required for independent research, but a bachelor's degree is sufficient for some jobs in applied research or product development; temporary postdoctoral research positions are common.
- Competition for independent research positions in academia is expected.

Nature of the Work

Biological scientists study living organisms and their relationship to the environment. They perform research to gain a better understanding of fundamental life processes and apply that understanding to developing new products or processes. Research can be broken down into two categories: basic and applied. Basic research is conducted without any intended aim; the goal is simply to expand on human knowledge. Applied research is directed towards solving a particular problem. Most biological scientists specialize in one area of biology, such as zoology (the study of animals) or microbiology (the study of microscopic organisms). (Medical scientists, whose work is closely related to that of biological scientists, are discussed elsewhere in this book.)

Basic research in biological sciences advances our knowledge of living organisms so that we can develop solutions to human health problems and improve the natural environment. These biological scientists mostly work in government, university, or private industry laboratories, often exploring new areas of research. Many expand on specialized research they started in graduate school.

Many biological scientists involved in basic research must submit grant proposals to obtain funding for their projects. Colleges and universities, private foundations, and federal government agencies, such as the National Institutes of Health and the National Science Foundation, contribute to the support of scientists whose research proposals are determined to be financially feasible and to have the potential to advance new ideas or processes.

Biological scientists who work in applied research or product development apply knowledge gained through basic research to develop new drugs, treatments, and medical diagnostic tests; increase crop yields; and develop new biofuels. They usually have less freedom than basic researchers do to choose the emphasis of their research, and they spend more time working on marketable treatments to meet the business goals of their employers. Biological scientists doing applied research and product development often work in teams, interacting with engineers, scientists of other disciplines, business

managers, and technicians. Those working in private industry may be required to describe their research plans or results to nonscientists who are in a position to veto or approve their ideas. These scientists must consider the business effects of their work. Some biological scientists also work with customers or suppliers and manage budgets.

Scientists usually conduct research in laboratories using a wide variety of other equipment. Some conduct experiments involving animals or plants. This is particularly true of botanists, physiologists, and zoologists. Some biological research also takes place outside the laboratory. For example, a botanist might do field research in tropical rain forests to see which plants grow there, or an ecologist might study how a forest area recovers after a fire. Some marine biologists also work outdoors, often on research vessels from which they study fish, plankton, or other marine organisms.

Swift advances in knowledge of genetics and organic molecules spurred growth in the field of biotechnology, transforming the industries in which biological scientists work. Biological scientists can now manipulate the genetic material of animals and plants, attempting to make organisms more productive or resistant to disease. Those working on various genome (chromosomes with their associated genes) projects isolate genes and determine their function. This work continues to lead to the discovery of genes associated with specific diseases and inherited health risks, such as sickle cell anemia. Advances in biotechnology have created research opportunities in almost all areas of biology, with commercial applications in areas such as medicine, agriculture, and environmental remediation.

Most biological scientists specialize in the study of a certain type of organism or in a specific activity, although recent advances have blurred some traditional classifications.

Aquatic biologists study micro-organisms, plants, and animals living in water. *Marine biologists* study salt water organisms, and *limnologists* study fresh water organisms. Much of the work of marine biology centers on molecular biology, the study of the biochemical processes that take place inside living cells. Marine biologists are sometimes called oceanographers, a broader field that also includes the study of the physical characteristics of oceans and the ocean floor.

Biochemists study the chemical composition of living things. They analyze the complex chemical combinations and reactions involved in metabolism, reproduction, and growth. Biochemists do most of their work in biotechnology, which involves understanding the complex chemistry of life.

Biophysicists study how physics, such as electrical and mechanical energy, relates to living cells and organisms. They perform research in fields such as neuroscience or bioinformatics (the use of computers to process biological information, usually at the molecular level).

Microbiologists investigate the growth and characteristics of microscopic organisms such as bacteria, algae, or fungi. Most microbiologists specialize in environmental, food, agricultural, or industrial microbiology; virology (the study of viruses); immunology (the study of mechanisms that fight infections); or bioinformatics. Many microbiologists use biotechnology to advance knowledge of cell reproduction and human disease.

Physiologists study life functions of plants and animals, both in the whole organism and at the cellular or molecular level, under normal and abnormal conditions. Physiologists often specialize in functions such as growth, reproduction, photosynthesis, respiration, or movement, or in the physiology of a certain area or system of the organism.

Botanists study plants and their environments. Some study all aspects of plant life, including algae, fungi, lichens, mosses, ferns, conifers, and flowering plants; others specialize in areas such as identification and classification of plants, the structure and function of plant parts, the biochemistry of plant processes, the causes and cures of plant diseases, the interaction of plants with other organisms and the environment, and the geological record of plants.

Zoologists and wildlife biologists study animals and wildlife—their origin, behavior, diseases, and life processes. Some experiment with live animals in controlled or natural surroundings, while others dissect dead animals to study their structure. Zoologists and wildlife biologists also may collect and analyze biological data to determine the environmental effects of current and potential uses of land and water areas. Zoologists are usually identified by the animal group they study—ornithologists study birds, for example, mammalogists study mammals, herpetologists study reptiles, and ichthyologists study fish.

Ecologists investigate the relationships among organisms and between organisms and their environments. They examine the effects of population size, pollutants, rainfall, temperature, and altitude. Using knowledge of various scientific disciplines, ecologists may collect, study, and report data on the quality of air, food, soil, and water.

Work environment. Most biologists spend their time in laboratories conducting research and in offices writing up results and keeping up with the latest research discoveries. Some biological scientists, particularly botanists, ecologists, and zoologists, do field studies that involve strenuous physical activity and primitive living conditions for extended periods of time. Biological scientists in the field may work in warm or cold climates, in all kinds of weather. Biological scientists usually are not exposed to unsafe or unhealthy conditions. Those who work with dangerous organisms or toxic substances in the laboratory must follow strict safety procedures to avoid contamination.

Many biological scientists, particularly those employed in academic settings, depend on grant money to support their research. They may be under pressure to meet deadlines and to conform to rigid grant-writing specifications when preparing proposals to seek new or extended funding.

Biological scientists typically work regular hours. While the 40-hour workweek is common, some biological scientists work longer hours. Some researchers may be required to work odd hours in laboratories or other locations (especially while in the field), depending on the nature of their research.

Training, Other Qualifications, and Advancement

Most biological scientists need a Ph.D. in biology or one of its subfields to work in independent research or development positions.

Other positions are available to those with a master's or bachelor's degree in the field.

Education and training. A Ph.D. is usually necessary for independent research, particularly in academia, as well as for advancement to administrative positions. A bachelor's or master's degree is sufficient for some jobs in applied research, product development, management, or inspection; it also may be sufficient to work as a research technician or a teacher. Many with a bachelor's degree in biology enter medical, dental, veterinary, or other health profession schools, or find jobs as high school science teachers. (See the statement on teachers—kindergarten, elementary, middle, and secondary.)

In addition to required courses in chemistry and biology, undergraduate biological science majors usually study allied disciplines such as mathematics, physics, engineering, and computer science. Computer courses are beneficial for modeling and simulating biological processes, operating some laboratory equipment, and performing research in the emerging field of bioinformatics. Those interested in studying the environment also should take courses in environmental studies and become familiar with applicable legislation and regulations.

Most colleges and universities offer bachelor's degrees in biological science, and many offer advanced degrees. Advanced degree programs often emphasize a subfield, such as microbiology or botany, but not all universities offer curricula in all subfields. Larger universities frequently have separate departments specializing in different areas of biological science. For example, a program in botany might cover agronomy, horticulture, or plant pathology. Advanced degree programs typically include classroom and fieldwork, laboratory research, and a thesis or dissertation. A master's degree generally takes 2 years, and a doctoral degree 5–6 years of full-time study.

Biological scientists with a Ph.D. often take temporary postdoctoral positions that provide specialized research experience. Postdoctoral positions may offer the opportunity to publish research findings. A solid record of published research is essential in obtaining a permanent position performing basic research, especially for those seeking a permanent college or university faculty position.

Other qualifications. Biological scientists should be able to work independently or as part of a team and be able to communicate clearly and concisely, both orally and in writing. Those in private industry, especially those who aspire to management or administrative positions, should possess strong business and communication skills and be familiar with regulatory issues and marketing and management techniques. Those doing field research in remote areas must have physical stamina. Biological scientists also must have patience and self-discipline to conduct long and detailed research projects.

Advancement. As they gain experience, biological scientists typically gain greater control over their research and may advance to become lead researchers directing a team of scientists and technicians. Some work as consultants to businesses or to government agencies. However, those dependent on research grants are still constrained by funding agencies, and may spend much of their time writing grant proposals. Others choose to move into managerial positions and become natural science managers. They may plan and administer programs for testing foods and drugs, for example, or direct activities at zoos or botanical gardens. Those who pursue management careers spend much of their time preparing budgets and schedules. Some leave biology for nontechnical managerial, administrative, or sales jobs.

Employment

Biological scientists held about 91,300 jobs in 2008. In addition, many biological scientists held biology faculty positions in colleges and universities but are not included in these numbers. Those whose primary work involves teaching and research are considered postsecondary teachers. (See the description for teachers—postsecondary elsewhere in this book.)

About 40 percent of all biological scientists were employed by federal, state, and local governments. Federal biological scientists worked mainly for the U.S. Departments of Agriculture, Interior, and Defense and for the National Institutes of Health. Most of the rest worked in scientific research and testing laboratories, the pharmaceutical and medicine manufacturing industry, or educational institutions.

Job Outlook

Employment of biological scientists is expected to increase much faster than the average for all occupations although there will continue to be competition for some basic research positions.

Employment change. Employment of biological scientists is projected to grow 21 percent over the 2008–2018 decade, much faster than the average for all occupations, as biotechnological research and development continues to drive job growth. Biological scientists enjoyed very rapid employment gains over the past few decades—reflecting, in part, the growth of the biotechnology industry. Employment growth will moderate somewhat as the biotechnology industry matures, with fewer new firms being founded and existing firms merging or being absorbed by larger biotechnology or pharmaceutical firms. However, much of the basic biological research done in recent years has resulted in new knowledge, including the isolation and identification of genes. Biological scientists will be needed to take this knowledge to the next stage, understanding how certain genes function within an entire organism, so that medical treatments can be developed to treat various diseases. Even pharmaceutical and other firms not solely engaged in biotechnology use biotechnology techniques extensively, spurring employment for biological scientists. For example, biological scientists are continuing to help farmers increase crop yields by pinpointing genes that can help crops, such as wheat, grow in more extreme climate conditions.

In addition, efforts to discover new and improved ways to clean up and preserve the environment will continue to add to job growth. More biological scientists will be needed to determine the environmental impact of industry and government actions and to prevent or correct environmental problems, such as the negative effects of pesticide use. Some biological scientists will find opportunities in environmental regulatory agencies, while others will use their expertise to advise lawmakers on legislation to save environmentally sensitive areas. New industrial applications of biotechnology, such as new methods for producing biofuels, also will spur demand for biological scientists.

The federal government is a major source of funding for basic research and development, including many areas of medical research that relate to biological science. Large budget increases at the National Institutes of Health in the early part of the decade led to increases in federal basic research and development expenditures, with research grants growing both in number and dollar amount. However, the increase in expenditures slowed substantially in recent years. Going forward, the level of federal funding will continue to impact competition for winning and renewing research grants.

There will continue to be demand for biological scientists specializing in botany, zoology, and marine biology, but opportunities will be limited because of the small size of these fields. Marine biology, despite its attractiveness as a career, is a very small specialty within biological science.

Job prospects. Doctoral degree holders are expected to face competition for basic research positions in academia. Furthermore, should the number of advanced degrees awarded continue to grow, applicants for research grants are likely to face even more competition. Currently, about 1 in 4 grant proposals are approved for long-term research projects. In general, applied research positions in private industry are somewhat easier to obtain, but may become more competitive if increasing numbers of scientists seek jobs in private industry because of the difficulty finding positions in colleges and universities.

Prospective marine biology students should be aware that those who would like to enter this specialty far outnumber the very few openings that occur each year for the type of glamorous research jobs that many would like to obtain. Almost all marine biologists who do basic research have a Ph.D.

People with bachelor's and master's degrees are expected to have more opportunities in nonscientist jobs related to biology, in fields like sales, marketing, publishing, and research management. Non-Ph.D.s also may fill positions as science or engineering technicians or as medical health technologists and technicians. Some become high school biology teachers.

Biological scientists are less likely to lose their jobs during recessions than those in other occupations, because many are employed on long-term research projects. However, an economic downturn could influence the amount of money allocated to new research and development efforts, particularly in areas of risky or innovative research. An economic downturn also could limit the possibility of extension or renewal of existing projects.

Earnings

Median annual wages of biochemists and biophysicists were $82,840 in May 2008. The middle 50 percent earned between $59,260 and $108,950. The lowest 10 percent earned less than $44,320, and the highest 10 percent earned more than $139,440. Median annual wages of biochemists and biophysicists employed in scientific research and development services were $85,870 in May 2008.

Median annual wages of microbiologists were $64,350 in May 2008. The middle 50 percent earned between $48,330 and $87,040. The lowest 10 percent earned less than $38,240, and the highest 10 percent earned more than $111,300.

Projections Data from the National Employment Matrix

Occupational title	SOC Code	Employment, 2008	Projected employment, 2018	Change, 2008–2018	
				Number	Percent
Biological scientists.................................... 19-1020	19-1020	91,300	110,500	19,200	21
Biochemists and biophysicists............................. 19-1021	19-1021	23,200	31,900	8,700	37
Microbiologists 19-1022	19-1022	16,900	18,900	2,100	12
Zoologists and wildlife biologists 19-1023	19-1023	19,500	22,000	2,500	13
Biological scientists, all other............................. 19-1029	19-1029	31,700	37,600	5,900	19

NOTE: Data in this table are rounded.

Median annual wages of zoologists and wildlife biologists were $55,290 in May 2008. The middle 50 percent earned between $43,060 and $70,500. The lowest 10 percent earned less than $33,550, and the highest 10 percent earned more than $90,850.

According to the National Association of Colleges and Employers, beginning salary offers in July 2009 averaged $33,254 a year for bachelor's degree recipients in biological and life sciences.

In the federal government in March 2009, microbiologists earned an average annual salary of $97,264; ecologists, $84,283; physiologists, $109,323; geneticists, $99,752; zoologists, $116,908; and botanists, $72,792.

Related Occupations

Other life science research occupations include agricultural and food scientists; conservation scientists and foresters; engineering and natural sciences managers; epidemiologists; medical scientists; and teachers—postsecondary.

Other health-related specialists with similar levels of education include dentists; physicians and surgeons; and veterinarians.

Sources of Additional Information

For information on careers in the biological sciences, contact

▸ American Institute of Biological Sciences, 1444 I St. NW, Suite 200, Washington, DC 20005. Internet: www.aibs.org

▸ Federation of American Societies for Experimental Biology, 9650 Rockville Pike, Bethesda, MD 20814. Internet: www.faseb.org

For information on careers in biochemistry or molecular biology, contact

▸ American Society for Biochemistry and Molecular Biology, 9650 Rockville Pike, Bethesda, MD 20814. Internet: www.asbmb.org

For information on careers in botany, contact

▸ The Botanical Society of America, P.O. Box 299, St. Louis, MO 63166. Internet: www.botany.org

For information on careers in cell biology, contact

▸ American Society for Cell Biology, 8120 Woodmont Ave., Suite 750, Bethesda, MD 20814. Internet: www.ascb.org

For information on careers in ecology, contact

▸ Ecological Society of America, 1990 M St. NW, Suite 700, Washington, DC 20036. Internet: www.esa.org

For information on careers in microbiology, contact

▸ American Society for Microbiology, Career Information—Education Department, 1752 N St. NW, Washington, DC 20036. Internet: www.asm.org

For information on careers in physiology, contact

▸ American Physiology Society, 9650 Rockville Pike, Bethesda, MD 20814. Internet: www.the-aps.org

Information on obtaining a biological scientist position with the federal government is available from the Office of Personnel Management through USAJOBS, the federal government's official employment information system. This resource for locating and applying for job opportunities can be accessed through the Internet at www.usajobs.opm.gov or through an interactive voice response telephone system at (703) 724-1850 or TDD (978) 461-8404. These numbers are not toll free, so charges may result.

Bookkeeping, Accounting, and Auditing Clerks

(O*NET 43-3031.00)

Significant Points

■ Bookkeeping, accounting, and auditing clerks held about 2.1 million jobs in 2008 and are employed in nearly every industry.

■ A high school degree is the minimum requirement; however, postsecondary education is increasingly important, and an associate degree in business or accounting is required for some positions.

■ The large size of this occupation ensures plentiful job openings, including many opportunities for temporary and part-time work.

Nature of the Work

Bookkeeping, accounting, and auditing clerks are financial record-keepers. They update and maintain accounting records, including those which calculate expenditures, receipts, accounts payable and receivable, and profit and loss. These workers have a wide range of skills from full-charge bookkeepers, who can maintain an entire company's books, to accounting clerks who handle specific tasks. All these clerks make numerous computations each day and must be comfortable using computers to calculate and record data.

In small businesses, *bookkeepers and bookkeeping clerks* often have responsibility for some or all the accounts, known as the general ledger. They record all transactions and post debits (costs) and credits (income). They also produce financial statements and prepare reports and summaries for supervisors and managers. Bookkeepers prepare bank deposits by compiling data from cashiers, verifying and balancing receipts, and sending cash, checks, or other forms of payment to the bank. Additionally, they may handle payroll, make purchases, prepare invoices, and keep track of overdue accounts.

In large companies, *accounting clerks* have more specialized tasks. Their titles, such as *accounts payable clerk* or *accounts receivable clerk*, often reflect the type of accounting they do. In addition, their responsibilities vary by level of experience. Entry-level accounting clerks post details of transactions, total accounts, and compute interest charges. They also may monitor loans and accounts to ensure that payments are up to date. More advanced accounting clerks may total, balance, and reconcile billing vouchers; ensure the completeness and accuracy of data on accounts; and code documents according to company procedures.

Auditing clerks verify records of transactions posted by other workers. They check figures, postings, and documents to ensure that they are mathematically accurate, and properly coded. They also correct or note errors for accountants or other workers to fix.

As organizations continue to computerize their financial records, many bookkeeping, accounting, and auditing clerks use specialized accounting software, spreadsheets, and databases. Most clerks now enter information from receipts or bills into computers, and the information is then stored electronically. The widespread use of computers also has enabled bookkeeping, accounting, and auditing clerks to take on additional responsibilities, such as payroll, procurement, and billing. Many of these functions require these clerks to write letters and make phone calls to customers or clients.

Work environment. Bookkeeping, accounting, and auditing clerks work in an office environment. They may experience eye and muscle strain, backaches, headaches, and repetitive motion injuries from using computers on a daily basis. Clerks may have to sit for extended periods while reviewing detailed data.

Many bookkeeping, accounting, and auditing clerks work regular business hours and a standard 40-hour week, although some may work occasional evenings and weekends. About 1 out of 4 clerks worked part time in 2008.

Bookkeeping, accounting, and auditing clerks may work longer hours to meet deadlines at the end of the fiscal year, during tax time, or when monthly or yearly accounting audits are performed. Additionally, those who work in hotels, restaurants, and stores may put in overtime during peak holiday and vacation seasons.

Training, Other Qualifications, and Advancement

Employers usually require bookkeeping, accounting, and auditing clerks to have at least a high school diploma and some accounting coursework or relevant work experience. Clerks should also have good communication skills, be detail oriented, and trustworthy.

Education and training. Most bookkeeping, accounting, and auditing clerks are required to have a high school degree at a minimum.

However, having some postsecondary education is increasingly important and an associate degree in business or accounting is required for some positions. Although a bachelor's degree is rarely required, graduates may accept bookkeeping, accounting, and auditing clerk positions to get into a particular company or to enter the accounting or finance field with the hope of eventually being promoted.

Once hired, bookkeeping, accounting, and auditing clerks usually receive on-the-job training. Under the guidance of a supervisor or another experienced employee, new clerks learn company procedures. Some formal classroom training also may be necessary, such as training in specialized computer software.

Other qualifications. Bookkeeping, accounting, and auditing clerks must be careful, orderly, and detail-oriented to avoid making errors and to recognize errors made by others. These workers also should be discreet and trustworthy, because they frequently come in contact with confidential material. They should also have good communication skills, because they increasingly work with customers. In addition, all bookkeeping, accounting, and auditing clerks should have a strong aptitude for numbers.

Experience in a related job and working in an office environment is recommended. Workers must be able to use computers, and knowledge of specialized bookkeeping or accounting software is especially valuable.

Certification and advancement. Bookkeeping, accounting, and auditing clerks, particularly those who handle all the recordkeeping for a company, may find it beneficial to become certified. The Certified Bookkeeper (CB) designation, awarded by the American Institute of Professional Bookkeepers, demonstrates that individuals have the skills and knowledge needed to carry out all bookkeeping functions, including overseeing payroll and balancing accounts, according to accepted accounting procedures. For certification, candidates must have at least two years of bookkeeping experience, pass a four-part examination, and adhere to a code of ethics. Several colleges and universities offer a preparatory course for certification; some offer courses online. Additionally, certified bookkeepers are required to meet a continuing education requirement every three years to maintain certification.

Bookkeeping, accounting, and auditing clerks usually advance by taking on more duties for higher pay or by transferring to a closely related occupation. Most companies fill office and administrative support supervisory and managerial positions by promoting individuals from within their organizations, so clerks who acquire additional skills, experience, and training improve their advancement opportunities. With appropriate experience and education, some bookkeeping, accounting, and auditing clerks may become accountants or auditors.

Employment

Bookkeeping, accounting, and auditing clerks held about 2.1 million jobs in 2008. They work in nearly all industries and at all levels of government. State and local government, educational services, health care, and the accounting, tax preparation, bookkeeping, and payroll services industries are among the individual industries employing the largest numbers of these clerks.

Projections Data from the National Employment Matrix

Occupational title	SOC Code	Employment, 2008	Projected employment, 2018	Change, 2008–2018	
				Number	Percent
Bookkeeping, accounting, and auditing clerks 43-3031		2,063,800	2,276,200	212,400	10

NOTE: Data in this table are rounded.

Job Outlook

Job growth is projected to be about as fast as the average. The large size of this occupation ensures plentiful job opportunities, as many bookkeeping, accounting, and auditing clerks are expected to retire or transfer to other occupations.

Employment change. Employment of bookkeeping, accounting, and auditing clerks is projected to grow by 10 percent during the 2008–2018 decade, which is about as fast as the average for all occupations. This occupation is one of the largest growth occupations in the economy, with about 212,400 new jobs expected over the projections decade.

A growing economy will result in more financial transactions and other activities that require recordkeeping by these workers. Additionally, an increased emphasis on accuracy, accountability, and transparency in the reporting of financial data for public companies will increase the demand for these workers. Also, new regulations and reporting methods, including the use of International Financial Reporting Standards, should result in additional demand for clerks involved in accounting and auditing. However, growth will be limited by improvements in accounting software and document-scanning technology that make it easier to record, track, audit, and file financial information, including transactions and reports. Moreover, companies will continue to outsource their bookkeeping, accounting, and, in some cases, auditing functions to third party contractors located both domestically and abroad.

Job prospects. While many job openings are expected to result from job growth, even more openings will stem from the need to replace existing workers who leave. Each year, numerous jobs will become available, as clerks transfer to other occupations or leave the labor force. The large size of this occupation ensures plentiful job openings, including many opportunities for temporary and part-time work.

Clerks who can carry out a wider range of bookkeeping and accounting activities will be in greater demand than specialized clerks. For example, demand for full-charge bookkeepers is expected to increase, because they can perform a wider variety of financial transactions, including payroll and billing. Certified Bookkeepers (CBs) and those with several years of accounting or bookkeeping experience who have demonstrated that they can handle a range of tasks will have the best job prospects.

Earnings

In May 2008, the median annual wages of bookkeeping, accounting, and auditing clerks were $32,510. The middle half of the occupation earned between $26,350 and $40,130. The top 10 percent of bookkeeping, accounting, and auditing clerks earned more than $49,260, and the bottom 10 percent earned less than $20,950.

Related Occupations

Bookkeeping, accounting, and auditing clerks work with financial records. Other workers who perform similar duties include accountants and auditors; billing and posting clerks and machine operators; brokerage clerks; credit authorizers, checkers, and clerks; payroll and timekeeping clerks; and procurement clerks.

Sources of Additional Information

For information on the Certified Bookkeeper designation, contact

▸ American Institute of Professional Bookkeepers, 6001 Montrose Rd., Suite 500, Rockville, MD 20852. Internet: www.aipb.org

Cargo and Freight Agents

(O*NET 43-5011.00 and 43-5011.01)

Significant Points

- Cargo and freight agents need no more than a high school diploma and learn their duties informally on the job.
- Much-faster-than-average employment growth is expected.
- Job prospects are expected to be good.

Nature of the Work

Cargo and freight agents help transportation companies manage incoming and outgoing shipments in airline, train, or trucking terminals or on shipping docks. Agents expedite shipments by determining a route, preparing all necessary documents, and arranging for the pickup of freight or cargo and its delivery to loading platforms. They may also keep records of the cargo, including its amount, type, weight, dimensions, destination, and time of shipment. They also keep a tally of missing items and record the condition of damaged items.

Cargo and freight agents arrange cargo according to destination. They also determine any shipping rates and other applicable charges. For imported or exported freight, they verify that the proper customs paperwork is in order. Cargo and freight agents often track shipments electronically, using bar codes, and answer customers' questions about the status of their shipments.

Work environment. Cargo and freight agents work in a wide variety of environments. Some work in warehouses, stockrooms, or shipping and receiving rooms that may not be temperature controlled. Others may spend time in cold storage rooms or outside on loading platforms, where they are exposed to the weather.

Projections Data from the National Employment Matrix

Occupational title	SOC Code	Employment, 2008	Projected employment, 2018	Change, 2008–2018	
				Number	Percent
Cargo and freight agents	43-5011	85,900	106,500	20,600	24

NOTE: Data in this table are rounded.

Most jobs for cargo and freight agents involve frequent standing, bending, walking, and stretching. Some lifting and carrying of small items may be involved. Although automated devices have lessened the physical demands of this occupation, not every employer has these devices. The work still can be strenuous, even though mechanical material-handling equipment is used to move heavy items.

The typical workweek is Monday through Friday. However, evening and weekend hours are common in jobs involving large shipments.

Training, Other Qualifications, and Advancement

Cargo and freight agents need no more than a high school diploma and learn their duties informally on the job.

Education and training. Many jobs are entry level and most require a high school diploma. Cargo and freight agents undergo informal on-the-job training. For example, they may start out by checking items to be shipped and making sure that addresses are correct.

Other qualifications. Employers prefer to hire people who are comfortable using computers. Typing, filing, recordkeeping, and other clerical skills also are important.

Advancement. Advancement opportunities for cargo and freight agents are usually limited, but some agents may become team leaders or use their experience to switch to other clerical occupations in the businesses where they work. Some may move to higher paying transportation industry jobs, such as freight brokering.

Employment

Cargo and freight agents held about 85,900 jobs in 2008. Most agents were employed in transportation. Approximately 52 percent worked for firms engaged in support activities for the transportation industry, 19 percent were in the air transportation industry, 8 percent worked for courier businesses, and 7 percent were in the truck transportation industry.

Job Outlook

Employment is expected to grow much faster than average; job prospects are expected to be good.

Employment change. Employment of cargo and freight agents is expected to increase by 24 percent during the 2008–2018 decade, which is much faster than the average for all occupations. As the overall economy continues to grow, more agents will be needed to handle the growing number of shipments resulting from increases in cargo traffic. Additionally, as shipments require multiple modes of transportation to reach their final destinations, such as freight trucking and air, a greater number of agents will be needed to manage the process. The growing popularity of online shopping and same day delivery may also spur employment growth.

Job prospects. A combination of job growth and turnover are expected to result in good job prospects for cargo and freight agents. However, employment of cargo and freight agents is sensitive to the fluctuations of the economy, and workers may experience high levels of unemployment when the overall level of economic activity falls.

Earnings

Median hourly wages of cargo and freight agents in May 2008 were $17.92. The middle 50 percent earned between $13.67 and $22.92. The lowest 10 percent earned less than $10.65, and the highest 10 percent earned more than $27.70. Median hourly wages in the industries employing the largest numbers of cargo and freight agents in May 2008 were as follows:

Scheduled air transportation	$18.39
Freight transportation arrangement	18.34
Couriers and express delivery services	18.08
General freight trucking	17.99
Support activities for air transportation	11.48

These workers usually receive the same benefits as most other workers. If uniforms are required, employers generally provide them or offer an allowance to purchase them.

Related Occupations

Cargo and freight agents coordinate shipments of cargo by airlines, trains, and trucks. Others who do similar work are postal service clerks; postal service mail sorters, processors, and processing machine operators; shipping, receiving, and traffic clerks; and weighers, measurers, checkers, and samplers, recordkeeping.

Sources of Additional Information

Information about the freight and cargo industry, including training opportunities, is available from

▸ Transportation Intermediaries Association (TIA). 1625 Prince St., Suite 200, Alexandria, VA 22314. Internet: www.tianet.org

Carpenters

(O*NET 47-2031.00, 47-2031.01, and 47-2031.02)

Significant Points

■ About 32 percent of all carpenters are self-employed.

■ Job opportunities should be best for those with the most training and skills.

■ Carpenters can learn their craft through on-the-job training, vocational schools or technical colleges, or formal apprenticeship programs, which often takes three to four years.

Nature of the Work

Carpenters construct, erect, install, and repair structures and fixtures made from wood and other materials. Carpenters are involved in many different kinds of construction, from the building of highways and bridges to the installation of kitchen cabinets.

Each carpentry task is somewhat different, but most involve the same basic steps. Working from blueprints or instructions from supervisors, carpenters first do the layout—measuring, marking, and arranging materials—in accordance with local building codes. They cut and shape wood, plastic, fiberglass, or drywall using hand and power tools, such as chisels, planes, saws, drills, and sanders. They then join the materials with nails, screws, staples, or adhesives. In the last step, carpenters do a final check of the accuracy of their work with levels, rules, plumb bobs, framing squares, and surveying equipment, and make any necessary adjustments. Some materials come prefabricated, allowing for easier and faster installation.

Carpenters may do many different carpentry tasks, or they may specialize in one or two. Carpenters who remodel homes and other structures, for example, need a broad range of carpentry skills. As part of a single job, they might frame walls and partitions, put in doors and windows, build stairs, install cabinets and molding, and complete many other tasks. Well-trained carpenters are able to switch from residential building to commercial construction or remodeling work, depending on which offers the best work opportunities.

Carpenters who work for large construction contractors or specialty contractors may perform only a few regular tasks, such as constructing wooden forms for pouring concrete, or erecting scaffolding. Some carpenters build tunnel bracing, or brattices, in underground passageways and mines to control the circulation of air through the passageways and to worksites. Others build concrete forms for tunnel, bridge, or sewer construction projects.

Carpenters employed outside the construction industry perform a variety of installation and maintenance work. They may replace panes of glass, ceiling tiles, and doors, as well as repair desks, cabinets, and other furniture. Depending on the employer, carpenters install partitions, doors, and windows; change locks; and repair broken furniture. In manufacturing firms, carpenters may assist in moving or installing machinery.

Work environment. As is true of other building trades, carpentry work is sometimes strenuous. Prolonged standing, climbing, bending, and kneeling often are necessary. Carpenters risk injury working with sharp or rough materials, using sharp tools and power equipment, and working in situations where they might slip or fall. Consequently, workers in this occupation experience a very high incidence of nonfatal injuries and illnesses. Additionally, carpenters who work outdoors are subject to variable weather conditions.

Many carpenters work a standard 40 hour week; however, some work more. About 7 percent worked part time.

Training, Other Qualifications, and Advancement

Carpenters can learn their craft through on-the-job training, vocational schools or technical colleges, or formal apprenticeship programs, which often takes 3 to 4 years.

Education and training. Learning to be a carpenter can start in high school. Classes in English, algebra, geometry, physics, mechanical drawing, blueprint reading, and general shop will prepare students for the further training they will need.

After high school, there are a number of different ways to obtain the necessary training. Some people get a job as a carpenter's helper, assisting more experienced workers. At the same time, the helper might attend a trade or vocational school, or community college to receive further trade-related training and eventually become a carpenter.

Some employers offer employees formal apprenticeships. These programs combine on-the-job training with related classroom instruction. Apprentices usually must be at least 18 years old and meet local requirements. Apprenticeship programs usually last 3 to 4 years, but new rules may allow apprentices to complete programs sooner as competencies are demonstrated.

On the job, apprentices learn elementary structural design and become familiar with common carpentry jobs, such as layout, form building, rough framing, and outside and inside finishing. They also learn to use the tools, machines, equipment, and materials of the trade. In the classroom, apprentices learn safety, first aid, blueprint reading, freehand sketching, basic mathematics, and various carpentry techniques. Both in the classroom and on the job, they learn the relationship between carpentry and the other building trades.

The number of apprenticeship programs is limited, however, so only a small proportion of carpenters learn their trade through these programs. Most apprenticeships are offered by commercial and industrial building contractors, along with construction unions.

Some people who are interested in carpentry careers choose to receive classroom training before seeking a job. There are a number of public and private vocational-technical schools and training academies affiliated with unions and contractors that offer training to become a carpenter. Employers often look favorably upon these students and usually start them at a higher level than those without this training.

Other qualifications. Carpenters need manual dexterity, good eye-hand coordination, physical fitness, and a good sense of balance. The ability to solve mathematical problems quickly and accurately also is required. In addition, military service or a good work history is viewed favorably by employers.

Certification and advancement. Carpenters who complete formal apprenticeship programs receive certification as journeypersons. Some carpenters earn other certifications in scaffold building, high torque bolting, or pump work. These certifications prove that carpenters are able to perform these tasks, which can lead to additional responsibilities.

Carpenters usually have more opportunities than most other construction workers to become general construction supervisors, because carpenters are exposed to the entire construction process. For those who would like to advance, it is increasingly important

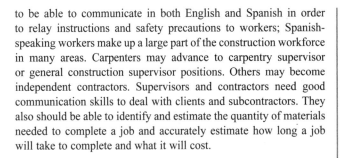

to be able to communicate in both English and Spanish in order to relay instructions and safety precautions to workers; Spanish-speaking workers make up a large part of the construction workforce in many areas. Carpenters may advance to carpentry supervisor or general construction supervisor positions. Others may become independent contractors. Supervisors and contractors need good communication skills to deal with clients and subcontractors. They also should be able to identify and estimate the quantity of materials needed to complete a job and accurately estimate how long a job will take to complete and what it will cost.

Employment

Carpenters are employed throughout the country in almost every community and make up the second largest building trades occupation. They held about 1.3 million jobs in 2008.

About 32 percent worked in the construction of buildings industry, and about 22 percent worked for specialty trade contractors. Most of the rest of wage and salary carpenters worked for manufacturing firms, government agencies, retail establishments, and a wide variety of other industries. About 32 percent of all carpenters were self-employed. Some carpenters change employers each time they finish a construction job. Others alternate between working for a contractor and working as contractors themselves on small jobs, depending on where the work is available.

Job Outlook

As-fast-as-average job growth, coupled with replacement needs, will create a large number of openings each year. Job opportunities should be best for those with the most training and skills.

Employment change. Employment of carpenters is expected to increase by 13 percent during the 2008–2018 decade, as fast as the average for all occupations. Population growth over the next decade will stimulate some growth in the construction industry over the long run to meet people's housing and other basic needs. Energy conservation will also stimulate demand for buildings that are more energy efficient, particularly in the industrial sector. The home remodeling market also will create demand for carpenters. Moreover, construction of roads and bridges should increase the demand for carpenters in the coming decade. Much will depend on spending by the federal and state governments, as they attempt to upgrade and repair existing infrastructure, such as highways, bridges, and public buildings.

Some of the demand for carpenters, however, will be offset by expected productivity gains resulting from the increasing use of prefabricated components and improved fasteners and tools. Prefabricated wall panels, roof assemblies, and stairs, as well as prehung doors and windows can be installed very quickly. Instead of having

to be built on the worksite, prefabricated walls, partitions, and stairs can be lifted into place in one operation; beams and, in some cases, entire roof assemblies, are lifted into place using a crane. As prefabricated components become more standardized, builders will use them more often. New and improved tools, equipment, techniques, and materials also are making carpenters more versatile, allowing them to perform more carpentry tasks.

Job prospects. Job opportunities will be good for those with the most training and skills. The need to replace carpenters who retire or leave the occupation for other reasons should result in a large number of openings. Carpenters with specialized or all-around skills will have better opportunities for steady work than carpenters who can perform only a few relatively simple, routine tasks.

Employment of carpenters, like that of many other construction workers, is sensitive to the fluctuations of the economy. Workers in these trades may experience periods of unemployment when the overall level of construction falls. On the other hand, shortages of these workers may occur in some areas during peak periods of building activity.

Job opportunities for carpenters also vary by geographic area. Construction activity parallels the movement of people and businesses and reflects differences in local economic conditions. The areas with the largest population increases will also provide the best opportunities for jobs as carpenters and for apprenticeships for people seeking to become carpenters.

Earnings

In May 2008, median hourly wages of wage and salary carpenters were $18.72. The middle 50 percent earned between $14.42 and $25.37. The lowest 10 percent earned less than $11.66, and the highest 10 percent earned more than $33.34. Median hourly wages in the industries employing the largest numbers of carpenters were as follows:

Nonresidential building construction	$21.08
Building finishing contractors	19.37
Residential building construction	18.24
Foundation, structure, and building exterior contractors	17.67
Employment services	15.81

Earnings can be reduced on occasion, because carpenters lose work-time in bad weather and during recessions when jobs are unavailable. Earnings may be increased by overtime during busy periods.

Some carpenters are members of the United Brotherhood of Carpenters and Joiners of America. About 19 percent of all carpenters were members of unions or covered by union contracts, higher than the average for all occupations.

Projections Data from the National Employment Matrix

Occupational title	SOC Code	Employment, 2008	Projected employment, 2018	Change, 2008–2018	
				Number	Percent
Carpenters	47-2031	1,284,900	1,450,300	165,400	13

NOTE: Data in this table are rounded.

Related Occupations

Carpenters are skilled construction workers. Other skilled construction occupations include brickmasons, blockmasons, and stonemasons; cement masons, concrete finishers, segmental pavers, and terrazzo workers; construction equipment operators; drywall and ceiling tile installers, tapers, plasterers, and stucco masons; electricians; and plumbers, pipelayers, pipefitters, and steamfitters.

Sources of Additional Information

For information about carpentry apprenticeships or other work opportunities in this trade, contact local carpentry contractors, locals of the union mentioned above, local joint union-contractor apprenticeship committees, or the nearest office of the state employment service or apprenticeship agency. You can also find information on the registered apprenticeship system with links to state apprenticeship programs on the U.S. Department of Labor web site: www.doleta.gov/OA/eta_default.cfm. Apprenticeship information is also available from the U.S. Department of Labor toll-free helpline: (877) 872-5627.

For information on training opportunities and carpentry in general, contact

- Associated Builders and Contractors, 4250 N. Fairfax Dr., 9th Floor, Arlington, VA 22203-1607. Internet: www.trytools.org
- Associated General Contractors of America, Inc., 2300 Wilson Blvd., Suite 400, Arlington, VA 22201-5426. Internet: www.agc.org
- National Center for Construction Education and Research, 3600 NW 43rd St., Bldg. G, Gainesville, FL, 32606-8134. Internet: www.nccer.org
- National Association of Home Builders, Home Builders Institute, 1201 15th St. NW, Washington, DC 20005-2842. Internet: www.hbi.org
- United Brotherhood of Carpenters and Joiners of America, Carpenters Training Fund, 101 Constitution Ave. NW, Washington, DC 20001-2192. Internet: www.carpenters.org

For general information on apprenticeships and how to get them, see the *Occupational Outlook Quarterly* article "Apprenticeships: Career training, credentials—and a paycheck in your pocket," online at www.bls.gov/opub/ooq/2002/summer/art01.pdf and in print at many libraries and career centers.

Child Care Workers

(O*NET 39-9011.00 and 39-9011.01)

Significant Points

- About 33 percent of child care workers are self-employed, most of whom provided child care in their homes.
- Training requirements range from a high school diploma to a college degree, although some jobs require less than a high school diploma.
- Many workers leave these jobs every year, creating good job opportunities.

Nature of the Work

Child care workers nurture, teach, and care for children who have not yet entered kindergarten. They also supervise older children before and after school. These workers play an important role in children's development by caring for them when their parents are at work or are away for other reasons or when the parents place their children in care to help them socialize with children their age. In addition to attending to children's health, safety, and nutrition, child care workers organize activities and implement curricula that stimulate children's physical, emotional, intellectual, and social growth. They help children explore individual interests, develop talents and independence, build self-esteem, learn how to get along with others, and prepare for more formal schooling.

Child care workers generally are classified into three different groups based on where they work: private household workers, who care for children at the children's homes; family child care providers, who care for children in the providers' homes; and child care workers who work at child care centers, which include Head Start, Early Head Start, full-day and part-day preschool, and other early childhood programs.

Private household workers who are employed on an hourly basis usually are called *babysitters.* These child care workers bathe, dress, and feed children; supervise their play; wash their clothes; and clean their rooms. Babysitters also may put children to bed and wake them, read to them, involve them in educational games, take them for doctors' visits, and discipline them. Those who are in charge of infants prepare bottles and change diapers. Babysitters may work for many different families. Workers who are employed by one family are often called nannies. They generally take care of children from birth to age 12, tending to the child's early education, nutrition, health, and other needs. They also may perform the duties of a housekeeper, including cleaning and doing the laundry.

Family child care providers often work alone with a small group of children, although some work in larger settings they work in groups or teams. Child care centers generally have more than one adult per group of children; in groups of children aged 3 to 5 years, a child care worker may assist a more experienced preschool teacher.

Most child care workers perform a combination of basic care and teaching duties, but the majority of their time is spent on caregiving activities. However, there is an increasing focus on preparing children aged 3 to 5 years for school. Workers whose primary responsibility is teaching are classified as preschool teachers. (Preschool teachers are covered elsewhere in this book.) However, many basic care activities also are opportunities for children to learn. For example, a worker who shows a child how to tie a shoelace teaches the child while providing for that child's basic needs.

Child care workers spend most of their day working with children. However, they do maintain contact with parents or guardians through informal meetings or scheduled conferences to discuss each child's progress and needs. Many child care workers keep records of each child's progress and suggest ways in which parents can stimulate their child's learning and development at home. Some child care centers and before- and afterschool programs actively recruit parent volunteers to work with the children and participate in administrative decisions and program planning.

Young children learn mainly through playing, solving problems, questioning, and experimenting. Child care workers recognize that fact and capitalize on children's play and other experiences to further their language development (through storytelling and acting games), improve their social skills (by having them work together to build a neighborhood in a sandbox), and introduce scientific and mathematical concepts (by balancing and counting blocks when building a bridge or mixing colors when painting). Often, a less structured approach, including small-group lessons; one-on-one instruction; and creative activities such as art, dance, and music, is used to teach young children. Child care workers play a vital role in preparing children to build the skills they will need in school.

Child care workers in child care centers, schools, or family child care homes greet young children as they arrive, help them with their jackets, and select an activity of interest. When caring for infants, they feed and change them. To ensure a well-balanced program, child care workers prepare daily and long-term schedules of activities. Each day's activities balance individual and group play, as well as quiet time and time for physical activity. Children are given some freedom to participate in activities they are interested in. As children age, child care workers may provide more guided learning opportunities, particularly in the areas of math and reading.

Concern over school-aged children being home alone before and after school has spurred many parents to seek alternative ways for their children to spend their time constructively. The purpose of before- and after-school programs is to watch over school-aged children during the gap between school hours and the end of their parents' daily work hours. These programs also may operate during the summer and on weekends. Workers in before- and after-school programs may help students with their homework or engage them in extracurricular activities, including field trips, sports, learning about computers, painting, photography, and other subjects. Some child care workers are responsible for taking children to school in the morning and picking them up from school in the afternoon. Before- and after-school programs may be operated by public school systems, local community centers, or other private organizations.

Helping to keep children healthy is another important part of the job. Child care workers serve nutritious meals and snacks and teach good eating habits and personal hygiene. They ensure that children have proper rest periods. They identify children who may not feel well, and they may help parents locate programs that will provide basic health services. Child care workers also watch for children who show signs of emotional or developmental problems. Upon identifying such a child, they discuss the child's situation with their supervisor and the child's parents. Early identification of children with special needs—such as those with behavioral, emotional, physical, or learning disabilities—is important in improving their future learning ability. Special education teachers often work with preschool children to provide the individual attention they need. (Special education teachers are discussed elsewhere in this book.)

Work environment. Helping children grow, learn, and gain new skills can be very rewarding. The work is sometimes routine, but new activities and challenges mark each day. Child care can be physically and emotionally taxing as workers constantly stand, walk, bend, stoop, and lift to attend to each child's interests and problems. These workers experienced a larger than average number of work-related injuries or illnesses.

States regulate child care facilities, the number of children per child care worker, the qualifications of the staff, and the health and safety of the children. To ensure that children in child care centers receive proper supervision, state or local regulations may require a certain ratio of workers to children. The ratio varies with the age of the children. For infants (children under 1 year old), child care workers may be responsible for 3 or 4 children. For toddler's (children 1 to 2 years old), workers may be responsible for 4 to 10 children, and for preschool-aged children (those between 3 and 5 years old), workers may be responsible for 8 to 25 children. However, these regulations vary greatly from state to state. In before- and after-school programs, workers may be responsible for many school-aged children at a time.

Family child care providers work out of their own homes, an arrangement that provides convenience, but also requires that their homes be accommodating to young children. Private household workers usually work in the homes or apartments of their employers. Most live in their own homes and travel to work, although some live in the home of their employer and generally are provided with their own room and bath. They often come to feel like part of their employer's family.

The work hours of child care workers vary widely. Child care centers usually are open year round, with long hours so that parents can drop off and pick up their children before and after work. Some centers employ full-time and part-time staff with staggered shifts to cover the entire day. Some workers are unable to take regular breaks during the day due to limited staffing. Public and many private preschool programs operate during the typical 9- or 10-month school year, employing both full-time and part-time workers. Family child care providers have flexible hours and daily routines, but they may work long or unusual hours to fit parents' work schedules. Live-in nannies usually work longer hours than do child care workers who live in their own homes. However, although nannies may work evenings or weekends, they usually get other time off. About 36 percent worked part time.

Training, Other Qualifications, and Advancement

Licensure and training requirements vary greatly by state, but some jobs require less than a high school diploma.

Education and training. The training and qualifications required of child care workers vary widely. Each state has its own licensing requirements that regulate caregiver training. These requirements range from less than a high school diploma, to a national Child Development Associate (CDA) credential, to community college courses or a college degree in child development or early childhood education. State requirements are generally higher for workers at child care centers than for family child care providers.

Child care workers in private settings who care for only a few children often are not regulated by states at all. Child care workers generally can obtain some form of employment with less than a high school diploma and little or no experience, but certain private firms and publicly funded programs have more demanding training and education requirements. Different public funding streams may set other education and professional development requirements. For example, many states have separate funding for prekindergarten

Projections Data from the National Employment Matrix

Occupational title	SOC Code	Employment, 2008	Projected employment, 2018	Change, 2008–2018	
				Number	Percent
Child care workers... 39-9011		1,301,900	1,443,900	142,100	11

NOTE: Data in this table are rounded.

programs for 4-year-old children. In accordance with the regulations that accompany the funding, these states typically set higher education degree requirements for those workers than do ordinary state child care licensing requirements.

Some employers prefer workers who have taken secondary or postsecondary courses in child development and early childhood education or who have work experience in a child care setting. Other employers require their own specialized training. An increasing number of employers are requiring an associate degree in early childhood education

Licensure. Many states require child care centers, including those in private homes, to be licensed if they care for more than a few children. In order to obtain their license, child care centers may require child care workers to pass a background check, get immunizations, and meet a minimum training requirement.

Other qualifications. Child care workers must anticipate and prevent problems, deal with disruptive children, provide fair but firm discipline, and be enthusiastic and constantly alert. They must communicate effectively with the children and their parents, as well as with teachers and other child care workers. Workers should be mature, patient, understanding, and articulate and have energy and physical stamina. Skills in music, art, drama, and storytelling also are important. Self-employed child care workers must have business sense and management abilities.

Certification and advancement. Some employers prefer to hire child care workers who have earned a nationally recognized Child Development Associate (CDA) credential or the Child Care Professional (CCP) designation from the Council for Professional Recognition and the National Child Care Association, respectively. Requirements include child care experience and coursework, such as college courses or employer-provided seminars.

Opportunities for advancement are limited. However, as child care workers gain experience, some may advance to supervisory or administrative positions in large child care centers or preschools. Often, these positions require additional training, such as a bachelor's or master's degree. Other workers move on to work in resource and referral agencies, consulting with parents on available child care services. A few workers become involved in policy or advocacy work related to child care and early childhood education. With a bachelor's degree, workers may become preschool teachers or become certified to teach in public or private schools. Some workers set up their own child care businesses.

Employment

Child care workers held about 1.3 million jobs in 2008. About 33 percent of child care workers were self-employed; most of these were family child care providers.

Child day care services employed about 19 percent of all child care workers, and about 19 percent worked for private households. The remainder worked primarily in educational services; nursing and residential care facilities; amusement and recreation industries; civic and social organizations; and individual and family services. Some child care programs are for-profit centers, which may be affiliated with a local or national company. A very small percentage of private-industry establishments operate onsite child care centers for the children of their employees.

Job Outlook

Child care workers are expected to experience job growth that is about as fast as the average for all occupations. Job prospects will be good because of the many workers who leave the occupation and need to be replaced.

Employment change. Employment of child care workers is projected to increase by 11 percent between 2008 and 2018, which is about as fast as the average for all occupations. An increasing emphasis on early childhood education programs will increase demand for these workers. Child care workers often work alongside preschool teachers as assistants. Therefore, increased demand for formal preschool programs will create growth for child care workers. Although only a few states currently provide targeted or universal preschool programs, many more are considering or starting such programs. A rise in enrollment in private preschools is likely as the value of formal education before kindergarten becomes more widely accepted. More states moving toward universal preschool education could increase employment growth for child care workers. However, growth will be moderated by relatively slow growth in the population of children under the age of five, who are generally cared for by these workers.

Job prospects. High replacement needs should create good job opportunities for child care workers. Qualified persons who are interested in this work should have little trouble finding and keeping a job. Many child care workers must be replaced each year as they leave the occupation to fulfill family responsibilities, to study, or for other reasons. Others leave because they are interested in pursuing other occupations or because of low wages.

Earnings

Pay depends on the educational attainment of the worker and the type of establishment. Although the pay generally is very low, more education usually means higher earnings. Median hourly wages of child care workers were $9.12 in May 2008. The middle 50 percent earned between $7.75 and $11.30. The lowest 10 percent earned less than $7.04, and the highest 10 percent earned more than $13.98. Median hourly wages in the industries employing the largest numbers of child care workers in May 2008 were as follows:

Other residential care facilities............................ $10.56
Elementary and secondary schools 10.53
Civic and social organizations 8.53
Other amusement and recreation industries.............. 8.41
Child day care services 8.39

Earnings of self-employed child care workers vary with the number of hours worked, the number and ages of the children, and the geographic location.

Benefits vary, but are minimal for most child care workers. Many employers offer free or discounted child care to employees. Some offer a full benefits package, including health insurance and paid vacations, but others offer no benefits at all. Some employers offer seminars and workshops to help workers learn new skills. A few are willing to cover the cost of courses taken at community colleges or technical schools. Live-in nannies receive free room and board.

Related Occupations

Child care work requires patience; creativity; an ability to nurture, motivate, teach, and influence children; and leadership, organizational, and administrative skills. Others who work with children and need these qualities and skills include teacher assistants; teachers—kindergarten, elementary, middle, and secondary; teachers—preschool, except special education; and teachers—special education.

Sources of Additional Information

For an electronic question-and-answer service on child care, for information on becoming a child care provider, and for information on other resources, contact

▸ National Child Care Information Center, 10530 Rosehaven St., Suite 400, Fairfax, VA 22030. Internet: www.nccic.org

For eligibility requirements and a description of the Child Development Associate credential, contact

▸ Council for Professional Recognition, 2460 16th St. NW, Washington, DC 20009-3547. Internet: www.cdacouncil.org

For eligibility requirements and a description of the Child Care Professional designation, contact

▸ National Child Care Association, 1325 G St. NW, Suite 500, Washington, DC 20005. Internet: www.nccanet.org

For information about early childhood education, contact

▸ National Association for the Education of Young Children, 1313 L St. NW, Suite 500 Washington, DC 20005. Internet: www.naeyc.org

For information about a career as a nanny, contact

▸ International Nanny Association, PO Box 1299, Hyannis, MA 02601. Internet: www.nanny.org

State departments of human services or social services can supply state regulations and training requirements for child care workers.

Clinical Laboratory Technologists and Technicians

(O*NET 29-2011.00, 29-2011.01, 29-2011.02, 29-2011.03, and 29-2012.00)

Significant Points

■ Excellent job opportunities are expected.

■ Clinical laboratory technologists usually have a bachelor's degree with a major in medical technology or in one of the life sciences; clinical laboratory technicians generally need either an associate degree or a certificate.

■ Most jobs will continue to be in hospitals, but employment will grow rapidly in other settings, as well.

Nature of the Work

Clinical laboratory testing plays a crucial role in the detection, diagnosis, and treatment of disease. *Clinical laboratory technologists*, also referred to as *clinical laboratory scientists* or *medical technologists*, and *clinical laboratory technicians*, also known as *medical technicians* or *medical laboratory technicians*, perform most of these tests.

Clinical laboratory personnel examine and analyze body fluids, and cells. They look for bacteria, parasites, and other microorganisms; analyze the chemical content of fluids; match blood for transfusions; and test for drug levels in the blood that show how a patient is responding to treatment. Technologists also prepare specimens for examination, count cells, and look for abnormal cells in blood and body fluids. They use microscopes, cell counters, and other sophisticated laboratory equipment. They also use automated equipment and computerized instruments capable of performing a number of tests simultaneously. After testing and examining a specimen, they analyze the results and relay them to physicians.

With increasing automation and the use of computer technology, the work of technologists and technicians has become less hands-on and more analytical. The complexity of tests performed, the level of judgment needed, and the amount of responsibility workers assume depend largely on the amount of education and experience they have. Clinical laboratory technologists usually do more complex tasks than clinical laboratory technicians do.

Clinical laboratory technologists perform complex chemical, biological, hematological, immunologic, microscopic, and bacteriological tests. Technologists microscopically examine blood and other body fluids. They make cultures of body fluid and tissue samples, to determine the presence of bacteria, fungi, parasites, or other microorganisms. Technologists analyze samples for chemical content or a chemical reaction and determine concentrations of compounds such as blood glucose and cholesterol levels. They also type and cross match blood samples for transfusions.

Clinical laboratory technologists evaluate test results, develop and modify procedures, and establish and monitor programs, to ensure the accuracy of tests. Some technologists supervise clinical laboratory technicians.

Technologists in small laboratories perform many types of tests, whereas those in large laboratories generally specialize. *Clinical chemistry technologists*, for example, prepare specimens and analyze the chemical and hormonal contents of body fluids. *Microbiology technologists* examine and identify bacteria and other microorganisms. *Blood bank technologists*, or *immunohematology technologists*, collect, type, and prepare blood and its components for transfusions. *Immunology technologists* examine elements of the human immune system and its response to foreign bodies. *Cytotechnologists* prepare slides of body cells and examine these cells microscopically for abnormalities that may signal the beginning of a cancerous growth. *Molecular biology technologists* perform complex protein and nucleic acid testing on cell samples.

Clinical laboratory technicians perform less complex tests and laboratory procedures than technologists do. Technicians may prepare specimens and operate automated analyzers, for example, or they may perform manual tests in accordance with detailed instructions. They usually work under the supervision of medical and clinical laboratory technologists or laboratory managers. Like technologists, clinical laboratory technicians may work in several areas of the clinical laboratory or specialize in just one. *Phlebotomists* collect blood samples, for example, and *histotechnicians* cut and stain tissue specimens for microscopic examination by pathologists.

Work environment. Clinical laboratory personnel are trained to work with infectious specimens. When proper methods of infection control and sterilization are followed, few hazards exist. Protective masks, gloves, and goggles often are necessary to ensure the safety of laboratory personnel.

Working conditions vary with the size and type of employment setting. Laboratories usually are well lighted and clean; however, specimens, solutions, and reagents used in the laboratory sometimes produce fumes. Laboratory workers may spend a great deal of time on their feet.

Hours of clinical laboratory technologists and technicians vary with the size and type of employment setting. In large hospitals or in independent laboratories that operate continuously, personnel usually work the day, evening, or night shift and may work weekends and holidays. Laboratory personnel in small facilities may work on rotating shifts, rather than on a regular shift. In some facilities, laboratory personnel are on call several nights a week or on weekends, in case of an emergency.

Training, Other Qualifications, and Advancement

Clinical laboratory technologists generally require a bachelor's degree in medical technology or in one of the life sciences; clinical laboratory technicians usually need an associate degree or a certificate.

Education and training. The usual requirement for an entry-level position as a clinical laboratory technologist is a bachelor's degree with a major in medical technology or one of the life sciences; however, it is possible to qualify for some jobs with a combination of education and on-the-job and specialized training. Universities and hospitals offer medical technology programs.

Bachelor's degree programs in medical technology include courses in chemistry, biological sciences, microbiology, mathematics, and statistics, as well as specialized courses devoted to knowledge and skills used in the clinical laboratory. Many programs also offer or require courses in management, business, and computer applications. The Clinical Laboratory Improvement Act requires technologists who perform highly complex tests to have at least an associate degree.

Medical and clinical laboratory technicians generally have either an associate degree from a community or junior college or a certificate from a hospital, a vocational or technical school, or the Armed Forces. A few technicians learn their skills on the job.

The National Accrediting Agency for Clinical Laboratory Sciences (NAACLS) fully accredits about 479 programs for medical and clinical laboratory technologists, medical and clinical laboratory technicians, histotechnologists and histotechnicians, cytogenetic technologists, and diagnostic molecular scientists. NAACLS also approves about 60 programs in phlebotomy and clinical assisting. Other nationally recognized agencies that accredit specific areas for clinical laboratory workers include the Commission on Accreditation of Allied Health Education Programs and the Accrediting Bureau of Health Education Schools.

Licensure. Some states require laboratory personnel to be licensed or registered. Licensure of technologists often requires a bachelor's degree and the passing of an exam, but requirements vary by state and specialty. Information on licensure is available from state departments of health or boards of occupational licensing.

Certification and other qualifications. Many employers prefer applicants who are certified by a recognized professional association. Associations offering certification include the Board of Registry of the American Society for Clinical Pathology, the American Medical Technologists, the National Credentialing Agency for Laboratory Personnel, and the Board of Registry of the American Association of Bioanalysts. These agencies have different requirements for certification and different organizational sponsors.

In addition to certification, employers seek clinical laboratory personnel with good analytical judgment and the ability to work under pressure. Technologists in particular are expected to be good at problem solving. Close attention to detail is also essential for laboratory personnel because small differences or changes in test substances or numerical readouts can be crucial to a diagnosis. Manual dexterity and normal color vision are highly desirable, and with the widespread use of automated laboratory equipment, computer skills are important.

Advancement. Technicians can advance and become technologists through additional education and experience. Technologists may advance to supervisory positions in laboratory work or may become chief medical or clinical laboratory technologists or laboratory managers in hospitals. Manufacturers of home diagnostic testing kits and laboratory equipment and supplies also seek experienced technologists to work in product development, marketing, and sales.

Professional certification and a graduate degree in medical technology, one of the biological sciences, chemistry, management, or education usually speeds advancement. A doctorate usually is needed to become a laboratory director. Federal regulation requires directors of moderately complex laboratories to have either a master's degree

Projections Data from the National Employment Matrix

Occupational title	SOC Code	Employment, 2008	Projected employment, 2018	Change, 2008–2018	
				Number	Percent
Clinical laboratory technologists and technicians 29-2010		328,100	373,600	45,600	14
Medical and clinical laboratory technologists 29-2011		172,400	193,000	20,500	12
Medical and clinical laboratory technicians 29-2012		155,600	180,700	25,000	16

NOTE: Data in this table are rounded.

or a bachelor's degree, combined with the appropriate amount of training and experience.

Employment

Clinical laboratory technologists and technicians held about 328,100 jobs in 2008. More than half of jobs were in hospitals. Most of the remaining jobs were in offices of physicians and in medical and diagnostic laboratories. A small proportion was in educational services and in all other ambulatory health-care services.

Job Outlook

Rapid job growth and excellent job opportunities are expected. Most jobs will continue to be in hospitals, but employment will grow rapidly in other settings, as well.

Employment change. Employment of clinical laboratory workers is expected to grow by 14 percent between 2008 and 2018, faster than the average for all occupations. The volume of laboratory tests continues to increase with both population growth and the development of new types of tests.

Technological advances will continue to have opposing effects on employment. On the one hand, new, increasingly powerful diagnostic tests and advances in genomics—the study of the genetic information of a cell or organism—will encourage additional testing and spur employment. On the other hand, research and development efforts targeted at simplifying and automating routine testing procedures may enhance the ability of nonlaboratory personnel—physicians and patients in particular—to perform tests now conducted in laboratories.

Although hospitals are expected to continue to be the major employer of clinical laboratory workers, employment is expected also to grow rapidly in medical and diagnostic laboratories, offices of physicians, and all other ambulatory health-care services.

Job prospects. Job opportunities are expected to be excellent because the number of job openings is expected to continue to exceed the number of jobseekers. Although significant, job growth will not be the only source of opportunities. As in most occupations, many additional openings will result from the need to replace workers who transfer to other occupations, retire, or stop working for some other reason. Willingness to relocate will further enhance one's job prospects.

Earnings

Median annual wages of medical and clinical laboratory technologists were $53,500 in May 2008. The middle 50 percent earned

between $44,560 and $63,420. The lowest 10 percent earned less than $36,180, and the highest 10 percent earned more than $74,680. Median annual wages in the industries employing the largest numbers of medical and clinical laboratory technologists were as follows:

Federal Executive Branch	$59,800
General medical and surgical hospitals	54,220
Medical and diagnostic laboratories	53,360
Offices of physicians	49,080
Colleges, universities, and professional schools	47,890

Median annual wages of medical and clinical laboratory technicians were $35,380 in May 2008. The middle 50 percent earned between $28,420 and $44,310. The lowest 10 percent earned less than $23,480, and the highest 10 percent earned more than $53,520. Median annual wages in the industries employing the largest numbers of medical and clinical laboratory technicians were as follows:

General medical and surgical hospitals	$36,840
Colleges, universities, and professional schools	36,290
Offices of physicians	33,980
Medical and diagnostic laboratories	32,630
Other ambulatory health care services	31,320

According to the American Society for Clinical Pathology, median hourly wages of staff clinical laboratory technologists and technicians, in various specialties and laboratory types, in 2007 were as follows:

Specialty	Hospital	Private clinic	Physician office laboratory
Cytotechnologist	$27.55	$28.75	$26.24
Histotechnologist	22.93	23.35	25.00
Medical technologist	23.45	23.00	20.00
Histotechnician	20.00	20.00	21.00
Medical laboratory technician	18.54	17.00	16.96
Phlebotomist	12.50	12.50	13.00

Related Occupations

Clinical laboratory technologists and technicians analyze body fluids, tissue, and other substances, using a variety of tests. Similar or related procedures are performed by chemists and materials scientists; science technicians; and veterinary technologists and technicians.

Sources of Additional Information

For a list of accredited and approved educational programs for clinical laboratory personnel, contact

▶ National Accrediting Agency for Clinical Laboratory Sciences, 5600 N. River Rd., Suite 720, Rosemont, IL 60018. Internet: www.naacls. org

Information on certification is available from

▶ American Association of Bioanalysts, Board of Registry, 906 Olive St., Suite 1200, St. Louis, MO 63101. Internet: www.aab.org

▶ American Medical Technologists, 10700 W. Higgins Rd., Suite 150, Rosemont, IL 60018. Internet: www.amt1.com

▶ American Society for Clinical Pathology, 33 W. Monroe St., Suite 1600, Chicago, IL 60603. Internet: www.ascp.org

▶ National Credentialing Agency for Laboratory Personnel, P.O. Box 15945-289, Lenexa, KS 66285. Internet: www.nca-info.org

Additional career information is available from

▶ American Association of Blood Banks, 8101 Glenbrook Rd., Bethesda, MD 20814. Internet: www.aabb.org

▶ American Society for Clinical Laboratory Science, 6701 Democracy Blvd., Suite 300, Bethesda, MD 20817. Internet: www.ascls.org

▶ American Society for Cytopathology, 100 W. 10th St., Suite 605, Wilmington, DE 19801. Internet: www.cytopathology.org

▶ Clinical Laboratory Management Association, 993 Old Eagle School Rd., Suite 405, Wayne, PA 19087. Internet: www.clma.org

Computer and Information Systems Managers

(O*NET 11-3021.00)

Significant Points

■ Employment is expected to grow faster than the average for all occupations.

■ A bachelor's degree in a computer-related field usually is required for management positions, although employers often prefer a graduate degree, especially an MBA with technology as a core component.

■ Many managers possess advanced technical knowledge gained from working in a computer occupation.

■ Job prospects should be excellent.

Nature of the Work

In the modern workplace, it is imperative that Information Technology (IT) work both effectively and reliably. *Computer and information systems managers* play a vital role in the implementation and administration of technology within their organizations. They plan, coordinate, and direct research on the computer-related activities of firms. In consultation with other managers, they help determine the goals of an organization and then implement technology to meet those goals. They oversee all technical aspect of an organization, such as software development, network security, and Internet operations.

Computer and information systems managers direct the work of other IT professionals, such as computer software engineers and computer programmers, computer systems analysts, and computer support specialists. They plan and coordinate activities such as installing and upgrading hardware and software, programming and systems design, the implementation of computer networks, and the development of Internet and intranet sites. They are increasingly involved with the upkeep, maintenance, and security of networks. They analyze the computer and information needs of their organizations from an operational and strategic perspective and determine immediate and long-range personnel and equipment requirements. They assign and review the work of their subordinates and stay abreast of the latest technology to ensure that the organization remains competitive.

Computer and information systems managers can have additional duties, depending on their role within an organization. *Chief technology officers (CTOs)*, for example, evaluate the newest and most innovative technologies and determine how these can help their organizations. They develop technical standards, deploy technology, and supervise workers who deal with the daily information technology issues of the firm. When a useful new tool has been identified, the CTO determines one or more possible implementation strategies, including cost-benefit and return on investment analyses, and presents those strategies to top management, such as the *chief information officer (CIO)*.

Management information systems (MIS) directors or *information technology (IT) directors* manage computing resources for their organizations. They often work under the chief information officer and plan and direct the work of subordinate information technology employees. These managers ensure the availability, continuity, and security of data and information technology services in their organizations. In this capacity, they oversee a variety of technical departments, develop and monitor performance standards, and implement new projects.

IT project managers develop requirements, budgets, and schedules for their firm's information technology projects. They coordinate such projects from development through implementation, working with their organization's IT workers, as well as clients, vendors, and consultants. These managers are increasingly involved in projects that upgrade the information security of an organization.

Work environment. Computer and information systems managers generally work in clean, comfortable offices. Long hours are common, and some may have to work evenings and weekends to meet deadlines or solve unexpected problems; in 2008, about 25 percent worked more than 50 hours per week. Some computer and information systems managers may experience considerable pressure in meeting technical goals with short deadlines or tight budgets. As networks continue to expand and more work is done remotely, computer and information systems managers have to communicate with and oversee offsite employees using laptops, e-mail, and the Internet.

Injuries in this occupation are uncommon, but like other workers who spend considerable time using computers, computer and information systems managers are susceptible to eyestrain, back discomfort, and hand and wrist problems such as carpal tunnel syndrome.

Training, Other Qualifications, and Advancement

Computer and information systems managers generally have technical expertise from working in a computer occupation, as well as an understanding of business and management principles. A strong educational background and experience in a variety of technical fields is needed.

Education and training. A bachelor's degree in a computer-related field usually is required for management positions, although employers often prefer a graduate degree, especially an MBA with technology as a core component. Common majors for undergraduate degrees are computer science, information science, and management information systems (MIS).

A bachelor's degree in a computer-related field generally takes four years to complete and includes courses in computer science, computer programming, computer engineering, mathematics, and statistics. Most also include general education courses such as English and communications. MIS programs usually are part of the business school or college and contain courses such as finance, marketing, accounting, and management, as well as systems design, networking, database management, and systems security.

MBA programs usually require two years of study beyond the undergraduate degree and, like undergraduate business programs, include courses on finance, marketing, accounting, and management, as well as database management, electronic business, and systems management and design.

A few computer and information systems managers attain their positions with only an associate or trade school degree, but they must have sufficient experience and must have acquired additional skills on the job. To aid their professional advancement, many managers with an associate degree eventually earn a bachelor's or master's degree while working.

Certification and other qualifications. Computer and information systems managers need a broad range of skills. Employers look for individuals who can demonstrate an understanding of the specific software or technology used on the job. Generally, this knowledge is gained through years of experience working with that particular product. Another way to demonstrate this trait is with professional certification. Although not required for most computer and information system management positions, certification demonstrates an area of expertise and can increase an applicant's chances of employment. These high-level certifications are often product-specific and are generally administered by software or hardware companies rather than independent organizations.

Computer and information systems managers also need a thorough understanding of business practices. Because information technology is a central component of many organizations, these workers often must make important business decisions. Consequently, many firms seek managers with a background in business management, consulting, or sales. These workers also must possess good leadership and communication skills, as one of their main duties is to assign work and monitor employee performance. They also must be able to explain technical subjects to people without technical expertise, such as clients or managers of other departments.

Advancement. Computer and information systems managers may advance to progressively higher leadership positions in an information technology department. A project manager, for instance, might be promoted to the chief technology officer position and then to chief information officer. On occasion, some may become managers in non-technical areas such as marketing, human resources, or sales because in high-technology firms, an understanding of technical issues is helpful in those areas.

Employment

Computer and information systems managers held about 293,000 jobs in 2008. About 16 percent worked in the computer systems design and related services industry. This industry provides IT services on a contract basis, including custom computer programming services, computer systems design and integration services, and computer facilities management services. Other large employers include insurance and financial firms, government agencies, business management organizations, and manufacturers.

Job Outlook

Faster-than-average employment growth is expected, and job prospects should be excellent.

Employment change. Employment of computer and information systems managers is expected to grow 17 percent over the 2008–2018 decade, which is faster than the average for all occupations. New applications of technology in the workplace will continue to drive demand for workers, fueling the need for more managers. To remain competitive, firms will continue to install sophisticated computer networks and set up more complex intranets and Web sites. They will need to adopt the most efficient software and systems and troubleshoot problems when they occur. Computer and information systems managers will be needed to oversee these functions.

Because so much business is carried out over computer networks, security will continue to be an important issue for businesses and other organizations and will lead to strong growth for computer managers. Firms will increasingly hire security experts to fill key leadership roles in their information technology departments because the integrity of their computing environments is of utmost importance.

The growth of computer and information systems managers should be closely related to the growth of the occupations they supervise.

Among computer and information system managers, job growth is expected to be the fastest in computer systems design establishments; software publishing firms; data processing and hosting companies; management, scientific, and technical consulting services; and health-care organizations. Increased consolidation of IT services may reduce growth to some extent in other industries.

Job prospects. Prospects for qualified computer and information systems managers should be excellent. Workers with specialized technical knowledge and strong communications and business skills, as well as those with an MBA with a concentration in information systems, will have the best prospects. Job openings will be the result of employment growth and the need to replace workers who transfer to other occupations or leave the labor force.

Projections Data from the National Employment Matrix

Occupational title	SOC Code	Employment, 2008	Projected employment, 2018	Change, 2008–2018	
				Number	Percent
Computer and information systems managers............... 11-3021		293,000	342,500	49,500	17

NOTE: Data in this table are rounded.

Earnings

Wages of computer and information systems managers vary by specialty and level of responsibility. Median annual wages of these managers in May 2008 were $112,210. The middle 50 percent earned between $88,240 and $141,890. Median annual wages in the industries employing the largest numbers of computer and information systems managers in May 2008 were as follows:

Software publishers	$126,840
Computer systems design and related services	118,120
Management of companies and enterprises	115,150
Depository credit intermediation	113,380
Insurance carriers...	109,810

In addition to salaries, computer and information systems managers, especially those at higher levels, often receive employment-related benefits, such as expense accounts, stock option plans, and bonuses.

Related Occupations

Other occupations that manage workers, deal with information technology, or make business or technical decisions include advertising, marketing, promotions, public relations, and sales managers; computer network, systems, and database administrators; computer scientists; computer software engineers and computer programmers; computer support specialists; computer systems analysts; engineering and natural sciences managers; financial managers; and top executives.

Sources of Additional Information

Additional information on a career in information technology is available from the following organizations:

▸ Association for Computing Machinery (ACM), 2 Penn Plaza, Suite 701, New York, NY 10121-0701. Internet: http://computingcareers.acm.org

▸ Institute of Electrical and Electronics Engineers Computer Society, Headquarters Office, 2001 L St. NW, Suite 700, Washington, DC 20036-4910. Internet: www.computer.org

▸ National Workforce Center for Emerging Technologies, 3000 Landerholm Circle SE, Bellevue, WA 98007. Internet: www.nwcet.org

▸ University of Washington Computer Science and Engineering Department, AC101 Paul G. Allen Center, Box 352350, 185 Stevens Way, Seattle, WA 98195-2350. Internet: www.cs.washington.edu/WhyCSE

▸ National Center for Women and Information Technology, University of Colorado, Campus Box 322 UCB, Boulder, CO 80309-0322. Internet: www.ncwit.org

Computer Network, Systems, and Database Administrators

(O*NET 15-1061.00, 15-1071.00, 15-1071.01, 15-1081.00, 15-1081.01, 15-1099.00, 15-1099.01, 15-1099.02, 15-1099.03, 15-1099.04, 15-1099.05, 15-1099.06, 15-1099.07, 15-1099.08, 15-1099.09, 15-1099.10, 15-1099.11, 15-1099.12, 15-1099.13, and 15-1099.14)

Significant Points

■ Employment is projected to grow much faster than the average for all occupations and add 286,600 new jobs over the 2008–2018 decade.

■ Excellent job prospects are expected.

■ Workers can enter this field with many different levels of formal education, but relevant computer skills are always needed.

Nature of the Work

Information technology (IT) has become an integral part of modern life. Among its most important functions are the efficient transmission of information and the storage and analysis of information. The workers described in this section all help individuals and organizations share and store information through computer networks and systems, the Internet, and computer databases.

Network architects or *network engineers* are the designers of computer networks. They set up, test, and evaluate systems such as local area networks (LANs), wide area networks (WANs), the Internet, intranets, and other data communications systems. Systems are configured in many ways and can range from a connection between two offices in the same building to globally distributed networks, voice mail, and e-mail systems of a multinational organization. Network architects and engineers perform network modeling, analysis, and planning, which often require both hardware and software solutions. For example, setting up a network may involve the installation of several pieces of hardware, such as routers and hubs, wireless adaptors, and cables, as well as the installation and configuration of software, such as network drivers. These workers may also research related products and make necessary hardware and software recommendations, as well as address information security issues.

Network and computer systems administrators design, install, and support an organization's computer systems. They are responsible for LANs, WANs, network segments, and Internet and intranet systems. They work in a variety of environments, including large corporations, small businesses, and government organizations. They install and maintain network hardware and software, analyze problems, and monitor networks to ensure their availability to users.

These workers gather data to evaluate a system's performance, identify user needs, and determine system and network requirements.

Systems administrators are responsible for maintaining system efficiency. They ensure that the design of an organization's computer system allows all of the components, including computers, the network, and software, to work properly together. Administrators also troubleshoot problems reported by users and by automated network monitoring systems and make recommendations for future system upgrades. Many of these workers are also responsible for maintaining network and system security.

Database administrators work with database management software and determine ways to store, organize, analyze, use, and present data. They identify user needs and set up new computer databases. In many cases, database administrators must integrate data from old systems into a new system. They also test and coordinate modifications to the system when needed and troubleshoot problems when they occur. An organization's database administrator ensures the performance of the system, understands the platform on which the database runs, and adds new users to the system. Because many databases are connected to the Internet, database administrators also must plan and coordinate security measures with network administrators. Some database administrators may also be responsible for database design, but this task is usually performed by *database designers* or *database analysts*.

Computer security specialists plan, coordinate, and maintain an organization's information security. These workers educate users about computer security, install security software, monitor networks for security breaches, respond to cyber attacks, and, in some cases, gather data and evidence to be used in prosecuting cyber crime. The responsibilities of computer security specialists have increased in recent years as cyber attacks have become more sophisticated.

Telecommunications specialists focus on the interaction between computer and communications equipment. These workers design voice, video, and data-communication systems; supervise the installation of the systems; and provide maintenance and other services to clients after the systems are installed. They also test lines and oversee equipment repair, and they may compile and maintain system records.

Web developers are responsible for the technical aspects of Web site creation. Using software languages and tools, they create applications for the Web. They identify a site's users and oversee its production and implementation. They determine the information that the site will contain and how it will be organized, and they may use Web development software to integrate databases and other information systems. Some of these workers may be responsible for the visual appearance of Web sites. Using design software, they create pages that appeal to the tastes of the site's users.

Webmasters or *Web administrators* are responsible for maintaining Web sites. They oversee issues such as availability to users and speed of access, and they are responsible for approving the content of the site. Webmasters also collect and analyze data on Web activity, traffic patterns, and other metrics, as well as monitor and respond to user feedback.

Work environment. Network and computer systems administrators, network architects, database administrators, computer security specialists, Web administrators, and Web developers normally work in well-lighted, comfortable offices or computer laboratories. Most work about 40 hours a week. However, about 15 percent of network and systems administrators, 14 percent of database administrators, and about 16 percent of network systems and data communications analysts (which includes network architects, telecommunications specialists, Web administrators, and Web developers) worked more than 50 hours per week in 2008. In addition, some of these workers may be required to be "on call" outside of normal business hours in order to resolve system failures or other problems.

As computer networks expand, more of these workers may be able to perform their duties from remote locations, reducing or eliminating the need to travel to the customer's workplace.

Injuries in these occupations are uncommon, but like other workers who spend long periods in front of a computer terminal typing on a keyboard, these workers are susceptible to eyestrain, back discomfort, and hand and wrist problems such as carpal tunnel syndrome.

Training, Other Qualifications, and Advancement

Training requirements vary by occupation. Workers can enter this field with many different levels of formal education, but relevant computer skills are always needed. Certification may improve an applicant's chances for employment and can help workers maintain adequate skill levels throughout their careers.

Education and training. Network and computer systems administrators often are required to have a bachelor's degree, although an associate degree or professional certification, along with related work experience, may be adequate for some positions. Most of these workers begin as computer support specialists before advancing into network or systems administration positions. (Computer support specialists are covered elsewhere in this book.) Common majors for network and systems administrators are computer science, information science, and management information systems (MIS), but a degree in any field, supplemented with computer courses and experience, may be adequate. A bachelor's degree in a computer-related field generally takes four years to complete and includes courses in computer science, computer programming, computer engineering, mathematics, and statistics. Most programs also include general education courses such as English and communications. MIS programs usually are part of the business school or college and contain courses such as finance, marketing, accounting, and management, as well as systems design, networking, database management, and systems security.

For network architect and database administrator positions, a bachelor's degree in a computer-related field generally is required, although some employers prefer applicants with a master's degree in business administration (MBA) with a concentration in information systems. MBA programs usually require two years of study beyond the undergraduate degree, and, like undergraduate business programs, include courses on finance, marketing, accounting, and management, as well as database management, electronic business, and systems management and design. In addition to formal education, network architects may be required to have several years of relevant work experience.

For Webmasters, an associate degree or certification is sufficient, although more advanced positions might require a computer-related bachelor's degree. For telecommunications specialists, employers prefer applicants with an associate degree in electronics or a related field, but for some positions, experience may substitute for formal education. Applicants for security specialist and Web developer positions generally need a bachelor's degree in a computer-related field, but for some positions, related experience and certification may be adequate.

Certification and other qualifications. Workers in these occupations must have strong problem-solving, analytical, and communication skills. Because they often deal with a number of tasks simultaneously, the ability to concentrate and pay close attention to detail also is important. Although these workers sometimes work independently, they frequently work in teams on large projects. As a result, they must be able to communicate effectively with other computer workers, such as programmers and managers, as well as with users or other staff who may have no computer background.

Jobseekers can enhance their employment opportunities by earning certifications, which are offered through product vendors, computer associations, and other training institutions. Many employers regard these certifications as the industry standard, and some require their employees to be certified. In some cases, applicants without formal education may use certification and experience to qualify for some positions.

Because technology changes rapidly, computer specialists must continue to acquire the latest skills. Many organizations offer intermediate and advanced certification programs that pertain to the most recent technological advancements.

Advancement. Entry-level network and computer systems administrators are involved in routine maintenance and monitoring of computer systems. After gaining experience and expertise, they are often able to advance to more senior-level positions. They may also advance to supervisory positions.

Database administrators and network architects may advance into managerial positions, such as chief technology officer, on the basis of their experience. Computer specialists with work experience and considerable expertise in a particular area may find opportunities as independent consultants.

Computer security specialists can advance into supervisory positions or may move into other occupations, such as computer systems analysts.

Employment

Computer network, systems, and database administrators held about 961,200 jobs in 2008. Of these, 339,500 were network and computer systems administrators, 120,400 were database administrators, and 292,000 were network and data communications analysts. In addition, about 209,300 were classified as "computer specialists, all other," a residual category.

These workers were employed in a wide range of industries. About 14 percent of all computer network, systems, and database administrators were in computer systems design and related services. Substantial numbers of these workers were also employed in telecommunications companies, financial firms and insurance provid-

ers, business management organizations, schools, and government agencies. About 7 percent were self-employed.

Job Outlook

Employment is expected to grow much faster than the average, and job prospects should be excellent.

Employment change. Overall employment of computer network, systems, and database administrators is projected to increase by 30 percent from 2008 to 2018, much faster than the average for all occupations. In addition, this occupation will add 286,600 new jobs over that period. Growth, however, will vary by specialty.

Employment of network and computer systems administrators is expected to increase by 23 percent from 2008 to 2018, much faster than the average for all occupations. Computer networks are an integral part of business, and demand for these workers will increase as firms continue to invest in new technologies. The increasing adoption of mobile technologies means that more establishments will use the Internet to conduct business online. This growth translates into a need for systems administrators who can help organizations use technology to communicate with employees, clients, and consumers. Growth will also be driven by the increasing need for information security. As cyber attacks become more sophisticated, demand will increase for workers with security skills.

Employment of database administrators is expected to grow by 20 percent from 2008 to 2018, much faster than the average. Demand for these workers is expected to increase as organizations need to store, organize, and analyze increasing amounts of data. In addition, as more databases are connected to the Internet and as data security becomes increasingly important, a growing number of these workers will be needed to protect databases from attack.

Employment of network systems and data communications analysts is projected to increase by 53 percent from 2008 to 2018, which is much faster than the average and places it among the fastest growing of all occupations. This occupational category includes network architects and engineers, as well as Web administrators and developers. Demand for network architects and engineers will increase as organizations continue to upgrade their IT capacity and incorporate the newest technologies. The growing reliance on wireless networks will result in a need for many more of these workers. Workers with knowledge of information security also will be in demand as computer networks transmit an increasing amount of sensitive data.

Demand for Web administrators and Web developers will also be strong. More of these workers will be needed to accommodate the increasing amount of data sent over the Internet, as well as the growing number of Internet users. In addition, as the number of services provided over the Internet expands, Web administrators and developers will continue to see employment increases.

Growth in computer network, systems, and database administrators will be rapid in the computer systems design, data processing and hosting, software publishing, and technical consulting industries as these types of establishments utilize or provide an increasing array of IT services. Growth will also be rapid in health care as these organizations look to increase their efficiency and improve patient care through the use of information systems and other technology.

Projections Data from the National Employment Matrix

Occupational title	SOC Code	Employment, 2008	Projected employment, 2018	Change, 2008–2018	
				Number	Percent
Computer network, systems, and database administrators..—		961,200	1,247,800	286,600	30
Database administrators 15-1061		120,400	144,700	24,400	20
Network and computer systems administrators................15-1071		339,500	418,400	78,900	23
Network systems and data communications analysts.........15-1081		292,000	447,800	155,800	53
All other computer specialists 15-1099		209,300	236,800	27,500	13

NOTE: Data in this table are rounded.

Growth in this occupation may be tempered somewhat by off-shore outsourcing as firms transfer work to countries with lower-prevailing wages and highly skilled work forces. In addition, the consolidation of IT services may increase efficiency, reducing the demand for workers.

Job prospects. Computer network, systems, and database administrators should continue to enjoy excellent job prospects. In general, applicants with a college degree and certification will have the best opportunities. However, for some of these occupations, opportunities will be available for applicants with related work experience. Job openings in these occupations will be the result of strong employment growth, as well as the need to replace workers who transfer to other occupations or leave the labor force.

Earnings

Median annual wages of network and computer systems administrators were $66,310 in May 2008. The middle 50 percent earned between $51,690 and $84,110. The lowest 10 percent earned less than $41,000, and the highest 10 percent earned more than $104,070. Median annual wages in the industries employing the largest numbers of network and computer systems administrators in May 2008 were as follows:

Management of companies and enterprises	$70,680
Computer systems design and related services	70,490
Wired telecommunications carriers	66,950
Colleges, universities, and professional schools	57,380
Elementary and secondary schools	56,320

Median annual wages of database administrators were $69,740 in May 2008. The middle 50 percent earned between $52,340 and $91,850. The lowest 10 percent earned less than $39,900, and the highest 10 percent earned more than $111,950. In May 2008, median annual wages of database administrators employed in computer systems design and related services were $78,510, and for those in management of companies and enterprises, wages were $74,730.

Median annual wages of network systems and data communication analysts were $71,100 in May 2008. The middle 50 percent earned between $54,330 and $90,740. The lowest 10 percent earned less than $41,660, and the highest 10 percent earned more than $110,920. These wages encompass network architects, telecommunications specialists, Webmasters, and Web developers. Median annual wages in the industries employing the largest numbers of

network systems and data communications analysts in May 2008 were as follows:

Wired telecommunications carriers	$75,930
Insurance carriers	74,910
Management of companies and enterprises	73,720
Computer systems design and related services	72,410
Local government	64,230

Related Occupations

Other occupations that work with information technology include computer and information systems managers, computer scientists, computer software engineers and computer programmers, computer support specialists, and computer systems analysts.

Sources of Additional Information

For additional information about a career as a computer network, systems, or database administrator, contact

▸ The League of Professional System Administrators, 15000 Commerce Pkwy., Suite C, Mount Laurel, NJ 08054. Internet: www.lopsa.org

▸ Data Management International, 19239 N. Dale Mabry Hwy. #132, Lutz, FL 33548. Internet: www.dama.org

Additional information on a career in information technology is available from the following organizations:

▸ Association for Computing Machinery (ACM), 2 Penn Plaza, Suite 701, New York, NY 10121-0701. Internet: http://computingcareers.acm.org

▸ Institute of Electrical and Electronics Engineers Computer Society, Headquarters Office, 2001 L St. NW, Suite 700, Washington, DC 20036-4910. Internet: www.computer.org

▸ National Workforce Center for Emerging Technologies, 3000 Landerholm Circle SE, Bellevue, WA 98007. Internet: www.nwcet.org

▸ University of Washington Computer Science and Engineering Department, AC101 Paul G. Allen Center, Box 352350, 185 Stevens Way, Seattle, WA 98195-2350. Internet: www.cs.washington.edu/WhyCSE

▸ National Center for Women and Information Technology, University of Colorado, Campus Box 322 UCB, Boulder, CO 80309-0322. Internet: www.ncwit.org

Computer Software Engineers and Computer Programmers

(O*NET 15-1021.00, 15-1031.00, and 15-1032.00)

Significant Points

- Computer software engineers are among the occupations projected to grow the fastest and add the most new jobs over the 2008–2018 decade, resulting in excellent job prospects.

- Employment of computer programmers is expected to decline by 3 percent through 2018.

- Job prospects will be best for applicants with a bachelor's or higher degree and relevant experience.

Nature of the Work

Computer software engineers design and develop software. They apply the theories and principles of computer science and mathematical analysis to create, test, and evaluate the software applications and systems that make computers work. The tasks performed by these workers evolve quickly, reflecting changes in technology and new areas of specialization as well as the changing practices of employers.

Software engineers design and develop many types of software, including computer games, business applications, operating systems, network control systems, and middleware. They must be experts in the theory of computing systems, the structure of software, and the nature and limitations of hardware to ensure that the underlying systems will work properly.

Computer software engineers begin by analyzing users' needs and then design, test, and develop software to meet those needs. During this process, they create flowcharts, diagrams, and other documentation and may also create the detailed sets of instructions, called algorithms, that actually tell the computer what to do. They also may be responsible for converting these instructions into a computer language, a process called programming or coding, but this usually is the responsibility of computer programmers.

Computer software engineers can generally be divided into two categories: applications engineers and systems engineers. *Computer applications software engineers* analyze end users' needs and design, construct, deploy, and maintain general computer applications software or specialized utility programs. These workers use different programming languages, depending on the purpose of the program and the environment in which the program runs. The programming languages most often used are C, C++, Java, and Python. Some software engineers develop packaged computer applications, but most create or adapt customized applications for business and other organizations. Some of these workers also develop databases.

Computer systems software engineers coordinate the construction, maintenance, and expansion of an organization's computer systems. Working with the organization, they coordinate each department's computer needs—ordering, inventory, billing, and payroll record-keeping, for example—and make suggestions about its technical direction. They also might set up the organization's intranets—networks that link computers within the organization and ease communication among various departments. Often, they are also responsible for the design and implementation of system security and data assurance.

Systems software engineers also work for companies that configure, implement, and install the computer systems of other organizations. These workers may be members of the marketing or sales staff serving as the primary technical resource for sales workers or providing logistical and technical support. Since the selling of complex computer systems often requires substantial customization to meet the needs of the purchaser, software engineers help to identify and explain needed changes. In addition, systems software engineers are responsible for ensuring security across the systems they are configuring.

Computer programmers write programs. After computer software engineers and systems analysts design software programs, the programmer converts that design into a logical series of instructions that the computer can follow. (A description of computer systems analysts appears elsewhere in this book.) The programmer codes these instructions in any of a number of programming languages, depending on the need. The most common languages are C++ and Python.

Computer programmers also update, repair, modify, and expand existing programs. Some, especially those working on large projects that involve many programmers, use computer-assisted software engineering (CASE) tools to automate much of the coding process. These tools enable a programmer to concentrate on writing the unique parts of a program. Programmers working on smaller projects often use "programmer environments," applications that increase productivity by combining compiling, code walk-through, code generation, test data generation, and debugging functions. Programmers also use libraries of basic code that can be modified or customized for a specific application. This approach yields more reliable and consistent programs and increases programmers' productivity by eliminating some routine steps.

As software design has continued to advance and some programming functions have become automated, programmers have begun to assume some of the responsibilities that were once performed only by software engineers. As a result, some computer programmers now assist software engineers in identifying user needs and designing certain parts of computer programs, as well as other functions.

Work environment. Computer software engineers and programmers normally work in clean, comfortable offices or in laboratories in which computer equipment is located. Software engineers who work for software vendors and consulting firms frequently travel to meet with customers. Telecommuting is becoming more common as technological advances allow more work to be done from remote locations.

Most software engineers and programmers work 40 hours a week, but about 15 percent of software engineers and 11 percent of programmers worked more than 50 hours a week in 2008. Injuries in these occupations are rare. However, like other workers who spend long periods in front of a computer terminal typing at a keyboard, engineers and programmers are susceptible to eyestrain, back discomfort, and hand and wrist problems such as carpal tunnel syndrome.

Training, Other Qualifications, and Advancement

A bachelor's degree commonly is required for software engineering jobs, although a master's degree is preferred for some positions. A bachelor's degree also is required for many computer programming jobs, although a two-year degree or certificate may be adequate in some cases. Employers favor applicants who already have relevant skills and experience. Workers who keep up to date with the latest technology usually have good opportunities for advancement.

Education and training. For software engineering positions, most employers prefer applicants who have at least a bachelor's degree and broad knowledge of, and experience with, a variety of computer systems and technologies. The usual college majors for applications software engineers are computer science, software engineering, or mathematics. Systems software engineers often study computer science or computer information systems. Graduate degrees are preferred for some of the more complex jobs.

Many programmers require a bachelor's degree, but a two-year degree or certificate may be adequate for some positions. Some computer programmers hold a college degree in computer science, mathematics, or information systems, whereas others have taken special courses in computer programming to supplement their degree in a field such as accounting, finance, or another area of business.

Employers who use computers for scientific or engineering applications usually prefer college graduates who have a degree in computer or information science, mathematics, engineering, or the physical sciences. Employers who use computers for business applications prefer to hire people who have had college courses in management information systems and business and who possess strong programming skills. A graduate degree in a related field is required for some jobs.

In addition to educational attainment, employers highly value relevant programming skills and experience. Students seeking software engineering or programming jobs can enhance their employment opportunities by participating in internships. Some employers, such as large computer and consulting firms, train new employees in intensive company-based programs.

As technology advances, employers will need workers with the latest skills. To help keep up with changing technology, workers may take continuing education and professional development seminars offered by employers, software vendors, colleges and universities, private training institutions, and professional computing societies. Computer software engineers also need skills related to the industry in which they work. Engineers working for a bank, for example, should have some expertise in finance so that they understand banks' computing needs.

Certification and other qualifications. Certification is a way to demonstrate a level of competence and may provide a jobseeker with a competitive advantage. Certification programs are generally offered by product vendors or software firms, which may require professionals who work with their products to be certified. Voluntary certification also is available through various other organizations, such as professional computing societies.

Computer software engineers and programmers must have strong problem-solving and analytical skills. Ingenuity and creativity are particularly important in order to design new, functional software programs. The ability to work with abstract concepts and to do technical analysis is especially important for systems engineers because they work with the software that controls the computer's operation. Engineers and programmers also must be able to communicate effectively with team members, other staff, and end users. Because they often deal with a number of tasks simultaneously, they must be able to concentrate and pay close attention to detail. Business skills are also important, especially for those wishing to advance to managerial positions.

Advancement. For skilled workers who keep up to date with the latest technology, prospects for advancement are good. Advancement opportunities for computer software engineers increase with experience. Eventually, they may become a project manager, manager of information systems, or chief information officer, especially if they have business skills and training. Some computer software engineers with several years of experience or expertise can find lucrative opportunities working as systems designers or independent consultants, particularly in specialized fields such as business-to-business transactions or security and data assurance.

In large organizations, programmers may be promoted to lead programmer and be given supervisory responsibilities. Some applications programmers may move into systems programming after they gain experience and take courses in systems software. With general business experience, programmers may become programmer-analysts or systems analysts or may be promoted to managerial positions. Programmers with specialized knowledge and experience with a language or operating system may become computer software engineers. As employers increasingly contract with outside firms to do programming jobs, more opportunities should arise for experienced programmers with expertise in a specific area to work as consultants.

Employment

Computer software engineers and computer programmers held about 1.3 million jobs in 2008. Approximately 514,800 were computer applications software engineers, about 394,800 were computer systems software engineers, and about 426,700 were computer programmers. Although computer software engineers and computer programmers can be found in a wide range of industries, about 32 percent were employed in computer systems design and related services. Many also worked for software publishers, manufacturers of computers and related electronic equipment, financial institutions, and insurance providers. About 48,200 computer software engineers and computer programmers were self-employed in 2008.

Job Outlook

Overall, employment of computer software engineers and computer programmers is projected to increase much faster than the average for all occupations. Job prospects should be best for those with a bachelor's degree and relevant experience.

Employment change. Overall, employment of computer software engineers and computer programmers is projected to increase by 21 percent from 2008 to 2018, much faster than the average for all

occupations. This will be the result of rapid growth among computer software engineers, as employment of computer programmers is expected to decline.

Employment of computer software engineers is expected to increase by 32 percent from 2008 to 2018, which is much faster than the average for all occupations. In addition, this occupation will see a large number of new jobs, with more than 295,000 created between 2008 and 2018. Demand for computer software engineers will increase as computer networking continues to grow. For example, expanding Internet technologies have spurred demand for computer software engineers who can develop Internet, intranet, and Web applications. Likewise, electronic data-processing systems in business, telecommunications, health care, government, and other settings continue to become more sophisticated and complex. Implementing, safeguarding, and updating computer systems and resolving problems will fuel the demand for growing numbers of systems software engineers.

New growth areas will also continue to arise from rapidly evolving technologies. The increasing uses of the Internet, the proliferation of Web sites, and mobile technology such as wireless Internet have created a demand for a wide variety of new products. As more software is offered over the Internet, and as businesses demand customized software to meet their specific needs, applications and systems software engineers will be needed in greater numbers. In addition, the growing use of handheld computers will create demand for new mobile applications and software systems. As these devices become a larger part of the business environment, it will be necessary to integrate current computer systems with this new, more mobile technology.

In addition, information security concerns have given rise to new software needs. Concerns over "cyber security" should result in the continued investment in software that protects computer networks and electronic infrastructure. The expansion of this technology over the next 10 years will lead to an increased need for software engineers to design and develop secure applications and systems and integrate them into older systems.

As with other information technology jobs, offshore outsourcing may temper employment growth of computer software engineers. Firms may look to cut costs by shifting operations to foreign countries with lower prevailing wages and highly educated workers. Jobs in software engineering are less prone to being offshored than are jobs in computer programming, however, because software engineering requires innovation and intense research and development.

Employment of computer programmers is expected to decline slowly, decreasing by 3 percent from 2008 to 2018. Advances in programming languages and tools, the growing ability of users to write and implement their own programs, and the offshore outsourcing of programming jobs will contribute to this decline.

Because they can transmit their programs digitally, computer programmers can perform their job function from anywhere in the world, allowing companies to employ workers in countries that have lower prevailing wages. Computer programmers are at a much higher risk of having their jobs offshored than are workers involved in more complex and sophisticated information technology functions, such as software engineering. Much of the work of computer programmers requires little localized or specialized knowledge and can be made routine once knowledge of a particular programming language is mastered.

Nevertheless, employers will continue to need some local programmers, especially those who have strong technical skills and who understand an employer's business and its programming requirements. This means that programmers will have to keep abreast of changing programming languages and techniques. Furthermore, a recent trend of domestic sourcing may help to keep a number of programming jobs onshore. Instead of hiring workers in foreign locations, some organizations have begun to contract with programmers in low-cost areas of the United States. This allows them to reduce payroll expenses while eliminating some of the logistical issues that arise with offshore outsourcing.

Job prospects. As a result of rapid employment growth over the 2008 to 2018 decade, job prospects for computer software engineers should be excellent. Those with practical experience and at least a bachelor's degree in a computer-related field should have the best opportunities. Employers will continue to seek computer professionals with strong programming, systems analysis, interpersonal, and business skills. In addition to jobs created through employment growth, many job openings will result from the need to replace workers who move into managerial positions, transfer to other occupations, or leave the labor force. Consulting opportunities for computer software engineers also should continue to grow as businesses seek help to manage, upgrade, and customize their increasingly complicated computer systems.

Although employment of computer programmers is projected to decline, numerous job openings will result from the need to replace workers who leave the labor force or transfer to other occupations. Prospects for these openings should be best for applicants with a bachelor's degree and experience with a variety of programming languages and tools. As technology evolves, however, and

Projections Data from the National Employment Matrix

Occupational title	SOC Code	Employment, 2008	Projected employment, 2018	Change, 2008–2018	
				Number	Percent
Computer software engineers and computer programmers..........—		1,336,300	1,619,300	283,000	21
Computer programmers 15-1021		426,700	414,400	−12,300	−3
Computer software engineers 15-1030		909,600	1,204,800	295,200	32
Computer software engineers, applications.............15-1031		514,800	689,900	175,100	34
Computer software engineers, systems software 15-1032		394,800	515,000	120,200	30

NOTE: Data in this table are rounded.

newer, more sophisticated tools emerge, programmers will need to update their skills in order to remain competitive. Obtaining vendor-specific or language-specific certification also can provide a competitive edge.

Earnings

In May 2008, median annual wages of wage-and-salary computer applications software engineers were $85,430. The middle 50 percent earned between $67,790 and $104,870. The lowest 10 percent earned less than $53,720, and the highest 10 percent earned more than $128,870. Median annual wages in the industries employing the largest numbers of computer applications software engineers in May 2008 were as follows:

Professional and commercial equipment and supplies merchant wholesalers	$93,740
Software publishers	87,710
Management of companies and enterprises	85,990
Computer systems design and related services	84,610
Insurance carriers	80,370

In May 2008, median annual wages of wage-and-salary computer systems software engineers were $92,430. The middle 50 percent earned between $73,200 and $113,960. The lowest 10 percent earned less than $57,810, and the highest 10 percent earned more than $135,780. Median annual wages in the industries employing the largest numbers of computer systems software engineers in May 2008 were as follows:

Scientific research and development services	$102,090
Computer and peripheral equipment manufacturing	101,270
Software publishers	93,590
Navigational measuring electromedical and control instruments manufacturing	91,720
Computer systems design and related services	91,610

Median annual wages of wage-and-salary computer programmers were $69,620 in May 2008. The middle 50 percent earned between $52,640 and $89,720 a year. The lowest 10 percent earned less than $40,080, and the highest 10 percent earned more than $111,450. Median annual wages in the industries employing the largest numbers of computer programmers in May 2008 are shown here:

Software publishers	$81,780
Management of companies and enterprises	71,040
Computer systems design and related services	70,270
Employment services	70,070
Insurance carriers	69,790

According to the National Association of Colleges and Employers, starting salary offers for graduates with a bachelor's degree in computer science averaged $61,407 in July 2009.

Related Occupations

Other professional workers who deal extensively with computer technology or data include actuaries; computer network, systems, and database administrators; computer scientists; computer support specialists; computer systems analysts; engineers; mathematicians; operations research analysts; and statisticians.

Sources of Additional Information

State employment service offices can provide information about job openings for computer programmers. Municipal chambers of commerce are an additional source of information on an area's largest employers.

Further information about computer careers is available from

▸ Association for Computing Machinery, 2 Penn Plaza, Suite 701, New York, NY 10121-0701. Internet: http://computingcareers.acm.org

▸ Institute of Electrical and Electronics Engineers Computer Society, Headquarters Office, 2001 L St. NW, Suite 700, Washington, DC 20036-4910. Internet: www.computer.org

▸ National Workforce Center for Emerging Technologies, 3000 Landerholm Circle SE, Bellevue, WA 98007. Internet: www.nwcet.org

▸ University of Washington Computer Science and Engineering Department, AC101 Paul G. Allen Center, Box 352350, 185 Stevens Way, Seattle, WA 98195-2350. Internet: www.cs.washington.edu/WhyCSE

▸ National Center for Women and Information Technology, University of Colorado, Campus Box 322 UCB, Boulder, CO 80309-0322. Internet: www.ncwit.org

Computer Support Specialists

(O*NET 15-1041.00)

Significant Points

■ Job growth is projected to be faster than the average for all occupations.

■ A bachelor's degree is required for some jobs, while an associate degree or certification is adequate for others.

■ Job prospects should be good, especially for college graduates with relevant skills and experience.

Nature of the Work

Computer support specialists provide technical assistance, support, and advice to individuals and organizations that depend on information technology. They work within organizations that use computer systems; for computer hardware or software vendors; or for third-party organizations that provide support services on a contract basis, such as help-desk service firms. Support specialists are usually differentiated between *technical support specialists* and *help-desk technicians*.

Technical support specialists respond to inquiries from their organizations' computer users and may run automatic diagnostics programs to resolve problems. In addition, they may write training manuals and train computer users in the use of new computer hardware and software. These workers also oversee the daily performance of their company's computer systems, resolving technical problems with Local Area Networks (LAN), Wide Area Networks (WAN), and other systems.

Help-desk technicians respond to telephone calls and e-mail messages from customers looking for help with computer problems. In responding to these inquiries, help-desk technicians must listen carefully to the customer, ask questions to diagnose the nature of the problem, and then patiently walk the customer through the problem-solving steps. They also install, modify, clean, and repair computer hardware and software. Many computer support specialists start out at the help desk.

Help-desk technicians deal directly with customer issues, and their employers value them as a source of feedback on their products and services. They are consulted for information about what gives customers the most trouble, as well as other customer concerns.

Work environment. Computer support specialists normally work in well-lighted, comfortable offices or computer laboratories. Most work about 40 hours a week. Those who work for third-party support firms often are away from their offices, spending considerable time working at a client's location. As computer networks expand, more computer support specialists may be able to provide technical support from remote locations. This capability would reduce or eliminate travel to the customer's workplace and may allow some support specialists to work from home.

Injuries in this occupation are uncommon, but like other workers who type on a keyboard for long periods, computer support specialists are susceptible to eyestrain, back discomfort, and hand and wrist problems such as carpal tunnel syndrome.

Training, Other Qualifications, and Advancement

A college degree is required for some computer support specialist positions, but an associate degree or certification may be sufficient for others. Strong problem-solving and communication skills are essential.

Education and training. Because of the wide range of skills required, there are many paths of entry to a job as a computer support specialist. Training requirements for computer support specialist positions vary, but many employers prefer to hire applicants with some formal college education. A bachelor's degree in computer science, computer engineering, or information systems is a prerequisite for some jobs; other jobs, however, may require only a computer-related associate degree. Some employers will hire applicants with a college degree in any field, as long as the applicant has the necessary technical skills. For some jobs, relevant computer experience and certifications may substitute for formal education.

Most support specialists receive on-the-job training after being hired. This training can last anywhere from one week to one year, but a common length is about three months. Many computer support specialists, in order to keep up with changes in technology, continue to receive training throughout their careers by attending professional training programs offered by employers, hardware and software vendors, colleges and universities, and private training institutions.

Certification and other qualifications. For some jobs, professional certification may qualify an applicant for employment. Certification can demonstrate proficiency in a product or process and help applicants obtain some entry-level positions. Some hardware and software vendors require their computer support specialists to be certified, and many of these will fund this training after an applicant is hired. Voluntary certification programs are offered by a wide variety of organizations, including product vendors and training institutions, and are available across the nation.

People interested in becoming a computer support specialist must have strong problem-solving, analytical, and communication skills because troubleshooting and helping others are vital parts of the job. The constant interaction with other computer personnel, customers, and employees requires computer support specialists to communicate effectively via e-mail, over the phone, or in person. Strong writing skills are useful in writing e-mail responses and preparing manuals for employees and customers.

Advancement. Entry-level computer support specialists generally work directly with customers or in-house users. They may advance into positions that handle products or problems with higher levels of technical complexity. Some may advance into management roles. Some computer support specialists may find opportunities in other occupations, such as computer programmers or software engineers, designing products rather than assisting users. Promotions depend heavily on job performance, but formal education and professional certification can improve advancement opportunities. Advancement opportunities in hardware and software companies can occur quickly, sometimes within months.

Employment

Computer support specialists held about 565,700 jobs in 2008. Although they worked in a wide range of industries, about 18 percent were employed in the computer systems design and related services industry. Substantial numbers of these workers were also employed in administrative and support services companies, financial institutions, insurance companies, government agencies, educational institutions, software publishers, telecommunications organizations, and health-care organizations.

Job Outlook

Employment is expected to increase faster than the average. Job prospects should be good, especially for those with a college degree and relevant skills.

Employment change. Employment of computer support specialists is expected to increase by 14 percent from 2008 to 2018, which is faster than the average for all occupations. Demand for these workers will result as organizations and individuals continue to adopt the newest forms of technology. As technology becomes more complex and widespread, support specialists will be needed in greater numbers to resolve the technical problems that arise. Businesses, especially, will demand greater levels of support, as information technology has become essential in the business environment.

Job growth will be fastest in several industries that rely heavily on technology. These include the computer systems design and related services industry; the data processing, hosting, and related services industry; the software publishing industry; and the management, scientific, and technical consulting industry. These industries will employ a growing number of support specialists as they utilize and provide an increasing array of IT services. Health-care and related establishments, in addition, may see substantial growth as these organizations look to improve their efficiency and patient care through the use of information systems and other technology.

Overall growth may be dampened, to a certain extent, as some jobs are outsourced to offshore locations. Advances in technology

Projections Data from the National Employment Matrix

Occupational title	SOC Code	Employment, 2008	Projected employment, 2018	Change, 2008–2018	
				Number	Percent
Computer support specialists	15-1041	565,700	643,700	78,000	14

NOTE: Data in this table are rounded.

increasingly allow computer support specialists to provide assistance remotely. Some employers may seek to reduce expenses by hiring workers in areas that have lower prevailing wages.

Job prospects. Job prospects are expected to be good; those who possess a bachelor's degree, relevant technical and communication skills, and previous work experience should have even better opportunities than applicants with an associate degree or professional certification.

Earnings

Median annual wages of wage-and-salary computer support specialists were $43,450 in May 2008. The middle 50 percent earned between $33,680 and $55,990. The lowest 10 percent earned less than $26,580, and the highest 10 percent earned more than $70,750. Median annual wages in the industries employing the largest numbers of computer support specialists in May 2008 were as follows:

Professional and commercial equipment
  and supplies merchant wholesalers $48,580
Management of companies and enterprises 45,200
Colleges, universities, and professional schools 43,130
Computer systems design and related services 43,080
Elementary and secondary schools 40,550

Related Occupations

Other occupations that deal with technology or respond to customer inquiries include broadcast and sound engineering technicians and radio operators; computer and information systems managers; computer network, systems, and database administrators; computer software engineers and computer programmers; and customer service representatives.

Sources of Additional Information

For additional information about a career as a computer support specialist, contact

▶ Association of Support Professionals, 122 Barnard Ave., Watertown, MA 02472. Internet: http://asponline.com

▶ HDI, 102 S. Tejon, Suite 1200, Colorado Springs, CO 80903. Internet: www.thinkhdi.com

For additional information about computer careers, contact

▶ Association for Computing Machinery, 2 Penn Plaza, Suite 701, New York, NY 10121-0701. Internet: http://computingcareers.acm.org

▶ Institute of Electrical and Electronics Engineers Computer Society, Headquarters Office, 2001 L St. NW, Suite 700, Washington, DC 20036-4910. Internet: www.computer.org

▶ National Workforce Center for Emerging Technologies, 3000 Landerholm Circle SE, Bellevue, WA 98007. Internet: www.nwcet.org

▶ University of Washington Computer Science and Engineering Department, AC101 Paul G. Allen Center, Box 352350, 185 Stevens Way, Seattle, WA 98195-2350. Internet: www.cs.washington.edu/WhyCSE

▶ National Center for Women and Information Technology, University of Colorado, Campus Box 322 UCB, Boulder, CO 80309-0322. Internet: www.ncwit.org

Computer Systems Analysts

(O*NET 15-1051.00 and 15-1051.01)

Significant Points

■ Employment is expected to increase much faster than average.

■ Excellent job prospects are expected as organizations continue to adopt increasingly sophisticated technologies.

■ Employers generally prefer applicants who have at least a bachelor's degree; relevant work experience also is very important.

Nature of the Work

Nearly all organizations rely on computer and information technology (IT) to conduct business and operate efficiently. *Computer systems analysts* use IT tools to help enterprises of all sizes achieve their goals. They may design and develop new computer systems by choosing and configuring hardware and software, or they may devise ways to apply existing systems' resources to additional tasks.

Most systems analysts work with specific types of computer systems—for example, business, accounting, and financial systems or scientific and engineering systems—that vary with the kind of organization. Analysts who specialize in helping an organization select the proper system hardware and software are often called *system architects* or *system designers.* Analysts who specialize in developing and fine-tuning systems often have the more general title of *systems analysts.*

To begin an assignment, systems analysts consult with an organization's managers and users to define the goals of the system and then design a system to meet those goals. They specify the inputs that the system will access, decide how the inputs will be processed, and format the output to meet users' needs. Analysts use techniques such as structured analysis, data modeling, information engineering, mathematical model building, sampling, and a variety of accounting principles to ensure their plans are efficient and complete. They also may prepare cost-benefit and return-on-investment analyses to help management decide whether implementing the proposed technology would be financially feasible.

When a system is approved, systems analysts oversee the implementation of the required hardware and software components. They coordinate tests and observe the initial use of the system to ensure that it performs as planned. They prepare specifications, flow charts, and process diagrams for computer programmers to follow; then they work with programmers to "debug," or eliminate errors, from the system. Systems analysts who do more in-depth testing may be called *software quality assurance analysts*. In addition to running tests, these workers diagnose problems, recommend solutions, and determine whether program requirements have been met. After the system has been implemented, tested, and debugged, computer systems analysts may train its users and write instruction manuals.

In some organizations, *programmer-analysts* design and update the software that runs a computer. They also create custom applications tailored to their organization's tasks. Because they are responsible for both programming and systems analysis, these workers must be proficient in both areas. (A separate description of computer software engineers and computer programmers appears elsewhere in this book.) As this dual proficiency becomes more common, analysts are increasingly working with databases, object-oriented programming languages, client-server applications, and multimedia and Internet technology.

One challenge created by expanding computer use is the need for different computer systems to communicate with each other. Many systems analysts are involved with "networking," connecting all the computers within an organization or across organizations, as when setting up e-commerce networks to facilitate business between companies.

Work environment. Computer systems analysts work in offices or laboratories in comfortable surroundings. Many work about 40 hours a week, but some work more than 50 hours a week. Some analysts telecommute, using computers to work from remote locations.

Injuries in this occupation are uncommon, but computer systems analysts, like other workers who spend long periods typing on a computer, are susceptible to eyestrain, back discomfort, and hand and wrist problems such as carpal tunnel syndrome.

Training, Other Qualifications, and Advancement

Training requirements for computer systems analysts vary depending on the job, but many employers prefer applicants who have a bachelor's degree. Relevant work experience also is very important. Advancement opportunities are good for those with the necessary skills and experience.

Education and training. When hiring computer systems analysts, employers usually prefer applicants who have at least a bachelor's degree. For more technically complex jobs, people with graduate degrees are preferred. For jobs in a technical or scientific environment, employers often seek applicants who have at least a bachelor's degree in a technical field, such as computer science, information science, applied mathematics, engineering, or the physical sciences. For jobs in a business environment, employers often seek applicants with at least a bachelor's degree in a business-related field such as management information systems (MIS). Increasingly, employers are seeking individuals who have a master's degree in business administration (MBA) with a concentration in information systems.

Despite the preference for technical degrees, however, people who have degrees in other areas may find employment as systems analysts if they also have technical skills. Courses in computer science or related subjects combined with practical experience can qualify people for some jobs in the occupation.

Employers generally look for people with expertise relevant to the job. For example, systems analysts who wish to work for a bank may need some expertise in finance, and systems analysts who wish to work for a hospital may need some knowledge of health management. Furthermore, business enterprises generally prefer individuals with information technology, business, and accounting skills and frequently assist employees in obtaining these skills.

Technological advances come so rapidly in the computer field that continuous study is necessary to remain competitive. Employers, hardware and software vendors, colleges and universities, and private training institutions offer continuing education to help workers attain the latest skills. Additional training may come from professional development seminars offered by professional computing societies.

Other qualifications. Employers usually look for people who have broad knowledge and experience related to computer systems and technologies, strong problem-solving and analytical skills, and the ability to think logically. In addition, the ability to concentrate and pay close attention to detail is important because computer systems analysts often deal with many tasks simultaneously. Although these workers sometimes work independently, they frequently work in teams on large projects. Therefore, they must have good interpersonal skills and be able to communicate effectively with computer personnel, users, and other staff who may have no technical background.

Advancement. With experience, systems analysts may be promoted to senior or lead analyst. Those who possess leadership ability and good business skills also can become computer and information systems managers or can advance into executive positions such as chief information officer. Those with work experience and considerable expertise in a particular subject or application may find lucrative opportunities as independent consultants, or they may choose to start their own computer consulting firms.

Employment

Computer systems analysts held about 532,200 jobs in 2008. Although they are employed in many industries, 24 percent of these workers were in the computer systems design and related services industry. Computer systems analysts also were employed by governments; insurance companies; financial institutions; and business management firms. About 30,300 computer systems analysts were self-employed in 2008.

Job Outlook

Employment is expected to grow much faster than the average for all occupations, and job prospects should be excellent.

Employment change. Employment of computer systems analysts is expected to grow by 20 percent from 2008 to 2018, which is much faster than the average for all occupations. Demand for these workers will increase as organizations continue to adopt and integrate

Projections Data from the National Employment Matrix

Occupational title	SOC Code	Employment, 2008	Projected employment, 2018	Change, 2008–2018	
				Number	Percent
Computer systems analysts..........................	15-1051	532,200	640,300	108,100	20

NOTE: Data in this table are rounded.

increasingly sophisticated technologies and as the need for information security grows.

As information technology becomes an increasingly important aspect of the business environment, the demand for computer networking, Internet, and intranet functions will drive demand for computer systems analysts. The increasing adoption of the wireless Internet, known as WiFi, and of personal mobile computers has created a need for new systems that can integrate these technologies into existing networks. Explosive growth in these areas is expected to fuel demand for analysts who are knowledgeable about systems development and integration. In addition, as sensitive data continues to be transmitted and stored electronically, the need for information security specialists is expected to grow rapidly. Furthermore, the health-care industry is expected to increase its use of information technology and will demand the services of this occupation. The adoption of e-prescribing, electronic health records, and other IT platforms will drive this trend, creating a large number of new jobs.

As with other information technology jobs, employment growth may be tempered somewhat by offshoring. Firms may look to cut costs by shifting operations to foreign countries with lower prevailing wages and highly skilled workers. However, due to the high level of expertise that is required, as well as the frequent need to be near the job site, systems analysts are less likely to be offshored than other IT occupations.

Job prospects. Job prospects should be excellent. Job openings will occur as a result of strong job growth and from the need to replace workers who move into other occupations or who leave the labor force.

Earnings

Median annual wages of wage and salary computer systems analysts were $75,500 in May 2008. The middle 50 percent earned between $58,460 and $95,810 a year. The lowest 10 percent earned less than $45,390, and the highest 10 percent earned more than $118,440. Median annual wages in the industries employing the largest numbers of computer systems analysts in May 2008 were as follows:

Professional and commercial equipment and supplies merchant wholesalers	$89,670
Computer systems design and related services	78,680
Data processing, hosting, and related services.......	78,010
Management of companies and enterprises	76,070
Insurance carriers..	74,610

Related Occupations

Other workers who use computers extensively and who use logic and creativity to solve business and technical problems include actuaries; computer and information systems managers; computer network, systems, and database administrators; computer software engineers and computer programmers; engineers; management analysts; mathematicians; operations research analysts; and statisticians.

Sources of Additional Information

Further information about computer careers is available from

▸ Association for Computing Machinery (ACM), 2 Penn Plaza, Suite 701, New York, NY 10121-0701. Internet: http://computingcareers. acm.org/

▸ Institute of Electrical and Electronics Engineers Computer Society, Headquarters Office, 2001 L St. NW, Suite 700, Washington, DC 20036-4910. Internet: www.computer.org

▸ National Workforce Center for Emerging Technologies, 3000 Landerholm Circle SE, Bellevue, WA 98007. Internet: www.nwcet.org

▸ University of Washington Computer Science and Engineering Department, AC101 Paul G. Allen Center, Box 352350, 185 Stevens Way, Seattle, WA 98195-2350. Internet: www.cs.washington.edu/ WhyCSE

▸ National Center for Women and Information Technology, University of Colorado, Campus Box 322 UCB, Boulder, CO 80309-0322. Internet: www.ncwit.org

Construction Equipment Operators

(O*NET 47-2071.00, 47-2072.00, and 47-2073.00)

Significant Points

■ Construction equipment operators are trained either through a formal apprenticeship program, through on-the-job training, through a paid training program, or a combination of these programs.

■ Job opportunities are expected to be good.

■ Hourly pay is relatively high, but operators of some types of equipment cannot work in inclement weather, so total annual earnings may be reduced.

Nature of the Work

Construction equipment operators use machinery to move construction materials, earth, and other heavy materials at construction sites and mines. They operate equipment that clears and grades land to prepare it for construction of roads, buildings, and bridges, as well as airport runways, power generation facilities, dams, levees, and other structures. They use machines to dig trenches to lay or repair sewer and other utilities, and hoist heavy construction materials. They even may work offshore constructing oil rigs. Construction equipment operators also operate machinery that spreads asphalt and concrete on roads and other structures.

These workers also help set up and inspect the equipment, make adjustments, and perform some maintenance and minor repairs. Construction equipment is more technologically advanced than it was in the past. For example, global positioning system (GPS) technology is now being used to help with grading and leveling activities.

Included in the construction equipment operator occupation are operating engineers and other construction equipment operators; paving and surfacing equipment operators; and piledriver operators. *Operating engineers* and *other construction equipment operators* work with one or several types of power construction equipment. They may operate excavation and loading machines equipped with scoops, shovels, or buckets that dig sand, gravel, earth, or similar materials and load it into trucks or onto conveyors. In addition operating to the familiar bulldozers, they operate trench excavators, road graders, and similar equipment. Sometimes, they may drive and control industrial trucks or tractors equipped with forklifts or booms for lifting materials or with hitches for pulling trailers. They also may operate and maintain air compressors, pumps, and other power equipment at construction sites.

Paving and surfacing equipment operators operate machines that spread and level asphalt or spread and smooth concrete for roadways or other structures. *Asphalt spreader operators* turn valves to regulate the temperature and flow of asphalt onto the roadbed. They must take care that the machine distributes the paving material evenly and without voids, and they must make sure that there is a constant flow of asphalt going into the hopper. Concrete paving machine operators control levers and turn handwheels to move attachments that spread, vibrate, and level wet concrete in forms. They must observe the surface of the concrete to identify low spots into which workers must add concrete. They use other attachments to smooth the surface of the concrete, spray on a curing compound, and cut expansion joints. Tamping equipment operators operate tamping machines that compact earth and other fill materials for roadbeds or other construction sites. They also may operate machines with interchangeable hammers to cut or break up old pavement and drive guardrail posts into the earth.

Piledriver operators use large machines mounted on skids, barges, or cranes to hammer piles into the ground. Piles are long, heavy beams of wood or steel driven into the ground to support retaining walls, bulkheads, bridges, piers, or building foundations. Some piledriver operators work on offshore oil rigs. Piledriver operators move hand and foot levers and turn valves to activate, position, and control the pile-driving equipment.

Work environment. Construction equipment operators work outdoors in nearly every type of climate and weather condition, although in many areas of the country some types of construction operations must be suspended in winter. Bulldozers, scrapers, and especially piledrivers are noisy and shake or jolt the operator. Operating heavy construction equipment can be dangerous, and this occupation incurs injuries and illnesses at a higher-than-average rate. As with most machinery, accidents generally can be avoided by observing proper operating procedures and safety practices.

Construction equipment operators often get dirty, greasy, muddy, or dusty. Some operators work in remote locations on large construction projects, such as highways and dams, or in factory or mining operations.

Operators may have irregular hours because work on some construction projects continues around the clock or must be performed late at night or early in the morning.

Training, Other Qualifications, and Advancement

Construction equipment operators are trained either through a formal apprenticeship program, through on-the-job training, through a paid training program, or a combination of these programs.

Education and training. Employers of construction equipment operators generally prefer to hire high school graduates, although some employers may train nongraduates to operate some types of equipment. High school courses in automobile mechanics are helpful because workers may perform maintenance on their machines. Also useful are courses in science and mechanical drawing. With the development of GPS, construction equipment operators need more experience with computers than in the past.

On the job, workers may start by operating light equipment under the guidance of an experienced operator. Later, they may operate heavier equipment, such as bulldozers. Technologically advanced construction equipment with computerized controls and improved hydraulics and electronics requires more skill to operate. Operators of such equipment may need more training and some understanding of electronics.

It is generally accepted that formal training provides more comprehensive skills. Some construction equipment operators train in formal operating engineer apprenticeship programs administered by union-management committees of the International Union of Operating Engineers (IUOE). Because apprentices learn to operate a wider variety of machines than do other beginners, they usually have better job opportunities. Apprenticeship programs consist of at least 3 years, or 6,000 hours, of paid on-the-job training together with 144 hours of related classroom instruction each year.

Private vocational schools offer instruction in the operation of certain types of construction equipment. Completion of such programs may help a person get a job. However, people considering this kind of training should check the school's reputation among employers in the area and find out if the school offers the opportunity to work on actual machines in realistic situations. A large amount of information can be learned in classrooms, but to become a skilled construction equipment operator, a worker needs to actually perform the various tasks. Many training facilities, including IUOE apprenticeship programs, incorporate sophisticated simulators into their training, allowing beginners to familiarize themselves with the equipment in a controlled environment.

Certification and other qualifications. Mechanical aptitude and experience operating related mobile equipment, such as farm tractors or heavy equipment, in the Armed Forces or elsewhere is an asset. Construction equipment operators often need a commercial driver's license to haul their equipment to the various jobsites. Commercial driver's licenses are issued by states according to each state's rules and regulations. Operators also need to be in good physical condition and have a good sense of balance, the ability to judge distance, and eye-hand-foot coordination. Some operator positions require the ability to work at heights.

Certification or training from the right school can improve opportunities for jobseekers; some employers may require operators to be certified. While attending some vocational schools, or by fulfilling the requirements of related professional associations, operators can qualify for various certifications. These certifications prove to potential employers that an operator is able to handle specific types of equipment.

Advancement. Construction equipment operators can advance to become supervisors. Some operators choose to pass on their knowledge and teach in training facilities. Other operators start their own contracting businesses, although doing so may be difficult because of high startup costs.

Employment

Construction equipment operators held about 469,300 jobs in 2008. Jobs were found in every section of the country and were distributed among various types of operators as follows:

Operating engineers and other construction
    equipment operators......................................404,500
Paving, surfacing, and tamping equipment
    operators 60,200
Pile-driver operators 4,600

About 63 percent of construction equipment operators worked in the construction industry. Many equipment operators worked in heavy and civil engineering construction, building highways, bridges, or railroads. About 16 percent of construction equipment operators worked in local government. Others—mostly grader, bulldozer, and scraper operators—worked in mining. Some also worked for manufacturing or utility companies. About 3 percent of construction equipment operators were self-employed.

Job Outlook

Average job growth is projected. The need to fill jobs and replace workers who leave the occupation should result in good job opportunities for construction equipment operators.

Employment change. Employment of construction equipment operators is expected to increase 12 percent between 2008 and 2018, about as fast as the average for all occupations. The likelihood of increased spending by the federal government on infrastructure to improve roads and bridges, railroads, the electric transmission system, and water and sewer systems, which are in great need of repair across the country, will generate numerous jobs for construction equipment operators who work primarily in these areas. In addition, population increases and the need for construction projects, such as new roads and sewer lines to service the increased population, will generate more jobs. However, without the extra spending on infrastructure by the federal government, employment may be flat as states and localities struggle with reduced taxes and budget shortfalls to pay for road and other improvements.

An expected rise in energy production is expected to increase work on oil rigs, smart grids, windmill farms, pipeline construction, and other types of power-generating facilities. Also, increased output of mines and rock and gravel quarries will generate jobs in the mining industry.

Job prospects. Job opportunities for construction equipment operators are expected to be good because the occupation often does not attract enough qualified candidates to fill jobs. Some workers' reluctance to work in construction makes it easier for willing workers to get operator jobs.

In addition, many job openings will arise from job growth and from the need to replace experienced construction equipment operators who transfer to other occupations, retire, or leave the job for other reasons. Construction equipment operators who can use a wide variety of equipment will have the best prospects. Operators with pipeline experience will have especially good opportunities if, as expected, natural-gas companies expand work on their infrastructure.

Employment of construction equipment operators, like that of many other construction workers, is sensitive to fluctuations in the economy. Workers in these trades may experience periods of unemployment when the overall level of construction falls. However, shortages of these workers may occur in some areas during peak periods of building activity.

Earnings

Wages for construction equipment operators vary. In May 2008, median hourly wages of wage and salary operating engineers and other construction equipment operators were $18.88. The middle 50 percent earned between $14.78 and $25.49. The lowest 10 percent earned less than $12.47, and the highest 10 percent earned more than $33.34. Median hourly wages in the industries employing the largest numbers of operating engineers were as follows:

Projections Data from the National Employment Matrix

Occupational title	SOC Code	Employment, 2008	Projected employment, 2018	Change, 2008–2018	
				Number	Percent
Construction equipment operators...................................47-2070		469,300	525,500	56,200	12
Paving, surfacing, and tamping equipment operators ...47-2071		60,200	67,200	6,900	12
Pile-driver operators 47-2072		4,600	5,200	600	13
Operating engineers and other construction equipment operators 47-2073		404,500	453,200	48,700	12

NOTE: Data in this table are rounded.

Nonresidential building construction $21.45
Highway, street, and bridge construction 21.20
Utility system construction 19.79
Other specialty trade contractors 18.61
Local government 17.19

Median hourly wages of wage and salary paving, surfacing, and tamping equipment operators were $16.00 in May 2008. The middle 50 percent earned between $12.94 and $20.75. The lowest 10 percent earned less than $10.77, and the highest 10 percent earned more than $26.70. Median hourly wages in the industries employing the largest numbers of paving, surfacing, and tamping equipment operators were as follows:

Other specialty trade contractors $16.16
Highway, street, and bridge construction 16.13
Local government 15.94

In May 2008, median hourly wages of wage and salary piledriver operators were $23.01. The middle 50 percent earned between $17.52 and $32.94. The lowest 10 percent earned less than $14.25, and the highest 10 percent earned more than $38.01. Median hourly wages in the industries employing the largest numbers of piledriver operators were as follows:

Other specialty trade contractors $26.07
Other heavy and civil engineering construction 23.24
Nonresidential building construction 20.46
Utility system construction 19.54

Hourly pay is relatively high, particularly in large metropolitan areas. However, annual earnings of some workers may be lower than hourly rates would indicate because worktime may be limited by bad weather. About 27 percent of construction equipment operators belong to a union.

Related Occupations

Other workers who operate mechanical equipment include the following agricultural equipment operators; logging equipment operators; material moving occupations; and truck drivers, heavy and tractor-trailer.

Sources of Additional Information

For further information about apprenticeships or work opportunities for construction equipment operators, contact a local of the International Union of Operating Engineers, a local apprenticeship committee, or the nearest office of the state apprenticeship agency or employment service. You also can find information on the registered apprenticeship system, with links to state apprenticeship programs, on the U.S. Department of Labor's web site: www.doleta.gov/OA/eta_default.cfm. In addition, apprenticeship information is available from the U.S. Department of Labor's toll free help line: (877) 872-5627.

For general information about the work of construction equipment operators, contact

▸ Associated General Contractors of America, 2300 Wilson Blvd., Suite 400, Arlington, VA 22201-5426. Internet: www.agc.org

▸ International Union of Operating Engineers, 1125 17th St. NW, Washington, DC 20036-4786. Internet: www.iuoe.org

▸ National Center for Construction Education and Research, 3600 NW 43rd St., Building G, Gainesville, FL 32606-8134. Internet: www.nccer.org

▸ Pile Driving Contractors Association, P.O. Box 66208, Orange Park, FL 32065-0021. Internet: www.piledrivers.org

For general information on apprenticeships and how to get them, see the *Occupational Outlook Quarterly* article "Apprenticeships: Career training, credentials—and a paycheck in your pocket," online at www.bls.gov/opub/ooq/2002/summer/art01.pdf and in print at many libraries and career centers.

Construction Laborers

(O*NET 47-2061.00)

Significant Points

■ Many construction laborer jobs require a variety of basic skills, but others require specialized training and experience.

■ Most construction laborers learn on the job, but formal apprenticeship programs provide the most thorough preparation.

■ Job opportunities vary by locality, but in many areas there will be competition, especially for jobs requiring limited skills.

■ Laborers who have specialized skills or who can relocate near new construction projects should have the best opportunities.

Nature of the Work

Construction laborers can be found on almost all construction sites, performing a wide range of tasks from the very easy to the hazardous. They can be found at building, highway, and heavy construction sites; residential and commercial sites; tunnel and shaft excavations; and demolition sites. Many of the jobs they perform require physical strength, training, and experience. Other jobs require little skill and can be learned quickly. Although most construction laborers specialize in a type of construction, such as highway or tunnel construction, some are generalists who perform many different tasks during all stages of construction. Construction laborers who work in underground construction, such as in tunnels, or in demolition are more likely to specialize in only those areas.

Construction laborers clean and prepare construction sites. They remove trees and debris; tend pumps, compressors, and generators; and erect and disassemble scaffolding and other temporary structures. They load, unload, identify, and distribute building materials to the appropriate location according to project plans and specifications. Laborers also tend machines; for example, they may use a portable mixer to mix concrete or tend a machine that pumps concrete, grout, cement, sand, plaster, or stucco through a spray gun for application to ceilings and walls. They often help other craftworkers, including carpenters, plasterers, operating engineers, and masons.

Construction laborers are responsible for the installation and maintenance of traffic control devices and patterns. At highway construction sites, this work may include clearing and preparing highway work zones and rights-of-way; installing traffic barricades, cones, and markers; and controlling traffic passing near, in, and around work zones. Construction laborers also dig trenches; install sewer, water, and storm drainpipes; and place concrete and asphalt on roads. Other highly specialized tasks include operating laser guidance equipment to place pipes; operating air, electric, and pneumatic drills; and transporting and setting explosives for the construction of tunnels, shafts, and roads.

Some construction laborers help with the removal of hazardous materials, such as asbestos, lead, or chemicals.

Construction laborers operate a variety of equipment, including pavement breakers; jackhammers; earth tampers; concrete, mortar, and plaster mixers; electric and hydraulic boring machines; torches; small mechanical hoists; laser beam equipment; and surveying and measuring equipment. They may use computers and other high-tech input devices to control robotic pipe cutters and cleaners. To perform their jobs effectively, construction laborers must be familiar with the duties of other craftworkers and with the materials, tools, and machinery they use, as all of these workers work as part of a team, jointly carrying out assigned construction tasks.

Work environment. Most construction laborers do physically demanding work. Some work at great heights or outdoors in all weather conditions. Some jobs expose workers to harmful materials or chemicals, fumes, odors, loud noises, or dangerous machinery. Some laborers may be exposed to lead-based paint, asbestos, or other hazardous substances during their work, especially when they work in confined spaces. Workers in this occupation experience one of the highest rates of nonfatal injuries and illnesses; consequently, the work requires constant attention to safety on the job. To avoid injury, workers in these jobs wear safety clothing, such as gloves, hardhats, protective chemical suits, and devices to protect their eyes, respiratory system, or hearing. While working underground, construction laborers must be especially alert in order to follow procedures safely and must deal with a variety of hazards.

A standard 40 hour work week is the most common work week for construction laborers. About 1 in 7 has a variable schedule, as overnight work may be required in highway work. In some parts of the country, construction laborers may work only during certain seasons. They also may experience weather-related work stoppages at any time of the year.

Training, Other Qualifications, and Advancement

Many construction laborer jobs require a variety of basic skills, but others require specialized training and experience. Most construction laborers learn on the job, but formal apprenticeship programs provide the most thorough preparation.

Education and training. Although some construction laborer jobs have no specific educational qualifications or entry-level training, apprenticeships for laborers usually require a high school diploma or the equivalent. High school classes in English, mathematics, physics, mechanical drawing, blueprint reading, welding, and general shop can be helpful.

Most workers start by getting a job with a contractor who provides on-the-job training. Increasingly, construction laborers are finding work through temporary-help agencies that send laborers to construction sites for short-term work. Entry-level workers generally help more experienced workers, by performing routine tasks such as cleaning and preparing the worksite and unloading materials. When the opportunity arises, they learn from experienced construction trades workers how to do more difficult tasks, such as operating tools and equipment. Construction laborers also may choose or be required to attend a trade or vocational school, association training class, or community college to receive further trade-related training.

Some laborers receive more formal training in the form of an apprenticeship. These programs include between 2 and 4 years of classroom and on-the-job training. In the first 200 hours, workers learn basic construction skills, such as blueprint reading, the correct use of tools and equipment, and safety and health procedures. The remainder of the curriculum consists of specialized skills training in three of the largest segments of the construction industry: building construction, heavy and highway construction, and environmental remediation, such as lead or asbestos abatement and mold or hazardous waste remediation. Training in "green," energy-efficient construction, an area of growth in the construction industry, is now available and can help workers find employment.

Workers who use dangerous equipment or handle toxic chemicals usually receive specialized safety training. Laborers who remove hazardous materials are required to take union- or employer-sponsored Occupational Safety and Health Administration safety training.

Apprenticeship applicants usually must be at least 18 years old and meet local requirements. Because the number of apprenticeship programs is limited, however, only a small proportion of laborers learn their trade in this way.

Other qualifications. Laborers need manual dexterity, eye-hand coordination, good physical fitness, a good sense of balance, and an ability to work as a member of a team. The ability to solve arithmetic problems quickly and accurately may be required. In addition, military service or a good work history is viewed favorably by contractors.

Certification and advancement. Laborers may earn certifications in welding, scaffold erecting, and concrete finishing. These certifications help workers prove that they have the knowledge to perform more complex tasks.

Through training and experience, laborers can move into other construction occupations. Laborers may also advance to become construction supervisors or general contractors. For those who would like to advance, it is increasingly important to be able to communicate in both English and Spanish in order to relay instructions and safety precautions to workers with limited understanding of English; Spanish-speaking workers make up a large part of the construction workforce in many areas. Supervisors and contractors need good communication skills to deal with clients and subcontractors.

In addition, supervisors and contractors should be able to identify and estimate the quantity of materials needed to complete a job and accurately estimate how long a job will take to complete and what it will cost. Computer skills also are important for advancement as construction becomes increasingly mechanized and computerized.

Projections Data from the National Employment Matrix

Occupational title	SOC Code	Employment, 2008	Projected employment, 2018	Change, 2008–2018	
				Number	Percent
Construction laborers 47-2061		1,248,700	1,504,600	255,900	20

NOTE: Data in this table are rounded.

Employment

Construction laborers held about 1.2 million jobs in 2008. They worked throughout the country, but like the general population, were concentrated in metropolitan areas. About 62 percent of construction laborers worked in the construction industry, including 27 percent who worked for specialty trade contractors. About 21 percent were self-employed in 2008.

Job Outlook

Employment is expected to grow much faster than the average. In many areas, there will be competition for jobs, especially those requiring limited skills. Laborers who have specialized skills or who can relocate near new construction projects should have the best opportunities.

Employment change. Employment of construction laborers is expected to grow by 20 percent between 2008 and 2018, much faster than the average for all occupations. Because of the large variety of tasks that laborers perform, demand for laborers will mirror the level of overall construction activity. However, some jobs may be adversely affected by automation as they are replaced by new machinery and equipment that improves productivity and quality.

Increasing job prospects for construction laborers, however, is the expected additional government funding for the repair and reconstruction of the nation's infrastructure, such as roads, bridges, public buildings, and water lines. The occupation should experience an increase in demand because laborers make up a significant portion of workers on these types of projects.

New emphasis on green construction also should help lead to better employment prospects as many green practices require more labor on construction sites. Additional duties resulting from practicing green construction include having to segregate materials that can be used again from those which cannot, and the actual reuse of such materials. In addition, these workers will be needed for the construction of any new projects to harness wind or solar power.

Job prospects. In many geographic areas, construction laborers—especially for those with limited skills—will experience competition because of a plentiful supply of workers who are willing to work as day laborers. Overall opportunities will be best for those with experience and specialized skills and for those who can relocate to areas with new construction projects. Opportunities also will be better for laborers specializing in road construction.

Employment of construction laborers, like that of many other construction workers, is sensitive to the fluctuations of the economy. On the one hand, workers in these trades may experience periods of unemployment when the overall level of construction falls. On the other hand, shortages of these workers may occur in some areas during peak periods of building activity.

Earnings

Median hourly wages of wage and salary construction laborers in May 2008 were $13.71. The middle 50 percent earned between $10.74 and $18.57. The lowest 10 percent earned less than $8.67, and the highest 10 percent earned more than $25.98. Median hourly wages in the industries employing the largest number of construction laborers were as follows:

Nonresidential building construction	$14.95
Other specialty trade contractors	13.81
Residential building construction	13.79
Foundation, structure, and building exterior contractors	13.35
Employment services	10.80

Earnings for construction laborers can be reduced by poor weather or by downturns in construction activity, which sometimes result in layoffs. Apprentices or helpers usually start out earning about 60 percent of the wage paid to experienced workers. Pay increases as apprentices gain experience and learn new skills.

Some laborers—about 14 percent—belong to a union, mainly the Laborers' International Union of North America.

Related Occupations

The work of construction laborers is closely related to that of other construction occupations, as well as that of others who perform similar physical work, such as the following assemblers and fabricators; brickmasons, blockmasons, and stonemasons; forest and conservation workers; grounds maintenance workers; highway maintenance workers; logging workers; material moving occupations; refractory materials repairers, except brickmasons; and roustabouts, oil and gas.

Sources of Additional Information

For information about jobs as a construction laborer, contact local building or construction contractors, local joint labor-management apprenticeship committees, apprenticeship agencies, or the local office of your State Employment Service. You also can find information on the registered apprenticeships, together with links to state apprenticeship programs, on the U.S. Department of Labor's web site: www.doleta.gov/OA/eta_default.cfm. Apprenticeship information also is available from the U.S. Department of Labor's toll-free help line: (877) 872-5627.

For general information on apprenticeships and how to get them, see the *Occupational Outlook Quarterly* article "Apprenticeships: Career training, credentials—and a paycheck in your pocket," online at www.bls.gov/opub/ooq/2002/summer/art01.pdf and in print at many libraries and career centers.

For information on education programs for laborers, contact

▸ Laborers-AGC Education and Training Fund, 37 Deerfield Rd., P.O. Box 37, Pomfret Center, CT 06258-0037.

▸ National Center for Construction Education and Research, 3600 NW 43rd St., Bldg. G, Gainesville, FL 32606. Internet: www.nccer.org

Construction Managers

(O*NET 11-9021.00)

Significant Points

■ About 61 percent of construction managers are self-employed.

■ Jobseekers who combine construction work experience with a bachelor's degree in a construction-related field should enjoy the best prospects.

■ Certification, although not required, is increasingly important for construction managers.

Nature of the Work

Construction managers plan, direct, coordinate, and budget a wide variety of construction projects, including the building of all types of residential, commercial, and industrial structures, roads, bridges, wastewater treatment plants, schools, and hospitals. Construction managers may supervise an entire project or just part of one. They schedule and coordinate all design and construction processes, including the selection, hiring, and oversight of specialty trade contractors, such as carpentry, plumbing, or electrical, but they usually do not do any actual construction of the structure.

Construction managers are salaried or self-employed managers who oversee construction supervisors and personnel. They are often called *project managers, constructors, construction superintendents, project engineers, construction supervisors,* or *general contractors.* Construction managers may be owners or salaried employees of a construction management or contracting firm, or they may work under contract or as a salaried employee of the property owner, developer, or contracting firm managing the construction project.

These managers coordinate and supervise the construction process from the conceptual development stage through final construction, making sure that the project gets completed on time and within budget. They often work with owners, engineers, architects, and others who are involved in the process. Given the designs for buildings, roads, bridges, or other projects, construction managers supervise the planning, scheduling, and implementation of those designs.

Large construction projects, such as an office building or an industrial complex, are often too complicated for one person to manage. Accordingly, these projects are divided into various segments: site preparation, including clearing and excavation of the land, installing sewage systems, and landscaping and road construction; building construction, including laying foundations and erecting the struc-

tural framework, floors, walls, and roofs; and building systems, including protecting against fire and installing electrical, plumbing, air-conditioning, and heating systems. Construction managers may be in charge of one or several of these activities.

Construction managers determine the best way to get materials to the building site and the most cost-effective plan and schedule for completing the project. They divide all required construction site activities into logical steps, estimating and budgeting the time required to meet established deadlines. Doing this may require sophisticated scheduling and cost-estimating techniques using computers with specialized software.

Construction managers also manage the selection of general contractors and trade contractors to complete specific phases of the project, which could include everything from structural metalworking and plumbing to painting to installing electricity and carpeting. Construction managers determine the labor requirements of the project and, in some cases, supervise or monitor the hiring and dismissal of workers. They oversee the performance of all trade contractors and are responsible for ensuring that all work is completed on schedule.

Construction managers direct and monitor the progress of construction activities, occasionally through construction supervisors or other construction managers. They are responsible for obtaining all necessary permits and licenses and, depending upon the contractual arrangements, for directing or monitoring compliance with building and safety codes, other regulations, and requirements set by the project's insurers. They also oversee the delivery and use of materials, tools, and equipment; worker safety and productivity; and the quality of the construction.

Work environment. Working out of a main office or out of a field office at the construction site, construction managers monitor the overall construction project. Decisions regarding daily construction activities generally are made at the jobsite. Managers might travel considerably when the construction site is not close to their main office or when they are responsible for activities at two or more sites. Management of overseas construction projects usually entails temporary residence in the country in which the project is being carried out.

Often on call 24 hours a day, construction managers deal with delays, such as the effects of bad weather, or emergencies at the jobsite. More than one-third worked a standard 40-hour week in 2008, and some construction projects continue around the clock. Construction managers may need to work this type of schedule for days or weeks to meet special project deadlines, especially if there are delays.

Although the work usually is not inherently dangerous, injuries can occur and construction managers must be careful while performing onsite services.

Training, Other Qualifications, and Advancement

Employers increasingly are hiring construction managers with a bachelor's degree in a construction-related field, although it is also possible for construction workers to become construction managers after many years of experience. Construction managers must understand contracts, plans, specifications, and regulations. Certification, although not required, is increasingly important.

Education and training. For construction manager jobs, a bachelor's degree in construction science, construction management, building science, or civil engineering, plus work experience, is becoming the norm. However, years of experience, in addition to taking classes in the field or getting an associate degree, can substitute for a bachelor's degree. Practical construction experience is very important for entering this occupation, whether earned through an internship, a cooperative education program, a job in the construction trades, or another job in the industry. Some people advance to construction management positions after having substantial experience as construction craftworkers—carpenters, masons, plumbers, or electricians, for example—or after having worked as construction supervisors or as owners of independent specialty contracting firms. However, as construction processes become increasingly complex, employers are placing more importance on specialized education after high school.

More than 100 colleges and universities offer bachelor's degree programs in construction science, building science, and construction engineering. These programs include courses in project control and development, site planning, design, construction methods, construction materials, value analysis, cost estimating, scheduling, contract administration, accounting, business and financial management, safety, building codes and standards, inspection procedures, engineering and architectural sciences, mathematics, statistics, and information technology. Graduates from four-year degree programs usually are hired as assistants to project managers, field engineers, schedulers, or cost estimators. An increasing number of graduates in related fields—engineering or architecture, for example—also enter construction management, often after acquiring substantial experience on construction projects.

Several colleges and universities offer a master's degree program in construction management or construction science. Master's degree recipients, especially those with work experience in construction, typically become construction managers in very large construction or construction management companies. Often, individuals who hold a bachelor's degree in an unrelated field seek a master's degree in construction management or construction science to work in the construction industry. Some construction managers obtain a master's degree in business administration or finance to further their career prospects.

A number of two-year colleges throughout the country offer construction management or construction technology programs. Many individuals also attend training and educational programs sponsored by industry associations, often in collaboration with postsecondary institutions.

Other qualifications. Construction managers should be flexible and work effectively in a fast-paced environment. They should be decisive and work well under pressure, particularly when faced with unexpected events or delays. The ability to manage several major activities at once, while analyzing and resolving specific problems, is essential, as is an understanding of engineering, architectural, and other construction drawings. Familiarity with computers and software programs for job costing, online collaboration, scheduling, and estimating also is important.

Good oral and written communication skills are important as well, as are leadership skills. Managers must be able to establish a good working relationship with many different people, including owners, other managers, designers, supervisors, and craftworkers. The ability to converse fluently in Spanish is increasingly becoming an asset, because Spanish is the first language of many workers in the construction industry.

Certification and advancement. There is a growing movement toward certification of construction managers. Although certification is not required to work in the construction industry, it can be valuable because it provides evidence of competence and experience. Both the American Institute of Constructors and the Construction Management Association of America have established voluntary certification programs for construction managers. Requirements combine written examinations with verification of education and professional experience. The American Institute of Constructors awards the Associate Constructor (AC) and Certified Professional Constructor (CPC) designations to candidates who meet its requirements and pass the appropriate construction examinations. The Construction Management Association of America awards the Certified Construction Manager (CCM) designation to workers who have the required experience and who pass a technical examination. Applicants for this designation also must complete a self-study course that covers the professional role of a construction manager, legal issues, the allocation of risk, and other topics related to construction management.

Advancement opportunities for construction managers vary with the individual's performance and the size and type of company for which the person works. Within large firms, managers may eventually become top-level managers or executives. Highly experienced individuals may become independent consultants; some serve as expert witnesses in court or as arbitrators in disputes. Those with the required capital may establish their own construction management services, specialty contracting, or general contracting firms.

Employment

Construction managers held 551,000 jobs in 2008. About 61 percent were self-employed, many as owners of general or specialty trade construction firms. Most salaried construction managers were employed in the construction industry—11 percent by specialty trade contractor businesses (for example, plumbing, heating, air-conditioning, and electrical contractors), 10 percent in nonresidential building construction, and 7 percent in residential building construction. Others were employed by architectural, engineering, and related services firms.

Job Outlook

Faster-than-average employment growth is expected. Jobseekers who combine construction work experience with a bachelor's degree in a construction-related field should enjoy the best prospects.

Employment change. Employment of construction managers is projected to increase by 17 percent during the 2008–2018 decade, faster than the average for all occupations. Construction managers will be needed as the level and variety of construction activity expands, but at a slower rate than in the past. Modest population and business growth will result in new and renovated construction of residential

Projections Data from the National Employment Matrix

Occupational title	SOC Code	Employment, 2008	Projected employment, 2018	Change, 2008–2018	
				Number	Percent
Construction managers	11-9021	551,000	645,800	94,800	17

NOTE: Data in this table are rounded.

dwellings, office buildings, retail outlets, hospitals, schools, restaurants, and other structures that require construction managers. A growing emphasis on making buildings more energy efficient should create additional jobs for construction managers involved in retrofitting buildings. In addition, the need to replace portions of the nation's infrastructure, such as roads, bridges, and water and sewer pipes, along with the need to increase energy supply lines, will further increase demand for construction managers.

The increasing complexity of construction projects requires specialized management-level personnel within the construction industry. Sophisticated technology; the proliferation of laws setting standards for buildings and construction materials, worker safety, energy efficiency, and environmental protection; and the potential for adverse litigation have complicated the construction process. In addition, advances in building materials, technology, and construction methods require continual learning and expertise.

Job prospects. Prospects should be best for people who have a bachelor's or higher degree in construction science, construction management, or civil engineering, plus practical work experience in construction. A strong background in building technology is beneficial as well. Construction managers also will have many opportunities to start their own firms.

In addition to job openings arising from employment growth, many openings should result annually from the need to replace workers who transfer to other occupations or leave the labor force for other reasons. A number of seasoned managers are expected to retire over the next decade, resulting in a number of job openings.

Employment of construction managers, like that of many other construction workers, is sensitive to the fluctuations of the economy. On the one hand, workers in these trades may experience periods of unemployment when the overall level of construction falls. On the other hand, shortages of these workers may occur in some areas during peak periods of building activity.

Earnings

Wages of salaried construction managers and self-employed independent construction contractors vary with the size and nature of the construction project, its geographic location, and economic conditions. In addition to receiving typical benefits, many salaried construction managers earn bonuses and are allowed the use of company motor vehicles.

Median annual wages of salaried construction managers in May 2008 were $79,860. The middle 50 percent earned between $60,650 and $107,140. The lowest-paid 10 percent earned less than $47,000, and the highest-paid 10 percent earned more than $145,920. Median annual wages in the industries employing the largest numbers of construction managers were as follows:

Building equipment contractors	$81,590
Nonresidential building construction	79,950
Other specialty trade contractors	78,410
Foundation, structure, and building exterior contractors	76,880
Residential building construction	74,770

The earnings of self-employed workers are not included in these numbers.

According to a July 2009 salary survey by the National Association of Colleges and Employers, people with a bachelor's degree in construction science or construction management received job offers averaging $53,199 a year.

Related Occupations

Construction managers participate in the conceptual development of a construction project and oversee its organization, scheduling, and implementation. Other workers who perform similar functions include the following: architects, except landscape and naval; engineers; cost estimators; engineering and natural sciences managers; and landscape architects.

Sources of Additional Information

For information about constructor certification, contact

▸ American Institute of Constructors, P.O. Box 26334, Alexandria, VA 22314. Internet: www.aicnet.org

For information about construction management and construction manager certification, contact

▸ Construction Management Association of America, 7926 Jones Branch Dr., Suite 800, McLean, VA 22102. Internet: www.cmaanet.org

Information on accredited construction science and management educational programs is available from

▸ American Council for Construction Education, 1717 North Loop 1604 E, Suite 320, San Antonio, TX 78232. Internet: www.acce-hq.org

▸ National Center for Construction Education and Research, 3600 NW 43rd St., Bldg. G, Gainesville, FL 32606. Internet: www.nccer.org

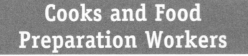

Cooks and Food Preparation Workers

(O*NET 35-2011.00, 35-2012.00, 35-2013.00, 35-2014.00, 35-2015.00, 35-2019.00, and 35-2021.00)

Significant Points

■ Many cooks and food preparation workers are young—35 percent are below the age of 24.

■ One-third of these workers are employed part time.

■ Job openings are expected to be plentiful because many of these workers will leave the occupation for full-time employment or better wages.

Nature of the Work

Cooks and food preparation workers prepare, season, and cook a wide range of foods—from soups, snacks, and salads to entrees, side dishes, and desserts. They work in a variety of restaurants, as well as other places where food is served, such as grocery stores, schools and hospitals. Cooks prepare and cook meals while food preparation workers assist cooks by performing tasks, such as peeling and cutting vegetables, trimming meat, preparing poultry, and keeping work areas clean and monitoring temperatures of ovens and stovetops.

Specifically, *cooks* measure, mix, and cook ingredients according to recipes, using a variety of equipment, including pots, pans, cutlery, ovens, broilers, grills, slicers, grinders, and blenders. *Food preparation workers* perform routine, repetitive tasks under the direction of chefs, head cooks, or food preparation and serving supervisors. These workers prepare the ingredients for complex dishes by slicing and dicing vegetables, and making salads and cold items. They weigh and measure ingredients, retrieve pots and pans, and stir and strain soups and sauces. Food preparation workers may also cut and grind meats, poultry, and seafood in preparation for cooking. They also clean work areas, equipment, utensils, dishes, and silverware.

Larger restaurants and food service establishments tend to have varied menus and larger kitchen staffs. Teams of restaurant cooks, sometimes called *assistant or line cooks*, each work an assigned station that is equipped with the types of stoves, grills, pans, and ingredients needed for the foods prepared at that station. Job titles often reflect the principal ingredient prepared or the type of cooking performed—*vegetable cook*, *fry cook*, or *grill cook*, for example. Chefs, head cooks, or food preparation and serving supervisors generally direct the work of cooks and food preparation workers.

The number, type, and responsibilities of cooks vary depending on where they work, the size of the facility, and the complexity and level of service offered. *Institution and cafeteria cooks*, for example, work in the kitchens of schools, cafeterias, businesses, hospitals, and other institutions. For each meal, they prepare a large quantity of a limited number of entrees, vegetables, and desserts according to preset menus. Meals are generally prepared in advance so diners seldom get the opportunity to special order a meal. *Restaurant cooks* usually prepare a wider selection of dishes, cooking most orders individually. *Short-order cooks* prepare foods in restaurants and coffee shops that emphasize fast service and quick food preparation. They grill and garnish hamburgers, prepare sandwiches, fry eggs, and cook French fries, often working on several orders at the same time. *Fast food cooks* prepare a limited selection of menu items in fast-food restaurants. They cook and package food, such as hamburgers and fried chicken, to be kept warm until served.

Work environment. Many restaurant and institutional kitchens have modern equipment, convenient work areas, and air conditioning, but kitchens in older and smaller eating places are often not as well designed. Kitchen staffs invariably work in small quarters against hot stoves and ovens. They are under constant pressure to prepare meals quickly, while ensuring quality is maintained and safety and sanitation guidelines are observed. Because the pace can be hectic during peak dining times, workers must be able to communicate clearly so that food orders are completed correctly.

Working conditions vary with the type and quantity of food prepared and the local laws governing food service operations. Workers usually must stand for hours at a time, lifting heavy pots and kettles, and working near hot ovens and grills. The incidence of reported injuries for institution and cafeteria cooks, restaurant cooks, and food preparation workers was comparatively high compared to all occupations, but job hazards, such as falls, cuts, and burns, are seldom serious.

Work hours in restaurants may include early mornings, late evenings, holidays, and weekends. Work schedules of cooks and food preparation workers in factory and school cafeterias may be more regular. In 2008, 31 percent of cooks and almost half of food preparation workers had part-time schedules, compared to 16 percent of workers throughout the economy. Work schedules in fine-dining restaurants, however, tend to be longer because of the time required to prepare ingredients in advance.

The wide range in dining hours and the need for fully-staffed kitchens during all open hours creates work opportunities for students, youth, and other individuals seeking supplemental income, flexible work hours, or variable schedules. Sixteen percent of cooks and food preparation workers were 16 to 19 years old in 2008 and another 18 percent were aged 20 to 24. Kitchen workers employed by schools may work during the school year only, usually for 9 or 10 months. Similarly, resort establishments usually only offer seasonal employment.

Training, Other Qualifications, and Advancement

On-the-job training is the most common method of learning for cooks and food preparation workers; however, restaurant cooks and other cooks who want to take on more advanced cooking duties often attend cooking school. Vocational training programs are available to many high school students and may lead to positions in restaurants. Experience, enthusiasm, and a desire to learn are the most common requirements for advancement to higher skilled cooking jobs or positions in higher paying restaurants.

Education and training. A high school diploma is not required for beginning jobs but is recommended for those planning a career in food services. Most fast-food or short-order cooks and food preparation workers learn their skills on the job. Training generally starts with basic sanitation and workplace safety regulations and continues with instruction on food handling, preparation, and cooking procedures.

Although most cooks and food preparation workers learn on the job, students with an interest in food service may be able to take high school or vocational school courses in kitchen basics and food safety and handling procedures. Additional training opportunities are also offered by many state employment services agencies and local job counseling centers. For example, many school districts, in cooperation with state departments of education, provide on-the-job training and summer workshops for cafeteria kitchen workers who aspire to become cooks.

When hiring restaurant cooks, employers usually prefer applicants who have training after high school. These training programs range from a few months to 2 years or more. Vocational or trade-school programs typically offer basic training in food handling and sanitation procedures, nutrition, slicing and dicing methods for various kinds of meats and vegetables, and basic cooking techniques, such as baking, broiling, and grilling. Longer certificate or degree granting programs, through independent cooking schools, professional culinary institutes, or college degree programs, train cooks who aspire to more responsible positions in fine-dining or upscale restaurants. They offer a wider array of training specialties, such as advanced cooking techniques; cooking for banquets, buffets, or parties; and cuisines and cooking styles from around the world. Some large hotels, restaurants, and the Armed Forces operate their own training and job-placement programs.

Professional culinary institutes, industry associations, and trade unions may also sponsor formal apprenticeship programs for cooks in coordination with the U.S. Department of Labor. The American Culinary Federation accredits more than 200 formal academic training programs and sponsors apprenticeship programs around the country. Typical apprenticeships last 2 years and combine classroom training and work experience. Accreditation is an indication that a culinary program meets recognized standards regarding course content, facilities, and quality of instruction.

Other qualifications. Cooks and food preparation workers must be efficient, quick, and work well as part of a team. Manual dexterity is helpful for cutting, chopping, and plating. These workers also need creativity and a keen sense of taste and smell. Personal cleanliness is essential because most states require health certificates indicating that workers are free from communicable diseases. Knowledge of a foreign language can be an asset because it may improve communication with other restaurant staff, vendors, and the restaurant's clientele.

Certification and advancement. The American Culinary Federation certifies chefs in different skill levels. For cooks seeking certification and advancement to higher-level chef positions, certification can help to demonstrate accomplishment and lead to higher-paying positions.

Advancement opportunities for cooks and food preparation workers depend on their training, work experience, and ability to perform more responsible and sophisticated tasks. Many food preparation workers, for example, may move into assistant or line cook positions or take on more complex food preparation tasks. Cooks who demonstrate an eagerness to learn new cooking skills and to accept greater responsibility may also advance and be asked to train or supervise lesser skilled kitchen staff. Some may become head cooks, chefs, or food preparation and serving supervisors. Others may find it necessary to move to other restaurants, often larger or more prestigious ones, in order to advance.

Employment

Cooks and food preparation workers held 3.0 million jobs in 2008. The distribution of jobs among the various types of cooks and food preparation workers was as follows:

Cooks, restaurant	914,200
Food preparation workers	891,900
Cooks, fast food	566,000
Cooks, institution and cafeteria	391,800
Cooks, short order	171,400
Cooks, private household	4,900
Cooks, all other	18,000

Two-thirds of all cooks and food preparation workers were employed in restaurants and other food services and drinking places. About 16 percent worked in institutions such as schools, universities, hospitals, and nursing care facilities. Grocery stores and hotels employed most of the remainder.

Job Outlook

Job opportunities for cooks and food preparation workers are expected to be good because of high turnover and the need to replace the workers who leave these occupations. The enjoyment of eating out and a preference for ready-made meals from a growing population will cause employment of these workers to increase, but slower than the average rate for all occupations over the 2008–2018 decade.

Employment change. Employment of cooks and food preparation workers is expected to increase by 6 percent over the 2008–2018 decade, more slowly than the average for all occupations. People will continue to enjoy eating out and taking meals home. In response, more restaurants will open and nontraditional food service operations, such as those found inside grocery and convenience stores, will serve more prepared food items. Other places that have dining rooms and cafeterias—such as schools, hospitals, and residential care facilities for the elderly—will open new or expanded food service operations to meet the needs of their growing customer base.

Among food services and drinking places, special food services, which include caterers and food service operators who often provide meals in hospitals, office buildings, or sporting venues on a contract basis, are expected to grow the fastest during the projection period. These companies typically employ large numbers of cafeteria and institution cooks and other cooks who perform cooking duties; employment in these occupations is expected to grow 10 percent (about as fast as the average) and 16 percent (faster than the average), respectively.

Full-service restaurants also will continue to attract patrons and grow in number, but not as fast as the previous decade. As restaurants increase their focus on the carryout business, cooks and food preparation workers will be needed to compete with limited service

Projections Data from the National Employment Matrix

Occupational title	SOC Code	Employment, 2008	Projected employment, 2018	Change, 2008–2018	
				Number	Percent
Cooks and food preparation workers 35-2000		2,958,100	3,149,600	191,500	6
Cooks 35-2010		2,066,200	2,220,000	153,800	7
Cooks, fast food 35-2011		566,000	608,400	42,400	7
Cooks, institution and cafeteria 35-2012		391,800	429,700	37,900	10
Cooks, private household 35-2013		4,900	5,100	200	4
Cooks, restaurant... 35-2014		914,200	984,400	70,300	8
Cooks, short order 35-2015		171,400	171,500	100	0
Cooks, all other... 35-2019		18,000	20,900	2,900	16
Food preparation workers 35-2021		891,900	929,600	37,800	4

NOTE: Data in this table are rounded.

restaurants and grocery stores. Employment of restaurant cooks is expected to show average growth (8 percent).

Limited service eating places, such as fast-food restaurants, sandwich and coffee shops, and other eating places without table service, also are expected to grow during the projection period, as people place greater emphasis on value, quick service, and carryout capability. This will generate greater demand for fast-food cooks. Employment of fast food cooks is expected to increase by 7 percent (average growth).

Employment of private household cooks should grow 4 percent, or more slowly than the average for all occupations, and employment of short-order cooks is expected to grow by less than 1 percent, which represents little to no change.

Food preparation workers are expected to grow more slowly than the average for all occupations, or 4 percent. As restaurants and quick service eating places find more efficient ways of preparing meals–such as at central kitchens that may serve multiple outlets or in wholesale and distribution facilities that wash, portion, and season ingredients—food preparation will become simpler, allowing these lower-skilled workers to take on more varied tasks in a growing number of eating places. Additionally, foods requiring simple preparation will increasingly be sold at convenience stores, snack shops, and in grocery stores, which also will employ food preparation workers.

Job prospects. In spite of slower-than-average employment growth, job opportunities for cooks and food preparation workers are expected to be good, primarily because of the very large number of workers that will need to be replaced because of high turnover. Because many of these jobs are part time, people often leave for full-time positions. Individuals seeking full-time positions at high-end restaurants might encounter competition as the number of job applicants exceeds the number of job openings. Generally, there is lower turnover for full-time jobs and at established restaurants that pay well.

Earnings

Earnings of cooks and food preparation workers vary greatly by region and the type of employer. Earnings usually are highest in fine dining restaurants and nicer hotels that have more exacting work standards. These restaurants are usually found in greater numbers in major metropolitan and resort areas.

Median annual wages of cooks, private household were $24,070 in May 2008. The middle 50 percent earned between $19,030 and $36,590. The lowest 10 percent earned less than $16,230, and the highest 10 percent earned more than $56,280.

Median annual wages of institution and cafeteria cooks were $22,210 in May 2008. The middle 50 percent earned between $17,850 and $27,460. The lowest 10 percent earned less than $15,220, and the highest 10 percent earned more than $33,050. Median annual wages in the industries employing the largest numbers of institution and cafeteria cooks were as follows:

General medical and surgical hospitals	$25,070
Special food services...	23,550
Community care facilities for the elderly...............	22,910
Nursing care facilities	22,140
Elementary and secondary schools	20,460

Median annual wages of restaurant cooks were $21,990 in May 2008. The middle 50 percent earned between $18,230 and $26,150. The lowest 10 percent earned less than $15,880, and the highest 10 percent earned more than $31,330. Median annual wages in the industries employing the largest numbers of restaurant cooks were as follows:

Traveler accommodation	$25,570
Other amusement and recreation industries...........	24,760
Special food services...	24,180
Drinking places (alcoholic beverages)...................	22,210
Full-service restaurants	21,770
Limited-service eating places	19,060

Median annual wages of short-order cooks were $19,260 in May 2008. The middle 50 percent earned between $16,280 and $23,450. The lowest 10 percent earned less than $14,740, and the highest 10 percent earned more than $27,630. Median annual wages in the industries employing the largest numbers of short-order cooks were as follows:

Full-service restaurants	$19,600
Drinking places (alcoholic beverages)...................	19,550
Grocery stores..	19,540

Other amusement and recreation industries........... 18,720

Limited-service eating places 17,910

Median annual wages of food preparation workers were $18,630 in May 2008. The middle 50 percent earned between $16,180 and $22,500. The lowest 10 percent earned less than $14,730, and the highest 10 percent earned more than $27,440. Median annual wages in the industries employing the largest number of food preparation workers were as follows:

Grocery stores..$19,580

Full-service restaurants 18,580

Limited-service eating places 16,790

Median annual wages of fast-food cooks were $16,880 in May 2008. The middle 50 percent earned between $15,470 and $19,240. The lowest 10 percent earned less than $14,090, and the highest 10 percent earned more than $22,080. Median annual wages in the industries employing the largest number of fast-food cooks were as follows:

Grocery stores..$19,180

Full-service restaurants 17,250

Limited-service eating places 16,820

Gasoline stations.. 16,640

Some employers provide employees with uniforms and free meals, but federal law permits employers to deduct from their employees' wages the cost or fair value of any meals or lodging provided, and some employers do so. Cooks and food preparation workers who work full time often receive typical benefits, but part-time and hourly workers usually do not.

In some large hotels and restaurants, kitchen workers belong to unions. The principal unions are the Hotel Employees and Restaurant Employees International Union and the Service Employees International Union.

Related Occupations

Other occupations in the food service industry include bakers; butchers and meat cutters; chefs, head cooks, and food preparation and serving supervisors; food and beverage serving and related workers; and food service managers.

Sources of Additional Information

Information about job opportunities may be obtained from local employers and local offices of the state employment service.

Career information for cooks and other kitchen workers, including a directory of 2- and 4-year colleges that offer courses or training programs, is available from

▸ National Restaurant Association, 1200 17th St. NW, Washington, DC 20036. Internet: www.restaurant.org

Information on the American Culinary Federation's apprenticeship and certification programs for cooks and a list of accredited culinary programs is available from

▸ American Culinary Federation, 180 Center Place Way, St. Augustine, FL 32095. Internet: www.acfchefs.org

For information about culinary apprenticeship programs registered with the U.S. Department of Labor, contact the local office of your state employment service agency or check the department's apprenticeship web site: www.doleta.gov/OA/eta_default.cfm, or call the toll free helpline: (877) 872-5627.

Correctional Officers

(O*NET 33-1011.00, 33-3011.00, and 33-3012.00)

Significant Points

■ The work can be stressful and hazardous; correctional officers have one of the highest rates of nonfatal on-the-job injuries.

■ Most jobs are in state and local government prisons and jails.

■ Job opportunities are expected to be favorable.

Nature of the Work

Correctional officers, also known as *detention officers* when they work in pretrial detention facilities, are responsible for overseeing individuals who have been arrested and are awaiting trial or who have been convicted of a crime and sentenced to serve time in a jail, reformatory, or penitentiary.

The jail population changes constantly as some prisoners are released, some are convicted and transferred to prison, and new offenders are arrested and enter the system. Correctional officers in local jails admit and process about 13 million people a year, with nearly 800,000 offenders in jail at any given time. Correctional officers in state and Federal prisons watch over the approximately 1.6 million offenders who are incarcerated there at any given time. Typically, offenders serving time at county jails are sentenced to a year or less. Those serving a year or more are usually housed in state or federal prisons.

Correctional officers maintain security and inmate accountability to prevent disturbances, assaults, and escapes. Officers have no law enforcement responsibilities outside of the institution where they work.

Regardless of the setting, correctional officers maintain order within the institution and enforce rules and regulations. To help ensure that inmates are orderly and obey rules, correctional officers monitor the activities and supervise the work assignments of inmates. Sometimes, officers must search inmates and their living quarters for contraband like weapons or drugs, settle disputes between inmates, and enforce discipline. Correctional officers periodically inspect the facilities, checking cells and other areas of the institution for unsanitary conditions, contraband, fire hazards, and any evidence of infractions of rules. In addition, they routinely inspect locks, window bars, grilles, doors, and gates for signs of tampering. Finally, officers inspect mail and visitors for prohibited items.

Correctional officers report orally and in writing on inmate conduct and on the quality and quantity of work done by inmates. Officers also report security breaches, disturbances, violations of rules, and any unusual occurrences. They usually keep a daily log or record of their activities. Correctional officers cannot show favoritism and must report any inmate who violates the rules. If a crime is committed within their institution or an inmate escapes, they help the responsible law enforcement authorities investigate or search for the escapee. In jail and prison facilities with direct supervision of cellblocks, officers work unarmed. They are equipped with communications devices so that they can summon help if necessary. These officers often work in a cellblock alone, or with another officer, among the 50 to 100 inmates who reside there. The officers enforce regulations primarily through their interpersonal communication skills and through the use of progressive sanctions, such as the removal of some privileges.

In the highest security facilities, where the most dangerous inmates are housed, correctional officers often monitor the activities of prisoners from a centralized control center with closed-circuit television cameras and a computer tracking system. In such an environment, the inmates may not see anyone but officers for days or weeks at a time and may leave their cells only for showers, solitary exercise time, or visitors. Depending on the offenders' security classification, correctional officers may have to restrain inmates in handcuffs and leg irons to safely escort them to and from cells and other areas and to see authorized visitors. Officers also escort prisoners between the institution and courtrooms, medical facilities, and other destinations.

Bailiffs, also known as *marshals* or *court officers*, are law enforcement officers who maintain safety and order in courtrooms. Their duties, which vary by location, include enforcing courtroom rules, assisting judges, guarding juries from outside contact, delivering court documents, and providing general security for courthouses.

Work environment. Working in a correctional institution can be stressful and hazardous. Every year, correctional officers are injured in confrontations with inmates. Correctional officers and jailers have one of the highest rates of nonfatal on-the-job injuries. First-line supervisors/managers of correctional officers also face the risk of work-related injury. Correctional officers may work indoors or outdoors. Some correctional institutions are well lighted, temperature controlled, and ventilated, but others are old, overcrowded, hot, and noisy. Although both jails and prisons can be dangerous places to work, prison populations are more stable than jail populations, and correctional officers in prisons know the security and custodial requirements of the prisoners with whom they are dealing. Consequently, they tend to be safer places to work.

Correctional officers usually work an 8-hour day, 5 days a week, on rotating shifts. Some correctional facilities have longer shifts and more days off between scheduled work weeks. Because prison and jail security must be provided around the clock, officers work all hours of the day and night, weekends, and holidays. In addition, officers may be required to work paid overtime.

Training, Other Qualifications, and Advancement

Correctional officers go through a training academy and then are assigned to a facility where they learn most of what they need to know for their work through on-the-job training. Qualifications vary by agency, but all agencies require a high school diploma or equivalent, and some also require some college education or full-time work experience. Military experience is often seen as a plus for corrections employment.

Education and training. A high school diploma or graduation equivalency degree is required by all employers. The Federal Bureau of Prisons requires entry-level correctional officers to have at least a bachelor's degree; three years of full-time experience in a field providing counseling, assistance, or supervision to individuals; or a combination of the two. Some state and local corrections agencies require some college credits, but law enforcement or military experience may be substituted to fulfill this requirement.

Federal, state, and some local departments of corrections provide training for correctional officers based on guidelines established by the American Correctional Association and the American Jail Association. Some states have regional training academies that are available to local agencies. At the conclusion of formal instruction, all state and local correctional agencies provide on-the-job training, including training on legal restrictions and interpersonal relations. Many systems require firearms proficiency and self-defense skills. Officer trainees typically receive several weeks or months of training in an actual job setting under the supervision of an experienced officer. However, on-the-job training varies widely from agency to agency.

Academy trainees generally receive instruction in a number of subjects, including institutional policies, regulations, and operations, as well as custody and security procedures. New federal correctional officers must undergo 200 hours of formal training within the first year of employment. They also must complete 120 hours of specialized training at the U.S. Federal Bureau of Prisons residential training center at Glynco, Georgia, within 60 days of their appointment. Experienced officers receive annual in-service training to keep abreast of new developments and procedures.

Correctional officers that are members of prison tactical response teams are trained to respond to disturbances, riots, hostage situations, forced cell moves, and other potentially dangerous confrontations. Team members practice disarming prisoners wielding weapons, protecting themselves and inmates against the effects of chemical agents, and other tactics.

Other qualifications. All institutions require correctional officers to be at least 18 to 21 years of age, be a U.S. citizen or permanent resident, and have no felony convictions. New applicants for federal corrections positions must be appointed before they are 37 years old. Some institutions require previous experience in law enforcement or the military, but college credits can be substituted to fulfill this requirement. Others require a record of previous job stability; usually accomplished through 2 years of work experience, which need not be related to corrections or law enforcement.

Correctional officers must be in good health. Candidates for employment are generally required to meet formal standards of physical fitness, eyesight, and hearing. In addition, many jurisdictions use standard tests to determine applicant suitability to work in a correctional environment. Good judgment and the ability to think and act quickly are indispensable. Applicants are typically screened for drug abuse, subject to background checks, and required to pass a written examination.

Advancement. Qualified officers may advance to the position of correctional sergeant. Correctional sergeants supervise correctional officers and usually are responsible for maintaining security and directing the activities of other officers during an assigned shift or in an assigned area. Ambitious and qualified correctional officers can be promoted to supervisory or administrative positions all the way up to warden. In some jurisdictions, corrections officers are given

Projections Data from the National Employment Matrix

Occupational title	SOC Code	Employment, 2008	Projected employment, 2018	Change, 2008–2018	
				Number	Percent
Correctional officers.. —		518,200	566,500	48,300	9
First-line supervisors/managers of correctional officers.. 33-1011		43,500	47,200	3,700	9
Bailiffs, correctional officers, and jailers 33-3010		474,800	519,400	44,600	9
Bailiffs.. 33-3011		20,200	21,900	1,700	8
Correctional officers and jailers 33-3012		454,500	497,500	42,900	9

NOTE: Data in this table are rounded.

the opportunity to "bid" for a specialty assignment, such as working in correctional industries, correctional health or correctional counseling, and receive additional training. Promotion prospects may be enhanced by attending college. Officers sometimes transfer to related jobs, such as probation officer, parole officer, and correctional treatment specialist.

Employment

Correctional officers and jailors held about 454,500 jobs in 2008, while first-line supervisors and managers of correctional officers held about 43,500 jobs. An additional 20,200 workers were employed as bailiffs. The vast majority of correctional officers and jailors and their supervisors were employed by state and local government in correctional institutions such as prisons, prison camps, and youth correctional facilities.

Job Outlook

Employment growth is expected to be as fast as the average for all occupations, and job opportunities are expected to be favorable.

Employment change. Employment of correctional officers is expected to grow 9 percent between 2008 and 2018, about as fast as the average for all occupations. Increasing demand for correctional officers will stem from population growth and rising rates of incarceration. Mandatory sentencing guidelines calling for longer sentences and reduced parole for inmates are a primary reason for increasing incarceration rates. Some states are reconsidering mandatory sentencing guidelines because of budgetary constraints, court decisions, and doubts about their effectiveness. Some employment opportunities also will arise in the private sector, as public authorities contract with private companies to provide and staff corrections facilities. Both state and federal corrections agencies are increasingly using private prisons.

Job prospects. Job opportunities for correctional officers are expected to be favorable. The need to replace correctional officers who transfer to other occupations, retire, or leave the labor force, coupled with rising employment demand, will generate job openings. In the past, some local and state corrections agencies have experienced difficulty in attracting and keeping qualified applicants, largely because of low salaries, shift work, and the concentration of jobs in rural locations. This situation is expected to continue.

Earnings

Median annual wages of correctional officers and jailers were $38,380 in May 2008. The middle 50 percent earned between $29,660 and $51,000. The lowest 10 percent earned less than $25,300, and the highest 10 percent earned more than $64,110. Median annual wages in the public sector were $50,830 in the federal government, $38,850 in state government, and $37,510 in local government. In the facilities support services industry, where the relatively small number of officers employed by privately operated prisons is classified, median annual wages were $28,790.

Median annual wages of first-line supervisors/managers of correctional officers were $57,380 in May 2008. The middle 50 percent earned between $41,740 and $73,630. The lowest 10 percent earned less than $32,300, and the highest 10 percent earned more than $86,970. Median annual wages were $57,050 in state government and $57,300 in local government.

Median annual wages of bailiffs were $37,820 in May 2008. The middle 50 percent earned between $26,730 and $51,470. The lowest 10 percent earned less than $18,750, and the highest 10 percent earned more than $61,500. Median annual wages were $32,690 in local government.

In March 2009, the average salary for federal correctional officers was $53,459. Federal salaries were slightly higher in areas where prevailing local pay levels were higher.

In addition to typical benefits, correctional officers employed in the public sector are usually provided with uniforms or a clothing allowance to purchase their own uniforms. Civil service systems or merit boards cover officers employed by the federal government and most state governments. Their retirement coverage entitles correctional officers to retire at age 50 after 20 years of service or at any age with 25 years of service. Unionized correctional officers often have slightly higher wages and benefits.

Related Occupations

Other protective service occupations include police and detectives; probation officers and correctional treatment specialists; and security guards and gaming surveillance officers.

Sources of Additional Information

Further information about correctional officers is available from

▸ American Correctional Association, 206 N. Washington St., Suite 200, Alexandria, VA 22314. Internet: www.aca.org

▸ American Jail Association, 1135 Professional Ct., Hagerstown, MD 21740. Internet: www.corrections.com/aja

▸ Information on entrance requirements, training, and career opportunities for correctional officers at the federal level may be obtained from the Federal Bureau of Prisons. Internet: www.bop. gov

Information on obtaining a position as a correctional officer with the federal government is available from the Office of Personnel Management through USAJOBS, the federal government's official employment information system. This resource for locating and applying for job opportunities can be accessed through the Internet at www.usajobs.opm.gov or through an interactive voice response telephone system at (703) 724-1850 or TDD (978) 461-8404. These numbers are not toll free, so charges may result.

Cost Estimators

(O*NET 13-1051.00)

Significant Points

■ About 59 percent of cost estimators work in the construction industry, and another 15 percent are employed by manufacturers.

■ Good job opportunities are expected; those with industry work experience and a bachelor's degree in a related field will have the best prospects.

■ Voluntary certification can be beneficial to cost estimators; some employers may require professional certification for employment.

Nature of the Work

Accurately forecasting the cost, size, and duration of future projects is vital to the survival of any business. *Cost estimators* develop the cost information that business owners and managers need to make a bid for a contract or to decide on the profitability of a proposed new project or product. They also determine which endeavors are making a profit.

Regardless of the industry in which they work, estimators collect and analyze data on all of the factors that can affect costs, such as materials; labor; location; duration of the project; and special machinery requirements, including computer hardware and software. Job duties vary widely depending on the type and size of the project.

The methods for estimating costs can also differ greatly by industry. On a large construction project, for example, the estimating process begins with the decision to submit a bid. After reviewing various preliminary drawings and specifications, the estimator visits the site of the proposed project. The estimator gathers information on access to the site; surface topography and drainage; and the availability of electricity, water, and other services. The estimator records this information, which may go in the final project estimate.

After the site visit, the estimator determines the quantity of materials and the labor required to complete the firm's part of the project. This process, called the quantity survey or "takeoff," involves completing standard estimating forms by filling in dimensions, numbers of units, and other information. A cost estimator working for a general contractor, for example, estimates the costs of all of the items that the contractor must provide. Although subcontractors estimate their costs as part of their own bidding process, the general contractor's cost estimator often analyzes bids made by subcontractors. Also during the takeoff process, the estimator must make decisions concerning equipment needs, the sequence of operations, the size of the crew required, and physical constraints at the site. Allowances for wasted materials, inclement weather, shipping delays, and other factors that may increase costs also must be incorporated in the estimate.

After completing the quantity surveys, the estimator prepares a cost summary for the entire project, which includes the costs of labor, equipment, materials, subcontractors, overhead, taxes, insurance, markup, and any additional costs that may affect the project. The chief estimator then prepares the bid proposal for submission to the owner. On large construction projects, there may be several estimators, each specializing in one area, such as electrical work or excavation, concrete, and forms.

Construction cost estimators also may be employed by the project's architect, engineering firm, or owner to help establish a budget, manage and control project costs, and track actual costs relative to bid specifications as the project develops. During construction, estimators may be employed to manage the cost of change orders and negotiate and settle extra costs or mitigate potential claims. Estimators may also be called upon as expert witness on cost in a construction dispute case.

In manufacturing, cost estimators usually are assigned to the engineering, cost, or pricing department. The estimator's goal is to accurately estimate the costs associated with developing and producing products. The job may begin when management requests an estimate of the costs associated with a major redesign of an existing product or the development of a new product or production process. For example, when estimating the cost of manufacturing a new product, the estimator works with engineers, first reviewing blueprints or conceptual drawings to determine the machining operations, tools, gauges, and materials that will be required. The estimator then prepares a parts list and determines whether it would be more efficient to produce or purchase the parts. To do this, the estimator asks for price information from potential suppliers. The next step is to determine the cost of manufacturing each component of the product. Some high-technology products require a considerable amount of computer programming during the design phase. The cost of software development is one of the fastest-growing and most difficult activities to estimate. As a result, some cost estimators now specialize in estimating only computer software development and related costs.

Thereafter, the cost estimator prepares time-phase charts and learning curves. Time-phase charts indicate the time required for tool design and fabrication, tool "debugging"—finding and correcting all problems, manufacturing of parts, assembly, and testing. Learning curves graphically represent the rate at which the performance of workers producing parts for the new product improves with practice.

These curves are commonly called "cost reduction" curves because many problems—such as engineering changes, rework, shortages of parts, and lack of operator skills—diminish as the number of units produced increases, resulting in lower unit costs.

Using all of this information, the estimator then calculates the standard labor hours necessary to produce a specified number of units. Standard labor hours are then converted to dollar values, to which are added factors for waste, overhead, and profit to yield the unit cost in dollars. The estimator compares the cost of purchasing parts with the firm's estimated cost of manufacturing them to determine which is less expensive.

Computers play a vital role in cost estimation because the process often involves complex mathematical calculations and requires advanced mathematical techniques. For example, to undertake a parametric analysis (a process used to estimate costs per unit based on square footage or other specific requirements of a project), cost estimators use a computer database containing information on the costs and conditions of many other similar projects. Although computers cannot be used for the entire estimating process, they can relieve estimators of much of the drudgery associated with routine, repetitive, and time-consuming calculations. New and improved cost estimating software has led to more efficient computations, leaving estimators more time to visit and analyze projects.

Operations research, production control, cost, and price analysts who work for government agencies may do significant amounts of cost estimating in the course of their usual duties. In addition, the duties of construction managers may include estimating costs. (For more information, see the statements on operations research analysts and construction managers elsewhere in this book.)

Work environment. Estimators spend most of their time in offices, but visits to construction worksites and factory floors are often needed for their work. In some industries, there may be frequent travel between a firm's headquarters, its subsidiaries, and subcontractors.

Estimators usually work a 40-hour week, but overtime is common. Cost estimators often work under pressure and stress, especially when facing bid deadlines. Inaccurate estimating can cause a firm to lose a bid or to lose money on a job that was not accurately estimated.

Training, Other Qualifications, and Advancement

Job entry requirements for cost estimators will vary by industry. In the construction and manufacturing industries, employers increasingly prefer to hire cost estimators with a bachelor's degree in a related field, although it is also possible for experienced construction workers to become cost estimators. Voluntary certification can be beneficial to cost estimators; some employers, including the federal government, may require professional certification for employment.

Education and training. In the construction industry, employers increasingly prefer individuals with a degree in construction management, building science, or construction science, all of which usually include several courses in cost estimating. Most construction estimators also have considerable construction experience gained through work in the industry, internships, or cooperative education programs, and for some estimators, years of experience can substitute for a degree in addition to taking classes in the field or getting an associate degree. Applicants with a thorough knowledge of construction materials, costs, and procedures in areas ranging from heavy construction to electrical work, plumbing systems, or masonry work have a competitive edge.

In manufacturing industries, employers prefer to hire individuals with a degree in engineering, physical science, operations research, mathematics, or statistics or in accounting, finance, business, economics, or a related subject. In most industries, experience in quantitative techniques is important.

Many colleges and universities include cost estimating as part of bachelor's and associate degree curriculums in civil engineering, industrial engineering, information systems development, and construction management or construction engineering technology. In addition, cost estimating is often part of master's degree programs in construction science or construction management. Organizations representing cost estimators, such as the American Society of Professional Estimators (ASPE), the Association for the Advancement of Cost Engineering (AACE International) and the Society of Cost Estimating and Analysis (SCEA), also sponsor educational and professional development programs. These programs help students, estimators-in-training, and experienced estimators learn about changes affecting the profession. Specialized courses and programs in cost-estimating techniques and procedures also are offered by many technical schools, community colleges, and universities.

Estimators also receive long-term training on the job because every company has its own way of handling estimates. Working with an experienced estimator, newcomers become familiar with each step in the process. Those with no experience reading construction specifications or blueprints first learn that aspect of the work. Subsequently, they may accompany an experienced estimator to the construction site or shop floor, where they observe the work being done, take measurements, or perform other routine tasks. As they become more knowledgeable, estimators learn how to tabulate quantities and dimensions from drawings and how to select the appropriate prices for materials.

Other qualifications. Cost estimators need to have an aptitude for mathematics; be able to analyze, compare, and interpret detailed but sometimes poorly defined information; and be able to make sound and accurate judgments based on this information. The ability to focus on details while analyzing and managing larger obstacles is vital. Assertiveness and self-assurance in presenting and supporting conclusions are also important, as are strong communications and interpersonal skills, because estimators may work as part of a team alongside managers, owners, engineers, and design professionals. Cost estimators also need to be proficient with computers and have skills in programming. Familiarity with cost-estimation software, including commercial and Building Information Modeling (BIM) software, is beneficial. BIM software technology takes standard blueprints and creates three-dimensional models on the computer, allowing for better estimates of the building process. Proficiency in project management and the ability to incorporate work breakdown structure (WBS) techniques are increasingly important in cost-estimating complex development projects.

Projections Data from the National Employment Matrix

Occupational title	SOC Code	Employment, 2008	Projected employment, 2018	Change, 2008–2018	
				Number	Percent
Cost estimators 13-1051		217,800	272,900	55,200	25

NOTE: Data in this table are rounded.

Certification and advancement. Voluntary certification can be beneficial to cost estimators because it provides professional recognition of the estimator's competence and experience. In some instances, individual employers may even require professional certification for employment. The ASPE, AACE International, and SCEA administer certification programs. To become certified, estimators usually must have between two and eight years of estimating experience and must pass a written examination. In addition, certification requirements may include the publication of at least one article or paper in the field.

For most estimators, advancement takes the form of higher pay and prestige. Some move into management positions, such as project manager for a construction firm, program manager for a government contractor, or manager of the industrial engineering department for a manufacturer. Others may go into business for themselves as consultants, providing estimating services for a fee to government or to construction or manufacturing firms.

Employment

Cost estimators held about 217,800 jobs in 2008. About 59 percent of estimators were in the construction industry, and another 15 percent were employed in manufacturing. The remainder worked in a wide range of other industries.

Cost estimators work throughout the country, usually in or near major industrial, commercial, and government centers and in cities and suburban areas experiencing rapid change or development.

Job Outlook

Employment is projected to grow much faster than average. Overall, good job opportunities are expected; those with industry work experience and a bachelor's degree in a related field will have the best prospects.

Employment change. Employment of cost estimators is expected to grow by 25 percent between 2008 and 2018, much faster than the average for all occupations. Growth in the construction industry will account for most new jobs in this occupation. In particular, construction and repair of highways, streets, bridges, subway systems, airports, water and sewage systems, and electric power plants and transmission lines will stimulate the need for more cost estimators. Similarly, an increasing population will result in more construction of residential homes, hospitals, schools, restaurants, and other structures that require cost estimators. As the population ages, the demand for nursing and extended-care facilities will also increase. The growing complexity of construction projects will also boost demand for cost estimators as more workers specialize in a particular area of construction.

Job prospects. Because there are no formal bachelor's degree programs in cost estimating, some employers have difficulty recruiting qualified cost estimators, resulting in good employment opportunities. Job prospects in construction should be best for those who have a degree in construction science, construction management, or building science or have years of practical experience in the various phases of construction or in a specialty craft area. Knowledge of Building Information Modeling software would also be helpful. For cost estimating jobs in manufacturing, those who have degrees in mathematics, statistics, engineering, accounting, business administration, or economics and are familiar with cost-estimation software should have the best job prospects.

In addition to job openings arising from employment growth, many additional openings should result annually from the need to replace workers who transfer to other occupations because of the sometimes stressful nature of the work, retire, or leave the occupation for other reasons.

Employment of cost estimators, like that of many other construction workers, is sensitive to the fluctuations of the economy. Workers in these trades may experience periods of unemployment when the overall level of construction falls. On the other hand, shortages of these workers may occur in some areas during peak periods of building activity.

Earnings

Salaries of cost estimators vary widely by experience, education, size of firm, and industry. Median annual wages of wage and salary cost estimators in May 2008 were $56,510. The middle 50 percent earned between $42,720 and $74,320. The lowest 10 percent earned less than $33,150, and the highest 10 percent earned more than $94,470. Median annual wages in the industries employing the largest numbers of cost estimators were the following:

Nonresidential building construction	$65,410
Building equipment contractors	60,510
Building finishing contractors	55,430
Residential building construction	55,390
Foundation, structure, and building exterior contractors	54,670

Related Occupations

Other workers who quantitatively analyze cost information include accountants and auditors; budget analysts; claims adjusters, appraisers, examiners, and investigators; construction managers; economists; financial analysts; financial managers; industrial production managers; insurance underwriters; loan officers; market and survey researchers; operations research analysts; and personal financial advisors.

Sources of Additional Information

Information about career opportunities, certification, educational programs, and cost-estimating techniques may be obtained from

▶ AACE International, 209 Prairie Ave., Suite 100, Morgantown, WV 26501. Internet: www.aacei.org

▶ American Society of Professional Estimators (ASPE), 2525 Perimeter Place Dr., Suite 103, Nashville, TN 37214. Internet: www. aspenational.org

▶ Society of Cost Estimating and Analysis, 527 Maple Ave. E., Suite 301, Vienna, VA 22180. Internet: www.sceaonline.org

Counselors

(O*NET 21-1011.00, 21-1012.00, 21-1013.00, 21-1014.00, 21-1015.00, and 21-1019.00)

Significant Points

■ People interested in counseling should have a strong desire to help others and should be able to inspire respect, trust, and confidence.

■ Education and training requirements vary by state and specialty, but a master's degree is required to become a licensed counselor.

■ Projected job growth varies by specialty, but job opportunities should be favorable as job openings are expected to exceed the number of graduates from counseling programs.

Nature of the Work

Counselors work in diverse community settings designed to provide a variety of counseling, rehabilitation, and support services. Their duties vary greatly, depending on their specialty, which is determined by the setting in which they work and the population they serve. Although the specific setting may have an implied scope of practice, counselors frequently are challenged with children, adolescents, adults, or families that have multiple issues, such as mental health disorders and addiction, disability and employment needs, school problems or career counseling needs, and trauma. Counselors must recognize these issues in order to provide their clients with appropriate counseling and support.

Educational, vocational, and school counselors provide individuals and groups with career, personal, social and educational counseling. School counselors assist students of all levels, from elementary school to postsecondary education. They advocate for students and work with other individuals and organizations to promote the academic, career, personal, and social development of children and youth. School counselors help students evaluate their abilities, interests, talents, and personalities to develop realistic academic and career goals. Counselors use interviews, counseling sessions, interest and aptitude assessment tests, and other methods to evaluate and advise students. They also operate career information centers and career education programs. Often, counselors work with students who have academic and social development problems or other special needs.

Elementary school counselors provide individual, small-group, and classroom guidance services to students. Counselors observe children during classroom and play activities and confer with their teachers and parents to evaluate the children's strengths, problems, or special needs. In conjunction with teachers and administrators, they make sure that the curriculum addresses both the academic and the developmental needs of students. Elementary school counselors do less vocational and academic counseling than high school counselors do.

High school counselors advise students regarding college majors, admission requirements, entrance exams, financial aid, trade or technical schools, and apprenticeship programs. They help students develop job search skills, such as resume writing and interviewing techniques. College career planning and placement counselors assist alumni or students with career development and job-hunting techniques.

School counselors at all levels help students to understand and deal with social, behavioral, and personal problems. These counselors emphasize preventive and developmental counseling to enhance students' personal, social, and academic growth and to provide students with the life skills needed to deal with problems before they worsen. Counselors provide special services, including alcohol and drug prevention programs and conflict resolution classes. They also try to identify cases of domestic abuse and other family problems that can affect a student's development.

Counselors interact with students individually, in small groups, or as an entire class. They consult and collaborate with parents, teachers, school administrators, school psychologists, medical professionals, and social workers to develop and implement strategies to help students succeed.

Vocational counselors, also called *employment counselors* or *career counselors*, usually provide career counseling outside the school setting. Their chief focus is helping individuals with career decisions. Vocational counselors explore and evaluate the client's education, training, work history, interests, skills, and personality traits. They may arrange for aptitude and achievement tests to help the client make career decisions. They also work with individuals to develop their job-search skills and assist clients in locating and applying for jobs. In addition, career counselors provide support to people experiencing job loss, job stress, or other career transition issues.

Rehabilitation counselors help people deal with the personal, social, and vocational effects of disabilities. They counsel people with both physical and emotional disabilities resulting from birth defects, illness or disease, accidents, or other causes. They evaluate the strengths and limitations of individuals, provide personal and vocational counseling, offer case management support, and arrange for medical care, vocational training, and job placement. Rehabilitation counselors interview both individuals with disabilities and their families, evaluate school and medical reports, and confer with physicians, psychologists, employers, and physical, occupational, and speech therapists to determine the capabilities and skills of the individual. They develop individual rehabilitation programs by conferring with the client. These programs often include training to help individuals develop job skills, become employed, and provide opportunities for community integration. Rehabilitation counselors are trained to recognize and to help lessen environmental and attitudinal barriers. Such help may include providing education, and advocacy services to individuals, families, employers, and others in the community. Rehabilitation counselors work toward increasing the person's capacity to live independently by facilitating and coordinating with other service providers.

Mental health counselors work with individuals, families, and groups to address and treat mental and emotional disorders and to promote mental health. They are trained in a variety of therapeutic techniques used to address issues such as depression, anxiety, addiction and substance abuse, suicidal impulses, stress, trauma, low self-esteem, and grief. They also help with job and career concerns, educational decisions, mental and emotional health issues, and relationship problems. In addition, they may be involved in community outreach, advocacy, and mediation activities. Some specialize in delivering mental health services for the elderly. Mental health counselors often work closely with other mental health specialists, such as psychiatrists, psychologists, clinical social workers, psychiatric nurses, and school counselors.

Substance abuse and behavioral disorder counselors help people who have problems with alcohol, drugs, gambling, and eating disorders. They counsel individuals to help them to identify behaviors and problems related to their addiction. Counseling can be done on an individual basis, but is frequently done in a group setting and can include crisis counseling, daily or weekly counseling, or drop-in counseling supports. Counselors are trained to assist in developing personalized recovery programs that help to establish healthy behaviors and provide coping strategies. Often, these counselors also will work with family members who are affected by the addictions of their loved ones. Some counselors conduct programs and community outreach aimed at preventing addiction and educating the public. Counselors must be able to recognize how addiction affects the entire person and those around him or her.

Marriage and family therapists apply family systems theory, principles, and techniques to address and treat mental and emotional disorders. In doing so, they modify people's perceptions and behaviors, enhance communication and understanding among family members, and help to prevent family and individual crises. They may work with individuals, families, couples, and groups. Marriage and family therapy differs from traditional therapy because less emphasis is placed on an identified client or internal psychological conflict. The focus is on viewing and understanding their clients' symptoms and interactions within their existing environment. Marriage and family therapists also may make appropriate referrals to psychiatric resources, perform research, and teach courses in human development and interpersonal relationships.

Work environment. The work environment can vary greatly, depending on the occupational specialty. School counselors work predominantly in schools, where they usually have an office but also may work in classrooms. Other counselors may work in a private practice, community health organizations, day treatment programs, or hospitals. Many counselors work in an office where they see clients throughout the day, although counselors may frequently be required to provide services out in the community.

Training, Other Qualifications, and Advancement

Education and training requirements for counselors are often very detailed and vary by state and specialty, but a master's degree usually is required to become a licensed counselor. Prospective counselors should check with state and local governments, prospective employers, and national voluntary certification organizations to determine which requirements apply.

Education and training. Education requirements vary with the occupational specialty and state licensure and certification requirements. A master's degree usually is required to be licensed or certified as a counselor. Counselor education programs in colleges and universities often are found in departments of education, psychology, or human services. Fields of study may include college student affairs, elementary or secondary school counseling, education, gerontological counseling, marriage and family therapy, substance abuse or addictions counseling, rehabilitation counseling, agency or community counseling, clinical mental health counseling, career counseling, and related fields. Courses frequently are grouped into core areas, including human growth and development, social and cultural diversity, relationships, group work, career development, counseling techniques, assessment, research and program evaluation, and professional ethics and identity. In an accredited master's degree program, 48 to 60 semester hours of graduate study, including a period of supervised clinical experience in counseling, typically are required.

Some employers provide training for newly hired counselors. Others may offer time off or tuition assistance to complete a graduate degree. Often, counselors must participate in graduate studies, workshops, and personal studies to maintain their certificates and licenses.

Licensure. Licensure requirements differ greatly by state, occupational specialty, and work setting. Some states require school counselors to hold a state school counseling certification and to have completed at least some graduate coursework; most require the completion of a master's degree. Some states require school counselors to be licensed, which generally entails completing continuing education credits. Some states require public school counselors to have both counseling and teaching certificates and to have had some teaching experience.

For counselors based outside of schools, 49 states and the District of Columbia have some form of counselor licensure that governs the practice of counseling. In addition, all 50 states and the District of Columbia have some licensure requirement for marriage and family therapists. Requirements for both counselors and marriage and family therapists typically include the completion of a master's degree in counseling or marriage and family therapy, the accumulation of 2 years or 3,000 hours of supervised clinical experience beyond the master's degree level, the passage of a state-recognized exam, adherence to ethical codes and standards, and the completion of annual continuing education credits. However, counselors working in certain settings or in a particular specialty may face different licensure requirements. For example, a career counselor working in private practice may need a license, but a counselor working for a college career center may not. In addition, substance abuse and behavior disorder counselors generally are governed by a different state agency or board than are other counselors. The criteria for their licensure can vary greatly, and in some cases these counselors may need only a high school diploma and certification. Those interested in entering the field must research state and specialty requirements to determine what qualifications are necessary.

Other qualifications. People interested in counseling should have a strong desire to help others and should be able to inspire respect, trust, and confidence. They should be able to work independently or as part of a team. Counselors must follow the code of ethics associated with their respective certifications and licenses.

Counselors must possess high physical and emotional energy to handle the array of problems that they address. Dealing daily with these problems can cause stress.

Certification and advancement. Some counselors elect to be certified by the National Board for Certified Counselors, which grants a general practice credential of National Certified Counselor. This national certification is voluntary and is distinct from state licensing. However, in some states, those who pass the national exam are exempt from taking a state certification exam. The board also offers specialty certifications in school, clinical mental health, and addiction counseling.

The Commission on Rehabilitation Counselor Certification offers voluntary national certification for rehabilitation counselors. Many state and local governments and other employers require rehabilitation counselors to have this certification. To become certified, rehabilitation counselors usually must graduate from an accredited educational program, complete an internship, and pass a written examination. Certification requirements vary, however, according to an applicant's educational history. Employment experience, for example, is required for those with a counseling degree in a specialty other than rehabilitation. To maintain their certification, counselors must successfully retake the certification exam or complete 100 credit hours of acceptable continuing education every 5 years.

Other counseling organizations also offer certification in particular counseling specialties. Usually, becoming certified is voluntary, but having certification may enhance one's job prospects.

Prospects for advancement vary by counseling field. School counselors can become directors or supervisors of counseling, guidance, or pupil personnel services; or, usually with further graduate education, they may become counselor educators, counseling psychologists, or school administrators. Some counselors choose to work for a state's department of education.

Some marriage and family therapists, especially those with doctorates in family therapy, become supervisors, teachers, researchers, or advanced clinicians in the discipline. Counselors also may become supervisors or administrators in their agencies. Some counselors move into research, consulting, or college teaching or go into private or group practice. Some may choose to pursue a doctoral degree to improve their chances for advancement.

Employment

Counselors held about 665,500 jobs in 2008. Employment was distributed among the counseling specialties as follows:

Educational, vocational, and school counselors.....275,800
Rehabilitation counselors 129,500
Mental health counselors....................................113,300
Substance abuse and behavioral disorder
    counselors.. 86,100
Marriage and family therapists 27,300
Counselors, all other... 33,400

A growing number of counselors are self-employed and work in group practices or private practice, due in part to laws allowing counselors to be paid for their services by insurance companies and to the growing recognition that counselors are well-trained, effective professionals.

Job Outlook

Employment is expected to grow faster than the average for all occupations. Projected job growth varies by specialty, but job opportunities should be favorable because job openings are expected to exceed the number of graduates from counseling programs, especially in rural areas.

Employment change. Overall employment of counselors is expected to increase by 18 percent between 2008 and 2018, which is faster than the average for all occupations. However, growth is expected to vary by specialty.

Employment of substance abuse and behavioral disorder counselors is expected to grow by 21 percent, which is much faster than the average for all occupations. As society becomes more knowledgeable about addiction, more people are seeking treatment. Furthermore, drug offenders are increasingly being sent to treatment programs rather than to jail.

Employment for educational, vocational, and school counselors is expected to grow by 14 percent, which is faster than the average for all occupations. Demand for vocational or career counselors should grow as multiple job and career changes become common and as workers become increasingly aware of counseling services. States require elementary schools to employ counselors. Expansion of the responsibilities of school counselors also is likely to lead to increases in their employment. For example, counselors are becoming more involved in crisis and preventive counseling, helping students deal with issues ranging from drug and alcohol abuse to death and suicide. Although schools and governments realize the value of counselors in helping their students to achieve academic success, budget constraints at every school level will dampen the job growth of school counselors. Federal grants and subsidies may help to offset tight budgets and allow the reduction in student-to-counselor ratios to continue.

Employment of mental health counselors is expected to grow by 24 percent, which is much faster than the average for all occupations. Under managed care systems, insurance companies increasingly are providing for reimbursement of counselors as a less costly alternative to psychiatrists and psychologists. In addition, there has been increased demand for mental health services as individuals become more willing to seek help.

Jobs for rehabilitation counselors are expected to grow by 19 percent, which is faster than the average for all occupations. The number of people who will need rehabilitation counseling will increase as the size of the elderly population, whose members become

Projections Data from the National Employment Matrix

Occupational title	SOC Code	Employment, 2008	Projected employment, 2018	Change, 2008–2018	
				Number	Percent
Counselors	21-1010	665,500	782,200	116,800	18
Substance abuse and behavioral disorder counselors	21-1011	86,100	104,200	18,100	21
Educational, vocational, and school counselors	21-1012	275,800	314,400	38,600	14
Marriage and family therapists	21-1013	27,300	31,300	3,900	14
Mental health counselors	21-1014	113,300	140,400	27,200	24
Rehabilitation counselors	21-1015	129,500	154,100	24,500	19
Counselors, all other	21-1019	33,400	37,800	4,400	13

NOTE: Data in this table are rounded.

injured or disabled at a higher rate than other age groups, increases and as treatment for mental health related disabilities increases.

Marriage and family therapists will experience growth of 14 percent, which is faster than the average for all occupations, in part because of an increased recognition of the field. It is becoming more common for people to seek help for their marital and family problems than it was in the past.

Job prospects. Job opportunities should be favorable because job openings are expected to exceed the number of graduates from counseling programs, particularly in rural areas. Substance abuse counselors should enjoy particularly good job prospects.

Earnings

Median annual wages of educational, vocational, and school counselors in May 2008 were $51,050. The middle 50 percent earned between $38,740 and $65,360. The lowest 10 percent earned less than $29,360, and the highest 10 percent earned more than $82,330. School counselors can earn additional income by working summers in the school system or in other jobs. Median annual wages in the industries employing the largest numbers of educational, vocational, and school counselors were as follows:

```
Elementary and secondary schools ...................$57,800
Junior colleges................................................ 50,440
Colleges, universities, and professional schools ..... 43,980
Vocational rehabilitation services ....................... 35,220
Individual and family services ............................ 33,780
```

Median annual wages of substance abuse and behavioral disorder counselors in May 2008 were $37,030. The middle 50 percent earned between $29,410 and $47,290. The lowest 10 percent earned less than $24,240, and the highest 10 percent earned more than $59,460. Median annual wages in the industries employing the largest numbers of substance abuse and behavioral disorder counselors were as follows:

```
General medical and surgical hospitals ................$44,130
Local government............................................. 41,660
Outpatient care centers.................................... 36,650
Individual and family services ............................ 35,210
Residential mental retardation, mental health
    and substance facilities ................................. 31,300
```

Median annual wages of mental health counselors in May 2008 were $36,810. The middle 50 percent earned between $28,930 and

$48,580. The lowest 10 percent earned less than $23,580, and the highest 10 percent earned more than $63,100. Median annual wages in the industries employing the largest numbers of mental health counselors were as follows:

```
Local government............................................$45,510
Offices of other health practitioners..................... 40,880
Outpatient care centers..................................... 37,590
Individual and family services ............................ 36,130
Residential mental retardation, mental health
    and substance abuse facilities......................... 29,950
```

Median annual wages of rehabilitation counselors in May 2008 were $30,930. The middle 50 percent earned between $24,110 and $41,240. The lowest 10 percent earned less than $20,150, and the highest 10 percent earned more than $56,550. Median annual wages in the industries employing the largest numbers of rehabilitation counselors were as follows:

```
State government............................................$45,350
Local government............................................. 38,800
Vocational rehabilitation services ....................... 29,060
Individual and family services ............................ 28,290
Residential mental retardation, mental health
    and substance facilities ................................. 25,950
```

Median annual wages of marriage and family therapists in May 2008 were $44,590. The middle 50 percent earned between $34,840 and $56,320. The lowest 10 percent earned less than $27,810, and the highest 10 percent earned more than $70,830. Median annual wages in the industries employing the largest numbers of marriage and family therapists were as follows:

```
State government............................................$50,770
Local government............................................. 48,220
Outpatient care centers..................................... 46,830
Offices of other health practitioners..................... 41,220
Individual and family services ............................ 39,690
```

Self-employed counselors who have well-established practices, as well as counselors employed in group practices, usually have the highest earnings.

Related Occupations

Counselors help people evaluate their interests, abilities, and disabilities and deal with personal, social, academic, and career problems. Others who help people in similar ways include human resources, training, and labor relations managers and specialists; occupational therapists; physicians and surgeons; psychologists; registered nurses; social and human service assistants; social workers; teachers—kindergarten, elementary, middle, and secondary; and teachers—special education.

Sources of Additional Information

For general information about counseling, as well as information on specialties such as school, college, mental health, rehabilitation, multicultural, career, marriage and family, and gerontological counseling, contact

▸ American Counseling Association, 5999 Stevenson Ave., Alexandria, VA 22304. Internet: www.counseling.org

For information on school counselors, contact

▸ American School Counselors Association, 1101 King St., Suite 625, Alexandria, VA 22314. Internet: www.schoolcounselor.org

For information on mental health counselors, contact

▸ American Mental Health Counselors Association, 801 N. Fairfax St., Suite 304, Alexandria, VA 22314. Internet: www.amhca.org

For information on marriage and family therapists, contact

▸ American Association for Marriage and Family Therapy, 112 S. Alfred St., Alexandria, VA 22314. Internet: www.aamft.org

For information on accredited counseling and related training programs, contact

▸ Council for Accreditation of Counseling and Related Educational Programs, American Counseling Association, 1001 N. Fairfax St., Suite 510, Alexandria, VA 22314. Internet: www.cacrep.org

For information on national certification requirements for counselors, contact

▸ National Board for Certified Counselors, Inc, 3 Terrace Way, Greensboro, NC 27403. Internet: www.nbcc.org

State departments of education can supply information on colleges and universities offering guidance and counseling training that meets state certification and licensure requirements.

State employment service offices have information about job opportunities and entrance requirements for counselors.

Customer Service Representatives

(O*NET 43-4051.00 and 43-4051.03)

Significant Points

■ Customer service representatives held about 2.3 million jobs in 2008, ranking among the largest occupations.

■ Most companies require a high school diploma and will provide job training.

■ Employment is projected to grow faster than average, and job prospects should be good.

Nature of the Work

Customer service representatives provide a valuable link between customers and the companies who produce the products they buy and the services they use. They are responsible for responding to customer inquiries and making sure that any problems they are experiencing are resolved. Although most customer service representatives do their work by telephone in call centers, some interact with customers by e-mail, fax, post, or face-to-face.

Many customer service inquiries involve simple questions or requests. For instance, a customer may want to know the status of an order or wish to change his or her address in the company's file. However, some questions may be somewhat more difficult, and may require additional research or help from an expert. In some cases, a representative's main function may be to determine who in the organization is best suited to answer a customer's questions.

Some customer inquiries are complaints, which generally must be handled in accordance with strict company policies. In some cases, representatives may try to fix problems or suggest solutions. They may have the authority to reverse erroneous fees or send replacement products. Other representatives act as gatekeepers who make sure that complaints are valid before accepting customer returns.

Although selling products and services is not the primary function of a customer service representative, some customer services representatives may provide information that helps customers to make purchasing decisions. For instance, a representative may point out a product or service that would fulfill a customer's needs.

Customer service representatives use computers, telephones, and other technology extensively in their work. When the customer has an account with the company, a representative will usually open his or her file in the company's computer system. Representatives use this information to solve problems and may be able to make specific changes as necessary. They also have access to responses for the most commonly asked questions and specific guidelines for dealing with requests or complaints. In the event that the representative does not know the answer or is unable to solve a specific problem, a supervisor or other experienced worker may provide assistance.

Many customer service workers are located in call centers, where they spend the entire day speaking on the telephone. Companies usually keep statistics on their workers to make sure they are working efficiently. This helps them to keep up with their call volume and ensures that customers do not have to wait on hold for extended periods of time. Supervisors may listen in on or tape calls to ensure customers are getting quality service.

Almost every industry employs customer service representatives, and their duties may vary greatly depending on the nature of the organization. For instance, representatives who work in banks may have similar duties to tellers, whereas those in insurance companies may be required to handle paperwork, such as changes to policies or renewals. Those who work for utility and communication companies may assist customers with service problems, such as outages. Representatives who work in retail stores often handle returns and help customers to find items in their stores.

Work environment. Although customer service representatives work in a variety of settings, most work in areas that are clean and well lit. Those who work in call centers generally have their own workstations or cubicle spaces equipped with telephones, headsets, and computers. Because many call centers are open extended hours or are staffed around the clock, these positions may require workers to take on early morning, evening, or late night shifts. Weekend or holiday work is also common. Because peak times may not last for a full shift, many workers are part-time or work a split shift. As a result, the occupation is well suited to flexible work schedules. Many companies hire additional employees at certain times of year when higher call volumes are expected.

Call centers may be crowded and noisy, and work may be repetitious and stressful, with little time between calls. Also, long periods spent sitting, typing, or looking at a computer screen may cause eye and muscle strain, backaches, headaches, and repetitive motion injuries. A growing number of employers are hiring telecommuters, who provide customer service from their own homes. Although this remains somewhat rare, it can be a major advantage for workers who need to remain in their homes during the day.

Customer service representatives working in retail stores may have customers approach them in person or contact them by telephone. They may be required to work later in the evenings or on weekends, as stores are generally open during those times. Evenings and weekends tend to be peak hours for customer traffic.

Customer service representatives may have to deal with difficult or irate customers, which can be challenging. However, the ability to resolve customers' problems has the potential to be very rewarding.

Training, Other Qualifications, and Advancement

Most jobs require at least a high school diploma. Employers provide training to workers before they begin serving customers.

Education and training. Most customer service representative jobs require a high school diploma. However, because employers are demanding a more skilled workforce, some customer service jobs now require associate or bachelor's degrees. High school and college level courses in computers, English, or business are helpful in preparing for a job in customer service.

Training requirements vary by industry. Almost all customer service representatives are provided with some training prior to beginning work. This training generally focuses on the company and its products, the most commonly asked questions, the computer and telephone systems they will be using, and basic people skills. Length of training varies, but often lasts several weeks. Some customer service representatives are expected to update their training regularly. This is particularly true of workers in industries such as banking, in which regulations and products are continually changing.

Other qualifications. Because customer service representatives constantly interact with the public, good communication and problem-solving skills are essential. Verbal communication and listening skills are especially important. Companies prefer to hire individuals who have a pleasant speaking voice and are easy to understand. For workers who communicate through e-mail, good typing, spelling, and grammar skills are necessary. Basic to intermediate computer knowledge and good interpersonal skills are also important.

Customer service representatives play a critical role in providing an interface between customers and companies. As a result, employers seek out people who are friendly and possess a professional manner. The ability to deal patiently with problems and complaints and to remain courteous when faced with difficult or angry people is critical. Also, a customer service representative often must be able to work independently within specified time constraints.

Advancement. Customer service jobs are often good introductory positions into a company or an industry. In some cases, experienced workers can move into supervisory or managerial positions or they may move into areas such as product development, in which they can use their knowledge to improve products and services. Some people work in call centers with the hope of transferring to a position in another department.

Employment

Customer service representatives held about 2.3 million jobs in 2008, ranking among the largest occupations. They can be found in almost every industry, although about 23 percent worked in the finance and insurance industry. Another 15 percent worked in the administrative and support services industry, which includes third party telephone call centers.

Job Outlook

Customer service representatives are expected to experience faster-than-average growth. Furthermore, job prospects should be good as many workers who leave this very large occupation will need to be replaced.

Employment change. Employment of customer service representatives is expected to grow by about 18 percent over the 2008–2018 period, faster than the average for all occupations. Providing quality customer service is important to nearly every company in the economy; in addition, companies are expected to place increasing emphasis on customer relationships, resulting in increased demand for customer service representatives. This very large occupation is projected to provide about 400,000 new jobs over the next decade.

Customer service representatives are especially prevalent in the finance and insurance industry, as many customer interactions do not require physical contact. Employment of customer service representatives in this industry is expected to increase 9 percent over the 2008–2018 period.

Although technology has tempered growth of this occupation to some degree, it has also created many opportunities for growth. For instance, online banking has reduced the need for telephone banking services. At the same time, however, it has increased the need for customer service representatives who assist users with banking Web sites. Additionally, online services create many new opportunities for customer support representatives as companies that operate on the Internet provide customer service by telephone.

In the past, many companies chose to relocate their customer service call centers in foreign countries, which led to layoffs in some industries. Although many companies continue to offshore some of their customer service jobs, this is becoming less prevalent than in the past. While it continues to be less expensive to hire workers overseas, many companies have found that foreign workers do not

Projections Data from the National Employment Matrix

Occupational title	SOC Code	Employment, 2008	Projected employment, 2018	Change, 2008–2018	
				Number	Percent
Customer service representatives................................ 43-4051		2,252,400	2,651,900	399,500	18

NOTE: Data in this table are rounded.

have the same cultural sensitivity as those located within the United States.

Job prospects. Prospects for obtaining a job in this field are expected to be good, with more job openings than jobseekers. In particular, bilingual jobseekers should enjoy excellent opportunities. Rapid job growth, coupled with a large number of workers who leave the occupation each year, should make finding a job as a customer service representative relatively easy.

While jobs in some industries may be affected by economic downturns, customer service representatives are not as vulnerable to layoffs as some other workers. This is, in part, because many customer service representatives work in industries where customers have accounts. While customers may have less money to spend, and as a result may choose to purchase fewer goods or services, they continue to have customer service needs. For instance, during an economic downturn, individuals may have less money in their bank accounts, but they continue to need banking services and customer service from their banks. Nevertheless, companies do attempt to cut costs during such times, so downsizing is still a possibility.

Earnings

In May 2008, median hourly wages of customer service representatives were $14.36. The middle 50 percent earned between $11.34 and $18.27. The lowest 10 percent earned less than $9.15, and the highest 10 percent earned more than $23.24.

Earnings for customer service representatives vary according to level of skill required, experience, training, location, and size of firm. Median hourly wages in the industries employing the largest numbers of these workers in May 2008 were as follows:

Insurance carriers...	$15.74
Agencies, brokerages, and other insurance related activities..	15.28
Depository credit intermediation	14.56
Employment services...	12.73
Business support services	11.56

In addition to receiving an hourly wage, full-time customer service representatives who work evenings, nights, weekends, or holidays may receive shift differential pay. Also, because call centers are often open during extended hours, or even 24 hours a day, some customer service representatives have the benefit of being able to work a schedule that does not conform to the traditional workweek. Other benefits can include life and health insurance, pensions, bonuses, employer-provided training, and discounts on the products and services the company offers.

Related Occupations

Customer service representatives interact with customers to provide information in response to inquiries about products and services and to handle and resolve complaints. Other occupations in which workers have similar dealings with customers and the public include bill and account collectors; computer support specialists; insurance sales agents; retail salespersons; securities, commodities, and financial services sales agents; and tellers.

Sources of Additional Information

For more information on customer service positions, contact your state employment office or

▸ International Customer Service Association. 24 Wernik Pl., Metuchen, NJ 08840. Internet: www.icsatoday.org

Dental Assistants

(O*NET 31-9091.00)

Significant Points

■ Job prospects should be excellent.

■ Dentists are expected to hire more assistants to perform routine tasks so dentists may devote their time to more complex procedures.

■ Many assistants learn their skills on the job, although an increasing number are trained in dental-assisting programs; most programs take one year or less to complete.

■ More than one-third of dental assistants worked part time in 2008.

Nature of the Work

Dental assistants perform a variety of patient care, office, and laboratory duties. They sterilize and disinfect instruments and equipment, prepare and lay out the instruments and materials required to treat each patient, and obtain and update patients' dental records. Assistants make patients comfortable in the dental chair and prepare them for treatment. During dental procedures, assistants work alongside the dentist to provide assistance. They hand instruments and materials to dentists and keep patients' mouths dry and clear by using suction hoses or other devices. They also instruct patients on postoperative and general oral health care.

Dental assistants may prepare materials for impressions and restorations, and process dental X-rays as directed by a dentist. They also may remove sutures, apply topical anesthetics to gums or cavity-preventive agents to teeth, remove excess cement used in the filling process, and place dental dams to isolate teeth for treatment. Many states are expanding dental assistants' duties to include tasks such as coronal polishing and restorative dentistry functions for those assistants who meet specific training and experience requirements.

Dental assistants with laboratory duties make casts of the teeth and mouth from impressions, clean and polish removable appliances, and make temporary crowns. Those with office duties schedule and confirm appointments, receive patients, keep treatment records, send bills, receive payments, and order dental supplies and materials.

Dental assistants must work closely with, and under the supervision of, dentists. Additionally, dental assistants should not be confused with dental hygienists, who are licensed to perform a different set of clinical tasks.

Work environment. Dental assistants work in a well-lighted, clean environment. Their work area is usually near the dental chair so that they can arrange instruments, materials, and medication and hand them to the dentist when needed. Dental assistants must wear gloves, masks, eyewear, and protective clothing to protect themselves and their patients from infectious diseases. Assistants also follow safety procedures to minimize the risks associated with the use of X-ray machines.

Almost half of dental assistants had a 35- to 40-hour workweek in 2008. More than one-third worked part time, or less than 35 hours per week, and many others have variable schedules. Depending on the hours of the dental office where they work, assistants may have to work on Saturdays or evenings. Some dental assistants hold multiple jobs by working at dental offices that are open on different days or by scheduling their work at a second office around the hours they work at their primary office.

Training, Other Qualifications, and Advancement

Many assistants learn their skills on the job, although an increasing number are trained in dental-assisting programs offered by community and junior colleges, trade schools, technical institutes, or the Armed Forces. Most programs take 1 year to complete. For assistants to perform more advanced functions, or to have the ability to complete radiological procedures, many states require assistants to obtain a license or certification.

Education and training. In most states, there are no formal education or training requirements to become an entry-level dental assistant. High school students interested in a career as a dental assistant should take courses in biology, chemistry, health, and office practices. For those wishing to pursue further education, the Commission on Dental Accreditation (CODA) approved 281 dental-assisting training programs in 2009. Programs include classroom, laboratory, and preclinical instruction in dental-assisting skills and related theory. Most programs take close to 1 year to complete and lead to a certificate or diploma. Two-year programs offered in community and junior colleges lead to an associate degree. All programs require a high school diploma or its equivalent, and some require science or computer-related courses for admission. A number of private vocational schools offer 4- to 6-month courses in dental assisting, but the Commission on Dental Accreditation does not accredit these programs.

A large number of dental assistants learn through on-the-job training. In these situations, the employing dentist or other dental assistants in the dental office teach the new assistant dental terminology, the names of the instruments, how to perform daily duties, how to interact with patients, and other things necessary to help keep the dental office running smoothly. While some things can be picked up easily, it may be a few months before new dental assistants are completely knowledgeable about their duties and comfortable doing all their tasks without assistance.

A period of on-the-job training is often required even for those who have completed a dental-assisting program or have some previous experience. Different dentists may have their own styles of doing things that need to be learned before an assistant can be comfortable working with them. Office-specific information, such as where files and instruments are kept, will need to be learned at each new job. Also, as dental technology changes, dental assistants need to stay familiar with the instruments and procedures that they will be using or helping dentists to use. On-the-job training may be sufficient to keep assistants up-to-date on these matters.

Licensure and certification. Most states regulate the duties that dental assistants are allowed to perform. Some states require licensure or registration to perform expanded functions or to perform radiological procedures within a dentist's office. Licensure may include attending an accredited dental assisting program and passing a written or practical examination. Many states also require continuing education to maintain licensure or registration. However, a few states allow dental assistants to perform any function delegated to them by the dentist. Since requirements vary widely by state, it is recommended to contact the appropriate state board directly for specific requirements.

The Certified Dental Assistant (CDA) credential, administered by the Dental Assisting National Board (DANB), is recognized or required in more than 37 states toward meeting various requirements. Candidates may qualify to take the DANB certification examination by graduating from a CODA-accredited dental assisting education program or by having 2 years of full-time, or 4 years of part-time, experience as a dental assistant. In addition, applicants must have current certification in cardiopulmonary resuscitation. For annual recertification, individuals must earn continuing education credits. Other organizations offer registration, most often at the state level.

Individual states have also adopted different standards for dental assistants who perform certain advanced duties. In some states, dental assistants who perform radiological procedures must complete additional training distinct from that required to perform other expanded functions. Completion of the Radiation Health and Safety examination or the Certified Dental Assistant examination offered by Dental Assisting National Board (DANB) meets the standards in 30 states and the District of Columbia. Some states require completion of a state-approved course in radiology as well. Twelve states have no formal requirements to perform radiological procedures.

Other qualifications. Dental assistants must be a second pair of hands for a dentist; therefore, dentists look for people who are reliable, work well with others, and have good manual dexterity.

Certification and advancement. Without further education, advancement opportunities are limited. Some dental assistants become office managers, dental-assisting instructors, dental product sales

Projections Data from the National Employment Matrix

Occupational title	SOC Code	Employment, 2008	Projected employment, 2018	Change, 2008–2018	
				Number	Percent
Dental assistants	31-9091	295,300	400,900	105,600	36

NOTE: Data in this table are rounded.

representatives, or insurance claims processors for dental insurance companies. Others go back to school to become dental hygienists. For many, this entry-level occupation provides basic training and experience and serves as a steppingstone to more highly skilled and higher paying jobs. Assistants wishing to take on expanded functions or perform radiological procedures may choose to complete coursework in those functions allowed under state regulation or, if required, obtain a state-issued license.

Employment

Dental assistants held about 295,300 jobs in 2008. About 93 percent of all jobs for dental assistants were in offices of dentists. A small number of jobs were in the federal, state, and local governments or in offices of physicians.

Job Outlook

Employment is expected to increase much faster than average; job prospects are expected to be excellent.

Employment change. Employment is expected to grow 36 percent from 2008 to 2018, which is much faster than the average for all occupations. In fact, dental assistants are expected to be among the fastest growing occupations over the 2008–2018 projection period. Population growth, greater retention of natural teeth by middle-aged and older people, and an increased focus on preventative dental care for younger generations will fuel demand for dental services. Older dentists, who have been less likely to employ assistants or have employed fewer, are leaving the occupation and will be replaced by recent graduates, who are more likely to use one or more assistants. In addition, as dentists' workloads increase, they are expected to hire more assistants to perform routine tasks, so that they may devote their own time to more complex procedures.

Job prospects. Job prospects should be excellent, as dentists continue to need the aid of qualified dental assistants. There will be many opportunities for entry-level positions, but some dentists prefer to hire experienced assistants, those who have completed a dental-assisting program, or have met state requirements to take on expanded functions within the office.

In addition to job openings due to employment growth, some job openings will arise out of the need to replace assistants who transfer to other occupations, retire, or leave for other reasons.

Earnings

Median annual wages of dental assistants were $32,380 in May 2008. The middle 50 percent earned between $26,980 and $38,960. The lowest 10 percent earned less than $22,270, and the highest 10 percent earned more than $46,150.

Benefits vary substantially by practice setting and may be contingent upon full-time employment. According to a 2008 survey conducted by the Dental Assisting National Board (DANB), 86 percent of Certified Dental Assistants (CDA) reported receiving paid vacation from their employers, and more than half of CDAs received health benefits.

Related Occupations

Other workers support health practitioners, including dental hygienists; medical assistants; occupational therapist assistants and aides; pharmacy technicians and aides; physical therapist assistants and aides; and surgical technologists.

Sources of Additional Information

Information about career opportunities and accredited dental assistant programs is available from

▸ Commission on Dental Accreditation, American Dental Association, 211 E. Chicago Ave., Suite 1900, Chicago, IL 60611. Internet: www.ada.org/prof/ed/accred/commission/index.asp

For information on becoming a Certified Dental Assistant and a list of state boards of dentistry, contact

▸ Dental Assisting National Board, Inc., 444 N. Michigan Ave., Suite 900, Chicago, IL 60611. Internet: www.danb.org

For more information on a career as a dental assistant and general information about continuing education, contact

▸ American Dental Assistants Association, 35 E. Wacker Dr., Suite 1730, Chicago, IL 60601. Internet: www.dentalassistant.org

Dental Hygienists

(O*NET 29-2021.00)

Significant Points

■ A degree from an accredited dental hygiene school and a state license are required for this job.

■ Dental hygienists rank among the fastest-growing occupations.

■ Job prospects are expected to be favorable in most areas, but strong competition for jobs is likely in some areas.

■ About half of all dental hygienists work part time, and flexible scheduling is a distinctive feature of this job.

Nature of the Work

Dental hygienists remove soft and hard deposits from teeth, teach patients how to practice good oral hygiene, and provide other preventive dental care. They examine patients' teeth and gums, recording the presence of diseases or abnormalities.

Dental hygienists use an assortment of tools to complete their tasks. Hand and rotary instruments and ultrasonic devices are used to clean and polish teeth, which includes removing tartar, stains, and plaque. Hygienists use X-ray machines to take dental pictures, and sometimes develop the film. They may use models of teeth to explain oral hygiene, perform root planning as a periodontal therapy, or apply cavity-preventative agents such as fluorides and pit and fissure sealants.

Other tasks hygienists may perform vary by state. In some states, hygienists are allowed to administer anesthetics, while in others they administer local anesthetics using syringes. Some states also allow hygienists to place and carve filling materials, temporary fillings, and periodontal dressings; remove sutures; and smooth and polish metal restorations.

Dental hygienists also help patients develop and maintain good oral health. For example, they may explain the relationship between diet and oral health or inform patients how to select toothbrushes and show them how to brush and floss their teeth.

Hygienists sometimes make a diagnosis and other times prepare clinical and laboratory diagnostic tests for the dentist to interpret. Hygienists sometimes work chair-side with the dentist during treatment.

Work environment. Dental hygienists work in clean, well-lighted offices. Important health safeguards include strict adherence to proper radiological procedures and the use of appropriate protective devices when administering anesthetic gas. Dental hygienists also wear safety glasses, surgical masks, and gloves to protect themselves and patients from infectious diseases. Dental hygienists also should be careful to avoid possible shoulder and neck injury from sitting for long periods of time while working with patients.

Flexible scheduling is a distinctive feature of this job. Full-time, part-time, evening, and weekend schedules are common. Dentists frequently hire hygienists to work only 2 or 3 days a week, so hygienists may hold jobs in more than one dental office. In 2008, about half of all dental hygienists worked part time—less than 35 hours a week.

Training, Other Qualifications, and Advancement

A degree from an accredited dental hygiene school and a state license are required for this job.

Education and training. A high school diploma and college entrance test scores are usually required for admission to a dental hygiene program. High school students interested in becoming dental hygienists should take courses in biology, chemistry, and mathematics. Some dental hygiene programs also require applicants to have completed at least one year of college. Specific entrance requirements typically vary from one school to another.

In 2008, there were 301 dental hygiene programs accredited by the Commission on Dental Accreditation. Most dental hygiene programs grant an associate degree, although some also offer a certificate, a bachelor's degree, or a master's degree. A minimum of an associate degree or certificate in dental hygiene is generally required

for practice in a private dental office. A bachelor's or master's degree usually is required for research, teaching, or clinical practice in public or school health programs.

Schools offer laboratory, clinical, and classroom instruction in subjects such as anatomy, physiology, chemistry, microbiology, pharmacology, nutrition, radiography, histology (the study of tissue structure), periodontology (the study of gum diseases), pathology, dental materials, clinical dental hygiene, and social and behavioral sciences.

Licensure. Dental hygienists must be licensed by the state in which they practice. Nearly all states require candidates to graduate from an accredited dental hygiene school and pass both a written and clinical examination. The American Dental Association's (ADA) Joint Commission on National Dental Examinations administers the written examination, which is accepted by all states and the District of Columbia. State or regional testing agencies administer the clinical examination. In addition, most states require an examination on the legal aspects of dental hygiene practice. Alabama is the only state that does not require candidates to take the ADA written exam. Instead, they require that candidates meet the requirements of the Alabama Dental Hygiene Program, which mandates taking courses, completing on-the-job training at a dentist's office, and passing a separate state administered licensing examination.

Other qualifications. Dental hygienists should work well with others because they work closely with dentists and dental assistants, as well as dealing directly with patients. Hygienists also need good manual dexterity, because they use dental instruments within patients' mouths, with little room for error.

Advancement. Advancement opportunities usually come from working outside a typical dentist's office, and usually require a bachelor's or master's degree in dental hygiene. Some dental hygienists may choose to pursue a career teaching at a dental hygiene program, working in public health, or working in a corporate setting.

Employment

Dental hygienists held about 174,100 jobs in 2008. Because multiple job holding is common in this field, the number of jobs exceeds the number of hygienists. About 51 percent of dental hygienists worked part time. Almost all jobs for dental hygienists—about 96 percent—were in offices of dentists. A very small number worked for employment services, in physicians' offices, or in other industries.

Job Outlook

Dental hygienists rank among the fastest-growing occupations. Job prospects are expected to be favorable in most areas, but competition for jobs is likely in some areas.

Employment change. Employment of dental hygienists is expected to grow 36 percent through 2018, which is much faster than the average for all occupations. This projected growth ranks dental hygienists among the fastest growing occupations, in response to increasing demand for dental care and more use of hygienists.

The demand for dental services will grow because of population growth, older people increasingly retaining more teeth, and a growing emphasis on preventative dental care. To help meet this demand, facilities that provide dental care, particularly dentists' offices, will

Projections Data from the National Employment Matrix

Occupational title	SOC Code	Employment, 2008	Projected employment, 2018	Change, 2008–2018	
				Number	Percent
Dental hygienists..	29-2021	174,100	237,000	62,900	36

NOTE: Data in this table are rounded.

increasingly employ dental hygienists, often to perform services that have been performed by dentists in the past. Ongoing research indicating a link between oral health and general health also will spur the demand for preventative dental services, which are typically provided by dental hygienists.

Job prospects. Job prospects are expected to be favorable in most areas, but will vary by geographical location. Because graduates are permitted to practice only in the state in which they are licensed, hygienists wishing to practice in areas that have an abundance of dental hygiene programs may experience strong competition for jobs.

Older dentists, who have been less likely to employ dental hygienists, are leaving the occupation and will be replaced by recent graduates, who are more likely to employ one or more hygienists. In addition, as dentists' workloads increase, they are expected to hire more hygienists to perform preventive dental care, such as cleaning, so that they may devote their own time to more complex procedures.

Earnings

Median annual wages of dental hygienists were $66,570 in May 2008. The middle 50 percent earned between $55,220 and $78,990. The lowest 10 percent earned less than $44,180, and the highest 10 percent earned more than $91,470.

Earnings vary by geographic location, employment setting, and years of experience. Dental hygienists may be paid on an hourly, daily, salary, or commission basis.

Benefits vary substantially by practice setting and may be contingent upon full-time employment. According to a 2009 survey conducted by the American Dental Hygienist Association, about half of all hygienists reported receiving some form of employment benefits. Of those receiving benefits, paid vacation, sick leave, and retirement plans were the most common.

Related Occupations

Other workers supporting health practitioners in an office setting include dental assistants; medical assistants; occupational therapist assistants and aides; physical therapist assistants and aides; physician assistants; and registered nurses.

Others who work with radiation technology include radiation therapists.

Sources of Additional Information

For information on a career in dental hygiene, including educational requirements, and on available accredited programs, contact

‣ American Dental Hygienists Association, 444 N. Michigan Ave., Suite 3400, Chicago, IL 60611. Internet: www.adha.org

For information about accredited programs and educational requirements, contact

‣ Commission on Dental Accreditation, American Dental Association, 211 E. Chicago Ave., Chicago, IL 60611. Internet: www.ada.org/prof/ed/accred/commission/index.asp

The State Board of Dental Examiners in each state can supply information on licensing requirements.

Dentists

(O*NET 29-1021.00, 29-1022.00, 29-1023.00, 29-1024.00, and 29-1029.00)

Significant Points

■ About 3 out of 4 dentists are solo practitioners.

■ Dentists must graduate from an accredited dental school and pass written and practical examinations; competition for admission to dental school is keen.

■ Faster-than-average employment growth is projected.

■ Job prospects should be good, reflecting the need to replace the large number of dentists expected to retire.

Nature of the Work

Dentists diagnose and treat problems with teeth and tissues in the mouth, along with giving advice and administering care to help prevent future problems. They provide instruction on diet, brushing, flossing, the use of fluorides, and other aspects of dental care. They remove tooth decay, fill cavities, examine X-rays, place protective plastic sealants on children's teeth, straighten teeth, and repair fractured teeth. They also perform corrective surgery on gums and supporting bones to treat gum diseases. Dentists extract teeth and make models and measurements for dentures to replace missing teeth. They also administer anesthetics and write prescriptions for antibiotics and other medications.

Dentists use a variety of equipment, including X-ray machines, drills, mouth mirrors, probes, forceps, brushes, and scalpels. Lasers, digital scanners, and other computer technologies also may be used. Dentists wear masks, gloves, and safety glasses to protect themselves and their patients from infectious diseases.

Dentists in private practice oversee a variety of administrative tasks, including bookkeeping and the buying of equipment and supplies. They may employ and supervise dental hygienists, dental assistants, dental laboratory technicians, and receptionists.

Most dentists are general practitioners, handling a variety of dental needs. Other dentists practice in any of nine specialty areas. *Orthodontists,* the largest group of specialists, straighten teeth by applying pressure to the teeth with braces or other appliances. The next largest group, *oral* and *maxillofacial surgeons*, operates on the mouth, jaws, teeth, gums, neck, and head. The remainder may specialize as *pediatric dentists* (focusing on dentistry for children and special-needs patients); *periodontists* (treating gums and bone supporting the teeth); *prosthodontists* (replacing missing teeth with permanent fixtures, such as crowns and bridges, or with removable fixtures such as dentures); *endodontists* (performing root-canal therapy); *oral pathologists* (diagnosing oral diseases); *oral* and *maxillofacial radiologists* (diagnosing diseases in the head and neck through the use of imaging technologies); or *dental public health specialists* (promoting good dental health and preventing dental diseases within the community).

Work environment. Most dentists are solo practitioners, meaning that they own their own businesses and work alone or with a small staff. Some dentists have partners, and a few work for other dentists as associate dentists.

Most dentists work 4 or 5 days a week. Some work evenings and weekends to meet their patients' needs. The number of hours worked varies greatly among dentists. Most full-time dentists work between 35 and 40 hours a week. However, others, especially those who are trying to establish a new practice, work more. Also, experienced dentists often work fewer hours. It is common for dentists to continue in part-time practice well beyond the usual retirement age.

Dentists usually work in the safety of an office environment. However, work-related injuries can occur, such as those resulting from the use of hand-held tools when performing dental work on patients.

Training, Other Qualifications, and Advancement

All 50 states and the District of Columbia require dentists to be licensed. To qualify for a license in most states, candidates must graduate from an accredited dental school and pass written and practical examinations.

Education and training. In 2008, there were 57 dental schools in the United States accredited by the American Dental Association's (ADA's) Commission on Dental Accreditation. Dental schools require a minimum of 2 years of college-level predental education prior to admittance. Most dental students have at least a bachelor's degree before entering dental school, although a few applicants are accepted to dental school after 2 or 3 years of college and complete their bachelor's degree while attending dental school. According to the ADA, 85 percent of dental students had a bachelor's degree prior to beginning their dental program in the 2006–2007 academic year.

High school and college students who want to become dentists should take courses in biology, chemistry, physics, health, and mathematics. College undergraduates planning on applying to dental school are required to take many science courses. Because of this, some choose a major in a science, such as biology or chemistry, whereas others take the required science coursework while pursuing a major in another subject.

All dental schools require applicants to take the Dental Admissions Test (DAT). When selecting students, schools consider scores earned on the DAT, applicants' grade point averages, and information gathered through recommendations and interviews. Competition for admission to dental school is keen.

Dental school usually lasts 4 academic years. Studies begin with classroom instruction and laboratory work in science, including anatomy, microbiology, biochemistry, and physiology. Beginning courses in clinical sciences, including laboratory techniques, are also completed. During the last 2 years, students treat patients, usually in dental clinics, under the supervision of licensed dentists. Most dental schools award the degree of Doctor of Dental Surgery (DDS). Others award an equivalent degree, Doctor of Dental Medicine (DMD).

Licensure. Licensing is required to practice as a dentist. In most states, licensure requires passing written and practical examinations in addition to having a degree from an accredited dental school. Candidates may fulfill the written part of the state licensing requirements by passing the National Board Dental Examinations. Individual states or regional testing agencies administer the written or practical examinations.

Individuals can be licensed to practice any of the 9 recognized specialties in all 50 states and the District of Columbia. Requirements include 2 to 4 years of postgraduate education and, in some cases, the completion of a special state examination. A postgraduate residency term also may be required, usually lasting up to 2 years. Most state licenses permit dentists to engage in both general and specialized practice.

Other qualifications. Dentistry requires diagnostic ability and manual skills. Dentists should have good visual memory; excellent judgment regarding space, shape, and color; a high degree of manual dexterity; and scientific ability. Good business sense, self-discipline, and good communication skills are helpful for success in private practice.

Advancement. Dentists and aspiring dentists who want to teach or conduct research full time usually spend an additional 2 to 5 years in advanced dental training, in programs operated by dental schools or hospitals. Many private practitioners also teach part time, including supervising students in dental school clinics.

Some dental school graduates work for established dentists as associates for 1 to 2 years to gain experience and save money to equip an office of their own. Most dental school graduates, however, purchase an established practice or open a new one immediately after graduation.

Employment

Dentists held about 141,900 jobs in 2008. Employment was distributed among general practitioners and specialists as follows:

Dentists, general	120,200
Orthodontists	7,700
Oral and maxillofacial surgeons	6,700
Prosthodontists	500
Dentists, all other specialists	6,900

Approximately 15 percent of all dentists were specialists. About 28 percent of dentists were self-employed and not incorporated.

Very few salaried dentists worked in hospitals and offices of physicians. Almost all dentists work in private practice. According to the American Dental Association, about 3 out of 4 dentists in private practice are solo proprietors, and almost 15 percent belonged to a partnership.

Job Outlook

Employment is projected to grow faster than the average. Job prospects should be good, reflecting the need to replace the large number of dentists expected to retire.

Employment change. Employment of dentists is projected to grow by 16 percent through 2018, which is faster than the average for all occupations. The demand for dental services is expected to continue to increase. The overall U.S. population is growing, and the elderly segment of the population is growing even faster; these phenomena will increase the demand for dental care. Many members of the baby-boom generation will need complicated dental work. In addition, elderly people are more likely to retain their teeth than were their predecessors, so they will require much more care than in the past. The younger generation will continue to need preventive checkups despite an overall increase in the dental health of the public over the last few decades. Recently, some private insurance providers have increased their dental coverage. If this trend continues, people with new or expanded dental insurance will be more likely to visit a dentist than in the past. Also, although they are currently a small proportion of dental expenditures, cosmetic dental services, such as providing teeth-whitening treatments, will become increasingly popular. This trend is expected to continue as new technologies allow these procedures to take less time and be much less invasive.

However, employment of dentists is not expected to keep pace with the increased demand for dental services. Productivity increases from new technology, as well as the tendency to assign more tasks to dental hygienists and assistants, will allow dentists to perform more work than they have in the past. As their practices expand, dentists are likely to hire more hygienists and dental assistants to handle routine services.

Dentists will increasingly provide care and instruction aimed at preventing the loss of teeth, rather than simply providing treatments such as fillings. Improvements in dental technology also will allow dentists to offer more effective and less painful treatment to their patients.

Job prospects. As an increasing number of dentists from the baby-boom generation reach retirement age, many of them will retire or work fewer hours and stop taking on new patients. Furthermore, the number of applicants to, and graduates from, dental schools has increased in recent years. Job prospects should be good, because younger dentists will be able to take over the work of older dentists who retire or cut back on hours, as well as provide dental services to accommodate the growing demand.

Demand for dental services tends to follow the business cycle, primarily because these services usually are paid for either by the patient or by private insurance companies. As a result, during slow times in the economy, demand for dental services can decrease; consequently, dentists may have difficulty finding employment, or if already in an established practice, they may work fewer hours because of reduced demand.

Earnings

Median annual wages of salaried general dentists were $142,870 in May 2008. Earnings vary according to number of years in practice, location, hours worked, and specialty. Self-employed dentists in private practice tend to earn more than salaried dentists.

Dentists who are salaried often receive benefits paid by their employer, with health insurance and malpractice insurance being among the most common. However, like other business owners, self-employed dentists must provide their own health insurance, life insurance, retirement plans, and other benefits.

Related Occupations

Dentists examine, diagnose, prevent, and treat diseases and abnormalities. Other workers who perform similar tasks include chiropractors; optometrists; physicians and surgeons; podiatrists; and veterinarians.

Sources of Additional Information

For information on dentistry as a career, a list of accredited dental schools, and a list of state boards of dental examiners, contact

▶ American Dental Association, Commission on Dental Accreditation, 211 E. Chicago Ave., Chicago, IL 60611. Internet: www.ada.org

For information on admission to dental schools, contact

▶ American Dental Education Association, 1400 K St. NW, Suite 1100, Washington, DC 20005. Internet: www.adea.org

Projections Data from the National Employment Matrix

Occupational title	SOC Code	Employment, 2008	Projected employment, 2018	Change, 2008–2018	
				Number	Percent
Dentists	29-1020	141,900	164,000	22,100	16
Dentists, general...........................	29-1021	120,200	138,600	18,400	15
Oral and maxillofacial surgeons............	29-1022	6,700	7,700	1,000	15
Orthodontists	29-1023	7,700	9,200	1,500	20
Prosthodontists............................	29-1024	500	700	100	28
Dentists, all other specialists............	29-1029	6,900	7,900	1,000	15

NOTE: Data in this table are rounded.

For more information on general dentistry or on a specific dental specialty, contact

- ▶ Academy of General Dentistry, 211 E. Chicago Ave., Suite 900, Chicago, IL 60611. Internet: www.agd.org
- ▶ American Association of Orthodontists, 401 N. Lindbergh Blvd., St. Louis, MO 63141. Internet: www.braces.org
- ▶ American Association of Oral and Maxillofacial Surgeons, 9700 W. Bryn Mawr Ave., Rosemont, IL 60018. Internet: www.aaoms.org
- ▶ American Academy of Pediatric Dentistry, 211 E. Chicago Ave., Suite 1700, Chicago, IL 60611. Internet: www.aapd.org
- ▶ American Academy of Periodontology, 737 N. Michigan Ave., Suite 800, Chicago, IL 60611. Internet: www.perio.org
- ▶ American Academy of Prosthodontists, 211 E. Chicago Ave., Suite 1000, Chicago, IL 60611. Internet: www.prosthodontics.org
- ▶ American Association of Endodontists, 211 E. Chicago Ave., Suite 1100, Chicago, IL 60611. Internet: www.aae.org
- ▶ American Academy of Oral and Maxillofacial Radiology, P.O. Box 1010, Evans, GA 30809. Internet: www.aaomr.org
- ▶ American Association of Public Health Dentistry, 3085 Stevenson Dr., Suite 200, Springfield, IL 62703. Internet: www.aaphd.org

People interested in practicing dentistry should obtain the requirements for licensure from the board of dental examiners of the state in which they plan to work.

To obtain information on scholarships, grants, and loans, including federal financial aid, prospective dental students should contact the office of student financial aid at the schools to which they apply.

Desktop Publishers

(O*NET 43-3021.00, 43-3021.01, 43-3021.02, and 43-3021.03)

Significant Points

- About 38 percent work for newspaper, periodical, book, and directory publishers; another 21 percent work in the printing industry.
- Employment is expected to decline rapidly.
- Most employers prefer to hire experienced desktop publishers; among persons without experience, opportunities should be best for those with certificates or degrees in desktop publishing or graphic design.

Nature of the Work

Desktop publishers use computer software to format and combine text, data, photographs, charts, and other graphic art or illustrations into prototypes of pages and other documents that are to be printed. They then may print the document on a high-resolution printer or send the materials to a commercial printer. Examples of materials produced by desktop publishers include books, brochures, calendars, magazines, newsletters, newspapers, and forms.

Desktop publishers typically design and create the graphics that accompany text, find and edit photographs and other digital images, and manipulate the text and images to display information in an attractive and readable format. They design page layouts, develop presentations and advertising campaigns, and do color separation of pictures and graphics material. Some desktop publishers may write some of the text or headlines used in newsletters or brochures.

Desktop publishers use the appropriate software to enter and select formatting properties, such as the size and style of type, column width, and spacing. Print formats are stored in the computer and displayed on its monitor. New information, such as charts, pictures, or more text, can be added. An entire newspaper, catalog, or book page, complete with artwork and graphics, can be created on the screen exactly as it will appear in print. Then, digital files are used to produce printing plates. Like photographers and multimedia artists and animators, desktop publishers can create special effects or other visual images with the use of film, video, computers, or other electronic media.

Computer software and printing technology continue to advance, making desktop publishing more economical and efficient than before. Other innovations in the occupation include digital color page-makeup systems, electronic page-layout systems, and off-press color proofing systems. In addition, most materials are reproduced on the Internet as well as printed; therefore, desktop publishers may need to know electronic publishing software, such as Hypertext Markup Language (HTML), and may be responsible for converting text and graphics to an Internet-ready format.

Some desktop publishers may write and edit, as well as layout and design pages. For example, in addition to laying out articles for a newsletter, desktop publishers may be responsible for copyediting content or for writing original content themselves. Desktop publishers' writing and editing responsibilities may vary widely from project to project and employer to employer. Smaller firms typically use desktop publishers to perform a wide range of tasks, while desktop publishers at larger firms may specialize in a certain part of the publishing process.

Desktop publishers also may be called publications specialists, electronic publishers, DTP operators, desktop publishing editors, electronic prepress technicians, electronic publishing specialists, image designers, typographers, compositors, layout artists, and Web publications designers. The exact name may vary with the specific tasks performed or simply by personal preference.

Work environment. Desktop publishers usually work in clean, air-conditioned office areas with little noise. They generally work a standard workweek; however, some may work night shifts, weekends, or holidays, depending upon the production schedule for the project or to meet deadlines.

These workers often are subject to stress and the pressures of short deadlines and tight work schedules. Like other workers who spend long hours working in front of a computer monitor, desktop publishers may be susceptible to eyestrain, back discomfort, and hand and wrist problems.

Training, Other Qualifications, and Advancement

Most desktop publishers learn their skills on the job. Experience is the best training, and many desktop publishers get started just by experimenting with the software and developing a knack for designing and laying out material for publication.

Projections Data from the National Employment Matrix

Occupational title	SOC Code	Employment, 2008	Projected employment, 2018	Change, 2008–2018	
				Number	Percent
Desktop publishers..	43-9031	26,400	20,400	−5,900	−23

NOTE: Data in this table are rounded.

Education and training. There is generally no educational requirement for the job of desktop publisher. Most people learn on the job or by taking classes online or through local learning centers that teach the latest software. For those who are interested in pursuing a career in desktop publishing, an associate degree or a bachelor's degree in graphic arts, graphic communications, or graphic design is preferred. Graphic arts programs are a good way to learn about the desktop publishing software used to format pages, assign type characteristics, and import text and graphics into electronic page layouts. Courses in other aspects of printing also are available at vocational institutes and private trade and technical schools.

Other qualifications. Although formal training is not always required, those with certificates or degrees will have the best job opportunities. Most employers prefer to hire people who have at least a high school diploma and who possess good communication abilities, basic computer skills, and a strong work ethic. Desktop publishers should be able to deal courteously with people, because they have to interact with customers and clients and be able to express design concepts and layout options with them. In addition, they may have to do simple math calculations and compute ratios to scale graphics and artwork and estimate job costs. A basic understanding of, and facility with, computers, printers, scanners, and other office equipment and technologies also is needed to work as a desktop publisher.

Desktop publishers need good manual dexterity, and they must be able to pay attention to detail and work independently. In addition, good eyesight, including visual acuity, depth perception, a wide field of view, color vision, and the ability to focus quickly, are assets. Artistic ability often is a plus. Employers also seek persons who are even tempered and adaptable—important qualities for workers who frequently must meet deadlines and learn how to operate new equipment.

Advancement. Workers with limited training and experience assist more experienced staff on projects while they learn the software and gain practical experience. They advance on the basis of their demonstrated mastery of skills. Some may move into supervisory or management positions. Other desktop publishers may start their own companies or work as independent consultants, while those with more artistic talent and further education may find job opportunities in graphic design or commercial art.

Employment

Desktop publishers held about 26,400 jobs in 2008. Approximately 38 percent worked for newspaper, periodical, book, and directory publishers, while 21 percent worked in the printing and related support activities industry. Other desktop publishers work for professional, scientific, and technical services firms and in many other industries that produce printed or published materials.

The printing and publishing industries are two of the most geographically dispersed industries in the United States, and desktop publishing jobs are found throughout the country. Although most jobs are in large metropolitan cities, electronic communication networks and the Internet allow some desktop publishers to work from other locations.

Job Outlook

Employment is expected to decline rapidly because more people are learning basic desktop publishing skills as a part of their regular job functions in other occupations and because more organizations are formatting materials for display on the Internet rather than designing pages for print publication.

Employment change. Employment of desktop publishers is expected to decline 23 percent between 2008 and 2018. Desktop publishing has become a frequently used and common tool for designing and laying out printed matter, such as advertisements, brochures, newsletters, and forms. However, increased computer-processing capacity and the widespread availability of more elaborate desktop publishing software will make it easier and more affordable for nonprinting professionals to use. As a result, there will be less need for people to specialize in desktop publishing.

In addition, organizations are increasingly moving their published material to the Internet to save the cost of printing and distributing materials. This change will slow the growth of desktop publishers, especially in smaller membership and trade organizations, which publish newsletters and brief reports. Companies that produce more extensive reports and rely on high-quality, high-resolution color and graphics within their publications, however, will continue to use desktop publishers to lay out publications for offset printing.

Job prospects. There will be some job opportunities for desktop publishers because of the need to replace workers who move into managerial positions, transfer to other occupations, or leave the labor force. However, job prospects will be better for those with experience; many employers prefer to hire experienced desktop publishers because of the long time it takes to become good at this type of work. Among individuals with little or no experience, opportunities should be best for those with computer backgrounds, those with certification in desktop publishing, or those who have completed a postsecondary program in desktop publishing, graphic design, or Web design.

Earnings

Wages for desktop publishers vary according to level of experience, training, geographic location, and company size. Median annual wages of desktop publishers were $36,600 in May 2008. The middle 50 percent earned between $28,140 and $47,870. The lowest 10 percent earned less than $21,860, and the highest 10 percent earned more than $59,210 a year. Median annual wages of desktop publishers in May 2008 were $39,870 in printing and related support services and $33,130 in newspaper, periodical, book, and directory publishers.

Related Occupations

Desktop publishers use artistic and editorial skills in their work. These skills also are essential for the following workers artists and related workers; commercial and industrial designers; graphic designers; and prepress technicians and workers.

Sources of Additional Information

Details about training programs may be obtained from local employers, such as newspapers and printing shops, or from local offices of the state employment service.

For information on careers and training in printing, desktop publishing, and graphic arts, write to

▸ Graphic Arts Education and Research Foundation, 1899 Preston White Dr., Reston, VA 20191-4367. Internet: www.gaerf.org

▸ Graphic Arts Information Network, 200 Deer Run Rd., Sewickley, PA 15143-2324. Internet: www.gain.net

Electricians

(O*NET 47-2111.00)

Significant Points

■ Job opportunities should be good, especially for those with the broadest range of skills.

■ Most electricians acquire their skills by completing an apprenticeship program usually lasting four years.

■ About 79 percent of electricians work in the construction industry or are self-employed, but there also will be opportunities for electricians in other industries.

Nature of the Work

Electricians install and maintain all of the electrical and power systems for our homes, businesses, and factories. They install and maintain the wiring and control equipment through which electricity flows. They also install and maintain electrical equipment and machines in factories and a wide range of other businesses.

Electricians generally focus on either construction or maintenance, although many do both. Electricians specializing in construction primarily install wiring systems into factories, businesses, and new homes. Electricians specializing in maintenance fix and upgrade existing electrical systems and repair electrical equipment. All electricians must follow state and local building codes and the National Electrical Code when performing their work.

Electricians usually start their work by reading blueprints—technical diagrams that show the locations of circuits, outlets, load centers, panel boards, and other equipment. After determining where all the wires and components will go, electricians install and connect the wires to circuit breakers, transformers, outlets, or other components and systems.

When installing wiring, electricians use handtools such as conduit benders, screwdrivers, pliers, knives, hacksaws, and wire strippers, as well as power tools such as drills and saws. Later, they use ammeters, ohmmeters, voltmeters, harmonics testers, and other equipment to test connections and ensure the compatibility and safety of components.

Maintenance electricians repair or replace electric and electronic equipment when it breaks. They make needed repairs as quickly as possible in order to minimize inconvenience. They may replace items such as circuit breakers, fuses, switches, electrical and electronic components, or wire.

Electricians also periodically inspect all equipment to ensure that it is operating properly and to correct problems before breakdowns occur.

Maintenance work varies greatly, depending on where an electrician works. Electricians who focus on residential work perform a wide variety of electrical work for homeowners. They may rewire a home and replace an old fuse box with a new circuit breaker box to accommodate additional appliances, or they may install new lighting and other electric household items, such as ceiling fans. These electricians also might do some construction and installation work.

Electricians in large factories usually do maintenance work that is more complex. These kinds of electricians may repair motors, transformers, generators, and electronic controllers on machine tools and industrial robots. They also advise management as to whether the continued operation of certain equipment could be hazardous. When working with complex electronic devices, they may consult with engineers, engineering technicians, line installers and repairers, or industrial machinery mechanics and maintenance workers.

Work environment. Electricians work indoors and out, at construction sites, in homes, and in businesses or factories. The work may be strenuous at times and may include bending conduit, lifting heavy objects, and standing, stooping, and kneeling for long periods. Electricians risk injury from electrical shock, falls, and cuts, and must follow strict safety procedures to avoid injuries. Data from the U.S. Bureau of Labor Statistics show that full-time electricians experienced a work-related injury and illness rate that was higher than the national average. When working outdoors, they may be subject to inclement weather. Some electricians may have to travel long distances to jobsites.

Most electricians work a standard 40-hour week, although overtime may be required. Those who do maintenance work may work nights or weekends and be on call to go to the worksite when needed. Electricians in industrial settings may have periodic extended overtime during scheduled maintenance or retooling periods. Companies that operate 24 hours a day may employ three shifts of electricians.

Training, Other Qualifications, and Advancement

Most electricians learn their trade through apprenticeship programs that combine on-the-job training with related classroom instruction.

Education and training. Apprenticeship programs combine paid on-the-job training with related classroom instruction. Joint training committees made up of local unions of the International Brotherhood of Electrical Workers and local chapters of the National Electrical Contractors Association; individual electrical contracting companies; or local chapters of the Associated Builders and Contractors and the Independent Electrical Contractors Association usually sponsor apprenticeship programs.

Because of the comprehensive training received, those who complete apprenticeship programs qualify to do both maintenance and construction work. Apprenticeship programs usually last 4 years. Each year includes at least 144 hours of classroom instruction and 2,000 hours of on-the-job training. In the classroom, apprentices learn electrical theory, blueprint reading, mathematics, electrical code requirements, and safety and first aid practices. They also may receive specialized training in soldering, communications, fire alarm systems, and cranes and elevators.

On the job, apprentices work under the supervision of experienced electricians. At first, they drill holes, set anchors and attach conduit. Later, they measure, fabricate, and install conduit and install, connect, and test wiring, outlets, and switches. They also learn to set up and draw diagrams for entire electrical systems. Eventually, they practice and master all of an electrician's main tasks.

Some people start their classroom training before seeking an apprenticeship. A number of public and private vocational-technical schools and training academies offer training to become an electrician. Employers often hire students who complete these programs and usually start them at a more advanced level than those without this training. A few people become electricians by first working as helpers—assisting electricians by setting up job sites, gathering materials, and doing other nonelectrical work—before entering an apprenticeship program. All apprentices need a high school diploma or a General Equivalency Diploma (G.E.D.). Electricians also may need additional classes in mathematics because they solve mathematical problems on the job.

Education continues throughout an electrician's career. Electricians may need to take classes to learn about changes to the National Electrical Code, and they often complete regular safety programs, manufacturer-specific training, and management training courses. Classes on such topics as low-voltage voice and data systems, telephone systems, video systems, and alternative energy systems such as solar energy and wind energy increasingly are being given as these systems become more prevalent. Other courses teach electricians how to become contractors.

Licensure. Most states and localities require electricians to be licensed. Although licensing requirements vary from state to state, electricians usually must pass an examination that tests their knowledge of electrical theory, the National Electrical Code, and local and state electric and building codes.

Electrical contractors who do electrical work for the public, as opposed to electricians who work for electrical contractors, often need a special license. In some states, electrical contractors need certification as master electricians. Most states require master electricians to have at least 7 years of experience as an electrician or a bachelor's degree in electrical engineering or a related field.

Other qualifications. Applicants for apprenticeships usually must be at least 18 years old and have a high school diploma or a G.E.D. They also may have to pass a test and meet other requirements.

Other skills needed to become an electrician include manual dexterity, eye-hand coordination, physical fitness, and a good sense of balance. Electricians also need good color vision because workers frequently must identify electrical wires by color. In addition, apprenticeship committees and employers view a good work history or military service favorably.

Advancement. Experienced electricians can advance to jobs as supervisors. In construction, they also may become project managers or construction superintendents. Those with sufficient capital and management skills can start their own contracting business, although doing so often requires a special electrical contractor's license. Supervisors and contractors should be able to identify and estimate costs and prices and the time and materials needed to complete a job. Many electricians also become electrical inspectors.

For those who seek to advance, it is increasingly important to be able to communicate in both English and Spanish in order to relay instructions and safety precautions to workers with limited understanding of English; Spanish-speaking workers make up a large part of the construction workforce in many areas. Spanish-speaking workers who want to advance in this occupation need very good English skills to understand electrician classes and installation instructions, which are usually written in English and are highly technical.

Employment

Electricians held about 694,900 jobs in 2008. About 65 percent of wage and salary workers were employed by electrical contracting firms, and the remainder worked as electricians in a variety of other industries. In addition, about 9 percent of electricians were self-employed.

Job Outlook

Average employment growth is expected. Job prospects should be good, particularly for workers with the widest range of skills, including voice, data, and video wiring.

Employment change. Employment of electricians should increase 12 percent between 2008 and 2018, about as fast as the average for all occupations. As the population grows, electricians will be needed to wire new homes, restaurants, schools, and other structures that will be built to accommodate the growing population. In addition, older buildings will require improvements to their electrical systems to meet modern codes and accommodate higher electricity consumption due to the greater use of electronic equipment in houses and workplaces.

New technologies also are expected to continue to spur demand for these workers. Robots and other automated manufacturing systems in factories will require the installation and maintenance of more complex wiring systems. In addition, efforts to boost conservation of energy in public buildings and in new construction will boost demand for electricians because electricians are key to installing some of the latest energy savers, such as solar panels and motion sensors for turning on lights.

Job prospects. In addition to jobs created by the increased demand for electrical work, openings are expected over the next decade as electricians retire. This will create good job opportunities, especially for those with the widest range of skills, including voice, data, and video wiring. Job openings for electricians will vary by location and specialty, however, and will be best in the fastest growing regions of the country.

Employment of electricians, like that of many other construction workers, is sensitive to the fluctuations of the economy. On the one hand, workers in these trades may experience periods of unemployment when the overall level of construction falls. On the other hand, shortages of these workers may occur in some areas during peak periods of building activity.

Although employment of maintenance electricians is steadier than that of construction electricians, those working in the automotive and other manufacturing industries that are sensitive to cyclical swings in the economy may experience layoffs during recessions. In addition, in many industries opportunities for maintenance electricians may be limited by increased contracting out for electrical services in an effort to reduce operating costs. However, increased job opportunities for electricians in electrical contracting firms should partially offset job losses in other industries.

Earnings

In May 2008, median hourly wages of wage and salary electricians were $22.32. The middle 50 percent earned between $17.00 and $29.88. The lowest 10 percent earned less than $13.54, and the highest 10 percent earned more than $38.18. Median hourly wages in the industries employing the largest numbers of electricians were as follows:

Electric power generation, transmission
    and distribution... $28.15
Local government... 25.66
Nonresidential building construction...................... 22.21
Building equipment contractors............................ 21.72
Employment services.. 18.32

Apprentices usually start at between 30 and 50 percent of the rate paid to fully trained electricians, depending on experience. As apprentices become more skilled, they receive periodic pay increases throughout their training.

About 32 percent of all electricians are members of a union, especially the International Brotherhood of Electrical Workers. Among unions representing maintenance electricians are the International Brotherhood of Electrical Workers; the International Union of Electronic, Electrical, Salaried, Machine, and Furniture Workers; the International Association of Machinists and Aerospace Workers; the International Union, United Automobile, Aircraft and Agricultural Implement Workers of America; and the United Steelworkers of America.

Related Occupations

Other occupations that combine manual skill and knowledge of electrical materials and concepts include the following computer, automated teller, and office machine repairers; electrical and electronics drafters; electrical and electronics engineering technicians; electrical and electronics installers and repairers; electronic home entertainment equipment installers and repairers; elevator installers and repairers; heating, air-conditioning, and refrigeration mechanics and installers; and line installers and repairers.

Sources of Additional Information

For details about apprenticeships or other work opportunities in this trade, contact the offices of the state employment service, the state apprenticeship agency, local electrical contractors or firms that employ maintenance electricians, or local union-management electrician apprenticeship committees. Apprenticeship information is available from the U.S. Department of Labor's toll free help line: (877) 872-5627. Internet: www.doleta.gov/OA/eta_default.cfm

Information may be available as well from local chapters of the Independent Electrical Contractors, Inc.; the National Electrical Contractors Association; the Home Builders Institute; the Associated Builders and Contractors trade association; and the International Brotherhood of Electrical Workers.

For information about union apprenticeship and training programs, contact

▸ National Joint Apprenticeship Training Committee, 301 Prince George's Blvd., Upper Marlboro, MD 20774-7410. Internet: www.njatc.org

▸ National Electrical Contractors Association, 3 Bethesda Metro Center, Suite 1100, Bethesda, MD 20814-6302. Internet: www.necanet.org

▸ International Brotherhood of Electrical Workers, 900 Seventh St. NW, Washington, DC 20001-3886. Internet: www.ibew.org

For information about independent apprenticeship programs, contact

▸ Associated Builders and Contractors, Workforce Development Department, 4250 N. Fairfax Dr., 9th Floor, Arlington, VA 22203-1607. Internet: www.trytools.org

▸ Independent Electrical Contractors, Inc., 4401 Ford Ave., Suite 1100, Alexandria, VA 22302-1464. Internet: www.ieci.org

▸ National Association of Home Builders, Home Builders Institute, 1201 15th St. NW, 6th Floor, Washington, DC 20005-2842. Internet: www.hbi.org

▸ National Center for Construction Education and Research, 3600 NW 43rd St., Bldg. G, Gainesville, FL 32606-8134. Internet: www.nccer.org

For general information on apprenticeships and how to get them, see the *Occupational Outlook Quarterly* article "Apprenticeships:

Projections Data from the National Employment Matrix

Occupational title	SOC Code	Employment, 2008	Projected employment, 2018	Change, 2008–2018	
				Number	Percent
Electricians.. 47-2111		694,900	777,900	83,000	12

NOTE: Data in this table are rounded.

Career training, credentials—and a paycheck in your pocket," online at www.bls.gov/opub/ooq/2002/summer/art01.pdf and in print at many libraries and career centers.

Engineers

(O*NET 17-2011.00, 17-2199.11, 17-2199.10, 17-2199.09, 17-2199.08, 17-2199.07, 17-2199.06, 17-2199.05, 17-2199.04, 17-2199.03, 17-2199.02, 17-2199.01, 17-2199.00, 17-2171.00, 17-2161.00, 17-2151.00, 17-2141.02, 17-2141.01, 17-2141.00, 17-2131.00, 17-2121.02, 17-2121.01, 17-2121.00, 17-2112.01, 17-2112.00, 17-2111.03, 17-2111.02, 17-2111.01, 17-2111.00, 17-2081.00, 17-2072.01, 17-2072.00, 17-2071.00, 17-2061.00, 17-2051.02, 17-2051.01, 17-2051.00, 17-2041.00, 17-2031.00, and 17-2021.00)

Significant Points

- Employment is projected to grow about as fast as the average for all occupations, although growth will vary by specialty; overall job opportunities for engineers are expected to be good.

- A bachelor's degree in engineering is required for most entry-level jobs, but some research positions may require a graduate degree.

- Starting salaries are among the highest of all college graduates.

- Continuing education is critical for engineers in order to keep up with improvements in technology.

Nature of the Work

Engineers apply the principles of science and mathematics to develop economical solutions to technical problems. Their work is the link between scientific discoveries and the commercial applications that meet societal and consumer needs.

Many engineers develop new products. During the process, they consider several factors. For example, in developing an industrial robot, engineers specify the functional requirements precisely; design and test the robot's components; integrate the components to produce the final design; and evaluate the design's overall effectiveness, cost, reliability, and safety. This process applies to the development of many different products, such as chemicals, computers, power plants, helicopters, and toys.

In addition to their involvement in design and development, many engineers work in testing, production, or maintenance. These engineers supervise production in factories, determine the causes of a component's failure, and test manufactured products to maintain quality. They also estimate the time and cost required to complete projects. Supervisory engineers are responsible for major components or entire projects.

Engineers use computers extensively to produce and analyze designs; to simulate and test how a machine, structure, or system operates; to generate specifications for parts; to monitor the quality of products; and to control the efficiency of processes. Nanotechnology, which involves the creation of high-performance materials and components by integrating atoms and molecules, also is introducing entirely new principles to the design process.

Most engineers specialize. Following are details on the 17 engineering specialties covered in the federal government's Standard Occupational Classification (SOC) system. Numerous other specialties are recognized by professional societies, and each of the major branches of engineering has numerous subdivisions. Civil engineering, for example, includes structural and transportation engineering, and materials engineering includes ceramic, metallurgical, and polymer engineering. Engineers also may specialize in one industry, such as motor vehicles, or in one type of technology, such as turbines or semiconductor materials.

Aerospace engineers design, test, and supervise the manufacture of aircraft, spacecraft, and missiles. Those who work with aircraft are called *aeronautical engineers,* and those working specifically with spacecraft are *astronautical engineers*. Aerospace engineers develop new technologies for use in aviation, defense systems, and space exploration, often specializing in areas such as structural design, guidance, navigation and control, instrumentation and communication, and production methods. They also may specialize in a particular type of aerospace product, such as commercial aircraft, military fighter jets, helicopters, spacecraft, or missiles and rockets, and may become experts in aerodynamics, thermodynamics, celestial mechanics, propulsion, acoustics, or guidance and control systems.

Agricultural engineers apply their knowledge of engineering technology and science to agriculture and the efficient use of biological resources. Accordingly, they also are referred to as *biological and agricultural engineers*. They design agricultural machinery, equipment, sensors, processes, and structures, such as those used for crop storage. Some engineers specialize in areas such as power systems and machinery design, structural and environmental engineering, and food and bioprocess engineering. They develop ways to conserve soil and water and to improve the processing of agricultural products. Agricultural engineers often work in research and development, production, sales, or management.

Biomedical engineers develop devices and procedures that solve medical and health-related problems by combining their knowledge of biology and medicine with engineering principles and practices. Many do research, along with medical scientists, to develop and evaluate systems and products such as artificial organs, prostheses (artificial devices that replace missing body parts), instrumentation, medical information systems, and health management and care delivery systems. Biomedical engineers also may design devices used in various medical procedures, imaging systems such as magnetic resonance imaging (MRI), and devices for automating insulin injections or controlling body functions. Most engineers in this specialty need a sound background in another engineering specialty, such as mechanical or electronics engineering, in addition to specialized biomedical training. Some specialties within biomedical engineering are biomaterials, biomechanics, medical imaging, rehabilitation engineering, and orthopedic engineering.

Chemical engineers apply the principles of chemistry to solve problems involving the production or use of chemicals and other products. They design equipment and processes for large-scale chemical manufacturing, plan and test methods of manufacturing products and treating byproducts, and supervise production. Chemical engineers also work in a variety of manufacturing industries other than chemical manufacturing, such as those producing energy,

electronics, food, clothing, and paper. In addition, they work in health care, biotechnology, and business services. Chemical engineers apply principles of physics, mathematics, and mechanical and electrical engineering, as well as chemistry. Some may specialize in a particular chemical process, such as oxidation or polymerization. Others specialize in a particular field, such as nanomaterials, or in the development of specific products. They must be aware of all aspects of chemical manufacturing and how the manufacturing process affects the environment and the safety of workers and consumers.

Civil engineers design and supervise the construction of roads, buildings, airports, tunnels, dams, bridges, and water supply and sewage systems. They must consider many factors in the design process, from the construction costs and expected lifetime of a project to government regulations and potential environmental hazards such as earthquakes and hurricanes. Civil engineering, considered one of the oldest engineering disciplines, encompasses many specialties. The major ones are structural, water resources, construction, transportation, and geotechnical engineering. Many civil engineers hold supervisory or administrative positions, from supervisor of a construction site to city engineer. Others may work in design, construction, research, and teaching.

Computer hardware engineers research, design, develop, test, and oversee the manufacture and installation of computer hardware, including computer chips, circuit boards, computer systems, and related equipment such as keyboards, routers, and printers. (Computer software engineers—often simply called computer engineers—design and develop the software systems that control computers.) The work of computer hardware engineers is similar to that of electronics engineers, in that they may design and test circuits and other electronic components; however, computer hardware engineers do that work only as it relates to computers and computer-related equipment. The rapid advances in computer technology are largely a result of the research, development, and design efforts of these engineers.

Electrical engineers design, develop, test, and supervise the manufacture of electrical equipment. Some of this equipment includes electric motors; machinery controls, lighting, and wiring in buildings; radar and navigation systems; communications systems; and power generation, control, and transmission devices used by electric utilities. Electrical engineers also design the electrical systems of automobiles and aircraft. Although the terms *electrical* and *electronics engineering* often are used interchangeably in academia and industry, electrical engineers traditionally have focused on the generation and supply of power, whereas electronics engineers have worked on applications of electricity to control systems or signal processing. Electrical engineers specialize in areas such as power systems engineering or electrical equipment manufacturing.

Electronics engineers, except computer, are responsible for a wide range of technologies, from portable music players to global positioning systems (GPSs), which can continuously provide the location of, for example, a vehicle. Electronics engineers design, develop, test, and supervise the manufacture of electronic equipment such as broadcast and communications systems. Many electronics engineers also work in areas closely related to computers. However, engineers whose work is related exclusively to computer hardware are considered computer hardware engineers. Electronics engineers specialize in areas such as communications, signal processing, and control systems or have a specialty within one of these areas—control systems or aviation electronics, for example.

Environmental engineers use the principles of biology and chemistry to develop solutions to environmental problems. They are involved in water and air pollution control, recycling, waste disposal, and public health issues. Environmental engineers conduct hazardous-waste management studies in which they evaluate the significance of the hazard, advise on its treatment and containment, and develop regulations to prevent mishaps. They design municipal water supply and industrial wastewater treatment systems, conduct research on the environmental impact of proposed construction projects, analyze scientific data, and perform quality-control checks. Environmental engineers are concerned with local and worldwide environmental issues. Some may study and attempt to minimize the effects of acid rain, global warming, automobile emissions, and ozone depletion. They also may be involved in the protection of wildlife. Many environmental engineers work as consultants, helping their clients to comply with regulations, prevent environmental damage, and clean up hazardous sites.

Health and safety engineers, except mining safety engineers and inspectors, prevent harm to people and property by applying their knowledge of systems engineering and mechanical, chemical, and human performance principles. Using this specialized knowledge, they identify and measure potential hazards, such as the risk of fires or the dangers involved in handling toxic chemicals. They recommend appropriate loss prevention measures according to their probability of harm and potential damage. Health and safety engineers develop procedures and designs to reduce the risk of illness, injury, or damage. Some work in manufacturing industries to ensure that the designs of new products do not create unnecessary hazards. They must be able to anticipate, recognize, and evaluate hazardous conditions, as well as develop hazard control methods.

Industrial engineers determine the most effective ways to use the basic factors of production—people, machines, materials, information, and energy—to make a product or provide a service. They are concerned primarily with increasing productivity through the management of people, methods of business organization, and technology. To maximize efficiency, industrial engineers study product requirements carefully and then design manufacturing and information systems to meet those requirements with the help of mathematical methods and models. They develop management control systems to aid in financial planning and cost analysis, and they design production planning and control systems to coordinate activities and ensure product quality. They also design or improve systems for the physical distribution of goods and services and determine the most efficient plant locations. Industrial engineers develop wage and salary administration systems and job evaluation programs. Many industrial engineers move into management positions because the work is closely related to the work of managers.

Marine engineers and naval architects are involved in the design, construction, and maintenance of ships, boats, and related equipment. They design and supervise the construction of everything from aircraft carriers to submarines and from sailboats to tankers. Naval architects work on the basic design of ships, including the form and stability of hulls. Marine engineers work on the propulsion, steering, and other systems of ships. Marine engineers and naval architects apply knowledge from a range of fields to the entire process by which water vehicles are designed and produced. Other workers who operate or supervise the operation of marine machinery on ships and other vessels sometimes may be called marine engineers or, more frequently, ship engineers, but they do different work.

Materials engineers are involved in the development, processing, and testing of the materials used to create a range of products, from computer chips and aircraft wings to golf clubs and snow skis. They work with metals, ceramics, plastics, semiconductors, and composites to create new materials that meet certain mechanical, electrical, and chemical requirements. They also are involved in selecting materials for new applications. Materials engineers have developed the ability to create and then study materials at an atomic level, using advanced processes to replicate the characteristics of those materials and their components with computers. Most materials engineers specialize in a particular material. For example, metallurgical engineers specialize in metals such as steel, and ceramic engineers develop ceramic materials and the processes for making them into useful products such as glassware or fiber-optic communication lines.

Mechanical engineers research, design, develop, manufacture, and test tools, engines, machines, and other mechanical devices. Mechanical engineering is one of the broadest engineering disciplines. Engineers in this discipline work on power-producing machines such as electric generators, internal combustion engines, and steam and gas turbines. They also work on power-using machines such as refrigeration and air-conditioning equipment, machine tools, material-handling systems, elevators and escalators, industrial production equipment, and robots used in manufacturing. Some mechanical engineers design tools that other engineers need for their work. In addition, mechanical engineers work in manufacturing or agriculture production, maintenance, or technical sales; many become administrators or managers.

Mining and geological engineers, including mining safety engineers, find, extract, and prepare coal, metals, and minerals for use by manufacturing industries and utilities. They design open-pit and underground mines, supervise the construction of mine shafts and tunnels in underground operations, and devise methods for transporting minerals to processing plants. Mining engineers are responsible for the safe, economical, and environmentally sound operation of mines. Some mining engineers work with geologists and metallurgical engineers to locate and appraise new ore deposits. Others develop new mining equipment or direct mineral-processing operations that separate minerals from the dirt, rock, and other materials with which they are mixed. Mining engineers frequently specialize in the mining of one mineral or metal, such as coal or gold. With increased emphasis on protecting the environment, many mining engineers are working to solve problems related to land reclamation and to water and air pollution. Mining safety engineers use their knowledge of mine design and practices to ensure the safety of workers and to comply with state and federal safety regulations. They inspect the surfaces of walls and roofs, monitor air quality, and examine mining equipment for compliance with safety practices.

Nuclear engineers research and develop the processes, instruments, and systems used to derive benefits from nuclear energy and radiation. They design, develop, monitor, and operate nuclear plants to generate power. They may work on the nuclear fuel cycle—the production, handling, and use of nuclear fuel and the safe disposal of waste produced by the generation of nuclear energy—or on the development of fusion energy. Some specialize in the development of nuclear power sources for naval vessels or spacecraft; others find industrial and medical uses for radioactive materials—for example, in equipment used to diagnose and treat medical problems.

Petroleum engineers design methods for extracting oil and gas from deposits below the earth. Once these resources have been discovered, petroleum engineers work with geologists and other specialists to understand the geologic formation and properties of the rock containing the reservoir, to determine the drilling methods to be used, and to monitor drilling and production operations. They design equipment and processes to achieve the maximum profitable recovery of oil and gas. Because only a small proportion of oil and gas in a reservoir flows out under natural forces, petroleum engineers develop and use various enhanced recovery methods, including injecting water, chemicals, gases, or steam into an oil reservoir to force out more of the oil and doing computer-controlled drilling or fracturing to connect a larger area of a reservoir to a single well. Because even the best techniques in use today recover only a portion of the oil and gas in a reservoir, petroleum engineers research and develop technology and methods for increasing the recovery of these resources and lowering the cost of drilling and production operations.

Work environment. Most engineers work in office buildings, laboratories, or industrial plants. Others may spend time outdoors at construction sites and oil and gas exploration and production sites, where they monitor or direct operations or solve onsite problems. Some engineers travel extensively to plants or worksites here and abroad.

Many engineers work a standard 40-hour week. At times, deadlines or design standards may bring extra pressure to a job, requiring engineers to work longer hours.

Training, Other Qualifications, and Advancement

Engineers typically enter the occupation with a bachelor's degree in an engineering specialty, but some basic research positions may require a graduate degree. Engineers offering their services directly to the public must be licensed. Continuing education to keep current with rapidly changing technology is important for engineers.

Education and training. A bachelor's degree in engineering is required for almost all entry-level engineering jobs. College graduates with a degree in a natural science or mathematics occasionally may qualify for some engineering jobs, especially in specialties that are in high demand. Most engineering degrees are granted in electrical and electronics engineering, mechanical engineering, and civil engineering. However, engineers trained in one branch may work in related branches. For example, many aerospace engineers have training in mechanical engineering. This flexibility allows employers to meet staffing needs in new technologies and specialties in which engineers may be in short supply. It also allows engineers to shift to fields with better employment prospects or to those which more closely match their interests.

Most engineering programs involve a concentration of study in an engineering specialty, along with courses in both mathematics and the physical and life sciences. Many programs also include courses in general engineering. A design course, sometimes accompanied by a computer or laboratory class or both, is part of the curriculum of most programs. Often, general courses not directly related to engineering, such as those in the social sciences or humanities, also are required.

In addition to the standard engineering degree, many colleges offer two-year or four-year degree programs in engineering technology. These programs, which usually include various hands-on laboratory classes that focus on current issues in the application of engineering principles, prepare students for practical design and production work, rather than for jobs that require more theoretical and scientific knowledge. Graduates of four-year technology programs may get jobs similar to those obtained by graduates with a bachelor's degree in engineering. Engineering technology graduates, however, are not qualified to register as professional engineers under the same terms as graduates with degrees in engineering. Some employers regard technology program graduates as having skills between those of a technician and an engineer.

Graduate training is essential for engineering faculty positions and some research and development programs, but is not required for the majority of entry-level engineering jobs. Many experienced engineers obtain graduate degrees in engineering or business administration to learn new technology and broaden their education. Numerous high-level executives in government and industry began their careers as engineers.

The Accreditation Board for Engineering and Technology (ABET) accredits college and university programs in engineering and engineering technology. ABET accreditation is based on a program's faculty, curriculum, and facilities; the achievement of a program's students; program improvements; and institutional commitment to specific principles of quality and ethics. Graduation from an ABET-accredited program may be required for engineers who need to be licensed.

Although most institutions offer programs in the major branches of engineering, only a few offer programs in the smaller specialties. Also, programs with the same title may vary in content. For example, some programs emphasize industrial practices, preparing students for a job in industry, whereas others are more theoretical and are designed to prepare students for graduate work. Therefore, students should investigate curricula and check accreditations carefully before selecting a college.

Admissions requirements for undergraduate engineering schools include a solid background in mathematics (algebra, geometry, trigonometry, and calculus) and science (biology, chemistry, and physics), in addition to courses in English, social studies, and humanities. Bachelor's degree programs in engineering typically are designed to last four years, but many students find that it takes between four and five years to complete their studies. In a typical four-year college curriculum, the first two years are spent studying mathematics, basic sciences, introductory engineering, humanities, and social sciences. In the last two years, most courses are in engineering, usually with a concentration in one specialty. Some programs offer a general engineering curriculum; students then specialize on the job or in graduate school.

Some engineering schools have agreements with two-year colleges whereby the college provides the initial engineering education and the engineering school automatically admits students for their last two years. In addition, a few engineering schools have arrangements that allow students who spend three years in a liberal arts college studying preengineering subjects and two years in an engineering school studying core subjects to receive a bachelor's degree from each school. Some colleges and universities offer five-year master's degree programs. Some five-year or even six-year cooperative plans combine classroom study with practical work, permitting students to gain valuable experience and to finance part of their education.

Licensure. All 50 states and the District of Columbia require licensure for engineers who offer their services directly to the public. Engineers who are licensed are called professional engineers (PEs). This licensure generally requires a degree from an ABET-accredited engineering program, four years of relevant work experience, and completion of a state examination. Recent graduates can start the licensing process by taking the examination in two stages. The initial Fundamentals of Engineering (FE) examination can be taken upon graduation. Engineers who pass this examination commonly are called engineers in training (EITs) or engineer interns (EIs). After acquiring suitable work experience, EITs can take the second examination, called the Principles and Practice of Engineering exam. Several states have imposed mandatory continuing education requirements for relicensure. Most states recognize licensure from other states, provided that the manner in which the initial license was obtained meets or exceeds their own licensure requirements. Many civil, mechanical, and chemical engineers are licensed PEs. Independently of licensure, various certification programs are offered by professional organizations to demonstrate competency in specific fields of engineering.

Other qualifications. Engineers should be creative, inquisitive, analytical, and detail oriented. They should be able to work as part of a team and to communicate well, both orally and in writing. Communication abilities are becoming increasingly important as engineers interact more frequently with specialists in a wide range of fields outside engineering.

Engineers who work for the federal government usually must be U.S. citizens. Some engineers, particularly nuclear engineers and aerospace and other engineers working for defense contractors, may need to hold a security clearance.

Certification and advancement. Beginning engineering graduates usually work under the supervision of experienced engineers and, in large companies, also may receive formal classroom or seminar-type training. As new engineers gain knowledge and experience, they are assigned more difficult projects with greater independence to develop designs, solve problems, and make decisions. Engineers may advance to become technical specialists or to supervise a staff or team of engineers and technicians. Some eventually may become engineering managers or enter other managerial or sales jobs. In sales, an engineering background enables them to discuss a product's technical aspects and assist in product planning, installation, and use.

Numerous professional certifications for engineers exist and may be beneficial for advancement to senior technical or managerial positions. Many certification programs are offered by the professional societies listed as sources of additional information for engineering specialties at the end of this statement.

Employment

In 2008, engineers held about 1.6 million jobs. Following is the distribution of employment by engineering specialty:

Civil engineers	278,400
Mechanical engineers	238,700
Industrial engineers	214,800
Electrical engineers	157,800
Electronics engineers, except computer	143,700
Computer hardware engineers	74,700
Aerospace engineers	71,600
Environmental engineers	54,300
Chemical engineers	31,700
Health and safety engineers, except mining safety engineers and inspectors	25,700
Materials engineers	24,400
Petroleum engineers	21,900
Nuclear engineers	16,900
Biomedical engineers	16,000
Marine engineers and naval architects	8,500
Mining and geological engineers, including mining safety engineers	7,100
Agricultural engineers	2,700
Engineers, all other	183,200

About 36 percent of engineering jobs were found in manufacturing industries, and another 30 percent were in the professional, scientific, and technical services industries, primarily in architectural, engineering, and related services. Many engineers also worked in the construction, telecommunications, and wholesale trade industries.

Federal, state, and local governments employed about 12 percent of engineers in 2008. About 6 percent were in the federal government, mainly in the U.S. Departments of Defense, Transportation, Agriculture, Interior, and Energy, and in the National Aeronautics and Space Administration. Many engineers in state and local government agencies worked in highway and public works departments. In 2008, about 3 percent of engineers were self-employed, many as consultants.

Engineers are employed in every state, in small and large cities and in rural areas. Some branches of engineering are concentrated in particular industries and geographic areas; for example, petroleum engineering jobs tend to be located in states with sizable petroleum deposits, such as Texas, Louisiana, Oklahoma, Alaska, and California. Other branches, such as civil engineering, are widely dispersed, and engineers in these fields often move from place to place to work on different projects.

Job Outlook

Employment of engineers is expected to grow about as fast as the average for all occupations over the next decade, but growth will vary by specialty. Biomedical engineers should experience the fastest growth, while civil engineers should see the largest employment increase. Overall job opportunities in engineering are expected to be good.

Overall employment change. Overall engineering employment is expected to grow by 11 percent over the 2008–2018 decade, about as fast as the average for all occupations. Engineers traditionally have been concentrated in slower growing or declining manufacturing industries, in which they will continue to be needed to design, build, test, and improve manufactured products. However, increasing employment of engineers in engineering, research and development, and consulting services industries should generate most of the employment growth. The job outlook varies by engineering specialty, as discussed later.

Competitive pressures and advancing technology will force companies to improve and update product designs and to optimize their manufacturing processes. Employers will rely on engineers to increase productivity and expand output of goods and services. New technologies continue to improve the design process, enabling engineers to produce and analyze various product designs much more rapidly than in the past. Unlike the situation in some other occupations, however, technological advances are not expected to substantially limit employment opportunities in engineering, because engineers are needed to provide the ideas that lead to improved products and more productive processes.

The continued globalization of engineering work will likely dampen domestic employment growth to some degree. There are many well-trained, often English-speaking, engineers available around the world who are willing to work at much lower salaries than U.S. engineers. The rise of the Internet has made it relatively easy for part of the engineering work previously done by engineers in this country to be done by engineers in other countries, a factor that will tend to hold down employment growth. Even so, there will always be a need for onsite engineers to interact with other employees and clients.

Overall job prospects. Overall job opportunities in engineering are expected to be good, and, indeed, prospects will be excellent in certain specialties. In addition to openings from job growth, many openings will be created by the need to replace current engineers who retire; transfer to management, sales, or other occupations; or leave engineering for other reasons.

Many engineers work on long-term research and development projects or in other activities that continue even during economic slowdowns. In industries such as electronics and aerospace, however, large cutbacks in defense expenditures and in government funding for research and development have resulted in significant layoffs of engineers in the past. The trend toward contracting for engineering work with engineering services firms, both domestic and foreign, also has made engineers more vulnerable to layoffs during periods of lower demand.

It is important for engineers, as it is for workers in other technical and scientific occupations, to continue their education throughout their careers, because much of their value to their employer depends on their knowledge of the latest technology. Engineers in high-technology areas, such as biotechnology or information technology, may find that their technical knowledge will become outdated rapidly. By keeping current in their field, engineers will be able to deliver the best solutions and greatest value to their employers. Engineers who have not kept current in their field may find themselves at a disadvantage when seeking promotions or during layoffs.

Employment change and job outlook by engineering specialty. Aerospace engineers are expected to have 10 percent growth in employment over the projections decade, about as fast as the average for all occupations. New technologies and new designs for commercial and military aircraft and spacecraft produced during the next decade should spur demand for aerospace engineers. The employment outlook for aerospace engineers appears favorable. Although the number of degrees granted in aerospace engineering has begun to increase after many years of declines, new graduates continue to be needed to replace aerospace engineers who retire or leave the occupation for other reasons.

Agricultural engineers are expected to have employment growth of 12 percent over the projections decade, about as fast as the average for all occupations. Employment growth should result from the need to increase crop yields to feed an expanding population and to produce crops used as renewable energy sources. Moreover, engineers will be needed to develop more efficient agricultural production and to conserve resources. In addition, engineers will be needed to meet the increasing demand for biosensors, used to determine the optimal treatment of crops.

Biomedical engineers are expected to have employment growth of 72 percent over the projections decade, much faster than the average for all occupations. The aging of the population and a growing focus on health issues will drive demand for better medical devices and equipment designed by biomedical engineers. Along with the demand for more sophisticated medical equipment and procedures, an increased concern for cost-effectiveness will boost demand for biomedical engineers, particularly in pharmaceutical manufacturing and related industries. Because of the growing interest in this field, the number of degrees granted in biomedical engineering has increased greatly. Many biomedical engineers, particularly those employed in research laboratories, need a graduate degree.

Chemical engineers are expected to have an employment decline of 2 percent over the projections decade. Overall employment in the chemical manufacturing industry is expected to continue to decline, although chemical companies will continue to employ chemical engineers to research and develop new chemicals and more efficient processes to increase output of existing chemicals. However, there will be employment growth for chemical engineers in service-providing industries, such as professional, scientific, and technical services, particularly for research in energy and the developing fields of biotechnology and nanotechnology.

Civil engineers are expected to have employment growth of 24 percent over the projections decade, much faster than the average for all occupations. Spurred by general population growth and the related need to improve the nation's infrastructure, more civil engineers will be needed to design and construct or expand transportation, water supply, and pollution control systems, and buildings and building complexes. They also will be needed to repair or replace existing roads, bridges, and other public structures. Because construction industries and architectural, engineering, and related services employ many civil engineers, employment opportunities will vary by geographic area and may decrease during economic slowdowns, when construction is often curtailed.

Computer hardware engineers are expected to have employment growth of 4 percent over the projections decade, slower than the average for all occupations. Although the use of information technology continues to expand rapidly, the manufacture of computer hardware is expected to be adversely affected by intense foreign competition. As computer and semiconductor manufacturers contract out more of their engineering needs to both domestic and foreign design firms, much of the growth in employment of hardware engineers is expected to take place in the computer systems design and related services industry.

Electrical engineers are expected to have employment growth of 2 percent over the projections decade. Although strong demand for electrical devices—including electric power generators, wireless phone transmitters, high-density batteries, and navigation systems—should spur job growth, international competition and the use of engineering services performed in other countries will limit employment growth. Electrical engineers working in firms providing engineering expertise and design services to manufacturers should have better job prospects.

Electronics engineers, except computer, are expected to experience little to no employment change over the projections decade. Although rising demand for electronic goods—including communications equipment, defense-related equipment, medical electronics, and consumer products—should continue to increase demand for electronics engineers, foreign competition in electronic products development and the use of engineering services performed in other countries will limit employment growth. Growth is expected to be fastest in service-providing industries—particularly in firms that provide engineering and design services.

Environmental engineers are expected to have employment growth of 31 percent over the projections decade, much faster than the average for all occupations. More environmental engineers will be needed to help companies comply with environmental regulations and to develop methods of cleaning up environmental hazards. A shift in emphasis toward preventing problems rather than controlling those which already exist, as well as increasing public health concerns resulting from population growth, also are expected to spur demand for environmental engineers. Because of this employment growth, job opportunities should be favorable.

Health and safety engineers, except mining safety engineers and inspectors, are expected to have employment growth of 10 percent over the projections decade, about as fast as the average for all occupations. Because health and safety engineers make production processes and products as safe as possible, their services should be in demand as concern increases for health and safety within work environments. As new technologies for production or processing are developed, health and safety engineers will be needed to ensure that they are safe.

Industrial engineers are expected to have employment growth of 14 percent over the projections decade, faster than the average for all occupations. As firms look for new ways to reduce costs and raise productivity, they increasingly will turn to industrial engineers to develop more efficient processes and reduce costs, delays, and waste. This focus should lead to job growth for these engineers, even in some manufacturing industries with declining employment overall. Because their work is similar to that done in management occupations, many industrial engineers leave the occupation to

Projections Data from the National Employment Matrix

Occupational title	SOC Code	Employment, 2008	Projected employment, 2018	Change, 2008–2018	
				Number	Percent
Engineers	17-2000	1,571,900	1,750,300	178,300	11
Aerospace engineers	17-2011	71,600	79,100	7,400	10
Agricultural engineers	17-2021	2,700	3,000	300	12
Biomedical engineers	17-2031	16,000	27,600	11,600	72
Chemical engineers	17-2041	31,700	31,000	−600	−2
Civil engineers	17-2051	278,400	345,900	67,600	24
Computer hardware engineers....................	17-2061	74,700	77,500	2,800	4
Electrical and electronics engineers	17-2070	301,500	304,600	3,100	1
Electrical engineers	17-2071	157,800	160,500	2,700	2
Electronics engineers, except computer	17-2072	143,700	144,100	400	0
Environmental engineers	17-2081	54,300	70,900	16,600	31
Industrial engineers, including health and safety........	17-2110	240,400	273,700	33,200	14
Health and safety engineers, except mining safety engineers and inspectors	17-2111	25,700	28,300	2,600	10
Industrial engineers	17-2112	214,800	245,300	30,600	14
Marine engineers and naval architects....................	17-2121	8,500	9,000	500	6
Materials engineers.................................	17-2131	24,400	26,600	2,300	9
Mechanical engineers...............................	17-2141	238,700	253,100	14,400	6
Mining and geological engineers, including mining safety engineers........................	17-2151	7,100	8,200	1,100	15
Nuclear engineers....................................	17-2161	16,900	18,800	1,900	11
Petroleum engineers	17-2171	21,900	25,900	4,000	18
All other engineers.................................	17-2199	183,200	195,400	12,200	7

NOTE: Data in this table are rounded.

become managers. Numerous openings will be created by the need to replace industrial engineers who transfer to other occupations or leave the labor force.

Marine engineers and naval architects are expected to have employment growth of 6 percent over the projections decade, slower than the average for all occupations. Continued demand for naval vessels and recreational small craft should more than offset the long-term decline in the domestic design and construction of large oceangoing vessels. Good prospects are expected for marine engineers and naval architects because of growth in employment, the need to replace workers who retire or take other jobs, and the limited number of students pursuing careers in this occupation.

Materials engineers are expected to have employment growth of 9 percent over the projections decade, about as fast as the average for all occupations. Growth should result from increased use of composite and other nontraditional materials developed through biotechnology and nanotechnology research. As manufacturing firms contract for their materials engineering needs, most employment growth is expected in professional, scientific, and technical services industries.

Mechanical engineers are expected to have employment growth of 6 percent over the projections decade, slower than the average for all occupations. Mechanical engineers are involved in the production of a wide range of products, and continued efforts to improve those products will create continued demand for their services. In addition, some new job opportunities will be created through the effects

of emerging technologies in biotechnology, materials science, and nanotechnology. Additional opportunities outside of mechanical engineering will exist because the skills acquired through earning a degree in mechanical engineering often can be applied in other engineering specialties.

Mining and geological engineers, including mining safety engineers, are expected to have employment growth of 15 percent over the projections decade, faster than the average for all occupations. Following a lengthy period of decline, strong growth in demand for minerals is expected to create some employment growth over the 2008–2018 period. Moreover, many currently employed mining engineers are approaching retirement age, a factor that should create additional job openings. Furthermore, relatively few schools offer mining engineering programs, resulting in good job opportunities for graduates. The best opportunities may require frequent travel or even living overseas for extended periods as mining operations around the world recruit graduates of U.S. mining engineering programs.

Nuclear engineers are expected to have employment growth of 11 percent over the projections decade, about as fast as the average for all occupations. Most job growth will be in research and development and engineering services. Although no commercial nuclear power plants have been built in the United States for many years, increased interest in nuclear power as an energy source will spur demand for nuclear engineers to research and develop new designs for reactors. They also will be needed to work in defense-related

Table 1. Earnings distribution by engineering specialty, May 2008

Specialty	Lowest 10%	Lowest 25%	Median	Highest 25%	Highest 10%
Aerospace engineers	$58,130	$72,390	$92,520	$114,530	$134,570
Agricultural engineers	43,150	55,430	68,730	86,400	108,470
Biomedical engineers	47,640	59,420	77,400	98,830	121,970
Chemical engineers	53,730	67,420	84,680	105,000	130,240
Civil engineers	48,140	58,960	74,600	94,470	115,630
Computer hardware engineers	59,170	76,250	97,400	122,750	148,590
Electrical engineers	52,990	64,910	82,160	102,520	125,810
Electronics engineers, except computer	55,330	68,400	86,370	106,870	129,920
Environmental engineers	45,310	56,980	74,020	94,280	115,430
Health and safety engineers, except mining safety engineers and inspectors	43,540	56,190	72,490	90,740	106,220
Industrial engineers	47,720	59,120	73,820	91,020	107,270
Marine engineers and naval architects	43,070	57,060	74,140	94,840	118,630
Materials engineers	51,420	63,830	81,820	102,040	124,470
Mechanical engineers	47,900	59,230	74,920	94,400	114,740
Mining and geological engineers, including mining safety engineers	45,020	57,970	75,960	96,030	122,750
Nuclear engineers	68,300	82,540	97,080	115,170	136,880
Petroleum engineers	57,820	80,040	108,020	148,700	>166,400
Engineers, all other	49,270	67,360	88,570	110,310	132,070

areas, to develop nuclear medical technology, and to improve and enforce waste management and safety standards. Nuclear engineers are expected to have good employment opportunities because the small number of nuclear engineering graduates is likely to be in rough balance with the number of job openings.

Petroleum engineers are expected to have employment growth of 18 percent over the projections decade, faster than the average for all occupations. Petroleum engineers increasingly will be needed to develop new resources, as well as new methods of extracting more from existing sources. Excellent opportunities are expected for petroleum engineers because the number of job openings is likely to exceed the relatively small number of graduates. Petroleum engineers work around the world, and in fact, the best employment opportunities may include some work in other countries.

Earnings

Earnings for engineers vary significantly by specialty, industry, and education. Variation in median earnings and in the earnings distributions for engineers in a number of specialties is especially significant. Table 1 shows wage distributions in May 2008 for engineers in specialties covered in this statement.

In the federal government, mean annual salaries for engineers ranged from $81,085 in agricultural engineering to $126,788 in ceramic engineering in March 2009.

As a group, engineers earn some of the highest average starting salaries among those holding bachelor's degrees. Average starting salary offers for graduates of bachelor's degree programs in engineering, according to a July 2009 survey by the National Association of Colleges and Employers, were as follows:

Petroleum	$83,121
Chemical	64,902
Mining and Mineral	64,404
Computer	61,738
Nuclear	61,610
Electrical/electronics and communications	60,125
Mechanical	58,766
Industrial/manufacturing	58,358
Materials	57,349
Aerospace/aeronautical/astronautical	56,311
Agricultural	54,352
Bioengineering and biomedical	54,158
Civil	52,048

Related Occupations

Engineers apply the principles of natural science and mathematics in their work. Other workers who use scientific and mathematical principles include the following: agricultural and food scientists; architects, except landscape and naval; atmospheric scientists; biological scientists; chemists and materials scientists; computer and information systems managers; computer scientists; computer software engineers and computer programmers; drafters; engineering and natural sciences managers; engineering technicians; environmental scientists and specialists; geoscientists and hydrologists; mathematicians; physicists and astronomers; sales engineers; and science technicians.

Sources of Additional Information

Information about careers in engineering is available from

▸ JETS, 1420 King St., Suite 405, Alexandria, VA 22314. Internet: www.jets.org

Information on ABET-accredited engineering programs is available from

▶ ABET, Inc., 111 Market Place, Suite 1050, Baltimore, MD 21202. Internet: www.abet.org

Those interested in information on the Professional Engineer licensure should contact

▶ National Council of Examiners for Engineering and Surveying, P.O. Box 1686, Clemson, SC 29633. Internet: www.ncees.org

▶ National Society of Professional Engineers, 1420 King St., Alexandria, VA 22314. Internet: www.nspe.org

Information on general engineering education and career resources is available from

▶ American Society for Engineering Education, 1818 N St. NW, Suite 600, Washington, DC 20036. Internet: www.asee.org

Information on obtaining engineering positions with the federal government is available from the Office of Personnel Management through USAJOBS, the federal government's official employment information system. This resource for locating and applying for job opportunities can be accessed through the Internet at www.usajobs.opm.gov or through an interactive voice response telephone system at (703) 724-1850 or TDD (978) 461-8404. These numbers are not toll free, and charges may result. For advice on how to find and apply for federal jobs, see the *Occupational Outlook Quarterly* article "How to get a job in the federal government," online at www.bls.gov/opub/ooq/2004/summer/art01.pdf.

For more detailed information on an engineering specialty, contact societies representing the individual branches of engineering. Each can provide information about careers in the particular branch.

Aerospace engineers

▶ American Institute of Aeronautics and Astronautics, Inc., 1801 Alexander Bell Dr., Suite 500, Reston, VA 20191. Internet: www.aiaa.org

Agricultural engineers

▶ American Society of Agricultural and Biological Engineers, 2950 Niles Rd., St. Joseph, MI 49085. Internet: www.asabe.org

Biomedical engineers

▶ Biomedical Engineering Society, 8401 Corporate Dr., Suite 140, Landover, MD 20785. Internet: www.bmes.org

Chemical engineers

▶ American Chemical Society, Department of Career Services, 1155 16th St. NW, Washington, DC 20036. Internet: www.chemistry.org

▶ American Institute of Chemical Engineers, 3 Park Ave., New York, NY 10016. Internet: www.aiche.org

Civil engineers

▶ American Society of Civil Engineers, 1801 Alexander Bell Dr., Reston, VA 20191. Internet: www.asce.org

Computer hardware engineers

▶ IEEE Computer Society, 2001 L St. NW, Suite 700, Washington, DC 20036. Internet: www.computer.org

Electrical and electronics engineers

▶ IEEE–USA, 2001 L St. NW, Suite 700, Washington, DC 20036. Internet: www.ieeeusa.org

Environmental engineers

▶ American Academy of Environmental Engineers, 130 Holiday Court, Suite 100, Annapolis, MD 21401. Internet: www.aaee.net

Health and safety engineers

▶ American Society of Safety Engineers, 1800 E Oakton St., Des Plaines, IL 60018. Internet: www.asse.org

Industrial engineers

▶ Institute of Industrial Engineers, 3577 Parkway Lane, Suite 200, Norcross, GA 30092. Internet: www.iienet.org

Marine engineers and naval architects

▶ Society of Naval Architects and Marine Engineers, 601 Pavonia Ave., Jersey City, NJ 07306. Internet: www.sname.org

Materials engineers

▶ ASM International, 9639 Kinsman Rd., Materials Park, OH 44073. Internet: www.asminternational.org

▶ Minerals, Metals, and Materials Society, 184 Thorn Hill Rd., Warrendale, PA 15086. Internet: www.tms.org

Mechanical engineers

▶ American Society of Mechanical Engineers, 3 Park Ave., New York, NY 10016. Internet: www.asme.org

▶ SAE International, 400 Commonwealth Dr., Warrendale, PA 15096. Internet: www.sae.org

Mining and geological engineers, including mining safety engineers

▶ Society for Mining, Metallurgy, and Exploration, Inc., 8307 Shaffer Parkway, Littleton, CO 80127. Internet: www.smenet.org

Nuclear engineers

▶ American Nuclear Society, 555 N. Kensington Ave., La Grange Park, IL 60526. Internet: www.ans.org

Petroleum engineers

▶ Society of Petroleum Engineers, 222 Palisades Creek Dr., Richardson, TX 75080. Internet: www.spe.org

Environmental Scientists and Specialists

(O*NET 19-2041.00, 19-2041.01, 19-2041.02, and 19-2041.03)

Significant Points

■ Federal, state, and local governments employ 44 percent of all environmental scientists and specialists.

■ A bachelor's degree in any life or physical science is generally sufficient for most entry-level positions, although many employers prefer a master's degree.

■ Job prospects are expected to be favorable, particularly for environmental health workers in state and local government.

Nature of the Work

Environmental scientists and specialists use their knowledge of the natural sciences to protect the environment by identifying problems and finding solutions that minimize hazards to the health of the environment and the population. They analyze measurements or observations of air, food, water, and soil to determine the way to clean and preserve the environment. Understanding the issues involved in protecting the environment—degradation, conservation, recycling, and replenishment—is central to the work of environmental scientists. They often use this understanding to design and monitor waste disposal sites, preserve water supplies, and reclaim contaminated land and water. They also write risk assessments, describing the likely affect of construction and other environmental changes; write technical proposals; and give presentations to managers and regulators.

The federal government and most state and local governments enact regulations to ensure that there is clean air to breathe, safe water to drink, and no hazardous materials in the soil. The regulations also place limits on development, particularly near sensitive parts of the ecosystem, such as wetlands. Many environmental scientists and specialists work for the government, ensuring that these regulations are followed and limiting the impact of human activity on the environment. Others monitor environmental impacts on the health of the population, checking for risks of disease and providing information about health hazards.

Environmental scientists also work with private companies to help them comply with environmental regulations and policies. They are usually hired by consulting firms to solve problems. Most consulting firms fall into two categories—large multidisciplinary engineering companies, the largest of which may employ thousands of workers, and small niche firms that may employ only a few workers. When looking for jobs, environmental scientists should consider the type of firm and the scope of the projects it undertakes. In larger firms, environmental scientists are more likely to engage in large, long-term projects in which they will work with people in other scientific disciplines. In smaller specialty firms, however, they work more often with business professionals and clients in government and the private sector.

Environmental scientists who work on policy formation may help identify ways that human behavior can be modified in the future to avoid such problems as ground-water contamination and depletion of the ozone layer. Some environmental scientists work in managerial positions, usually after spending some time performing research or learning about environmental laws and regulations.

Many environmental scientists do work and have training that is similar to other physical or life scientists, but they focus on environmental issues. Many specialize in subfields such as environmental ecology and conservation, environmental chemistry, environmental biology, or fisheries science. Specialties affect the specific activities that environmental scientists perform, although recent understandings of the interconnectedness of life processes have blurred some traditional classifications. For example, *environmental ecologists* study the relationships between organisms and their environments and the effects of factors such as population size, pollutants, rainfall, temperature, and altitude, on both. They may collect, study, and report data on air, soil, and water using their knowledge of various scientific disciplines. *Ecological modelers* study ecosystems, pollution control, and resource management using mathematical modeling, systems analysis, thermodynamics, and computer techniques. *Environmental chemists* study the toxicity of various chemicals, that is, how those chemicals affect plants, animals, and people.

Environmental scientists in research positions with the federal government or in colleges and universities often have to find funding for their work by writing grant proposals. Consultants face similar pressures to market their skills and write proposals so that they will have steady work.

Work environment. Many entry-level environmental scientists and specialists spend a significant amount of time in the field, while more experienced workers generally devote more time to office or laboratory work. Some environmental scientists, such as environmental ecologists and environmental chemists, often take field trips that involve physical activity. Environmental scientists in the field may work in warm or cold climates, in all kinds of weather. Travel often is required to meet with prospective clients.

Researchers and consultants might face stress when looking for funding. Occasionally, those who write technical reports to business clients and regulators may be under pressure to meet deadlines and thus have to work long hours.

Training, Other Qualifications, and Advancement

A bachelor's degree is sufficient for most jobs in government and private sector companies, although a master's degree is often preferred. A Ph.D. is usually only necessary for jobs in college teaching or research.

Education and training. A bachelor's degree in an earth science is adequate for entry-level positions, although many companies prefer to hire environmental scientists with a master's degree in environmental science or a related natural science. A doctoral degree generally is necessary only for college teaching and some research positions. Some environmental scientists and specialists have a degree in environmental science, but many earn degrees in biology, chemistry, physics, or the geosciences and then apply their education to the environment. They often need research or work experience related to environmental science.

A bachelor's degree in environmental science offers an interdisciplinary approach to the natural sciences, with an emphasis on biology, chemistry, and geology. Undergraduate environmental science majors typically focus on data analysis and physical geography, which are particularly useful in studying pollution abatement, water resources, or ecosystem protection, restoration, and management. Understanding the geochemistry of inorganic compounds is becoming increasingly important in developing remediation goals. Students interested in working in the environmental or regulatory fields, either in environmental consulting firms or for federal or state governments, should take courses in hydrology, hazardous-waste management, environmental legislation, chemistry, fluid mechanics, and geologic logging, which is the gathering of geologic data. An understanding of environmental regulations and government permit issues also is valuable.

For environmental scientists and specialists who consult, courses in business, finance, marketing, or economics may be useful. In addition, combining environmental science training with other disciplines such as engineering or business, qualifies these scientists for the widest range of jobs.

Other qualifications. Computer skills are essential for prospective environmental scientists. Students who have some experience with computer modeling, data analysis and integration, digital mapping, remote sensing, and Geographic Information Systems (GIS) will be the most prepared to enter the job market.

Environmental scientists and specialists usually work as part of a team with other scientists, engineers, and technicians, and they must

Projections Data from the National Employment Matrix

Occupational title	SOC Code	Employment, 2008	Projected employment, 2018	Change, 2008–2018	
				Number	Percent
Environmental scientists and specialists, including health..	19-2041	85,900	109,800	23,900	28

NOTE: Data in this table are rounded.

often write technical reports and research proposals that communicate their research results or ideas to company managers, regulators, and the public. Environmental health specialists also work closely with the public, providing and collecting information on public health risks. As a result, strong oral and written communication skills are essential.

Advancement. Environmental scientists and specialists often begin their careers as field analysts or as research assistants or technicians in laboratories or offices. They are given more difficult assignments and more autonomy as they gain experience. Eventually, they may be promoted to project leader, program manager, or some other management and research position.

Employment

Environmental scientists and specialists held about 85,900 jobs in 2008. An additional 6,200 jobs were held by environmental science faculty.

About 37 percent of environmental scientists were employed in state and local governments; 21 percent in management, scientific, and technical consulting services; 15 percent in architectural, engineering and related services; and 7 percent in the federal government, primarily in the Environmental Protection Agency (EPA) and the Department of Defense.

Job Outlook

Employment is expected to grow much faster than the average for all occupations. Job prospects are expected to be favorable, particularly in state and local government.

Employment change. Employment of environmental scientists and specialists is expected to increase by 28 percent between 2008 and 2018, much faster than the average for all occupations. Job growth should be strongest in private-sector consulting firms. Growth in employment will be spurred largely by the increasing demands placed on the environment by population growth and increasing awareness of the problems caused by environmental degradation. Further demand should result from the need to comply with complex environmental laws and regulations, particularly those regarding ground-water decontamination and clean air.

Much job growth will result from a continued need to monitor the quality of the environment, to interpret the impact of human actions on terrestrial and aquatic ecosystems, and to develop strategies for restoring ecosystems. In addition, environmental scientists will be needed to help planners develop and construct buildings, transportation corridors, and utilities that protect water resources and reflect efficient and beneficial land use.

Many environmental scientists and specialists work in consulting. Consulting firms have hired these scientists to help businesses and government address issues related to underground tanks, land disposal areas, and other hazardous-waste-management facilities. Currently, environmental consulting is evolving from investigations to creating remediation and engineering solutions. At the same time, the regulatory climate is moving from a rigid structure to a more flexible risk-based approach. These factors, coupled with new federal and state initiatives that integrate environmental activities into the business process itself, will result in a greater focus on waste minimization, resource recovery, pollution prevention, and the consideration of environmental effects during product development. This shift in focus to preventive management will provide many new opportunities for environmental scientists in consulting roles.

Job prospects. In addition to job openings due to growth, there will be additional demand for new environmental scientists to replace those who retire, advance to management positions, or change careers. Job prospects for environmental scientists will be good, particularly for jobs in state and local government.

During periods of economic recession, layoffs of environmental scientists and specialists may occur in consulting firms, particularly when there is a slowdown in new construction; layoffs are much less likely in government.

Earnings

Median annual wages of environmental scientists and specialists were $59,750 in May 2008. The middle 50 percent earned between $45,340 and $78,980. The lowest 10 percent earned less than $36,310, and the highest 10 percent earned more than $102,610.

According to the National Association of Colleges and Employers, beginning salary offers in July 2009 for graduates with bachelor's degrees in an environmental science averaged $39,160 a year.

Related Occupations

Other occupations that deal with preserving or researching the natural environment include atmospheric scientists; biological scientists; chemists and materials scientists; conservation scientists and foresters; engineering technicians; engineers; epidemiologists; geoscientists and hydrologists; physicists and astronomers; science technicians; and surveyors, cartographers, photogrammetrists, and surveying and mapping technicians.

Sources of Additional Information

Information on training and career opportunities for environmental scientists and specialists is available from

▶ American Geological Institute, 4220 King St., Alexandria, VA 22302. Internet: www.agiweb.org

Information on obtaining a position as an environmental protection specialist with the federal government is available from the Office of Personnel Management through USAJOBS, the federal government's official employment information system. This resource for locating and applying for job opportunities can be accessed through the Internet at www.usajobs.opm.gov or through an interactive voice response telephone system at (703) 724-1850 or TDD (978) 461-8404. These numbers are not toll free, and charges may result.

Financial Analysts

(O*NET 13-2051.00)

Significant Points

- Financial analyst positions require a bachelor's or master's degree.
- Positions may also require professional licenses and certifications.
- Keen competition is anticipated for these highly paid positions.
- Financial analysts earn high wages.

Nature of the Work

Financial analysts provide guidance to businesses and individuals making investment decisions. Financial analysts assess the performance of stocks, bonds, commodities, and other types of investments. Also called *securities analysts* and *investment analysts*, they work for banks, insurance companies, mutual and pension funds, securities firms, the business media, and other businesses, making investment decisions or recommendations. Financial analysts study company financial statements and analyze commodity prices, sales, costs, expenses, and tax rates to determine a company's value by projecting its future earnings. They often meet with company officials to gain a better insight into the firms' prospects and management.

Financial analysts can be divided into two categories: *buy side analysts* and *sell side analysts*. Analysts on the buy side work for companies that have a great deal of money to invest. These companies, called institutional investors, include mutual funds, hedge funds, insurance companies, independent money managers, and nonprofit organizations with large endowments. Buy side financial analysts devise investment strategies. Conversely, sell side analysts help securities dealers, such as banks and other firms, sell stocks, bonds, and other investments. The business media hire financial advisors that are supposed to be impartial and occupy a role somewhere in the middle.

Financial analysts generally focus on trends impacting a specific industry, region, or type of product. For example, an analyst will focus on a subject area such as the utilities industry, an area such as Latin America, or the options market. Firms with larger research departments assign analysts even narrower subject areas. They must understand how new regulations, policies, and political and economic trends may impact the investments they are watching. *Risk*

analysts evaluate the risk in portfolio decisions, project potential losses, and determine how to limit potential losses and volatility, using diversification, currency futures, derivatives, short selling, and other investment decisions.

Some experienced analysts called *portfolio managers* supervise a team of analysts and select the mix of products, industries, and regions for their company's investment portfolio. Hedge fund and mutual fund managers are called *fund managers*. Fund and portfolio managers frequently make split-second buy or sell decisions in reaction to quickly changing market conditions. These managers are not only responsible for the overall portfolio, but are also expected to explain investment decisions and strategies in meetings with investors.

Ratings analysts evaluate the ability of companies or governments to pay their debts, including bonds. On the basis of their evaluation, a management team rates the risk of a company or government defaulting on its bonds. Other financial analysts perform budget, cost, and credit analysis as part of their responsibilities.

Financial analysts use spreadsheet and statistical software packages to analyze financial data, spot trends, create portfolios, and develop forecasts. Analysts also use the data they find to measure the financial risks associated with making a particular investment decision. On the basis of their results, they recommend whether to buy, hold, or sell particular investments.

Work environment. Financial analysts usually work in offices. They may work long hours, travel frequently to visit companies or potential investors, and face the pressure of deadlines. Much of their research must be done after office hours because their days are filled with telephone calls and meetings.

Training, Other Qualifications, and Advancement

Financial analysts must have a bachelor's degree. Many positions require a master's degree in finance or a Master of Business Administration (MBA). Positions may also require professional licenses and certifications. However, licenses and certifications are generally only earned after someone is hired.

Education and training. A bachelor's or graduate degree is required for financial analysts. Most companies require a bachelor's degree in a related field, such as finance, business, accounting, statistics, or economics. An understanding of statistics, economics, and business is essential, and knowledge of accounting policies and procedures, corporate budgeting, and financial analysis methods is recommended. An MBA or a master's degree in finance is often required. Advanced courses or knowledge of options pricing, bond valuation, and risk management are important.

Licensure. The Financial Industry Regulatory Authority (FINRA) is the main licensing organization for the securities industry. Depending on an individual's work, different licenses may be required, although buy side analysts are less likely to need licenses. The majority of these licenses require sponsorship by an employer, so companies do not expect individuals to have these licenses before starting a job. Experienced workers who change jobs will need to have their licenses renewed with the new company.

Projections Data from the National Employment Matrix

Occupational title	SOC Code	Employment, 2008	Projected employment, 2018	Change, 2008–2018	
				Number	Percent
Financial analysts	13-2051	250,600	300,300	49,600	20

NOTE: Data in this table are rounded.

Other qualifications. Strong math, analytical, and problem-solving skills are essential qualifications for financial analysts. Good communication skills are necessary because these workers must present complex financial concepts and strategies. Self-confidence, maturity, and the ability to work independently are important. Financial analysts must be detail-oriented; motivated to seek out obscure information; and familiar with the workings of the economy, tax laws, and money markets. Although much of the software they use is proprietary, financial analysts must be comfortable working with spreadsheets and statistical packages.

With the increasing global diversification of investments, companies are assigning more financial analysts to cover foreign markets. These analysts normally specialize in one country, such as Brazil, or one region, such as Latin America. Companies prefer financial analysts to have the international experience necessary to understand the language, culture, business environment, and political conditions in the country or region that they cover.

Certification and advancement. Although not always required, certifications enhance professional standing and are recommended by employers. Certifications are becoming increasingly common. Financial analysts can earn the Chartered Financial Analyst (CFA) designation, sponsored by the CFA Institute. To qualify for this designation, applicants need a bachelor's degree and four years of related work experience and must pass three exams. Applicants can take the exams while they are obtaining the required work experience. Passing the exams requires several hundred hours of self-study. These exams cover subjects such as accounting, economics, securities analysis, financial markets and instruments, corporate finance, asset valuation, and portfolio management. Additional certifications are helpful for financial analysts who specialize in specific areas, such as risk management.

Financial analysts advance by moving into positions where they are responsible for larger or more important products. They may supervise teams of financial analysts. They may become portfolio managers or fund managers, directing the investment portfolios of their companies or funds.

Employment

Financial analysts held 250,600 jobs in 2008. Many financial analysts work at large financial institutions based in New York City or other major financial centers. About 47 percent of financial analysts worked in the finance and insurance industries, including securities and commodity brokers, banks and credit institutions, and insurance carriers. Others worked throughout private industry and government.

Job Outlook

Employment of financial analysts is expected to grow much faster than the average for all occupations. However, keen competition will continue for these well-paid jobs, especially for new entrants.

Employment change. As the level of investment increases, overall employment of financial analysts is expected to increase by 20 percent during the 2008–2018 decade, which is much faster than the average for all occupations. Primary factors for this growth are increasing complexity and global diversification of investments and growth in the overall amount of assets under management. As the number and type of mutual and hedge funds and the amount of assets invested in these funds increase, companies will need more financial analysts to research and recommend investments. As the international investment increases, companies will need more analysts to cover the global range of investment options.

Job prospects. Despite employment growth, keen competition is expected for these high-paying jobs. Growth in financial services will create new positions, but there are still far more people who would like to enter the occupation. For those aspiring to financial analyst jobs, a strong academic background, including courses such as finance, accounting, and economics, is essential. Certifications and graduate degrees, such as a CFA certification or a master's degree in business or finance, significantly improve an applicant's prospects.

Earnings

Median annual wages, excluding bonuses, of wage and salary financial analysts were $73,150 in May 2008, which is more than double the national median wage. The middle 50 percent earned between $54,930 and $99,100. The lowest 10 percent earned less than $43,440, and the highest 10 percent earned more than $141,070. Annual performance bonuses are quite common and can be a significant part of their total earnings.

Related Occupations

Other jobs requiring expertise in finance and investment include accountants and auditors; actuaries; budget analysts; financial managers; insurance sales agents; insurance underwriters; personal financial advisors; and securities, commodities, and financial services sales agents.

Sources of Additional Information

For general information on securities industry employment, contact

▸ Financial Industry Regulatory Authority (FINRA), 1735 K St. NW, Washington, DC 20006. Internet: www.finra.org

▶ Securities Industry and Financial Markets Association, 120 Broadway, 35th Floor, New York, NY 10271. Internet: www.sifma.org

For information on financial analyst careers and training, contact

▶ American Academy of Financial Management, 200 L&A Rd., Suite B, Metairie, LA 70001. Internet: www.aafm.us

For information on financial analyst careers and CFA certification, contact

▶ CFA Institute, 560 Ray C. Hunt Dr., Charlottesville, VA 22903. Internet: www.cfainstitute.org

For additional career information, see the *Occupational Outlook Quarterly* article "Financial analysts and personal financial advisors" online at www.bls.gov/opub/ooq/2000/summer/art03.pdf and in print at many libraries and career centers.

Fire Fighters

(O*NET 33-1021.00, 33-1021.01, 33-1021.02, 33-2011.00, 33-2011.01, and 33-2011.02)

Significant Points

■ Fire fighting involves hazardous conditions and long, irregular hours.

■ About 9 out of 10 fire fighters are employed by local governments.

■ Applicants generally must pass written, physical, and medical examinations, and candidates with some postsecondary education are increasingly preferred.

■ Keen competition for jobs is expected because this occupation attracts many qualified candidates.

Nature of the Work

Every year, fires and other emergencies take thousands of lives and destroy property worth billions of dollars. *Fire fighters* help protect the public against these dangers by responding to fires and a variety of other emergencies. Although they put out fires, fire fighters more frequently respond to other emergencies. They are often the first emergency personnel at the scene of a traffic accident or medical emergency and may be called upon to treat injuries or perform other vital functions.

During duty hours, fire fighters must be prepared to respond immediately to a fire or other emergency. Fighting fires is complex and dangerous and requires organization and teamwork. At every emergency scene, fire fighters perform specific duties assigned by a superior officer. At fires, they connect hose lines to hydrants and operate a pump to send water to high-pressure hoses. Some carry hoses, climb ladders, and enter burning buildings—using systematic and careful procedures—to put out fires. At times, they may need to use tools to make their way through doors, walls, and debris, sometimes with the aid of information about a building's floor plan. Some find and rescue occupants who are unable to leave the building safely without assistance. They also provide emergency medical attention, ventilate smoke-filled areas and attempt to salvage the contents of buildings. Fire fighters' duties may change several times while the company is in action. Sometimes they remain at the site of

a disaster for days at a time, rescuing trapped survivors, and assisting with medical treatment.

Fire fighters work in a variety of settings, including metropolitan areas, rural areas, airports, chemical plants and other industrial sites. They also have assumed a range of responsibilities, including providing emergency medical services. In fact, most calls to which fire fighters respond involve medical emergencies. In addition, some fire fighters work in hazardous materials units that are specially trained for the control, prevention, and cleanup of hazardous materials, such as oil spills or accidents involving the transport of chemicals.

Workers specializing in forest fires utilize methods and equipment different from those of other fire fighters. When fires break out, crews of fire fighters are brought in to suppress the blaze with heavy equipment and water hoses. Fighting forest fires, like fighting urban fires, is rigorous work. One of the most effective means of fighting a forest fire is creating fire lines—cutting down trees and digging out grass and all other combustible vegetation in the path of the fire in order to deprive it of fuel. Elite fire fighters called *smoke jumpers* parachute from airplanes to reach otherwise inaccessible areas. This tactic, however, can be extremely hazardous.

When they aren't responding to fires and other emergencies, fire fighters clean and maintain equipment, learn additional skills related to their jobs, conduct practice drills, and participate in physical fitness activities. They also prepare written reports on fire incidents and review fire science literature to stay informed about technological developments and changing administrative practices and policies.

Work environment. Fire fighters spend much of their time at fire stations, which are usually similar to dormitories. When an alarm sounds, fire fighters respond, regardless of the weather or hour. Fire fighting involves a high risk of death or injury. Common causes include floors caving in, walls toppling, traffic accidents, and exposure to flame and smoke. Fire fighters also may come into contact with poisonous, flammable, or explosive gases and chemicals and radioactive materials, all of which may have immediate or long-term effects on their health. For these reasons, they must wear protective gear that can be very heavy and hot.

Work hours of fire fighters are longer and more varied than the hours of most other workers. Many fire fighters work about 50 hours a week, and sometimes they may work longer. In some agencies, fire fighters are on duty for 24 hours, then off for 48 hours, and receive an extra day off at intervals. In others, they work a day shift of 10 hours for 3 or 4 days, work a night shift of 14 hours for 3 or 4 nights, have 3 or 4 days off, and then repeat the cycle. In addition, fire fighters often work extra hours at fires and other emergencies and are regularly assigned to work on holidays. Fire lieutenants and fire captains frequently work the same hours as the fire fighters they supervise.

Training, Other Qualifications, and Advancement

Applicants for fire fighting jobs usually are required to have at least a high school diploma, but candidates with some postsecondary education are increasingly being preferred. Most municipal jobs require passing written and physical tests. All fire fighters receive extensive training after being hired.

Education and training. Most fire fighters have a high school diploma; however, the completion of community college courses or, in some cases, an associate degree, in fire science may improve an applicant's chances for a job. A number of colleges and universities offer courses leading to 2-year or 4-year degrees in fire engineering or fire science. In recent years, an increasing proportion of new fire fighters have had some education after high school.

As a rule, entry-level workers in large fire departments are trained for several weeks at the department's training center or academy. Through classroom instruction and practical training, the recruits study fire fighting techniques, fire prevention, hazardous materials control, local building codes, and emergency medical procedures, including first aid and cardiopulmonary resuscitation (CPR). They also learn how to use axes, chain saws, fire extinguishers, ladders, and other fire fighting and rescue equipment. After successfully completing training, the recruits are assigned to a fire company, where they undergo a period of probation.

Many fire departments have accredited apprenticeship programs lasting up to 4 years, including programs in fighting forest fires. These programs combine formal instruction with on-the-job training under the supervision of experienced fire fighters.

Almost all departments require fire fighters to be certified as emergency medical technicians. Although most fire departments require the lowest level of certification, Emergency Medical Technician-Basic (EMT-Basic), larger departments in major metropolitan areas increasingly are requiring paramedic certification. Some departments include this training in the fire academy, whereas others prefer that recruits earn EMT certification on their own, but will give them up to one year to do it.

In addition to participating in training programs conducted by local fire departments, some fire fighters attend training sessions sponsored by the U.S. National Fire Academy. These training sessions cover topics such as executive development, antiarson techniques, disaster preparedness, hazardous materials control, and public fire safety and education. Some states also have mandatory or voluntary fire fighter training and certification programs. Many fire departments offer fire fighters incentives, such as tuition reimbursement or higher pay, for completing advanced training.

Other qualifications. Applicants for municipal fire fighting jobs usually must pass a written exam; tests of strength, physical stamina, coordination, and agility; and a medical examination that includes a drug screening. Workers may be monitored on a random basis for drug use after accepting employment. Examinations are generally open to people who are at least 18 years of age and have a high school education or its equivalent. Those who receive the highest scores in all phases of testing have the best chances of being hired.

Among the personal qualities fire fighters need are mental alertness, self-discipline, courage, mechanical aptitude, endurance, strength, and a sense of public service. Initiative and good judgment also are extremely important, because fire fighters make quick decisions in emergencies. Members of a crew live and work closely together under conditions of stress and danger for extended periods, so they must be dependable and able to get along well with others. Leadership qualities are necessary for officers, who must establish and maintain discipline and efficiency, as well as direct the activities of the fire fighters in their companies.

Advancement. Most experienced fire fighters continue studying to improve their job performance and prepare for promotion examinations. To progress to higher level positions, they acquire expertise in advanced fire fighting equipment and techniques, building construction, emergency medical technology, writing, public speaking, management and budgeting procedures, and public relations.

Opportunities for promotion depend upon the results of written examinations, as well as job performance, interviews, and seniority. Hands-on tests that simulate real-world job situations also are used by some fire departments.

Usually, fire fighters are first promoted to engineer, then lieutenant, captain, battalion chief, assistant chief, deputy chief, and, finally, chief. For promotion to positions higher than battalion chief, many fire departments now require a bachelor's degree, preferably in fire science, public administration, or a related field. An associate degree is required for executive fire officer certification from the National Fire Academy.

Employment

In 2008, total paid employment in fire fighting occupations was about 365,600. Fire fighters held about 310,400 jobs, and first-line supervisors/managers of fire fighting and prevention workers held about 55,200. These employment figures include only paid career fire fighters—they do not cover volunteer fire fighters, who perform the same duties and may constitute the majority of fire fighters in a residential area. According to the U.S. Fire Administration, about 70 percent of fire companies were staffed entirely by volunteer fire fighters in 2007.

About 91 percent of fire fighting workers were employed by local governments. Some local and regional fire departments are being consolidated into countywide establishments to reduce administrative staffs, cut costs, and establish consistent training standards and work procedures. Some large cities have thousands of career fire fighters, while many small towns have only a few. Most of the fire fighters not employed by local governments worked in fire departments on federal and state installations, including airports. Private fire fighting companies employ a small number of fire fighters.

Job Outlook

Although employment is expected to grow faster than the average for all jobs, candidates for these positions are expected to face keen competition because these positions are highly attractive and sought after.

Employment change. Employment of fire fighters is expected to grow by 19 percent over the 2008–2018 decade, which is faster than the average for all occupations. Most job growth will stem from volunteer fire fighting positions being converted to paid positions. In recent years, it has become more difficult for volunteer fire departments to recruit and retain volunteers, perhaps because of the considerable amount of training and time commitment required. Furthermore, a trend toward more people living in and around cities has increased the demand for fire fighters. When areas develop and become more densely populated, emergencies and fires affect more buildings and more people and, therefore, require more fire fighters.

Projections Data from the National Employment Matrix

Occupational title	SOC Code	Employment, 2008	Projected employment, 2018	Change, 2008–2018	
				Number	Percent
Fire fighting occupations.. —		365,600	427,600	62,100	17
First-line supervisors/managers of fire fighting and prevention workers.. 33-1021		55,200	59,700	4,500	8
Fire fighters 33-2011		310,400	367,900	57,500	19

NOTE: Data in this table are rounded.

Job prospects. Prospective fire fighters are expected to face keen competition for available job openings. Many people are attracted to fire fighting because it is challenging and provides the opportunity to perform an essential public service, a high school education is usually sufficient for entry, and a pension is usually guaranteed after 25 years of service. Consequently, the number of qualified applicants in most areas far exceeds the number of job openings, even though the written examination and physical requirements eliminate many applicants. This situation is expected to persist in coming years. Applicants with the best chances are those who are physically fit and score the highest on physical-conditioning and mechanical aptitude exams. Those who have completed some fire fighter education at a community college and have EMT or paramedic certification will have an additional advantage.

Earnings

Median annual wages of fire fighters were $44,260 in May 2008. The middle 50 percent earned between $31,180 and $58,440. The lowest 10 percent earned less than $22,440, and the highest 10 percent earned more than $72,210. Median annual wages were $44,800 in local government, $45,610 in the federal government, $25,300 in other support services, and $37,870 in state governments.

Median annual wages of first-line supervisors/managers of fire fighting and prevention workers were $67,440 in May 2008. The middle 50 percent earned between $53,820 and $86,330. The lowest 10 percent earned less than $40,850, and the highest 10 percent earned more than $108,930. First-line supervisors/managers of fire fighting and prevention workers employed in local government earned a median of about $69,000 a year.

According to the International City-County Management Association, average salaries in 2008 for sworn full-time positions were as follows:

Position	Minimum annual base salary	Maximum annual base salary
Fire chief................................	$78,672	$104,780
Deputy chief	69,166	88,571
Battalion chief.........................	66,851	81,710
Assistant fire chief	65,691	83,748
Fire captain	60,605	72,716
Fire lieutenant	50,464	60,772
Engineer..................................	48,307	62,265

Fire fighters who average more than a certain number of work hours per week are required to be paid overtime. The threshold is deter-

mined by the department. Fire fighters often work extra shifts to maintain minimum staffing levels and during special emergencies.

In 2008, 66 percent of all fire fighters were union members or covered by a union contract. Fire fighters receive benefits that usually include medical and liability insurance, vacation and sick leave, and some paid holidays. Almost all fire departments provide protective clothing (helmets, boots, and coats) and breathing apparatus, and many also provide dress uniforms. Fire fighters generally are covered by pension plans, often offering retirement at half pay after 25 years of service or if the individual is disabled in the line of duty.

Related Occupations

Other occupations that involve protecting the public and property are emergency medical technicians and paramedics; fire inspectors and investigators; and police and detectives.

Sources of Additional Information

Information about a career as a fire fighter may be obtained from local fire departments and from either of the following organizations:

▸ International Association of Fire Fighters, 1750 New York Ave. NW, Washington, DC 20006. Internet: www.iaff.org

▸ U.S. Fire Administration, 16825 S. Seton Ave., Emmitsburg, MD 21727. Internet: www.usfa.dhs.gov

Information about professional qualifications and a list of colleges and universities offering two-year or four-year degree programs in fire science or fire prevention may be obtained from

▸ National Fire Academy, 16825 S. Seton Ave., Emmitsburg, MD 21727. Internet: www.usfa.dhs.gov/nfa

Fitness Workers

(O*NET 39-9031.00)

Significant Points

■ Many fitness and personal training jobs are part time, but many workers increase their hours by working at several different facilities or at clients' homes.

■ Most fitness workers need to be certified.

■ Employment is expected to grow much faster than the average.

■ Job prospects are expected to be good.

Nature of the Work

Fitness workers lead, instruct, and motivate individuals or groups in exercise activities, including cardiovascular exercise, strength training, and stretching. They work in health clubs, country clubs, hospitals, universities, yoga and Pilates studios, resorts, and clients' homes. Fitness workers also are found in workplaces, where they organize and direct health and fitness programs for employees. Although gyms and health clubs offer a variety of exercise activities, such as weight lifting, yoga, cardiovascular training, and karate, fitness workers typically specialize in only a few areas.

Personal trainers work one-on-one or with two or three clients, either in a gym or in the clients' homes. They help clients assess their level of physical fitness and set and reach fitness goals. *Trainers* also demonstrate various exercises and help clients improve their exercise techniques. They may keep records of their clients' exercise sessions to monitor the clients' progress toward physical fitness. They also may advise their clients on how to modify their lifestyles outside of the gym to improve their fitness.

Group exercise instructors conduct group exercise sessions that usually include aerobic exercise, stretching, and muscle conditioning. Cardiovascular conditioning classes often are set to music. *Instructors* select the music and choreograph a corresponding exercise sequence. Two increasingly popular conditioning methods taught in exercise classes are Pilates and yoga. In these classes, instructors demonstrate the different moves and positions of the particular method; they also observe students and correct those who are doing the exercises improperly. Group exercise instructors are responsible for ensuring that their classes are motivating, safe, and challenging, yet not too difficult for the participants.

Fitness directors oversee the fitness-related aspects of a health club or fitness center. They create and oversee programs that meet the needs of the club's members, including new-member orientations, fitness assessments, and workout incentive programs. They also select fitness equipment; coordinate personal training and group exercise programs; hire, train, and supervise fitness staff; and carry out administrative duties.

Fitness workers in smaller facilities with few employees may perform a variety of functions in addition to their fitness duties, such as tending the front desk, signing up new members, giving tours of the fitness center, writing newsletter articles, creating posters and flyers, and supervising the weight-training and cardiovascular equipment areas. In larger commercial facilities, personal trainers often are required to sell their services to members and to make a specified number of sales. Some fitness workers may combine the duties of group exercise instructors and personal trainers; in smaller facilities, the fitness director may teach classes and do personal training.

Work environment. Most fitness workers spend their time indoors at fitness or recreation centers and health clubs. Fitness directors and supervisors, however, typically spend most of their time in an office. In some fitness centers, workers may split their time among doing office work, engaging in personal training, and teaching classes. Nevertheless, fitness workers at all levels risk suffering injuries during physical activities.

Since most fitness centers are open long hours, fitness workers often work nights and weekends and even occasional holidays. In 2008, about 40 percent of fitness workers were part-time employees. Some may travel from place to place throughout the day, to different gyms or to clients' homes, to maintain a full work schedule.

Fitness workers generally enjoy a lot of autonomy. Group exercise instructors choreograph or plan their own classes, and personal trainers have the freedom to design and implement their clients' workout routines.

Training, Other Qualifications, and Advancement

For most fitness workers, certification is critical. Personal trainers usually must be certified to begin working with clients or with members of a fitness facility. Group fitness instructors may begin without a certification, but they are often encouraged or required by their employers to become certified.

Education and training. The education and training required depends on the specific type of fitness work: personal training, group fitness, and a specialization such as Pilates or yoga each need different preparation. Personal trainers often start out by taking classes to become certified. Then they may begin by working alongside an experienced trainer before being allowed to train clients alone. Group fitness instructors often get started by participating in exercise classes until they are ready to audition as instructors and, if the audition is successful, begin teaching classes. They also may improve their skills by taking training courses or attending fitness conventions. Most employers require instructors to work toward becoming certified.

Fitness workers usually do not receive much on-the-job training; they are expected to know how to do their jobs when they are hired. Workers may receive some organizational training to learn about the operations of their new employer. Occasionally, they receive specialized training if they are expected to teach or lead a specific method of exercise or focus on a particular age or ability group. Because requirements vary from employer to employer, before pursuing training it may be helpful to contact local fitness centers or other potential employers to find out what background they prefer.

An increasing number of employers are requiring fitness workers to have a bachelor's degree in a field related to health or fitness, such as exercise science or physical education. Some employers allow workers to substitute a college degree for certification, but most employers who require a bachelor's degree also require certification.

Training for Pilates and yoga instructors has changed. When interest in these forms of exercise exploded, the demand for teachers grew faster than the ability to train them properly. Inexperienced teachers contributed to student injuries, leading to a push toward more standardized, rigorous requirements for teacher training.

Pilates and yoga teachers now need specialized training in their particular method of exercise. For Pilates, training options range from weekend-long workshops to yearlong programs, but the trend is toward requiring even more training. The Pilates Method Alliance has established training standards that recommend at least 200 hours of training; the group also has standards for training schools and maintains a list of training schools that meet the requirements. However, some Pilates teachers are certified group exercise instructors who attend short Pilates workshops; currently, many fitness centers hire people with minimal Pilates training if the applicants have a fitness certification and group fitness experience.

Training requirements for yoga teachers are similar to those for Pilates teachers. Training programs range from a few days to more than 2 years. Many people get their start by taking yoga; eventually, their teachers may consider them ready to assist or to substitute teach. Some students may begin teaching their own classes when their yoga teachers think that they are ready; the teachers may even provide letters of recommendation. Those who wish to pursue teaching more seriously usually seek formal teacher training.

Currently, there are many training programs throughout the yoga community, as well as programs throughout the fitness industry. The Yoga Alliance has established training standards requiring at least 200 training hours, with a specified number of hours in techniques, teaching methodology, anatomy, physiology, philosophy, and other areas. The Yoga Alliance also registers schools that train students to its standards. Because some schools may meet the standards but not be registered, prospective students should check the requirements and decide whether particular schools meet them.

Certification and other qualifications. The most important characteristic that an employer looks for in a new fitness instructor is the ability to plan and lead a class that is motivating and safe. Group fitness instructors do not necessarily require certification to begin working. However, most organizations encourage their group instructors to become certified over time, and many require it.

In the fitness field, there are many organizations that offer certification. Getting certified by one of the top certification organizations is becoming increasingly important, especially for personal trainers. One way to ensure that a certifying organization is reputable is to make sure that it is accredited by the National Commission for Certifying Agencies.

Most certifying organizations require candidates to have a high school diploma, be certified in cardiopulmonary resuscitation (CPR), and pass an exam. All certification exams have a written component, and some also have a practical component. The exams measure knowledge of human physiology, understanding of proper exercise techniques, assessment of client fitness levels, and development of appropriate exercise programs. There is no particular training program required for certification; candidates may prepare however they prefer. Certifying organizations do offer study materials, including books, CD-ROMs, other audio and visual materials, and exam preparation workshops and seminars, but candidates are not required to purchase materials to take exams.

Certification generally is good for 2 years, after which workers must become recertified by attending continuing education classes or conferences, writing articles, or giving presentations. Some organizations offer more advanced certification that requires an associate or bachelor's degree in an exercise-related subject for individuals who are interested in training athletes, working with people who are injured or ill, or advising clients on general health.

Pilates and yoga instructors usually do not need group exercise certification to maintain their employment. It is more important that they have specialized training in their particular method of exercise. However, the Pilates Method Alliance does offer certification. Pilates certification requires 450 hours of documented training or 720 hours of full-time work the previous 12 months.

People planning fitness careers should be outgoing, excellent communicators, good at motivating people, and sensitive to the needs of others. Excellent health and physical fitness are important because of the physical nature of the job. Those who wish to be personal trainers in a large commercial fitness center should have strong sales skills. All personal trainers should have the personality and motivation to attract and retain clients.

Advancement. A bachelor's degree in exercise science, physical education, kinesiology (the study of the mechanics of human motion, including the role of the muscles), or a related area, along with experience, usually is required to advance to management positions in a health club or fitness center. Some organizations require a master's degree. As in other occupations, managerial skills also are needed to advance to supervisory or managerial positions. College courses in management, business administration, accounting, and personnel management may be helpful, but many fitness companies have corporate universities in which they train employees for management positions.

Personal trainers may advance to head trainer, with responsibility for hiring and overseeing the personal training staff and for bringing in new personal-training clients. Group fitness instructors may be promoted to group exercise director, a position responsible for hiring instructors and coordinating exercise classes. Later, a worker might become the fitness director of an organization, managing the fitness budget and staff. A worker also might become the general manager, whose main focus is the financial aspects of the organization, particularly setting and achieving sales goals; in a small fitness center, however, the general manager usually is involved with all aspects of running the facility. Some workers go into business for themselves and open their own fitness centers.

Employment

Fitness workers held about 261,100, jobs in 2008. About 61 percent of all personal trainers and group exercise instructors worked in fitness and recreational sports centers, including health clubs. Another 13 percent worked in civic and social organizations. About 9 percent of fitness workers were self-employed; many of these were personal trainers, while others were group fitness instructors working on a contract basis with fitness centers. Many fitness jobs are part time, and many workers hold multiple jobs, teaching or doing personal training at several different fitness centers and at clients' homes.

Job Outlook

Jobs for fitness workers are expected to increase much faster than the average for all occupations. Fitness workers should have good opportunities because of continued job growth in health clubs, fitness facilities, and other settings in which fitness workers are concentrated.

Employment change. Employment of fitness workers is expected to increase 29 percent over the 2008–2018 decade, which is much faster than the average for all occupations. These workers are expected to gain jobs because an increasing number of people are spending time and money on fitness and more businesses are recognizing the benefits of health and fitness programs for their employees.

Aging baby boomers, one group that increasingly is becoming concerned with staying healthy and physically fit, will be the main

Projections Data from the National Employment Matrix

Occupational title	SOC Code	Employment, 2008	Projected employment, 2018	Change, 2008–2018	
				Number	Percent
Fitness trainers and aerobics instructors 39-9031		261,100	337,900	76,800	29

NOTE: Data in this table are rounded.

driver of employment growth in fitness workers. An additional factor is the combination of a reduction in the number of physical education programs in schools with parents' growing concern about childhood obesity. This factor will increase the need for fitness workers to work with children in nonschool settings, such as health clubs. Increasingly, parents also are hiring personal trainers for their children, and the number of weight-training gyms for children is expected to continue to grow. Health club membership among young adults has grown steadily as well, driven by concern with physical fitness and by rising incomes.

As health clubs strive to provide more personalized service to keep their members motivated, they will continue to offer personal training and a wide variety of group exercise classes. Participation in yoga and Pilates is expected to continue to increase, driven partly by the aging population, which demands low-impact forms of exercise and seeks relief from arthritis and other ailments.

Job prospects. Opportunities are expected to be good for fitness workers because demand for these workers is expected to remain strong in health clubs, fitness facilities, and other settings in which fitness workers are concentrated. In addition, many job openings will stem from the need to replace the large numbers of workers who leave these occupations each year. Part-time jobs will be easier to find than full-time jobs. People with degrees in fitness-related subjects will have better opportunities because clients prefer to work with people they perceive as higher quality trainers. Trainers who incorporate new technology and wellness issues as part of their services may be in more demand.

Earnings

Median annual wages of fitness trainers and aerobics instructors in May 2008 were $29,210. The middle 50 percent earned between $19,610 and $44,420. The bottom 10 percent earned less than $16,120, while the top 10 percent earned $60,760 or more. These figures do not include the earnings of the self-employed. Earnings of successful self-employed personal trainers can be much higher. Median annual wages in the industries employing the largest numbers of fitness workers in May 2008 were as follows:

General medical and surgical hospitals $32,140
Fitness and recreational sports centers................. 30,610
Local government... 30,200
Civic and social organizations 25,110
Other schools and instruction 24,230

Because many fitness workers work part time, they often do not receive benefits such as health insurance or retirement plans from their employers. They are able to use fitness facilities at no cost, however.

Related Occupations

Other occupations that focus on health and physical fitness include the following athletes, coaches, umpires, and related workers; dietitians and nutritionists; physical therapists; and recreation workers.

Sources of Additional Information

For more information about fitness careers and about universities and other institutions offering programs in health and fitness, contact

▶ National Strength and Conditioning Association, 1885 Bob Johnson Dr., Colorado Springs, CO 80906. Internet: www.nsca-lift.org

For information about personal trainer and group fitness instructor certifications, contact

▶ American College of Sports Medicine, P.O. Box 1440, Indianapolis, IN 46206-1440. Internet: www.acsm.org

▶ American Council on Exercise, 4851 Paramount Dr., San Diego, CA 92123. Internet: www.acefitness.org

▶ National Academy of Sports Medicine, 26632 Agoura Rd., Calabasas, CA 91302. Internet: www.nasm.org

▶ NSCA Certification Commission, 1885 Bob Johnson Dr., Colorado Springs, CO 80906. Internet: www.nsca-cc.org

For information about Pilates certification and training programs, contact

▶ Pilates Method Alliance, P.O. Box 37096, Miami, FL 33137-0906. Internet: www.pilatesmethodalliance.org

For information on yoga teacher training programs, contact

▶ Yoga Alliance, 1701 Clarendon Boulevard, Suite 110, Arlington, VA 22209. Internet: www.yogaalliance.org

For information about health clubs and sports clubs, contact

▶ International Health, Racquet, and Sportsclub Association, Seaport Center, 70 Fargo St., Boston, MA 02210. Internet: http://cms.ihrsa.org

Food and Beverage Serving and Related Workers

(O*NET 35-3011.00, 35-3021.00, 35-3022.00, 35-3022.01, 35-3031.00, 35-3041.00, 35-9011.00, 35-9021.00, 35-9031.00, and 35-9099.00)

Significant Points

■ Most jobs are part time and have few educational requirements, attracting many young people to the occupation—21 percent of these workers were 16 to 19 years old in 2008, about six times the proportion for all workers.

- Job openings are expected to be abundant through 2018, which will create excellent opportunities for jobseekers.

- Tips comprise a major portion of earnings for servers, so keen competition is expected for jobs in fine dining and more popular restaurants where potential tips are greatest.

Nature of the Work

Food and beverage serving and related workers are the front line of customer service in full-service restaurants, casual dining eateries, and other food service establishments. These workers greet customers, escort them to seats and hand them menus, take food and drink orders, and serve food and beverages. They also answer questions, explain menu items and specials, and keep tables and dining areas clean and set for new diners. Most work as part of a team, helping coworkers to improve workflow and customer service.

Waiters and waitresses, also called *servers*, are the largest group of these workers. They take customers' orders, serve food and beverages, prepare itemized checks, and sometimes accept payment. Their specific duties vary considerably, depending on the establishment. In casual-dining restaurants serving routine, straightforward fare, such as salads, soups, and sandwiches, servers are expected to provide fast, efficient, and courteous service. In fine dining restaurants, where more complicated meals are prepared and often served over several courses, waiters and waitresses provide more formal service emphasizing personal, attentive treatment at a more leisurely pace. Waiters and waitresses may meet with managers and chefs before each shift to discuss the menu and any new items or specials, review ingredients for potential food allergies, or talk about any food safety concerns. They also discuss coordination between the kitchen and the dining room and any customer service issues from the previous day or shift. In addition, waiters and waitresses usually check the identification of patrons to ensure they meet the minimum age requirement for the purchase of alcohol and tobacco products wherever those items are sold.

Waiters and waitresses sometimes perform the duties of other food and beverage service workers, including escorting guests to tables, serving customers seated at counters, clearing and setting up tables, or operating a cash register. However, full-service restaurants frequently hire other staff, such as hosts and hostesses, cashiers, or dining room attendants, to perform these duties.

Bartenders fill drink orders either taken directly from patrons at the bar or through waiters and waitresses who place drink orders for dining room customers. Bartenders check the identification of customers seated at the bar to ensure they meet the minimum age requirement for the purchase of alcohol and tobacco products. They prepare mixed drinks, serve bottled or draught beer, and pour wine or other beverages. Bartenders must know a wide range of drink recipes and be able to mix drinks accurately, quickly, and without waste. Some establishments, especially those with higher volume, use equipment that automatically measures, pours, and mixes drinks at the push of a button. Bartenders who use this equipment, however, still must work quickly to handle a large volume of drink orders and be familiar with the ingredients for special drink requests. Much of a bartender's work still must be done by hand.

Besides mixing and serving drinks, bartenders stock and prepare garnishes for drinks; maintain an adequate supply of ice, glasses, and other bar supplies; and keep the bar area clean for customers. They also may collect payment, operate the cash register, wash glassware and utensils, and serve food to customers who dine at the bar. Bartenders usually are responsible for ordering and maintaining an inventory of liquor, mixers, and other bar supplies.

Hosts and hostesses welcome guests and maintain reservation and waiting lists. They may direct patrons to coatrooms, restrooms, or to a place to wait until their table is ready. Hosts and hostesses assign guests to tables suitable for the size of their group, escort patrons to their seats, and provide menus. They also enter reservations, arrange parties, and assist with other special requests. In some restaurants, they act as cashiers.

Dining room and cafeteria attendants and bartender helpers— sometimes referred to collectively as the *bus staff*—assist waiters, waitresses, and bartenders by cleaning and setting tables, removing dirty dishes, and keeping serving areas stocked with supplies. They may also assist waiters and waitresses by bringing meals out of the kitchen, distributing dishes to individual diners, filling water glasses, and delivering condiments. *Cafeteria attendants* stock serving tables with food, trays, dishes, and silverware. They may carry trays to dining tables for patrons. *Bartender helpers* keep bar equipment clean and glasses washed. *Dishwashers* clean dishes, cutlery, and kitchen utensils and equipment.

Food also is prepared and served in limited-service eateries, which don't employ servers and specialize in simpler preparations that often are made in advance. Two occupations with large numbers of workers are common in these types of establishments: *combined food preparation and serving workers, including fast food*; and *counter attendants, cafeteria, food concession, and coffee shop.* Combined food preparation and serving workers are employed primarily by fast food restaurants. They take food and beverage orders, retrieve items when ready, fill drink cups, and accept payment. They also may heat food items and assemble salads and sandwiches, which constitutes food preparation. Counter attendants take orders and serve food in snack bars, cafeterias, movie theatres, and coffee shops over a counter or steam table. They may fill cups with coffee, soda, and other beverages and may prepare fountain specialties, such as milkshakes and ice cream sundaes. Counter attendants take carryout orders from diners and wrap or place items in containers. They clean counters, write itemized bills, and sometimes accept payment. Other workers, referred to as *foodservers, nonrestaurant*, serve food to patrons outside of a restaurant environment. They might deliver room service meals in hotels or meals to hospital rooms or act as carhops, bringing orders to parked cars.

Work environment. Food and beverage service workers are on their feet most of the time and often carry heavy trays of food, dishes, and glassware. During busy dining periods, they are under pressure to serve customers quickly and efficiently. The work is relatively safe, but injuries from slips, cuts, and burns often result from hurrying or mishandling sharp tools. Three occupations—food servers, nonrestaurant; dining room and cafeteria attendants and bartender helpers; and dishwashers—reported higher incident rates than many occupations throughout the economy.

Part-time work is more common among food and beverage serving and related workers than among workers in almost any other occupation. In 2008, those on part-time schedules included half of all waiters and waitresses and almost three-fourths of all hosts and hostesses.

Food service and drinking establishments typically maintain long dining hours and offer flexible and varied work opportunities. Many food and beverage serving and related workers work evenings, weekends, and holidays. The long business hours allow for more flexible schedules that appeal to many teenagers who can gain valuable work experience. More than one-fifth of all food and beverage serving and related workers were 16 to 19 years old in 2008—about six times the proportion for all workers.

Training, Other Qualifications, and Advancement

Most food and beverage service jobs are entry level and require a high school diploma or less. Generally, training is received on the job; however, those who wish to work at more upscale restaurants, where income from tips is greater and service standards are higher, may need previous experience or vocational training.

Education and training. There are no specific educational requirements for most food and beverage service jobs. Many employers prefer to hire high school graduates for waiter and waitress, bartender, and host and hostess positions, but completion of high school usually is not required for fast-food workers, counter attendants, dishwashers, and dining room attendants and bartender helpers. Many entrants to these jobs are in their late teens or early twenties and have a high school education or less. Usually, they have little or no work experience. Food and beverage service jobs are a major source of part-time employment for high school and college students, multiple job holders, and those seeking supplemental incomes.

All new employees receive some training from their employer. They learn safe food handling procedures and sanitation practices, for example. Some employers, particularly those in fast-food restaurants, teach new workers using self-study programs, on-line programs, audiovisual presentations, and instructional booklets that explain food preparation and service skills. But most food and beverage serving and related workers pick up their skills by observing and working with more experienced workers. Some full-service restaurants also provide new dining room employees with some form of classroom training that alternates with periods of on-the-job work experience. These training programs communicate the operating philosophy of the restaurant, help establish a personal rapport with other staff, teach formal serving techniques, and instill a desire to work as a team. They also provide an opportunity to discuss customer service situations and the proper ways to handle unpleasant circumstances or unruly patrons.

Some food serving workers can acquire more skills by attending relevant classes offered by public or private vocational schools, restaurant associations, or large restaurant chains. Some bartenders acquire their skills through formal vocational training either by attending a school for bartending or a vocational and technical school where bartending classes are taught. These programs often include instruction on state and local laws and regulations, cocktail recipes, proper attire and conduct, and stocking a bar. Some of these schools help their graduates find jobs. Although few employers require any minimum level of educational attainment, some specialized training is usually needed in food handling and legal issues surrounding serving alcoholic beverages. Employers are more likely to hire and promote employees based on people skills and personal qualities than education.

Other qualifications. Restaurants rely on good food and customer service to retain loyal customers and succeed in a competitive industry. Food and beverage serving and related workers who exhibit excellent personal qualities—such as a neat appearance, an ability to work as part of a team, and a natural rapport with customers—will be highly sought after. Most states require workers who serve alcoholic beverages to be at least 18 years of age, but some states require servers to be older. For bartender jobs, many employers prefer to hire people who are 25 or older. All servers that serve alcohol need to be familiar with state and local laws concerning the sale of alcoholic beverages.

Waiters and waitresses need a good memory to avoid confusing customers' orders and to recall faces, names, and preferences of frequent patrons. Knowledge of a foreign language can be helpful to communicate with a diverse clientele and staff. Restaurants and hotels that have rigid table service standards often offer higher wages and have greater income potential from tips, but they may also have stiffer employment requirements, such as prior table service experience or higher education attainment than other establishments.

Advancement. Due to the relatively small size of most food-serving establishments, opportunities for promotion are limited. After gaining experience, some dining room and cafeteria attendants and bartender helpers advance to waiter, waitress, or bartender jobs. For waiters, waitresses, and bartenders, advancement usually is limited to finding a job in a busier or more expensive restaurant or bar where prospects for tip earnings are better. Some bartenders, hosts and hostesses, and waiters and waitresses advance to supervisory jobs, such as dining room supervisor, maitre d', assistant manager, or restaurant general manager. A few bartenders open their own businesses. In larger restaurant chains, food and beverage service workers who excel often are invited to enter the company's formal management training program.

Employment

Food and beverage serving and related workers held 7.7 million jobs in 2008. The distribution of jobs among the various food and beverage serving occupations was as follows:

Combined food preparation and serving workers, including fast food	2,701,700
Waiters and waitresses	2,381,600
Counter attendants, cafeteria, food concession, and coffee shop	525,400
Dishwashers	522,900
Bartenders	508,700
Dining room and cafeteria attendants and bartender helpers	420,700

Projections Data from the National Employment Matrix

Occupational title	SOC Code	Employment, 2008	Projected employment, 2018	Change, 2008–2018	
				Number	Percent
Food and beverage serving and related workers........................—		7,652,400	8,413,100	760,700	10
Food and beverage serving workers............................35-3000		6,307,200	6,962,300	655,100	10
Bartenders..35-3011		508,700	549,500	40,800	8
Fast food and counter workers.............................35-3020		3,227,100	3,670,400	443,300	14
Combined food preparation and serving workers, including fast food 35-3021		2,701,700	3,096,000	394,300	15
Counter attendants, cafeteria, food concession, and coffee shop.........................35-3022		525,400	574,400	49,000	9
Waiters and waitresses 35-3031		2,381,600	2,533,300	151,600	6
Food servers, nonrestaurant 35-3041		189,800	209,100	19,300	10
Other food preparation and serving related workers 35-9000		1,345,200	1,450,800	105,600	8
Dining room and cafeteria attendants and bartender helpers 35-9011		420,700	444,000	23,300	6
Dishwashers..35-9021		522,900	583,400	60,400	12
Hosts and hostesses, restaurant, lounge, and coffee shop 35-9031		350,700	373,400	22,800	6
Food preparation and serving related workers, all other...35-9099		50,900	50,000	–900	–2

NOTE: Data in this table are rounded.

Hosts and hostesses, restaurant, lounge, and coffee shop 350,700	
Food servers, nonrestaurant 189,800	
All other food preparation and serving related workers 50,900	

The overwhelming majority of jobs for food and beverage serving and related workers were found in food services and drinking places, such as restaurants, fast food outlets, bars, and catering or contract food service operations. Other jobs were in hotels, motels, and other traveler accommodation establishments; amusement, gambling, and recreation establishments; educational services; nursing care facilities; and civic and social organizations.

Jobs are located throughout the country but are more plentiful in larger cities and tourist areas. Vacation resorts offer seasonal employment.

Job Outlook

Average employment growth is expected, and job opportunities should be excellent for food and beverage serving and related workers as turnover is generally very high among these workers, but job competition is often keen for jobs at upscale restaurants.

Employment change. Overall employment of these workers is expected to increase by 10 percent over the 2008–2018 decade, which is about as fast as the average for all occupations. Food and beverage serving and related workers are projected to have one of the largest numbers of new jobs arise, about 761,000, over this period. The growth in jobs is expected to increase as the population continues to expand. However, employment will grow more slowly than in the past as people change their dining habits. The growing popularity of take-out food and the growing number and variety of

places that offer carryout options, including at many full-service restaurants, will slow the growth of waiters and waitresses and other serving workers.

Projected employment growth will vary by job type. Employment of combined food preparation and serving workers, which includes fast-food workers, is expected to increase faster than the average for all occupations. The limited service segment of the food services and drinking places industry has a low price advantage, fast service, and has been adding healthier foods. Slower than average employment growth is expected for waiters and waitresses, hosts and hostesses, and dining room and cafeteria attendants and bartender helpers, as more people use take-out service. Employment of bartenders, dishwashers, and counter attendants, cafeteria, food concession, and coffee shop will grow about as fast as average. Nonrestaurant servers, such as those who deliver food trays in hotels, hospitals, residential care facilities, or catered events, are expected to have average employment growth.

Job prospects. Job opportunities at most eating and drinking places will be excellent because many people in these occupations change jobs frequently, which creates a large number of openings. Keen competition is expected, however, for jobs in popular restaurants and fine dining establishments, where potential earnings from tips are greatest.

Earnings

Food and beverage serving and related workers derive their earnings from a combination of hourly wages and customer tips. Earnings vary greatly, depending on the type of job and establishment. For example, fast-food workers and hosts and hostesses usually do not receive tips, so their wage rates may be higher than those of waiters and waitresses and bartenders in full-service restaurants, but their overall earnings might be lower. In many full-service restaurants, tips are higher than wages. In some restaurants, workers contribute all or a portion of their tips to a tip pool, which is distributed among qualifying workers. Tip pools allow workers who don't usually receive tips directly from customers, such as dining room attendants, to feel a part of a team and to share in the rewards of good service.

In May 2008, median hourly wages (including tips) of waiters and waitresses were $8.01. The middle 50 percent earned between $7.32 and $10.35. The lowest 10 percent earned less than $6.73, and the highest 10 percent earned more than $14.26 an hour. For most waiters and waitresses, higher earnings are primarily the result of receiving more in tips rather than higher hourly wages. Tips usually average between 10 percent and 20 percent of guests' checks; waiters and waitresses working in busy or expensive restaurants earn the most.

Bartenders had median hourly wages (including tips) of $8.54. The middle 50 percent earned between $7.53 and $10.98. The lowest 10 percent earned less than $7.00, and the highest 10 percent earned more than $14.93 an hour. Like waiters and waitresses, bartenders employed in public bars may receive more than half of their earnings as tips. Service bartenders often are paid higher hourly wages to offset their lower tip earnings.

Median hourly wages (including tips) of dining room and cafeteria attendants and bartender helpers were $8.05. The middle 50 percent earned between $7.39 and $9.44. The lowest 10 percent earned less than $6.82, and the highest 10 percent earned more than $11.67 an hour. Most received over half of their earnings as wages; the rest of their income was a share of the proceeds from tip pools.

Median hourly wages of hosts and hostesses were $8.42. The middle 50 percent earned between $7.50 and $9.70. The lowest 10 percent earned less than $6.88, and the highest 10 percent earned more than $11.89 an hour. Wages comprised the majority of their earnings. In some cases, wages were supplemented by proceeds from tip pools.

Median hourly wages of combined food preparation and serving workers, including fast food, were $7.90. The middle 50 percent earned between $7.26 and $9.12. The lowest 10 percent earned less than $6.67, and the highest 10 percent earned more than $10.67 an hour. Although some combined food preparation and serving workers receive a part of their earnings as tips, fast-food workers usually do not.

Median hourly wages of counter attendants in cafeterias, food concessions, and coffee shops (including tips) were $8.42. The middle 50 percent earned between $7.57 and $9.64 an hour. The lowest 10 percent earned less than $6.97, and the highest 10 percent earned more than $11.73 an hour.

Median hourly wages of dishwashers were $8.19. The middle 50 percent earned between $7.47 and $9.35. The lowest 10 percent earned less than $6.90, and the highest 10 percent earned more than $10.74 an hour.

Median hourly wages of food servers outside of restaurants were $9.32. The middle 50 percent earned between $7.93 and $11.64. The lowest 10 percent earned less than $7.20, and the highest 10 percent earned more than $14.69 an hour.

Many beginning or inexperienced workers earn the federal minimum wage ($7.25 per hour as of July 24, 2009), but many states set minimum wages higher than the federal minimum. Also, various minimum wage exceptions apply under specific circumstances to disabled workers, full-time students, youth under age 20 in their first 90 days of employment, tipped employees, and student-learners. Tipped employees are those who customarily and regularly receive more than $30 a month in tips. The employer may consider tips as part of wages, but the employer must pay at least $2.13 an hour in direct wages.

Many employers provide free meals and furnish uniforms, but some may deduct from wages the cost, or fair value, of any meals or lodging provided. Food and beverage service workers who work full time often receive typical benefits, but part-time workers usually do not. In some large restaurants and hotels, food and beverage serving and related workers belong to unions—principally the Unite HERE and the Service Employees International Union.

Related Occupations

Other workers who prepare or serve food and drink for diners include cashiers; chefs, head cooks, and food preparation and serving supervisors; cooks and food preparation workers; flight attendants; and retail salespersons.

Sources of Additional Information

Information about job opportunities may be obtained from local employers and local offices of state employment services agencies.

A guide to careers in restaurants plus a list of 2- and 4-year colleges offering food service programs and related scholarship information is available from

▸ National Restaurant Association, 1200 17th St. NW, Washington, DC 20036. Internet: www.restaurant.org

For general information on hospitality careers, contact

▸ International Council on Hotel, Restaurant, and Institutional Education, 2810 N. Parham Rd., Suite 230, Richmond, VA 23294. Internet: www.chrie.org

Graphic Designers

(O*NET 27-1024.00)

Significant Points

■ Employment is expected to grow about as fast as the average, with many new jobs associated with interactive media.

■ A bachelor's degree in graphic design is usually required.

■ Jobseekers are expected to face keen competition; individuals with Web site design and animation experience will have the best opportunities.

Nature of the Work

Graphic designers—or *graphic artists*—plan, analyze, and create visual solutions to communications problems. They find the most effective way to get messages across in print and electronic media using color, type, illustration, photography, animation, and various print and layout techniques. Graphic designers develop the overall layout and production design of magazines, newspapers, journals, corporate reports, and other publications. They also produce promotional displays, packaging, and marketing brochures for products and services, design distinctive logos for products and businesses, and develop signs and signage systems—called environmental graphics—for business and government. An increasing number of graphic designers also develop material for Internet Web pages, interactive media, and multimedia projects. Graphic designers also may produce the credits that appear before and after television programs and movies.

The first step in developing a new design is to determine the needs of the client, the message the design should portray, and its appeal to customers or users. Graphic designers consider cognitive, cultural, physical, and social factors in planning and executing designs for the target audience. Designers gather relevant information by meeting with clients, creative or art directors, and by performing their own research. Identifying the needs of consumers is becoming increasingly important for graphic designers as they continue to develop corporate communication strategies in addition to creating designs and layouts.

Graphic designers prepare sketches or layouts—by hand or with the aid of a computer—to illustrate their vision for the design. They select colors, sound, artwork, photography, animation, style of type, and other visual elements for the design. Designers also select the size and arrangement of the different elements on the page or screen. They may create graphs and charts from data for use in publications, and they often consult with copywriters on any text that accompanies the design. Designers then present the completed design to their clients or art or creative director for approval. In printing and publishing firms, graphic designers also may assist the printers by selecting the type of paper and ink for the publication and reviewing the mock-up design for errors before final publication.

Graphic designers use specialized computer software packages to help them create layouts and design elements and to program animated graphics.

Graphic designers sometimes supervise assistants who follow instructions to complete parts of the design process. Designers who run their own businesses also may devote a considerable time to developing new business contacts, choosing equipment, and performing administrative tasks, such as reviewing catalogues and ordering samples. The need for up-to-date computer and communications equipment is an ongoing consideration for graphic designers.

Work environment. Working conditions and places of employment vary. Graphic designers employed by large advertising, publishing, or design firms generally work regular hours in well-lighted and comfortable settings. Designers in smaller design consulting firms and those who freelance generally work on a contract, or job, basis. They frequently adjust their workday to suit their clients' schedules and deadlines. Consultants and self-employed designers tend to work longer hours and in smaller, more congested, environments.

Designers may work in their own offices or studios or in clients' offices. Designers who are paid by the assignment are under pressure to please existing clients and to find new ones to maintain a steady income. All designers sometimes face frustration when their designs are rejected or when their work is not as creative as they wish. Graphic designers may work evenings or weekends to meet production schedules, especially in the printing and publishing industries where deadlines are shorter and more frequent.

Training, Other Qualifications, and Advancement

A bachelor's degree in graphic design is usually required. Creativity, communication, and problem-solving skills are important, as are a familiarity with computer graphics and design software.

Education and training. A bachelor's degree in graphic design is usually required for most entry-level and advanced graphic design positions. Bachelor's degree programs in fine arts or graphic design are offered at many colleges, universities, and private design schools. Most curriculums include studio art, principles of design, computerized design, commercial graphics production, printing techniques, and Web site design. In addition to design courses, a liberal arts education that includes courses in art history, writing, psychology, sociology, foreign languages and cultural studies, marketing, and business are useful in helping designers work effectively.

Associate degrees and certificates in graphic design also are available from 2-year and 3-year professional schools, and graduates of these programs normally qualify as assistants to graphic designers or for positions requiring technical skills only. Creative individuals who wish to pursue a career in graphic design—and who already possess a bachelor's degree in another field—can complete a 2-year or 3-year program in graphic design to learn the technical requirements.

The National Association of Schools of Art and Design accredits about 300 postsecondary institutions with programs in art and design. Most of these schools award a degree in graphic design. Many schools do not allow formal entry into a bachelor's degree program until a student has successfully finished a year of basic art and design courses, which can be completed in high school. Applicants may be required to submit sketches and other examples of their artistic ability.

Graphic designers must keep up with new and updated computer graphics and design software, either on their own or through formal software training programs.

Other qualifications. In addition to postsecondary training in graphic design, creativity, communication, and problem-solving skills are crucial. Graphic designers must be creative and able to communicate their ideas visually, verbally, and in writing. They also must have an eye for details. Designers show employers these traits by putting together a portfolio—a collection of examples of a person's best work. A good portfolio often is the deciding factor in getting a job.

Because consumer tastes can change fairly quickly, designers also need to be well read, open to new ideas and influences, and quick to react to changing trends. The abilities to work independently and under pressure are equally important traits. People in this field need self-discipline to start projects on their own, to budget their time, and to meet deadlines and production schedules. Good business sense and sales ability also are important, especially for those who freelance or run their own firms.

Advancement. Beginning graphic designers usually need 1 to 3 years of working experience before they can advance to higher posi-

Projections Data from the National Employment Matrix

Occupational title	SOC Code	Employment, 2008	Projected employment, 2018	Change, 2008–2018	
				Number	Percent
Graphic designers	27-1024	286,100	323,100	36,900	13

NOTE: Data in this table are rounded.

tions. Experienced graphic designers in large firms may advance to chief designer, art or creative director, or other supervisory positions. Some designers leave the occupation to become teachers in design schools or in colleges and universities. Many faculty members continue to consult privately or operate small design studios to complement their classroom activities. Some experienced designers open their own firms or choose to specialize in one area of graphic design.

Employment

Graphic designers held about 286,100 jobs in 2008. Most graphic designers worked in specialized design services; advertising and related services; printing and related support activities; or newspaper, periodical, book, and directory publishers. A small number of designers produced computer graphics for computer systems design firms.

Some designers do freelance work—full time or part time—in addition to holding a salaried job in design or in another occupation.

Job Outlook

Employment is expected grow about as fast as average. Keen competition for jobs is expected; individuals with Web site design and animation experience will have the best opportunities.

Employment change. Employment of graphic designers is expected to grow 13 percent, as fast as the average for all occupations from 2008 to 2018, as demand for graphic design continues to increase from advertisers and computer design firms.

Moreover, graphic designers with Web site design and animation experience will especially be needed as demand increases for design projects for interactive media—Web sites, mobile phones, and other technology. Demand for graphic designers also will increase as advertising firms create print and Web marketing and promotional materials for a growing number of products and services. Growth in Internet advertising, in particular, is expected to increase the number of designers. However, growth may be tempered by reduced demand in the print publishing, where many graphic designers are employed.

Job prospects. Graphic designers are expected to face keen competition for available positions. Many talented individuals are attracted to careers as graphic designers. Individuals with Web site design and animation experience will have the best opportunities.

Graphic designers with a broad liberal arts education and experience in marketing and business management will be best suited for positions developing communication strategies.

Earnings

Median annual wages for graphic designers were $42,400 in May 2008. The middle 50 percent earned between $32,600 and $56,620. The lowest 10 percent earned less than $26,110, and the highest 10 percent earned more than $74,660. May 2008 median annual wages in the industries employing the largest numbers of graphic designers were as follows:

Computer systems design and related services	$47,860
Specialized design services	45,870
Advertising, public relations and related services	43,540
Newspaper, periodical, book, and directory publishers	36,910
Printing and related support activities	36,100

According to the American Institute of Graphic Arts, median annual cash compensation for entry-level designers was $35,000 in 2008. Staff-level graphic designers earned a median of $45,000. Senior designers, who may supervise junior staff or have some decision-making authority that reflects their knowledge of graphic design, earned a median of $60,000. Solo designers who freelanced or worked under contract to another company reported median earnings of $57,000. Design directors, the creative heads of design firms or in-house corporate design departments, earned $95,000. Graphic designers with ownership or partnership interests in a firm or who were principals of the firm in some other capacity earned $95,000.

Related Occupations

Workers in other occupations in the art and design field include artists and related workers; commercial and industrial designers; fashion designers; floral designers; and interior designers.

Other occupations that require computer-aided design skills include computer software engineers and computer programmers; desktop publishers; and drafters.

Other occupations involved in the design, layout, and copy of publications include advertising, marketing, promotions, public relations, and sales managers; authors, writers, and editors; photographers; and prepress technicians and workers.

Sources of Additional Information

For general information about art and design and a list of accredited college-level programs, contact

▸ National Association of Schools of Art and Design, 11250 Roger Bacon Dr., Suite 21, Reston, VA 20190-5248. Internet: http://nasad.arts-accredit.org

For information about various design careers, contact

▸ American Institute of Graphic Arts, 164 Fifth Ave., New York, NY 10010. Internet: www.aiga.org

For information on workshops, scholarships, internships, and competitions for graphic design students interested in advertising careers, contact

▸ Art Directors Club, 106 W. 29th St., New York, NY 10001. Internet: www.adcglobal.org

Grounds Maintenance Workers

(O*NET 37-1012.00, 37-3011.00, 37-3012.00, 37-3013.00, and 37-3019.00)

Significant Points

■ Most grounds maintenance workers need no formal education and are trained on the job; however, some workers may require formal education.

■ Occupational characteristics include full-time and part-time jobs, seasonal jobs, physically demanding work, and low earnings.

■ Job opportunities are expected to be good.

Nature of the Work

Grounds maintenance workers perform a variety of tasks necessary to achieve a pleasant and functional outdoor environment. They mow lawns, rake leaves, trim hedges and trees; plant flowers; and otherwise ensure that the grounds of houses, businesses, and parks are attractive, orderly, and healthy. They also care for indoor gardens and plantings in commercial and public facilities, such as malls, hotels, and botanical gardens.

These workers use handtools such as shovels, rakes, pruning and handsaws, hedge and brush trimmers, and axes. They also use power lawnmowers, chain saws, leaf blowers, and electric clippers. Some use equipment such as tractors and twin-axle vehicles.

Grounds maintenance workers can be divided into several specialties, including landscaping workers, groundskeeping workers, pesticide handlers, tree trimmers, and grounds maintenance supervisors. In general, these specialties have varying job duties, but in many cases their responsibilities overlap.

Landscaping workers create new functional outdoor areas and upgrade existing landscapes, but also may help maintain landscapes. Their duties include planting bushes, trees, sod, and other forms of vegetation, as well as, edging, trimming, fertilizing, watering, and mulching lawns and grounds. They also grade property by creating or smoothing hills and inclines; install lighting or sprinkler systems; and build walkways, terraces, patios, decks, and fountains. Landscaping workers provide their services in a variety of residential and commercial settings, such as homes, apartment buildings, office buildings, shopping malls, and hotels and motels.

Groundskeeping workers, also called *groundskeepers*, usually focus on maintaining existing grounds. In addition to caring for sod, plants, and trees, they rake and mulch leaves, clear snow from walkways and parking lots, and use irrigation methods to adjust water consumption and prevent waste. These individuals work on athletic fields, golf courses, cemeteries, university campuses, and parks, as well as many of the same settings as landscaping workers. They also see to the proper upkeep and repair of sidewalks, parking lots, groundskeeping equipment, pools, fountains, fences, planters, and benches.

Groundskeeping workers who care for athletic fields keep natural and artificial turf in top condition, mark out boundaries, and paint turf with team logos and names before events. They mow, water, fertilize, and aerate the fields regularly. They must make sure that the underlying soil on fields with natural turf has the required composition to allow proper drainage and to support the grasses used on the field. In sports venues, they vacuum and disinfect synthetic turf after its use to prevent the growth of harmful bacteria, and they remove the turf and replace the cushioning pad periodically.

Groundskeepers in parks and recreation facilities care for lawns, trees, and shrubs; maintain playgrounds; clean buildings; and keep parking lots, picnic areas, and other public spaces free of litter. They also may erect and dismantle snow fences, and maintain swimming pools. These workers inspect buildings and equipment, make needed repairs, and keep everything freshly painted.

Workers who maintain golf courses are called *greenskeepers*. Greenskeepers do many of the same things as other groundskeepers, but they also periodically relocate the holes on putting greens to prevent uneven wear of the turf and to add interest and challenge to the game. Greenskeepers also keep canopies, benches, ball washers, and tee markers repaired and freshly painted.

Some groundskeepers specialize in caring for cemeteries and memorial gardens. They dig graves to specified depths, generally using a backhoe. They mow grass regularly, apply fertilizers and other chemicals, prune shrubs and trees, plant flowers, and remove debris from graves.

Pesticide handlers, sprayers, and applicators, vegetation mix herbicides, fungicides, or insecticides and apply them through sprays, dusts, or vapors into the soil or onto plants. Those working for chemical lawn service firms are more specialized, inspecting lawns for problems and applying fertilizers, pesticides, and other chemicals to stimulate growth and prevent or control weeds, diseases, or insect infestation. Many practice integrated pest-management techniques.

Tree trimmers and pruners, sometimes called *arborists,* cut away dead or excess branches from trees or shrubs to clear roads, sidewalks, or utilities' equipment, or to improve the appearance, health, and value of trees. Some specialize in diagnosing and treating tree diseases, and in performing preventive measures to keep trees healthy. Some may plant trees. Some of these workers also specialize in pruning, trimming and shaping ornamental trees and shrubs for private residences, golf courses, or other institutional grounds. Tree trimmers and pruners use handsaws, pole saws, shears, and clippers. When trimming near power lines, they usually work on truck-mounted lifts and use power pruners.

Supervisors of landscaping and groundskeeping workers oversee grounds maintenance work. They prepare cost estimates, schedule work for crews on the basis of weather conditions or the availability of equipment, perform spot checks to ensure the quality of the service, and suggest changes in work procedures. In addition, supervisors train workers; keep employees' time records and record work performed; and may assist workers when deadlines are near. Supervisors who own their own business are also known as *landscape contractors*. They also often call themselves *landscape designers* if they create landscape design plans. Landscape designers also design exterior floral displays by planting annual or perennial flowers. Some work with landscape architects. (Landscape architects create more technical architectural plans and usually work on larger projects.) Supervisors of workers on golf courses are known as *superintendents*.

Work environment. Many grounds maintenance jobs are seasonal, available mainly in the spring, summer, and fall, when most planting, mowing, trimming, and cleanup are necessary. Most of the work is performed outdoors in all kinds of weather. It can be physically demanding and repetitive, involving bending, lifting, and shoveling. This occupation offers opportunities for both part-time and full-time work.

According to BLS data, full-time landscaping and groundskeeping workers, tree trimmers and pruners, and the supervisors of these workers experienced a much higher than average rate of work-related injury and illness. Those who work with pesticides, fertilizers, and other chemicals, as well as dangerous equipment and tools such as power lawnmowers and chain saws, must exercise safety precautions. Workers who use motorized equipment must take care to protect their hearing.

Training, Other Qualifications, and Advancement

Most grounds maintenance workers need no formal education and are trained on the job. However, some workers may require formal education in areas such as landscape design, horticulture, or business management.

Education and training. There usually are no minimum educational requirements for entry-level positions in grounds maintenance. In 2008, most workers had no education beyond high school. A short period of on-the-job training generally is sufficient to teach new hires the necessary skills, which often include planting and maintenance procedures; the operation of mowers, trimmers, leaf blowers, small tractors and other equipment; and proper safety procedures. Large institutional employers such as golf courses or municipalities may supplement on-the-job training with coursework in subjects like horticulture or small engine repair. A bachelor's degree may be needed for those who want to become specialists.

Supervisors may need a high school diploma, and may receive several months of on-the-job training. Formal training in landscape design, horticulture, arboriculture, or business may improve an applicant's chances for employment. Landscape designers may be required to obtain such training.

Licensure. Most states require licensure or certification for workers who apply pesticides. Requirements vary but usually include passing a test on the proper use and disposal of insecticides, herbicides, and fungicides. Some states also require that landscape contractors be licensed.

Other qualifications. Employers look for responsible, self-motivated individuals because grounds maintenance workers often work with little supervision. Employers want people who can learn quickly and follow instructions accurately so that time is not wasted and plants are not damaged. Driving a vehicle is often needed for these jobs. If driving is required, preference is given to applicants with a driver's license, a good driving record, and experience driving a truck.

Certification and advancement. Laborers who demonstrate a proficiency in the work and have good communication skills may advance to crew leader or other supervisory positions. Becoming a grounds manager or landscape contractor may require some formal education beyond high school in addition to several years of experience. Some workers with groundskeeping backgrounds may start their own businesses after several years of experience.

Certification from a professional organization may improve a worker's chances for advancement. The Professional Grounds Management Society offers voluntary certification to grounds managers who have a bachelor's degree in a relevant major with at least four years of experience, including two years as a supervisor; an associate degree in a relevant major with six years of experience, including 3 years as a supervisor; or eight years of experience including four years as a supervisor, and no degree. Additionally, candidates for certification must pass two examinations covering subjects such as insects and diseases, soils, trees and shrubs, turf management, irrigation, and budgets and finances. This organization also offers certification for grounds technicians. Candidates for this program must have a high school diploma or GED as well as two years of work experience as a grounds technician.

The Professional Landcare Network offers six certifications for individuals with varying levels of experience, in landscaping and grounds maintenance. Each of these programs requires applicants to pass an examination, and some require self-study course work. The Tree Care Industry Association offers five levels of credentials. Currently available credentials include Tree Care Apprentice, Ground Operations Specialist, Tree Climber Specialist, Aerial Lift Specialist and Tree Care Specialist, as well as a certification program in safety. These programs are available to individuals with varying levels of experience, and require applicants to pass training courses.

Employment

Grounds maintenance workers held about 1.5 million jobs in 2008. Employment was distributed as follows:

Landscaping and groundskeeping workers 1,205,800
First-line supervisors/managers of
    landscaping, lawn service, and
    groundskeeping workers 217,900
Tree trimmers and pruners 45,000
Pesticide handlers, sprayers, and applicators,
    vegetation 30,800
Grounds maintenance workers, all other 21,100

About 36 percent of all grounds maintenance workers were employed in companies providing landscaping services to buildings and dwellings. Others worked for educational institutions, public and private. Some were employed by local governments, installing and maintaining landscaping for parks, hospitals, and other public facilities. Around 402,000 grounds maintenance workers were self-employed, providing landscape maintenance directly to customers on a contract basis.

Job Outlook

Employment is expected to grow faster than average, and job opportunities should be good.

Employment change. Employment of grounds maintenance workers is expected to increase by 18 percent during the 2008–2018 decade, which is faster than the average for all occupations. In addition, grounds maintenance workers will be among the occupations with largest numbers of new jobs, with around 269,200. More workers will be needed to keep up with increasing demand for lawn care and landscaping services both from large institutions and from individual homeowners.

Major institutions, such as universities and corporate headquarters, recognize the importance of good landscape design in attracting personnel and clients and are expected to continue to use grounds maintenance services to maintain and upgrade their properties. Homeowners are also a growing source of demand for grounds maintenance workers. Many two-income households lack the time to take care of their lawns so they increasingly hire people to maintain them. Also, as the population ages, more elderly homeowners will require lawn care services to help maintain their yards.

Employment of tree trimmers and pruners should grow by 26 percent from 2008 to 2018, which is much faster than the average. In order to improve the environment, municipalities across the country are planting more trees in urban areas, increasing demand for these workers.

Job prospects. Job opportunities are expected to be good. Openings will arise from faster-than-average growth and the need to replace workers who leave this large occupation.

Job opportunities for nonseasonal work are best in regions with temperate climates, where landscaping and lawn services are required all year. Opportunities may vary with local economic conditions.

Earnings

Wages of grounds maintenance workers are low. Median hourly wages of landscaping and groundskeeping workers were $11.13 in May 2008. The middle 50 percent earned between $9.09 and $14.01 per hour. The lowest 10 percent earned less than $7.98 per hour, and the highest 10 percent earned more than $17.57. Median hourly wages in the largest employing industries of landscaping and groundskeeping workers in May 2008 were as follows:

Elementary and secondary schools $13.70
Local government 12.65
Services to buildings and dwellings........................ 11.11
Other amusement and recreation industries............. 10.01
Employment services.. 9.92

Median hourly wages of pesticide handlers, sprayers, and applicators, vegetation were $14.31 in May 2008. The middle 50 percent earned between $11.61 and $17.86 per hour. The lowest 10 percent earned less than $9.53 per hour, and the highest 10 percent earned more than $21.59. Median hourly wages in the services to buildings and dwellings industry were $14.51 in May 2008.

Median hourly wages of tree trimmers and pruners were $14.41 in May 2008. The middle 50 percent earned between $11.50 and $18.18 per hour. The lowest 10 percent earned less than $9.62 per hour, and the highest 10 percent earned more than $22.34. Median hourly wages in the services to buildings and dwellings industry were $14.04 in May 2008.

Median hourly wages of first-line supervisors/manages of landscaping, lawn service, and groundskeeping workers were $19.19 in May 2008. The middle 50 percent earned between $15.22 and $24.90 per hour. The lowest 10 percent earned less than $12.57 per hour, and the highest 10 percent earned more than $31.33. Median hourly wages in the largest employing industries of first-line supervisors/managers of landscaping, lawn service, and groundskeeping workers in May 2008 were as follows:

Local government $22.84
Other amusement and recreation industries............. 20.82
Services to buildings and dwellings........................ 18.50

Related Occupations

Other occupations that work with plants and soils include agricultural workers, other; farmers, ranchers, and agricultural managers; forest and conservation workers; landscape architects; and logging workers.

Projections Data from the National Employment Matrix

Occupational title	SOC Code	Employment, 2008	Projected employment, 2018	Change, 2008–2018	
				Number	Percent
Grounds maintenance workers .... —		1,520,600	1,789,900	269,200	18
First-line supervisors/managers of landscaping, lawn service, and groundskeeping workers........... 37-1012		217,900	250,300	32,400	15
Grounds maintenance workers.............................. 37-3000		1,302,700	1,539,500	236,800	18
Landscaping and groundskeeping workers 37-3011		1,205,800	1,422,900	217,100	18
Pesticide handlers, sprayers, and applicators, vegetation... 37-3012		30,800	36,300	5,400	18
Tree trimmers and pruners 37-3013		45,000	56,800	11,800	26
Grounds maintenance workers, all other............. 37-3019		21,100	23,600	2,500	12

NOTE: Data in this table are rounded.

Sources of Additional Information

For career and certification information on tree trimmers and pruners, contact

▶ Tree Care Industry Association, 136 Harvey Rd., Suite 101, Londonderry, NH 03053. Internet: www.treecareindustry.org

For information on work as a landscaping and groundskeeping worker, contact the following organizations:

▶ Professional Grounds Management Society, 720 Light St., Baltimore, MD 21230. Internet: www.pgms.org

▶ Professional Landcare Network, 950 Herndon Pkwy., Suite 450, Herndon, VA 20170. Internet: www.landcarenetwork.org

For information on becoming a licensed pesticide applicator, contact your state's Department of Agriculture or Department of Environmental Protection or Conservation.

Heating, Air-Conditioning, and Refrigeration Mechanics and Installers

(O*NET 49-9021.00, 49-9021.01, and 49-9021.02)

Significant Points

■ Job prospects are expected to be excellent.

■ Employment is projected to grow much faster than the average.

■ Employers prefer to hire those who have completed technical school training or a formal apprenticeship.

Nature of the Work

Heating and air-conditioning systems control the temperature, humidity, and the total air quality in residential, commercial, industrial, and other buildings. By providing a climate controlled environment, refrigeration systems make it possible to store and transport food, medicine, and other perishable items. *Heating, air-conditioning, and refrigeration mechanics and installers*—also called *technicians*—install, maintain, and repair such systems. Because heating, ventilation, air-conditioning, and refrigeration systems often are referred to as HVACR systems, these workers also may be called HVACR technicians.

Heating, air-conditioning, and refrigeration systems consist of many mechanical, electrical, and electronic components, such as motors, compressors, pumps, fans, ducts, pipes, thermostats, and switches. In central forced air heating systems, for example, a furnace heats air, which is then distributed through a system of metal or fiberglass ducts. Technicians maintain, diagnose, and correct problems throughout the entire system. To do this, they adjust system controls to recommended settings and test the performance of the system using special tools and test equipment.

Technicians often specialize in either installation or maintenance and repair, although they are trained to do both. They also may specialize in doing heating work or air-conditioning or refrigeration work. Some specialize in one type of equipment—for example,

hydronics (water-based heating systems), solar panels, or commercial refrigeration.

Technicians are often required to sell service contracts to their clients. Service contracts provide for regular maintenance of the heating and cooling systems, and they help to reduce the seasonal fluctuations of this type of work.

Technicians follow blueprints or other specifications to install oil, gas, electric, solid-fuel, and multiple-fuel heating systems and air-conditioning systems. After putting the equipment in place, they install fuel and water supply lines, air ducts and vents, pumps, and other components. They may connect electrical wiring and controls and check the unit for proper operation. To ensure the proper functioning of the system, furnace installers often use combustion test equipment, such as carbon dioxide testers, carbon monoxide testers, combustion analyzers, and oxygen testers. These tests ensure that the system will operate safely and at peak efficiency.

After a furnace or air-conditioning unit has been installed, technicians often perform routine maintenance and repair work to keep the systems operating efficiently. They may adjust burners and blowers and check for leaks. If the system is not operating properly, technicians check the thermostat, burner nozzles, controls, or other parts to diagnose and correct the problem.

Technicians also install and maintain heat pumps, which are similar to air conditioners but can be reversed so that they both heat and cool a home. Because of the added complexity, and the fact that they run both in summer and winter, these systems often require more maintenance and need to be replaced more frequently than traditional furnaces and air conditioners.

During the summer, when heating systems are not being used, heating equipment technicians do maintenance work, such as replacing filters, ducts, and other parts of the system that may accumulate dust and impurities during the operating season. During the winter, air-conditioning mechanics inspect the systems and do required maintenance, such as overhauling compressors.

Refrigeration mechanics install, service, and repair industrial and commercial refrigerating systems and a variety of refrigeration equipment. They follow blueprints, design specifications, and manufacturers' instructions to install motors, compressors, condensing units, evaporators, piping, and other components. They connect this equipment to the ductwork, refrigerant lines, and electrical power source. After making the connections, refrigerator mechanics charge the system with refrigerant, check it for proper operation and leaks, and program control systems.

When air-conditioning and refrigeration technicians service equipment, they must use care to conserve, recover, and recycle the refrigerants used in air-conditioning and refrigeration systems. The release of these refrigerants can be harmful to the environment. Technicians conserve the refrigerant by making sure that there are no leaks in the system; they recover it by venting the refrigerant into proper cylinders; they recycle it for reuse with special filter-dryers; or they ensure that the refrigerant is properly disposed of.

Heating, air-conditioning, and refrigeration mechanics and installers are adept at using a variety of tools to work with refrigerant lines and air ducts, including hammers, wrenches, metal snips, electric drills, pipe cutters and benders, measurement gauges, and acetylene torches. They use voltmeters, thermometers, pressure gauges, manometers, and other testing devices to check airflow, refrigerant pressure, electrical circuits, burners, and other components.

Other craft workers sometimes install or repair cooling and heating systems. For example, on a large air-conditioning installation job, especially where workers are covered by union contracts, ductwork might be done by sheet metal workers and duct installers; electrical work by electricians; and installation of piping, condensers, and other components by pipelayers, plumbers, pipefitters, and steamfitters. Home appliance repairers usually service room air-conditioners and household refrigerators.

Work environment. Heating, air-conditioning, and refrigeration mechanics and installers work in homes, retail establishments, hospitals, office buildings, and factories—anywhere there is climate-control equipment that needs to be installed, repaired, or serviced. They may be assigned to specific job sites at the beginning of each day or may be dispatched to a variety of locations if they are making service calls.

Technicians may work outside in cold or hot weather, or in buildings that are uncomfortable because the air-conditioning or heating equipment is broken. In addition, technicians might work in awkward or cramped positions, and sometimes they are required to work in high places. Hazards include electrical shock, burns, muscle strains, and other injuries from handling heavy equipment. Appropriate safety equipment is necessary when handling refrigerants because contact can cause skin damage, frostbite, or blindness. When working in tight spaces, inhalation of refrigerant is a possible hazard.

The majority of mechanics and installers work at least 40 hours per week. During peak seasons, they often work overtime or irregular hours. Maintenance workers, including those who provide maintenance services under contract, often work evening or weekend shifts and are on call. Most employers try to provide a full workweek year-round by scheduling both installation and maintenance work, and many manufacturers and contractors now provide or even require year-round service contracts. In most shops that service both heating and air-conditioning equipment, employment is stable throughout the year.

Training, Other Qualifications, and Advancement

Because of the increasing sophistication of heating, air-conditioning, and refrigeration systems, employers prefer to hire those who have completed technical school training or a formal apprenticeship. Some mechanics and installers, however, still learn the trade informally on the job.

Education and training. Many heating, air-conditioning, and refrigeration mechanics and installers receive their primary training in secondary and postsecondary technical and trade schools and junior and community colleges that offer programs in heating, air-conditioning, and refrigeration. These programs can take between 6 months and 2 years to complete. Others get their training in the Armed Forces.

High school students interested in some initial training for this industry should take courses in shop math, mechanical drawing, applied physics and chemistry, electronics, blueprint reading, and computer applications. Some knowledge of plumbing or electrical work and a basic understanding of electronics are beneficial for an HVACR technician. Secondary and postsecondary students studying HVACR learn about theory of temperature control, equipment design and construction, and electronics. They also learn the basics of installation, maintenance, and repair.

Three accrediting agencies have set academic standards for HVACR programs: HVAC Excellence; the National Center for Construction Education and Research; and the Partnership for Air-Conditioning, Heating, and Refrigeration Accreditation. After completing these programs, new technicians generally need between 6 months to 2 years of field experience before they are considered proficient.

Many other technicians train through apprenticeships. Apprenticeship programs frequently are run by joint committees representing local chapters of the Air-Conditioning Contractors of America, the Mechanical Contractors Association of America, Plumbing-Heating-Cooling Contractors—National Association, and locals of the Sheet Metal Workers' International Association or the United Association of Journeymen and Apprentices of the Plumbing and Pipefitting Industry of the United States and Canada. Local chapters of the Associated Builders and Contractors and the National Association of Home Builders sponsor other apprenticeship programs. Formal apprenticeship programs normally last 3 to 5 years and combine paid on-the-job training with classroom instruction. Classes include subjects such as safety practices, the use and care of tools, blueprint reading, and the theory and design of heating, ventilation, air-conditioning, and refrigeration systems. In addition to understanding how systems work, technicians must learn about refrigerant products and the legislation and regulations that govern their use.

Applicants for apprenticeships must have a high school diploma or equivalent. Math and reading skills are essential. After completing an apprenticeship program, technicians are considered skilled trades workers and capable of working alone. These programs are also a pathway to certification and, in some cases, college credits.

Those who acquire their skills on the job usually begin by assisting experienced technicians. They may begin by performing simple tasks such as carrying materials, insulating refrigerant lines, or cleaning furnaces. In time, they move on to more difficult tasks, such as cutting and soldering pipes and sheet metal and checking electrical and electronic circuits.

Licensure. Heating, air-conditioning, and refrigeration mechanics and installers are required to be licensed by some states and localities. Requirements for licensure vary greatly, but all states or localities that require a license have a test that must be passed. The contents of these tests vary by state or locality, with some requiring extensive knowledge of electrical codes and others focusing more on HVACR-specific knowledge. Completion of an apprenticeship program or 2 to 5 years of experience are also common requirements.

In addition, all technicians who purchase or work with refrigerants must be certified in their proper handling. To become certified to purchase and handle refrigerants, technicians must pass a written examination specific to the type of work in which they specialize. The three possible areas of certification are: Type I—servicing small appliances; Type II—high-pressure refrigerants; and Type III—low-pressure refrigerants. Exams are administered by organizations approved by the U.S. Environmental Protection Agency, such as trade schools, unions, contractor associations, or building groups.

Other qualifications. Because technicians frequently deal directly with the public, they should be courteous and tactful, especially when dealing with an aggravated customer. They should be in good physical condition because they sometimes have to lift and move heavy equipment.

Certification and advancement. Throughout the learning process, technicians may have to take a number of tests that measure their skills. For those with relevant coursework and less than 2 years of experience, the industry has developed a series of exams to test basic competency in residential heating and cooling, light commercial heating and cooling, and commercial refrigeration. These are referred to as "Entry-level" certification exams and are commonly conducted at both secondary and postsecondary technical and trade schools.

Additionally, HVACR technicians who have at least 1 year of experience performing installations and 2 years of experience performing maintenance and repair can take a number of different tests to certify their competency in working with specific types of equipment, such as oil-burning furnaces. The Air Conditioning, Heating, and Refrigeration Institute offers an Industry Competency Exam; HVAC Excellence offers both a Secondary Employment Ready Exam and a Secondary Heat and Heat Plus exams; and National Occupational Competency Testing Institute offers a secondary exam; and the Refrigeration Service Engineers Society offers two levels of certification, as well. Employers increasingly recommend taking and passing these tests and obtaining certification; doing so may increase advancement opportunities.

Another way to increase advancement opportunities is to take advantage of any courses that will improve competency with computers; these courses are useful because of the increasing complexity of automated computer controls in larger buildings.

Advancement usually takes the form of higher wages. Some technicians, however, may advance to positions as supervisor or service manager. Others may move into sales and marketing. Still others may become building superintendents, cost estimators, system test and balance specialists, or, with the necessary certification, teachers. Those with sufficient money and managerial skill can open their own contracting business.

Employment

Heating, air-conditioning, and refrigeration mechanics and installers held about 308,200 jobs in 2008; about 54 percent worked for plumbing, heating, and air-conditioning contractors. The rest were employed in a variety of industries throughout the country, reflecting a widespread dependence on climate-control systems. Some worked for refrigeration and air-conditioning service and repair shops, schools, and stores that sell heating and air-conditioning systems. Local governments, the federal government, hospitals, office buildings, and other organizations that operate large air-conditioning, refrigeration, or heating systems also employed these workers. About 16 percent of these workers were self-employed.

Job Outlook

With much-faster-than-average job growth and numerous expected retirements, heating, air-conditioning, and refrigeration mechanics and installers should have excellent employment opportunities.

Employment change. Employment of heating, air-conditioning, and refrigeration mechanics and installers is projected to increase 28 percent during the 2008–2018 decade, much faster than the average for all occupations. As the population and stock of buildings grows, so does the demand for residential, commercial, and industrial climate-control systems. Residential HVACR systems generally need replacement after 10 to 15 years; the large number of homes built in recent years will enter this replacement timeframe by 2018. The increased complexity of HVACR systems, which increases the possibility that equipment may malfunction, also will create opportunities for service technicians. A growing focus on improving indoor air quality and the increasing use of refrigerated equipment by a rising number of stores and gasoline stations that sell food should also create more jobs for heating, air-conditioning, and refrigeration technicians.

Concern for the environment and the need to reduce energy consumption overall has prompted the development of new energy-saving heating and air-conditioning systems. This emphasis on better energy management is expected to lead to the replacement of older systems and the installation of newer, more efficient systems in existing homes and buildings. Also, demand for maintenance and service work should rise as businesses and homeowners strive to keep increasingly complex systems operating at peak efficiency. Regulations prohibiting the discharge and production of older types of refrigerants that pollute the atmosphere should continue to result in the need to replace many existing air conditioning systems or to modify them to use new environmentally safe refrigerants. The pace of replacement in the commercial and industrial sectors will quicken if Congress or individual states change tax rules designed to encourage companies to buy new HVACR equipment.

Job prospects. Job prospects for heating, air-conditioning, and refrigeration mechanics and installers are expected to be excellent, particularly for those who have completed training from an accredited technical school or a formal apprenticeship. A growing number of retirements of highly skilled technicians are expected to generate many more job openings. Many contractors have reported problems finding enough workers to meet the demand for service and installation of HVACR systems.

Technicians who specialize in installation work may experience periods of unemployment when the level of new construction activity declines, but maintenance and repair work usually remains relatively stable. People and businesses depend on their climate-control or refrigeration systems and must keep them in good working order, regardless of economic conditions.

In light of the complexity of new computer-controlled HVACR systems in modern high-rise buildings, prospects should be best for those who can acquire and demonstrate computer competency. Training in new techniques that improve energy efficiency will also make it much easier to enter the occupation.

Projections Data from the National Employment Matrix

Occupational title	SOC Code	Employment, 2008	Projected employment, 2018	Change, 2008–2018	
				Number	Percent
Heating, air conditioning, and refrigeration mechanics and installers.. 49-9021		308,200	394,800	86,600	28

NOTE: Data in this table are rounded.

Earnings

Median hourly wages of heating, air-conditioning, and refrigeration mechanics and installers were $19.08 in May 2008. The middle 50 percent earned between $14.94 and $24.84 an hour. The lowest 10 percent earned less than $12.19, and the top 10 percent earned more than $30.59. Median hourly wages in the industries employing the largest numbers of heating, air-conditioning, and refrigeration mechanics and installers were as follows:

Local government..	$22.79
Hardware, and plumbing and heating equipment and supplies merchant wholesalers.......	22.18
Commercial and industrial machinery and equipment (except automotive and electronic) repair and maintenance	20.83
Direct selling establishments.................................	20.03
Building equipment contractors............................	18.26

Apprentices usually earn about 50 percent of the wage rate paid to experienced workers. As they gain experience and improve their skills, they receive periodic increases until they reach the wage rate of experienced workers.

Heating, air-conditioning, and refrigeration mechanics and installers generally receive a variety of employer-sponsored benefits. In addition to typical benefits such as health insurance and pension plans, some employers pay for work-related training and provide uniforms, company vans, and tools.

About 15 percent of heating, air-conditioning, and refrigeration mechanics and installers are members of a union. The unions to which the greatest numbers of mechanics and installers belong are the Sheet Metal Workers International Association and the United Association of Journeymen and Apprentices of the Plumbing and Pipefitting Industry of the United States and Canada.

Related Occupations

Heating, air-conditioning, and refrigeration mechanics and installers work with sheet metal and piping, and repair machinery, such as electrical motors, compressors, and burners. Other workers who have similar duties include boilermakers; electricians; home appliance repairers; plumbers, pipelayers, pipefitters, and steamfitters; and sheet metal workers.

Sources of Additional Information

For more information about opportunities for training, certification, and employment in this trade, contact local vocational and technical schools; local heating, air-conditioning, and refrigeration contractors; a local of the unions or organizations previously mentioned;

a local joint union-management apprenticeship committee; or the nearest office of the state employment service or apprenticeship agency. You can also find information on the registered apprenticeship system with links to state apprenticeship programs on the U.S. Department of Labor's web site: www.doleta.gov/OA/eta_default.cfm. Apprenticeship information is also available from the U.S. Department of Labor's toll free helpline: (877) 872-5627.

For information on career opportunities, training, and technician certification, contact

▸ Air-Conditioning Contractors of America, 2800 Shirlington Rd., Suite 300, Arlington, VA 22206-3607. Internet: www.acca.org

▸ Air-Conditioning, Heating, and Refrigeration Institute, 2111 Wilson Blvd., Suite 500, Arlington, VA 22201-3001. Internet: www.ahrinet.org

▸ Associated Builders and Contractors, Workforce Development Department, 4250 N. Fairfax Dr., 9th Floor, Arlington, VA 22203-1607. Internet: www.trytools.org

▸ Carbon Monoxide Safety Association, P.O. Box 669, Eastlake, CO 80614-0669. Internet: www.cosafety.org

▸ Green Mechanical Council 1701 Pennsylvania, Ave. NW, Suite 300, Washington, DC 20006-5813. Internet: www.greenmech.org

▸ Home Builders Institute, National Association of Home Builders, 1201 15th St. NW, 6th Floor, Washington, DC 20005-2842. Internet: www.hbi.org

▸ HVAC Excellence, P.O. Box 491, Mt. Prospect, IL 60056-0521. Internet: www.hvacexcellence.org

▸ Mechanical Contractors Association of America, Mechanical Service Contractors of America, 1385 Piccard Dr., Rockville, MD 20850-4329. Internet: www.mcaa.org

▸ National Center for Construction Education and Research, 3600 NW 43rd St., Bldg. G, Gainesville, FL 32606-8134. Internet: www.nccer.org

▸ National Occupational Competency Testing Institute, 500 N. Bronson Ave., Big Rapids, MI 49307-2737. Internet: www.nocti.org

▸ North American Technician Excellence, 2111 Wilson Blvd., Suite 510, Arlington, VA 22201-3051. Internet: www.natex.org

▸ Plumbing-Heating-Cooling Contractors, 180 S. Washington St., P.O. Box 6808, Falls Church, VA 22046-6808. Internet: www.phccweb.org

▸ Radiant Panel Association, P.O. Box 717, Loveland, CO 80539-0717. Internet: www.radiantpanelassociation.org

▸ Refrigeration Service Engineers Society, 1666 Rand Rd., Des Plaines, IL 60016-3552. Internet: www.rses.org

▸ Sheet Metal and Air-Conditioning Contractors National Association, 4201 Lafayette Center Dr., Chantilly, VA 20151-1209. Internet: www.smacna.org

▸ United Association of Journeymen and Apprentices of the Plumbing and Pipefitting Industry, United Association Bldg., 3 Park Place, Annapolis, MD 21401-3687. Internet: www.ua.org

Home Health Aides and Personal and Home Care Aides

(O*NET 31-1011.00 and 39-9021.00)

Significant Points

■ Job opportunities are expected to be excellent because of rapid growth in home health care and high replacement needs.

■ Training requirements vary from state to state, the type of home services agency, and funding source covering the costs of services.

■ Many of these workers work part time and weekends or evenings to suit the needs of their clients.

Nature of the Work

Home health aides and personal and home care aides help people who are disabled, chronically ill, or cognitively impaired and older adults, who many need assistance, live in their own homes or in residential facilities instead of in health facilities or institutions. They also assist people in hospices and day programs and help individuals with disabilities go to work and remain engaged in their communities. Most aides work with elderly or physically or mentally disabled clients who need more care than family or friends can provide. Others help discharge hospital patients who have relatively short-term needs.

Aides provide light housekeeping and homemaking tasks such as laundry, change bed linens, shop for food, plan and prepare meals. Aides also may help clients get out of bed, bathe, dress, and groom. Some accompany clients to doctors' appointments or on other errands.

Home health aides and personal and home care aides provide instruction and psychological support to their clients. They may advise families and patients on nutrition, cleanliness, and household tasks.

Aides' daily routine may vary. They may go to the same home every day or week for months or even years and often visit four or five clients on the same day. However, some aides may work solely with one client who is in need of more care and attention. In some situations, this may involve working with other aides in shifts so that the client has an aide throughout the day and night. Aides also work with clients, particularly younger adults at schools or at the client's work site.

In general, home health aides and personal and home care aides have similar job duties. However, there are some small differences.

Home health aides typically work for certified home health or hospice agencies that receive government, funding and therefore must comply with regulations from to receive funding. This means that they must work under the direct supervision of a medical professional, usually a nurse. These aides keep records of services performed and of clients' condition and progress. They report changes in the client's condition to the supervisor or case manager. Aides also work with therapists and other medical staff.

Home health aides may provide some basic health-related services, such as checking patients' pulse rate, temperature, and respiration rate. They also may help with simple prescribed exercises and assist with medications administration. Occasionally, they change simple dressings, give massage, provide skin care, or assist with braces and artificial limbs. With special training, experienced home health aides also may assist with medical equipment such as ventilators, which help patients breathe.

Personal and home care aides—also called *homemakers, caregivers, companions,* and *personal attendants*—work for various public and private agencies that provide home care services. In these agencies, caregivers are likely supervised by a licensed nurse, social worker, or other non-medical managers. Aides receive detailed instructions explaining when to visit clients and what services to perform for them. However, personal and home care aides work independently, with only periodic visits by their supervisors. These caregivers may work with only one client each day or five or six clients once a day every week or every 2 weeks.

Some aides are hired directly by the patient or the patient's family. In these situations, personal and home care aides are supervised and assigned tasks directly by the patient or the patient's family.

Aides may also work with individuals who are developmentally or intellectually disabled. These workers are often called direct support professionals and they may assist in implementing a behavior plan, teaching self-care skills and providing employment support, as well as providing a range of other personal assistance services.

Work environment. Work as an aide can be physically demanding. Aides must guard against back injury because they may have to move patients into and out of bed or help them to stand or walk. Aides also may face hazards from minor infections and exposure to communicable diseases, such as hepatitis, but can avoid infections by following proper procedures. Because mechanical lifting devices available in institutional settings are not as frequently available in patients' homes, home health aides must take extra care to avoid injuries resulting from overexertion when they assist patients. These workers experienced a larger than average number of work-related injuries or illnesses

Aides also perform tasks that some may consider unpleasant, such as emptying bedpans and changing soiled bed linens. The patients they care for may be disoriented, irritable, or uncooperative. Although their work can be emotionally demanding, many aides gain satisfaction from assisting those in need.

Most aides work with a number of different patients, each job lasting a few hours, days, or weeks. They often visit multiple patients on the same day. Surroundings differ by case. Some homes are neat and pleasant, whereas others are untidy and depressing. Some clients are pleasant and cooperative; others are angry, abusive, depressed, or otherwise difficult.

Home health aides and personal and home care aides generally work alone, with periodic visits from their supervisor. They receive detailed instructions explaining when to visit patients and what services to perform. Aides are responsible for getting to patients' homes, and they may spend a good portion of the work day traveling from one patient to another.

Many of these workers work part time and weekends or evenings to suit the needs of their clients.

Training, Other Qualifications, and Advancement

Home health aides must receive formal training and pass a competency test to work for certified home health or hospice agencies that receive reimbursement from Medicare or Medicaid. Personal and home care aides, however, face a wide range of requirements, which vary from state to state.

Education and training. Home health aides and personal and home care aides are generally not required to have a high school diploma. They usually are trained on the job by registered nurses, licensed practical nurses, experienced aides, or their supervisor. Aides are instructed on how to cook for a client, including on special diets. Furthermore, they may be trained in basic housekeeping tasks, such as making a bed and keeping the home sanitary and safe for the client. Generally, they are taught how to respond to an emergency, learning basic safety techniques. Employers also may train aides to conduct themselves in a professional and courteous manner while in a client's home. Some clients prefer that tasks are done a certain way and will teach the aide. A competency evaluation may be required to ensure that the aide can perform the required tasks.

Licensure. Home health aides who work for agencies that receive reimbursement from Medicare or Medicaid must receive a minimum level of training. They must complete both a training program consisting of a minimum of 75 hours and a competency evaluation or state certification program. Training includes information regarding personal hygiene, safe transfer techniques, reading and recording vital signs, infection control, and basic nutrition. Aides may take a competency exam to become certified without taking any of the training. At a minimum, 16 hours of supervised practical training are required before an aide has direct contact with a resident. These certification requirements represent the minimum, as outlined by the federal government. Some states may require additional hours of training to become certified.

Personal and home care aides are not required to be certified.

Other qualifications. Aides should have a desire to help people. They should be responsible, compassionate, patient, emotionally stable, and cheerful. In addition, aides should be tactful, honest, and discreet, because they work in private homes. Aides also must be in good health. A physical examination, including state-mandated tests for tuberculosis and other diseases, may be required. A criminal background check and a good driving record also may be required for employment.

Certification and advancement. The National Association for Home Care and Hospice (NAHC) offers national certification for aides. Certification is a voluntary demonstration that the individual has met industry standards. Certification requires the completion of 75 hours of training; observation and documentation of 17 skills for competency, assessed by a registered nurse; and the passing of a written exam developed by NAHC.

Advancement for home health aides and personal and home care aides is limited. In some agencies, workers start out performing homemaker duties, such as cleaning. With experience and training, they may take on more personal care duties. Some aides choose to receive additional training to become nursing aides, licensed practical nurses, or registered nurses. Some may start their own home care agency or work as a self-employed aide. Self-employed aides have no agency affiliation or supervision and accept clients, set fees, and arrange work schedules on their own.

Employment

Home health aides and personal and home care aides held about 1.7 million jobs in 2008. The majority of jobs were in home health-care services, individual and family services, residential care facilities, and private households.

Job Outlook

Excellent job opportunities are expected for this occupation because rapid employment growth and high replacement needs are projected to produce a large number of job openings.

Employment change. Employment of home health aides is projected to grow by 50 percent between 2008 and 2018, which is much faster than the average for all occupations. Employment of personal and home care aides is expected to grow by 46 percent from 2008 to 2018, which is much faster than the average for all occupations. For both occupations, the expected growth is due, in large part, to the projected rise in the number of elderly people, an age group that often has mounting health problems and that needs some assistance with daily activities. The elderly and other clients, such as the mentally disabled, increasingly rely on home care.

This trend reflects several developments. Inpatient care in hospitals and nursing homes can be extremely expensive, so more patients return to their homes from these facilities as quickly as possible in order to contain costs. Patients, who need assistance with everyday tasks and household chores rather than medical care, can reduce medical expenses by returning to their homes. Furthermore, most patients—particularly the elderly—prefer care in their homes rather than in nursing homes or other in-patient facilities. This develop-

Projections Data from the National Employment Matrix

Occupational title	SOC Code	Employment, 2008	Projected employment, 2018	Change, 2008–2018	
				Number	Percent
Home health aides and personal and home care aides........... —		1,738,800	2,575,600	836,700	48
Home health aides 31-1011		921,700	1,382,600	460,900	50
Personal and home care aides.............................. 39-9021		817,200	1,193,000	375,800	46

Data in this table are rounded.

ment is aided by the realization that treatment can be more effective in familiar surroundings.

Job prospects. In addition to job openings created by the increased demand for these workers, replacement needs are expected to lead to many openings. The relatively low skill requirements, low pay, and high emotional demands of the work result in high replacement needs. For these same reasons, many people are reluctant to seek jobs in the occupation. Therefore, persons who are interested in and suited for this work—particularly those with experience or training as personal care, home health, or nursing aides—should have excellent job prospects.

Earnings

Median hourly wages of wage-and-salary personal and home care aides were $9.22 in May 2008. The middle 50 percent earned between $7.81 and $10.98 an hour. The lowest 10 percent earned less than $6.84, and the highest 10 percent earned more than $12.33 an hour. Median hourly wages in the industries employing the largest numbers of personal and home care aides were as follows:

Individual and family services	$9.77
Employment services	9.76
Residential mental retardation, mental health and substance abuse facilities	9.70
Vocational rehabilitation services	9.58
Home health care services	7.94

Median hourly wages of home health aides were $9.84 in May 2008. The middle 50 percent earned between $8.52 and $11.69 an hour. The lowest 10 percent earned less than $7.65, and the highest 10 percent earned more than $13.93 an hour. Median hourly wages in the industries employing the largest numbers of home health aides in May 2008 were as follows:

Nursing care facilities	$10.20
Residential mental retardation, mental health and substance abuse facilities	10.02
Home health care services	9.70
Individual and family services	9.48
Community care facilities for the elderly	9.44

Aides receive slight pay increases with experience and added responsibility. Usually, they are paid only for the time worked in the home, not for travel time between jobs, and must pay for their travel costs from their earnings. Most employers hire only on-call hourly workers.

Related Occupations

Home health aides and personal and home care aides combine the duties of caregivers and social service workers. Workers in related occupations that involve personal contact to help others include child care workers; licensed practical and licensed vocational nurses; medical assistants; nursing and psychiatric aides; occupational therapist assistants and aides; physical therapist assistants and aides; radiation therapists; registered nurses; and social and human service assistants.

Sources of Additional Information

Information on licensing requirements for nursing and home health aides, as well as lists of state-approved nursing aide programs, are available from state departments of public health, departments of occupational licensing, boards of nursing, and home care associations.

For information about voluntary credentials for personal and home care aides, contact

▸ National Association for Home Care and Hospice, 228 Seventh St. SE, Washington, DC 20003. Internet: www.nahc.org

Hotel, Motel, and Resort Desk Clerks

(O*NET 43-4081.00)

Nature of the Work

Hotel, motel, and resort desk clerks are the first line of customer service for a lodging property. They register arriving guests, assign rooms, and answer guests' questions on hotel services and other matters. At other times, they check out guests and report problems with guest rooms or public areas to the housekeeping or maintenance staff. Night and weekend work is common and approximately 1 in 4 desk clerks works part time.

Training, Other Qualifications, and Advancement

Most hotel, motel, and resort desk clerks learn their job through short-term on-the-job training, which describes their job duties, familiarizes them with the hotel's facilities, and provides instruction on how to use the computerized reservation, room assignment, and billing systems. Postsecondary education is not required for this job, but some background or coursework in hospitality is helpful. Most importantly, employers look for people who are friendly and customer-service oriented, well groomed, and display maturity and good judgment.

Job Outlook

Current and Projected Employment

2008 Employment	230,200
2018 Employment	261,700
Employment Change	31,500
Growth Rate	14%

Employment change. Employment of hotel, motel, and resort desk clerks is expected to grow faster than the average. As developers open new hotels, jobs for hotel, motel, and resort desk clerks should become available. The recent trend toward smaller limited-service hotels, which are more efficient to operate and require less staff, however, will mean fewer desk clerks for each hotel. In addition, jobs will be created as consumers begin traveling again after the hiatus brought on by the recent economic downturn.

Job prospects. Workers in this occupation will likely face competition. During recessions, vacation and business travel declines, and hotels and motels need fewer desk clerks; however, newly opened hotels and the need to replace the many desk clerks who leave this occupation each year will offer some new opportunities.

Earnings

Median annual wages for hotel, motel, and resort desk clerks were $19,480 in May 2008.

For current wage data, visit the Occupational Employment Statistics program's Occupational Profile for hotel, motel, and resort desk clerks.

Related Occupations

Counter and rental clerks; customer service representatives; lodging managers; retail salespersons.

Sources of Additional Information

▸ American Hotel & Lodging Association, 1201 New York Ave. NW, Suite 600, Washington, DC 20005. Internet: www.ahla.com

Human Resources, Training, and Labor Relations Managers and Specialists

(O*NET 11-3041.00, 11-3042.00, 11-3049.00, 13-1071.00, 13-1071.01, 13-1071.02, 13-1072.00, 13-1073.00, and 13-1079.00)

Significant Points

■ The educational backgrounds of these workers vary considerably, reflecting the diversity of duties and levels of responsibility.

■ College graduates and those who have earned certification should have the best job and advancement opportunities.

■ Human resources occupations require strong interpersonal skills.

■ Much-faster-than-average growth is expected during the projection period.

Nature of the Work

Every organization wants to attract, motivate, and retain the most qualified employees and match them to jobs for which they are best suited. *Human resources, training, and labor relations managers and specialists* provide this connection. In the past, these workers performed the administrative function of an organization, such as handling employee benefits questions or recruiting, interviewing, and hiring new staff in accordance with policies established by top management. Today's human resources workers manage these tasks, but increasingly they consult with top executives regarding strategic planning. They have moved from behind-the-scenes staff work to leading the company in suggesting and changing policies.

In an effort to enhance morale and productivity, limit job turnover, and help organizations increase performance and improve results, these workers also help their companies effectively use employee skills, provide training and development opportunities to improve those skills, and increase employees' satisfaction with their jobs and working conditions. Although some jobs in the human resources field require only limited contact with people outside the human resources office, dealing with people is an important part of the job.

There are many types of human resources, training, and labor relations managers and specialists. In a small organization, a *human resources generalist* may handle all aspects of human resources work and thus require an extensive range of knowledge. The responsibilities of human resources generalists can vary widely, depending on their employer's needs.

In a large corporation, the *director of human resources* may supervise several departments, each headed by an experienced manager who most likely specializes in one human resources activity, such as employment and placement, compensation and benefits, training and development, or labor relations. The director may report to a top human resources executive.

Employment and placement. *Employment and placement managers* supervise the recruitment, hiring, and separation of employees. They also supervise employment, recruitment, and placement specialists, including employment interviewers. *Employment, recruitment, and placement specialists* recruit and place workers.

Recruitment specialists maintain contacts within the community and may travel considerably, often to job fairs and college campuses, to search for promising job applicants. Recruiters screen, interview, and occasionally test applicants. They also may check references and extend job offers. These workers must be thoroughly familiar with their organization, the work that is done, and the human resources policies of their company in order to discuss wages, working conditions, and advancement opportunities with prospective employees. They also must stay informed about equal employment opportunity (EEO) and affirmative action guidelines and laws, such as the Americans with Disabilities Act.

Employment interviewers—whose many job titles include *human resources consultants*, *human resources development specialists*, and *human resources coordinators*—help to match employers with qualified jobseekers. Similarly, *employer relations representatives*, who usually work in government agencies or college career centers, maintain working relationships with prospective employers and promote the use of public employment programs and services.

Compensation, benefits, and job analysis. *Compensation, benefits, and job analysis specialists* administer compensation programs for employers and may specialize in specific areas such as pensions or position classifications. For example, *job analysts*, occasionally called *position classifiers*, collect and examine detailed information about job duties in order to prepare job descriptions. These descriptions explain the duties, training, and skills that each job requires. Whenever a large organization introduces a new job or reviews existing jobs, it calls upon the expert knowledge of job analysts.

Occupational analysts research occupational classification systems and study the effects of industry and occupational trends on worker relationships. They may serve as technical liaisons between companies or departments, government, and labor unions.

Establishing and maintaining a firm's pay structure is the principal job of *compensation managers*. Assisted by compensation analysts or specialists, compensation managers devise ways to ensure fair and equitable pay rates. They may participate in or purchase salary surveys to see how their firm's pay compares with others, and they ensure that the firm's pay scale complies with changing laws and regulations. In addition, compensation managers often oversee the compensation side of their company's performance management system. They may design reward systems such as pay-for-performance plans, which might include setting merit pay guidelines and bonus or incentive pay criteria. Compensation managers also might administer executive compensation programs or determine commission rates and other incentives for corporate sales staffs.

Employee benefits managers and specialists administer a company's employee benefits program, most notably its health insurance and retirement plans. Expertise in designing, negotiating, and administering benefits programs continues to take on importance as employer-provided benefits account for a growing proportion of overall compensation costs and as benefit plans increase in number and complexity. For example, retirement benefits might include defined benefit pension plans; defined contribution plans, such as 401(k) or thrift savings plans; and profit-sharing or stock ownership plans. Health benefits might include medical, dental, and vision insurance and protection against catastrophic illness. Familiarity with health benefits is a top priority for employee benefits managers and specialists because of the rising cost of providing health-care benefits to employees and retirees. In addition to health insurance and retirement coverage, many firms offer employees life and accidental death and dismemberment insurance; disability insurance; and benefits designed to meet the needs of a changing workforce, such as parental leave, long-term nursing or home care insurance, wellness programs, and flexible benefits plans. Benefits managers must keep abreast of changing federal and state regulations and legislation that may affect employee benefits. Working with employee assistance plan managers or work-life coordinators, many benefits managers work to integrate the growing number of programs that deal with mental and physical health, such as employee assistance, obesity, and smoking cessation, into their health benefits programs.

Employee assistance plan managers, also called *employee welfare managers* or *work-life managers*, are responsible for a wide array of programs to enhance employee safety and wellness and improve work-life balance. These may include occupational safety and health standards and practices; health promotion and physical fitness; medical examinations; and minor health treatment, such as first aid, flexible work schedules, food service and recreation activities, carpooling and transportation programs such as transit subsidies, employee suggestion systems, child care and elder care, and counseling services. Child care and elder care are increasingly significant because of growth in the number of dual-income households and the older population. Counseling may help employees deal with emotional disorders; alcoholism; or marital, family, consumer, legal, and financial problems. Some employers offer career counseling and outplacement services. In some companies, certain programs, such as those dealing with physical security or information technology, may be coordinated in separate departments by other managers.

Training and development. *Training and development managers and specialists* create, procure, and conduct training and development programs for employees. Managers typically supervise specialists and make budget-impacting decisions in exchange for a reduced training portfolio. Increasingly, executives recognize that training offers a way of developing skills, enhancing productivity and quality of work, and building worker loyalty. Enhancing employee skills can increase individual and organizational performance and help to achieve business results. Increasingly, executives realize that developing the skills and knowledge of their workforce is a business imperative that can give them a competitive edge in recruiting and retaining high-quality employees and can lead to business growth.

Other factors involved in determining whether training is needed include the complexity of the work environment, the rapid pace of organizational and technological change, and the growing number of jobs in fields that constantly generate new knowledge and, thus, require new skills. In addition, advances in learning theory have provided insights into how people learn and how training can be organized most effectively.

Training managers oversee development of training programs, contracts, and budgets. They may perform needs assessments of the types of training needed, determine the best means of delivering training, and create the content. They may provide employee training in a classroom, computer laboratory, or onsite production facility or through a training film, Web video-on-demand, or self-paced or self-guided instructional guides. For live or in-person training, training managers ensure that teaching materials are prepared and the space appropriately set, training and instruction stimulate the class, and completion certificates are issued at the end of training. For computer-assisted or recorded training, trainers ensure that cameras, microphones, and other necessary technology platforms are functioning properly and that individual computers or other learning devices are configured for training purposes. They also have the responsibility for the entire learning process and its environment to ensure that the course meets its objectives and is measured and evaluated to understand how learning impacts performance.

Training specialists plan, organize, and direct a wide range of training activities. Trainers consult with training managers and employee supervisors to develop performance improvement measures, conduct orientation sessions, and arrange on-the-job training for new employees. They help employees maintain and improve their job skills and prepare for jobs requiring greater skill. They work with supervisors to improve their interpersonal skills and to deal effectively with employees. They may set up individualized training plans to strengthen employees' existing skills or teach new ones. Training specialists also may set up leadership or executive development programs for employees who aspire to move up in the organization. These programs are designed to develop or "groom" leaders to replace those leaving the organization and as part of a corporate succession plan. Trainers also lead programs to assist employees with job transitions as a result of mergers or consolidation, as well as retraining programs to develop new skills that may result from technological changes in the workplace. In government-supported job-training programs, training specialists serve as case managers and provide basic job skills to prepare participants to function in the labor force. They assess the training needs of clients and guide them through the most appropriate training. After training, clients may either be referred to employer relations representatives or receive job placement assistance.

Planning and program development is an essential part of the training specialist's job. In order to identify and assess training needs, trainers may confer with managers and supervisors or conduct surveys. They also evaluate training effectiveness to ensure that employees actually learn and that the training they receive helps the organization meet its strategic goals and achieve results.

Depending on the size, goals, and nature of the organization, trainers may differ considerably in their responsibilities and in the methods they use. Training methods also vary by whether the training predominantly is knowledge-based or skill-based or is sometimes a combination of the two. For example, much knowledge-based training is conducted in a classroom setting. Most skill training provides some combination of hands-on instruction, demonstration, and practice at doing something and usually is conducted on a shop floor, in a studio, or in a laboratory where trainees gain experience and confidence. Some on-the-job training methods could apply equally to knowledge or skill training, and formal apprenticeship training programs combine classroom training and work experience. Increasingly, training programs involve interactive Internet-based training modules that can be downloaded for either individual or group instruction, for dissemination to a geographically dispersed class, or to be coordinated with other multimedia programs. These technologies allow participants to take advantage of distance learning alternatives and to attend conferences and seminars through satellite or Internet communications hookups or use other computer-aided instructional technologies, such as those for the hearing-impaired or sight-impaired.

Employee relations. An organization's *director of industrial relations* forms labor policy, oversees industrial labor relations, negotiates collective bargaining agreements, and coordinates grievance procedures to handle complaints resulting from management disputes with employees. The director of industrial relations also advises and collaborates with the director of human resources, other managers, and members of their staffs because all aspects of human resources policy—such as wages, benefits, pensions, and work practices—may be involved in drawing up new or revised work rules that comply with a union contract.

Labor relations managers and their staffs implement industrial labor relations programs. Labor relations specialists prepare information for management to use during collective bargaining agreement negotiations, a process that requires the specialist to be familiar with economic and wage data and to have extensive knowledge of labor law and collective bargaining procedures. The labor relations staff interprets and administers the contract with respect to grievances, wages and salaries, employee welfare, health care, pensions, union and management practices, and other contractual stipulations. In the absence of a union, industrial relations personnel may work with employees individually or with employee association representatives.

Dispute resolution—attaining tacit or contractual agreements—has become increasingly significant as parties to a dispute attempt to avoid costly litigation, strikes, or other disruptions. Dispute resolution also has become more complex, involving employees, management, unions, other firms, and government agencies. Specialists involved in dispute resolution must be highly knowledgeable and experienced and often report to the director of industrial relations. *Mediators* advise and counsel labor and management to prevent and, when necessary, resolve disputes over labor agreements or other labor relations issues. *Arbitrators,* occasionally called umpires or referees, decide disputes that bind both labor and management to specific terms and conditions of labor contracts. Labor relations specialists who work for unions perform many of the same functions on behalf of the union and its members.

EEO officers, representatives, or *affirmative action coordinators* handle equal employment opportunity matters. They investigate and resolve EEO grievances, examine corporate practices for possible violations, and compile and submit EEO statistical reports.

Other emerging specialties in human resources include *international human resources managers*, who handle human resources issues related to a company's overseas operations; *human resources information system specialists*, who develop and apply computer programs to process human resources information, match jobseekers with job openings, and handle other human resources matters; and *total compensation* or *total rewards specialists*, who determine an appropriate mix of compensation, benefits, and incentives.

Work environment. Human resources personnel usually work in clean, pleasant, and comfortable office settings. Arbitrators and mediators, many of whom work independently, may work out of home offices. Although most human resources, training, and labor relations managers and specialists work in the office, some travel extensively. For example, recruiters regularly attend professional meetings, participate in job fairs, and visit college campuses to interview prospective employees. Arbitrators and mediators often must travel to the site chosen for negotiations. Trainers and other specialists may travel to regional, satellite, or international offices of a company to meet with employees who work outside of the main corporate office.

Many human resources, training, and labor relations managers and specialists work a standard 40-hour week. However, longer hours might be necessary for some workers—for example, labor relations managers and specialists, arbitrators, and mediators—when contract agreements or dispute resolutions are being negotiated.

Training, Other Qualifications, and Advancement

The educational backgrounds of human resources, training, and labor relations managers and specialists vary considerably, reflecting the diversity of duties and levels of responsibility. In filling entry-level jobs, many employers seek college graduates who have majored in human resources, human resources administration, or industrial and labor relations. Other employers look for college graduates with a technical or business background or a well-rounded liberal arts education.

Education and training. Although a bachelor's degree is a typical path of entry into these occupations, many colleges and universities do not offer degree programs in personnel administration, human resources, or labor relations until the graduate degree level. However, many offer individual courses in these subjects at the undergraduate level in addition to concentrations in human resources administration or human resources management, training and development, organizational development, and compensation and benefits.

Because an interdisciplinary background is appropriate in this field, a combination of courses in the social sciences, business administration, and behavioral sciences is useful. Some jobs may require more technical or specialized backgrounds in engineering, science, finance, or law. Most prospective human resources specialists should take courses in principles of management, organizational structure, and industrial psychology; however, courses in accounting or finance are becoming increasingly important. Courses in labor law, collective bargaining, labor economics, and labor history also provide a valuable background for the prospective labor relations specialist. As in many other fields, knowledge of computers and information systems is useful.

An advanced degree is increasingly important for some jobs. Many labor relations jobs require graduate study in industrial or labor relations. A strong background in industrial relations and law is highly desirable for contract negotiators, mediators, and arbitrators; in fact, many people in these specialties have law degrees. A master's degree in human resources, labor relations, or in business administration with a concentration in human resources management is highly recommended for those seeking general and top management positions.

The duties given to entry-level workers will vary, depending on whether the new workers have a degree in human resource management, have completed an internship, or have some other type of human resources-related experience. Entry-level employees commonly learn by performing administrative duties—helping to enter data into computer systems, compiling employee handbooks, researching information for a supervisor, or answering phone calls and handling routine questions. Entry-level workers often enter on-the-job training programs in which they learn how to classify jobs, interview applicants, or administer employee benefits; they then are assigned to specific areas in the human resources department to gain experience. Later, they may advance to supervisory positions, overseeing a major element of the human resources program—compensation or training, for example.

Other qualifications. Experience is an asset for many specialties in the human resources area and is essential for advancement to senior-level positions, including managers, arbitrators, and mediators. Many employers prefer entry-level workers who have gained some experience through an internship or work-study program while in school. Employees in human resources administration and human resources development need the ability to work well with individuals and a commitment to organizational goals. This field demands skills that people may have developed elsewhere—teaching, supervising, and volunteering, among others. Human resources work also offers clerical workers opportunities to advance to more responsible or professional positions. Some positions occasionally are filled by experienced individuals from other backgrounds, including business, government, education, social services administration, and the military.

The human resources field demands a range of personal qualities and skills. Human resources, training, and labor relations managers and specialists must speak and write effectively. Ever-changing technologies and the growing complexities inherent to the many services human resources personnel provide require that they be knowledgeable about computer systems, storage and retrieval software, and how to use a wide array of digital communications devices.

The growing diversity of the workforce requires that human resources managers and specialists work with or supervise people of various ages, cultural backgrounds, levels of education, and experience. Ability to speak a foreign language is an asset, especially if working in an industry with a large immigrant workforce or for a company with many overseas operations. Human resources employees must be able to cope with conflicting points of view; function under pressure; and demonstrate discretion, integrity, fairmindedness, and a persuasive, genial personality. Because much of the information collected by these employees is confidential, they must also show the character and responsibility of dealing with sensitive employee information.

Certification and advancement. Most professional associations that specialize in human resources offer classes intended to enhance the skills of their members. Some organizations offer certification programs, which are signs of competence and credibility and can enhance advancement opportunities. For example, the International Foundation of Employee Benefit Plans confers a designation in three distinct areas of specialization—group benefit, retirement, and compensation—to persons who complete a series of college-level courses and pass exams. Candidates can earn a designation in each of the specialty tracks and, simultaneously, receive credit toward becoming a Certified Employee Benefits Specialist (CEBS). The American Society for Training and Development (ASTD) Certification Institute offers professional certification in the learning and performance field. Addressing nine areas of expertise, certification requires passing a knowledge-based exam and successful work experience. In addition, ASTD offers 16 short-term certificate and workshop programs covering a broad range of professional training and development topics. The Society for Human Resource Management offers two levels of certification, including the Professional in Human Resources (PHR) and the Senior Professional in Human Resources (SPHR). Additionally, the organization offers the Global Professional in Human Resources certification for those with international and cross-border responsibilities and the California Certification in Human Resources for those who plan to work in that state and become familiar with California's labor and human resources laws. All designations require experience and a passing score on a comprehensive exam. The WorldatWork Society of Certified Professionals offers four distinct designations in the areas of compensation, benefits, work-life, and global remuneration that comprise the total rewards management practice. Candidates obtain the designations of Certified Compensation Professional (CCP), Certified Benefits Professional (CBP), Global Remuneration Professional (GRP), and Work-Life Certified Professional (WLCP). Certification is achieved after passing a series of knowledge-based exams within each designation. Additionally, WorldatWork offers online and classroom education covering a broad range of total rewards topics.

Exceptional human resources workers may be promoted to director of human resources or industrial relations, which can eventually lead to a top managerial or executive position. Others may join a consulting or outsourcing firm or open their own business. A Ph.D. is an asset for teaching, writing, or consulting work.

Employment

Human resources, training, and labor relations managers and specialists held about 904,900 jobs in 2008. The following tabulation shows the distribution of jobs by occupational specialty:

Training and development specialists 216,600
Employment, recruitment, and placement
    specialists..207,900
Compensation, benefits, and job analysis
    specialists..121,900
Compensation and benefits managers.................. 40,500
Training and development managers 30,400
Human resources, training, and labor relations
    specialists, all other......................................224,600
Human resources managers, all other 63,100

Human resources, training, and labor relations managers and specialists were employed in virtually every industry. About 13 percent of human resources, training, and labor relations managers and specialists were employed in administrative and support services, 11 percent in professional, scientific, and technical services, 10 percent in health care and social assistance, and 9 percent in finance and insurance firms. About 12,900 managers and specialists were self-employed, working as consultants to public and private employers.

Job Outlook

Employment is expected to grow much faster than the average for all occupations. College graduates and those who have earned certification should have the best job opportunities.

Employment change. Overall employment is projected to grow by 22 percent between 2008 and 2018, much faster than the average for all occupations. Legislation and court rulings revising standards in various areas—occupational safety and health, equal employment opportunity, wages, health care, retirement plans, and family leave, among others—will increase demand for human resources, training, and labor relations experts. Rising health-care costs and a growing number of health-care coverage options should continue to spur demand for specialists to develop creative compensation and benefits packages that companies can offer prospective employees.

Employment of labor relations staff, including arbitrators and mediators, should grow as companies attempt to resolve potentially costly labor-management disputes out of court. Additional job growth may stem from increasing demand for specialists in international human resources management and human resources information systems.

Job growth could be limited by the widespread use of computerized human resources information systems that make workers more productive. Like other workers, employment of human resources, training, and labor relations managers and specialists, particularly in larger companies, may be adversely affected by corporate downsizing, restructuring, and mergers; however, as companies once again expand operations, additional workers may be needed to manage company growth.

Demand may be particularly strong for certain specialists. For example, employers are expected to devote greater resources to job-specific training programs in response to the increasing complexity of many jobs and technological advances that can leave employees with obsolete skills. Additionally, as highly trained and skilled baby boomers retire, there should be strong demand for training and development specialists to impart needed skills to their replacements. In addition, increasing efforts throughout industry to recruit and retain quality employees should create many jobs for employment, recruitment, and placement specialists.

Among industries, firms involved in management, consulting, and employment services should offer many job opportunities as businesses increasingly contract out human resources functions or hire human resources specialists on a temporary basis to deal with increasing costs and complexity of training and development programs. Demand for specialists also should increase in outsourcing firms that develop and administer complex employee benefits and compensation packages for other organizations.

Job prospects. College graduates and those who have earned certification should have the best job opportunities, particularly graduates with a bachelor's degree in human resources, human resources administration, or industrial and labor relations. Those with a techni-

Projections Data from the National Employment Matrix

Occupational title	SOC Code	Employment, 2008	Projected employment, 2018	Change, 2008–2018	
				Number	Percent
Human resources, training, and labor relations managers and specialists.. —		904,900	1,102,300	197,400	22
Human resources managers............................ 11-3040		133,900	146,800	12,900	10
Compensation and benefits managers....................... 11-3041		40,500	43,900	3,400	9
Training and development managers....................... 11-3042		30,400	34,000	3,600	12
All other human resources managers 11-3049		63,100	68,900	5,800	9
Human resources, training, and labor relations specialists.. 13-1070		770,900	955,500	184,500	24
Employment, recruitment, and placement specialists ... 13-1071		207,900	265,900	58,000	28
Compensation, benefits, and job analysis specialists.... 13-1072		121,900	150,600	28,700	24
Training and development specialists 13-1073		216,600	267,100	50,500	23
Human resources, training, and labor relations specialists, all other 13-1079		224,600	271,900	47,200	21

NOTE: Data in this table are rounded.

cal or business background or a well-rounded liberal arts education also should find opportunities. Demand for human resources, training, and labor relations managers and specialists depends on general economic conditions and the business cycle as well as staffing needs of the companies in which they work. A rapidly expanding business is likely to hire additional human resources workers—either as permanent employees or consultants—while businesses that have consolidated operations or merged with another company may require fewer of these workers. Also, as human resources management becomes increasingly important to the success of an organization, some small and medium-size businesses that do not have separate human resources departments may assign various human resources responsibilities to some employees in addition to their usual responsibilities; others may contract with consulting firms to establish formal procedures and train current employees to administer programs on a long-term basis.

In addition to new human resources management and specialist jobs created over the 2008–2018 projection period, many job openings will arise from the need to replace workers who transfer to other occupations, retire, or leave the labor force for other reasons.

Earnings

Annual salary rates for human resources workers vary according to occupation, level of experience, training, location, and firm size.

Median annual wages of compensation and benefits managers were $86,500 in May 2008. The middle 50 percent earned between $64,930 and $113,480. The lowest 10 percent earned less than $49,350, and the highest 10 percent earned more than $147,050. Median annual wages in the industries employing the largest numbers of compensation and benefits managers were the following:

```
Computer systems design and related services ......$97,630
Insurance carriers............................................. 94,340
Management of companies and enterprises ........... 94,230
General medical and surgical hospitals ................. 86,060
Depository credit intermediation ......................... 84,980
```

Median annual wages of training and development managers were $87,700 in May 2008. The middle 50 percent earned between $64,770 and $115,570. The lowest 10 percent earned less than $48,280, and the highest 10 percent earned more than $149,050. Median annual wages in the industries employing the largest numbers of training and development managers were the following:

```
Management of companies and enterprises .........$93,140
Insurance carriers............................................. 92,210
General medical and surgical hospitals ................. 86,820
Local government.............................................. 70,430
Employment services......................................... 69,170
```

Median annual wages of human resources managers, all other were $96,130 in May 2008. The middle 50 percent earned between $73,480 and $126,050. The lowest 10 percent earned less than $56,770, and the highest 10 percent earned more than $163,220. Median annual wages in the industries employing the largest numbers of human resources managers, all other were the following:

```
Management of companies and enterprises ....... $107,280
General medical and surgical hospitals ................. 91,580
Local government.............................................. 89,240
```

```
Colleges, universities, and professional schools ..... 86,920
State government.............................................. 76,570
```

Median annual wages of employment, recruitment, and placement specialists were $45,470 in May 2008. The middle 50 percent earned between $35,020 and $63,110. The lowest 10 percent earned less than $28,030, and the highest 10 percent earned more than $85,760. Median annual wages in the industries employing the largest numbers of employment, recruitment, and placement specialists were the following:

```
Management, scientific, and technical
    consulting services........................................$56,110
Computer systems design and related services ....... 55,600
Management of companies and enterprises ........... 51,320
Local government.............................................. 42,950
Employment services......................................... 42,670
State government.............................................. 38,970
```

Median annual wages of compensation, benefits, and job analysis specialists were $53,860 in May 2008. The middle 50 percent earned between $42,050 and $67,730. The lowest 10 percent earned less than $34,080, and the highest 10 percent earned more than $84,310. Median annual wages in the industries employing the largest numbers of compensation, benefits, and job analysis specialists were the following:

```
Management, scientific, and technical
    consulting services........................................$59,810
Local government.............................................. 56,930
Management of companies and enterprises ........... 54,930
Agencies, brokerages, and other insurance-
    related activities............................................ 53,490
Insurance carriers............................................. 51,890
State government.............................................. 43,880
```

Median annual wages of training and development specialists were $51,450 in May 2008. The middle 50 percent earned between $38,550 and $67,450. The lowest 10 percent earned less than $29,470, and the highest 10 percent earned more than $85,160. Median annual wages in the industries employing the largest numbers of training and development specialists were the following:

```
Computer systems design and related services ......$61,110
General medical and surgical hospitals ................. 56,540
Insurance carriers............................................. 55,190
Management of companies and enterprises ........... 54,800
Local government.............................................. 52,080
State government.............................................. 48,480
```

According to a July 2009 salary survey conducted by the National Association of Colleges and Employers, bachelor's degree candidates majoring in human resources, including labor and industrial relations, received starting offers averaging $45,170 a year.

Related Occupations

Human resources occupations require strong interpersonal skills. Other occupations that demand these skills include counselors, education administrators, lawyers, psychologists, public relations specialists, social and human service assistants, and social workers.

Sources of Additional Information

For information about human resource management careers and certification, contact

▸ Society for Human Resource Management, 1800 Duke St., Alexandria, VA 22314. Internet: www.shrm.org

For information about careers in employee training and development and certification, contact

▸ American Society for Training and Development, 1640 King St., Box 1443, Alexandria, VA 22313-2043. Internet: www.astd.org

For information about careers and certification in employee compensation and benefits, contact

▸ International Foundation of Employee Benefit Plans, 18700 W. Bluemound Rd., Brookfield, WI 53045. Internet: www.ifebp.org

▸ WorldatWork, 14040 N. Northsight Blvd., Scottsdale, AZ 85260. Internet: www.worldatwork.org

Instructional Coordinators

(O*NET 25-9031.00 and 25-9031.01)

Significant Points

■ Many instructional coordinators have experience as teachers or education administrators.

■ A master's degree is required for positions in public schools and preferred for jobs in other settings.

■ Employment is projected to grow much faster than average, reflecting the need to meet new educational standards, train teachers, and develop new materials.

■ Favorable job prospects are expected.

Nature of the Work

Instructional coordinators—also known as *curriculum specialists, personnel development specialists, instructional coaches,* or *directors of instructional material*—play a large role in improving the quality of education in the classroom. They develop curricula, select textbooks and other materials, train teachers, and assess educational programs for quality and adherence to regulations and standards. They also assist in implementing new technology in the classroom. At the primary and secondary school levels, instructional coordinators often specialize in a specific subject, such as reading, language arts, mathematics, or science.

Instructional coordinators evaluate how well a school or training program's curriculum, or plan of study, meets students' needs. Based on their research and observations of instructional practice, they recommend improvements. They research teaching methods and techniques and develop procedures to ensure that instructors are implementing the curriculum successfully and meeting program goals. To aid in their evaluation, they may meet with members of educational committees and advisory groups to explore how curriculum materials relate to occupations and meet students' needs. Coordinators also may develop questionnaires and interview school staff about the curriculum.

Some instructional coordinators review textbooks, software, and other educational materials to make recommendations. They monitor the ways in which teachers use materials in the classroom and supervise workers who catalogue, distribute, and maintain a school's educational materials and equipment.

Some instructional coordinators find ways to use technology to enhance student learning and monitor the introduction of new technology into a school's curriculum. In addition, instructional coordinators might recommend educational software, such as interactive books and exercises designed to enhance student literacy and develop math skills. Instructional coordinators may invite experts to help integrate technological materials into the curriculum.

Besides developing curriculum and instructional materials, many of these workers plan and provide onsite education for teachers and administrators. Instructional coordinators mentor new teachers and train experienced ones in the latest instructional methods. This role becomes especially important when a school district introduces new content, programs, or a different organizational structure. For example, when a state or school district introduces standards or tests that students must pass, instructional coordinators often advise teachers on the content of those standards and provide instruction on how to implement them in the classroom.

Work environment. Many instructional coordinators work long hours. They often work year round. Some spend much of their time traveling between schools and meeting with teachers and administrators. The opportunity to shape and improve instructional curricula and work in an academic environment can be satisfying. However, some instructional coordinators find the work stressful because they are continually accountable to school administrators.

Training, Other Qualifications, and Advancement

The minimum educational requirement for most instructional coordinator positions in public schools is a master's degree or higher—usually in education—plus a state teacher or administrator license. A master's degree also is preferred for positions in other settings.

Education and training. Instructional coordinators should have training in curriculum development and instruction or in the specific field for which they are responsible, such as mathematics or history. Courses in research design teach how to create and implement research studies to determine the effectiveness of a given method of instruction or curriculum and how to measure and improve student performance.

Instructional coordinators are usually required to take continuing education courses to keep their skills current. Topics may include teacher evaluation techniques, curriculum training, new teacher orientation, consulting and teacher support, and observation and analysis of teaching.

Licensure. Instructional coordinators must be licensed to work in public schools. Some states require a teaching license, whereas others require an education administrator license.

Other qualifications. Instructional coordinators must have a good understanding of how to teach specific groups of students and expertise in developing educational materials. As a result, many people become instructional coordinators after working for several

Projections Data from the National Employment Matrix

Occupational title	SOC Code	Employment, 2008	Projected employment, 2018	Change, 2008–2018	
				Number	Percent
Instructional coordinators..	25-9031	133,900	165,000	31,100	23

NOTE: Data in this table are rounded.

years as teachers. Also beneficial is work experience in an education administrator position, such as a principal or assistant principal, or in another advisory role, such as a master teacher, department chair or lead teacher.

Instructional coordinators must be able to make sound decisions about curriculum options and to organize and coordinate work efficiently. They should have strong interpersonal and communication skills. Familiarity with computer technology also is important for instructional coordinators, who are increasingly involved in gathering technical information for students and teachers.

Advancement. Depending on experience and educational attainment, instructional coordinators may advance to higher administrative positions in a school system or to management or executive positions in private industry.

Employment

Instructional coordinators held about 133,900 jobs in 2008. About 70 percent worked in public or private educational institutions. Other employing industries included state and local government, individual and family services, and child day care services.

Job Outlook

Much-faster-than-average job growth is projected. Job opportunities should be favorable, particularly for those with experience in math and reading curriculum development.

Employment change. The number of instructional coordinators is expected to grow by 23 percent over the 2008–2018 decade, which is much faster than the average for all occupations. These workers will be instrumental in developing new curricula to meet the demands of a changing society and in training teachers. Although budget constraints may limit employment growth to some extent, a continuing emphasis on improving the quality of education should result in an increasing demand for these workers. The emphasis on accountability also should increase at all levels of government and cause more schools to focus on improving standards of educational quality and student performance. Growing numbers of coordinators will be needed to incorporate the new standards into existing curricula and ensure that teachers and administrators are informed of changes.

Additional job growth for instructional coordinators will stem from an increasing emphasis on lifelong learning and on programs for students with special needs, including those for whom English is a second language. These students often require more educational resources and consolidated planning and management within the educational system.

Job prospects. Favorable job prospects are expected. Opportunities should be best for those who specialize in subjects targeted for

improvement by the No Child Left Behind Act—reading, math, and science. There also will be a need for more instructional coordinators to show teachers how to use technology in the classroom.

Earnings

Median annual wages of instructional coordinators in May 2008 were $56,880. The middle 50 percent earned between $42,070 and $75,000. The lowest 10 percent earned less than $31,800, and the highest 10 percent earned more than $93,250.

Related Occupations

Instructional coordinators are professionals involved in education, training, and development. Occupations with similar characteristics include counselors; education administrators; human resources, training, and labor relations managers and specialists; teachers—kindergarten, elementary, middle, and secondary; teachers—postsecondary; teachers—preschool, except special education; and teachers—special education.

Sources of Additional Information

Information on requirements and job opportunities for instructional coordinators is available from local school systems and state departments of education.

Insurance Sales Agents

(O*NET 41-3021.00)

Significant Points

- In addition to offering insurance policies, agents increasingly sell mutual funds, annuities, and securities and offer comprehensive financial planning services, including retirement and estate planning services, some designed specifically for the elderly.

- Agents must obtain a license in the states where they sell.

- Job opportunities should be best for college graduates who have sales ability, excellent interpersonal skills, and expertise in a wide range of insurance and financial services.

Nature of the Work

Most people have their first contact with an insurance company through an insurance sales agent. These workers help individuals, families, and businesses select insurance policies that provide the best protection for their lives, health, and property.

Insurance sales agents, commonly referred to as "producers" in the insurance industry, sell one or more types of insurance, such as property and casualty, life, health, disability, and long-term care. Property and casualty insurance agents sell policies that protect individuals and businesses from financial loss resulting from automobile accidents, fire, theft, storms, and other events that can damage property. For businesses, property and casualty insurance can also cover injured workers' compensation, product liability claims, or medical malpractice claims.

Life insurance agents specialize in selling policies that pay beneficiaries when a policyholder dies. Depending on the policyholder's circumstances, a cash-value policy can be designed to provide retirement income, funds for the education of children, and other benefits, as well. Life insurance agents also sell annuities that promise a retirement income. Health insurance agents sell health insurance policies that cover the costs of medical care and loss of income due to illness or injury. They also may sell dental insurance and short-term and long-term-disability insurance policies. Agents may specialize in any one of these products, or function as generalists, providing multiple products to a single customer.

An increasing number of insurance sales agents offer their clients advice on how to minimize risk as well as comprehensive financial planning services, especially to those approaching retirement. These services include retirement planning, estate planning, and assistance in setting up pension plans for businesses. As a result, many insurance agents are involved in "cross-selling" or "total account development." Besides offering insurance, these agents may become licensed to sell mutual funds, variable annuities, and other securities. This practice is most common with life insurance agents who already sell annuities, but many property and casualty agents also sell financial products.

Insurance sales agents also prepare reports, maintain records, and seek out new clients. In the event that policy holders experience a loss, agents help them settle their insurance claims. Insurance sales agents working exclusively for one insurance company are referred to as *captive agents*. These agents typically have a contractual agreement with the carrier, and are usually an employee of the carrier. Independent insurance agents, or *brokers*, are mostly facilitators who represent several companies. They match insurance policies for their clients with the company that offers the best rate and coverage.

Technology—specifically, the Internet—has greatly affected the insurance business, making the tasks of obtaining price quotes and processing applications and service requests faster and easier. The Internet has made it easier for agents to take on more clients and to be better informed about new products. It has also altered the relationship between agent and client. Agents formerly used to devote much of their time to marketing and selling products to new clients. Now, clients are increasingly obtaining insurance quotes from a company's Web site and then contacting the company directly to purchase policies. This interaction gives the client a more active role in selecting their policy, while reducing the amount of time agents spend seeking new clients. Insurance sales agents also obtain many new accounts through referrals, so it is important that they maintain regular contact with their clients to ensure that the client's financial needs are being met. Developing a satisfied clientele that will recommend an agent's services to other potential customers is a key to success for agents.

Increasing competition in the insurance industry has spurred carriers to find new ways to keep their clients satisfied. One solution is hiring customer service representatives who are accessible 24 hours a day, 7 days a week to handle routine tasks such as answering questions, making changes in policies, processing claims, and selling more products to clients. The opportunity to cross-sell new products to clients will help an agent's business grow. The use of customer service representatives also allows agents to concentrate their efforts on seeking out new clients and maintaining relationships with old ones.

Work environment. Most insurance sales agents work in offices. Since some agencies are small, agents may work alone or with only a few others. Some independent agents, or brokers, however, may spend much of their time traveling to meet with clients, close sales, or investigate claims. Agents usually determine their own hours of work and often schedule evening and weekend appointments for the convenience of clients. Some sales agents meet with clients during business hours and then spend evenings doing paperwork and preparing presentations to prospective clients. Although most agents work a 40-hour week, some may work much longer.

Training, Other Qualifications, and Advancement

Every sales agent involved in the solicitation, selling, or negotiation of insurance must have a state-issued license. Licensure requirements vary by state but typically require some insurance-related coursework and the passing of several exams. Although some agents are hired right out of college, many are hired by insurance companies as customer service representatives and are later promoted to sales agent.

Education and training. For insurance sales agent jobs, many companies and independent agencies prefer to hire college graduates—especially those who have majored in business, finance, or economics. High school graduates may be hired if they have proven sales ability or have been successful in other types of work.

College training can help agents grasp the technical aspects of insurance policies as well as the fundamentals of the insurance industry. Many colleges and universities offer courses in insurance, and a few schools offer a bachelor's degree in the field. College courses in finance, mathematics, accounting, economics, business law, marketing, and business administration enable insurance sales agents to understand how social and economic conditions relate to the insurance industry. Courses in psychology, sociology, and public speaking can prove useful in improving sales techniques. In addition, familiarity with popular software packages has become very important because computers provide instantaneous information on a wide variety of financial products and greatly improve an agent's efficiency.

Agents learn many of their job duties on the job from other agents. Many employers have their new agents shadow an experienced agent for a period of time. This allows the agent to learn how to conduct their business, how the agency interacts with clients, and how to write policies.

Employers also are placing greater emphasis on continuing professional education as the diversity of financial products sold by insurance agents increases. It is important for insurance agents to keep up to date on issues concerning clients. Changes in tax laws, government benefits programs, and other state and federal regulations can affect the insurance needs of clients and the way in which agents conduct business. Agents can enhance their selling skills and broaden their knowledge of insurance and other financial services by taking courses at colleges and universities and by attending institutes, conferences, and seminars sponsored by insurance organizations.

Licensure. Insurance sales agents must obtain a license in the states where they plan to work. Separate licenses are required for agents to sell life and health insurance and property and casualty insurance. In most states, licenses are issued only to applicants who complete specified prelicensing courses and who pass state examinations covering insurance fundamentals and state insurance laws. Most state licensing authorities also have mandatory continuing education requirements every 2 years, focusing on insurance laws, consumer protection, ethics, and the technical details of various insurance policies.

As the demand for financial products and financial planning increases, many insurance agents choose to gain the proper licensing and certification to sell securities and other financial products. Doing so, however, requires substantial study and passing an additional examination—either the Series 6 or Series 7 licensing exam, both of which are administered by the National Association of Securities Dealers (NASD). The Series 6 exam is for individuals who wish to sell only mutual funds and variable annuities, whereas the Series 7 exam is the main NASD series license that qualifies agents as general securities sales representatives.

Other qualifications. Previous experience in sales or insurance jobs can be very useful in becoming an insurance sales agent. In selling commercial insurance, technical experience in a particular field can help sell policies to those in the same profession. As a result, these agents tend to be older than entrants in many other occupations.

Insurance sales agents should be flexible, enthusiastic, confident, disciplined, hard working, and willing to solve problems. They should communicate effectively and inspire customer confidence. Because they usually work without supervision, sales agents must have good time-management skills and the initiative to locate new clients.

Certification and advancement. A number of organizations offer professional designation programs that certify an agent's expertise in specialties such as life, health, and property and casualty insurance, as well as financial consulting. For example, The National Alliance for Insurance Education and Research offers a wide variety of courses in health, life and property, and casualty insurance for independent insurance agents. Although voluntary, such programs assure clients and employers that an agent has a thorough understanding of the relevant specialty. Agents who complete certification are usually required to fulfill a specified number of hours of continuing education to retain their designation, as determined by the Alliance.

In the area of financial planning, many agents find it worthwhile to demonstrate competency by earning the certified financial planner or chartered financial consultant designation. The Certified Financial Planner credential, issued by the Certified Financial Planner Board of Standards, requires relevant experience, completion of education requirements, passing a comprehensive examination, and adherence to an enforceable code of ethics. The exam tests the candidate's knowledge of the financial planning process, insurance and risk management, employee benefits planning, taxes and retirement planning, and investment and estate planning.

The Chartered Financial Consultant (ChFC) and the Chartered Life Underwriter (CLU) designations, issued by the American College in Bryn Mawr, Pennsylvania, typically require professional experience and the completion of an eight-course program of study. For those new to the industry, however, the American College offers the Life Underwriter Training Council Fellow (FUTCF), an introductory course that teaches basic insurance concepts. Many property and casualty insurance agents obtain the Chartered Property Casualty Underwriter (CPCU) designation, offered by the American Institute for Chartered Property Casualty Underwriter. The majority of professional designations in insurance have continuing education requirements.

An insurance sales agent who shows ability and leadership may become a sales manager in a local office. A few advance to managerial or executive positions. However, many who have established a client base prefer to remain in sales work. Some—particularly in the property and casualty field—launch their own independent agencies or brokerage firms.

Employment

Insurance sales agents held about 434,800 jobs in 2008. About 51 percent of insurance sales agents work for insurance agencies and brokerages. About 21 percent work directly for insurance carriers. Although most insurance agents specialize in life and health insurance or property and casualty insurance, a growing number of "multiline" agents sell all lines of insurance. A small number of agents work for banks and securities brokerages as a result of the increasing integration of the finance and insurance industries. Approximately 22 percent of insurance sales agents are self-employed.

The majority of insurance sales agents are employed in local offices or independent agencies, but some work in the headquarters of insurance companies.

Job Outlook

Employment is expected to grow about as fast as average for all occupations. Opportunities will be best for college graduates who have sales ability, excellent interpersonal skills, and expertise in a wide range of insurance and financial services.

Employment change. Employment of insurance sales agents is expected to increase by 12 percent over the 2008–2018 period, which is about as fast as average for all occupations. Future demand for insurance sales agents depends largely on the variety of financial products and volume of sales. Sales of health insurance, long-term-care insurance, and other comprehensive financial planning services designed specifically for the elderly are expected to rise sharply as the population ages. In addition, a growing population will increase demand for insurance for automobiles, homes, and high-priced valuables and equipment. As new businesses emerge and existing firms expand their insurance coverage, sales of commercial insurance

Projections Data from the National Employment Matrix

Occupational title	SOC Code	Employment, 2008	Projected employment, 2018	Change, 2008–2018	
				Number	Percent
Insurance sales agents 41-3021		434,800	486,400	51,600	12

NOTE: Data in this table are rounded.

also should increase, including coverage such as product liability, workers' compensation, employee benefits, and pollution liability insurance.

Employment of agents will not keep up with the rising level of insurance sales, however. Many insurance carriers are trying to contain costs and are shedding their captive agents—those agents working directly for insurance carriers. Instead carriers are relying more on independent agents or brokers.

It is unlikely that the Internet will threaten the jobs of these agents. The automation of policy and claims processing allows insurance agents to take on more clients. Most clients value their relationship with their agent and prefer personal service, discussing their policies directly with their agents, rather than through a computer. Insurance law and investments are becoming more complex, and many people and businesses lack the time and expertise to buy insurance without the advice of an agent.

Job prospects. College graduates who have sales ability, excellent interpersonal skills, and expertise in a wide range of insurance and financial services should enjoy the best prospects. Multilingual agents should have an advantage, because they can serve a wider range of customers. Additionally, insurance language tends to be quite technical, so agents who have a firm understanding of relevant technical and legal terms will also be desirable to employers. Many beginning agents fail to earn enough from commissions to meet their income goals and eventually transfer to other careers. Many job openings are likely to result from the need to replace agents who leave the occupation or retire.

Agents may face some competition from traditional securities brokers and bankers, as they also sell insurance policies. Insurance sales agents will need to expand the products and services they offer as consolidation increases among insurance companies, banks, and brokerage firms and as demands increase from clients for more comprehensive financial planning.

Independent agents who incorporate new technology into their existing businesses will remain competitive. Agents who use the Internet to market their products will reach a broader client base and expand their business. Agents who offer better customer service also will remain competitive.

Earnings

The median annual wages of wage and salary insurance sales agents were $45,430 in May 2008. The middle 50 percent earned between $33,070 and $68,730. The lowest 10 percent had earnings of $26,120 or less, while the highest 10 percent earned more than $113,930. Median annual wages in May 2008 in the two industries employing the largest number of insurance sales agents were $48,150 for insurance carriers, and $44,450 for agencies, brokerages, and other insurance related activities.

Many independent agents are paid by commission only, whereas sales workers who are employees of an agency or an insurance carrier may be paid in one of three ways: salary only, salary plus commission, or salary plus bonus. In general, commissions are the most common form of compensation, especially for experienced agents. The amount of the commission depends on the type and amount of insurance sold and on whether the transaction is a new policy or a renewal. Bonuses usually are awarded when agents meet their sales goals or when an agency meets its profit goals. Some agents involved with financial planning receive a fee for their services, rather than a commission.

Company-paid benefits to insurance sales agents usually include continuing education, training to qualify for licensing, group insurance plans, office space, and clerical support services. Some companies also may pay for automobile and transportation expenses, attendance at conventions and meetings, promotion and marketing expenses, and retirement plans. Independent agents working for insurance agencies receive fewer benefits, but their commissions may be higher to help them pay for marketing and other expenses.

Related Occupations

Other workers who provide or sell financial products or services include financial analysts; financial managers; personal financial advisors; real estate brokers and sales agents; and securities, commodities, and financial services sales agents.

Other sales workers include advertising sales agents; customer service representatives; and sales representatives, wholesale and manufacturing.

Other occupations in the insurance industry include claims adjusters, appraisers, examiners, and investigators; and insurance underwriters.

Sources of Additional Information

Occupational information about insurance sales agents is available from the home office of many insurance companies. Information on state licensing requirements may be obtained from the department of insurance at any state capital.

For information about insurance sales careers and training, contact

▶ National Association of Professional Insurance Agents, 400 N. Washington St., Alexandria, VA 22314. Internet: www.pianet.org

For information about health insurance sales careers, contact

▶ National Association of Health Underwriters, 2000 N. 14th St., Suite 450, Arlington, VA 22201. Internet: www.nahu.org

For general information on the property and casualty field, contact

▸ Insurance Information Institute, 110 William St., New York, NY 10038. Internet: www.iii.org

For information about professional designation programs, contact

▸ The American Institute for Chartered Property and Casualty Under-writers/Insurance Institute of America, 720 Providence Rd., Suite 100, Malvern, PA 19355-3433. Internet: www.aicpcu.org

▸ The American College, 270 S. Bryn Mawr Ave., Bryn Mawr, PA 19010-2195. Internet: www.theamericancollege.edu

For information on financial planning careers, contact

▸ Certified Financial Planner Board of Standards, Inc., 1425 K St. NW, Suite 500, Washington, DC 20005. Internet: www.cfp.net

Interviewers, Except Eligibility and Loan

(O*NET 43-4111.00)

Nature of the Work

Interviewers obtain and verify information from individuals and businesses by mail, telephone, or in person for the purpose of completing forms, applications, and questionnaires, such as market research surveys, Census forms, college admission applications, and medical histories. They review the answers for completeness and accuracy and record the information.

Training, Other Qualifications, and Advancement

Most employers prefer applicants with a high school diploma or its equivalent or a mix of education and related experience. New employees generally are trained on the job.

Job Outlook

Current and Projected Employment

2008 Employment	233,400
2018 Employment	269,900
Employment Change	36,500
Growth Rate	16%

Employment change. Employment is projected to grow faster than the average for all occupations. Rapid growth in the health-care and market research industries that employ the majority of these workers will generate jobs for interviewers. However, the expanding use of online surveys and questionnaires to conduct market research and the increasing use of digital health records will impede growth.

Job prospects. Job prospects are expected to be good. Turnover is generally high for this occupation where over a quarter of the jobs are part time. Applicants with good customer service and communications skills and those that are detail oriented should have the best prospects.

Earnings

Median annual wages for interviewers, except eligibility and loan, were $28,140 in May 2008.

For current wage data, visit the Occupational Employment Statistics program's Occupational Profile for interviewers, except eligibility and loan.

Related Occupations

Bill and account collectors; customer service representatives; and procurement clerks.

Lawyers

(O*NET 23-1011.00)

Significant Points

■ About 26 percent of lawyers are self-employed, either as partners in law firms or in solo practices.

■ Formal requirements to become a lawyer usually include a four-year college degree, three years of law school, and passing a written bar examination; however, some requirements may vary by state.

■ Competition for admission to most law schools is intense.

■ Competition for job openings should be keen because of the large number of students graduating from law school each year.

Nature of the Work

The legal system affects nearly every aspect of our society, from buying a home to crossing the street. *Lawyers* form the backbone of this system, linking it to society in numerous ways. They hold positions of great responsibility and are obligated to adhere to a strict code of ethics.

Lawyers, also called *attorneys*, act as both advocates and advisors in our society. As advocates, they represent one of the parties in criminal and civil trials by presenting evidence and arguing in court to support their client. As advisors, lawyers counsel their clients about their legal rights and obligations and suggest particular courses of action in business and personal matters. Whether acting as an advocate or an advisor, all attorneys research the intent of laws and judicial decisions and apply the law to the specific circumstances faced by their clients.

The more detailed aspects of a lawyer's job depend upon his or her field of specialization and position. Although all lawyers are licensed to represent parties in court, some appear in court more frequently than others. Trial lawyers spend the majority of their time outside the courtroom, conducting research, interviewing clients and witnesses, and handling other details in preparation for a trial.

Lawyers may specialize in a number of areas, such as bankruptcy, probate, international, elder, or environmental law. Those specializing in for example, environmental law may represent interest groups, waste disposal companies, or construction firms in their dealings with the U.S. Environmental Protection Agency and other federal and state agencies. These lawyers help clients prepare and file for licenses and applications for approval before certain activities are permitted to occur. Some lawyers specialize in the growing field of intellectual property, helping to protect clients' claims to copyrights, artwork under contract, product designs, and computer programs. Other lawyers advise insurance companies about the legality of insurance transactions, guiding the company in writing insurance policies to conform to the law and to protect the companies from unwarranted claims. When claims are filed against insurance companies, these attorneys review the claims and represent the companies in court.

Most lawyers are in private practice, concentrating on criminal or civil law. In criminal law, lawyers represent individuals who have been charged with crimes and argue their cases in courts of law. Attorneys dealing with civil law assist clients with litigation, wills, trusts, contracts, mortgages, titles, and leases. Other lawyers handle only public-interest cases—civil or criminal—concentrating on particular causes and choosing cases that might have an impact on the way law is applied. Lawyers sometimes are employed full time by a single client. If the client is a corporation, the lawyer is known as "house counsel" and usually advises the company concerning legal issues related to its business activities. These issues might involve patents, government regulations, contracts with other companies, property interests, or collective-bargaining agreements with unions.

A significant number of attorneys are employed at the various levels of government. Some work for state attorneys general, prosecutors, and public defenders in criminal courts. At the federal level, attorneys investigate cases for the U.S. Department of Justice and other agencies. Government lawyers also help develop programs, draft and interpret laws and legislation, establish enforcement procedures, and argue civil and criminal cases on behalf of the government.

Other lawyers work for legal aid societies—private, nonprofit organizations established to serve disadvantaged people. These lawyers generally handle civil, rather than criminal, cases.

Lawyers are increasingly using various forms of technology to perform more efficiently. Although all lawyers continue to use law libraries to prepare cases, most supplement conventional printed sources with computer sources, such as the Internet and legal databases. Software is used to search this legal literature automatically and to identify legal texts relevant to a specific case. In litigation involving many supporting documents, lawyers may use computers to organize and index materials. Lawyers must be geographically mobile and able to reach their clients in a timely matter, so they might use electronic filing, Web and videoconferencing, mobile electronic devices, and voice-recognition technology to share information more effectively.

Work environment. Lawyers do most of their work in offices, law libraries, and courtrooms. They sometimes meet in clients' homes or places of business and, when necessary, in hospitals or prisons. They may travel to attend meetings, gather evidence, and appear before courts, legislative bodies, and other authorities. They also may face particularly heavy pressure when a case is being tried. Preparation for court includes understanding the latest laws and judicial decisions.

Salaried lawyers usually have structured work schedules. Lawyers who are in private practice or those who work for large firms may work irregular hours, including weekends, while conducting research, conferring with clients, or preparing briefs during nonoffice hours. Lawyers often work long hours; of those who work full time, about 33 percent work 50 or more hours per week.

Training, Other Qualifications, and Advancement

Formal requirements to become a lawyer usually include a 4-year college degree, 3 years of law school, and passing a written bar examination; however, some requirements vary by state. Competition for admission to most law schools is intense. Federal courts and agencies set their own qualifications for those practicing before or in them.

Education and training. Becoming a lawyer usually takes 7 years of full-time study after high school—4 years of undergraduate study, followed by 3 years of law school. Law school applicants must have a bachelor's degree to qualify for admission. To meet the needs of students who can attend only part time, a number of law schools have night or part-time divisions.

Although there is no recommended "prelaw" undergraduate major, prospective lawyers should develop proficiency in writing and speaking, reading, researching, analyzing, and thinking logically—skills needed to succeed both in law school and in the law. Regardless of major, a multidisciplinary background is recommended. Courses in English, foreign languages, public speaking, government, philosophy, history, economics, mathematics, and computer science, among others, are useful. Students interested in a particular aspect of law may find related courses helpful. For example, prospective patent lawyers need a strong background in engineering or science, and future tax lawyers must have extensive knowledge of accounting.

Acceptance by most law schools depends on the applicant's ability to demonstrate an aptitude for the study of law, usually through undergraduate grades, the Law School Admission Test (LSAT), the quality of the applicant's undergraduate school, any prior work experience, and sometimes, a personal interview. However, law schools vary in the weight they place on each of these and other factors.

All law schools approved by the American Bar Association (ABA) require applicants to take the LSAT. As of June 2008, there were 200 ABA-accredited law schools; others were approved by state authorities only. Nearly all law schools require applicants to have certified transcripts sent to the Law School Data Assembly Service, which then submits the applicants' LSAT scores and their standardized records of college grades to the law schools of their choice. The Law School Admission Council administers both this service and the LSAT. Competition for admission to many law schools—especially the most prestigious ones—is usually intense, with the number of applicants greatly exceeding the number that can be admitted.

During the first year or year and a half of law school, students usually study core courses, such as constitutional law, contracts, property law, torts, civil procedure, and legal writing. In the remaining time, they may choose specialized courses in fields such as tax, labor, or corporate law. Law students often gain practical experience by participating in school-sponsored legal clinics; in the school's moot court competitions, in which students conduct appellate arguments; in practice trials under the supervision of experienced lawyers and judges; and through research and writing on legal issues for the school's law journals.

A number of law schools have clinical programs in which students gain legal experience through practice trials and projects under the supervision of lawyers and law school faculty. Law school clinical programs might include work in, for example, legal-aid offices or on legislative committees. Part-time or summer clerkships in law firms, government agencies, and corporate legal departments also provide valuable experience. Such training can lead directly to a job after graduation and can help students decide what kind of practice best suits them. Law school graduates receive the degree of *juris doctor* (J.D.), a first professional degree.

Advanced law degrees may be desirable for those planning to specialize, perform research, or teach. Some law students pursue joint degree programs, which usually require an additional semester or year of study. Joint degree programs are offered in a number of areas, including business administration or public administration.

After graduation, lawyers must keep informed about legal and nonlegal developments that affect their practices. In 2008, 46 states and jurisdictions required lawyers to participate in mandatory continuing legal education. Many law schools and state and local bar associations provide continuing education courses that help lawyers stay abreast of recent developments. Some states allow continuing education credits to be obtained through participation in seminars on the Internet.

Licensure. To practice law in the courts of any state or other jurisdiction, a person must be licensed, or admitted to its bar, under rules established by the jurisdiction's highest court. All states require that applicants for admission to the bar pass a written bar examination; most states also require applicants to pass a separate written ethics examination. Lawyers who have been admitted to the bar in one state occasionally may be admitted to the bar in another without taking another examination if they meet the latter jurisdiction's standards of good moral character and a specified period of legal experience. In most cases, however, lawyers must pass the bar examination in each state in which they plan to practice. Federal courts and agencies set their own qualifications for those practicing before or in them.

To qualify for the bar examination in most states, an applicant must earn a college degree and graduate from a law school accredited by the ABA or the proper state authorities. ABA accreditation signifies that the law school—particularly its library and faculty—meets certain standards. With certain exceptions, graduates of schools not approved by the ABA are restricted to taking the bar examination and practicing in the state or other jurisdiction in which the school is located; most of these schools are in California.

Although there is no nationwide bar examination, 48 states, the District of Columbia, Guam, the Northern Mariana Islands, Puerto Rico, and the Virgin Islands require the 6-hour Multistate Bar Examination (MBE) as part of their overall bar examination; the MBE is not required in Louisiana or Washington. The MBE covers a broad range of issues, and sometimes a locally prepared state bar examination is given in addition to it. The 3-hour Multistate Essay Examination (MEE) is used as part of the bar examination in several states. States vary in their use of MBE and MEE scores.

Many states also require the Multistate Performance Test to test the practical skills of beginning lawyers. Requirements vary by state, although the test usually is taken at the same time as the bar exam and is a one-time requirement.

In 2008, law school graduates in 52 jurisdictions were required to pass the Multistate Professional Responsibility Examination (MPRE), which tests their knowledge of the ABA codes on professional responsibility and judicial conduct. In some states, the MPRE may be taken during law school, usually after completing a course on legal ethics.

Other qualifications. The practice of law involves a great deal of responsibility. Individuals planning careers in law should like to work with people and be able to win the respect and confidence of their clients, associates, and the public. Perseverance, creativity, and reasoning ability also are essential to lawyers, who often analyze complex cases and handle new and unique legal problems.

Trial lawyers, who specialize in trial work, must be able to think quickly and speak with ease and authority. In addition, familiarity with courtroom rules and strategy is particularly important in trial work.

Advancement. Most beginning lawyers start in salaried positions. Newly hired attorneys usually start as associates and work with more experienced lawyers or judges. After several years, some lawyers are admitted to partnership in their firm, which means that they are partial owners of the firm, or go into practice for themselves. Some experienced lawyers are nominated or elected to judgeships. Others become full-time law school faculty or administrators; a growing number of these lawyers have advanced degrees in other fields as well.

Some attorneys use their legal training in administrative or managerial positions in various departments of large corporations. A transfer from a corporation's legal department to another department is often viewed as a way to gain administrative experience and rise in the ranks of management.

Employment

Lawyers held about 759,200 jobs in 2008. Approximately 26 percent of lawyers were self-employed, practicing either as partners in law firms or in solo practices. Most salaried lawyers held positions in government, in law firms or other corporations, or in nonprofit organizations. Most government-employed lawyers worked at the local level. In the federal government, lawyers worked for many different agencies, but were concentrated in the Departments of Justice, Treasury, and Defense. Many salaried lawyers working outside of government were employed as house counsel by public utilities, banks, insurance companies, real-estate agencies, manufacturing firms, and other business firms and nonprofit organizations. Some also had part-time independent practices, while others worked part time as lawyers and full time in another occupation.

A relatively small number of trained attorneys work in law schools and are not included in the employment estimate for lawyers. Most are faculty members who specialize in one or more subjects; however, some serve as administrators. Others work full time in nonacademic settings and teach part time.

Projections Data from the National Employment Matrix

Occupational title	SOC Code	Employment, 2008	Projected employment, 2018	Change, 2008–2018	
				Number	Percent
Lawyers	23-1011	759,200	857,700	98,500	13

NOTE: Data in this table are rounded.

Job Outlook

About-as-fast-as-the-average employment growth is projected, but job competition is expected to be keen.

Employment change. Employment of lawyers is expected to grow 13 percent during the 2008–2018 decade, about as fast as the average for all occupations. Growth in the population and in the level of business activity is expected to create more legal transactions, civil disputes, and criminal cases. Job growth among lawyers also will result from increasing demand for legal services in such areas as health care, intellectual property, bankruptcy, corporate and security litigation, antitrust law, and environmental law. In addition, the wider availability and affordability of legal clinics should result in increased use of legal services by middle-income people. However, growth in demand for lawyers will be constrained as businesses increasingly use large accounting firms and paralegals to perform some of the same functions that lawyers do. For example, accounting firms may provide employee-benefit counseling, process documents, or handle various other services previously performed by a law firm. Also, mediation and dispute resolution are increasingly being used as alternatives to litigation.

Job growth for lawyers will continue to be concentrated in salaried jobs as businesses and all levels of government employ a growing number of staff attorneys. Most salaried positions are in urban areas where government agencies, law firms, and big corporations are concentrated. The number of self-employed lawyers is expected to grow slowly, reflecting the difficulty of establishing a profitable new practice in the face of competition from larger, established law firms. Moreover, the growing complexity of the law, which encourages specialization, along with the cost of maintaining up-to-date legal research materials, favors larger firms.

Job prospects. Competition for job openings should continue to be keen because of the large number of students graduating from law school each year. Graduates with superior academic records from highly regarded law schools will have the best job opportunities. Perhaps as a result of competition for attorney positions, lawyers are increasingly finding work in less traditional areas for which legal training is an asset, but not normally a requirement—for example, administrative, managerial, and business positions in banks, insurance firms, real estate companies, government agencies, and other organizations. Employment opportunities are expected to continue to arise in these organizations at a growing rate.

As in the past, some graduates may have to accept positions outside of their field of interest or for which they feel overqualified. Some recent law school graduates who have been unable to find permanent positions are turning to the growing number of temporary staffing firms that place attorneys in short-term jobs. This service allows companies to hire lawyers on an "as-needed" basis and permits beginning lawyers to develop practical skills.

Because of the keen competition for jobs, a law graduate's geographic mobility and work experience are assuming greater importance. Willingness to relocate may be an advantage in getting a job, but to be licensed in another state, a lawyer may have to take an additional state bar examination. In addition, employers increasingly are seeking graduates who have advanced law degrees and experience in a specialty, such as tax, patent, or admiralty law.

Job opportunities often are adversely affected by cyclical swings in the economy. During recessions, demand declines for some discretionary legal services, such as planning estates, drafting wills, and handling real estate transactions. Also, corporations are less likely to litigate cases when declining sales and profits restrict their budgets. Some corporations and law firms will not hire new attorneys until business improves, and these establishments may even cut staff to contain costs. Several factors, however, mitigate the overall impact of recessions on lawyers; during recessions, for example, individuals and corporations face other legal problems, such as bankruptcies, foreclosures, and divorces—all requiring legal action.

For lawyers who wish to work independently, establishing a new practice will probably be easiest in small towns and expanding suburban areas. In such communities, competition from larger, established law firms is likely to be less than in big cities, and new lawyers may find it easier to establish a reputation among potential clients.

Earnings

In May 2008, the median annual wages of all wage-and-salaried lawyers were $110,590. The middle half of the occupation earned between $74,980 and $163,320. Median annual wages in the industries employing the largest numbers of lawyers in May 2008 were the following:

Management of companies and enterprises	$145,770
Federal Executive Branch	126,080
Legal services	116,550
Local government	82,590
State government	78,540

Salaries of experienced attorneys vary widely according to the type, size, and location of their employer. Lawyers who own their own practices usually earn less than those who are partners in law firms. Lawyers starting their own practice may need to work part time in other occupations to supplement their income until their practice is well established.

Median salaries of lawyers 9 months after graduation from law school in 2007 varied by type of work, as indicated in table 1.

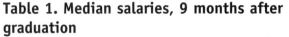

Table 1. Median salaries, 9 months after graduation

Employer	Salary
All graduates	$68,500
Private practice	108,500
Business	69,100
Government	50,000
Academic/judicial clerkships	48,000

SOURCE: National Association of Law Placement

Most salaried lawyers are provided health and life insurance, and contributions are made to retirement plans on their behalf. Lawyers who practice independently are covered only if they arrange and pay for such benefits themselves.

Related Occupations

Legal training is necessary in many other occupations, including judges, magistrates, and other judicial workers; law clerks; paralegals and legal assistants; and title examiners, abstractors, and searchers.

Sources of Additional Information

Information on law schools and a career in law may be obtained from the following organizations:

▸ American Bar Association, 321 N. Clark St., Chicago, IL 60654. Internet: www.abanet.org

▸ National Association for Law Placement, 1025 Connecticut Ave. NW, Suite 1110, Washington, DC 20036. Internet: www.nalp.org

Information on the LSAT, the Law School Data Assembly Service, the law school application process, and financial aid available to law students may be obtained from

▸ Law School Admission Council, 662 Penn St., Newtown, PA 18940. Internet: www.lsac.org

Information on obtaining positions as lawyers with the federal government is available from the Office of Personnel Management through USAJOBS, the federal government's official employment information system. This resource for locating and applying for job opportunities can be accessed through the Internet at www.usajobs. opm.gov or through an interactive voice response telephone system at (703) 724-1850 or TDD (978) 461-8404. These numbers are not toll free, and charges may result. For advice on how to find and apply for federal jobs, see the *Occupational Outlook Quarterly* article "How to get a job in the federal government," online at www. bls.gov/opub/ooq/2004/summer/art01.pdf.

The requirements for admission to the bar in a particular state or other jurisdiction may be obtained at the state capital, from the clerk of the Supreme Court, or from the administrator of the State Board of Bar Examiners.

Licensed Practical and Licensed Vocational Nurses

(O*NET 29-2061.00)

Significant Points

■ Most training programs last about one year and are offered by vocational or technical schools or community or junior colleges.

■ Overall job prospects are expected to be very good, but job outlook varies by industry.

■ Replacement needs will be a major source of job openings as many workers leave the occupation permanently.

Nature of the Work

Licensed practical nurses (*LPNs*), or *licensed vocational nurses* (*LVNs*), care for people who are sick, injured, convalescent, or disabled under the direction of physicians and registered nurses. The nature of the direction and supervision required varies by state and job setting.

LPNs care for patients in many ways. Often, they provide basic bedside care. Many LPNs measure and record patients' vital signs such as height, weight, temperature, blood pressure, pulse, and respiration. They also prepare and give injections and enemas, monitor catheters, dress wounds, and give alcohol rubs and massages. To help keep patients comfortable, they assist with bathing, dressing, and personal hygiene, moving in bed, standing, and walking. They might also feed patients who need help eating. Experienced LPNs may supervise nursing assistants and aides.

As part of their work, LPNs collect samples for testing, perform routine laboratory tests, and record food and fluid intake and output. They clean and monitor medical equipment. Sometimes, they help physicians and registered nurses perform tests and procedures. Some LPNs help to deliver, care for, and feed infants.

LPNs also monitor their patients and report adverse reactions to medications or treatments. LPNs gather information from patients, including their health history and how they are currently feeling. They may use this information to complete insurance forms, preauthorizations, and referrals, and they share information with registered nurses and doctors to help determine the best course of care for a patient. LPNs often teach family members how to care for a relative or teach patients about good health habits.

Most LPNs are generalists and will work in any area of health care. However, some work in a specialized setting, such as a nursing home, a doctor's office, or in home health care. LPNs in nursing care facilities help to evaluate residents' needs, develop care plans, and supervise the care provided by nursing aides. In doctors' offices and clinics, they may be responsible for making appointments, keeping records, and performing other clerical duties. LPNs who work in home health care may prepare meals and teach family members simple nursing tasks.

In some states, LPNs are permitted to administer prescribed medicines, start intravenous fluids, and provide care to ventilator-dependent patients.

Work environment. Most licensed practical nurses work a 40-hour week. In some work setting where patients need round-the-clock care, LPNs may have to work nights, weekends, and holidays. About 18 percent of LPNs and LVN's worked part-time in 2008. They often stand for long periods and help patients move in bed, stand, or walk.

LPNs may face hazards from caustic chemicals, radiation, and infectious diseases. They are subject to back injuries when moving patients. They often must deal with the stress of heavy workloads. In addition, the patients they care for may be confused, agitated, or uncooperative.

Training, Other Qualifications, and Advancement

Most practical nursing training programs last about 1 year, and are offered by vocational and technical schools or community or junior colleges. LPNs must be licensed to practice.

Education and training. LPNs must complete a state-approved training program in practical nursing to be eligible for licensure. Contact your state's board of nursing for a list of approved programs. Most training programs are available from technical and vocational schools or community and junior colleges. Other programs are available through high schools, hospitals, and colleges and universities. A high school diploma or its equivalent usually is required for entry, although some programs accept candidates without a diploma, and some programs are part of a high school curriculum.

Most year-long practical nursing programs include both classroom study and supervised clinical practice (patient care). Classroom study covers basic nursing concepts and subjects related to patient care, including anatomy, physiology, medical-surgical nursing, pediatrics, obstetrics nursing, pharmacology, nutrition, and first aid. Clinical practice usually is in a hospital but sometimes includes other settings.

Licensure. The National Council Licensure Examination, or NCLEX-PN, is required in order to obtain licensure as an LPN. The exam is developed and administered by the National Council of State Boards of Nursing. The NCLEX-PN is a computer-based exam and varies in length. The exam covers four major *Client Needs* categories: safe and effective care environment, health promotion and maintenance, psychosocial integrity, and physiological integrity. Eligibility for licensure may vary by state; for details, contact your state's board of nursing.

Other qualifications. LPNs should have a caring, sympathetic nature. They should be emotionally stable because working with the sick and injured can be stressful. They also need to be observant, and to have good decision-making and communication skills. As part of a health-care team, they must be able to follow orders and work under close supervision.

LPNs should enjoy learning because continuing education credits are required by some states and/or employers at regular intervals. Career-long learning is a distinct reality for LPNs.

Advancement. In some employment settings, such as nursing homes, LPNs can advance to become charge nurses who oversee the work of other LPNs and nursing aides.

LPNs may become credentialed in specialties like IV therapy, gerontology, long-term care, and pharmacology.

Some LPNs also choose to become registered nurses through LPN-to-RN training programs.

Employment

Licensed practical and licensed vocational nurses held about 753,600 jobs in 2008. About 25 percent of LPNs worked in hospitals, 28 percent in nursing care facilities, and another 12 percent in offices of physicians. Others worked for home health-care services; employment services; residential care facilities; community care facilities for the elderly; outpatient care centers; and federal, state, and local government agencies.

Job Outlook

Employment of LPNs is projected to grow much faster than average. Overall job prospects are expected to be very good, but job outlook varies by industry. The best job opportunities will occur in nursing care facilities and home health-care services.

Employment change. Employment of LPNs is expected to grow by 21 percent between 2008 and 2018, much faster than the average for all occupations, in response to the long-term care needs of an increasing elderly population and the general increase in demand for health-care services.

Demand for LPNs will be driven by the increase in the share of the older population. Older persons have an increased incidence of injury and illness, which will increase their demand for health-care services. In addition, with better medical technology, people are living longer, increasing the demand for long-term health care. Job growth will occur over all health-care settings but especially those that service the geriatric population like nursing care facilities, community care facilities, and home health-care services.

In order to contain health-care costs, many procedures once performed only in hospitals are being performed in physicians' offices and in outpatient care centers, largely because of advances in technology. As a result, the number of LPNs should increase faster in these facilities than in hospitals. Nevertheless, hospitals will continue to demand the services of LPNs and will remain one of the largest employers of these workers.

Job prospects. In addition to projected job growth, job openings will result from replacement needs, as many workers leave the occupa-

Projections Data from the National Employment Matrix

Occupational title	SOC Code	Employment, 2008	Projected employment, 2018	Change, 2008–2018	
				Number	Percent
Licensed practical and licensed vocational nurses	29-2061	753,600	909,200	155,600	21

NOTE: Data in this table are rounded.

tion permanently. Very good job opportunities are expected. Rapid employment growth is projected in most health-care industries, with the best job opportunities occurring in nursing care facilities and in home health-care services. There is a perceived inadequacy of available health care in many rural areas, so LPNs willing to locate in rural areas should have good job prospects.

Earnings

Median annual wages of licensed practical and licensed vocational nurses were $39,030 in May 2008. The middle 50 percent earned between $33,360 and $46,710. The lowest 10 percent earned less than $28,260, and the highest 10 percent earned more than $53,580. Median annual wages in the industries employing the largest numbers of licensed practical and licensed vocational nurses in May 2008 were as follows:

Employment services	$44,690
Nursing care facilities	40,580
Home health care services	39,510
General medical and surgical hospitals	38,080
Offices of physicians	35,020

Related Occupations

LPNs work closely with people while helping them. Other health-care occupations that work closely with patients include athletic trainers; emergency medical technicians and paramedics; home health aides and personal and home care aides; medical assistants; nursing and psychiatric aides; and registered nurses.

Sources of Additional Information

For information about practical nursing and specialty credentialing, contact the following organizations:

▸ National Association for Practical Nurse Education and Service, Inc., 1940 Duke St., Suite 200, Alexandria, VA 22314. Internet: www.napnes.org

▸ National Federation of Licensed Practical Nurses, Inc., 605 Poole Dr., Garner, NC 27529. Internet: www.nflpn.org

▸ National League for Nursing, 61 Broadway, 33rd floor, New York, NY 10006. Internet: www.nln.org

Information on the NCLEX-PN licensing exam is available from

▸ National Council of State Boards of Nursing, 111 E. Wacker Dr., Suite 2900, Chicago, IL 60601. Internet: www.ncsbn.org

Lists of state-approved LPN programs are available from individual state boards of nursing.

Maintenance and Repair Workers, General

(O*NET 49-9042.00)

Significant Points

■ General maintenance and repair workers are employed in almost every industry.

■ Many workers learn their skills informally on the job; obtaining certification may result in better advancement opportunities in higher paying industries.

■ Job growth and turnover in this large occupation should result in excellent job opportunities, especially for people with experience in maintenance and related fields.

Nature of the Work

Most craft workers specialize in one kind of work, such as plumbing or carpentry. *General maintenance and repair workers*, however, have skills in many different crafts. They repair and maintain machines, mechanical equipment, and buildings and work on plumbing, electrical, and air-conditioning and heating systems. They build partitions, make plaster or drywall repairs, and fix or paint roofs, windows, doors, floors, woodwork, and other parts of building structures. They also maintain and repair specialized equipment and machinery found in cafeterias, laundries, hospitals, stores, offices, and factories.

Typical duties include troubleshooting and fixing faulty electrical switches, repairing air-conditioning motors, and unclogging drains. New buildings sometimes have computer-controlled systems that allow maintenance workers to make adjustments in building settings and monitor for problems from a central location. For example, they can remotely control light sensors that turn off lights automatically after a set amount of time or identify a broken ventilation fan that needs to be replaced.

General maintenance and repair workers inspect and diagnose problems and determine the best way to correct them, frequently checking blueprints, repair manuals, and parts catalogs. They obtain supplies and repair parts from distributors or storerooms. Using common hand and power tools such as screwdrivers, saws, drills, wrenches, and hammers, as well as specialized equipment and electronic testing devices, these workers replace or fix worn or broken parts, where necessary, or make adjustments to correct malfunctioning equipment and machines.

General maintenance and repair workers also perform routine preventive maintenance and ensure that machines continue to run smoothly, building systems operate efficiently, and the physical condition of buildings does not deteriorate. Following a checklist, they may inspect drives, motors, and belts, check fluid levels, replace filters, and perform other maintenance actions. Maintenance and repair workers keep records of their work.

Employees in small establishments, where they are often the only maintenance worker, make all repairs, except for very large or difficult jobs. In larger establishments, duties may be limited to the maintenance of everything in a single workshop or a particular area.

Work environment. General maintenance and repair workers often carry out many different tasks in a single day, at any number of locations, including indoor and outdoor. They may work inside a single building, such as a hotel or hospital, or be responsible for the maintenance of many buildings, such as those in an apartment complex or college campus. They may have to stand for long periods, lift heavy objects, and work in uncomfortably hot or cold environments, in awkward and cramped positions, or on ladders. Those employed in small establishments often work with only limited supervision.

Those in larger establishments frequently work under the direct supervision of an experienced worker. Some tasks put workers at risk of electrical shock, burns, falls, cuts, and bruises. Data from the U.S. Bureau of Labor Statistics show that full-time general maintenance workers experienced a work-related injury and illness rate that was much higher than the national average. Most general maintenance workers work a 40-hour week. Some work evening, night, or weekend shifts or are on call for emergency repairs.

Training, Other Qualifications, and Advancement

Many general maintenance and repair workers learn their skills informally on the job as helpers to other repairers or to carpenters, electricians, and other construction workers. Certification is available for entry-level workers, as well as experienced workers seeking advancement.

Education and training. General maintenance and repair workers often learn their skills informally on the job. They start as helpers, watching and learning from skilled maintenance workers. Helpers begin by performing simple jobs, such as fixing leaky faucets and replacing light bulbs, and progress to more difficult tasks, such as overhauling machinery or building walls. Some learn their skills by working as helpers to other types of repair or construction workers, including machinery repairers, carpenters, or electricians.

Several months of on-the-job training are required to become fully qualified, depending on the skill level required. Some jobs require a year or more to become fully qualified. Because a growing number of new buildings rely on computers to control their systems, general maintenance and repair workers may need basic computer skills, such as how to log onto a central computer system and navigate through a series of menus. Companies that install computer-controlled equipment usually provide on-site training for general maintenance and repair workers.

Many employers prefer to hire high school graduates. High school courses in mechanical drawing, electricity, woodworking, blueprint reading, science, mathematics, and computers are useful. Because of the wide variety of tasks performed by maintenance and repair workers, technical education is an important part of their training. Maintenance and repair workers often need to do work that involves electrical, plumbing, and heating and air-conditioning systems, or painting and roofing tasks. Although these basic tasks may not require a license to do the work, a good working knowledge of many repair and maintenance tasks is required. Many maintenance and repair workers learn some of these skills in high school shop classes and postsecondary trade or vocational schools or community colleges.

Licensure. Licensing requirements vary by state and locality. In some cases, workers may need to be licensed in a particular specialty such as electrical or plumbing work.

Other qualifications. Technical and mechanical aptitude, the ability to use shop mathematics, and manual dexterity are important attributes. Good health is necessary because the job involves much walking, climbing, standing, reaching, and heavy lifting. Difficult jobs require problem-solving ability, and many positions require the ability to work without direct supervision.

Certification and advancement. The International Management Institute (IMI) offers certification for three levels of competence, focusing on a broad range of topics, including blueprints, mathematics, basic electricity, piping systems, landscape maintenance, and troubleshooting skills. The lowest level of certification is Certified Maintenance Technician, the second level is Certified Maintenance Professional, and the highest level of certification is Certified Maintenance Manager. To become certified, applicants must meet several prerequisites and pass a comprehensive written examination.

Many general maintenance and repair workers in large organizations advance to maintenance supervisor or become craftworkers such as electricians, heating and air-conditioning mechanics, or plumbers. Within small organizations, promotion opportunities may be limited. Obtaining IMI certification may lead to better advancement opportunities in higher paying industries.

Employment

General maintenance and repair workers held about 1.4 million jobs in 2008. They were employed in almost every industry. Around 18 percent worked in manufacturing industries, while about 11 percent worked for Government. Others worked for wholesale and retail firms and for real estate firms that operate office and apartment buildings.

Job Outlook

Average employment growth is expected. Job growth and the need to replace those who leave this large occupation should result in excellent job opportunities, especially for those with experience in maintenance and related fields.

Employment change. Employment of general maintenance and repair workers is expected to grow 11 percent during the 2008–2018 decade, about as fast as the average for all occupations. Employment is related to the number of buildings—for example, office and apartment buildings, stores, schools, hospitals, hotels, and factories—and the amount of equipment needing maintenance and repair. One factor limiting job growth is that computers allow buildings to be monitored more efficiently, partially reducing the need for workers.

Projections Data from the National Employment Matrix

Occupational title	SOC Code	Employment, 2008	Projected employment, 2018	Change, 2008–2018	
				Number	Percent
Maintenance and repair workers, general....................	49-9042	1,361,300	1,509,200	147,900	11

NOTE: Data in this table are rounded.

Job prospects. Job opportunities should be excellent, especially for those with experience in maintenance or related fields. Those who obtain certification will also face excellent opportunities. General maintenance and repair is a large occupation, generating many job openings due to growth and the need to replace those who leave the occupation. Many job openings are expected to result from the retirement of experienced maintenance workers over the next decade.

Earnings

Median hourly wages of general maintenance and repair workers were $16.21 in May 2008. The middle 50 percent earned between $12.44 and $21.09. The lowest 10 percent earned less than $9.78, and the highest 10 percent earned more than $25.94. Median hourly wages in the industries employing the largest numbers of general maintenance and repair workers in May 2008 are shown in the following tabulation:

Local government	$17.11
Elementary and secondary schools	16.86
Activities related to real estate	14.41
Lessors of real estate	13.91
Traveler accommodation	12.65

About 15 percent of general maintenance and repair workers are members of unions, including the American Federation of State, County, and Municipal Employees and the United Auto Workers.

Related Occupations

Some duties of general maintenance and repair workers are similar to those of boilermakers; carpenters; electricians; heating, air-conditioning, and refrigeration mechanics and installers; and plumbers, pipelayers, pipefitters, and steamfitters.

Other, more specific, duties are similar to those of coin, vending, and amusement machine servicers and repairers; electrical and electronics installers and repairers; electronic home entertainment equipment installers and repairers; and radio and telecommunications equipment installers and repairers.

Sources of Additional Information

Information about job opportunities may be obtained from local employers and local offices of the state.

For information related to training and certification, contact

▸ International Maintenance Institute, P.O. Box 751896, Houston, TX 77275-1896. Internet: www.imionline.org

▸ Society for Maintenance and Reliability Professionals, 8400 West-park Dr., 2nd Floor, McLean, VA 22102-3570. Internet: www.smrp.org/

Management Analysts

(O*NET 13-1111.00)

Significant Points

■ Despite 24-percent employment growth, keen competition is expected for jobs; opportunities should be best for those with a graduate degree, specialized expertise, and a talent for salesmanship and public relations.

■ About 26 percent, three times the average for all occupations, are self-employed.

■ A bachelor's degree is sufficient for many entry-level government jobs; many positions in private industry require a master's degree, specialized expertise, or both.

Nature of the Work

As business becomes more complex, firms are continually faced with new challenges. They increasingly rely on *management analysts* to help them remain competitive amidst these changes. Management analysts, often referred to as *management consultants* in private industry, analyze and propose ways to improve an organization's structure, efficiency, or profits.

For example, a small but rapidly growing company might employ a consultant who is an expert in just-in-time inventory management to help improve its inventory-control system. In another case, a large company that has recently acquired a new division may hire management analysts to help reorganize the corporate structure and eliminate duplicate or nonessential jobs. In recent years, information technology and electronic commerce have provided new opportunities for management analysts. Companies hire consultants to develop strategies for entering and remaining competitive in the new electronic marketplace.

Management analysts might be single practitioners or part of large international organizations employing thousands of other consultants. Some analysts and consultants specialize in a specific industry, such as health care or telecommunications, while others specialize by type of business function, such as human resources, marketing, logistics, or information systems. In government, management analysts tend to specialize by type of agency. The work of management analysts and consultants varies with each client or employer and from project to project. Some projects require a team of consultants, each specializing in one area. In other projects, consultants work independently with the organization's managers. In all cases, analysts and consultants collect, review, and analyze information in order to make recommendations to managers.

Both public and private organizations use consultants for a variety of reasons. Some lack the internal resources needed to handle a project, while others need a consultant's expertise to determine what resources will be required and what problems may be encountered if they pursue a particular opportunity. To retain a consultant, a company first solicits proposals from a number of consulting firms specializing in the area in which it needs assistance. These proposals include the estimated cost and scope of the project, staffing requirements, references from previous clients, and a completion deadline. The company then selects the proposal that best suits its needs. Some firms, however, employ internal management consulting groups rather than hiring outside consultants.

After obtaining an assignment or contract, management analysts first define the nature and extent of the problem that they have been asked to solve. During this phase, they analyze relevant data—which may include annual revenues, employment, or expenditures—and interview managers and employees while observing their operations. The analysts or consultants then develop solutions to the problem. While preparing their recommendations, they take into account the nature of the organization, the relationship it has with others in the industry, and its internal organization and culture. Insight into the problem often is gained by building and solving mathematical models, such as one that shows how inventory levels affect costs and product delivery times.

Once they have decided on a course of action, consultants report their findings and recommendations to the client. Their suggestions usually are submitted in writing, but oral presentations regarding findings are also common. For some projects, management analysts are retained to help implement their suggestions.

Like their private-sector colleagues, management analysts in government agencies try to increase efficiency and worker productivity and control costs. For example, if an agency is planning to purchase personal computers, it must first determine which type to buy, given its budget and data-processing needs. In this case, management analysts would assess the prices and characteristics of various machines and determine which ones best meet the agency's needs. Analysts may manage contracts for a wide range of goods and services to ensure quality performance and to prevent cost overruns.

Work environment. Management analysts usually divide their time between their offices and the client's site. In either situation, much of an analyst's time is spent indoors in clean, well-lit offices. Because they must spend a significant portion of their time with clients, analysts travel frequently.

Analysts and consultants generally work at least 40 hours a week. Uncompensated overtime is common, especially when project deadlines are approaching. Analysts may experience a great deal of stress when trying to meet a client's demands, often on a tight schedule.

Self-employed consultants can set their workload and hours and work at home. On the other hand, their livelihood depends on their ability to maintain and expand their client base. Salaried consultants also must impress potential clients to get and keep clients for their company.

Training, Other Qualifications, and Advancement

Entry requirements for management analysts vary. For some entry-level positions, a bachelor's degree is sufficient. For others, a master's degree or specialized expertise is required.

Education and training. Educational requirements for entry-level jobs in this field vary between private industry and government. Many employers in private industry generally seek individuals with a master's degree in business administration or a related discipline. Some employers also require additional years of experience in the field or industry in which the worker plans to consult. Other firms hire workers with a bachelor's degree as research analysts or associates and promote them to consultants after several years. Some government agencies require experience, graduate education, or both, but many also hire people with a bachelor's degree and little work experience for entry-level management analyst positions.

Few universities or colleges offer formal programs in management consulting; however, many fields of study provide a suitable educational background for this occupation because of the wide range of areas addressed by management analysts. Common fields of study include business, management, accounting, marketing, economics, statistics, computer and information science, and engineering. Most analysts also have years of experience in management, human resources, information technology, or other specialties. Analysts also routinely attend conferences to keep abreast of current developments in their field.

Other qualifications. Management analysts often work with minimal supervision, so they need to be self-motivated and disciplined. Analytical skills, the ability to get along with a wide range of people, strong oral and written communication skills, good judgment, time-management skills, and creativity are other desirable qualities. The ability to work in teams also is an important attribute as consulting teams become more common.

Certification and advancement. As consultants gain experience, they often become solely responsible for specific projects, taking on more responsibility and managing their own hours. At the senior level, consultants may supervise teams working on more complex projects and become more involved in seeking out new business. Those with exceptional skills may eventually become partners in the firm and focus on attracting new clients and bringing in revenue. Senior consultants who leave their consulting firms often move to senior management positions at non-consulting firms. Others with entrepreneurial ambition may open their own firms.

A high percentage of management consultants are self-employed, in part because business startup and overhead costs are low. Since many small consulting firms fail each year because of lack of managerial expertise and clients, persons interested in opening their own firm must have good organizational and marketing skills. Several years of consulting experience are also helpful.

The Institute of Management Consultants USA, Inc., offers the Certified Management Consultant (CMC) designation to those who meet minimum levels of education and experience, submit client reviews, and pass an interview and exam covering the IMC USA's Code of Ethics. Management consultants with a CMC designation must be recertified every three years. Certification is not mandatory for management consultants, but it may give a jobseeker a competitive advantage.

Employment

Management analysts held about 746,900 jobs in 2008. About 26 percent of these workers, three times the average for all occupations, were self-employed. Management analysts are found throughout the country, but employment is concentrated in large metropolitan areas. Management analysts work in a range of industries, including management, scientific, and technical consulting firms; computer systems design and related services firms; and federal, state, and local governments.

Job Outlook

Employment of management analysts is expected to grow 24 percent, much faster than the average for all occupations. Despite projected rapid employment growth, keen competition is expected for jobs as management analysts because the independent and chal-

Projections Data from the National Employment Matrix

Occupational title	SOC Code	Employment, 2008	Projected employment, 2018	Change, 2008–2018	
				Number	Percent
Management analysts 13-1111		746,900	925,200	178,300	24

NOTE: Data in this table are rounded.

lenging nature of the work and the high earnings potential make this occupation attractive to many.

Employment change. Employment of management analysts is expected to grow by 24 percent, much faster than the average, over the 2008–2018 decade as industry and government increasingly rely on outside expertise to improve the performance of their organizations. Job growth is projected in very large consulting firms with international expertise and in smaller consulting firms that specialize in specific areas, such as biotechnology, health care, information technology, human resources, engineering, and marketing. Growth in the number of individual practitioners may be hindered by increasing use of consulting teams that are often more versatile.

Job growth for management analysts will be driven by a number of changes in the business environment that have forced firms to take a closer look at their operations. These changes include regulatory changes, developments in information technology, and the growth of electronic commerce. In addition, as firms try to solve regulatory changes due to the current economic credit and housing crisis, consultants will be hired to render advice on the recovery process. Firms will also hire information technology consultants who specialize in "green" or environmentally safe use of technology management consulting to help lower energy consumption and implement "green" initiatives. Traditional companies hire analysts to help design intranets or company Web sites or to establish online businesses. New Internet startup companies hire analysts not only to design Web sites but also to advise them in traditional business practices, such as pricing strategies, marketing, and inventory and human resource management.

To offer clients better quality and a wider variety of services, consulting firms are partnering with traditional computer software and technology firms. Also, many computer firms are developing consulting practices of their own to take advantage of this expanding market. Although information technology consulting should remain one of the fastest-growing consulting areas, employment in the computer services industry can be volatile, and so the most successful management analysts may also consult in other business areas.

The growth of international business will also contribute to an increase in demand for management analysts. As U.S. firms expand their business abroad, many will hire management analysts to help them form the right strategy for entering the market; to advise them on legal matters pertaining to specific countries; or to help them with organizational, administrative, and other issues, especially if the U.S. company is involved in a partnership or merger with a local firm. These trends provide management analysts with more opportunities to travel or work abroad but also require them to have a more comprehensive knowledge of international business and foreign cultures and languages. Just as globalization creates new

opportunities for management analysts, it also allows U.S. firms to hire management analysts in other countries; however, because international work is expected to increase the total amount of work, this development is not expected to adversely affect employment in this occupation.

Furthermore, as international and domestic markets become more competitive, firms will need to use resources more efficiently. Management analysts will be increasingly sought to help reduce costs, streamline operations, and develop marketing strategies. As this process expands and as businesses downsize, even more opportunities will be created for analysts to perform duties that were previously handled internally. Finally, more management analysts will also be needed in the public sector as federal, state, and local government agencies seek to improve efficiency.

Job prospects. Despite rapid employment growth, keen competition is expected. The pool of applicants from which employers can draw is quite large, since analysts can have very diverse educational backgrounds and work experience. Furthermore, the independent and challenging nature of the work, combined with high earnings potential, makes this occupation attractive to many. Job opportunities are expected to be best for those with a graduate degree, specialized expertise, and a talent for salesmanship and public relations.

Economic downturns can also have adverse effects on employment for some management consultants. In these times, businesses look to cut costs, and consultants may be considered an excess expense. On the other hand, some consultants might experience an increase in work during recessions because they advise businesses on how to cut costs and remain profitable.

Earnings

Salaries for management analysts vary widely by years of experience and education, geographic location, specific expertise, and size of employer. Generally, management analysts employed in large firms or in metropolitan areas have the highest salaries. Median annual wages of wage and salary management analysts in May 2008 were $73,570. The middle 50 percent earned between $54,890 and $99,700. The lowest 10 percent earned less than $41,910, and the highest 10 percent earned more than $133,850. Median annual wages in the industries employing the largest numbers of management analysts were the following:

Computer systems and design related services $82,090
Management, scientific, and technical
    consulting services 81,670
Federal Executive Branch 79,830
Management of companies and enterprises 73,760
State government 55,590

Salaried management analysts usually receive common benefits, such as health and life insurance, a retirement plan, vacation, and sick leave, as well as less common benefits, such as profit sharing and bonuses for outstanding work. In addition, all travel expenses usually are reimbursed by the employer. Self-employed consultants have to maintain their own office and provide their own benefits.

Related Occupations

Management analysts collect, review, and analyze data; make recommendations; and implement their ideas. Occupations with similar duties include accountants and auditors, budget analysts, cost estimators, economists, financial analysts, market and survey researchers, operations research analysts, and personal financial advisors.

Some management analysts specialize in information technology and work with computers, similar to computer scientists and computer systems analysts.

Most management analysts also have managerial experience similar to that of administrative services managers; advertising, marketing, promotions, public relations, and sales managers; financial managers; human resources, training, and labor relations managers and specialists; industrial production managers; and top executives.

Sources of Additional Information

Information about career opportunities in management consulting is available from

▶ Association of Management Consulting Firms, 370 Lexington Ave., Suite 2209, New York, NY 10017. Internet: www.amcf.org

Information about the Certified Management Consultant designation can be obtained from

▶ Institute of Management Consultants USA, Inc., 2025 M St. NW, Suite 800, Washington, DC 20036. Internet: www.imcusa.org

Information on obtaining a management analyst position with the federal government is available from the Office of Personnel Management (OPM) through USAJOBS, the federal government's official employment information system. This resource for locating and applying for job opportunities can be accessed through the Internet at www.usajobs.opm.gov or through an interactive voice response telephone system at (703) 724-1850 or TDD (978) 461-8404. These numbers are not toll free, and charges may result. For advice on how to find and apply for federal jobs, see the *Occupational Outlook Quarterly* article "How to get a job in the federal government," online at www.bls.gov/opub/ooq/2004/summer/art01.pdf.

Market and Survey Researchers

(O*NET 19-3021.00 and 19-3022.00)

Significant Points

■ Market and survey researchers can enter the occupation with a bachelor's degree, but those with a master's or Ph.D. in marketing or a social science should enjoy the best opportunities.

■ Researchers need strong quantitative skills and, increasingly, knowledge of conducting web-based surveys.

■ Employment is expected to grow much faster than average.

Nature of the Work

Market and survey researchers gather information about what people think. Market research analysts help companies understand what types of products people want, determine who will buy them and at what price. Gathering statistical data on competitors and examining prices, sales, and methods of marketing and distribution, they analyze data on past sales to predict future sales.

Market research analysts devise methods and procedures for obtaining the data they need by designing surveys to assess consumer preferences. While a majority of surveys are conducted through the Internet and telephone, other methods may include focus group discussions, mail responses, or setting up booths in public places, such as shopping malls, for example. Trained interviewers usually conduct the surveys under a market research analyst's direction.

Market opinion research has contributed greatly to a higher standard of living as most products and services consumers purchase are available with the aid of market research. By making recommendations to their client or employer, market research analysts provide companies with vital information to help them make decisions on the promotion, distribution, and design of products or services. For example, child proof closures on medicine bottles exist because research helped define the most workable design; and the growing variety of ready to cook meals, such as microwaveable soups and prepackaged meat products, exist because of increasing public demand for fast and convenient meals. The information also may be used to determine whether the company should add new lines of merchandise, open new branches, or otherwise diversify the company's operations. Market research analysts also help develop advertising brochures and commercials, sales plans, and product promotions such as rebates and giveaways based on their knowledge of the consumer being targeted.

Survey researchers also gather information about people and their opinions, but these workers focus exclusively on designing and conducting surveys. They work for a variety of clients—such as corporations, government agencies, political candidates—gathering information to help make fiscal or policy decisions, measure the effectiveness of those decisions, and improve customer satisfaction. Survey researchers may conduct opinion research to determine public attitudes on various issues; the research results may help political or business leaders measure public support for their electoral prospects or social policies. Like market research analysts, survey researchers may use a variety of mediums to conduct surveys, such as the Internet, telephone interviews, or questionnaires sent through the mail. They also may supervise interviewers who conduct surveys in person or over the telephone.

Survey researchers design surveys in many different formats, depending upon the scope of their research and the method of collection. Interview surveys, for example, are common because they can increase participation rates. Survey researchers may consult with economists, statisticians, market research analysts, or other data users in order to design surveys. They also may present survey results to clients.

Work environment. Market and survey researchers generally have structured work schedules. They often work alone, writing reports and preparing statistical charts on computers, but they sometimes may be part of a research team. Market researchers who conduct personal interviews have frequent contact with the public. Most work under pressure of deadlines and tight schedules, which may require overtime. Travel may be necessary.

Training, Other Qualifications, and Advancement

While a bachelor's degree is often sufficient for entry-level market and survey research jobs, higher degrees are usually required for advancement and more technical positions. Strong quantitative skills and keeping current with the latest methods of developing, conducting, and analyzing surveys and other data also are important for advancement.

Education and training. A bachelor's degree is the minimum educational requirement for many market and survey research jobs. However, a master's degree is usually required for more technical positions.

In addition to completing courses in business, marketing, and consumer behavior, prospective market and survey researchers should take social science courses, including economics, psychology and sociology. Because of the importance of quantitative skills to market and survey researchers, courses in mathematics, statistics, sampling theory and survey design, and computer science are extremely helpful. Market and survey researchers often earn advanced degrees in business administration, marketing, statistics, communications, or other closely related disciplines.

While in college, aspiring market and survey researchers should gain experience gathering and analyzing data, conducting interviews or surveys, and writing reports on their findings. This experience can prove invaluable toward obtaining a full-time position in the field, because much of the work may center on these duties. Some schools help graduate students find internships or part-time employment in government agencies, consulting firms, financial institutions, or marketing research firms prior to graduation.

Other qualifications. Market and survey researchers spend a lot of time performing precise data analysis, so being detail-oriented is critical. Patience and persistence are also necessary qualities because these workers devote long hours to independent study and problem solving. At the same time, they must work well with others as market and survey researchers sometimes oversee the interviewing of individuals. Communication skills are important, too, because the wording of surveys is critical, and researchers must be able to present their findings both orally and in writing.

Certification and advancement. Market research analysts often begin their careers by assisting others prior to being assigned independent research projects. With experience, continuing education, and advanced degrees, they may advance to more responsible positions in this occupation. Those with expertise in marketing or survey research may choose to teach. While a master's degree is often sufficient to teach as a marketing or survey research instructor

in junior and community colleges, most colleges and universities require instructors to hold a Ph.D. A Ph.D. and extensive publications in academic journals are needed for professorship, tenure, and promotion. Others advance to supervisory or managerial positions. Many corporation and government executives have a strong background in marketing.

Advancement in this occupation may be helped by obtaining certification. The Marketing Research Association (MRA) offers a certification program for professional researchers who wish to demonstrate their expertise. The Professional Researcher Certification (PRC) is awarded for two levels of knowledge: practitioner and expert. Prior to gaining certification, each level of knowledge requires certain criteria to be met, consisting largely of education and experience, and also previous membership to at least one professional marketing research organization. Those who have been granted the PRC designation require continuing education within their particular discipline, and individuals must apply to renew their certification every 2 years.

Employment

Market and survey researchers held about 273,200 jobs in 2008, most of which—249,800—were held by market research analysts. Because of the applicability of market research to many industries, market research analysts are employed throughout the economy. The industries that employed the largest number of market research analysts in 2008 were management, scientific, and technical consulting services; management of companies and enterprises; computer systems design and related services; insurance carriers; and other professional, scientific, and technical services—which includes marketing research and public opinion polling.

Survey researchers held about 23,400 jobs in 2008. Most were employed primarily by firms in other professional, scientific, and technical services—which include market research and public opinion polling; scientific research and development services; and management, scientific, and technical consulting services. About 9 percent of survey researchers worked in educational services—which includes colleges, universities, and professional schools.

A number of market and survey researchers combine a full-time job in government, academia, or business with part-time consulting work in another setting. About 7 percent of market and survey researchers are self-employed.

Besides holding the previously mentioned jobs, many people who perform market and survey research held faculty positions in colleges and universities. These workers are counted as postsecondary teachers rather than market and survey researchers.

Job Outlook

Employment growth of market and survey researchers is projected to be much faster than average. Job opportunities should be best for jobseekers with a master's or Ph.D. degree in marketing or a social science and with strong quantitative skills.

Employment change. Overall employment of market and survey researchers is projected to grow 28 percent from 2008 to 2018, much faster than the average for all occupations. Market research analysts, the larger specialty, will experience much faster than average job

Projections Data from the National Employment Matrix

Occupational title	SOC Code	Employment, 2008	Projected employment, 2018	Change, 2008–2018	
				Number	Percent
Market and survey researchers 19-3020		273,200	350,500	77,200	28
Market research analysts 19-3021		249,800	319,900	70,100	28
Survey researchers... 19-3022		23,400	30,500	7,100	30

NOTE: Data in this table are rounded.

growth because competition between companies seeking to expand their market and sales of their products will generate a growing need for marketing professionals. Marketing research provides organizations valuable feedback from purchasers, allowing companies to evaluate consumer satisfaction and adjust their marketing strategies and plan more effectively for the future. Future locations of stores and shopping centers, for example, will be determined by marketing research, as will consumer preference of virtually all products and services. In addition, globalization of the marketplace creates a need for more market researchers to analyze foreign markets and competition.

Survey researchers, a much smaller specialty, will also increase much faster than average as public policy groups and all levels of governments increasingly use public opinion research to help determine a variety of issues, such as the best mass transit systems, social programs, and special services for school children and senior citizens that will be needed. Survey researchers will also be needed to meet the growing demand for market and opinion research as an increasingly competitive economy requires businesses and organizations to allocate advertising funds and other expenditures more effectively and efficiently.

Job prospects. Bachelor's degree holders may face competition for market research jobs, as many positions, especially technical ones, require a master's or doctoral degree. Among bachelor's degree holders, those with good quantitative skills, including a strong background in mathematics, statistics, survey design, and computer science, will have the best opportunities. Those with a background in consumer behavior or an undergraduate degree in a social science—psychology, sociology, or economics—may qualify for less technical positions, such as a public opinion researcher. Obtaining the Professional Researcher Certification also can be important as it demonstrates competence and professionalism among potential candidates. Overall, job opportunities should be best for jobseekers with a master's or Ph.D. degree in marketing or a related field and with strong quantitative skills. Market research analysts should have the best opportunities in consulting firms and marketing research firms as companies find it more profitable to contract for market research services rather than support their own marketing department. However, other organizations, including computer systems design companies, software publishers, financial services organizations, health-care institutions, advertising firms, and insurance companies, may also offer job opportunities for market research analysts. Increasingly, market research analysts not only collect and analyze information, but also help clients implement ideas and recommendations.

There will be fewer job opportunities for survey researchers since it is a relatively smaller occupation and a greater number of candidates qualify for these positions. The best prospects will come from growth in the market research and public opinion polling industry, which employs many survey researchers.

Earnings

Median annual wages of market research analysts in May 2008 were $61,070. The middle 50 percent earned between $43,990 and $85,510. The lowest 10 percent earned less than $33,770, and the highest 10 percent earned more than $112,410. Median annual wages in the industries employing the largest numbers of market research analysts in May 2008 were the following:

Computer systems design and related services	$77,170
Management of companies and enterprises	65,880
Other professional, scientific, and technical services	58,480
Advertising, public relations, and related services	56,730
Management, scientific, and technical consulting services	55,570

Median annual wages of survey researchers in May 2008 were $36,220. The middle 50 percent earned between $22,290 and $54,480. The lowest 10 percent earned less than $17,650, and the highest 10 percent earned more than $75,940. Median annual wages of survey researchers in other professional, scientific, and technical services were $26,440.

Related Occupations

Market and survey researchers perform research to find out how well the market will receive products, services, and ideas. This research may include planning, implementing, and analyzing surveys to determine the needs and preferences of people. Other jobs using these skills include economists; management analysts; operations research analysts; psychologists; sociologists and political scientists; statisticians; and urban and regional planners.

Market and survey researchers often work closely with advertising, marketing, promotions, public relations, and sales managers.

When analyzing data, market and survey researchers must use quantitative skills similar to those of actuaries; cost estimators; and mathematicians.

Market and survey researchers often are concerned with public opinion, as are public relations specialists.

Sources of Additional Information

For information about careers and certification in market research, contact

▸ Marketing Research Association, 110 National Dr., 2nd Floor, Glastonbury, CT 06033. Internet: www.mra-net.org

For information about careers in survey research, contact

▸ Council of American Survey Research Organizations, 170 North Country Rd., Suite 4, Port Jefferson, NY 11777. Internet: www.casro.org

Medical and Health Services Managers

(O*NET 11-9111.00, and 11-9111.01)

Significant Points

■ Job opportunities will be good, especially for applicants with work experience in health care and strong business and management skills.

■ A master's degree is the standard credential, although a bachelor's degree is adequate for some entry-level positions.

■ Medical and health services managers typically work long hours and may be called at all hours to deal with problems.

Nature of the Work

Health care is a business and, like every business, it needs good management to keep the business running smoothly. *Medical and health services managers*, also referred to as *health-care executives* or *health-care administrators*, plan, direct, coordinate, and supervise the delivery of health care. These workers are either specialists in charge of a specific clinical department or generalists who manage an entire facility or system.

The structure and financing of health care are changing rapidly. Future medical and health services managers must be prepared to deal with the integration of health-care delivery systems, technological innovations, an increasingly complex regulatory environment, restructuring of work, and an increased focus on preventive care. They will be called on to improve efficiency in health-care facilities and the quality of the care provided.

Large facilities usually have several *assistant administrators* who aid the top administrator and handle daily decisions. Assistant administrators direct activities in clinical areas, such as nursing, surgery, therapy, medical records, and health information.

In smaller facilities, top administrators handle more of the details of daily operations. For example, many *nursing home administrators* manage personnel, finances, facility operations, and admissions while also providing resident care.

Clinical managers have training or experience in a specific clinical area and, accordingly, have more specific responsibilities than do generalists. For example, directors of physical therapy are experienced physical therapists, and most health information and medical record administrators have a bachelor's degree in health information

or medical record administration. Clinical managers establish and implement policies, objectives, and procedures for their departments; evaluate personnel and work quality; develop reports and budgets; and coordinate activities with other managers.

Health information managers are responsible for the maintenance and security of all patient records. Recent regulations enacted by the federal government require that all health-care providers maintain electronic patient records and that these records be secure. As a result, health information managers must keep up with current computer and software technology, as well as with legislative requirements. In addition, as patient data become more frequently used for quality management and in medical research, health information managers must ensure that databases are complete, accurate, and available only to authorized personnel.

In group medical practices, managers work closely with physicians. Whereas an office manager might handle business affairs in small medical groups, leaving policy decisions to the physicians themselves, larger groups usually employ a full-time administrator to help formulate business strategies and coordinate day-to-day business.

A small group of 10 to 15 physicians might employ one administrator to oversee personnel matters, billing and collection, budgeting, planning, equipment outlays, and patient flow. A large practice of 40 to 50 physicians might have a chief administrator and several assistants, each responsible for a different area of expertise.

Medical and health services managers in managed care settings perform functions similar to those of their counterparts in large group practices, except that they could have larger staffs to manage. In addition, they might do more community outreach and preventive care than do managers of a group practice.

Some medical and health services managers oversee the activities of a number of facilities in health systems. Such systems might contain both inpatient and outpatient facilities and offer a wide range of patient services.

Work environment. Some managers work in comfortable, private offices; others share space with other staff. Many medical and health services managers work long hours. Nursing care facilities and hospitals operate around the clock; administrators and managers may be called at all hours to deal with problems. They also travel to attend meetings or to inspect satellite facilities.

Training, Other Qualifications, and Advancement

A master's degree in one of a number of fields is the standard credential for most generalist positions as a medical or health-care manager. A bachelor's degree is sometimes adequate for entry-level positions in smaller facilities and departments. In physicians' offices and some other facilities, on-the-job experience may substitute for formal education.

Education and training. Medical and health services managers must be familiar with management principles and practices. A master's degree in health services administration, long-term care administration, health sciences, public health, public administration, or business administration is the standard credential for most generalist positions in this field. However, a bachelor's degree is adequate for some entry-level positions in smaller facilities, at the departmental level within health-care organizations, and in health information management. Physicians' offices and some other facilities hire those with on-the-job experience instead of formal education.

Bachelor's, master's, and doctoral degree programs in health administration are offered by colleges; universities; and schools of public health, medicine, allied health, public administration, and business administration. In 2008, according to the Commission on Accreditation of Healthcare Management Education, there were 72 schools that had accredited programs leading to the master's degree in health services administration.

For people seeking to become heads of clinical departments, a degree in the appropriate field and work experience may be sufficient early in their career. However, a master's degree in health services administration or a related field might be required to advance. For example, nursing service administrators usually are chosen from among supervisory registered nurses with administrative abilities and graduate degrees in nursing or health services administration.

Health information managers require a bachelor's degree from an accredited program. In 2008, there were 48 accredited bachelor's degree programs and 5 master's degree programs in health information management, according to the Commission on Accreditation for Health Informatics and Information Management Education.

Some graduate programs seek students with undergraduate degrees in business or health administration; however, many graduate programs prefer students with a liberal arts or health profession background. Candidates with previous work experience in health care also may have an advantage. Competition for entry into these programs is keen, and applicants need above-average grades to gain admission. Graduate programs usually last between two and three years. They may include up to one year of supervised administrative experience and coursework in areas such as hospital organization and management, marketing, accounting and budgeting, human resources administration, strategic planning, law and ethics, biostatistics or epidemiology, health economics, and health information systems. Some programs allow students to specialize in one type of facility—hospitals, nursing care facilities, mental health facilities, or medical groups. Other programs encourage a generalist approach to health administration education.

Licensure. All states and the District of Columbia require nursing care facility administrators to have a bachelor's degree, pass a licensing examination, complete a state-approved training program, and pursue continuing education. Some states also require licenses for administrators in assisted-living facilities. A license is not required in other areas of medical and health services management.

Certification and other qualifications. Medical and health services managers often are responsible for facilities and equipment worth millions of dollars and for hundreds of employees. To make effective decisions, they need to be open to different opinions and good at analyzing contradictory information. They must understand finance and information systems and be able to interpret data. Motivating others to implement their decisions requires strong leadership abilities. Tact, diplomacy, flexibility, and communication skills are essential because medical and health services managers spend most of their time interacting with others.

Health information managers who have a bachelor's degree or post-baccalaureate degree from an approved program and who pass an exam can earn certification as a Registered Health Information Administrator from the American Health Information Management Association.

Advancement. Medical and health services managers advance by moving into more responsible and higher-paying positions, such as assistant or associate administrator, department head, or chief executive officer, or by moving to larger facilities. Some experienced managers also may become consultants or professors of health-care management.

New graduates with master's degrees in health services administration may start as department managers or as supervisory staff. The level of the starting position varies with the experience of the applicant and the size of the organization. Hospitals and other health facilities offer postgraduate residencies and fellowships, which usually are staff positions. Graduates from master's degree programs also take jobs in large medical group practices, clinics, mental health facilities, nursing care corporations, and consulting firms.

Graduates with bachelor's degrees in health administration usually begin as administrative assistants or assistant department heads in larger hospitals. They also may begin as department heads or assistant administrators in small hospitals or nursing care facilities.

Employment

Medical and health services managers held about 283,500 jobs in 2008. About 38 percent worked in hospitals, and another 19 percent worked in offices of physicians or in nursing and residential care facilities. Many of the remainder worked in home health-care services, federal government health-care facilities, outpatient care centers, insurance carriers, and community care facilities for the elderly.

Job Outlook

Employment is projected to grow faster than the average. Job opportunities should be good, especially for applicants with work experience in health care and strong business management skills.

Employment change. Employment of medical and health services managers is expected to grow 16 percent from 2008 to 2018, faster than the average for all occupations. The health-care industry will continue to expand and diversify, requiring managers to help ensure smooth business operations.

Managers in all settings will be needed to improve quality and efficiency of health care while controlling costs as insurance companies and Medicare demand higher levels of accountability. Managers also will be needed to oversee the computerization of patient records and to ensure their security as required by law. Additional demand for managers will stem from the need to recruit workers and increase employee retention, to comply with changing regulations, to implement new technology, and to help improve the health of their communities by emphasizing preventive care.

Hospitals will continue to employ the most medical and health services managers over the 2008–2018 decade. However, the number of new jobs created is expected to increase at a slower rate in hospitals than in many other industries because of the growing use

Projections Data from the National Employment Matrix

Occupational title	SOC Code	Employment, 2008	Projected employment, 2018	Change, 2008–2018	
				Number	Percent
Medical and health services managers 11-9111		283,500	328,800	45,400	16

NOTE: Data in this table are rounded.

of clinics and other outpatient care sites. Despite relatively slow employment growth in hospitals, a large number of new jobs will be created because of the industry's large size.

Employment will grow fast in offices of health practitioners. Many services previously provided in hospitals will continue to shift to these settings, especially as medical technologies improve. Demand in medical group practice management will grow as medical group practices become larger and more complex.

Medical and health services managers also will be employed by health-care management companies that provide management services to hospitals and other organizations and to specific departments such as emergency, information management systems, managed care contract negotiations, and physician recruiting.

Job prospects. Job opportunities will be good, especially for applicants with work experience in health care and strong business management skills. Medical and health services managers with experience in large hospital facilities will enjoy an advantage in the job market as hospitals become larger and more complex. Competition for jobs at the highest management levels will be keen because of the high pay and prestige.

Earnings

Median annual wages of wage and salary medical and health services managers were $80,240 in May 2008. The middle 50 percent earned between $62,170 and $104,120. The lowest 10 percent earned less than $48,300, and the highest 10 percent earned more than $137,800. Median annual wages in the industries employing the largest numbers of medical and health services managers in May 2008 were the following:

General medical and surgical hospitals	$87,040
Outpatient care centers	74,130
Offices of physicians	74,060
Home health care services	71,450
Nursing care facilities	71,190

Earnings of medical and health services managers vary by type and size of the facility and by level of responsibility. For example, the Medical Group Management Association reported that, in 2007, median salaries for administrators were $82,423 in practices with 6 or fewer physicians; $105,710 in practices with 7 to 25 physicians; and $119,000 in practices with 26 or more physicians.

According to a survey by the Professional Association of Health Care Office Management, 2009 average total compensation for office managers in specialty physicians' practices was $54,314 in gastroenterology; $54,201 in dermatology; $58,899 in cardiology; $48,793 in ophthalmology; and $44,910 in obstetrics and gynecology;

$51,263 in orthopedics; $51,466 in pediatrics; $48,814 in internal medicine; and $47,152 in family practice.

Related Occupations

Medical and health services managers have training or experience in both health and management. Other occupations requiring knowledge of both fields include insurance underwriters and social and community service managers.

Sources of Additional Information

Information about undergraduate and graduate academic programs in this field is available from

▶ Association of University Programs in Health Administration, 2000 N. 14th St., Suite 780, Arlington, VA 22201. Internet: www.aupha. org

For a list of accredited graduate programs in medical and health services administration, contact

▶ Commission on Accreditation of Healthcare Management Education, 2111 Wilson Blvd., Suite 700, Arlington, VA 22201. Internet: www. cahme.org

For information about career opportunities in health-care management, contact

▶ American College of Healthcare Executives, 1 N. Franklin St., Suite 1700, Chicago, IL 60606. Internet: www.healthmanagementcareers. org

For information about career opportunities in long-term care administration, contact

▶ American College of Healthcare Administrators, 1321 Duke St., Suite 400, Alexandria, VA 22314. Internet: www.achca.org

For information about career opportunities in medical group practices and ambulatory care management, contact

▶ Medical Group Management Association, 104 Inverness Terrace E., Englewood, CO 80112. Internet: www.mgma.org

For information about medical and health-care office managers, contact

▶ Professional Association of Health Care Office Management, 3755 Avocado Blvd., Suite 306, La Mesa, CA 91941. Internet: www. pahcom.com

For information about career opportunities in health information management, contact

▶ American Health Information Management Association, 233 N. Michigan Ave., 21st Floor, Chicago, IL 60601. Internet: www. ahima.org

Medical Assistants

(O*NET 31-9092.00)

Significant Points

■ Employment is projected to grow much faster than average, ranking medical assistants among the fastest-growing occupations over the 2008–2018 decade.

■ Job prospects should be excellent.

■ About 62 percent of medical assistants work in offices of physicians.

■ Some medical assistants are trained on the job, but many complete one-year or two-year programs.

Nature of the Work

Medical assistants perform administrative and clinical tasks to keep the offices of physicians, podiatrists, chiropractors, and other health practitioners running smoothly. The duties of medical assistants vary from office to office, depending on the location and size of the practice and the practitioner's specialty. In small practices, medical assistants usually do many different kinds of tasks, handling both administrative and clinical duties and reporting directly to an office manager, physician, or other health practitioner. Those in large practices tend to specialize in a particular area, under the supervision of department administrators. Medical assistants should not be confused with physician assistants, who examine, diagnose, and treat patients under the direct supervision of a physician.

Administrative medical assistants update and file patients' medical records, fill out insurance forms, and arrange for hospital admissions and laboratory services. They also perform tasks less specific to medical settings, such as answering telephones, greeting patients, handling correspondence, scheduling appointments, and handling billing and bookkeeping.

Clinical medical assistants have various duties, depending on state law. Some common tasks include taking medical histories and recording vital signs, explaining treatment procedures to patients, preparing patients for examinations, and assisting physicians during examinations. Medical assistants collect and prepare laboratory specimens and sometimes perform basic laboratory tests, dispose of contaminated supplies, and sterilize medical instruments. As directed by a physician, they might instruct patients about medications and special diets, prepare and administer medications, authorize drug refills, telephone prescriptions to a pharmacy, draw blood, prepare patients for X-rays, take electrocardiograms, remove sutures, and change dressings. Medical assistants also may arrange examining room instruments and equipment, purchase and maintain supplies and equipment, and keep waiting and examining rooms neat and clean.

Ophthalmic medical assistants, *optometric assistants*, and *podiatric medical assistants* are examples of specialized assistants who have additional duties. Ophthalmic medical assistants help ophthalmologists provide eye care. They conduct diagnostic tests, measure and record vision, and test eye muscle function. They apply eye dressings and also show patients how to insert, remove, and care for contact lenses. Under the direction of the physician, ophthalmic medical assistants may administer eye medications. They also maintain optical and surgical instruments and may assist the ophthalmologist in surgery. Optometric assistants also help provide eye care, working with optometrists. They provide chair-side assistance, instruct patients about contact lens use and care, conduct preliminary tests on patients, and otherwise provide assistance while working directly with an optometrist. Podiatric medical assistants make castings of feet, expose and develop X-rays, and assist podiatrists in surgery.

Work environment. Medical assistants work in well-lighted, clean environments. They constantly interact with other people and may have to handle several responsibilities at once. Most full-time medical assistants work a regular 40-hour week. However, medical assistants may work part time, evenings, or weekends.

Training, Other Qualifications, and Advancement

Some medical assistants are trained on the job, but many complete 1- or 2-year programs. Almost all medical assistants have at least a high school diploma, although there are no formal education or training requirements.

Education and training. Medical assisting programs are offered in vocational-technical high schools, postsecondary vocational schools, and community and junior colleges. Postsecondary programs usually last either 1 year and result in a certificate or diploma, or 2 years and result in an associate degree. Courses cover anatomy, physiology, and medical terminology, as well as keyboarding, transcription, recordkeeping, accounting, and insurance processing. Students learn laboratory techniques, clinical and diagnostic procedures, pharmaceutical principles, the administration of medications, and first aid. They study office practices, patient relations, medical law, and ethics. There are two accrediting bodies that accredit medical assisting programs. Accredited programs often include an internship that provides practical experience in physicians' offices or other health-care facilities.

Formal training in medical assisting, while generally preferred, is not required. Many medical assistants are trained on the job, and usually only need to have a high school diploma or the equivalent. Recommended high school courses include mathematics, health, biology, keyboarding, bookkeeping, computers, and office skills. Volunteer experience in the health-care field also is helpful. Medical assistants who are trained on the job usually spend their first few months attending training sessions and working closely with more experienced workers.

Some states allow medical assistants to perform more advanced procedures, such as giving injections or taking X-rays, after passing a test or taking a course.

Other qualifications. Medical assistants deal with the public; therefore, they must be neat and well groomed and have a courteous, pleasant manner and they must be able to put patients at ease and explain physicians' instructions. They must respect the confidential nature of medical information. Clinical duties require a reasonable level of manual dexterity and visual acuity.

Certification and advancement. Although not required, certification indicates that a medical assistant meets certain standards

Projections Data from the National Employment Matrix

Occupational title	SOC Code	Employment, 2008	Projected employment, 2018	Change, 2008–2018	
				Number	Percent
Medical assistants	31-9092	483,600	647,500	163,900	34

NOTE: Data in this table are rounded.

of knowledge. It may also help to distinguish an experienced or formally trained assistant from an entry-level assistant, which may lead to a higher salary or more employment opportunities. There are various associations—such as the American Association of Medical Assistants (AAMA) and Association of Medical Technologists (AMT)—that award certification credentials to medical assistants. The certification process varies by association. It is also possible to become certified in a specialty, such as podiatry, optometry, or ophthalmology.

Medical assistants may also advance to other occupations through experience or additional training. For example, some may go on to teach medical assisting, and others pursue additional education to become nurses or other health-care workers. Administrative medical assistants may advance to office managers, or qualify for a variety of administrative support occupations.

Employment

Medical assistants held about 483,600 jobs in 2008. About 62 percent worked in offices of physicians; 13 percent worked in public and private hospitals, including inpatient and outpatient facilities; and 11 percent worked in offices of other health practitioners, such as chiropractors and optometrists. Most of the remainder worked in other health-care industries, such as outpatient care centers and nursing and residential care facilities.

Job Outlook

Employment is projected to grow much faster than average, ranking medical assistants among the fastest growing occupations over the 2008–2018 decade. Job opportunities should be excellent, particularly for those with formal training or experience, and certification.

Employment change. Employment of medical assistants is expected to grow 34 percent from 2008 to 2018, much faster than the average for all occupations. As the health-care industry expands because of technological advances in medicine and the growth and aging of the population, there will be an increased need for all health-care workers. The increasing prevalence of certain conditions, such as obesity and diabetes, also will increase demand for health-care services and medical assistants. Increasing use of medical assistants to allow doctors to care for more patients will further stimulate job growth.

Helping to drive job growth is the increasing number of group practices, clinics, and other health-care facilities that need a high proportion of support personnel, particularly medical assistants who can handle both administrative and clinical duties. In addition, medical assistants work mostly in primary care, a consistently growing sector of the health-care industry.

Job prospects. Jobseekers who want to work as a medical assistant should find excellent job prospects. Medical assistants are projected to account for a very large number of new jobs, and many other opportunities will come from the need to replace workers leaving the occupation. Medical assistants with formal training or experience—particularly those with certification—should have the best job opportunities, since employers generally prefer to hire these workers.

Earnings

The earnings of medical assistants vary, depending on their experience, skill level, and location. Median annual wages of wage-and-salary medical assistants were $28,300 in May 2008. The middle 50 percent earned between $23,700 and $33,050. The lowest 10 percent earned less than $20,600, and the highest 10 percent earned more than $39,570. Median annual wages in the industries employing the largest numbers of medical assistants in May 2008 were as follows:

General medical and surgical hospitals $29,720
Colleges, universities, and professional schools 28,820
Offices of physicians 28,710
Outpatient care centers 28,570
Offices of other health practitioners 25,240

Related Occupations

Medical assistants perform work similar to the tasks completed by other workers in medical support occupations. Administrative medical assistants do work similar to that of medical records and health information technicians; medical secretaries; and medical transcriptionists.

Clinical medical assistants perform duties similar to those of dental assistants; dental hygienists; licensed practical and licensed vocational nurses; nursing and psychiatric aides; occupational therapist assistants and aides; pharmacy technicians and aides; physical therapist assistants and aides; and surgical technologists.

Sources of Additional Information

Information about career opportunities and certification for medical assistants is available from

▸ American Association of Medical Assistants, 20 N. Wacker Dr., Suite 1575, Chicago, IL 60606. Internet: www.aama-ntl.org

▸ American Medical Technologists, 10700 W. Higgins Rd., Suite 150, Rosemont, IL 60018. Internet: www.amt1.com

▸ National Healthcareer Association, 7 Ridgedale Ave., Suite 203, Cedar Knolls, NJ 07927. Internet: www.nhanow.com

For lists of accredited educational programs in medical assisting, contact

▶ Accrediting Bureau of Health Education Schools, 7777 Leesburg Pike, Suite 314 N, Falls Church, VA 22043. Internet: www.abhes.org

▶ Commission on Accreditation of Allied Health Education Programs, 1361 Park St., Clearwater, FL 33756. Internet: www.caahep.org

Information about career opportunities, training programs, and certification for ophthalmic medical personnel is available from

▶ Joint Commission on Allied Health Personnel in Ophthalmology, 2025 Woodlane Dr., St. Paul, MN 55125. Internet: www.jcahpo.org

Information about career opportunities, training programs, and certification for optometric assistants is available from

▶ American Optometric Association, 243 N. Lindbergh Blvd., St. Louis, MO 63141. Internet: www.aoa.org

Information about certification for podiatric assistants is available from

▶ American Society of Podiatric Medical Assistants, 2124 S. Austin Blvd., Cicero, IL 60804. Internet: www.aspma.org

Medical Equipment Repairers

(O*NET 49-9062.00)

Significant Points

■ Employment is projected to grow 27 percent, which is much faster than the average for all occupations.

■ Excellent job opportunities are expected.

■ Employers generally prefer applicants with an associate's degree in biomedical equipment technology or engineering; a bachelor's degree often is needed for advancement.

■ Repairers may be on call around the clock in case of emergencies.

Nature of the Work

Medical equipment repairers, also known as *biomedical equipment technicians* (BMET), maintain, adjust, calibrate, and repair a wide variety of electronic, electromechanical, and hydraulic equipment used in hospitals and other medical environments, including health practitioners' offices. They may work on patient monitors, defibrillators, medical imaging equipment (X-rays, CAT scanners, and ultrasound equipment), voice-controlled operating tables, electric wheelchairs, as well as other sophisticated dental, optometric, and ophthalmic equipment.

Medical equipment repairers use a wide variety of tools to conduct their work, including multimeters, specialized software, and computers designed to communicate with specific pieces of hardware. They may also use hand tools, soldering irons, and other electronic tools to fix or adjust malfunctioning equipment, such as a broken wheelchair. If a machine is not functioning to its potential, the repairer may have to adjust the mechanical or hydraulic components, or adjust the software to bring the equipment back into calibration. Most medical equipment is powered by electricity, but because many also have mechanical and hydraulic components, being familiar with all of these systems is critical.

In some cases, medical equipment repairers perform routine scheduled maintenance to ensure that all equipment is in good working order. Since many doctors, particularly specialty practitioners, regularly use complex medical devices to run tests and diagnose patients, they must be guaranteed that the readings are accurate. For less complicated equipment, such as electric hospital beds, many repairs may take place on an as-needed basis.

In a hospital setting, specialists must be comfortable working around patients because repairs occasionally must take place while equipment is being used. When this is the case, the repairer must take great care to ensure that repairs do not disturb patients.

Many medical equipment repairers are employed in hospitals. Some, however, work for electronic equipment repair and maintenance companies that service medical equipment used by other health practitioners, including gynecologists, orthodontists, veterinarians, and other diagnostic medical professionals. Whereas some medical equipment repairers are trained to fix a wide variety of equipment, others specialize and become proficient at repairing one or a small number of machines.

Work environment. Medical equipment repairers usually work daytime hours, but are often expected to be on call. Still, like other hospital employees, some repairers work irregular hours and may be required to work overtime if an important piece of medical equipment malfunctions. Medical equipment repairers often must work in a patient environment, which has the potential to expose them to diseases and other health risks. Because medical equipment is often used in life-saving therapies, diagnosing and repairing equipment can be urgent. Although this may be gratifying, it can also be very stressful. Those who work as contractors often have to travel— sometimes long distances—to perform needed repairs.

Training, Other Qualifications, and Advancement

Employers generally prefer candidates with an associate degree in biomedical technology or engineering; a bachelor's degree often is needed for advancement.

Education and training. Although education requirements vary depending on a worker's experience and area of specialization, the most common education path for repairers is an associate degree in biomedical equipment technology or engineering. Those who repair less complicated equipment, such as hospital beds or electric wheelchairs, may learn entirely through on-the-job training. Others, particularly those who work on more sophisticated equipment such as CAT scanners and defibrillators, may need a bachelor's degree. New workers generally start by observing and assisting experienced repairers over a period of 3 to 6 months, learning a single piece of equipment at a time. Gradually, they begin working more independently, while still under close supervision. Each piece of equipment is different, and medical equipment repairers must learn each one separately. In some cases, this requires careful study of a machine's technical specifications and manual. Medical device manufacturers also may provide training courses in a classroom or online.

Because medical equipment technology is rapidly evolving and new devices are frequently introduced, repairers must constantly update their skills and knowledge of equipment. As a result, they must

Projections Data from the National Employment Matrix

Occupational title	SOC Code	Employment, 2008	Projected employment, 2018	Change, 2008–2018	
				Number	Percent
Medical equipment repairers.................................... 49-9062		41,400	52,600	11,300	27

NOTE: Data in this table are rounded.

constantly learn new technologies and equipment through seminars, self-study, and certification exams.

Certification and other qualifications. Medical equipment repairers are problem solvers—diagnosing and repairing equipment, often under time constraints—therefore, being able to work under pressure is critical. As in most repair occupations, having mechanical and technical aptitude, as well as manual dexterity, is important.

Some associations offer certifications for medical equipment repairers. For example, the Association for the Advancement of Medical Instrumentation (AAMI) offers certification in three specialty areas—Certified Biomedical Equipment Technician (CBET), Certified Radiology Equipment Specialists (CRES), and Certified Laboratory Equipment Specialist (CLEB). Those who wish to become certified must satisfy a combination of education and experience requirements prior to taking the AAMI examination. Candidates who meet the necessary criteria can begin pursuing the desired certification on the basis of their qualifications. Certification demonstrates a level of competency and can make an applicant more attractive to employers, as well as increase one's opportunities for advancement. Most employers, particularly hospitals, often pay for their in-house medical repairers to become certified.

Advancement. Most medical equipment repairers advance by demonstrating competency at lower levels, which allows them to repair more complex equipment. Some may become supervisors or managers, but these positions usually require a bachelor's degree. Experienced repairers also may serve as mentors for new employees or teach training courses on specific products.

Employment

Medical equipment repairers held 41,400 jobs in May 2008. Industries employing the largest number of medical equipment repairers in 2008 were as follows:

Professional and commercial equipment and
    supplies merchant wholesalers 9,400
Hospitals, public and private................................ 7,100
Electronic and precision equipment repair and
    maintenance.. 5,700
Health and personal care stores............................ 2,300
Consumer goods rental.. 2,300

Job Outlook

Medical equipment repairers are projected to grow much faster than average between 2008 and 2018. Opportunities should be excellent for qualified job seekers.

Employment change. Employment of medical equipment repairers is expected to grow 27 percent over the 2008–2018 decade, which is

much faster than the average for all occupations. As the proportion of people in older age groups will grow faster than the total population between 2008 and 2018, demand for overall health care will increase. Increased demand for health-care services and increasing complexity of the medical equipment used in hospitals and by private practitioners will result in a greater need for repairers. For example, a growing number of hospital diagnostic, electromedical, and patient monitoring equipment including CAT scans, electrocardiogram, magnetic resonance imaging, ultrasound, and X-ray machines, as well as hospital furniture, such as full electric beds and wheelchairs, will all need to be maintained and repaired. Additionally, machines used by private practitioners and technicians to diagnose and treat vision, teeth, and other parts of the human body also are becoming increasingly sophisticated, and will further spur growth of medical equipment repairers.

Job prospects. A combination of employment growth and the need to replace workers leaving the occupation will result in excellent job prospects over the next decade. The number of job openings is expected to outnumber the number of qualified applicants; therefore, applicants should have little difficulty finding jobs. Candidates with an associate's degree in biomedical equipment technology or engineering should have the best prospects. Opportunities should be even more abundant for those who are willing to relocate because relatively few qualified applicants can be found in rural areas.

Earnings

Median annual wages for medical equipment repairers in May 2008 were $41,520. The middle 50 percent earned between $31,590 and $53,720. The lowest 10 percent earned less than $25,860, and the highest 10 percent earned more than $65,930.

Median annual wages for medical equipment repairers in the largest industries were as follows:

General medical and surgical hospitals $45,990
Electronic and precision equipment repair
    and maintenance 44,740
Professional and commercial equipment and
    supplies merchant wholesalers 42,950
Health and personal care stores.......................... 32,770
Consumer goods rental...................................... 29,020

Related Occupations

Other workers who repair precision mechanical and electronic equipment include coin, vending, and amusement machine servicers and repairers; computer, automated teller, and office machine repairers; and medical, dental, and ophthalmic laboratory technicians.

Sources of Additional Information

For information about medical equipment repairers and a list of schools with related programs of study, contact

▶ Association for the Advancement of Medical Instrumentation (AAMI), 1110 N. Glebe Rd., Suite 220, Arlington, VA 22201-4795. Internet: www.aami.org

Medical Records and Health Information Technicians

(O*NET 29-2071.00)

Significant Points

- Employment is expected to grow much faster than the average.
- Job prospects should be very good, particularly for technicians with strong computer software skills.
- Entrants usually have an associate degree.
- This is one of the few health-related occupations in which there is no direct hands-on patient care.

Nature of the Work

Medical records and health information technicians assemble patients' health information including medical history, symptoms, examination results, diagnostic tests, treatment methods, and all other health-care provider services. Technicians organize and manage health information data by ensuring its quality, accuracy, accessibility, and security. They regularly communicate with physicians and other health-care professionals to clarify diagnoses or to obtain additional information.

The increasing use of electronic health records (EHR) will continue to broaden and alter the job responsibilities of health information technicians. For example, with the use of EHRs, technicians must be familiar with EHR computer software, maintaining EHR security, and analyzing electronic data to improve health-care information. Health information technicians use EHR software to maintain data on patient safety, patterns of disease, and disease treatment and outcome. Technicians also may assist with improving EHR software usability and may contribute to the development and maintenance of health information networks.

Medical records and health information technicians' duties vary with the size of the facility where they work. Technicians can specialize in many aspects of health information.

Some medical records and health information technicians specialize in codifying patients' medical information for reimbursement purposes. Technicians who specialize in coding are called *medical coders* or *coding specialists*. Medical coders assign a code to each diagnosis and procedure by using classification systems software. The classification system determines the amount for which health-care providers will be reimbursed if the patient is covered by Medicare, Medicaid, or other insurance programs using the system. Coders may use several coding systems, such as those required for ambulatory settings, physician offices, or long-term care.

Medical records and health information technicians also may specialize in cancer registry. *Cancer* (or tumor) *registrars* maintain facility, regional, and national databases of cancer patients. Registrars review patient records and pathology reports, and assign codes for the diagnosis and treatment of different cancers and selected benign tumors. Registrars conduct annual followups to track treatment, survival, and recovery. This information is used to calculate survivor rates and success rates of various types of treatment, to locate geographic areas with high incidences of certain cancers, and to identify potential participants for clinical drug trials.

Work environment. Medical records and health information technicians work in pleasant and comfortable offices. This is one of the few health-related occupations in which there is no direct hands-on patient care.

Medical records and health information technicians usually work a typical 40-hour week. Some overtime may be required. In health facilities that are open 24 hours a day, 7 days a week, technicians may work day, evening, and night shifts. About 14 percent of technicians worked part-time in 2008.

Training, Other Qualifications, and Advancement

Entry-level medical records and health information technicians usually have an associate degree. Many employers favor technicians who have a Registered Health Information Technicians (RHIT) credential.

Education and training. Medical records and health information technicians generally have an associate degree. Typical coursework in health information technology includes medical terminology, anatomy and physiology, health data requirements and standards, clinical classification and coding systems, data analysis, health-care reimbursement methods, database security and management, and quality improvement methods. Applicants can improve their chances of admission into a postsecondary program by taking biology, math, chemistry, health, and computer science courses in high school.

Certification and other qualifications. Most employers prefer to hire credentialed medical record and health information technicians. A number of organizations offer credentials typically based on passing a credentialing exam. Most credentialing programs require regular recertification and continuing education to maintain the credential. Many coding credentials require an amount of time in coding experience in the work setting.

The American Health Information Management Association (AHIMA) offers credentialing as a Registered Health Information Technicians (RHIT). To obtain the RHIT credential, an individual must graduate from a 2-year associate degree program accredited by the Commission on Accreditation for Health Informatics and Information Management Education (CAHIIM) and pass an AHIMA-administered written examination. In 2008, there were more than 200 CAHIIM-accredited health information technology colleges and universities programs.

The American Academy of Professional Coders (AAPC) offers coding credentials. The Board of Medical Specialty Coding (BMSC) and Professional Association of Health care Coding Specialists

Projections Data from the National Employment Matrix

Occupational title	SOC Code	Employment, 2008	Projected employment, 2018	Change, 2008–2018	
				Number	Percent
Medical records and health information technicians 29-2071		172,500	207,600	35,100	20

NOTE: Data in this table are rounded.

(PAHCS) both offer credentialing in specialty coding. The National Cancer Registrars Association (NCRA) offers a credential as a Certified Tumor Registrar (CTR). To learn more about the credentials available and their specific requirements, contact the credentialing organization.

Health information technicians and coders should possess good oral and written communication skills as they often serve as liaisons between health-care facilities, insurance companies, and other establishments. Candidates proficient with computer software and technology will be appealing to employers as health-care facilities continue to adopt electronic health records. Medical records and health information technicians should enjoy learning, as continuing education is important in the occupation.

Advancement. Experienced medical records and health information technicians usually advance their careers by obtaining a bachelor's or master's degree or by seeking an advanced specialty certification. Technicians with a bachelor's or master's degree can advance and become a health information manager. (See the statement on *medical and health services managers* for more information on health information managers). Technicians can also obtain advanced specialty certification. Advanced specialty certification is typically experience-based, but may require additional formal education depending on the certifying organization.

Employment

Medical records and health information technicians held about 172,500 jobs in 2008. About 39 percent of jobs were in hospitals. Health information technicians work at a number of health-care providers such as offices of physicians, nursing care facilities, outpatient care centers, and home health-care services. Technicians also may be employed outside of health-care facilities, such as in federal government agencies.

Job Outlook

Employment is expected to grow much faster than the average. Job prospects should be very good; technicians with a strong understanding of technology and computer software will be in particularly high demand.

Employment change. Employment of medical records and health information technicians is expected to increase by 20 percent, much faster than the average for all occupations through 2018. Employment growth will result from the increase in the number of medical tests, treatments, and procedures that will be performed. As the population continues to age, the occurrence of health-related problems will increase. Cancer registrars should experience job growth as the incidence of cancer increases from an aging population.

In addition, with the increasing use of electronic health records, more technicians will be needed to complete the new responsibilities associated with electronic data management.

Job prospects. Job prospects should be very good. In addition to job growth, numerous openings will result from the need to replace medical record and health information technicians who retire or leave the occupation permanently. Technicians that demonstrate a strong understanding of technology and computer software will be in particularly high demand.

Earnings

The median annual wage of medical records and health information technicians was $30,610 in May 2008. The middle 50 percent earned between $24,290 and $39,490. The lowest 10 percent earned less than $20,440, and the highest 10 percent earned more than $50,060. Median annual wages in the industries employing the largest numbers of medical records and health information technicians in May 2008 were as follows:

Federal Executive Branch $42,760
General medical and surgical hospitals 32,600
Nursing care facilities 30,660
Outpatient care centers 29,160
Offices of physicians 26,210

Related Occupations

Health care occupations with similar responsibilities include medical and health services managers; and medical transcriptionists.

Sources of Additional Information

A list of accredited training programs is available from

▸ The Commission on Accreditation for Health Informatics and Information Management Education, 233 N. Michigan Ave., 21st Floor, Chicago, IL 60601-5800. Internet: www.cahiim.org

For information careers and credentialing, contact

▸ American Health Information Management Association, 233 N. Michigan Ave., 21st Floor, Chicago, IL 60601-5809. Internet: www.ahima.org or http://himcareers.ahima.org

▸ American Academy of Professional Coders, 2480 S. 3850 W., Suite B, Salt Lake City, UT 84120. Internet: www.aapc.com

▸ Practice Management Institute, 9501 Console Dr., Suite 100, San Antonio, TX 78229. Internet: www.pmimd.com

▸ Professional Association of Healthcare Coding Specialists, 218 E. Bearss Ave., #354, Tampa, FL 33613. Internet: www.pahcs.org

▸ National Cancer Registrars Association, 1340 Braddock Place, Suite 203, Alexandria, VA 22314. Internet: www.ncra-usa.org

Medical Scientists

(O*NET 19-1042.00)

Significant Points

■ Most medical scientists need a Ph.D. in a biological science; some also hold a medical degree.

■ Some medical scientists work in research laboratories at universities and hospitals; others work for pharmaceutical or biotechnology companies.

■ Medical scientists with both a Ph.D. and M.D. are likely to have the best opportunities.

Nature of the Work

Medical scientists research human diseases and conditions with the goal of improving human health. Most medical scientists conduct biomedical research and development to advance knowledge of life processes and of other living organisms that affect human health, including viruses, bacteria, and other infectious agents. Past research has resulted in advances in diagnosis, treatment, and prevention of many diseases. Basic medical research continues to build the foundation for new vaccines, drugs, and treatment procedures. Medical scientists engage in laboratory research, clinical investigation, technical writing, drug development, regulatory review, and related activities.

Medical scientists study biological systems to understand the causes of disease and other health problems. For example, some try to identify changes in cells or in chromosomes that signal the development of medical problems. They use this knowledge to develop treatments and design research tools and techniques that have medical applications. Medical scientists involved in cancer research may formulate a combination of drugs that will lessen the effects of the disease. They can then work with physicians to administer these drugs to patients in clinical trials, monitor their reactions, and observe the results. They may draw blood, excise tissue, or perform other invasive procedures. Medical scientists examine the results of clinical trials and adjust the dosage levels to reduce negative side effects or to induce better results. In addition to developing treatments for medical conditions, medical scientists attempt to discover ways to prevent health problems. For example, they may study the link between smoking and lung cancer or between alcoholism and liver disease.

Many medical scientists conduct independent research in university, hospital, or government laboratories, exploring new areas of research or expanding on specialized research that they began in graduate school. Medical scientists working in colleges and universities, hospitals, and nonprofit medical research organizations typically submit grant proposals to obtain funding for their projects. The federal government's National Institutes of Health (NIH) provides funding support for researchers whose proposals are determined to be financially feasible and to have the potential to advance new ideas or processes that benefit human health. Medical scientists who rely on grant money may be under pressure to meet deadlines and to conform to rigid grant-writing specifications when preparing proposals to seek new or extended funding.

Most medical scientists who work in private industry conduct applied research or support product development, using knowledge discovered through research to develop new drugs and medical treatments. They usually have less autonomy than do medical researchers in academia to choose the emphasis of their research. Medical scientists spend more time working on marketable treatments to meet the business goals of their employers. Medical scientists in private industry may also be required to explain their research plans or results to nonscientists who are in a position to reject or approve their ideas, potentially for business reasons rather than scientific merit. Medical scientists increasingly work as part of teams, interacting with engineers, scientists of other disciplines, business managers, and technicians.

Swift advances in basic medical knowledge related to genetics and organic molecules have spurred growth in the field of biotechnology. Discovery of important drugs, including human insulin and growth hormone, is the result of research using biotechnology techniques, such as recombining DNA. Many other substances not previously available in large quantities are now produced by biotechnological means; some may one day be useful in treating diseases such as Parkinson's or Alzheimer's. Today, many medical scientists are involved in the science of genetic engineering—isolating, identifying, and sequencing human genes to determine their functions. This work continues to lead to the discovery of genes associated with specific diseases and inherited health risks, such as sickle cell anemia. These advances in biotechnology have opened up research opportunities in almost all areas of medical science.

Work environment. Medical scientists who conduct research usually work in laboratories and use a wide variety of equipment. Some may work directly with individual patients or larger groups as they administer drugs and monitor patients during clinical trials. Often, these medical scientists also spend time working in clinics and hospitals. Medical scientists are not usually exposed to unsafe or unhealthy conditions; however, those scientists who work with dangerous organisms or toxic substances must follow strict safety procedures to avoid contamination.

Medical scientists typically work regular hours in offices or laboratories, but longer hours are not uncommon. Researchers may be required to work odd hours in laboratories or other locations, depending on the nature of their research.

Training, Other Qualifications, and Advancement

A Ph.D. in a biological science is the minimum education required for most prospective medical scientists. However, some medical scientists also earn medical degrees in order to perform clinical work. A period of postdoctoral work in the laboratory of a senior researcher is becoming increasingly common for medical scientists.

Education and training. A Ph.D. in the biological sciences typically qualifies people to research basic life processes or particular medical problems and to analyze the results of experiments. Some medical scientists obtain a medical degree, instead of a Ph.D., but do not become licensed physicians, because they prefer research to clinical practice. It is particularly helpful for medical scientists to earn both a Ph.D. and a medical degree.

Students planning careers as medical scientists should pursue a bachelor's degree in a biological science. In addition to required courses in chemistry and biology, undergraduates should study allied disciplines, such as mathematics, engineering, physics, and computer science. General humanities courses are also beneficial, as writing and communication skills are necessary for drafting grant proposals and publishing research results.

Once students have completed undergraduate studies, there are two main paths for prospective medical scientists. They can enroll in a university Ph.D. program in the biological sciences; these programs typically take about 6 years of study, and students specialize in one particular field, such as genetics, pathology, or bioinformatics. They can also enroll in a joint M.D.-Ph.D. program at a medical college; these programs typically take 7 to 8 years of study, where students learn both the clinical skills needed to be a physician and the research skills needed to be a scientist.

In addition to formal education, medical scientists usually spend some time in a postdoctoral position before they apply for permanent jobs. Postdoctoral work provides valuable laboratory experience, including experience in specific processes and techniques such as gene splicing, which is transferable to other research projects. In some institutions, the postdoctoral position can lead to a permanent job.

Licensure. Medical scientists who administer drug or gene therapy to human patients, or who otherwise interact medically with patients—drawing blood, excising tissue, or performing other invasive procedures—must be licensed physicians. To be licensed, physicians must graduate from an accredited medical school, pass a licensing examination, and complete 1 to 7 years of graduate medical education.

Other qualifications. Medical scientists should be able to work independently or as part of a team and be able to communicate clearly and concisely, both orally and in writing. Those in private industry, especially those who aspire to consulting and administrative positions, should possess strong communication skills so that they can provide instruction and advice to physicians and other health-care professionals.

Advancement. Advancement among medical scientists usually takes the form of greater independence in their work, larger budgets, or tenure in university positions. Others choose to move into managerial positions and become natural science managers. Those who pursue management careers spend more time preparing budgets and schedules.

Employment

Medical scientists held about 109,400 jobs in 2008. About 31 percent of medical scientists were employed in scientific research and development services firms. Another 27 percent were employed in educational services; 13 percent were employed in pharmaceutical and medicine manufacturing; and 10 percent were employed in hospitals.

Job Outlook

Medical scientists are expected to grow much faster than average over the coming decade. Those with both a Ph.D. and M.D. are likely to experience the best opportunities.

Employment change. Employment of medical scientists is expected to increase 40 percent over the 2008–2018 decade, much faster than the average for all occupations. Medical scientists have enjoyed rapid gains in employment since the 1980s—reflecting, in part, the growth of biotechnology as an industry. Much of the basic biological and medical research done in recent years has resulted in new knowledge, including the isolation and identification of genes. Medical scientists will be needed to take this knowledge to the next stage—understanding how certain genes function within an entire organism—so that medical treatments can be developed for various diseases. Even pharmaceutical and other firms not solely engaged in biotechnology have adopted biotechnology techniques, thus creating employment for medical scientists. However, job growth will moderate from its previous heights as the biotechnology industry matures and begins to grow at a slower rate. Some companies may also conduct more of their research and development in lower-wage countries, further limiting employment growth.

Employment growth should also occur as a result of the expected expansion in research related to illnesses such as AIDS, cancer, and avian flu, along with growing treatment problems, such as antibiotic resistance. Moreover, environmental conditions such as overcrowding and the increasing frequency of international travel will tend to spread existing diseases and give rise to new ones. Medical scientists will continue to be needed because they greatly contribute to the development of treatments and medicines that improve human health.

The federal government is a major source of funding for medical research. Large budget increases at the National Institutes of Health in the early part of the decade led to increases in federal basic research and development expenditures, with research grants growing both in number and dollar amount. However, the increase in expenditures slowed substantially in recent years. Going forward, the level of federal funding will continue to impact competition for winning and renewing research grants.

Job prospects. Medical scientists with both doctoral and medical degrees are likely to experience the best opportunities. Workers with both a biological and professional medical background will have a distinct advantage in competing for research funding, as certain opportunities are only open to those with both qualifications.

Projections Data from the National Employment Matrix

Occupational title	SOC Code	Employment, 2008	Projected employment, 2018	Change, 2008–2018	
				Number	Percent
Medical scientists, except epidemiologists	19-1042	109,400	153,600	44,200	40

NOTE: Data in this table are rounded.

Medical scientists are less likely to lose their jobs during recessions than workers in many other occupations because they are employed on long-term research projects. However, a recession could influence the amount of money allocated to new research and development, particularly in areas of risky or innovative medical research. A recession also could limit extensions or renewals of existing projects.

Earnings

Median annual wages of medical scientists, except epidemiologists, were $72,590 in May 2008. The middle 50 percent of these workers earned between $51,640 and $101,290. The lowest 10 percent earned less than $39,870, and the highest 10 percent earned more than $134,770. Median annual wages in the industries employing the largest numbers of medical scientists were as follows:

Drugs and druggists' sundries merchant
    wholesalers $90,640
Pharmaceutical and medicine manufacturing 87,500
Scientific research and development services......... 79,210
General medical and surgical hospitals 74,230
Colleges, universities, and professional schools 52,880

Earnings are lower and benefits limited for medical scientists in postdoctoral placements; workers in permanent positions typically receive higher wages and excellent benefits, in addition to job security.

Related Occupations

Other life science research occupations include agricultural and food scientists; biological scientists; epidemiologists; and teachers–postsecondary.

Other health specialists with similar levels of education include dentists; pharmacists; physicians and surgeons; and veterinarians.

Sources of Additional Information

For general information on medical scientists, contact

▶ Federation of American Societies for Experimental Biology, 9650 Rockville Pike, Bethesda, MD 20814. Internet: www.faseb.org

For information on and a listing of M.D.-Ph.D. programs, contact

▶ National Association of M.D.-Ph.D. Programs. Internet: www.aamc. org/students/considering/research/mdphd/

For information on pharmaceutical scientists, contact

▶ American Association of Pharmaceutical Scientists (AAPS), 2107 Wilson Blvd., Suite 700, Arlington, VA 22201. Internet: www. aapspharmaceutica.org

For information on careers in pharmacology, contact

▶ American Society for Pharmacology and Experimental Therapeutics, 9650 Rockville Pike, Bethesda, MD 20814. Internet: www.aspet.org

Information on obtaining a medical scientist position with the federal government is available from the Office of Personnel Management through USAJOBS, the federal government's official employment information system. This resource for locating and applying for job opportunities can be accessed through the Internet at www.usajobs. opm.gov or through an interactive voice response telephone system at (703) 724-1850 or TDD (978) 461-8404. These numbers are not

toll free, and charges may result. For advice on how to find and apply for federal jobs, see the *Occupational Outlook Quarterly* article "How to get a job in the federal government," online at www. bls.gov/opub/ooq/2004/summer/art01.pdf.

Nursing and Psychiatric Aides

(O*NET 31-1012.00 and 31-1013.00)

Significant Points

■ Numerous job openings and excellent job opportunities are expected.

■ Most jobs are in nursing and residential care facilities and in hospitals.

■ A high school diploma is required for many jobs; specific qualifications vary by occupation, state laws, and work setting.

■ This occupation is characterized by modest entry requirements, low pay, high physical and emotional demands, and limited advancement opportunities.

Nature of the Work

Nursing and psychiatric aides help care for physically or mentally ill, injured, disabled, or infirm individuals in hospitals, nursing care facilities, and mental health settings. Nursing aides and home health aides are among the occupations commonly referred to as direct care workers, due to their role in working with patients who need long-term care. The specific care they give depends on their specialty.

Nursing aides, also known as *nurse aides, nursing assistants, certified nursing assistants, geriatric aides, unlicensed assistive personnel, orderlies,* or *hospital attendants*, provide hands-on care and perform routine tasks under the supervision of nursing and medical staff. Specific tasks vary, with aides handling many aspects of a patient's care. They often help patients to eat, dress, and bathe. They also answer calls for help, deliver messages, serve meals, make beds, and tidy up rooms. Aides sometimes are responsible for taking a patient's temperature, pulse rate, respiration rate, or blood pressure. They also may help provide care to patients by helping them get out of bed and walk, escorting them to operating and examining rooms, or providing skin care. Some aides help other medical staff by setting up equipment, storing and moving supplies, and assisting with some procedures. Aides also observe patients' physical, mental, and emotional conditions and report any change to the nursing or medical staff.

Nursing aides employed in nursing care facilities often are the principal caregivers and have more contact with residents than do other members of the staff. Because some residents may stay in a nursing care facility for months or even years, aides develop positive, caring relationships with their patients.

Psychiatric aides, also known as *mental health assistants* or *psychiatric nursing assistants,* care for mentally impaired or emotionally disturbed individuals. They work under a team that may include psychiatrists, psychologists, psychiatric nurses, social workers, and therapists. In addition to helping patients to dress, bathe, groom themselves, and eat, psychiatric aides socialize with them and lead them in educational and recreational activities. Psychiatric aides may play card games or other games with patients, watch television with them, or participate in group activities, such as playing sports or going on field trips. They observe patients and report any physical or behavioral signs that might be important for the professional staff to know. They accompany patients to and from therapy and treatment. Because they have such close contact with patients, psychiatric aides can have a great deal of influence on their outlook and treatment.

Work environment. Work as an aide can be physically demanding. Aides spend many hours standing and walking, and they often face heavy workloads. Aides must guard against back injury, because they may have to move patients into and out of bed or help them stand or walk. It is important for aides to be trained in and to follow the proper procedures for lifting and moving patients. Aides also may face hazards from minor infections and major diseases, such as hepatitis, but can avoid infections by following proper procedures. Nursing aides, orderlies, and attendants and psychiatric aides have some of the highest non-fatal injuries and illness rates for all occupations, in the 98th and 99th percentiles in 2007.

Aides also perform tasks that some may consider unpleasant, such as emptying bedpans and changing soiled bed linens. The patients they care for may be disoriented, irritable, or uncooperative. Psychiatric aides must be prepared to care for patients whose illnesses may cause violent behavior. Although their work can be emotionally demanding, many aides gain satisfaction from assisting those in need.

Most full-time aides work about 40 hours per week, but because patients need care 24 hours a day, some aides work evenings, nights, weekends, and holidays. In 2008 about 24 percent of nursing aides, orderlies, and attendants and psychiatric aides worked part-time.

Training, Other Qualifications, and Advancement

In many cases, a high school diploma or equivalent is necessary for a job as a nursing or psychiatric aide. Specific qualifications vary by occupation, state laws, and work setting. Advancement opportunities are limited.

Education and training. Nursing and psychiatric aide training is offered in high schools, vocational-technical centers, some nursing care facilities, and some community colleges. Courses cover body mechanics, nutrition, anatomy and physiology, infection control, communication skills, and resident rights. Personal care skills, such as how to help patients bathe, eat, and groom themselves, also are taught. Hospitals may require previous experience as a nursing aide or home health aide. Some states also require psychiatric aides to complete a formal training program. However, most psychiatric aides learn their skills on the job from experienced workers.

Some employers provide classroom instruction for newly hired aides, while others rely exclusively on informal on-the-job instruction by a licensed nurse or an experienced aide. Such training may last from several days to a few months. Aides also may attend lectures, workshops, and in-service training.

Licensure and certification. Federal government requirements exist for nursing aides who work in nursing care facilities. These aides must complete a minimum of 75 hours of state-approved training and pass a competency evaluation. Aides who complete the program are known as certified nurse assistants (CNAs) and are placed on the state registry of nurse aides. Additional requirements may exist, but vary by state. Therefore, individuals should contact their state board directly for applicable information.

Other qualifications. Aides must be in good health. A physical examination, including state-regulated disease tests, may be required. A criminal background check also is usually required for employment.

Applicants should be tactful, patient, understanding, emotionally stable, and dependable and should have a desire to help people. They also should be able to work as part of a team, have good communication skills, and be willing to perform repetitive, routine tasks.

Advancement. Opportunities for advancement within these occupations are limited. Aides generally need additional formal training or education to enter other health occupations. The most common health-care occupations for former aides are licensed practical nurse, registered nurse, and medical assistant.

For some individuals, these occupations serve as entry-level jobs. For example, some high school and college students gain experience working in these occupations while attending school. And experience as an aide can help individuals decide whether to pursue a career in health care.

Employment

Nursing and psychiatric aides held about 1.5 million jobs in 2008. Nursing aides, orderlies, and attendants held the most jobs—approximately 1.5 million, and psychiatric aides held about 62,500 jobs. About 41 percent of nursing aides, orderlies, and attendants worked in nursing care facilities and another 29 percent worked in hospitals. About 50 percent of all psychiatric aides worked in hospitals. Others were employed in residential care facilities, government agencies, outpatient care centers, and individual and family services.

Job Outlook

Employment is projected to grow faster than the average. Excellent job opportunities are expected.

Employment change. Overall employment of nursing and psychiatric aides is projected to grow 18 percent between 2008 and 2018, faster than the average for all occupations. However, growth will vary for individual occupations. Employment for nursing aides, orderlies, and attendants will grow 19 percent, faster than the average for all occupations, predominantly in response to the long-term care needs of an increasing elderly population. Financial pressures on hospitals to discharge patients as soon as possible should boost admissions to nursing care facilities. As a result, new jobs will be more numerous in nursing and residential care facilities than in hospitals, and growth will be especially strong in community care facilities for the elderly. Modern medical technology will also drive demand for nursing aides, because as the technology saves and extends more lives, it increases the need for long-term care provided by aides. However, employment growth is not expected to be as fast as for other health-care support occupations, largely because nursing

Projections Data from the National Employment Matrix

Occupational title	SOC Code	Employment, 2008	Projected employment, 2018	Change, 2008–2018	
				Number	Percent
Nursing and psychiatric aides... —		1,532,300	1,811,800	279,600	18
Nursing aides, orderlies, and attendants................. 31-1012		1,469,800	1,745,800	276,000	19
Psychiatric aides... 31-1013		62,500	66,100	3,600	6

NOTE: Data in this table are rounded.

aides are concentrated in the relatively slower growing nursing and residential care facilities industry sector. In addition, growth will be hindered by nursing facilities' reliance on government funding, which does not increase as fast as the cost of patient care. Government funding limits the number of nursing aides nursing facilities can afford to have on staff.

Psychiatric aides are expected to grow 6 percent, more slowly than average. Psychiatric aides are a small occupation compared to nursing aides, orderlies, and attendants. Most psychiatric aides currently work in hospitals, but the industries most likely to see growth will be residential facilities for people with developmental disabilities, mental illness, and substance abuse problems. There is a long-term trend toward treating psychiatric patients outside of hospitals, because it is more cost effective and allows patients greater independence. Demand for psychiatric aides in residential facilities will rise in response to increases in the number of older persons, many of whom will require mental health services. Demand for these workers will also grow as an increasing number of mentally disabled adults, formerly cared for by their elderly parents, will need care. Job growth also could be affected by changes in government funding of programs for the mentally ill.

Job prospects. High replacement needs for nursing and psychiatric aides reflect modest entry requirements, low pay, high physical and emotional demands, and limited opportunities for advancement within the occupation. For these same reasons, the number of people looking to enter the occupation will be limited. Many aides leave the occupation to attend training programs for other health-care occupations. Therefore, people who are interested in, and suited for, this work should have excellent job opportunities.

Earnings

Median hourly wages of nursing aides, orderlies, and attendants were $11.46 in May 2008. The middle 50 percent earned between $9.71 and $13.76 an hour. The lowest 10 percent earned less than $8.34, and the highest 10 percent earned more than $15.97 an hour. Median hourly wages in the industries employing the largest numbers of nursing aides, orderlies, and attendants in May 2008 were as follows:

Employment services.. $12.10
General medical and surgical hospitals 12.05
Nursing care facilities 11.13
Community care facilities for the elderly................ 10.91
Home health care services 10.58

Median hourly wages of psychiatric aides were $12.77 in May 2008. The middle 50 percent earned between $10.00 and $15.63 an hour. The lowest 10 percent earned less than $8.35, and the highest 10 percent earned more than $18.77 an hour. Median hourly wages in the industries employing the largest numbers of psychiatric aides in May 2008 were as follows:

Psychiatric and substance abuse hospitals $13.43
General medical and surgical hospitals 13.29
Nursing care facilities 11.66
Individual and family services.............................. 10.78
Residential mental retardation, mental health
   and substance abuse facilities.............................9.89

Related Occupations

Other occupations that help people who need routine care or treatment include child care workers; home health aides and personal and home care aides; licensed practical and licensed vocational nurses; medical assistants; occupational therapist assistants and aides; registered nurses; and social and human service assistants.

Sources of Additional Information

Information about employment opportunities may be obtained from local hospitals, nursing care facilities, home health-care agencies, psychiatric facilities, state boards of nursing, and local offices of the state employment service. Information on licensing requirements for nursing aides, and lists of state-approved nursing aide programs are available from state departments of public health, departments of occupational licensing, and boards of nursing.

For more information on nursing aides, orderlies, and attendants, contact

▸ National Association of Health Care Assistants, 1201 L St. NW, Washington, DC 20005. Internet: www.nahcacares.org

▸ National Network of Career Nursing Assistants, 3577 Easton Rd., Norton, OH 44203. Internet: www.cna-network.org

For more information on the assisted living, nursing facility, developmentally-disabled, and subacute care provider industry, contact

▸ American Health Care Association, 1201 L St. NW, Washington, DC 20005. Internet: www.ahca.org/

Occupational Therapists

(O*NET 29-1122.00 and 29-1122.01)

Significant Points

- Employment is expected to grow much faster than average, and job opportunities should be good, especially for therapists treating the elderly.

- Occupational therapists are regulated in all 50 states; requirements vary by state.

- Occupational therapists are increasingly taking on supervisory roles, allowing assistants and aides to work more closely with clients under the guidance of a therapist.

Nature of the Work

Occupational therapists help patients improve their ability to perform tasks in living and working environments. They work with individuals who suffer from a mentally, physically, developmentally, or emotionally disabling condition. Occupational therapists use treatments to develop, recover, or maintain the daily living and work skills of their patients. The therapist helps clients not only to improve their basic motor functions and reasoning abilities, but also to compensate for permanent loss of function. The goal is to help clients have independent, productive, and satisfying lives.

Occupational therapists help clients to perform all types of activities, from using a computer to caring for daily needs such as dressing, cooking, and eating. Physical exercises may be used to increase strength and dexterity, while other activities may be chosen to improve visual acuity or the ability to discern patterns. For example, a client with short-term memory loss might be encouraged to make lists to aid recall, and a person with coordination problems might be assigned exercises to improve hand-eye coordination. Occupational therapists also use computer programs to help clients improve decision-making, abstract-reasoning, problem-solving, and perceptual skills, as well as memory, sequencing, and coordination—all of which are important for independent living.

Patients with permanent disabilities, such as spinal cord injuries, cerebral palsy, or muscular dystrophy, often need special instruction to master certain daily tasks. For these individuals, therapists demonstrate the use of adaptive equipment, including wheelchairs, orthoses, eating aids, and dressing aids. They also design or build special equipment needed at home or at work, including computer-aided adaptive equipment. They teach clients how to use the equipment to improve communication and control various situations in their environment.

Some occupational therapists treat individuals whose ability to function in a work environment has been impaired. These practitioners might arrange employment, evaluate the work space, plan work activities, and assess the client's progress. Therapists also may collaborate with the client and the employer to modify the work environment so that the client can succeed at work.

Assessing and recording a client's activities and progress is an important part of an occupational therapist's job. Accurate records are essential for evaluating clients, for billing, and for reporting to physicians and other health-care providers.

Occupational therapists may work exclusively with individuals in a particular age group or with a particular disability. In schools, for example, they evaluate children's capabilities, recommend and provide therapy, modify classroom equipment, and help children participate in school activities. A therapist may work with children individually, lead small groups in the classroom, consult with a teacher, or serve on an administrative committee. Some therapists provide early intervention therapy to infants and toddlers who have, or are at risk of having, developmental delays. Therapies may include facilitating the use of the hands and promoting skills for listening, following directions, social play, dressing, or grooming.

Other occupational therapists work with elderly patients. These therapists help the elderly lead more productive, active, and independent lives through a variety of methods. Therapists with specialized training in driver rehabilitation assess an individual's ability to drive using both clinical and on-the-road tests. The evaluations allow the therapist to make recommendations for adaptive equipment, training to prolong driving independence, and alternative transportation options. Occupational therapists also work with clients to assess their homes for hazards and to identify environmental factors that contribute to falls.

Occupational therapists in mental health settings treat individuals who are mentally ill, developmentally challenged, or emotionally disturbed. To treat these problems, therapists choose activities that help people learn to engage in and cope with daily life. Activities might include time management skills, budgeting, shopping, home-making, and the use of public transportation. Occupational therapists also work with individuals who are dealing with alcoholism, drug abuse, depression, eating disorders, or stress-related disorders.

Work environment. In large rehabilitation centers, therapists may work in spacious rooms equipped with machines, tools, and other devices generating noise. The work can be tiring because therapists are on their feet much of the time. Therapists also face hazards such as back strain from lifting and moving clients and equipment.

Occupational therapists working for one employer full-time usually work a 40-hour week. Around 31 percent of occupational therapists worked part-time. It is not uncommon for occupational therapists to work for more than one employer at multiple facilities, which may involve significant travel time. Those in schools may participate in meetings and other activities during and after the school day.

Training, Other Qualifications, and Advancement

Occupational therapists are regulated in all 50 states. Individuals pursuing a career as an occupational therapist usually need to earn a post-baccalaureate degree from an accredited college or university or education deemed equivalent.

Education and training. A master's degree or higher in occupational therapy is the typical minimum requirement for entry into the field. In addition, occupational therapists must attend an academic program accredited by the Accreditation Council for Occupational Therapy Education (ACOTE) in order to sit for the national certifying exam. In 2009, 150 master's degree programs or combined

bachelor's and master's degree programs were accredited, and 4 doctoral degree programs were accredited. Most schools have full-time programs, although a growing number are offering weekend or part-time programs as well. Coursework in occupational therapy programs include the physical, biological, and behavioral sciences as well as the application of occupational therapy theory and skills. All accredited programs require at least 24 weeks of supervised fieldwork as part of the academic curriculum.

People considering this profession should take high school courses in biology, chemistry, physics, health, art, and the social sciences. College admissions offices also look favorably on paid or volunteer experience in the health-care field. Relevant undergraduate majors include biology, psychology, sociology, anthropology, liberal arts, and anatomy.

Licensure. All states regulate the practice of occupational therapy. To obtain a license, applicants must graduate from an accredited educational program and pass a national certification examination. Those who pass the exam are awarded the title "Occupational Therapist Registered (OTR)." Specific eligibility requirements for licensure vary by state; contact your state's licensing board for details.

Some states have additional requirements for therapists who work in schools or early intervention programs. These requirements may include education-related classes, an education practice certificate, or early intervention certification.

Certification and other qualifications. Certification is voluntary. The National Board for Certifying Occupational Therapy certifies occupational therapists through a national certifying exam. Those who pass the test are awarded the title Occupational Therapist Registered (OTR). In some states, the national certifying exam meets requirements for regulation while other states have their own licensing exam.

Occupational therapists are expected to continue their professional development by participating in continuing education courses and workshops. In fact, a number of states require continuing education as a condition of maintaining licensure.

Occupational therapists need patience and strong interpersonal skills to inspire trust and respect in their clients. Patience is necessary because many clients may not show immediate improvement. Ingenuity and imagination in adapting activities to individual needs are assets. Those working in home health-care services also must be able to adapt to a variety of settings.

Advancement. Therapists are increasingly taking on supervisory roles in addition to their supervision of occupational therapy assistants and aides. Occupational therapists may advance their careers by taking on administrative duties at hospitals or rehabilitation centers.

Occupational therapists also can advance by specializing in a clinical area and gaining expertise in treating a certain type of patient or ailment. Therapists may specialize in gerontology, mental health, pediatrics, and physical rehabilitation. In addition, some occupational therapists choose to teach classes in accredited occupational therapy educational programs.

Employment

Occupational therapists held about 104,500 jobs in 2008. The largest number of occupational therapist jobs was in ambulatory health-care services, which employed about 29 percent of occupational therapists. Other major employers were hospitals, offices of other health practitioners (including offices of occupational therapists), public and private educational services, and nursing care facilities. Some occupational therapists were employed by home health-care services, outpatient care centers, offices of physicians, individual and family services, community care facilities for the elderly, and government agencies.

A small number of occupational therapists were self-employed in private practice. These practitioners treated clients referred by other health professionals. They also provided contract or consulting services to nursing care facilities, schools, adult day care programs, and home health-care agencies.

Job Outlook

Employment is expected to grow much faster than average. Job opportunities should be good, especially for occupational therapists treating the elderly.

Employment change. Employment of occupational therapists is expected to increase by 26 percent between 2008 and 2018, much faster than the average for all occupations. The increasing elderly population will drive growth in the demand for occupational therapy services. The demand for occupational therapists should continue to rise as a result of the increasing number of individuals with disabilities or limited function who require therapy services. Older persons have an increased incidence of heart attack and stroke, which will spur demand for therapeutic services. Growth in the population 75 years and older—an age group that suffers from high incidences of disabling conditions—also will increase demand for therapeutic services. In addition, medical advances now enable more patients with critical problems to survive—patients who ultimately may need extensive therapy. However, growth may be dampened by the impact of federal legislation imposing limits on reimbursement for therapy services.

Hospitals will continue to employ a large number of occupational therapists to provide therapy services to acutely ill inpatients. Hospitals also will need occupational therapists to staff their outpatient rehabilitation programs.

Employment growth in schools will result from the expansion of the school-age population and the federally funded extension of services for disabled students. Therapists will be needed to help children with disabilities prepare to enter special education programs.

Job prospects. Job opportunities should be good for licensed occupational therapists in all settings, particularly in acute hospital, rehabilitation, and orthopedic settings because the elderly receive most of their treatment in these settings. Occupational therapists with specialized knowledge in a treatment area also will have increased job prospects. Driver rehabilitation, training for the elderly, and ergonomic consulting are emerging practice areas for occupational therapy.

Projections Data from the National Employment Matrix

Occupational title	SOC Code	Employment, 2008	Projected employment, 2018	Change, 2008–2018	
				Number	Percent
Occupational therapists	29-1122	104,500	131,300	26,800	26

NOTE: Data in this table are rounded.

Earnings

Median annual wages of occupational therapists were $66,780 in May 2008. The middle 50 percent earned between $55,090 and $81,290. The lowest 10 percent earned less than $42,820, and the highest 10 percent earned more than $98,310. Median annual wages in the industries employing the largest numbers of occupational therapists in May 2008 were as follows:

Home health care services	$74,510
Nursing care facilities	72,790
Offices of other health care practitioners	69,360
General medical and surgical hospitals	68,100
Elementary and secondary schools	60,020

Related Occupations

Occupational therapists use specialized knowledge to help individuals perform daily living skills and achieve maximum independence. Other occupations performing similar duties include athletic trainers; physical therapists; recreational therapists; respiratory therapists; and speech-language pathologists.

Sources of Additional Information

For more information on occupational therapy as a career, contact

▸ American Occupational Therapy Association, 4720 Montgomery Lane, P.O. Box 31220, Bethesda, MD 20824-1220. Internet: www.aota.org

For information regarding the requirements to practice as an occupational therapist in schools, contact the appropriate occupational therapy regulatory agency for your state.

Office and Administrative Support Worker Supervisors and Managers

(O*NET 43-1011.00)

Nature of the Work

Office and administrative support supervisors and managers plan or supervise support staff to ensure that they can work efficiently. After allocating work assignments and issuing deadlines, office and administrative support supervisors and managers oversee the work to ensure that it is proceeding on schedule and meeting established quality standards.

Training, Other Qualifications, and Advancement

Many employers require office and administrative support supervisors and managers to have postsecondary training—and in some cases, an associate or even a bachelor's degree. Most firms fill office and administrative support supervisory and managerial positions by promoting office or administrative support workers from within their organizations.

Job Outlook

Current and Projected Employment

2008 Employment	1,457,200
2018 Employment	1,617,500
Employment Change	160,300
Growth Rate	11%

Employment change. Employment of office and administrative support supervisors and managers is expected to grow about as fast as the average for all occupations through the year 2018. Continuing advances in technology should increase office and administrative support workers' productivity and allow a wider variety of tasks to be performed by people in professional positions.

Job prospects. Keen competition is expected for jobs as the number of applicants greatly exceeds the number of job openings. Opportunities will continue to be best for those office and administrative support worker supervisors and managers who show leadership and team building skills, and who are able to multitask, communicate well, and keep abreast of technological advances.

Earnings

Median annual wages for office and administrative support worker supervisors and managers were $45,790 in May 2008.

For current wage data, visit the Occupational Employment Statistics program's Occupational Profile for first-line supervisors/managers of office and administrative support workers.

Related Occupations

Administrative services managers; education administrators; office clerks, general; and secretaries and administrative assistants.

Sources of Additional Information

▸ International Association of Administrative Professionals, P.O. Box 20404, Kansas City, MO 64195-0404. Internet: www.iaap-hq.org

Office Clerks, General

(O*NET 43-9061.00)

Significant Points

- Employment growth and high replacement needs in this large occupation will result in numerous job openings.
- Prospects should be best for those with knowledge of basic computer applications and office machinery.
- Part-time and temporary positions are common.

Nature of the Work

Rather than performing a single specialized task, *general office clerks* have responsibilities that often change daily with the needs of the specific job and the employer. Some clerks spend their days filing or keyboarding. Others enter data at a computer terminal. They also operate photocopiers, fax machines, and other office equipment; prepare mailings; proofread documents; and answer telephones and deliver messages.

The specific duties assigned to clerks vary significantly, depending on the type of office in which they work. An office clerk in a doctor's office, for example, would not perform the same tasks that a clerk in a large financial institution or in the office of an auto parts wholesaler would. Although all clerks may sort checks, keep payroll records, take inventory, and access information, they also perform duties unique to their employer. For example, a clerk in a doctor's office may organize medications, a corporate office clerk may help prepare materials for presentations, and a clerk employed by a wholesaler may fill merchandise orders.

Clerks' duties also vary by level of experience. Inexperienced employees may make photocopies, stuff envelopes, or record inquiries. Experienced clerks are usually given additional responsibilities. For example, they may maintain financial or other records, set up spreadsheets, verify statistical reports for accuracy and completeness, handle and adjust customer complaints, work with vendors, make travel arrangements, take inventory of equipment and supplies, answer questions on departmental services and functions, or help prepare invoices or budgetary requests. Senior office clerks may also be expected to monitor and direct the work of lower-level clerks.

Work environment. For the most part, general office clerks work in comfortable office settings. Those on full-time schedules usually work a standard 40-hour week; however, some work shifts or overtime during busy periods. About 24 percent of clerks worked part time in 2008. Many clerks also work in temporary positions.

Training, Other Qualifications, and Advancement

General office clerks often need to know how to use computers, word processing, and other business software and office equipment. Experience working in an office is helpful, but office clerks also learn skills on the job.

Education and training. Employers usually require a high school diploma or equivalent, and some require basic computer skills, including familiarity with word processing software, as well as other general office skills. Although most general office clerk jobs are entry-level positions, employers may prefer or require previous office or business experience.

Training for this occupation is available through business education programs offered in high schools, community and junior colleges, and postsecondary vocational schools. Courses in office practices, word processing, and other computer applications are particularly helpful.

Other qualifications. Because general office clerks usually work with other office staff, they should be cooperative and able to work as part of a team. Employers prefer individuals who can perform a variety of tasks and satisfy the needs of the many departments within a company. In addition, applicants should have good writing and other communication skills, be detail oriented, and be adaptable.

Advancement. General office clerks who exhibit strong communication, interpersonal, and analytical skills may be promoted to supervisory positions. Others may move into different, more senior administrative jobs, such as receptionist, secretary, or administrative assistant. After gaining some work experience or specialized skills, many workers transfer to jobs with higher pay or greater advancement potential. Advancement to professional occupations within an organization normally requires additional formal education, such as a college degree.

Employment

General office clerks held about 3.0 million jobs in 2008. Most are employed in relatively small businesses. Although they work in every sector of the economy, about one quarter worked in educational services and in health-care and social assistance.

Job Outlook

Employment growth and high replacement needs in this large occupation are expected to result in numerous job openings for general office clerks. Prospects should be best for those with knowledge of basic computer applications and office machinery.

Employment change. Employment of general office clerks is expected to grow by 12 percent between 2008 and 2018, which is about as fast as the average for all occupations. The employment outlook for these workers will continue to be affected by the increasing use of technology, expanding office automation, and the consolidation of administrative support tasks. These factors will lead to a consolidation of administrative support staffs and a diversification of job responsibilities. However, this consolidation will increase the demand for general office clerks because they perform a variety of administrative support tasks, as opposed to clerks with very specific functions. It will become increasingly common within businesses, especially those smaller in size, to find only general office clerks in charge of all administrative support work.

Job prospects. In addition to many full-time job openings for general office clerks, part-time and temporary positions are common. Prospects should be best for those who have knowledge of basic

Projections Data from the National Employment Matrix

Occupational title	SOC Code	Employment, 2008	Projected employment, 2018	Change, 2008–2018	
				Number	Percent
Office clerks, general	43-9061	3,024,400	3,383,100	358,700	12

NOTE: Data in this table are rounded.

computer applications and office machinery—such as computers, fax machines, telephone systems, and scanners—and good writing and other communication skills. Office clerks with previous business or office experience should also have good job prospects. As general administrative support duties continue to be consolidated, employers will increasingly seek well-rounded individuals with highly developed communication skills and the ability to perform multiple tasks.

Job opportunities may vary from year to year because the strength of the economy affects demand for general office clerks. Companies tend to employ more workers when the economy is strong. Industries least likely to be affected by economic fluctuations tend to be the most stable places for employment.

Earnings

Median annual wages of general office clerks were $25,320 in May 2008; the middle 50 percent earned between $19,620 and $31,980 annually. The lowest 10 percent earned less than $16,030, and the highest 10 percent earned more than $39,880. Median annual wages in the industries employing the largest numbers of general office clerks in May 2008 were as follows:

Local government	$28,750
General medical and surgical hospitals	27,700
Elementary and secondary schools	25,690
Colleges, universities, and professional schools	25,400
Employment services	23,840

Related Occupations

The duties of general office clerks can include a combination of bookkeeping, keyboarding, office machine operation, and filing. Other office and administrative support workers who perform similar duties include bookkeeping, accounting, and auditing clerks; communications equipment operators; customer service representatives; data entry and information processing workers; order clerks; receptionists and information clerks; secretaries and administrative assistants; stock clerks and order fillers; and tellers.

Non-clerical entry-level workers who perform these duties include cashiers; counter and rental clerks; and food and beverage serving and related workers.

Sources of Additional Information

State employment service offices and agencies can provide information about job openings for general office clerks.

For information related to administrative occupations, including educational programs and certified designations, contact

▶ International Association of Administrative Professionals, P.O. Box 20404, Kansas City, MO 64195-0404. Internet: www.iaap-hq.org

▶ American Management Association, 1601 Broadway, New York, NY 10019. Internet: www.amanet.org

▶ Association of Professional Office Managers, P.O. Box 1926, Rockville, MD 20849. Internet: www.apomonline.org

Operations Research Analysts

(O*NET 15-2031.00)

Significant Points

■ Candidates should have strong quantitative and computer skills; employers prefer workers who have completed advanced math courses.

■ Employment is projected to grow much faster than average.

■ Individuals with a master's or Ph.D. degree in operations research or management science should have excellent employment prospects; some entry-level positions are available to those with a bachelor's degree.

Nature of the Work

Operations research analysts formulate and apply mathematical modeling methods to develop and interpret information that assists management with policy formulation and other managerial functions. Using analytical techniques, operations research analysts help managers to make better decisions and solve problems. The procedures of operations research were first formalized by the military. They have been used in wartime to effectively deploy radar, search for enemy submarines, and get supplies to where they are most needed. In peacetime and in private enterprises, operations research is used in planning business ventures and analyzing options by using statistical analysis, data mining, simulation, computer modeling, linear programming, and other mathematical techniques.

In addition to the military, operations research analysts today are employed in almost every industry, as companies and organizations must effectively manage money, materials, equipment, people, and time. Operations research analysts reduce the complexity of these elements by applying analytical methods from mathematics, science, and engineering, to help companies make better decisions and improve efficiency. Using sophisticated software tools, operations research analysts are largely responsible for solving complex problems, such as setting up schedules for sports leagues or determining how to organize products in supermarkets. Presenting the pros and cons of each possible scenario, analysts present solutions to managers, who use the information to make decisions.

Analysts are often involved in top-level strategizing, planning, and forecasting. They help to allocate resources, measure performance, schedule, design production facilities and systems, manage the supply chain, set prices, coordinate transportation and distribution, or analyze large databases.

The duties of operations research analysts vary according to the structure and management of the organizations they are assisting. Some firms centralize operations research in one department; others use operations research in each division. Many analysts work with management consulting companies that perform contract work for other firms. Analysts working in these positions often have areas of specialization, such as transportation or finance. Because problems are very complex and often require expertise from many disciplines, most analysts work in teams.

Teams of analysts usually start projects by listening to managers describe problems. Analysts ask questions and search for data that may help to formally define a problem. For example, an operations research team for an auto manufacturer may be asked to determine the best inventory level for each of the parts needed on a production line and to determine the optimal number of windshields to be kept in stock. Too many windshields would be wasteful and expensive, whereas too few could halt production.

Analysts study the problem, breaking it into its components. Then they gather information from a variety of sources. To determine the optimal inventory, operations research analysts might talk with engineers about production levels, discuss purchasing arrangements with buyers, and examine storage-cost data provided by the accounting department. They might also find data on past inventory levels or other statistics that may help them to project their needs.

Relevant information in hand, the team determines the most appropriate analytical technique. Techniques used may include Monte Carlo simulations, linear and nonlinear programming, dynamic programming, queuing and other stochastic-process models, Markov decision processes, econometric methods, data envelopment analysis, neural networks, expert systems, decision analysis, and the analytic hierarchy process. Nearly all of these techniques involve the construction of mathematical models that attempt to describe the system. The problem of the windshields, for example, would be described as a set of equations that represent real-world conditions.

Using these models, the team can explicitly describe the different components and clarify the relationships among them. The model's inputs can then be altered to examine what might happen to the system under different circumstances. In most cases, a computer program is used to numerically evaluate the model.

A team will often run the model with a variety of different inputs to determine the results of each change. A model for airline flight scheduling, for example, might stipulate such things as connecting cities, the amount of fuel required to fly the routes, projected levels of passenger demand, varying ticket and fuel prices, pilot scheduling, and maintenance costs. Analysts may also use optimization techniques to determine the most cost effective or profit-maximizing solution for the airline.

Based on the results of the analysis, the operations research team presents recommendations to managers. Managers may ask analysts to modify and rerun the model with different inputs or change some aspect of the model before making their decisions. Once a manager reaches a final decision, the team usually works with others in the organization to ensure the plan's successful implementation.

Work environment. Operations research analysts generally work 40 hours a week; some, however, work longer. While most of their work is done in an office environment, they may spend time in the field, analyzing processes through direct observation. Because they work on projects that are of immediate interest to top managers, operations research analysts often are under pressure to meet deadlines.

Training, Other Qualifications, and Advancement

Some entry-level positions are available to those with a bachelor's degree in operations research, management science, or a related field, but higher degrees are required for many positions. Strong quantitative and computer skills are essential. Employers prefer workers who have completed advanced math courses.

Education and training. A bachelor's degree coupled with extensive coursework in mathematics and other quantitative subjects usually is the minimum education requirement. Many employers, however, prefer applicants with a master's degree in operations research, management science, or a closely related field—such as computer science, engineering, business, applied mathematics, or information systems. Dual graduate degrees in operations research and computer science are especially attractive to employers. There are numerous degree programs in operations research and closely related fields in colleges and universities across the United States.

Continuing education is important for operations research analysts. Keeping up to date with technological advances, software tools, and improvements in analytical methods is vital for maintaining their problem-solving skills.

Other qualifications. Those considering careers as operations research analysts should be able to pay attention to detail because much time is spent on data analysis. Candidates should also have strong computer and quantitative skills and be able to perform complex research. Employers prefer analysts who understand how to use advanced operations research software and statistical packages. Although not always required, having programming skills can be very helpful.

Since operations research is a multi-disciplinary field, a background in political science, economics, statistics, engineering, accounting, and management can also be useful. Operations research analysts must be able to think logically, work well with people, and write and speak well.

Advancement. Beginning analysts usually perform routine computational work under the supervision of more experienced analysts. As novices gain knowledge and experience, they are assigned more complex tasks and are given greater autonomy to design models and solve problems.

Operations research analysts can advance by becoming technical specialists or project team leaders. Analysts also gain valuable insights into the industry where they work and may assume higher level managerial or administrative positions. Operations research analysts with significant experience or expertise may become inde-

Projections Data from the National Employment Matrix

Occupational title	SOC Code	Employment, 2008	Projected employment, 2018	Change, 2008–2018	
				Number	Percent
Operations research analysts 15-2031		63,000	76,900	13,900	22

NOTE: Data in this table are rounded.

pendent consultants. Others may move into corporate management, where they eventually may become chief operating officers.

Employment

Operations research analysts held about 63,000 jobs in 2008. Major employers include computer systems design firms; insurance carriers and other financial institutions; management; telecommunications companies; and scientific, and technical consulting services firms. Most operations research analysts in the federal government work for the Department of Defense.

Job Outlook

Employment is projected to grow much faster than average. Individuals with a master's or Ph.D. degree in operations research or management science should have excellent job opportunities; some entry-level positions are available to those with a bachelor's degree.

Employment change. Employment of operations research analysts is expected to grow 22 percent over the 2008–2018 period, much faster than the average for all occupations. As technology advances and companies further emphasize efficiency, demand for operations research analysis should continue to grow. Technological advancements have extended the availability of data access and storage, making information more readily available. Advancements in computing capabilities and analytical software have made it cheaper and faster for analysts to solve problems. As problem solving becomes cheaper and faster with technological advances, more firms will have the ability to employ or consult with analysts.

Additionally, organizations increasingly will be faced with the pressure of growing domestic and international competition and must work to maximize organizational efficiency. As a result, businesses increasingly will rely on operations research analysts to optimize profits by improving productivity and reducing costs. As new technologies are introduced into the marketplace, operations research analysts will be needed to determine how to best use those new technologies.

Job prospects. Jobs for operations research analysts exist in almost every industry because of the diversity of applications for their work. As businesses and government agencies continue to contract out jobs to cut costs, opportunities for operations research analysts will be best in management, scientific, and technical consulting firms. The relatively small pool of qualified candidates will result in excellent opportunities for those with a master's or Ph.D. degree in operations research or management science. Operations research is not a particularly well-known field, which means there are fewer applicants competing for each job.

In addition to job growth, some openings will result from the need to replace analysts retiring or leaving the occupation for other reasons.

Earnings

Median annual wages of operations research analysts were $69,000 in May 2008. The middle 50 percent earned between $51,780 and $92,920. The lowest 10 percent had wages of less than $40,000, while the highest 10 percent earned more than $118,130. Median annual wages of operations research analysts working in management, scientific, and technical consulting services were $80,290 in May 2008. The average annual salary for operations research analysts in the federal government was $107,198 in March 2009.

Operations research analysts generally are paid fixed annual salaries with the possibility of bonuses. They also receive benefits typical of professional employees, such as medical and life insurance and 401(k) programs. Many employers offer training programs, including tuition reimbursement programs that allow analysts to attend advanced university classes.

Related Occupations

Operations research analysts apply advanced analytical methods to large, complicated problems, similar to computer software engineers and computer programmers; computer systems analysts; economists; engineers; management analysts; market and survey researchers; mathematicians; and statisticians.

Sources of Additional Information

For information on career opportunities and a list of degree programs for operations research analysts, contact

▸ Institute for Operations Research and the Management Sciences, 7240 Parkway Dr., Suite 300, Hanover, MD 21076. Internet: www.informs.org

For information on operations research careers and degree programs in the Armed Forces, contact

▸ Military Operations Research Society, 1703 N. Beauregard St., Suite 450, Alexandria, VA 22311. Internet: www.mors.org

Information on obtaining positions as operations research analysts with the federal government is available from the Office of Personnel Management through USAJOBS, the federal government's official employment information system. This resource for locating and applying for job opportunities can be accessed through the Internet at www.usajobs.opm.gov or through an interactive voice response telephone system at (703) 724-1850 or TDD (978) 461-8404. These numbers are not toll free, and charges may result. For advice on how to find and apply for federal jobs, see the *Occupational Outlook*

Quarterly article "How to get a job in the federal government," online at www.bls.gov/opub/ooq/2004/summer/art01.pdf.

Paralegals and Legal Assistants

(O*NET 23-2011.00)

Significant Points

■ Despite projected much-faster-than-average employment growth, competition for jobs is expected.

■ Formally trained, experienced paralegals should have the best employment opportunities.

■ Most entrants have an associate's degree in paralegal studies or a bachelor's degree in another field and a certificate in paralegal studies.

■ About 71 percent work for law firms.

Nature of the Work

Although lawyers assume ultimate responsibility for legal work, they often delegate many of their tasks to paralegals. In fact, *paralegals*—also called *legal assistants*—are continuing to assume new responsibilities in legal offices and perform many of the same tasks as lawyers. Nevertheless, they are explicitly prohibited from carrying out duties considered to be within the scope of practice of law, such as setting legal fees, giving legal advice, and presenting cases in court.

One of a paralegal's most important tasks is helping lawyers prepare for closings, hearings, trials, and corporate meetings. Paralegals might investigate the facts of cases and ensure that all relevant information is considered. They also identify appropriate laws, judicial decisions, legal articles, and other materials that are relevant to assigned cases. After they analyze and organize the information, paralegals may prepare written reports that attorneys use in determining how cases should be handled. If attorneys decide to file lawsuits on behalf of clients, paralegals may help prepare the legal arguments, draft pleadings and motions to be filed with the court, obtain affidavits, and assist attorneys during trials. Paralegals also organize and track files of all important case documents and make them available and easily accessible to attorneys.

In addition to this preparatory work, paralegals perform a number of other functions. For example, they help draft contracts, mortgages, and separation agreements. They also may assist in preparing tax returns, establishing trust funds, and planning estates. Some paralegals coordinate the activities of other law office employees and maintain financial office records.

Computer software packages and the Internet are used to search legal literature stored in computer databases and on CD-ROM. In litigation involving many supporting documents, paralegals usually use computer databases to retrieve, organize, and index various materials. Imaging software allows paralegals to scan documents directly into a database, while billing programs help them to track hours billed to clients. Computer software packages also are used to

perform tax computations and explore the consequences of various tax strategies for clients.

Paralegals are found in all types of organizations, but most are employed by law firms, corporate legal departments, and various government offices. In these organizations, they can work in many different areas of the law, including litigation, personal injury, corporate law, criminal law, employee benefits, intellectual property, labor law, bankruptcy, immigration, family law, and real estate. As the law becomes more complex, paralegals become more specialized. Within specialties, functions are often broken down further. For example, paralegals specializing in labor law may concentrate exclusively on employee benefits. In small and medium-size law firms, duties are often more general.

The tasks of paralegals differ widely according to the type of organization for which they work. *Corporate paralegals* often assist attorneys with employee contracts, shareholder agreements, stock-option plans, and employee benefit plans. They also may help prepare and file annual financial reports, maintain corporate minutes' record resolutions, and prepare forms to secure loans for the corporation. Corporate paralegals often monitor and review government regulations to ensure that the corporation is aware of new requirements and is operating within the law. Increasingly, experienced corporate paralegals or paralegal managers are assuming additional supervisory responsibilities, such as overseeing team projects.

The duties of paralegals who work in the public sector usually vary by agency. In general, *litigation paralegals* analyze legal material for internal use, maintain reference files, conduct research for attorneys, and collect and analyze evidence for agency hearings. They may prepare informative or explanatory material on laws, agency regulations, and agency policy for general use by the agency and the public. Paralegals employed in community legal-service projects help the poor, the aged, and others who are in need of legal assistance. They file forms, conduct research, prepare documents, and, when authorized by law, may represent clients at administrative hearings.

Work environment. Paralegals handle many routine assignments, particularly when they are inexperienced. As they gain experience, paralegals usually assume more varied tasks with additional responsibility. Paralegals do most of their work in offices and law libraries. Occasionally, they travel to gather information and perform other duties.

Paralegals employed by corporations and government usually work a standard 40-hour week. Although most paralegals work year round, some are temporarily employed during busy times of the year. Paralegals who work for law firms sometimes work very long hours when they are under pressure to meet deadlines.

Training, Other Qualifications, and Advancement

Most entrants have an associate degree in paralegal studies, or a bachelor's degree in another field and a certificate in paralegal studies. Some employers train paralegals on the job.

Education and training. There are several ways to become a paralegal. The most common is through a community college paralegal program that leads to an associate degree. Another common method of entry, mainly for those who already have a college degree, is earning a certificate in paralegal studies. A small number of schools offer bachelor's and master's degrees in paralegal studies. Finally, some employers train paralegals on the job.

Associate and bachelor's degree programs usually combine paralegal training with courses in other academic subjects. Certificate programs vary significantly, with some taking only a few months to complete. Most certificate programs provide intensive paralegal training for individuals who already hold college degrees.

More than 1,000 colleges and universities, law schools, and proprietary schools offer formal paralegal training programs. Approximately 260 paralegal programs are approved by the American Bar Association (ABA). Although not required by many employers, graduation from an ABA-approved program can enhance employment opportunities. Admission requirements vary. Some schools require certain college courses or a bachelor's degree, while others accept high school graduates or those with legal experience. A few schools require standardized tests and personal interviews.

The quality of paralegal training programs varies; some programs may include job placement services. If possible, prospective students should examine the experiences of recent graduates before enrolling in a paralegal program. Training programs usually include courses in legal research and the legal applications of computers. Many paralegal training programs also offer an internship, in which students gain practical experience by working for several months in a private law firm, the office of a public defender or attorney general, a corporate legal department, a legal aid organization, a bank, or a government agency. Internship experience is a valuable asset in seeking a job after graduation.

Some employers train paralegals on the job, hiring college graduates with no legal experience or promoting experienced legal secretaries. Some entrants have experience in a technical field that is useful to law firms, such as a background in tax preparation or criminal justice. Nursing or health administration experience is valuable in personal-injury law practices.

Certification and other qualifications. Although most employers do not require certification, earning voluntary certification from a professional national or local paralegal organization may offer advantages in the labor market. Many national and local paralegal organizations offer voluntary paralegal certifications by requiring students to pass an exam. Other organizations offer voluntary paralegal certifications by meeting certain criteria such as experience and education.

The National Association of Legal Assistants (NALA), for example, has established standards for certification that require various combinations of education and experience. Paralegals who meet these standards are eligible to take a 2-day examination. Those who pass the exam may use the Certified Legal Assistant (CLA) or Certified Paralegal (CP) credential. NALA certification is for a period of five years and 50 hours of continuing education is required for recertification. According to the NALA, as of September 4, 2009, there were 15,652 Certified Paralegals in the United States. NALA also offers the Advanced Paralegal Certification for experienced paralegals who want to specialize. The Advanced Paralegal Certification program is a curriculum-based program offered on the Internet.

The American Alliance of Paralegals, Inc., offers the American Alliance Certified Paralegal (AACP) credential, a voluntary certification

program. Paralegals seeking the AACP certification must possess at least five years of paralegal experience and meet one of three educational criteria. Certification must be renewed every two years, including the completion of 18 hours of continuing education.

In addition, the National Federation of Paralegal Associations (NFPA) offers the Registered Paralegal (RP) designation to paralegals with a bachelor's degree and at least two years of experience who pass an exam. To maintain the credential, workers must complete 12 hours of continuing education every two years. The National Association of Legal Secretaries (NALS) offers the Professional Paralegal (PP) certification to those who pass a four-part exam. Recertification requires 75 hours of continuing education.

Paralegals must be able to document and present their findings and opinions to their supervising attorney. They need to understand legal terminology and have good research and investigative skills. Familiarity with the operation and applications of computers in legal research and litigation support also is important. Paralegals should stay informed of new developments in the laws that affect their area of practice. Participation in continuing legal education seminars allows paralegals to maintain and expand their knowledge of the law. In fact, all paralegals in California must complete 4 hours of mandatory continuing education in either general law or a specialized area of law.

Because paralegals frequently deal with the public, they should be courteous and uphold the ethical standards of the legal profession. The NALA, the NFPA, and a few states have established ethical guidelines for paralegals to follow.

Advancement. Paralegals usually are given more responsibilities and require less supervision as they gain work experience. Experienced paralegals who work in large law firms, corporate legal departments, or government agencies may supervise and delegate assignments to other paralegals and clerical staff. Advancement opportunities also include promotion to managerial and other law-related positions within the firm or corporate legal department. However, some paralegals find it easier to move to another law firm when seeking increased responsibility or advancement.

Employment

Paralegals and legal assistants held about 263,800 jobs in 2008. Private law firms employed 71 percent; most of the remainder worked for corporate legal departments and various levels of government. Within the federal government, the U.S. Department of Justice is the largest employer, followed by the Social Security Administration and the U.S. Department of the Treasury. A small number of paralegals own their own businesses and work as freelance legal assistants, contracting their services to attorneys or corporate legal departments.

Job Outlook

Despite projected much-faster-than-average employment growth, competition for jobs is expected to continue as many people seek to go into this profession; experienced, formally trained paralegals should have the best employment opportunities.

Employment change. Employment of paralegals and legal assistants is projected to grow 28 percent between 2008 and 2018, much faster than the average for all occupations. Employers are trying to reduce costs and increase the availability and efficiency of legal services by hiring paralegals to perform tasks once done by lawyers. Paralegals are performing a wider variety of duties, making them more useful to businesses.

Demand for paralegals also is expected to grow as an expanding population increasingly requires legal services, especially in areas such as intellectual property, health care, international law, elder issues, criminal law, and environmental law. The growth of prepaid legal plans also should contribute to the demand for legal services.

Private law firms will continue to be the largest employers of paralegals, but a growing array of other organizations, such as corporate legal departments, insurance companies, real-estate and title insurance firms, and banks also hire paralegals. Corporations in particular are expected to increase their in-house legal departments to cut costs. The wide range of tasks paralegals can perform has helped to increase their employment in small and medium-size establishments of all types.

Job prospects. In addition to new jobs created by employment growth, more job openings will arise as people leave the occupation. There will be demand for paralegals who specialize in areas such as real estate, bankruptcy, medical malpractice, and product liability. Community legal service programs, which provide assistance to the poor, elderly, minorities, and middle-income families, will employ additional paralegals to minimize expenses and serve the most people. Job opportunities also are expected in federal, state, and local government agencies, consumer organizations, and the courts. However, this occupation attracts many applicants, creating competition for jobs. Experienced, formally trained paralegals should have the best job prospects.

To a limited extent, paralegal jobs are affected by the business cycle. During recessions, demand declines for some discretionary legal services, such as planning estates, drafting wills, and handling real estate transactions. Corporations are less inclined to initiate certain types of litigation when falling sales and profits lead to fiscal belt tightening. As a result, full-time paralegals employed in offices adversely affected by a recession may be laid off or have their work hours reduced. However, during recessions, corporations and individuals are more likely to face problems that require legal assistance, such as bankruptcies, foreclosures, and divorces. Paralegals, who provide many of the same legal services as lawyers at a lower cost, tend to fare relatively better in difficult economic conditions.

Earnings

Wages of paralegals and legal assistants vary greatly. Salaries depend on education, training, experience, the type and size of employer, and the geographic location of the job. In general, paralegals who work for large law firms or in large metropolitan areas earn more than those who work for smaller firms or in less populated regions. In May 2008, full-time wage-and-salary paralegals and legal assistants earned $46,120. The middle 50 percent earned between $36,080 and $59,310. The top 10 percent earned more than $73,450, and the bottom 10 percent earned less than $29,260. Median annual wages in the industries employing the largest numbers of paralegals were as follows:

Federal Executive Branch	$58,540
Management of companies and enterprises	55,910
Insurance carriers	52,200
Employment services	50,050
Legal services	44,480

In addition to earning a salary, many paralegals receive bonuses, in part to compensate them for sometimes having to work long hours. Paralegals also receive vacation, paid sick leave, a savings plan, life insurance, personal paid time off, dental insurance, and reimbursement for continuing legal education.

Related Occupations

Among the other occupations that call for a specialized understanding of the law, but that do not require the extensive training of a lawyer are claims adjusters, examiners, and investigators; law clerks; occupational health and safety specialists; occupational health and safety technicians; and title examiners, abstractors, and searchers.

Sources of Additional Information

General information on a career as a paralegal can be obtained from

▸ Standing Committee on Paralegals, American Bar Association, 321 N. Clark St., Chicago, IL 60654. Internet: www.abanet.org/legalservices/paralegals

For information on the Certified Legal Assistant exam, schools that offer training programs in a specific state, and standards and guidelines for paralegals, contact

▸ National Association of Legal Assistants, Inc., 1516 S. Boston St., Suite 200, Tulsa, OK 74119. Internet: www.nala.org

Information on the Paralegal Advanced Competency Exam, paralegal careers, paralegal training programs, job postings, and local associations is available from

▸ National Federation of Paralegal Associations, P.O. Box 2016, Edmonds, WA 98020. Internet: www.paralegals.org

Information on paralegal training programs, including the pamphlet *How to Choose a Paralegal Education Program*, may be obtained from

▸ American Association for Paralegal Education, 19 Mantua Rd., Mt. Royal, NJ 08061. Internet: www.aafpe.org

Projections Data from the National Employment Matrix

Occupational title	SOC Code	Employment, 2008	Projected employment, 2018	Change, 2008–2018	
				Number	Percent
Paralegals and legal assistants	23-2011	263,800	337,900	74,100	28

NOTE: Data in this table are rounded.

Information on paralegal careers, certification, and job postings is available from

▶ American Alliance of Paralegals, Inc., Suite 134-146, 4001 Kennett Pike, Wilmington, DE 19807. Internet: www.aapipara.org

For information on the Professional Paralegal exam, schools that offer training programs in a specific state, and standards and guidelines for paralegals, contact

▶ National Association of Legal Secretaries, 8159 E. 41st St., Tulsa, OK 74145. Internet: www.nals.org

Information on obtaining positions as a paralegal or legal assistant with the federal government is available from the Office of Personnel Management through USAJOBS, the federal government's official employment information system. This resource for locating and applying for job opportunities can be accessed through the Internet at www.usajobs.opm.gov or through an interactive voice response telephone system at (703) 724-1850 or TDD (978) 461-8404. These numbers are not toll free, and charges may result. For advice on how to find and apply for federal jobs, see the *Occupational Outlook Quarterly* article "How to get a job in the federal government," online at www.bls.gov/opub/ooq/2004/summer/art01.pdf.

Personal Financial Advisors

(O*NET 13-2052.00)

Significant Points

■ Most personal financial advisors have a bachelor's degree.

■ Math, analytical, and interpersonal skills are important.

■ Keen competition is anticipated for these highly paid positions, despite much-faster-than-average job growth.

■ About 29 percent of personal financial advisors are self-employed.

Nature of the Work

Personal financial advisors assess the financial needs of individuals and assist them with investments, tax laws, and insurance decisions. Advisors help their clients identify and plan for short-term and long-term goals. Advisors help clients plan for retirement, education expenses, and general investment choices. Many also provide tax advice or sell insurance. Although most planners offer advice on a wide range of topics, some specialize in areas such as retirement and estate planning or risk management.

Personal financial advisors usually work with many clients and often must find their own customers. Many personal financial advisors spend a great deal of their time marketing their services. Many advisors meet potential clients by giving seminars or through business and social networking. Finding clients and building a customer base is one of the most important aspects of becoming a successful financial advisor.

Financial advisors begin work with a client by setting up a consultation. This is usually an in-person meeting where the advisor obtains as much information as possible about the client's finances and goals. The advisor creates a comprehensive financial plan that identifies problem areas; makes recommendations for improvement; and selects appropriate investments compatible with the client's goals, attitude toward risk, and expectation or need for investment returns. Advisors sometimes seek advice from financial analysts, accountants, or lawyers.

Financial advisors usually meet with established clients at least once a year to update them on potential investments and adjust their financial plan to any life changes, such as marriage, disability, or retirement. Financial advisors also answer clients' questions regarding changes in benefit plans or the consequences of changing their job. Financial planners must educate their clients about risks and possible scenarios so that the clients don't harbor unrealistic expectations.

Many personal financial advisors are licensed to directly buy and sell financial products, such as stocks, bonds, derivatives, annuities, and insurance products. Depending upon the agreement they have with their clients, personal financial advisors may have their clients' permission to make decisions regarding the buying and selling of stocks and bonds.

Private bankers or *wealth managers* are personal financial advisors who work for people who have a lot of money to invest. Because they have so much capital, these clients resemble institutional investors and approach investing differently from the general public. Private bankers manage portfolios for these individuals using the resources of the bank, including teams of financial analysts, accountants, lawyers, and other professionals. Private bankers sell these services to wealthy individuals, generally spending most of their time working with a small number of clients. Private bankers normally directly manage their customers' finances.

Work environment. Personal financial advisors usually work in offices or their own homes. Personal financial advisors usually work standard business hours, but they also schedule meetings with clients in the evenings or on weekends. Many also teach evening classes or hold seminars to bring in more clients. Some personal financial advisors spend a fair amount of their time traveling to attend conferences or training sessions or to visit clients.

Private bankers also generally work during standard business hours, but because they work so closely with their clients, they may have to be available outside normal hours upon request.

Training, Other Qualifications, and Advancement

Personal financial advisors must have a bachelor's degree. Many also earn a master's degree in finance or business administration or get professional designations. Math, analytical, and interpersonal skills are important.

Education and training. A bachelor's or graduate degree is strongly preferred for personal financial advisors. Employers usually do not require a specific field of study for personal financial advisors, but a bachelor's degree in accounting, finance, economics, business, mathematics, or law provides good preparation for the occupation. Courses in investments, taxes, estate planning, and risk management are also helpful. Programs in financial planning are becoming more available in colleges and universities.

Projections Data from the National Employment Matrix

Occupational title	SOC Code	Employment, 2008	Projected employment, 2018	Change, 2008–2018	
				Number	Percent
Personal financial advisors.. 13-2052		208,400	271,200	62,800	30

NOTE: Data in this table are rounded.

Licensure. Personal financial advisors who directly buy or sell stocks, bonds, insurance policies, or specific investment advice need a combination of licenses that varies based upon the products they sell. In addition to those licenses, smaller firms that manage clients' investments must be registered with state regulators, and larger firms must be registered with the Securities and Exchange Commission. Personal financial advisors who choose to sell insurance need licenses issued by state boards. State licensing board information and requirements for registered investment advisors are available from the North American Securities Administrator Association.

Other qualifications. Personal financial advisors need strong math, analytical, and interpersonal skills. They need strong sales ability, including the ability to make a wide range of customers feel comfortable. Personal financial advisor training emphasizes the different types of investors and how to tailor advice to the investor's personality. They need the ability to present financial concepts to clients in easy-to-understand language. Some advisors have experience in a related occupation, such as accountant, auditor, insurance sales agent, or broker.

Private bankers may have previously worked as a financial analyst and need to understand and explain highly technical investment strategies and products.

Certification and advancement. Although not always required, certifications enhance professional standing and are recommended by employers. Personal financial advisors may obtain the Certified Financial Planner (CFP) credential. This certification, issued by the Certified Financial Planner Board of Standards, requires three years of relevant experience; the completion of education requirements, including a bachelor's degree; passing a comprehensive examination, and adherence to a code of ethics. The exam tests the candidate's knowledge of the financial planning process, insurance and risk management, employee benefits planning, taxes and retirement planning, and investment and estate planning. Candidates are also required to have a working knowledge of debt management, planning liability, emergency fund reserves, and statistical modeling.

Personal financial advisors have several different paths to advancement. Those who work in firms may move into managerial positions. Others may choose to open their own branch offices for securities firms and serve as independent registered representatives of those firms.

Employment

Personal financial advisors held 208,400 jobs in May 2008. Jobs were spread throughout the country, although a significant number are located in New York, California, and Florida. About 63 percent worked in finance and insurance industries, including securities and commodity brokers, banks, insurance carriers, and financial invest-

ment firms. About 29 percent of personal financial advisors were self-employed, operating small investment advisory firms.

Job Outlook

Employment of personal financial advisors is expected to grow much faster than the average for all occupations. Despite strong job growth, keen competition will continue for these well-paid jobs, especially for new entrants.

Employment change. Personal financial advisors are projected to grow by 30 percent over the 2008–2018 period, which is much faster than the average for all occupations. Growing numbers of advisors will be needed to assist the millions of workers expected to retire in the next 10 years. As more members of the large baby boom generation reach their peak years of retirement savings, personal investments are expected to increase and more people will seek the help of experts. Many companies also have replaced traditional pension plans with retirement savings programs, so more individuals are managing their own retirements than in the past, creating jobs for advisors. In addition, as people are living longer, they should plan to finance longer retirements.

The growing number and assets of very wealthy individuals will help drive growth of private bankers and wealth managers. The need for private bankers to explain and manage the increasing complexity of financial and investment products will continue to drive growth.

Job prospects. Personal financial advisors will face keen competition, as relatively low barriers to entry and high wages attract many new entrants. Many individuals enter the field by working for a bank or full-service brokerage. Because the occupation requires sales, people who have strong selling skills will ultimately be most successful. A college degree and certification can lend credibility.

Earnings

Median annual wages of wage and salary personal financial advisors were $69,050 in May 2008. The middle 50 percent earned between $46,390 and $119,290. Personal financial advisors who work for financial services firms are often paid a salary plus bonus. Bonuses are not included in the wage data listed here. Advisors who work for financial investment or planning firms or who are self-employed typically earn their money by charging a percentage of the clients' assets under management. They may also earn money by charging hourly fees for their services or through fees on stock and insurance purchases. Advisors generally receive commissions for financial products they sell in addition to charging a fee. Wages of self-employed workers are not included in the earnings given here.

Related Occupations

Other jobs requiring expertise in finance and investment or in the sale of financial products include accountants and auditors; actuaries; budget analysts; financial analysts; financial managers; insurance sales agents; insurance underwriters; real estate brokers and sales agents; and securities, commodities, and financial services sales agents.

Sources of Additional Information

For general information on securities industry employment, contact

▸ Financial Industry Regulatory Authority (FINRA), 1735 K St. NW, Washington, DC 20006. Internet: www.finra.org

▸ Securities Industry and Financial Markets Association, 120 Broadway, 35th Floor, New York, NY 10271. Internet: www.sifma.org

For information on state and federal investment advisor registration, contact

▸ North American Securities Administrator Association, 750 First St. NE, Suite 1140, Washington, DC 20002. Internet: www.nasaa.org

▸ Securities and Exchange Commission (SEC), 100 F St. NE, Washington, DC 20549. Internet: www.sec.gov

For information on personal financial advisor careers, contact

▸ Certified Financial Planner Board of Standards, Inc., 1425 K St. NW, Suite 500, Washington, DC 20005. Internet: www.cfp.net

▸ Financial Planning Association, 4100 E. Mississippi Ave., Suite 400, Denver, CO 80246-3053. Internet: www.fpanet.org

For additional career information, see the *Occupational Outlook Quarterly* article "Financial analysts and personal financial advisors" online at www.bls.gov/opub/ooq/2000/summer/art03.pdf and in print at many libraries and career centers.

Pharmacists

(O*NET 29-1051.00)

Significant Points

■ Excellent job opportunities are expected.

■ Earnings are relatively high, but some pharmacists are required to work nights, weekends, and holidays.

■ Pharmacists are becoming more involved in counseling patients and planning drug therapy programs.

■ Pharmacists must graduate from an accredited college of pharmacy and pass a series of examinations to be licensed.

Nature of the Work

Pharmacists distribute prescription drugs to individuals. They also advise their patients, physicians, and other health practitioners on the selection, dosages, interactions, and side effects of medications, as well as monitor the health and progress of those patients to ensure that they are using their medications safely and effectively. Compounding—the actual mixing of ingredients to form medications—is a small part of a pharmacist's practice, because most medicines are produced by pharmaceutical companies in standard dosages and drug delivery forms. Most pharmacists work in a community setting, such as a retail drugstore, or in a health-care facility, such as a hospital.

Pharmacists in community pharmacies dispense medications, counsel patients on the use of prescription and over-the-counter medications, and advise physicians about medication therapy. They also advise patients about general health topics, such as diet, exercise, and stress management, and provide information on products, such as durable medical equipment or home health-care supplies. In addition, they often complete third-party insurance forms and other paperwork. Those who own or manage community pharmacies may sell non-health-related merchandise, hire and supervise personnel, and oversee the general operation of the pharmacy. Some community pharmacists provide specialized services to help patients with conditions such as diabetes, asthma, smoking cessation, or high blood pressure. Some pharmacists are trained to administer vaccinations.

Pharmacists in health-care facilities dispense medications and advise the medical staff on the selection and effects of drugs. They may make sterile solutions to be administered intravenously. They also plan, monitor, and evaluate drug programs or regimens. They may counsel hospitalized patients on the use of drugs before the patients are discharged.

Some pharmacists specialize in specific drug therapy areas, such as intravenous nutrition support, oncology (cancer), nuclear pharmacy (used for chemotherapy), geriatric pharmacy, and psychiatric pharmacy (the use of drugs to treat mental disorders).

Most pharmacists keep confidential computerized records of patients' drug therapies to prevent harmful drug interactions. Pharmacists are responsible for the accuracy of every prescription that is filled, but they often rely upon pharmacy technicians to assist them in the dispensing medications. Thus, the pharmacist may delegate prescription-filling and administrative tasks and supervise their completion. Pharmacists also frequently oversee pharmacy students serving as interns.

Some pharmacists are involved in research for pharmaceutical manufacturers, developing new drugs and testing their effects. Others work in marketing or sales, providing clients with expertise on the use, effectiveness, and possible side effects of drugs. Some pharmacists work for health insurance companies, developing pharmacy benefit packages and carrying out cost-benefit analyses on certain drugs. Other pharmacists work for the government, managed care organizations, public health-care services, or the armed services. Finally, some pharmacists are employed full time or part time as college faculty, teaching classes and performing research in a wide range of areas.

Work environment. Pharmacists work in clean, well-lighted, and well-ventilated areas. Many pharmacists spend most of their workday on their feet. When working with sterile or dangerous pharmaceutical products, pharmacists wear gloves, masks, and other protective equipment.

Most pharmacists work about 40 hours a week, but about 12 percent worked more than 50 hours per week in 2008. In addition, about 19 percent of pharmacists worked part-time. Many community and hospital pharmacies are open for extended hours, so pharmacists may be required to work nights, weekends, and holidays. Consultant pharmacists may travel to health-care facilities to monitor patients' drug therapies.

Training, Other Qualifications, and Advancement

A license is required in all states and the District of Columbia, as well as in Guam, Puerto Rico, and the U.S. Virgin Islands. In order to obtain a license, pharmacists generally must earn a Doctor of Pharmacy (Pharm.D.) degree from a college of pharmacy and pass several examinations.

Education and training. Pharmacists who are trained in the United States must earn a Pharm.D. degree from an accredited college or school of pharmacy. The Pharm.D. degree has replaced the Bachelor of Pharmacy degree, which is no longer being awarded. To be admitted to a Pharm.D. program, an applicant must have completed at least two years of specific professional study. This requirement generally includes courses in mathematics and natural sciences, such as chemistry, biology, and physics, as well as courses in the humanities and social sciences. In addition, most applicants have completed 3 or more years at a college or university before moving on to a Pharm.D. program, although this is not specifically required.

Pharm.D. programs generally take four years to complete. The courses offered are designed to teach students about all aspects of drug therapy. In addition, students learn how to communicate with patients and other health-care providers about drug information and patient care. Students also learn professional ethics, concepts of public health, and business management. In addition to receiving classroom instruction, students in Pharm.D. programs spend time working with licensed pharmacists in a variety of practice settings.

Some Pharm.D. graduates obtain further training through one-year or two-year residency programs or fellowships. Pharmacy residencies are postgraduate training programs in pharmacy practice and usually require the completion of a research project. The programs are often mandatory for pharmacists who wish to work in a clinical setting. Pharmacy fellowships are highly individualized programs that are designed to prepare participants to work in a specialized area of pharmacy, such clinical practice or research laboratories. Some pharmacists who own their own pharmacy obtain a master's degree in business administration (MBA). Others may obtain a degree in public administration or public health.

Licensure. A license to practice pharmacy is required in all states and the District of Columbia, as well as in Guam, Puerto Rico, and the U.S. Virgin Islands. To obtain a license, a prospective pharmacist generally must obtain a Pharm.D. degree from a college of pharmacy that has been approved by the Accreditation Council for Pharmacy Education. After obtaining the Pharm.D. degree, the individual must pass a series of examinations. All states, U.S. territories, and the District of Columbia require the North American Pharmacist Licensure Exam (NAPLEX), which tests pharmacy skills and knowledge. Forty-four states and the District of Columbia also require the Multistate Pharmacy Jurisprudence Exam (MPJE), which tests pharmacy law. Both exams are administered by the National Association of Boards of Pharmacy (NABP). Each of the eight states and territories that do not require the MJPE has its own pharmacy law exam. Besides requiring the NAPLEX and law examination, some states and territories require additional exams

that are unique to their jurisdictions. All jurisdictions also require a specified number of hours of experience in a practice setting before a license is awarded. In most jurisdictions, this requirement can be met while obtaining the Pharm.D. In many states, applicants must meet an age requirement before a license can be obtained, and some states require a criminal background check.

All states and U.S. territories except Puerto Rico permit licensure for graduates of foreign pharmacy schools. These individuals must apply for certification from the Foreign Pharmacy Graduate Examination Committee (FPGEC). Once certified, they must pass the Foreign Pharmacy Graduate Equivalency Examination (FPGEE), Test of English as a Foreign Language (TOEFL) exam, and Test of Spoken English (TSE) exam. Then they must pass all of the exams required by the licensing jurisdiction, such as the NAPLEX and MJPE, and meet the requirements for practical experience. In some states, applicants who graduated from programs accredited by the Canadian Council for Accreditation of Pharmacy Programs (CCAPP) between 1993 and 2004 are exempt from FPGEC certification and examination requirements.

Other qualifications. Prospective pharmacists should have scientific aptitude, good interpersonal skills, and a desire to help others. They also must be conscientious and pay close attention to detail, because the decisions they make affect human lives.

Advancement. In community pharmacies, pharmacists usually begin at the staff level. Pharmacists in chain drugstores may be promoted to pharmacy supervisor or store manager. Some pharmacists may be promoted to manager at the district or regional level and, later, to an executive position within the chain's headquarters. Hospital pharmacists may advance to supervisory or administrative positions. Some pharmacists become owners or part owners of independent pharmacies. Pharmacists in the pharmaceutical industry may advance in marketing, sales, research, quality control, production, or other areas.

Employment

Pharmacists held about 269,900 jobs in 2008. About 65 percent worked in retail settings. Most of these were salaried employees, but a small number were self-employed owners. About 22 percent of pharmacists worked in hospitals. A small proportion worked in mail-order and Internet pharmacies, pharmaceutical wholesalers, offices of physicians, and the federal government.

Job Outlook

Employment is expected to increase faster than the average. As a result of job growth, the need to replace workers who leave the occupation, and the limited capacity of training programs, job prospects should be excellent.

Employment change. Employment of pharmacists is expected to grow by 17 percent between 2008 and 2018, which is faster than the average for all occupations. The increasing numbers of middle-aged and elderly people—who use more prescription drugs than younger people—will continue to spur demand for pharmacists throughout the projection period. In addition, as scientific advances lead to new drug products, and as an increasing number of people obtain

Projections Data from the National Employment Matrix

Occupational title	SOC Code	Employment, 2008	Projected employment, 2018	Change, 2008–2018	
				Number	Percent
Pharmacists	29-1051	269,900	315,800	45,900	17

NOTE: Data in this table are rounded.

prescription drug coverage, the need for these workers will continue to expand.

Pharmacists also are becoming more involved in patient care. As prescription drugs become more complex, and as the number of people taking multiple medications increases, the potential for dangerous drug interactions will grow. Pharmacists will be needed to counsel patients on the proper use of medication, assist in drug selection and dosage, and monitor complex drug regimens. This need will lead to rapid growth for pharmacists in medical care establishments, such as doctors' offices, outpatient care centers, and nursing care facilities.

Demand also will increase in mail-order pharmacies, which often are more efficient than pharmacies in other practice settings. Employment also will continue to grow in hospitals, drugstores, grocery stores, and mass retailers, because pharmacies in these settings will continue to process the majority of all prescriptions and increasingly will offer patient care services, such as the administration of vaccines.

Job prospects. Job prospects are expected to be excellent over the 2008–2018 period. Employers in many parts of the country report difficulty in attracting and retaining adequate numbers of pharmacists—primarily the result of the limited training capacity of Pharm.D. programs. In addition, as a larger percentage of pharmacists elects to work part time, more individuals will be needed to fill the same number of prescriptions. Job openings also will result from faster than average employment growth and from the need to replace workers who retire or leave the occupation for other reasons.

Earnings

Median annual wages of wage and salary pharmacists in May 2008 were $106,410. The middle 50 percent earned between $92,670 and $121,310 a year. The lowest 10 percent earned less than $77,390, and the highest 10 percent earned more than $131,440 a year.

Related Occupations

Other workers who are employed in pharmacies, work with pharmaceutical compounds, or are involved in patient care include biological scientists; medical scientists; pharmacy technicians and aides; physicians and surgeons; and registered nurses.

Sources of Additional Information

For information on pharmacy as a career, preprofessional and professional requirements, programs offered by colleges of pharmacy, and student financial aid, contact

▸ American Association of Colleges of Pharmacy, 1727 King St., Alexandria, VA 22314. Internet: www.aacp.org

General information on careers in pharmacy is available from

▸ American Society of Health-System Pharmacists, 7272 Wisconsin Ave., Bethesda, MD 20814. Internet: www.ashp.org

▸ National Association of Chain Drug Stores, 413 N. Lee St., Alexandria, VA 22313. Internet: www.nacds.org

▸ Academy of Managed Care Pharmacy, 100 N. Pitt St., Suite 400, Alexandria, VA 22314. Internet: www.amcp.org

▸ American Pharmacists Association, 2215 Constitution Ave. NW, Washington, DC 20037. Internet: www.pharmacist.com

Information on the North American Pharmacist Licensure Exam (NAPLEX) and the Multistate Pharmacy Jurisprudence Exam (MPJE) is available from

▸ National Association of Boards of Pharmacy, 1600 Feehanville Dr., Mount Prospect, IL 60056. Internet: www.nabp.net

State licensure requirements are available from each state's board of pharmacy. Information on specific college entrance requirements, curricula, and financial aid is available from any college of pharmacy.

Pharmacy Technicians and Aides

(O*NET 29-2052.00 and 31-9095.00)

Significant Points

■ Job opportunities are expected to be good, especially for those with certification or previous work experience.

■ Many technicians and aides work evenings, weekends, and holidays.

■ About 75 percent of jobs are in a retail setting.

Nature of the Work

Pharmacy technicians and aides help licensed pharmacists prepare prescription medications, provide customer service, and perform administrative duties within a pharmacy setting. *Pharmacy technicians* generally are responsible for receiving prescription requests, counting tablets, and labeling bottles, while *pharmacy aides* perform administrative functions such as answering phones, stocking shelves, and operating cash registers. In organizations that do not have aides, however, pharmacy technicians may be responsible for these clerical duties.

Pharmacy technicians who work in retail or mail-order pharmacies have various responsibilities, depending on state rules and regulations. Technicians receive written prescription requests from patients. They also may receive prescriptions sent electronically from doctors' offices, and in some states they are permitted to process requests by phone. They must verify that the information on the prescription is complete and accurate. To prepare the prescription, technicians retrieve, count, pour, weigh, measure, and sometimes mix the medication. Then they prepare the prescription labels, select the type of container, and affix the prescription and auxiliary labels to the container. Once the prescription is filled, technicians price and file the prescription, which must be checked by a pharmacist before it is given to the patient. Technicians may establish and maintain patient profiles, as well as prepare insurance claim forms. Technicians always refer any questions regarding prescriptions, drug information, or health matters to a pharmacist.

In hospitals, nursing homes, and assisted-living facilities, technicians have added responsibilities, including preparing sterile solutions and delivering medications to nurses or physicians. Technician may also record the information about the prescribed medication onto the patient's profile.

Pharmacy aides work closely with pharmacy technicians. They primarily perform administrative duties such as answering telephones, stocking shelves, and operating cash registers. They also may prepare insurance forms and maintain patient profiles. Unlike pharmacy technicians, pharmacy aides do not prepare prescriptions or mix medications.

Work environment. Pharmacy technicians and aides work in clean, organized, well-lighted, and well-ventilated areas. Most of their workday is spent on their feet. They may be required to lift heavy boxes or to use stepladders to retrieve supplies from high shelves.

Technicians and aides often have varying schedules that include nights, weekends, and holidays. In facilities that are open 24 hours a day, such as hospital pharmacies, technicians and aides may be required to work nights. Many technicians and aides work part time.

Training, Other Qualifications, and Advancement

There is no national training standard for pharmacy technicians, but employers favor applicants who have formal training, certification, or previous experience. There also are no formal training requirements for pharmacy aides, but a high school diploma may increase an applicant's prospects for employment.

Education and training. There are no standard training requirements for pharmacy technicians, but some states require a high school diploma or its equivalent. Although most pharmacy technicians receive informal on-the-job training, employers favor those who have completed formal training and certification. On-the-job training generally ranges between 3 and 12 months.

Formal technician education programs are available through a variety of organizations, including community colleges, vocational schools, hospitals, and the military. These programs range from 6 months to 2 years and include classroom and laboratory work. They cover a variety of subject areas, such as medical and pharmaceutical terminology, pharmaceutical calculations, pharmacy recordkeeping, pharmaceutical techniques, and pharmacy law and ethics. Technicians also are required to learn the names, actions, uses, and doses of the medications they work with. Many training programs include internships, in which students gain hands-on experience in actual pharmacies. After completion, students receive a diploma, a certificate, or an associate degree, depending on the program.

There are no formal education requirements for pharmacy aides, but employers may favor applicants with a high school diploma or its equivalent. Experience operating a cash register, interacting with customers, managing inventory, and using computers may be helpful. Pharmacy aides also receive informal on-the-job training that generally lasts less than 3 months.

Certification and other qualifications. In most states, pharmacy technicians must be registered with the state board of pharmacy. Eligibility requirements vary, but in some states applicants must possess a high school diploma or its equivalent and pay an application fee.

Most states do not require technicians to be certified, but voluntary certification is available through several private organizations. The Pharmacy Technician Certification Board (PTCB) and the Institute for the Certification of Pharmacy Technicians (ICPT) administer national certification examinations. Certification through such programs may enhance an applicant's prospects for employment and is required by some states and employers. To be eligible for either exam, candidates must have a high school diploma or its equivalent and no felony convictions of any kind. In addition, applicants for the PTCB exam must not have had any drug-related or pharmacy-related convictions, including misdemeanors. Many employers will reimburse the cost of the exams.

Under these programs, technicians must be recertified every 2 years. Recertification requires 20 hours of continuing education within the 2-year certification period. Continuing education hours can be earned from several different sources, including colleges, pharmacy associations, and pharmacy technician training programs. Up to 10 hours of continuing education also can be earned on the job under the direct supervision and instruction of a pharmacist.

Good customer service and communication skills are needed because pharmacy technicians and aides interact with patients, coworkers, and health-care professionals. Basic mathematics, spelling, and reading skills also are important, as technicians must interpret prescription orders and verify drug doses. Technicians also must be precise: details are sometimes a matter of life and death.

Advancement. Advancement opportunities generally are limited, but in large pharmacies and health systems pharmacy technicians and aides with significant training or experience can be promoted to supervisory positions. Some may advance into specialty positions such as chemotherapy technician or nuclear pharmacy technician. Others may move into sales. With a substantial amount of formal training, some technicians and aides go on to become pharmacists.

Employment

Pharmacy technicians and aides held about 381,200 jobs in 2008. Of these, about 326,300 were pharmacy technicians and about 54,900 were pharmacy aides. About 75 percent of jobs were in a retail setting, and about 16 percent were in hospitals.

Projections Data from the National Employment Matrix

Occupational title	SOC Code	Employment, 2008	Projected employment, 2018	Change, 2008–2018	
				Number	Percent
Pharmacy technicians and aides .... —		381,200	477,500	96,300	25
Pharmacy technicians 29-2052		326,300	426,000	99,800	31
Pharmacy aides.. 31-9095		54,900	51,500	–3,500	–6

NOTE: Data in this table are rounded.

Job Outlook

Employment is expected to increase much faster than the average, and job opportunities are expected to be good.

Employment change. Employment of pharmacy technicians and aides is expected to increase by 25 percent from 2008 to 2018, which is much faster than the average for all occupations. The increased number of middle-aged and elderly people—who use more prescription drugs than younger people—will spur demand for pharmacy workers throughout the projection period. In addition, as scientific advances lead to new drugs, and as more people obtain prescription drug coverage, pharmacy workers will be needed in growing numbers.

Employment of pharmacy technicians is expected to increase by 31 percent. As cost-conscious insurers begin to use pharmacies as patient-care centers and pharmacists become more involved in patient care, pharmacy technicians will continue to see an expansion of their role in the pharmacy. In addition, they will increasingly adopt some of the administrative duties that were previously performed by pharmacy aides, such as answering phones and stocking shelves. As a result of this development, demand for pharmacy aides should decrease, and employment is expected to decline moderately, decreasing by 6 percent over the projection period.

Job prospects. Job opportunities for pharmacy technicians are expected to be good, especially for those with previous experience, formal training, or certification. Job openings will result from employment growth, as well as the need to replace workers who transfer to other occupations or leave the labor force.

Despite declining employment, job prospects for pharmacy aides also are expected to be good. As people leave this occupation, new applicants will be needed to fill the positions that remain.

Earnings

Median hourly wages of wage and salary pharmacy technicians in May 2008 were $13.32. The middle 50 percent earned between $10.95 and $15.88. The lowest 10 percent earned less than $9.27, and the highest 10 percent earned more than $18.98.

Median hourly wages of wage and salary pharmacy aides were $9.66 in May 2008. The middle 50 percent earned between $8.47 and $11.62. The lowest 10 percent earned less than $7.69, and the highest 10 percent earned more than $14.26.

Certified technicians may earn more than non-certified technicians. Some technicians and aides belong to unions representing hospital or grocery store workers.

Related Occupations

Other occupations related to health care include the following dental assistants; medical assistants; medical records and health information technicians; medical transcriptionists; and pharmacists.

Sources of Additional Information

For information on pharmacy technician certification programs, contact

▸ Pharmacy Technician Certification Board, 2215 Constitution Ave. NW, Washington DC 20037-2985. Internet: www.ptcb.org

▸ Institute for the Certification of Pharmacy Technicians, 2536 S. Old Hwy. 94, Suite 224, St. Charles, MO 63303. Internet: www. nationaltechexam.org

For a list of accredited pharmacy technician training programs, contact

▸ American Society of Health-System Pharmacists, 7272 Wisconsin Ave., Bethesda, MD 20814. Internet: www.ashp.org

For pharmacy technician career information, contact

▸ National Pharmacy Technician Association, P.O. Box 683148, Houston, TX 77268. Internet: www.pharmacytechnician.org

Physical Therapist Assistants and Aides

(O*NET 31-2021.00 and 31-2022.00)

Significant Points

- Employment is projected to grow much faster than average.

- Physical therapist assistants should have very good job prospects; on the other hand, aides may face keen competition from the large pool of qualified applicants.

- Aides usually learn skills on the job, while physical therapist assistants have an associate degree; most states require licensing for assistants.

- Most jobs are in offices of other health practitioners and in hospitals.

Nature of the Work

Physical therapist assistants and aides help physical therapists to provide treatment that improves patient mobility, relieves pain, and prevents or lessens physical disabilities of patients. A physical therapist might ask a physical therapist assistant to help patients exercise or learn to use crutches, for example, or an aide to gather and prepare therapy equipment. Patients include accident victims and individuals with disabling conditions such as lower-back pain, arthritis, heart disease, fractures, head injuries, and cerebral palsy.

Physical therapist assistants assist physical therapists in providing care to patients. Under the direction and supervision of physical therapists, they provide exercise, instruction; therapeutic methods like electrical stimulation, mechanical traction, and ultrasound; massage; and gait and balance training. Physical therapist assistants record the patient's responses to treatment and report the outcome of each treatment to the physical therapist.

Physical therapist aides help make therapy sessions productive, under the direct supervision of a physical therapist or physical therapist assistant. They usually are responsible for keeping the treatment area clean and organized and for preparing for each patient's therapy. When patients need assistance moving to or from a treatment area, aides assist in their transport. Because they are not licensed, aides do not perform the clinical tasks of a physical therapist assistant in states where licensure is required.

The duties of aides include some clerical tasks, such as ordering depleted supplies, answering the phone, and filling out insurance forms and other paperwork. The extent to which an aide or an assistant performs clerical tasks depends on the needs and organization of the facility.

Work environment. Physical therapist assistants and aides need a moderate degree of strength because of the physical exertion required in assisting patients with their treatment. In some cases, assistants and aides need to lift patients. Frequent kneeling, stooping, bending, and standing for long periods also are part of the job.

The hours and days that physical therapist assistants and aides work vary with the facility. About 28 percent of all physical therapist assistants and aides work part-time. Many outpatient physical therapy offices and clinics have evening and weekend hours, to coincide with patients' personal schedules.

Training, Other Qualifications, and Advancement

Most physical therapy aides are trained on the job, while almost all physical therapist assistants earn an associate degree from an accredited physical therapist assistant program. Most states require licensing for physical therapist assistants.

Education and training. Employers typically require physical therapy aides to have a high school diploma. They are trained on the job, and most employers provide clinical on-the-job training.

In most states, physical therapist assistants are required by law to hold an associate degree. The American Physical Therapy Association's Commission on Accreditation in Physical Therapy Education accredits postsecondary physical therapy assistant programs. In 2009, there were 223 accredited programs, which usually last 2 years and culminate in an associate degree.

Programs are divided into academic coursework and hands-on clinical experience. Academic coursework includes algebra, English, anatomy and physiology, and psychology. Clinical work includes certifications in cardiopulmonary resuscitation (CPR) and other first aid, and field experience in treatment centers. Both educators

and prospective employers view clinical experience as essential to ensuring that students understand the responsibilities of a physical therapist assistant.

Licensure. Licensing is not required to practice as a physical therapy aide. However, most states regulate physical therapist assistants through licensure, registration, or certification. Most states require physical therapist assistants to graduate from an accredited education program and pass the National Physical Therapy Exam. Some states may require physical therapy assistants to pass state exams. Many states also require continuing education credits for physical therapist assistants to maintain licensure. Complete information on regulations can be obtained from state licensing boards.

Other qualifications. Physical therapist assistants and aides should be well-organized, detail oriented, and caring. They should be able to take direction and work well in a team situation. They usually have strong interpersonal skills and a desire to help people in need.

Advancement. Some physical therapist aides advance to become therapist assistants after gaining experience and completing an accredited education program.

Some physical therapist assistants advance their knowledge and skills in a variety of clinical areas after graduation. The American Physical Therapy Association recognizes physical therapist assistants who have gained additional skills in geriatric, pediatric, musculoskeletal, neuromuscular, integumentary, and cardiopulmonary physical therapy. Physical therapist assistants may also advance in non-clinical areas, like administrative positions. These positions might include organizing all the assistants in a large physical therapy organization or acting as the director for a specific department such as aquatic therapy. Physical therapist assistants may also pursue a career in teaching at an accredited physical therapist assistant academic program.

Employment

Physical therapist assistants and aides held about 109,900 jobs in 2008. Physical therapist assistants held about 63,800 jobs; physical therapist aides held 46,100. Both work with physical therapists in a variety of settings. About 72 percent of jobs were in offices of other health practitioners and in hospitals. Others worked primarily in nursing care facilities, home health-care services, and outpatient care centers.

Job Outlook

Employment is expected to grow much faster than average because of increasing demand for physical therapy services. Job prospects for physical therapist assistants are expected to be very good. Aides may experience keen competition for jobs.

Employment change. Employment of physical therapist assistants and aides is expected to grow by 35 percent from 2008 through 2018, much faster than the average for all occupations. Changes to restrictions on reimbursement for physical therapy services by third-party payers will increase patient access to services and, thus, increase demand. The increasing number of people who need therapy reflects, in part, the increasing elderly population. The elderly population is particularly vulnerable to chronic and debilitating conditions that require therapeutic services. These patients often

Projections Data from the National Employment Matrix

Occupational title	SOC Code	Employment, 2008	Projected employment, 2018	Change, 2008–2018	
				Number	Percent
Physical therapist assistants and aides 31-2020		109,900	147,800	37,900	35
Physical therapist assistants 31-2021		63,800	85,000	21,200	33
Physical therapist aides 31-2022		46,100	62,800	16,700	36

NOTE: Data in this table are rounded.

need additional assistance in their treatment, making the roles of assistants and aides vital. In addition, the large baby-boom generation is entering the prime age for heart attacks and strokes, further increasing the demand for cardiac and physical rehabilitation.

Medical and technological developments should permit an increased percentage of trauma victims and newborns with birth defects to survive, creating added demand for therapy and rehabilitative services.

Physical therapists are expected to increasingly use assistants and aides to reduce the cost of physical therapy services. Once a patient is evaluated and a treatment plan is designed by the physical therapist, the physical therapist assistant can provide many parts of the treatment, as directed by the therapist.

Job prospects. Opportunities for individuals interested in becoming physical therapist assistants are expected to be very good; with help from physical therapist assistants, physical therapists are able to manage more patients. However, physical therapy aides may face keen competition from the large pool of qualified individuals. In addition to employment growth, job openings will result from the need to replace workers who leave the occupation permanently. Job opportunities should be particularly good in acute hospital, skilled nursing, and orthopedic settings, where the elderly are most often treated. Job prospects should be especially favorable in rural areas, as many physical therapists tend to cluster in highly populated urban and suburban areas.

Earnings

Median annual wages of physical therapist assistants were $46,140 in May 2008. The middle 50 percent earned between $37,170 and $54,900. The lowest 10 percent earned less than $28,580, and the highest 10 percent earned more than $63,830. Median annual wages in the industries employing the largest numbers of physical therapist assistants in May 2008 were as follows:

Home health care services	$51,950
Nursing care facilities	51,090
General medical and surgical hospitals	45,510
Offices of other health practitioners.....................	44,580
Offices of physicians...	43,390

Median annual wages of physical therapy aides were $23,760 in May 2008. The middle 50 percent earned between $19,910 and $28,670. The lowest 10 percent earned less than $17,270, and the highest 10 percent earned more than $33,540. Median annual wages in the industries employing the largest numbers of physical therapy aides in May 2008 were as follows:

Nursing care facilities	$26,530
General medical and surgical hospitals	24,780
Specialty (except psychiatric and substance abuse) hospitals...	24,590
Offices of physicians...	23,730
Offices of other health practitioners.....................	22,550

Related Occupations

Physical therapist assistants and aides work under the supervision of physical therapists. Other workers in the health-care field who work under similar supervision include dental assistants; medical assistants; nursing and psychiatric aides; occupational therapist assistants and aides; and pharmacy technicians and aides.

Sources of Additional Information

Career information on physical therapist assistants and a list of schools offering accredited programs can be obtained from

▸ The American Physical Therapy Association, 1111 N. Fairfax St., Alexandria, VA 22314-1488. Internet: www.apta.org

Physical Therapists

(O*NET 29-1123.00)

Significant Points

- Employment is expected to grow much faster than average.
- Job opportunities should be good.
- Today's entrants to this profession need a post-baccalaureate degree from an accredited physical therapist program.
- About 60 percent of physical therapists work in hospitals or in offices of other health practitioners.

Nature of the Work

Physical therapists, sometimes referred to as simply *PTs*, are health-care professionals who diagnose and treat individuals of all ages, from newborns to the very oldest, who have medical problems or other health-related conditions, illnesses, or injuries that limits their abilities to move and perform functional activities as well as they would like in their daily lives. Physical therapists examine each individual and develop a plan using treatment techniques to promote the ability to move, reduce pain, restore function, and prevent disability. In addition, PTs work with individuals to prevent the loss of mobility before it occurs by developing fitness and wellness-oriented programs for healthier and more active lifestyles.

Physical therapists provide care to people of all ages who have functional problems resulting from, for example, back and neck injuries, sprains/strains and fractures, arthritis, burns, amputations, stroke, multiple sclerosis, conditions such as cerebral palsy and spina bifida, and injuries related to work and sports. Physical therapy care and services are provided by physical therapists and physical therapist assistants who work under the direction and supervision of a physical therapist. Physical therapists evaluate and diagnose movement dysfunction and use interventions to treat patient/clients. Interventions may include therapeutic exercise, functional training, manual therapy techniques, assistive and adaptive devices and equipment, and physical agents and electrotherapeutic modalities.

Physical therapists often consult and practice with a variety of other professionals, such as physicians, dentists, nurses, educators, social workers, occupational therapists, speech-language pathologists, and audiologists.

Work environment. Physical therapists practice in hospitals, outpatient clinics, and private offices that have specially equipped facilities. These jobs can be physically demanding, because therapists may have to stoop, kneel, crouch, lift, and stand for long periods. In addition, physical therapists move heavy equipment and lift patients or help them turn, stand, or walk.

In 2008, most full-time physical therapists worked a 40-hour week; some worked evenings and weekends to fit their patients' schedules. About 27 percent of physical therapists worked part-time.

Training, Other Qualifications, and Advancement

Today's entrants to this profession need a post-baccalaureate degree from an accredited physical therapy program. All states regulate the practice of physical therapy, which usually requires passing scores on national and state examinations.

Education and training. The American Physical Therapy Association's accrediting body, called the Commission on Accreditation of Physical Therapy Education (CAPTE), accredits entry-level academic programs in physical therapy. In 2009, there were 212 physical therapist education programs. Of these accredited programs, 12 awarded master's degrees; and 200 awarded doctoral degrees. Currently, only graduate degree physical therapist programs are accredited. Master's degree programs typically are 2 to 2.5 years in length, while doctoral degree programs last 3 years.

Physical therapist education programs include foundational science courses, such as biology, anatomy, physiology, cellular histology, exercise physiology, neuroscience, biomechanics, pharmacology, pathology, and radiology/imaging, as well as behavioral science courses, such as evidence-based practice and clinical reasoning. Some of the clinically-based courses include medical screening, examination tests and measures, diagnostic process, therapeutic interventions, outcomes assessment, and practice management. In addition to classroom and laboratory instruction, students receive supervised clinical experience.

Among the undergraduate courses that are useful when one applies to a physical therapist education program are anatomy, biology, chemistry, physics, social science, mathematics, and statistics. Before granting admission, many programs require volunteer experience in the physical therapy department of a hospital or clinic.

Licensure. All states regulate the practice of physical therapy. Eligibility requirements vary by state. Typical requirements for physical therapists include graduation from an accredited physical therapy education program; passing the National Physical Therapy Examination; and fulfilling state requirements such as jurisprudence exams. A number of states require continuing education as a condition of maintaining licensure.

Other qualifications. Physical therapists should have strong interpersonal and communication skills, so they can educate patients about their condition and physical therapy treatments and communicate with patients' families. Physical therapists also should be compassionate and possess a desire to help patients.

Advancement. Physical therapists are expected to continue their professional development by participating in continuing education courses and workshops. Some physical therapists become board certified in a clinical specialty. Opportunities for physical therapists exist in academia and research. Some become self-employed, providing contract services or opening a private practice.

Employment

Physical therapists held about 185,500 jobs in 2008. The number of physical therapist jobs is probably greater than the number of practicing physical therapists, because some physical therapists work part time, holding two or more jobs. For example, some may work in a private practice, but also work part time in another health-care facility.

About 60 percent of physical therapists worked in hospitals or in offices of other health practitioners. Other jobs were in the home health-care services industry, nursing care facilities, outpatient care centers, and offices of physicians. Some physical therapists were self-employed in private practices, seeing individual patients and contracting to provide services in hospitals, rehabilitation centers, nursing care facilities, home health-care agencies, adult day care programs, and schools. Physical therapists also teach in academic institutions and conduct research.

Job Outlook

Employment is expected to grow much faster than average. Job opportunities should be good.

Employment change. Employment of physical therapists is expected to grow by 30 percent from 2008 to 2018, much faster than the average for all occupations. Changes to restrictions on reimbursement for physical therapy services by third-party payers will increase patient access to services and, thus, increase demand. The increasing elderly population will drive growth in the demand for physical therapy services. The elderly population is particularly vulnerable to chronic and debilitating conditions that require therapeutic services. Also, the baby-boom generation is entering the prime age for heart attacks and strokes, increasing the demand for cardiac and physical rehabilitation. Medical and technological developments will permit a greater percentage of trauma victims and newborns with birth defects to survive, creating additional demand for rehabilitative

Projections Data from the National Employment Matrix

Occupational title	SOC Code	Employment, 2008	Projected employment, 2018	Change, 2008–2018	
				Number	Percent
Physical therapists...	29-1123	185,500	241,700	56,200	30

NOTE: Data in this table are rounded.

care. In addition, growth may result from advances in medical technology and the use of evidence-base practices, which could permit the treatment of an increasing number of disabling conditions that were untreatable in the past.

In addition, the federally mandated Individuals with Disabilities Education Act guarantees that students have access to services from physical therapists and other therapeutic and rehabilitative services. Demand for physical therapists will continue in schools.

Job prospects. Job opportunities will be good for licensed physical therapists in all settings. Job opportunities should be particularly good in acute hospital, skilled nursing, and orthopedic settings, where the elderly are most often treated. Job prospects should be especially favorable in rural areas as many physical therapists tend to cluster in highly populated urban and suburban areas.

Earnings

Median annual wages of physical therapists were $72,790 in May 2008. The middle 50 percent earned between $60,300 and $85,540. The lowest 10 percent earned less than $50,350, and the highest 10 percent earned more than $104,350. Median annual wages in the industries employing the largest numbers of physical therapists in May 2008 were as follows:

Home health care services	$77,630
Nursing care facilities	76,680
General medical and surgical hospitals	73,270
Offices of physicians	72,790
Offices of other health practitioners	71,400

Related Occupations

Physical therapists rehabilitate people with physical disabilities and provide wellness and prevention programs. Others who work in the rehabilitation field include audiologists; chiropractors; occupational therapists; recreational therapists; and speech-language pathologists.

Sources of Additional Information

Additional career information and a list of accredited educational programs in physical therapy are available from

▸ American Physical Therapy Association, 1111 N. Fairfax St., Alexandria, VA 22314-1488. Internet: www.apta.org

In addition, the American Physical Therapy Association has developed the PT Centralized Application Service (PTCAS) that allows one to apply to some of the accredited physical therapist programs. Internet: www.ptcas.org

Physician Assistants

(O*NET 29-1071.00 and 29-1071.01)

Significant Points

■ Requirements for admission to training programs vary; most applicants have a college degree and some health-related work experience.

■ Physician assistants must complete an accredited education program and pass a national exam in order to obtain a license.

■ Employment is projected to grow much faster than the average.

■ Job opportunities should be good, particularly in rural and inner-city health-care facilities.

Nature of the Work

Physician assistants (*PAs*) practice medicine under the supervision of physicians and surgeons. They should not be confused with medical assistants, who perform routine clinical and clerical tasks. PAs are formally trained to provide diagnostic, therapeutic, and preventive health-care services, as delegated by a physician. Working as members of a health-care team, they take medical histories, examine and treat patients, order and interpret laboratory tests and X-rays, and make diagnoses. They also treat minor injuries by suturing, splinting, and casting. PAs record progress notes, instruct and counsel patients, and order or carry out therapy. Physician assistants also may prescribe certain medications. In some establishments, a PA is responsible for managerial duties, such as ordering medical supplies or equipment and supervising medical technicians and assistants.

Physician assistants work under the supervision of a physician. However, PAs may be the principal care providers in rural or inner-city clinics where a physician is present for only 1 or 2 days each week. In such cases, the PA confers with the supervising physician and other medical professionals as needed and as required by law. PAs also may make house calls or go to hospitals and nursing care facilities to check on patients, after which they report back to the physician.

The duties of physician assistants are determined by the supervising physician and by state law. Aspiring PAs should investigate the laws and regulations in the states in which they wish to practice.

Many PAs work in primary care specialties, such as general internal medicine, pediatrics, and family medicine. Other specialty areas include general and thoracic surgery, emergency medicine, orthopedics, and geriatrics. PAs specializing in surgery provide preoperative and postoperative care and may work as first or second assistants during major surgery.

Work environment. Although PAs usually work in a comfortable, well-lighted environment, those in surgery often stand for long periods. At times, the job requires a considerable amount of walking.

PA's work schedules may vary according to the practice setting and often depend on the hours of the supervising physician. The workweek of hospital-based PAs may include weekends, nights, or early morning hospital rounds to visit patients. These workers also may be on call. PAs in clinics usually work about a 40-hour week.

Training, Other Qualifications, and Advancement

Requirements for admission to training programs vary; most applicants have a college degree and some health-related work experience. All states require physician assistants to complete an accredited, formal education program and pass a national exam to obtain a license.

Education and training. Physician assistant educational programs usually take at least two years to complete for full-time students. Most programs are at schools of allied health, academic health centers, medical schools, or 4-year colleges; a few are at community colleges, are part of the military, or are at hospitals. Many accredited PA programs have clinical teaching affiliations with medical schools.

In 2008, 142 education programs for physician assistants were accredited or provisionally accredited by the Accreditation Review Commission on Education for the Physician Assistant. Eighty percent, or 113, of these programs offered the option of a master's degree, 21 of them offered a bachelor's degree, 3 awarded associate degrees, and 5 awarded a certificate.

Most applicants to PA educational programs already have a college degree and some health-related work experience; however, admissions requirements vary from program to program. Many PAs have prior experience as registered nurses, emergency medical technicians, and paramedics.

PA education includes classroom and laboratory instruction in subjects like biochemistry, pathology, human anatomy, physiology, clinical pharmacology, clinical medicine, physical diagnosis, and medical ethics. PA programs also include supervised clinical training in several areas, including family medicine, internal medicine, surgery, prenatal care and gynecology, geriatrics, emergency medicine, and pediatrics. Sometimes, PA students serve in one or more of these areas under the supervision of a physician who is seeking to hire a PA. The rotation may lead to permanent employment in one of the areas where the student works.

Licensure. All states and the District of Columbia have legislation governing the practice of physician assistants. All jurisdictions require physician assistants to pass the Physician Assistant National Certifying Examination, administered by the National Commission on Certification of Physician Assistants (NCCPA) and open only to graduates of accredited PA education programs. Only those who have successfully completed the examination may use the credential "Physician Assistant-Certified." To remain certified, PAs must complete 100 hours of continuing medical education every 2 years. Every 6 years, they must pass a recertification examination or complete an alternative program combining learning experiences and a take-home examination.

Other qualifications. Physician assistants must have a desire to serve patients and be self-motivated. PAs also must have a good bedside manner, emotional stability, and the ability to make decisions in emergencies. Physician assistants should have an enthusiasm for lifelong learning, because their eligibility to practice depends on continuing education.

Advancement. Some PAs pursue additional education in a specialty. PA postgraduate educational programs are available in areas such as internal medicine, rural primary care, emergency medicine, surgery, pediatrics, neonatology, and occupational medicine. Candidates must be graduates of an accredited program and be certified by the NCCPA.

As they attain greater clinical knowledge and experience, PAs can earn new responsibilities and higher wages. However, by the very nature of the profession, clinically practicing PAs always are supervised by physicians.

Employment

Physician assistants held about 74,800 jobs in 2008. The number of jobs is greater than the number of practicing PAs because some hold two or more jobs. For example, some PAs work with a supervising physician but also work in another health-care facility. According to the American Academy of Physician Assistants, about 15 percent of actively practicing PAs worked in more than one clinical job concurrently in 2008.

More than 53 percent of jobs for PAs were in the offices of physicians. About 24 percent were in general medical and surgical hospitals, public or private. The rest were mostly in outpatient care centers, including health maintenance organizations; the federal government; and public or private colleges, universities, and professional schools. Very few were self-employed.

Job Outlook

Employment is expected to grow much faster than the average for all occupations. Job opportunities for PAs should be good, particularly in rural and inner-city health-care facilities.

Employment change. Employment of physician assistants is expected to grow by 39 percent from 2008 to 2018, much faster than the average for all occupations. Projected rapid job growth reflects the expansion of health-care industries and an emphasis on cost containment, which results in increasing use of PAs by health-care establishments.

Physicians and institutions are expected to employ more PAs to provide primary care and to assist with medical and surgical procedures because PAs are cost-effective and productive members of the health-care team. Physician assistants can relieve physicians of routine duties and procedures. Health-care providers will use more physician assistants as states continue to expand PAs' scope of practice by allowing them to perform more procedures.

Besides working in traditional office-based settings, PAs should find a growing number of jobs in institutional settings such as hospitals, academic medical centers, public clinics, and prisons.

Job prospects. Job opportunities for PAs should be good, particularly in rural and inner-city clinics because those settings have difficulty attracting physicians. Job openings will result both from

Projections Data from the National Employment Matrix

Occupational title	SOC Code	Employment, 2008	Projected employment, 2018	Change, 2008–2018	
				Number	Percent
Physician assistants...	29-1071	74,800	103,900	29,200	39

NOTE: Data in this table are rounded.

employment growth and from the need to replace physician assistants who retire or leave the occupation permanently. Opportunities will be best in states that allow PAs a wider scope of practice.

Earnings

The median annual wage of physician assistants was $81,230 in May 2008. The middle 50 percent of physician assistants earned between $68,210 and $97,070. The lowest 10 percent earned less than $51,360, and the highest 10 percent earned more than $110,240. Median annual wages in the industries employing the largest numbers of physician assistants in May 2008 were as follows:

General medical and surgical hospitals	$84,550
Outpatient care centers	84,390
Offices of physicians	80,440
Federal Executive Branch	78,200
Colleges, universities, and professional schools	74,200

According to the American Academy of Physician Assistants' 2008 Census Report, median income for physician assistants in full-time clinical practice was $85,710 in 2008; median income for first-year graduates was $74,470. Income varies by specialty, practice setting, geographical location, and years of experience. Employers often pay for their employees' professional liability insurance, registration fees with the Drug Enforcement Administration, state licensing fees, and credentialing fees.

Related Occupations

Occupations with similar educational backgrounds, health-care experience, and/or responsibilities include audiologists; occupational therapists; physical therapists; registered nurses; and speech-language pathologists.

Sources of Additional Information

For information on a career as a physician assistant, including a list of accredited programs, contact

▸ American Academy of Physician Assistants Information Center, 950 N. Washington St., Alexandria, VA 22314. Internet: www.aapa.org

For a list of accredited physician assistant programs, contact

▸ Accreditation Review Commission on Education for the Physician Assistants, 12000 Findley Rd., Suite 240, Johns Creek, Georgia 30097. Internet: www.arc-pa.org

For eligibility requirements and a description of the Physician Assistant National Certifying Examination, contact

▸ National Commission on Certification of Physician Assistants, Inc., 12000 Findley Rd., Suite 200, Duluth, GA 30097. Internet: www.nccpa.net

Physicians and Surgeons

(O*NET 29-1061.00, 29-1062.00, 29-1063.00, 29-1064.00, 29-1065.00, 29-1066.00, 29-1067.00, 29-1069.00, 29-1069.01, 29-1069.02, 29-1069.03, 29-1069.04, 29-1069.05, 29-1069.06, 29-1069.07, 29-1069.08, 29-1069.09, 29-1069.10, 29-1069.11, and 29-1069.12)

Significant Points

■ Many physicians and surgeons work long, irregular hours.

■ Acceptance to medical school is highly competitive.

■ Formal education and training requirements—typically four years of undergraduate school, four years of medical school, and three to eight years of internship and residency—are among the most demanding of any occupation, but earnings are among the highest.

■ Job opportunities should be very good, particularly in rural and low-income areas.

Nature of the Work

Physicians and surgeons diagnose illnesses and prescribe and administer treatment for people suffering from injury or disease. Physicians examine patients, obtain medical histories, and order, perform, and interpret diagnostic tests. They counsel patients on diet, hygiene, and preventive health care.

There are two types of physicians: *M.D.* (*Medical Doctor*) and *D.O.* (*Doctor of Osteopathic Medicine*). M.D.s also are known as *allopathic physicians*. While both M.D.s and D.O.s may use all accepted methods of treatment, including drugs and surgery, D.O.s place special emphasis on the body's musculoskeletal system, preventive medicine, and holistic patient care. D.O.s are most likely to be primary care specialists although they can be found in all specialties. About half of D.O.s practice general or family medicine, general internal medicine, or general pediatrics.

Physicians work in one or more of several specialties, including, but not limited to, anesthesiology, family and general medicine, general internal medicine, general pediatrics, obstetrics and gynecology, psychiatry, and surgery.

Anesthesiologists focus on the care of surgical patients and pain relief. Like other physicians, they evaluate and treat patients and direct the efforts of their staffs. Through continual monitoring and assessment, these critical care specialists are responsible for maintenance of the patient's vital life functions—heart rate, body temperature, blood pressure, breathing—during surgery. They also work outside of the operating room, providing pain relief in the intensive care unit, during labor and delivery, and for those who suffer from chronic pain. Anesthesiologists confer with other physicians and surgeons about appropriate treatments and procedures before, during, and after operations.

Family and general physicians often provide the first point of contact for people seeking health care, by acting as the traditional family physician. They assess and treat a wide range of conditions, from sinus and respiratory infections to broken bones. Family and general physician typically have a base of regular, long-term patients. These doctors refer patients with more serious conditions to specialists or other health-care facilities for more intensive care.

General internists diagnose and provide nonsurgical treatment for a wide range of problems that affect internal organ systems, such as the stomach, kidneys, liver, and digestive tract. Internists use a variety of diagnostic techniques to treat patients through medication or hospitalization. Like general practitioners, general internists commonly act as primary care specialists. They treat patients referred from other specialists and, in turn, they refer patients to other specialists when more complex care is required.

General pediatricians care for the health of infants, children, teenagers, and young adults. They specialize in the diagnosis and treatment of a variety of ailments specific to young people and track patients' growth to adulthood. Like most physicians, pediatricians work with different health-care workers, such as nurses and other physicians, to assess and treat children with various ailments. Most of the work of pediatricians involves treating day-to-day illnesses—minor injuries, infectious diseases, and immunizations—that are common to children, much as a general practitioner treats adults. Some pediatricians specialize in pediatric surgery or serious medical conditions, such as autoimmune disorders or serious chronic ailments.

Obstetricians and gynecologists (OB/GYNs) specialize in women's health. They are responsible for women's general medical care, and they also provide care related to pregnancy and the reproductive system. Like general practitioners, OB/GYNs attempt to prevent, diagnose, and treat general health problems, but they focus on ailments specific to the female anatomy, such as cancers of the breast or cervix, urinary tract and pelvic disorders, and hormonal disorders. OB/GYNs also specialize in childbirth, which includes treating and counseling women throughout their pregnancy, from giving prenatal diagnoses to assisting with delivery and providing postpartum care.

Psychiatrists are the primary mental health-care-givers. They assess and treat mental illnesses through a combination of psychotherapy, psychoanalysis, hospitalization, and medication. Psychotherapy involves regular discussions with patients about their problems; the psychiatrist helps them find solutions through changes in their behavioral patterns, the exploration of their past experiences, or group and family therapy sessions. Psychoanalysis involves long-term psychotherapy and counseling for patients. In many cases, medications are administered to correct chemical imbalances that cause emotional problems.

Surgeons specialize in the treatment of injury, disease, and deformity through operations. Using a variety of instruments, and with patients under anesthesia, a surgeon corrects physical deformities, repairs bone and tissue after injuries, or performs preventive surgeries on patients with debilitating diseases or disorders. Although a large number perform general surgery, many surgeons choose to specialize in a specific area. One of the most prevalent specialties is orthopedic surgery: the treatment of the musculoskeletal system. Others include neurological surgery (treatment of the brain and nervous system), cardiovascular surgery, otolaryngology (treatment of the ear, nose, and throat), and plastic or reconstructive surgery. Like other physicians, surgeons also examine patients, perform and interpret diagnostic tests, and counsel patients on preventive health care.

Other physicians and surgeons work in a number of other medical and surgical specialists, including allergists, cardiologists, dermatologists, emergency physicians, gastroenterologists, ophthalmologists, pathologists, and radiologists.

Work environment. Many physicians—primarily general and family practitioners, general internists, pediatricians, OB/GYNs, and psychiatrists—work in small private offices or clinics, often assisted by a small staff of nurses and other administrative personnel. Increasingly, physicians are practicing in groups or health-care organizations that provide backup coverage and allow for more time off. Physicians in a group practice or health-care organization often work as part of a team that coordinates care for a number of patients; they are less independent than the solo practitioners of the past. Surgeons and anesthesiologists usually work in well-lighted, sterile environments while performing surgery and often stand for long periods. Most work in hospitals or in surgical outpatient centers.

Many physicians and surgeons work long, irregular hours. In 2008, 43 percent of all physicians and surgeons worked 50 or more hours a week. Nine percent of all physicians and surgeons worked part-time. Physicians and surgeons travel between office and hospital to care for their patients. While on call, a physician will deal with many patients' concerns over the phone and make emergency visits to hospitals or nursing homes.

Training, Other Qualifications, and Advancement

The common path to practicing as a physician requires 8 years of education beyond high school and 3 to 8 additional years of internship and residency. All states, the District of Columbia, and U.S. territories license physicians.

Education and training. Formal education and training requirements for physicians are among the most demanding of any occupation—4 years of undergraduate school, 4 years of medical school, and 3 to 8 years of internship and residency, depending on the specialty selected. A few medical schools offer combined undergraduate and medical school programs that last 6 or 7 years rather than the customary 8 years.

Premedical students must complete undergraduate work in physics, biology, mathematics, English, and inorganic and organic chemistry. Students also take courses in the humanities and the social sciences. Some students volunteer at local hospitals or clinics to gain practical experience in the health professions.

The minimum educational requirement for entry into medical school is 3 years of college; most applicants, however, have at least a bachelor's degree, and many have advanced degrees. In 2008, there were 129 medical schools accredited by the Liaison Committee on Medical Education (LCME). The LCME is the national accrediting body for M.D. medical education programs. The American Osteopathic

Association accredits schools that award a D.O. degree; there were 25 schools accredited in 31 locations in 2008.

Acceptance to medical school is highly competitive. Most applicants must submit transcripts, scores from the Medical College Admission Test, and letters of recommendation. Schools also consider an applicant's character, personality, leadership qualities, and participation in extracurricular activities. Most schools require an interview with members of the admissions committee.

Students spend most of the first 2 years of medical school in laboratories and classrooms, taking courses such as anatomy, biochemistry, physiology, pharmacology, psychology, microbiology, pathology, medical ethics, and laws governing medicine. They also learn to take medical histories, examine patients, and diagnose illnesses. During their last 2 years, students work with patients under the supervision of experienced physicians in hospitals and clinics, learning acute, chronic, preventive, and rehabilitative care. Through rotations in internal medicine, family practice, obstetrics and gynecology, pediatrics, psychiatry, and surgery, they gain experience in the diagnosis and treatment of illness.

Following medical school, almost all M.D.s enter a residency— graduate medical education in a specialty that takes the form of paid on-the-job training, usually in a hospital. Most D.O.s serve a 12-month rotating internship after graduation and before entering a residency, which may last 2 to 6 years.

A physician's training is costly. According to the Association of American Medical Colleges, in 2007 85 percent of public medical school graduates and 86 percent of private medical school graduates were in debt for educational expenses.

Licensure and certification. To practice medicine as a physician, all states, the District of Columbia, and U.S. territories require licensing. All physicians and surgeons practicing in the United States must pass the United States Medical Licensing Examination (USMLE). To be eligible to take the USMLE in its entirety, physicians must graduate from an accredited medical school. Although physicians licensed in one state usually can get a license to practice in another without further examination, some states limit reciprocity. Graduates of foreign medical schools generally can qualify for licensure after passing an examination and completing a U.S. residency. For specific information on licensing in a given state, contact that state's medical board.

M.D.s and D.O.s seeking board certification in a specialty may spend up to 7 years in residency training, depending on the specialty. A final examination immediately after residency or after 1 or 2 years of practice is also necessary for certification by a member board of the American Board of Medical Specialists (ABMS) or the American Osteopathic Association (AOA). The ABMS represents 24 boards related to medical specialties ranging from allergy and immunology to urology. The AOA has approved 18 specialty boards, ranging from anesthesiology to surgery. For certification in a subspecialty, physicians usually need another 1 to 2 years of residency.

Other qualifications. People who wish to become physicians must have a desire to serve patients, be self-motivated, and be able to survive the pressures and long hours of medical education and practice. Physicians also must have a good bedside manner, emotional stability, and the ability to make decisions in emergencies. Prospective physicians must be willing to study throughout their career to keep up with medical advances.

Advancement. Some physicians and surgeons advance by gaining expertise in specialties and subspecialties and by developing a reputation for excellence among their peers and patients. Physicians and surgeons may also start their own practice or join a group practice. Others teach residents and other new doctors, and some advance to supervisory and managerial roles in hospitals, clinics, and other settings.

Employment

Physicians and surgeons held about 661,400 jobs in 2008; approximately 12 percent were self-employed. About 53 percent of wage-and-salary physicians and surgeons worked in offices of physicians, and 19 percent were employed by hospitals. Others practiced in federal, state, and local governments, educational services, and outpatient care centers.

According to 2007 data from the American Medical Association (AMA), 32 percent of physicians in patient care were in primary care, but not in a subspecialty of primary care. (See table 1.)

Table 1. Percent distribution of active physicians in patient care by specialty, 2007

Specialty	Percent
Internal medicine	20.1
Family medicine/general practice	12.4
Pediatrics	9.6
Obstetrics and gynecology	5.6
Anesthesiology	5.5
Psychiatry	5.2
General Surgery	5.0
Emergency Medicine	4.1

SOURCE: American Medical Association, 2009 Physician Characteristic and Distribution in the US.

A growing number of physicians are partners or wage-and-salary employees of group practices. Organized as clinics or as associations of physicians, medical groups can more easily afford expensive medical equipment, share support staff, and benefit from other business advantages.

According to the AMA, the New England and Middle Atlantic states have the highest ratios of physicians to population; the South Central and Mountain states have the lowest. Physicians tend to locate in urban areas, close to hospitals and education centers. AMA data showed that in 2007, about 75 percent of physicians in patient care were located in metropolitan areas while the remaining 25 percent were located in rural areas.

Job Outlook

Employment is expected to grow much faster than the average for all occupations. Job opportunities should be very good, particularly in rural and low-income areas.

Employment change. Employment of physicians and surgeons is projected to grow 22 percent from 2008 to 2018, much faster than

Projections Data from the National Employment Matrix

Occupational title	SOC Code	Employment, 2008	Projected employment, 2018	Change, 2008–2018	
				Number	Percent
Physicians and surgeons... 29-1060		661,400	805,500	144,100	22

NOTE: Data in this table are rounded.

the average for all occupations. Job growth will occur because of continued expansion of health-care-related industries. The growing and aging population will drive overall growth in the demand for physician services, as consumers continue to demand high levels of care using the latest technologies, diagnostic tests, and therapies. Many medical schools are increasing their enrollments based on perceived new demand for physicians.

Despite growing demand for physicians and surgeons, some factors will temper growth. For example, new technologies allow physicians to be more productive. This means physicians can diagnose and treat more patients in the same amount of time. The rising cost of health care can dramatically affect demand for physicians' services. Physician assistants and nurse practitioners, who can perform many of the routine duties of physicians at a fraction of the cost, may be increasingly used. Furthermore, demand for physicians' services is highly sensitive to changes in health-care reimbursement policies. If changes to health coverage result in higher out-of-pocket costs for consumers, they may demand fewer physician services.

Job prospects. Opportunities for individuals interested in becoming physicians and surgeons are expected to be very good. In addition to job openings from employment growth, openings will result from the need to replace the relatively high number of physicians and surgeons expected to retire over the 2008–2018 decade.

Job prospects should be particularly good for physicians willing to practice in rural and low-income areas because these medically underserved areas typically have difficulty attracting these workers. Job prospects will also be especially good for physicians in specialties that afflict the rapidly growing elderly population. Examples of such specialties are cardiology and radiology because the risks for heart disease and cancer increase as people age.

Earnings

Earnings of physicians and surgeons are among the highest of any occupation. According to the Medical Group Management Association's Physician Compensation and Production Survey, median total compensation for physicians varied by their type of practice. In 2008, physicians practicing primary care had total median annual compensation of $186,044, and physicians practicing in medical specialties earned total median annual compensation of $339,738.

Self-employed physicians—those who own or are part owners of their medical practice—generally have higher median incomes than salaried physicians. Earnings vary according to number of years in practice, geographic region, hours worked, skill, personality, and professional reputation. Self-employed physicians and surgeons must provide for their own health insurance and retirement.

Related Occupations

Physicians work to prevent, diagnose, and treat diseases, disorders, and injuries. Other health-care practitioners who need similar skills and who exercise critical judgment include chiropractors; dentists; optometrists; physician assistants; podiatrists; registered nurses; and veterinarians.

Sources of Additional Information

For a list of medical schools and residency programs, as well as general information on premedical education, financial aid, and medicine as a career contact

▸ Association of American Medical Colleges, Section for Student Services, 2450 N St. NW, Washington, DC 20037. Internet: www.aamc.org/students

For information on licensing, contact

▸ Federation of State Medical Boards, P.O. Box 619850, Dallas, TX 75261-9850. Internet: www.fsmb.org

For general information on physicians, contact

▸ American Medical Association, 515 N. State St., Chicago, IL 60654. Internet: www.ama-assn.org/go/becominganmd

▸ American Osteopathic Association, Department of Communications, 142 E. Ontario St., Chicago, IL 60611. Internet: www.osteopathic.org

For information about various medical specialties, contact

▸ American Academy of Family Physicians, Resident Student Activities Department, P.O. Box 11210, Shawnee Mission, KS 66207-1210. Internet: http://fmignet.aafp.org

▸ American Board of Medical Specialties, 222 N. LaSalle St., Suite 1500, Chicago, IL 60601. Internet: www.abms.org

▸ American College of Obstetricians and Gynecologists, P.O. Box 96920, Washington, DC 20090. Internet: www.acog.org

▸ American College of Surgeons, Division of Education, 633 N. Saint Clair St., Chicago, IL 60611. Internet: www.facs.org

▸ American Psychiatric Association, 1000 Wilson Blvd., Suite 1825, Arlington, VA 22209. Internet: www.psych.org

▸ American Society of Anesthesiologists, 520 N. Northwest Hwy., Park Ridge, IL 60068. Internet: www.asahq.org/career/homepage.htm

Information on federal scholarships and loans is available from the directors of student financial aid at schools of medicine. Information on licensing is available from state boards of examiners.

Plumbers, Pipelayers, Pipefitters, and Steamfitters

(O*NET 47-2151.00, 47-2152.00, 47-2152.01, and 47-2152.02)

Significant Points

- Job opportunities should be very good.
- These workers constitute one of the largest and highest paid construction occupations.
- Most states and localities require plumbers to be licensed.
- Most workers train in apprenticeship programs and in career or technical schools or community colleges.

Nature of the Work

Most people are familiar with plumbers who come to their home to unclog a drain or fix a leaking toilet. *Plumbers, pipelayers, pipefitters, and steamfitters* install, maintain, and repair many different types of pipe systems. Some of these systems move water from reservoirs to municipal water treatment plants and then to residential, commercial, and public buildings. Other systems dispose of waste, supply gas to stoves and furnaces, or provide for heating and cooling needs. Pipe systems in powerplants carry the steam that powers huge turbines. Pipes also are used in manufacturing plants to move material through the production process. Specialized piping systems are very important in both pharmaceutical and computer-chip manufacturing.

Although plumbing, pipelaying, pipefitting, and steamfitting are sometimes considered a single trade, workers generally specialize in one of five areas. *Plumbers* install and repair the water, waste disposal, drainage, and gas systems in homes and commercial and industrial buildings. Plumbers also install plumbing fixtures—bathtubs, showers, sinks, and toilets—and appliances such as dishwashers, waste disposers, and water heaters. *Pipelayers* lay clay, concrete, plastic, or cast-iron pipe for drains, sewers, water mains, and oil or gas lines. Before laying the pipe, pipelayers prepare and grade the trenches either manually or with machines. After laying the pipe, they weld, glue, cement, or otherwise join the pieces together. *Pipefitters* install and repair both high-pressure and low-pressure pipe systems used in manufacturing, in the generation of electricity, and in the heating and cooling of buildings. They also install automatic controls that are increasingly being used to regulate these systems. *Steamfitters* install pipe systems that move liquids or gases under high pressure. *Sprinklerfitters* install automatic fire sprinkler systems in buildings. Plumbers, pipelayers, pipefitters, and steamfitters use many different materials and construction techniques, depending on the type of project. Residential water systems, for example, incorporate copper, steel, and plastic pipe that can be handled and installed by one or two plumbers. Municipal sewerage systems, by contrast, are made of large cast-iron pipes; installation normally requires crews of pipefitters. Despite these differences, all plumbers, pipelayers, pipefitters, and steamfitters must be able to follow building plans or blueprints and instructions from supervisors, lay out the job, and work efficiently with the materials and tools of their trade. When plumbers working construction install piping in a new house, they work from blueprints or drawings that show the planned location of pipes, plumbing fixtures, and appliances. Recently, plumbers have become more involved in the design process. Their knowledge of codes and the operation of plumbing systems can cut costs. First they lay out the job to fit the piping into the structure of the house with the least waste of material. Then they measure and mark areas in which pipes will be installed and connected. Construction plumbers also check for obstructions such as electrical wiring and, if necessary, plan the pipe installation around the problem.

Sometimes, plumbers have to cut holes in walls, ceilings, and floors of a house. With some systems, they may hang steel supports from ceiling joists to hold the pipe in place. To assemble a system, plumbers—using saws, pipe cutters, and pipe-bending machines—cut and bend lengths of pipe. They connect the lengths of pipe with fittings, using methods that depend on the type of pipe used. For plastic pipe, plumbers connect the sections and fittings with adhesives. For copper pipe, they slide a fitting over the end of the pipe and solder it in place with a torch.

After the piping is in place in the house, plumbers install the fixtures and appliances and connect the system to the outside water or sewer lines. Finally, using pressure gauges, they check the system to ensure that the plumbing works properly.

Work environment. Plumbers work in commercial and residential settings where water and septic systems need to be installed and maintained. Pipefitters and steamfitters most often work in industrial and power plants. Pipelayers work outdoors, sometimes in remote areas, laying pipes that connect sources of oil, gas, and chemicals with the users of these resources. Sprinklerfitters work in all buildings that require the use of fire sprinkler systems.

Because plumbers, pipelayers, pipefitters, and steamfitters frequently must lift heavy pipes, stand for long periods, and sometimes work in uncomfortable or cramped positions, they need physical strength and stamina. They also may have to work outdoors in inclement weather. In addition, they are subject to possible falls from ladders, cuts from sharp tools, and burns from hot pipes or soldering equipment. Consequently, this occupation experiences rates of nonfatal injuries and illnesses that are much higher than average.

Plumbers, pipelayers, pipefitters, and steamfitters often work more than 40 hours per week and can be on call for emergencies nights and weekends. Some pipelayers may need to travel to and from worksites.

Training, Other Qualifications, and Advancement

Most plumbers, pipelayers, pipefitters, and steamfitters train on the job through jointly administered apprenticeships and in career or technical schools or community colleges.

Education and training. Plumbers, pipelayers, pipefitters, and steamfitters enter into the occupation in a variety of ways. Most plumbers, pipefitters, and steamfitters get their training in jointly administered apprenticeships or in technical schools and community colleges. Pipelayers typically receive their training on the job.

Apprenticeship programs generally provide the most comprehensive training available for these jobs. Such programs are, for the most part, administered jointly by union locals and their affiliated companies or by nonunion contractor organizations. Organizations that sponsor apprenticeships include the United Association of Journeymen and Apprentices of the Plumbing and Pipefitting Industry of the United States and Canada; local employers of either the Mechanical Contractors Association of America or the National Association of Plumbing-Heating-Cooling Contractors; a union associated with a member of the National Fire Sprinkler Association; the Associated Builders and Contractors; the National Association of Plumbing-Heating-Cooling Contractors; the American Fire Sprinkler Association; and the Home Builders Institute of the National Association of Home Builders.

Apprenticeships—both union and nonunion—consist of 4 or 5 years of paid on-the-job training and at least 144 hours of related classroom instruction per year. Classroom subjects include drafting and blueprint reading, mathematics, applied physics and chemistry, safety, and local plumbing codes and regulations. On the job, apprentices first learn basic skills, such as identifying grades and types of pipe, using the tools of the trade, and unloading materials safely. As apprentices gain experience, they learn how to work with various types of pipe and how to install different piping systems and plumbing fixtures. Apprenticeship gives trainees a thorough knowledge of all aspects of the trade. Although most plumbers, pipefitters, and steamfitters are trained through apprenticeships, some still learn their skills informally on the job or by taking classes on their own.

Licensure. Although there are no uniform national licensing requirements, most states and communities require plumbers to be licensed. Licensing requirements vary, but most localities require workers to have 2 to 5 years of experience and to pass an examination that tests their knowledge of the trade and of local plumbing codes before they are permitted to work independently. Several states require a special license to work on gas lines. A few states require pipefitters to be licensed. Licenses usually require a test, experience, or both.

Other qualifications. Applicants for union or nonunion apprentice jobs must be at least 18 years old and in good physical condition. A drug test may be required. Apprenticeship committees may require applicants to have a high school diploma or its equivalent. For jointly administered apprenticeships approved by the U.S. Department of Labor, a high school diploma is mandatory, because these programs can earn credit from community colleges and, in some cases, from 4-year colleges. Armed Forces training in plumbing, pipefitting, and steamfitting is considered very good preparation. In fact, people with this background may be given credit for previous experience when they enroll in a civilian apprenticeship program. High school or postsecondary courses in shop, plumbing, general mathematics, drafting, blueprint reading, computers, and physics also are good preparation.

Certification and advancement. With additional training, some plumbers, pipefitters, and steamfitters become supervisors for mechanical and plumbing contractors. Others, especially plumbers, go into business for themselves, often starting as a self-employed plumber working from home. Some eventually become owners of businesses employing many workers and may spend most of their time as managers rather than as plumbers. Others move into closely related areas such as construction management or building inspection.

For those who would like to advance, it is becoming increasingly important to be able to communicate in both English and Spanish in order to relay instructions and safety precautions to workers with limited understanding of English; Spanish-speaking workers make up a large part of the construction workforce in many areas. Supervisors and contractors need good communication skills to deal with clients and subcontractors.

In line with new opportunities arising from the growing need to conserve water, the Plumbing-Heating-Cooling Contractors—National Association has formed a partnership with GreenPlumbers USA to train and certify plumbers across the nation on water-saving technologies and energy efficiency. Attainment of this certification may help people trained in this area to get more jobs and advance more quickly.

Employment

Plumbers, pipelayers, pipefitters, and steamfitters constitute one of the largest construction occupations, holding about 555,900 jobs in 2008. About 56 percent worked for plumbing, heating, and air-conditioning contractors engaged in new construction, repair, modernization, or maintenance work. Others were employed by a variety of industrial, commercial, and government employers. Pipefitters, for example, were employed in the petroleum and chemical industries to maintain the pipes that carry industrial liquids and gases. About 12 percent of plumbers, pipelayers, pipefitters, and steamfitters were self-employed.

Job Outlook

Faster-than-average employment growth is projected. Job opportunities are expected to be very good.

Employment change. Employment of plumbers, pipelayers, pipefitters, and steamfitters is expected to grow 16 percent between 2008 and 2018, faster than the average for all occupations. Demand for plumbers will stem from new construction and from renovation of buildings. In addition, repair and maintenance of existing residential systems will keep plumbers employed. A growing emphasis on water conservation, particularly in dryer parts of the country, that will require retrofitting in order to conserve water in new ways will increase demand for plumbers. Demand for pipefitters and steamfitters will be driven by maintenance and construction of places such as powerplants, water and wastewater treatment plants, office buildings, and factories, all of which have extensive pipe systems. The stimulus package aimed at repairing the nation's infrastructure should help the employment picture immediately; long-term growth of pipelayer jobs will stem from the building of new water and sewer lines and of pipelines to new oil and gas fields. Demand for sprinklerfitters also should also increase, because of proposed changes to construction codes, set to take effect in 2011, that will require the installation of fire sprinkler systems in residential buildings where these systems had previously never been required.

Job prospects. Job opportunities are expected to be very good, with demand for skilled plumbers, pipelayers, pipefitters, and steamfitters expected to outpace the supply of well-trained workers in this craft. Some employers report difficulty finding workers with the right qualifications. In addition, many people currently working in these trades are expected to retire over the next 10 years, which will

Projections Data from the National Employment Matrix

Occupational title	SOC Code	Employment, 2008	Projected employment, 2018	Change, 2008–2018	
				Number	Percent
Pipelayers, plumbers, pipefitters, and steamfitters 47-2150		555,900	642,100	86,300	16
Pipelayers 47-2151		61,200	71,700	10,500	17
Plumbers, pipefitters, and steamfitters................... 47-2152		494,700	570,500	75,800	15

NOTE: Data in this table are rounded.

create additional job openings. Workers with welding experience should have especially good opportunities.

Traditionally, many organizations with extensive pipe systems have employed their own plumbers or pipefitters to maintain equipment and keep systems running smoothly. But, to reduce labor costs, a large number of these firms no longer employ full-time, in-house plumbers or pipefitters. Instead, when they need a plumber, they increasingly are relying on workers provided under service contracts by plumbing and pipefitting contractors.

Construction projects generally provide only temporary employment. When a project ends, some plumbers, pipelayers, pipefitters, and steamfitters may be unemployed until they can begin work on a new project, although most companies are trying to limit these periods of unemployment in order to retain workers. In addition, the jobs of plumbers, pipelayers, pipefitters, and steamfitters are generally less sensitive to changes in economic conditions than are jobs in other construction trades. Moreover, the coming emphasis on conservation of energy and water is opening up opportunities for those plumbers, pipefitters, and steamfitters who become proficient in new green technologies.

Earnings

Plumbers, pipelayers, pipefitters, and steamfitters are among the highest paid workers in construction occupations. Median hourly wages of wage and salary plumbers, pipefitters, and steamfitters were $21.94 in May 2008. The middle 50 percent earned between $16.63 and $29.66. The lowest 10 percent earned less than $13.22, and the highest 10 percent earned more than $37.93. Median hourly wages in the industries employing the largest numbers of plumbers, pipefitters, and steamfitters were as follows:

Natural gas distribution......................................	$26.27
Nonresidential building construction......................	23.14
Building equipment contractors............................	21.86
Utility system construction..................................	21.15
Local government..	20.65

In May 2008, median hourly wages of wage and salary pipelayers were $15.72. The middle 50 percent earned between $12.84 and $20.85. The lowest 10 percent earned less than $10.74, and the highest 10 percent earned more than $27.43.

Apprentices usually begin at about 50 percent of the wage rate paid to experienced workers. Wages increase periodically as skills improve. After an initial waiting period, apprentices receive the same benefits as experienced plumbers, pipelayers, pipefitters, and steamfitters.

About 31 percent of plumbers, pipelayers, pipefitters, and steamfitters belonged to a union. Many of these workers are members of the United Association of Journeymen and Apprentices of the Plumbing and Pipefitting Industry of the United States and Canada.

Related Occupations

Other workers who install and repair mechanical systems in buildings include the following boilermakers; electricians; elevator installers and repairers; heating, air-conditioning, and refrigeration mechanics and installers; industrial machinery mechanics and millwrights; sheet metal workers; and stationary engineers and boiler operators.

Other construction-related workers who need to know plumbing requirements include the following construction and building inspectors; and construction managers.

Sources of Additional Information

For information about apprenticeships or work opportunities in plumbing, pipelaying, pipefitting, and steamfitting, contact local plumbing, heating, and air-conditioning contractors; a local or state chapter of the Plumbing-Heating-Cooling Contractors; a local chapter of the Mechanical Contractors Association; a local chapter of the United Association of Journeymen and Apprentices of the Plumbing and Pipefitting Industry of the United States and Canada; or the nearest office of your state employment service or apprenticeship agency. Apprenticeship information also is available from the U.S. Department of Labor's toll-free help line: (877) 872-5627.

For information about apprenticeship opportunities for plumbers, pipefitters, and steamfitters, contact

▸ United Association of Journeymen and Apprentices of the Plumbing and Pipefitting Industry, Three Park Place, Annapolis, MD 21401-3687. Internet: www.ua.org

For general information about the work of pipelayers, plumbers, and pipefitters, contact

▸ Mechanical Contractors Association of America, 1385 Piccard Dr., Rockville, MD 20850-4329. Internet: www.mcaa.org
▸ National Center for Construction Education and Research, 3600 NW 43rd St., Bldg. G, Gainesville, FL 32606-8134. Internet: www.nccer.org
▸ Plumbing-Heating-Cooling Contractors—National Association, 180 S. Washington St., Falls Church, VA 22046-2935. Internet: www.phccweb.org

For general information about the work of sprinklerfitters, contact

▸ American Fire Sprinkler Association, Inc., 12750 Merit Dr., Suite 350, Dallas, TX 75251-1273. Internet: www.firesprinkler.org

▶ National Fire Sprinkler Association, 40 Jon Barrett Rd., Patterson, NY 12563-2164. Internet: www.nfsa.org

For general information on apprenticeships and how to get them, see the *Occupational Outlook Quarterly* article "Apprenticeships: Career training, credentials—and a paycheck in your pocket," online at www.bls.gov/opub/ooq/2002/summer/art01.pdf and in print at many libraries and career centers.

Police and Detectives

(O*NET 33-1012.00, 33-3021.00, 33-3021.01, 33-3021.02, 33-3021.03, 33-3021.05, 33-3021.06, 33-3031.00, 33-3051.00, 33-3051.01, 33-3051.03, and 33-3052.00)

Significant Points

■ Police work can be dangerous and stressful.

■ Education requirements range from a high school diploma to a college degree or higher.

■ Job opportunities in most local police departments will be favorable for qualified individuals, while competition is expected for jobs in state and federal agencies.

■ Bilingual applicants with college training in police science or with military police experience will have the best opportunities.

Nature of the Work

Police officers and *detectives* protect lives and property. *Law enforcement officers'* duties depend on the size and type of their organizations.

Police and detectives pursue and apprehend individuals who break the law and then issue citations or give warnings. A large proportion of their time is spent writing reports and maintaining records of incidents they encounter. Most police officers patrol their jurisdictions and investigate any suspicious activity they notice. They also respond to calls from individuals. Detectives, who often are called *agents* or *special agents*, perform investigative duties such as gathering facts and collecting evidence.

The daily activities of police and detectives vary with their occupational specialty—such as police officer, game warden, or detective—and whether they are working for a local, state, or federal agency. Duties also differ substantially among various federal agencies, which enforce different aspects of the law. Regardless of job duties or location, police officers and detectives at all levels must write reports and maintain meticulous records that will be needed if they testify in court.

State and Local Law Enforcement. *Uniformed police officers* have general law enforcement duties. They maintain regular patrols and respond to calls for service. Much of their time is spent responding to calls and doing paperwork. They may direct traffic at the scene of an accident, investigate a burglary, or give first aid to an accident victim. In large police departments, officers usually are assigned to a specific type of duty.

Many urban police agencies are involved in community policing—a practice in which an officer builds relationships with the citizens of local neighborhoods and mobilizes the public to help fight crime.

Police agencies are usually organized into geographic districts, with uniformed officers assigned to patrol a specific area. Officers in large agencies often patrol with a partner. They attempt to become familiar with their patrol area and remain alert for anything unusual. Suspicious circumstances and hazards to public safety are investigated or noted, and officers are dispatched to individual calls for assistance within their district. During their shift, they may identify, pursue, and arrest suspected criminals; resolve problems within the community; and enforce traffic laws.

Some agencies have special geographic jurisdictions and enforcement responsibilities. Public college and university police forces, public school district police, and agencies serving transportation systems and facilities are examples. Most law enforcement workers in special agencies are uniformed officers.

Some police officers specialize in a particular field, such as chemical and microscopic analysis, training and firearms instruction, or handwriting and fingerprint identification. Others work with special units, such as horseback, bicycle, motorcycle, or harbor patrol; canine corps; special weapons and tactics (SWAT); or emergency response teams. A few local and special law enforcement officers primarily perform jail-related duties or work in courts.

Sheriffs and *deputy sheriffs* enforce the law on the county level. Sheriffs usually are elected to their posts and perform duties similar to those of a local or county police chief. Sheriffs' departments tend to be relatively small, most having fewer than 50 sworn officers. Deputy sheriffs have law enforcement duties similar to those of officers in urban police departments. Police and sheriffs' deputies who provide security in city and county courts are sometimes called *bailiffs*.

State police officers, sometimes called *state troopers* or *highway patrol officers*, arrest criminals statewide and patrol highways to enforce motor vehicle laws and regulations. State police officers often issue traffic citations to motorists. At the scene of accidents, they may direct traffic, give first aid, and call for emergency equipment. They also write reports used to determine the cause of the accident. State police officers frequently are called upon to render assistance to other law enforcement agencies, especially those in rural areas or small towns.

State highway patrols operate in every state except Hawaii. Most full-time sworn personnel are uniformed officers who regularly patrol and respond to calls for service. Others work as investigators, perform court-related duties, or carry out administrative or other assignments.

Detectives are plainclothes investigators who gather facts and collect evidence for criminal cases. Some are assigned to interagency task forces to combat specific types of crime. They conduct interviews, examine records, observe the activities of suspects, and participate in raids or arrests. Detectives usually specialize in investigating one type of violation, such as homicide or fraud. They are assigned cases on a rotating basis and work on them until an arrest and conviction is made or until the case is dropped.

Fish and game wardens enforce fishing, hunting, and boating laws. They patrol hunting and fishing areas, conduct search and rescue operations, investigate complaints and accidents, and aid in prosecuting court cases.

Federal Law Enforcement. *Federal Bureau of Investigation (FBI) agents* are the government's principal investigators, responsible for investigating violations of more than 200 categories of federal law and conducting sensitive national security investigations. Agents may conduct surveillance, monitor court-authorized wiretaps, examine business records, investigate white-collar crime, or participate in sensitive undercover assignments. The FBI investigates a wide range of criminal activity, including organized crime, public corruption, financial crime, bank robbery, kidnapping, terrorism, espionage, drug trafficking, and cybercrime.

There are many other federal agencies that enforce particular types of laws. *U.S. Drug Enforcement Administration (DEA) agents* enforce laws and regulations relating to illegal drugs. *U.S. marshals and deputy marshals* provide security for the federal courts and ensure the effective operation of the judicial system. *Bureau of Alcohol, Tobacco, Firearms, and Explosives agents* enforce and investigate violations of federal firearms and explosives laws, as well as federal alcohol and tobacco tax regulations. The U.S. Department of State *Bureau of Diplomatic Security special agents* are engaged in the battle against terrorism.

The Department of Homeland Security also employs numerous law enforcement officers within several different agencies, including Customs and Border Protection, Immigration and Customs Enforcement, and the U.S. Secret Service. *U.S. Border Patrol agents* protect more than 8,000 miles of international land and water boundaries. *Immigration inspectors* interview and examine people seeking entry into the United States and its territories. *Customs inspectors* enforce laws governing imports and exports by inspecting cargo, baggage, and articles worn or carried by people, vessels, vehicles, trains, and aircraft entering or leaving the United States. *Federal Air Marshals* provide air security by guarding against attacks targeting U.S. aircraft, passengers, and crews. *U.S. Secret Service special agents* and *U.S. Secret Service uniformed officers* protect the President, the Vice President, their immediate families, and other public officials. Secret Service special agents also investigate counterfeiting, forgery of government checks or bonds, and fraudulent use of credit cards.

Other federal agencies employ police and special agents with sworn arrest powers and the authority to carry firearms. These agencies include the Postal Service, the Bureau of Indian Affairs Office of Law Enforcement, the Forest Service, and the National Park Service.

Work environment. Police and detective work can be very dangerous and stressful. Police officers and detectives have one of the highest rates of on-the-job injury and illness. In addition to the obvious dangers of confrontations with criminals, police officers and detectives need to be constantly alert and ready to deal appropriately with a number of other threatening situations. Many law enforcement officers witness death and suffering resulting from accidents and criminal behavior. A career in law enforcement may take a toll on their private lives.

Uniformed officers, detectives, agents, and inspectors usually are scheduled to work 40-hour weeks, but paid overtime is common.

Shift work is necessary because protection must be provided around the clock. Junior officers frequently work weekends, holidays, and nights. Police officers and detectives are required to work whenever they are needed and may work long hours during investigations. Officers in most jurisdictions, whether on or off duty, are expected to be armed and to exercise their authority when necessary.

The jobs of some federal agents, such as U.S. Secret Service and DEA special agents, require extensive travel, often on very short notice. These agents may relocate a number of times over the course of their careers. Some special agents, such as those in the U.S. Border Patrol, may work outdoors in rugged terrain and in all kinds of weather.

Training, Other Qualifications, and Advancement

Education requirements range from a high school diploma to a college degree or higher. Most police and detectives learn much of what they need to know on the job, often in their agency's training academy. Civil service regulations govern the appointment of police and detectives in most states, large municipalities, and special police agencies, as well as in many smaller jurisdictions. Candidates must be U.S. citizens, usually at least 21 years old, and meet rigorous physical and personal qualifications.

Education and training. Applicants usually must have at least a high school education, and some departments require 1 or 2 years of college coursework or, in some cases, a college degree. Physical education classes and participation in sports are also helpful in developing the competitiveness, stamina, and agility needed for many law enforcement positions. Knowledge of a foreign language is an asset in many federal agencies and urban departments.

State and local agencies encourage applicants to take courses or training related to law enforcement subjects after high school. Many entry-level applicants for police jobs have completed some formal postsecondary education, and a significant number are college graduates. Many junior colleges, colleges, and universities offer programs in law enforcement or administration of justice. Many agencies pay all or part of the tuition for officers to work toward degrees in criminal justice, police science, administration of justice, or public administration and pay higher salaries to those who earn one of those degrees.

Before their first assignments, officers usually go through a period of training. In state and large local police departments, recruits get training in their agency's police academy, often for 12 to 14 weeks. In small agencies, recruits often attend a regional or state academy. Training includes classroom instruction in constitutional law and civil rights, state laws and local ordinances, and accident investigation. Recruits also receive training and supervised experience in patrol, traffic control, use of firearms, self-defense, first aid, and emergency response. Police departments in some large cities hire high school graduates who are still in their teens as police cadets or trainees. They do clerical work and attend classes, usually for one to two years, until they reach the minimum age requirement and can be appointed to the regular force.

Fish and game wardens also must meet specific requirements. Most states require at least two years of college study. Once hired, fish and game wardens attend a training academy lasting from 3 to 12 months, sometimes followed by further training in the field.

Federal agencies require a bachelor's degree, related work experience, or a combination of the two. Federal law enforcement agents undergo extensive training, usually at the U.S. Marine Corps base in Quantico, Virginia, or the Federal Law Enforcement Training Center in Glynco, Georgia. The specific educational requirements, qualifications, and training information for a particular federal agency can be found on its Web site. Many of these agencies are listed as sources of additional information at the end of this statement.

To be considered for appointment as an FBI agent, an applicant must be a college graduate and have at least three years of professional work experience or must have an advanced degree plus two years of professional work experience. An applicant who meets these criteria also must have one of the following: a college major in accounting, electrical engineering, information technology, or computer science; fluency in a foreign language; a degree from an accredited law school; or three years of related full-time work experience. All new FBI agents undergo 18 weeks of training at the FBI Academy on the U.S. Marine Corps base in Quantico, Virginia.

Other qualifications. Civil service regulations govern the appointment of police and detectives in most states, large municipalities, and special police agencies, as well as in many smaller jurisdictions. Candidates must be U.S. citizens usually must be at least 21 years old, and must meet rigorous physical and personal qualifications. Physical examinations for entry into law enforcement often include tests of vision, hearing, strength, and agility. Eligibility for appointment usually depends on one's performance in competitive written examinations and previous education and experience.

Candidates should enjoy working with people and meeting the public. Because personal characteristics such as honesty, sound judgment, integrity, and a sense of responsibility are especially important in law enforcement, candidates are interviewed by senior officers and their character traits and backgrounds are investigated. A history of domestic violence may disqualify a candidate. In some agencies, candidates are interviewed by a psychiatrist or a psychologist or given a personality test. Most applicants are subjected to lie detector examinations or drug testing. Some agencies subject sworn personnel to random drug testing as a condition of continuing employment.

Although similar in nature, the requirements for federal agents are generally more stringent and the background checks are more thorough. There are polygraph tests as well as interviews with references. Jobs that require security clearances have additional requirements.

Advancement. Police officers usually become eligible for promotion after a probationary period ranging from six months to three years. In large departments, promotion may enable an officer to become a detective or to specialize in one type of police work, such as working with juveniles. Promotions to corporal, sergeant, lieutenant, and captain usually are made according to a candidate's position on a promotion list, as determined by scores on a written examination and on-the-job performance.

Federal agents often are on the General Services (GS) pay scale. Most begin at the GS-5 or GS-7 level. As agents meet time-in-grade and knowledge and skills requirements, they move up the GS scale.

Promotions at and above GS-13 are most often managerial positions. Many agencies hire internally for these supervisory positions. A few agents may be able to enter the Senior Executive Series ranks of upper management.

Continuing training helps police officers, detectives, and special agents improve their job performance. Through police department academies, regional centers for public safety employees established by the states, and federal agency training centers, instructors provide annual training in self-defense tactics, firearms, use-of-force policies, sensitivity and communications skills, crowd-control techniques, relevant legal developments, and advances in law enforcement equipment.

Employment

Police and detectives held about 883,600 jobs in 2008. About 79 percent were employed by local governments. State police agencies employed about 11 percent. Various federal agencies employ police and detectives.

According to the U.S. Bureau of Justice Statistics, police and detectives employed by local governments worked primarily in cities with more than 25,000 inhabitants. Some cities have very large police forces, while thousands of small communities employ fewer than 25 officers each.

Job Outlook

Job opportunities in most local police departments will be favorable for qualified individuals, whereas competition is expected for jobs in state and federal agencies. As-fast-as-average employment growth is expected.

Employment change. Employment of police and detectives is expected to grow 10 percent over the 2008–2018 decade, about as fast as the average for all occupations. Population growth is the main source of demand for police services.

Job prospects. Overall opportunities in local police departments will be favorable for individuals who meet the psychological, personal, and physical qualifications. In addition to openings from employment growth, many openings will be created by the need to replace workers who retire and those who leave local agencies for federal jobs and private-sector security jobs. Jobs in local police departments that offer relatively low salaries, or those in urban communities in which the crime rate is relatively high, may be the easiest to get. Some smaller departments may have fewer opportunities as budgets limit the ability to hire additional officers. Bilingual applicants with military experience or college training in police science will have the best opportunities in local and state departments.

There will be more competition for jobs in federal and state law enforcement agencies than for jobs in local agencies. Bilingual applicants with a bachelor's degree and several years of law enforcement or military experience, especially investigative experience, will have the best opportunities in federal agencies.

The level of government spending determines the level of employment for police and detectives. The number of job opportunities, therefore, can vary from year to year and from place to place. Layoffs are rare because retirements enable most staffing cuts to be handled through attrition. Trained law enforcement officers who

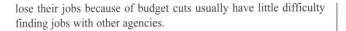

lose their jobs because of budget cuts usually have little difficulty finding jobs with other agencies.

Earnings

Police and sheriff's patrol officers had median annual wages of $51,410 in May 2008. The middle 50 percent earned between $38,850 and $64,940. The lowest 10 percent earned less than $30,070, and the highest 10 percent earned more than $79,680. Median annual wages were $46,620 in federal government, $57,270 in state government, $51,020 in local government and $43,350 in educational services.

In May 2008, median annual wages of police and detective supervisors were $75,490. The middle 50 percent earned between $59,320 and $92,700. The lowest 10 percent earned less than $46,000, and the highest 10 percent earned more than $114,300. Median annual wages were $89,930 in federal government, $75,370 in state government, and $74,820 in local government.

In May 2008, median annual wages of detectives and criminal investigators were $60,910. The middle 50 percent earned between $45,930 and $81,490. The lowest 10 percent earned less than $36,500, and the highest 10 percent earned more than $97,870. Median annual wages were $73,170 in federal government, $53,910 in state government, and $55,930 in local government.

In May 2008, median annual wages of fish and game wardens were $48,930. The middle 50 percent earned between $37,500 and $61,290. The lowest 10 percent earned less than $30,400, and the highest 10 percent earned more than $81,710. Median annual wages were $48,960 in federal government, $50,440 in state government, and $35,810 in local government.

In May 2008, median annual wages of parking enforcement workers were $32,390. The middle 50 percent earned between $25,400 and $42,000. The lowest 10 percent earned less than $20,510, and the highest 10 percent earned more than $50,470. Median annual wages were $33,130 in local government and $27,640 in educational services.

In May 2008, median annual wages of transit and railroad police were $46,670. The middle 50 percent earned between $37,640 and $57,830. The lowest 10 percent earned less than $31,300, and the highest 10 percent earned more than $72,700. Median annual wages

were $49,370 in state government, $43,720 in local government, and $56,300 in rail transportation.

Federal law provides special salary rates to federal employees who serve in law enforcement. Additionally, federal special agents and inspectors receive law enforcement availability pay (LEAP)—equal to 25 percent of the agent's grade and step—awarded because of the large amount of overtime that these agents are expected to work. Salaries were slightly higher in selected areas where the prevailing local pay level was higher. Because federal agents may be eligible for a special law enforcement benefits package, applicants should ask their recruiter for more information.

Total earnings for local, state, and special police and detectives frequently exceed the stated salary because of payments for overtime, which can be significant.

According to the International City-County Management Association's annual Police and Fire Personnel, Salaries, and Expenditures Survey, average salaries for sworn full-time positions in 2008 were as follows:

Position	Minimum salary	Maximum salary w/o longevity
Police chief	$90,570	$113,930
Deputy chief	74,834	96,209
Police captain	72,761	91,178
Police lieutenant	65,688	79,268
Police sergeant	58,739	70,349
Police corporal	49,421	61,173

In addition to the common benefits—paid vacation, sick leave, and medical and life insurance—most police and sheriffs' departments provide officers with special allowances for uniforms. Many police officers retire at half-pay after 20 years of service; others often are eligible to retire with 30 or fewer years of service.

Related Occupations

Other occupations that help protect and serve people are correctional officers; emergency medical technicians and paramedics; fire fighters; private detectives and investigators; probation officers and correctional treatment specialists; and security guards and gaming surveillance officers.

Projections Data from the National Employment Matrix

Occupational title	SOC Code	Employment, 2008	Projected employment, 2018	Change, 2008–2018	
				Number	Percent
Police and detectives	—	883,600	968,400	84,700	10
First-line supervisors/managers of police and detectives	33-1012	97,300	105,200	7,800	8
Detectives and criminal investigators	33-3021	112,200	130,900	18,700	17
Fish and game wardens	33-3031	8,300	9,000	700	8
Police officers	33-3050	665,700	723,300	57,500	9
Police and sheriff's patrol officers	33-3051	661,500	718,800	57,300	9
Transit and railroad police	33-3052	4,300	4,500	200	5

NOTE: Data in this table are rounded.

Sources of Additional Information

Information about entry requirements may be obtained from federal, state, and local law enforcement agencies.

To find federal, state, and local law enforcement job fairs and other recruiting events across the country, contact

- ▶ National Law Enforcement Recruiters Association, P.O. Box 17132, Arlington, VA 22216. Internet: www.nlera.org

For general information about sheriffs and to learn more about the National Sheriffs' Association scholarship, contact

- ▶ National Sheriffs' Association, 1450 Duke St., Alexandria, VA 22314. Internet: www.sheriffs.org

For information about chiefs of police, contact

- ▶ International Association of Chiefs of Police, 515 N. Washington St., Alexandria, VA 22314. Internet: www.theiacp.org

Information related to federal law enforcement:

- ▶ Information about qualifications for employment as a Federal Bureau of Investigation (FBI) Special Agent is available from the nearest state FBI office. The address and phone number are listed in the local telephone directory. Internet: www.fbi.gov

- ▶ Information on career opportunities, qualifications, and training for U.S. Secret Service Special Agents and Uniformed Officers is available from the Secret Service Personnel Division at (202) 406-5830, (888) 813-8777, (888) 813-USSS, or U.S. Secret Services, Recruitment and Hiring Coordination Center, 245 Murray Dr., Building 410, Washington, DC 20223. Internet: www.secretservice.gov/join

- ▶ Information about qualifications for employment as a Drug Enforcement Administration (DEA) Special Agent is available from the nearest DEA office, DEA Office of Personnel, 8701 Morrissette Dr., Springfield, VA 22152, or call (800) DEA-4288. Internet: www.usdoj.gov/dea

Information about jobs in other federal law enforcement agencies is available from

- ▶ U.S. Marshals Service, Human Resources Division—Law Enforcement Recruiting, Washington, DC 20530-1000. Internet: www.usmarshals.gov

- ▶ U.S. Bureau of Alcohol, Tobacco, Firearms, and Explosives, Office of Governmental and Public Affairs, 99 New York Ave. NE, Mail Stop 5S 144, Washington, DC 20226. Internet: www.atf.gov

- ▶ U.S. Customs and Border Protection, 1300 Pennsylvania Ave. NW, Washington, DC 20229. Internet: www.cbp.gov

- ▶ U.S. Department of Homeland Security, Washington, DC 20528. Internet: www.dhs.gov

Probation Officers and Correctional Treatment Specialists

(O*NET 21-1092.00)

Significant Points

- State and local governments employ most of these workers.

- A bachelor's degree in social work, criminal justice, psychology, or a related field is usually required.

- Employment growth, which is projected to be faster than the average, is dependent on government funding.

- Job opportunities are expected to be excellent.

Nature of the Work

Many people who are convicted of crimes are placed on probation, instead of being sent to prison. People who have served time in prison are often released on parole. During probation and parole, offenders must stay out of trouble and meet various other requirements. *Probation officers, parole officers, and correctional treatment specialists* work with and monitor offenders to prevent them from committing new crimes.

Probation officers, who are called *community supervision officers* in some states, supervise people who have been placed on probation. *Correctional treatment specialists*, who may also be known as *case managers* or *correctional counselors*, counsel offenders and create rehabilitation plans for them to follow when they are no longer in prison or on parole. *Parole officers* perform many of the same duties that probation officers perform. The difference is that parole officers supervise offenders who have been released from prison, whereas probation officers work with those who are sentenced to probation instead of prison. *Pretrial services officers* conduct pretrial investigations, the findings of which help determine whether suspects should be released before their trial. In most jurisdictions, probation is a county function and parole is a state function.

Probation and parole officers supervise offenders on probation or parole through personal contact with the offenders and their families. Instead of requiring offenders to come to them, many officers meet offenders in their homes and at their places of employment or therapy. Probation and parole agencies also seek the assistance of community organizations, such as religious institutions, neighborhood groups, and local residents, to monitor the behavior of many offenders. Some offenders are required to wear an electronic device so officers can monitor their location and movements. Probation and parole officers may arrange for offenders to get substance abuse rehabilitation or job training. Probation officers usually work with either adults or juveniles exclusively. Juvenile probation is also called aftercare. Only in small, usually rural, jurisdictions do probation officers counsel both adults and juveniles. In some states, the jobs of parole and probation officers are combined.

Probation officers also spend much of their time working for the courts. They investigate the backgrounds of the accused, write presentence reports, and recommend sentences. They review sentencing recommendations with offenders and their families before submitting them to the court. Probation officers may be required to testify in court as to their findings and recommendations. They also attend hearings to update the court on offenders' efforts at rehabilitation and compliance with the terms of their sentences.

Correctional treatment specialists work in jails, prisons, or parole or probation agencies. In jails and prisons, they monitor the progress of inmates. They may evaluate inmates using questionnaires and psychological tests. They also work with inmates, probation officers, and other agencies to develop parole and release plans. Their case reports, which discuss the inmate's history and likelihood of committing another crime, are provided to the appropriate parole board when their clients are eligible for release. In addition, correctional treatment specialists plan education and training programs to improve offenders' job skills and provide them with coping, anger management, and drug and sexual abuse counseling either individually or in groups. They usually write treatment plans and summaries for each client. Correctional treatment specialists working in parole and probation agencies perform many of the same duties as their counterparts who work in correctional institutions.

The number of cases a probation officer or correctional treatment specialist handles at one time depends on the needs of offenders and the risks they pose. Higher risk offenders and those who need more counseling usually command more of the officer's time and resources. Caseload size also varies by agency jurisdiction. Consequently, officers may handle from 20 to more than 100 active cases at a time.

Computers, telephones, and fax machines enable the officers to handle the caseload. Probation officers may telecommute from their homes. Other technological advancements, such as electronic monitoring devices, reporting kiosks, and drug screening, also assist probation officers and correctional treatment specialists in supervising and counseling offenders.

Pretrial services officers conduct pretrial investigations, the findings of which help determine whether suspects should be released before their trial. When suspects are released before their trial, pretrial services officers supervise them to make sure they adhere to the terms of their release and that they show up for trial. In most jurisdictions, including the federal courts system, probation officers perform the functions of pretrial services officers.

Work environment. Probation officers and correctional treatment specialists work with criminal offenders, some of whom may be dangerous. While supervising offenders, they usually interact with many other individuals, such as family members and friends of their clients, who may be angry, upset, or difficult to work with. Workers may be assigned to fieldwork in high-crime areas or in institutions where there is a risk of violence or communicable disease.

Probation officers and correctional treatment specialists are required to meet many court-imposed deadlines, which contribute to heavy workloads. In addition, extensive travel and fieldwork may be required to meet with offenders who are on probation or parole. Workers may be required to carry a firearm or other weapon for protection. They also may be required to collect and transport urine samples of offenders for drug testing. All of these factors make for a stressful work environment. Although the high stress levels can make these jobs very difficult at times, this work also can be very rewarding. Many workers obtain personal satisfaction from counseling members of their community and helping them become productive citizens.

Probation officers and correctional treatment specialists generally work a 40-hour week, but some may work longer. They may be on call 24 hours a day to supervise and assist offenders at any time.

Training, Other Qualifications, and Advancement

Qualifications vary by agency, but a bachelor's degree is usually required. Most employers require candidates to pass oral, written, and psychological examinations.

Education and training. A bachelor's degree in social work, criminal justice, psychology, or a related field is usually required. Some employers require a master's degree in criminal justice, social work, psychology, or a related field for candidates who do not have previous related experience. Different employers have different require-

ments for what counts as related experience. It may include work in probation, pretrial services, parole, corrections, criminal investigations, substance abuse treatment, social work, or counseling.

Most probation officers and some correctional treatment specialists are required to complete a training program sponsored by their state government or the federal government, after which a certification test may be required. Most probation officers and correctional treatment specialists work as trainees or on a probationary period for up to a year before being offered a permanent position.

Other qualifications. Applicants usually take written, oral, psychological, and physical examinations. Prospective probation officers or correctional treatment specialists should be in good physical and emotional condition. Most agencies require applicants to be at least 21 years old and, for federal employment, not older than 37. Those convicted of felonies may not be eligible for employment in this occupation. A valid driver's license is often required.

Familiarity with the use of computers is often required, due to the use of computer technology in probation and parole work. Candidates also should be knowledgeable about laws and regulations pertaining to corrections. Probation officers and correctional treatment specialists should have strong writing skills because they are required to prepare many reports. They should also have excellent listening and interpersonal skills to work effectively with offenders.

Advancement. A typical agency has probation and parole officers and correctional treatment specialists with varying amounts of experience, as well as supervisors. Advancement is primarily based on experience and performance. A graduate degree, such as a master's degree in criminal justice, social work, or psychology, may be helpful or required for advancement.

Employment

Probation officers and correctional treatment specialists held about 103,400 jobs in 2008. Most jobs are in state or local governments. Depending on the state, probation officers and correctional treatment specialists may be employed solely by state or local government, or they are employed at both levels. Jobs are more plentiful in urban areas than in rural ones. In the federal government, probation officers are employed by the U.S. courts, and correctional treatment specialists are employed by the U.S. Department of Justice's Bureau of Prisons.

Job Outlook

Employment of probation officers and correctional treatment specialists is projected to grow faster than the average for all occupations through 2018. Job opportunities are expected to be excellent.

Employment change. Employment of probation officers and correctional treatment specialists is projected to grow about 19 percent between 2008 and 2018, faster than the average for all occupations. Mandatory sentencing guidelines calling for longer sentences and reduced parole for inmates have resulted in a large increase in the prison population. However, mandatory sentencing guidelines are being reconsidered in many states because of budgetary constraints, court decisions, and doubts about the guidelines' effectiveness. Instead, there may be more emphasis in many states on rehabilitation and alternate forms of punishment, such as probation, that will

Projections Data from the National Employment Matrix

Occupational title	SOC Code	Employment, 2008	Projected employment, 2018	Change, 2008–2018	
				Number	Percent
Probation officers and correctional treatment specialists 21-1092		103,400	123,300	19,900	19

NOTE: Data in this table are rounded.

spur demand for probation and parole officers and correctional treatment specialists. Additionally, there will be a need for parole officers to supervise the large number of currently incarcerated people when they are released from prison.

However, employment growth depends primarily on the amount of government funding that is allocated to corrections, and especially to probation and parole systems. Although community supervision is far less expensive than keeping offenders in prison, a change in political trends toward more imprisonment and away from community supervision could result in reduced employment opportunities.

Job prospects. In addition to openings due to growth, many openings will be created by replacement needs, especially openings due to the large number of these workers who are expected to retire. This occupation is not attractive to some potential entrants due to relatively low earnings, heavy workloads, and high stress. For these reasons, job opportunities are expected to be excellent.

Earnings

Median annual wages of probation officers and correctional treatment specialists in May 2008 were $45,910. The middle 50 percent earned between $35,990 and $60,430. The lowest 10 percent earned less than $29,490, and the highest 10 percent earned more than $78,210. In May 2008, median annual wages for probation officers and correctional treatment specialists employed in state government were $46,580; those employed in local government earned $46,420. Higher wages tend to be found in urban areas.

Related Occupations

Other workers who help treat and care of people include counselors; social and human service assistants; and social workers.

Other workers who help protect communities include correctional officers; firefighters; and police and detectives.

Sources of Additional Information

For information about criminal justice job opportunities in your area, contact your state's department of corrections, criminal justice, or probation.

Further information about probation officers and correctional treatment specialists is available from

▶ American Probation and Parole Association, P.O. Box 11910, Lexington, KY 40578. Internet: www.appa-net.org

Public Relations Specialists

(O*NET 27-3031.00)

Significant Points

■ Although employment is projected to grow much faster than average, keen competition is expected for entry-level jobs.

■ Opportunities should be best for college graduates who combine a degree in public relations, journalism, or another communications-related field with a public relations internship or other related work experience.

■ Strong communication skills are essential.

Nature of the Work

An organization's reputation, profitability, and its continued existence can depend on the degree to which its targeted public supports its goals and policies. *Public relations specialists*—also referred to as *communications specialists* and *media specialists*, among other titles—serve as advocates for clients seeking to build and maintain positive relationships with the public. Their clients include businesses, nonprofit associations, universities, hospitals, and other organizations, and build and maintain positive relationships with the public. As managers recognize the link between good public relations and the success of their organizations, they increasingly rely on public relations specialists for advice on the strategy and policy of their communications.

Public relations specialists handle organizational functions, such as media, community, consumer, industry, and governmental relations; political campaigns; interest-group representation; conflict mediation; and employee and investor relations. Public relations specialists must understand the attitudes and concerns of community, consumer, employee, and public interest groups to establish and maintain cooperative relationships between them and representatives from print and broadcast journalism.

Public relations specialists draft press releases and contact people in the media who might print or broadcast their material. Many radio or television special reports, newspaper stories, and magazine articles start at the desks of public relations specialists. Sometimes, the subject of a press release is an organization and its policies toward employees or its role in the community. For example, a press release might describe a public issue, such as health, energy, or the environment, and what an organization does to advance that issue.

Public relations specialists also arrange and conduct programs to maintain contact between organization representatives and the public. For example, public relations specialists set up speaking engagements and prepare speeches for officials. These media specialists represent employers at community projects; make film, slide, and other visual presentations for meetings and school assemblies; and plan conventions.

In government, public relations specialists may be called *press secretaries*. They keep the public informed about the activities of agencies and officials. For example, *public affairs specialists* in the U.S. Department of State alert the public of travel advisories and of U.S. positions on foreign issues. A press secretary for a member of Congress informs constituents of the representative's accomplishments.

In large organizations, the key public relations executive, who often is a vice president, may develop overall plans and policies with other executives. In addition, public relations departments employ public relations specialists to write, research, prepare materials, maintain contacts, and respond to inquiries.

People who handle publicity for an individual or who direct public relations for a small organization may deal with all aspects of the job. These public relations specialists contact people, plan and research, and prepare materials for distribution. They also may handle advertising or sales promotion work to support marketing efforts.

Work environment. Public relations specialists work in busy offices. The pressures of deadlines and tight work schedules can be stressful.

Some public relations specialists work a standard 35- to 40-hour week, but overtime is common, and work schedules can be irregular and are frequently interrupted. Occasionally, they must be at the job or on call around the clock, especially if there is an emergency or crisis. Schedules often have to be rearranged so workers can meet deadlines, deliver speeches, attend meetings and community activities, and travel.

Training, Other Qualifications, and Advancement

A bachelor's degree in a communications-related field combined with public relations experience is excellent preparation for a person interested in public relations work.

Education and training. Many entry-level public relations specialists have a college degree in public relations, journalism, marketing, or communications. Some firms seek college graduates who have worked in electronic or print journalism. Other employers seek applicants with demonstrated communication skills and training or experience in a field related to the firm's business—information technology, health care, science, engineering, sales, or finance, for example.

Many colleges and universities offer bachelor's and postsecondary programs leading to a degree in public relations, usually in a journalism or communications department. In addition, many other colleges offer courses in this field. Courses in advertising, business administration, finance, political science, psychology, sociology, and creative writing also are helpful. Specialties may be offered in public relations for business, government, and nonprofit organizations.

Internships in public relations provide students with valuable experience and training and are the best route to finding entry-level employment. Membership in local chapters of the Public Relations Student Society of America (affiliated with the Public Relations Society of America) or in student chapters of the International Association of Business Communicators provides an opportunity for students to exchange views with public relations specialists and to make professional contacts that may help them to find a full-time job after graduation.

Some organizations, particularly those with large public relations staffs, have formal training programs for new employees. In smaller organizations, new employees work under the guidance of experienced staff members. Entry-level workers often maintain files of material about company activities, skim newspapers and magazines for appropriate articles to clip, and assemble information for speeches and pamphlets. New workers also may answer calls from the press and the public, prepare invitation lists and details for press conferences, or escort visitors and clients. After gaining experience, they write news releases, speeches, and articles for publication or plan and carry out public relations programs. Public relations specialists in smaller firms usually get well-rounded experience, whereas those in larger firms become more specialized.

Other qualifications. In addition to the ability to communicate thoughts clearly and simply, public relations specialists must show creativity, initiative, and good judgment. Decision-making, problem-solving, and research skills also are important. People who choose public relations as a career should have an outgoing personality, self-confidence, an understanding of human psychology, and an enthusiasm for motivating people. They should be assertive but able to participate as part of a team and be open to new ideas.

Certification and advancement. The Universal Accreditation Board accredits public relations specialists who are members of the Public Relations Society of America and who participate in the Examination for Accreditation in Public Relations process. This process includes both a readiness review and an examination, which are designed for candidates who have at least five years of full-time work or teaching experience in public relations and who have earned a bachelor's degree in a communications-related field. The readiness review includes a written submission by each candidate, a portfolio review, and dialogue between the candidate and a three-member panel. Candidates who successfully advance through readiness review and pass the computer-based examination earn the Accredited in Public Relations (APR) designation.

The International Association of Business Communicators (IABC) also has an accreditation program for professionals in the communications field, including public relations specialists. Those who meet all the requirements of the program earn the Accredited Business Communicator (ABC) designation. Candidates must have at least five years of experience and a bachelor's degree in a communications field and must pass written and oral examinations. They also must submit a portfolio of work samples that demonstrate involvement in a range of communications projects and a thorough understanding of communications planning.

Employers may consider professional recognition through accreditation as a sign of competence in this field, and such designations could be especially helpful in a competitive job market.

Projections Data from the National Employment Matrix

Occupational title	SOC Code	Employment, 2008	Projected employment, 2018	Change, 2008–2018	
				Number	Percent
Public relations specialists..	27-3031	275,200	341,300	66,200	24

NOTE: Data in this table are rounded.

Public relations specialists who show that they can handle more demanding assignments are more likely to be promoted to supervisory jobs than those who are unable to do so. In public relations firms, an entry-level worker might be hired as a junior account executive and be promoted over the course of a career to account executive, senior account executive, account manager, and, eventually, vice president. Specialists in corporate public relations follow a similar career path, although the job titles may differ.

Some experienced public relations specialists start their own consulting firms.

Employment

Public relations specialists held about 275,200 jobs in 2008. They are concentrated in service-providing industries, such as advertising and related services; health care and social assistance; educational services; and government. Others work for communications firms, financial institutions, and government agencies.

Public relations specialists are concentrated in large cities, where press services and other communications facilities are readily available and where many businesses and trade associations have their headquarters. Many public relations consulting firms, for example, are in New York, Los Angeles, San Francisco, Chicago, and Washington, D.C. There is a trend, however, toward public relations jobs to be dispersed throughout the nation, closer to clients.

Job Outlook

Employment is projected to grow much faster than average; however, keen competition is expected for entry-level jobs.

Employment change. Employment of public relations specialists is expected to grow 24 percent from 2008 to 2018, much faster than the average for all occupations. The need for good public relations in an increasingly competitive and global business environment should spur demand for these workers, especially those with specialized knowledge or international experience. Employees who possess additional language capabilities also are in great demand.

The recent emergence of social media in the public relations is expected to increase job growth as well. Many public relations firms are expanding their use of these tools, and specialists with skills in them will be needed.

Employment in public relations firms is expected to grow as firms hire contractors to provide public relations services, rather than support more full-time staff when additional work is needed.

Among detailed industries, the largest job growth will continue to be in advertising and related services.

Job prospects. Keen competition likely will continue for entry-level public relations jobs, as the number of qualified applicants is expected to exceed the number of job openings. Many people are attracted to this profession because of the high-profile nature of the work. Opportunities should be best for college graduates who combine a degree in journalism, public relations, or another communications-related field with a public relations internship or other related work experience. Applicants who do not have the appropriate educational background or work experience will face the toughest obstacles.

Additional job opportunities should result from the need to replace public relations specialists who retire or leave the occupation for other reasons.

Earnings

Median annual wages for salaried public relations specialists were $51,280 in May 2008. The middle 50 percent earned between $38,400 and $71,670; the lowest 10 percent earned less than $30,140, and the top 10 percent earned more than $97,910. Median annual wages in the industries employing the largest numbers of public relations specialists in May 2008 were as follows:

Management of companies and enterprises	$55,530
Business, professional, labor, political, and similar organizations	55,460
Advertising, public relations and related services	55,290
Local government	51,340
Colleges, universities, and professional schools	46,660

Related Occupations

Public relations specialists create favorable attitudes among various organizations, interest groups, and the public through effective communication. Other workers with similar jobs include advertising, marketing, promotions, public relations, and sales managers; demonstrators and product promoters; lawyers; market and survey researchers; news analysts, reporters, and correspondents; and sales representatives, wholesale and manufacturing.

Sources of Additional Information

A comprehensive directory of schools offering degree programs, a sequence of study in public relations, a brochure on careers in public relations, and an online brochure entitled *Where Shall I Go to Study Advertising and Public Relations?* are available from

▸ Public Relations Society of America, Inc., 33 Maiden Lane, New York, NY 10038-5150. Internet: www.prsa.org

For information on accreditation for public relations professionals and the IABC Student Web site, contact

▸ International Association of Business Communicators, 601 Montgomery St., Suite 1900, San Francisco, CA 94111.

Radiologic Technologists and Technicians

(O*NET 29-2034.00, 29-2034.01, and 29-2034.02)

Significant Points

■ Employment is projected to grow faster than average; those with knowledge of more than one diagnostic imaging procedure will have the best employment opportunities.

■ Formal training programs in radiography are offered in hospitals or colleges and universities and lead to a certificate, an associate degree, or a bachelor's degree.

■ Most states require licensure, and requirements vary.

■ Although hospitals will remain the primary employer, a number of new jobs will be found in physicians' offices and diagnostic imaging centers.

Nature of the Work

Radiologic technologists and technicians perform diagnostic imaging examination. Radiologic technicians perform imaging examinations like X-rays, while technologists use other imaging modalities such as computed tomography, magnetic resonance imaging, and mammography.

Radiologic technicians, sometimes referred to as *radiographers,* produce X-ray films (radiographs) of parts of the human body for use in diagnosing medical problems. They prepare patients for radiologic examinations by explaining the procedure, removing jewelry and other articles through which X-rays cannot pass, and positioning patients so that the parts of the body can be appropriately radiographed. To prevent unnecessary exposure to radiation, these workers surround the exposed area with radiation protection devices, such as lead shields, or limit the size of the X-ray beam. Radiographers position radiographic equipment at the correct angle and height over the appropriate area of a patient's body. Using instruments similar to a measuring tape they may measure the thickness of the section to be radiographed and set controls on the X-ray machine to produce radiographs of the appropriate density, detail, and contrast.

Radiologic technologists and technicians must follow physicians' orders precisely and conform to regulations concerning the use of radiation to protect themselves, their patients, and their coworkers from unnecessary exposure.

In addition to preparing patients and operating equipment, radiologic technologists and technicians keep patient records and adjust and maintain equipment. They also may prepare work schedules, evaluate purchases of equipment, or manage a radiology department.

Radiologic technologists perform more complex imaging procedures. When performing fluoroscopies, for example, radiologic technologists prepare a solution for the patient to drink, allowing the radiologist (a physician who interprets radiographs) to see soft tissues in the body.

Some radiologic technologists specialize in computed tomography (CT), as *CT technologists.* CT scans produce a substantial amount of cross-sectional X-rays of an area of the body. From those cross-sectional X-rays, a three-dimensional image is made. The CT uses ionizing radiation; therefore, it requires the same precautionary measures that are used with X-rays.

Radiologic technologists also can specialize in Magnetic Resonance Imaging (MR) as *MR technologists.* MR, like CT, produces multiple cross-sectional images to create a 3-dimensional image. Unlike CT and X-rays, MR uses non-ionizing radio frequency to generate image contrast.

Radiologic technologists might also specialize in mammography. Mammographers use low dose X-ray systems to produce images of the breast.

In addition to radiologic technologists, others who conduct diagnostic imaging procedures include cardiovascular technologists and technicians, diagnostic medical sonographers, and nuclear medicine technologists.

Work environment. Physical stamina is important in this occupation because technologists and technicians are on their feet for long periods and may lift or turn disabled patients. Technologists and technicians work at diagnostic machines but also may perform some procedures at patients' bedsides. Some travel to patients in large vans equipped with sophisticated diagnostic equipment.

Although radiation hazards exist in this occupation, they are minimized by the use of lead aprons, gloves, and other shielding devices, and by instruments monitoring exposure to radiation. Technologists and technicians wear badges measuring radiation levels in the radiation area, and detailed records are kept on their cumulative lifetime dose.

Most full-time radiologic technologists and technicians work about 40 hours a week. They may, however, have evening, weekend, or on-call hours. Some radiologic technologists and technicians work part time for more than one employer; for those, travel to and from facilities must be considered.

Training, Other Qualifications, and Advancement

There are multiple paths to entry into this profession offered in hospitals or colleges and universities. Most states require licensure, and requirements vary.

Education and training. Formal training programs in radiography lead to a certificate, an associate degree, or a bachelor's degree. An associate degree is the most prevalent form of educational attainment among radiologic technologists and technicians. Some may receive a certificate. Certificate programs typically last around 21–24 months.

The Joint Review Committee on Education in Radiologic Technology accredits formal training programs in radiography. The committee accredited 213 programs resulting in a certificate, 397 programs resulting in an associate degree, and 35 resulting in a bachelor's degree in 2009. The programs provide both classroom and clinical instruction in anatomy and physiology, patient care procedures, radiation physics, radiation protection, principles of imaging, medical terminology, positioning of patients, medical ethics, radiobiology, and pathology.

Students interested in radiologic technology should take high school courses in mathematics, physics, chemistry, and biology.

Licensure. Federal legislation protects the public from the hazards of unnecessary exposure to medical and dental radiation by ensuring that operators of radiologic equipment are properly trained. However, it is up to each state to require licensure of radiologic technologists. Most states require licensure for practicing radiologic technologists. Licensing requirements vary by state; for specific requirements contact your state's health board.

Certification and other qualifications. The American Registry of Radiologic Technologists (ARRT) offers voluntary certification for radiologic technologists. In addition, a number of states use ARRT-administered exams for state licensing purposes. To be eligible for certification, technologists must graduate from an ARRT-approved accredited program and pass an examination. Many employers prefer to hire certified radiologic technologists. In order to maintain an ARRT certification, 24 hours of continuing education must be completed every 2 years.

Radiologic technologists should be sensitive to patients' physical and psychological needs. They must pay attention to detail, follow instructions, and work as part of a team. In addition, operating complicated equipment requires mechanical ability and manual dexterity.

Advancement. With experience and additional training, staff technologists may become specialists, performing CT scanning, MR, mammography, or bone densitometry. Technologists also may advance, with additional education and certification, to become a radiologist assistant. The ARRT offers specialty certification in many radiologic specialties as well as a credentialing for radiologist assistants.

Experienced technologists also may be promoted to supervisor, chief radiologic technologist, and, ultimately, department administrator or director. Depending on the institution, courses or a master's degree in business or health administration may be necessary for the director's position.

Some technologists progress by specializing in the occupation to become instructors or directors in radiologic technology educational programs; others take jobs as sales representatives or instructors with equipment manufacturers.

Employment

Radiologic technologists held about 214,700 jobs in 2008. About 61 percent of all jobs were in hospitals. Most other jobs were in offices of physicians; medical and diagnostic laboratories, including diagnostic imaging centers; and outpatient care centers.

Job Outlook

Employment is projected to grow faster than average. Those with knowledge of more than one diagnostic imaging procedure—such as CT, MR, and mammography—will have the best employment opportunities.

Employment change. Employment of radiologic technologists is expected to increase by about 17 percent from 2008 to 2018, faster than the average for all occupations. As the population grows and ages, there will be an increasing demand for diagnostic imaging. With age comes increased incidence of illness and injury, which often requires diagnostic imaging for diagnosis. In addition to diagnosis, diagnostic imaging is used to monitor the progress of disease treatment. With the increasing success of medical technologies in treating disease, diagnostic imaging will increasingly be needed to monitor progress of treatment.

The extent to which diagnostic imaging procedures are performed depends largely on cost and reimbursement considerations. However, accurate early disease detection allows for lower cost of treatment in the long run, which many third-party payers find favorable.

Although hospitals will remain the principal employer of radiologic technologists, a number of new jobs will be found in offices of physicians and diagnostic imaging centers. As technology advances many imaging modalities are becoming less expensive and more feasible to have in a physician's office.

Job prospects. In addition to job growth, job openings also will arise from the need to replace technologists who leave the occupation. Those with knowledge of more than one diagnostic imaging procedure—such as CT, MR, and mammography—will have the best employment opportunities as employers seek to control costs by using multi-credentialed employees.

Demand for radiologic technologists and technicians can tend to be regional with some areas having large demand, while other areas are saturated. Technologists and technicians willing to relocate may have better job prospects.

CT is continuing to become a frontline diagnosis tool. Instead of taking x rays to decide whether a CT is needed, as was the practice before, it is often the first choice for imaging because of its accuracy. MR also is increasingly used. Technologists with credentialing in either of these specialties will be very marketable to employers.

Projections Data from the National Employment Matrix

Occupational title	SOC Code	Employment, 2008	Projected employment, 2018	Change, 2008–2018	
				Number	Percent
Radiologic technologists and technicians.................... 29-2034		214,700	251,700	37,000	17

NOTE: Data in this table are rounded.

Earnings

The median annual wage of radiologic technologists was $52,210 in May 2008. The middle 50 percent earned between $42,710 and $63,010. The lowest 10 percent earned less than $35,100, and the highest 10 percent earned more than $74,970. Median annual wages in the industries employing the largest numbers of radiologic technologists in 2008 were as follows:

Medical and diagnostic laboratories	$55,210
Federal Executive Branch	53,650
General medical and surgical hospitals	52,890
Outpatient care centers	50,840
Offices of physicians	48,530

Related Occupations

Radiologic technologists operate sophisticated equipment to help physicians, dentists, and other health practitioners diagnose and treat patients. Workers in related health-care occupations include cardiovascular technologists and technicians; diagnostic medical sonographers; nuclear medicine technologists; and radiation therapists.

Sources of Additional Information

For information on careers in radiologic technology, contact

▶ American Society of Radiologic Technologists, 15000 Central Ave. SE, Albuquerque, NM 87123. Internet: www.asrt.org

For the current list of accredited education programs in radiography, contact

▶ Joint Review Committee on Education in Radiologic Technology, 20 N. Wacker Dr., Suite 2850, Chicago, IL 60606-3182. Internet: www.jrcert.org

For certification information, contact

▶ American Registry of Radiologic Technologists, 1255 Northland Dr., St. Paul, MN 55120-1155. Internet: www.arrt.org

Real Estate Brokers and Sales Agents

(O*NET 41-9021.00 and 41-9022.00)

Significant Points

■ A license is required in every state and the District of Columbia.

■ Residential real estate brokers and sales agents often work evenings and weekends.

■ Although gaining a job may be relatively easy, beginning workers face competition from well-established, more experienced agents and brokers.

■ Employment is sensitive to swings in the economy, as well as interest rates; during periods of declining economic activity or rising interest rates, the volume of sales and the resulting demand for sales workers fall.

Nature of the Work

One of the most complex and significant financial events in peoples' lives is the purchase or sale of a home or investment property. Because of the complexity and importance of this transaction, people typically seek the help of *real estate brokers and sales agents* when buying or selling real estate.

Real estate brokers and sales agents have a thorough knowledge of the real estate market in their communities. They know which neighborhoods will best fit clients' needs and budgets. They are familiar with local zoning and tax laws and know where to obtain financing for the purchase of property.

Brokers and agents do the same type of work, but brokers are licensed to manage their own real estate businesses. Agents must work with a broker. They usually provide their services to a licensed real estate broker on a contract basis. In return, the broker pays the agent a portion of the commission earned from the agent's sale of the property. Brokers, as independent businesspeople, often sell real estate owned by others; they also may rent or manage properties for a fee.

When selling property, brokers and agents arrange for title searches to verify ownership and for meetings between buyers and sellers during which they agree to the details of the transactions. In a final meeting, the new owners take possession of the property. Agents and brokers also act as intermediaries in price negotiations between buyers and sellers. They may help to arrange financing from a lender for the prospective buyer, which may make the difference between success and failure in closing a sale. In some cases, brokers and agents assume primary responsibility for finalizing, or closing, sales, but typically this function is done by lenders or lawyers.

Agents and brokers spend a significant amount of time looking for properties to buy or sell. They obtain listings—agreements by owners to place properties for sale with the firm. When listing a property for sale, agents and brokers compare the listed property with similar properties that recently sold, to determine a competitive market price for the property. Following the sale of the property, both the agent who sold it and the agent who obtained the listing receive a portion of the commission. Thus, agents who sell a property that they themselves have listed can increase their commission.

Before showing residential properties to potential buyers, agents meet with them to get an idea of the type of home the buyers would like, and how much the buyers can afford to spend. They may also ask buyers to sign a loyalty contract, which states that the agent will be the only one to show houses to the buyer. An agent or broker then generates lists of properties for sale, their location and description, and available sources of financing. In some cases, agents and brokers use computers to give buyers a virtual tour of properties that interest them.

Agents may meet numerous times with prospective buyers to discuss and visit available properties. Agents identify and emphasize the most pertinent selling details. To a young family looking for a house, for example, they may emphasize the convenient floor plan, the area's low crime rate, and the proximity to schools and shopping. To a potential investor, they may point out the tax advantages of owning a rental property and finding a renter. If negotiation over price becomes necessary, agents must follow their client's instructions thoroughly and may present counteroffers to reach the final sales price.

Once the buyer and seller have signed a contract, the real estate broker or agent must ensure that all terms of the contract are met before the closing date. If the seller agrees to any repairs, the broker or agent ensures they are made. Increasingly, brokers and agents must deal with environmental issues as well, such as advising buyers about lead paint on the walls. In addition, the agent must make sure that any legally mandated or agreed-upon inspections, such as termite and radon inspections, take place. Loan officers, attorneys, and other people handle many details, but the agent must ensure that they are carried out.

Most real estate brokers and sales agents sell residential property. A small number—usually employed in large or specialized firms—sell commercial, industrial, agricultural, or other types of real estate. Every specialty requires knowledge of that particular type of property and clientele. Selling, buying, or leasing business property requires an understanding of leasing practices, business trends, and the location of the property. Agents who sell, buy, or lease industrial properties must know about the region's transportation, utilities, and labor supply. Whatever the type of property, the agent or broker must know how to meet the client's particular requirements.

Work environment. Real estate agents and brokers often work more than a standard 40-hour week, often working evenings and weekends for the convenience of clients. Although the hours are long and frequently irregular, most agents and brokers have the freedom to determine their own schedule.

Advances in telecommunications and the ability to retrieve data about properties over the Internet allow many real estate brokers and sales agents to work out of their homes instead of real estate offices. Even with this convenience, workers spend much of their time away from their desks—showing properties to customers, analyzing properties for sale, meeting with prospective clients, or researching the real estate market.

Training, Other Qualifications, and Advancement

In every state and the District of Columbia, real estate brokers and sales agents must be licensed. Prospective agents must be high school graduates, be at least 18 years old, and pass a written test administered by the state.

Education and training. Agents and brokers must be high school graduates. In fact, as real estate transactions have become more legally complex, many firms have turned to college graduates to fill positions. A large number of agents and brokers have some college training.

Most universities, colleges, and community colleges offer various courses in real estate. Some offer associate and bachelor's degrees in real estate, but mostly they offer certificate programs. Additionally, college courses in finance, business administration, statistics, economics, law, and English are also helpful. For those who intend to start their own company, business courses such as marketing and accounting are as important as courses in real estate or finance.

Many local real estate associations that are members of the National Association of Realtors sponsor courses covering the fundamentals and legal aspects of the field. Advanced courses in mortgage financing, property development and management, and other subjects also are available. Also, some brokerage firms offer formal training programs for both beginners and experienced agents. In addition, much of the training needed to learn the practical aspects of the trade happens on the job, under the direction of an experienced agent, who may demonstrate how to use a computer to locate or list available properties and identify sources of financing.

Licensure. In every state and the District of Columbia, real estate brokers and sales agents must be licensed. Prospective brokers and agents must pass a written examination. The examination—more comprehensive for brokers than for agents—includes questions on basic real estate transactions and the laws affecting the sale of property. Most states require candidates for the general sales license to complete between 30 and 90 hours of classroom instruction. To get a broker's license an individual needs between 60 and 90 hours of formal training and a specific amount of experience selling real estate, usually 1 to 3 years. Some states waive the experience requirements for the broker's license for applicants who have a bachelor's degree in real estate.

State licenses typically must be renewed every 1 or 2 years; usually, no examination is needed. However, many states require continuing education for license renewals. Prospective agents and brokers should contact the real estate licensing commission of the state in which they wish to work to verify the exact licensing requirements.

Other qualifications. Personality traits are as important as academic background. Brokers look for agents who have a pleasant personality and a neat appearance. They must be at least 18 years old. Maturity, good judgment, trustworthiness, honesty, and enthusiasm for the job are required to attract prospective customers in this highly competitive field. Agents should be well organized, be detail oriented, and have a good memory for names, faces, and business particulars. A good knowledge of the local area and its neighborhoods is a clear advantage.

Advancement. As agents gain knowledge and expertise, they become more efficient in closing a greater number of transactions and increase their income. In many large firms, experienced agents can advance to sales manager or general manager. People who earn their broker's license may open their own offices. Others with experience and training in estimating property values may become real estate appraisers, and people familiar with operating and maintaining rental properties may become property managers. Experienced agents and brokers with a thorough knowledge of business conditions and property values in their localities may enter mortgage financing or real estate investment counseling.

Employment

In 2008, real estate brokers and sales agents held about 517,800 jobs; real estate sales agents held approximately 76 percent of these jobs.

Many real estate brokers and sales agents worked part time, combining their real estate activities with other careers. About 59 percent of real estate brokers and sales agents were self-employed. Real estate is sold in all areas, but employment is concentrated in large urban areas and in rapidly growing communities.

Projections Data from the National Employment Matrix

Occupational title	SOC Code	Employment, 2008	Projected employment, 2018	Change, 2008–2018	
				Number	Percent
Real estate brokers and sales agents 41-9020		517,800	592,100	74,300	14
Real estate brokers... 41-9021		123,400	134,000	10,600	9
Real estate sales agents..................................... 41-9022		394,400	458,200	63,700	16

NOTE: Data in this table are rounded.

Most real estate firms are relatively small; indeed, some are one-person businesses. By contrast, some large real estate firms have several hundred agents operating out of numerous branch offices. Many brokers have franchise agreements with national or regional real estate organizations. Under this type of arrangement, the broker pays a fee in exchange for the privilege of using the more widely known name of the parent organization. Although franchised brokers often receive help in training sales staff and running their offices, they bear the ultimate responsibility for the success or failure of their firms.

Job Outlook

Employment of real estate brokers and agents is expected to grow faster than average. Beginning agents and brokers, however, will face competition from their well-established, more experienced counterparts.

Employment change. Employment of real estate brokers and sales agents is expected to grow 14 percent during the 2008–2018 decade, faster than average for all occupations. A growing population, particularly young adults who will be forming households in greater numbers, will require the services of real estate agents and brokers to buy their homes. Home sales will be sparked by the continuing desire for people to own their own homes and their perception that real estate will be a good investment over the long run. However, job growth will be somewhat limited by the increasing use of the Internet, which is improving the productivity of agents and brokers, and transforming the way they do business. For example, prospective customers often can perform their own searches for properties that meet their criteria by accessing real estate information on the Internet.

Job prospects. In addition to job growth, a large number of job openings will arise from the need to replace workers who transfer to other occupations or leave the labor force. Real estate brokers and sales agents are older, on average, than most other workers, and many are expected to leave the occupation over the next decade.

Employment of real estate brokers and sales agents is sensitive to swings in the economy, such as a recession. During periods of declining economic activity or rising interest rates, the volume of sales and the resulting demand for sales workers fall. As a result, the income of agents and brokers declines, and many work fewer hours or leave the occupation altogether. Over the coming decade, the opportunity for part-time work is expected to decline. Although the occupation is relatively easy to enter, increasingly complex legal and technological requirements are raising startup costs associated with becoming an agent and making it more difficult for part-time workers to enter the occupation.

Well-trained, ambitious people who enjoy selling—particularly those with extensive social and business connections in their communities—should have the best chance for success. However, beginning agents and brokers often face competition from their well-established, more experienced counterparts in obtaining listings and in closing an adequate number of sales.

Earnings

The median annual wages, including commissions, of salaried real estate sales agents were $40,150 in May 2008. The middle 50 percent earned between $27,390 and $64,820 a year. The lowest 10 percent earned less than $21,120, and the highest 10 percent earned more than $101,860. Median annual wages in the industries employing the largest number of real estate sales agents in May 2008 were as follows:

Residential building construction.........................$49,620
Land subdivision 44,410
Offices of real estate agents and brokers 41,320
Activities related to real estate 36,410
Lessors of real estate 32,150

Median annual wages, including commissions, of salaried real estate brokers were $57,500 in May 2008. The middle 50 percent earned between $36,420 and $93,970 a year. Median annual wages in the industries employing the largest number of real estate brokers in May 2008 were as follows:

Residential building construction.........................$63,280
Offices of real estate agents and brokers 59,710
Activities related to credit Intermediation 57,740
Activities related to real estate 56,140
Lessors of real estate 47,230

Commissions on sales are the main source of earnings of real estate agents and brokers. The rate of commission varies according to whatever the agent and broker agree on, the type of property, and its value. The percentage paid on the sale of farm and commercial properties or unimproved land is typically higher than the percentage paid for selling a home.

Commissions may be divided among several agents and brokers. The broker or agent who obtains a listing usually shares the commission with the broker or agent who sells the property and with the firms that employ each of them. Although an agent's share varies greatly from one firm to another, often it is about half of the total amount received by the firm. Agents who both list and sell a property maximize their commission.

Income usually increases as an agent gains experience, but individual motivation, economic conditions, and the type and location of the property also can affect income. Sales workers who are active in community organizations and in local real estate associations can broaden their contacts and increase their income. A beginner's earnings often are irregular because a few weeks or even months may go by without a sale. Although some brokers allow an agent to draw against future income from a special account, the practice is not common with new employees. The beginner, therefore, should have enough money to live for about 6 months or until commissions increase.

Related Occupations

Other occupations requiring knowledge of real estate include appraisers and assessors of real estate; and property, real estate, and community association managers.

Other sales workers who need these character traits include insurance sales agents; sales representatives, wholesale and manufacturing; and securities, commodities, and financial services sales agents.

Sources of Additional Information

Information on licensing requirements for real estate brokers and sales agents is available from most local real estate organizations or from the state real estate commission or board.

More information about opportunities in real estate is available on the Internet site of the following organization:

▸ National Association of Realtors. Internet: www.realtor.org

Receptionists and Information Clerks

(O*NET 43-4171.00)

Significant Points

■ Good interpersonal skills are critical.

■ A high school diploma or its equivalent is the most common educational requirement.

■ A large number of job openings are expected.

■ Opportunities should be best for persons with a wide range of clerical and technical skills, particularly those with related work experience.

Nature of the Work

Receptionists and information clerks are charged with a responsibility that may affect the success of an organization: making a good first impression. Receptionists and information clerks answer telephones, route and screen calls, greet visitors, respond to inquiries from the public, and provide information about the organization. Some are responsible for the coordination of all mail into and out of the office. In addition, they contribute to the security of an organization by helping to monitor the access of visitors—a function that has become increasingly important.

Whereas some tasks are common to most receptionists and information clerks, their specific responsibilities vary with the type of establishment in which they work. For example, receptionists and information clerks in hospitals and in doctors' offices may gather patients' personal and insurance information and direct them to the proper waiting rooms. In corporate headquarters, they may greet visitors and manage the scheduling of the board room or common conference area. In beauty or hair salons, they arrange appointments, direct customers to the hairstylist, and may serve as cashiers. In factories, large corporations, and government offices, receptionists and information clerks may provide identification cards and arrange for escorts to take visitors to the proper office. Those working for bus and train companies respond to inquiries about departures, arrivals, stops, and other related matters.

Receptionists and information clerks use the telephone, personal computers, and other electronic devices to send e-mail and fax documents, for example. Despite the widespread use of automated answering systems or voice mail, many receptionists and clerks still take messages and inform other employees of visitors' arrivals or cancellation of an appointment. When they are not busy with callers, most workers are expected to assist other administrative employees by performing a variety of office duties, including opening and sorting mail, collecting and distributing parcels, transmitting and delivering facsimiles, and performing Internet search tasks. Other duties include updating appointment calendars, preparing travel vouchers, and performing basic bookkeeping, word processing, and filing.

Companies sometimes hire off-site receptionists and information clerks, called *virtual receptionists*, to perform, or supplement, many of the duties done by the traditional receptionist. Virtual receptionists use software integrated into their phone system to instantly track their employer's location, inform them of every call, and relay vital information to their callers. Using fax mailbox services, employers can retrieve faxes from any location at any time. The service receives them for the employer in special mailboxes and then transfers them when the line is free.

Work environment. Receptionists and information clerks who greet customers and visitors usually work in areas that are highly visible and designed and furnished to make a good impression. Most work stations are clean, well lighted, and relatively quiet. Virtual receptionists work from home or at an off-site office building. The work performed by some receptionists and information clerks may be tiring, repetitive, and stressful as they may spend all day answering continuously ringing telephones and sometimes encounter difficult or irate callers. The work environment, however, may be very friendly and motivating for individuals who enjoy greeting customers face to face and making them feel comfortable. About 30 percent of receptionists and information clerks worked part time.

Training, Other Qualifications, and Advancement

A high school diploma or its equivalent is the most common educational requirement, although hiring requirements for receptionists and information clerks vary by industry and employer. Good

Projections Data from the National Employment Matrix

Occupational title	SOC Code	Employment, 2008	Projected employment, 2018	Change, 2008–2018	
				Number	Percent
Receptionists and information clerks 43-4171		1,139,200	1,312,100	172,900	15

NOTE: Data in this table are rounded.

interpersonal skills and being technologically proficient also are important to employers.

Education and training. Receptionists and information clerks generally need a high school diploma or equivalent as most of their training is received on the job. However, employers often look for applicants who already possess certain skills, such as knowledge of spreadsheet and word processing software or answering telephones. Some employers also may prefer some formal office education or training. On the job, they learn how to operate the telephone system and computers. They also learn the proper procedures for greeting visitors and for distributing mail, fax messages, and parcels. While many of these skills can be learned quickly, those who are charged with relaying information to visitors or customers may need several months to learn details about the organization.

Other qualifications. Good interpersonal and customer service skills—being courteous, professional, and helpful—are critical for this job. Being an active listener often is a key quality needed by receptionists and information clerks that requires the ability to listen patiently to the points being made, to wait to speak until others have finished, and to ask appropriate questions when necessary. In addition, the ability to relay information accurately to others is important.

The ability to operate a wide range of office technology also is helpful, as receptionists and information clerks are often asked to work on other assignments during the day.

Advancement. Advancement for receptionists generally comes about either by transferring to an occupation with more responsibility or by being promoted to a supervisory position. Receptionists with especially strong computer skills, a bachelor's degree, and several years of experience may advance to a better paying job as a secretary or an administrative assistant.

Employment

Receptionists and information clerks held about 1.1 million jobs in 2008. The health-care and social assistance industries—including offices of physicians, hospitals, nursing homes, and outpatient care facilities—employed about 36 percent of all receptionists and information clerks. Wholesale and retail trade, personal services, educational services, finance and insurance, employment services, religious organizations, and real estate industries also employed large numbers of receptionists and information clerks.

Job Outlook

Employment is projected to grow faster than the average for all occupations. Job growth, coupled with the need to replace workers who transfer to other occupations or leave the labor force, will generate a large number of job openings for receptionists and information clerks.

Employment change. Employment of receptionists and information clerks is expected to increase by 15 percent from 2008 to 2018, which is faster than the average for all occupations. Employment growth will result from growth in industries such as offices of physicians and in other health practitioners, legal services, personal care services, construction, and management and technical consulting.

Technology will have conflicting effects on employment growth for receptionists and information clerks. The increasing use of voice mail and other telephone automation reduces the need for receptionists by allowing one receptionist to perform work that formerly required several. At the same time, however, the increasing use of other technology has caused a consolidation of clerical responsibilities and growing demand for workers with diverse clerical and technical skills, such as virtual receptionists. Because receptionists and information clerks may perform a wide variety of clerical tasks, they should continue to be in demand. Further, they perform many tasks that are interpersonal in nature and are not easily automated, ensuring continued demand for their services in a variety of establishments.

Job prospects. In addition to job growth, numerous job opportunities will be created as receptionists and information clerks transfer to other occupations or leave the labor force altogether. Opportunities should be best for persons with a wide range of clerical and technical skills, particularly those with related work experience.

Earnings

Median hourly wages of receptionists and information clerks in May 2008 were $11.80. The middle 50 percent earned between $9.69 and $14.44. The lowest 10 percent earned less than $8.09, and the highest 10 percent earned more than $17.07. Median hourly wages in the industries employing the largest number of receptionists and information clerks in May 2008 were as follows:

Offices of dentists	$13.78
Offices of physicians	12.20
Employment services	11.63
Offices of other health practitioners......................	11.45
Personal care services	9.35

Related Occupations

Receptionists deal with the public and often direct people to others who can assist them. Other workers who perform similar duties include customer service representatives; dispatchers, except police, fire, and ambulance; and secretaries and administrative assistants.

Sources of Additional Information

State employment offices can provide information on job openings for receptionists.

For information related to administrative occupations, including educational programs and certified designations, contact

▶ International Association of Administrative Professionals, P.O. Box 20404, Kansas City, MO 64195-0404. Internet: www.iaap-hq.org

Recreation Workers

(O*NET 39-9032.00)

Significant Points

■ The recreation field offers an unusually large number of part-time and seasonal job opportunities.

■ Opportunities for part-time, seasonal, and temporary recreation jobs will be good, but competition will remain keen for full-time career positions.

■ Many recreation workers spend most of their time outdoors and may work in a variety of weather conditions.

Nature of the Work

As participation in organized recreational activities grows, *recreation workers* will be needed to plan, organize, and direct these activities in local playgrounds and recreation areas, parks, community and senior centers, nursing homes and other senior housing, camps, and tourist attractions. These workers lead groups in activities such as arts and crafts, sports, performing arts, camping, and other special interests. They make sure that participants abide by the rules of the camps and recreational facilities and that safety practices are adhered to so that no one gets injured. Recreation workers also are found in some businesses or business groups, where they direct leisure activities for employees, such as softball or bowling, and organize sports leagues.

Recreation workers hold a variety of positions at different levels of responsibility. Those who work directly with children in residential or day camps are called *camp counselors*. These workers lead and instruct children and teenagers in a variety of outdoor recreation activities, such as swimming, hiking, horseback riding, and camping. In addition, counselors who specialize may teach campers special subjects, such as archery, boating, music, drama, gymnastics, tennis, and computers. In residential camps, counselors also provide guidance and supervise daily living and socialization. *Camp directors* typically supervise camp counselors, plan camp activities or programs, and perform the various administrative functions of a camp.

Workers who provide instruction and coaching primarily in one activity, such as art, music, drama, swimming, or tennis, are called *activity specialists.* These workers can work in camps or anywhere else where there is interest in a single activity.

Recreation leaders are responsible for a recreation program's daily operation. They primarily organize and direct participants, schedule the use of facilities, keep records of equipment use, and ensure that recreation facilities and equipment are used properly. In addition, they may lead classes and provide instruction in a recreational activity.

Recreation supervisors oversee recreation leaders and plan, organize, and manage recreational activities to meet the needs of a variety of populations. These workers often serve as liaisons between the director of the park or recreation center and the recreation leaders. Recreation supervisors with more specialized responsibilities also may direct special activities or events or oversee a major activity, such as aquatics, gymnastics, or one or more performing arts.

Directors of recreation and parks develop and manage comprehensive recreation programs in parks, playgrounds, and other settings. Directors usually serve as technical advisors to state and local recreation and park commissions and may be responsible for recreation and park budgets.

Work environment. Recreation workers work in a variety of settings—for example, a cruise ship, a nature park, a summer camp, or a playground in the center of an urban community. Many recreation workers spend most of their time outdoors and may work in a variety of weather conditions. Recreation directors and supervisors, however, typically spend most of their time in an office, planning programs and special events. Directors and supervisors generally engage in less physical activity than do lower level recreation workers. Nevertheless, recreation workers at all levels risk suffering injuries during physical activities.

Some recreation workers work about 40 hours a week. However, many people entering this field, such as camp counselors, may have some night and weekend work, irregular hours, and seasonal employment. In 2008, about 40 percent of these workers worked part time.

Training, Other Qualifications, and Advancement

The educational and training requirements for recreation workers vary widely with on the type of job. Full-time career positions usually require a college degree. Many jobs, however, require demonstrated knowledge of the activity or can be learned with only a short period of on-the-job training.

Education and training. The educational needs for people entering into this occupational field vary widely depending on the job and level of responsibility. For activity specialists, it is more important to have experience and demonstrated competence in a particular activity, such as art or kayaking, than to have a degree. Camp counselors often are older teenagers or young adults who have experienced camping as a child and enjoy the camping experience. A degree is less important than the counselor's maturity level, ability to work well with children and teens, and ability to make sure that they stay safe.

Those working in administrative positions for large organizations or public recreation systems may need a bachelor's degree or higher. Full-time career professional positions usually require a college degree with a major in parks and recreation or leisure studies, but a bachelor's degree in any liberal arts field may be sufficient for some jobs in the private sector. In industrial recreation, or "employee services" as it is more commonly called, companies that offer recreational activities for their employees prefer to hire those with a bachelor's degree in recreation or leisure studies and a background in business administration.

Employers seeking candidates for some administrative positions favor those with at least a master's degree in parks and recreation, business administration, or public administration. Most require at least an associate degree in recreation studies or a related field.

An associate or bachelor's degree in a recreation-related discipline, along with experience, is preferred for most recreation supervisor jobs and is required for most higher level administrative jobs. Graduates of associate degree programs in parks and recreation, social work, and other human services disciplines also can enter some career recreation positions. High school graduates occasionally enter career positions, but doing so is not common.

Programs leading to an associate or bachelor's degree in parks and recreation, leisure studies, or related fields are offered at several hundred colleges and universities. Many also offer master's or doctoral degrees in the field. In 2009, 89 bachelor's degree programs in parks and recreation were accredited by the National Recreation and Park Association (NRPA). Accredited programs provide broad exposure to the history, theory, and practice of park and recreation management. Courses offered include community organization; supervision and administration; recreational needs of special populations, such as the elderly or disabled; and supervised fieldwork. Students may specialize in areas such as therapeutic recreation, park management, outdoor recreation, industrial or commercial recreation, and camp management.

Specialized training or experience in a particular field, such as art, music, drama, or athletics, is an asset for many jobs. Some jobs also require certification. For example, a lifesaving certificate is a prerequisite for teaching or coaching water-related activities.

The majority of seasonal and part-time workers learn through on-the-job training.

Licensure and certification. The NRPA certifies individuals for professional and technical jobs. Certified park and recreation professionals must pass an exam. In order to qualify to take the exam, individuals need to (1) have earned a bachelor's degree in a major such as recreation, park resources, or leisure services from a program accredited by the NRPA or have at least 1 year of experience if the program is not accredited; (2) have earned any other bachelor's degree and have at least 3 years of relevant full-time work experience; or (3) have at least 5 years of full-time experience in the field. Continuing education is necessary to remain certified.

Many cities and localities require lifeguards to be certified. Training and certification details vary from state to state and county to county. Information on lifeguards is available from local parks and recreation departments.

Other qualifications. People planning careers in recreation should be outgoing, good at motivating people, and sensitive to the needs of others. Excellent health and physical fitness often are required, due to the physical nature of some jobs. Time management and the ability to manage others also are important.

Advancement. Recreation workers start their careers working with people. As they gain experience, they may get promoted to positions with greater responsibilities. Recreation workers with experience and managerial skills may advance to supervisory or managerial positions. Eventually, they may become the director of a recreation department.

Employment

Recreation workers held about 327,500 jobs in 2008, and many additional workers held summer jobs in the occupation. About 31 percent of recreation workers worked for local governments, primarily in park and recreation departments. About 16 percent of recreation workers were employed by nursing and residential care facilities, and another 10 percent were employed in civic and social organizations, such as the Boy Scouts or Girl Scouts or the YMCA and YWCA.

Job Outlook

Faster-than-average growth is expected. Jobs opportunities for part-time, seasonal, and temporary recreation workers will be good, but competition will remain keen for career positions as recreation workers.

Employment change. Overall employment of recreation workers is projected to increase by 15 percent between 2008 and 2018, which is faster than the average for all occupations. Although people will spend more time and money on recreation, budget restrictions in state and local government will limit the number of jobs added. Many of the new jobs will be in social assistance organizations and in nursing and residential care facilities. Civic and social organizations and fitness and sports centers will also contribute to growth.

Growth will be driven by the growing numbers of young and older Americans. The large numbers of births in recent years likely will increase the demand for recreation services for children, and retiring baby boomers are expected to have more leisure time, higher disposable incomes, and more concern for health and fitness than previous generations had. The latter factors should lead to an increasing demand for recreation services for baby boomers.

Job prospects. Applicants for part-time, seasonal, and temporary recreation jobs should have good opportunities, but competition

Projections Data from the National Employment Matrix

Occupational title	SOC Code	Employment, 2008	Projected employment, 2018	Change, 2008–2018	
				Number	Percent
Recreation workers..	39-9032	327,500	375,700	48,200	15

NOTE: Data in this table are rounded.

will remain keen for career positions because the recreation field attracts many applicants and because the number of career positions is limited compared with the number of lower level seasonal jobs. Opportunities for staff positions should be best for people with formal training and experience in part-time or seasonal recreation jobs. Volunteer experience, part-time work during school, and a summer job are viewed favorably. Those with graduate degrees should have the best opportunities for supervisory or administrative positions. Job openings will stem from growth and the need to replace the large numbers of workers who leave the occupation each year.

Earnings

In May 2008, median annual wages of recreation workers who worked full time were $21,960. The middle 50 percent earned between $17,680 and $28,810. The lowest paid 10 percent earned less than $15,630, while the highest paid 10 percent earned $37,730 or more. However, earnings of recreation directors and others in supervisory or managerial positions can be substantially higher. Most public and private recreation agencies provide full-time recreation workers with typical benefits; part-time workers receive few, if any, benefits. In May 2008, median annual wages in the industries employing the largest numbers of recreation workers were as follows:

Nursing care facilities	$23,100
Individual and family services	22,260
Local government	21,890
Civic and social organizations	19,800
Other amusement and recreation industries	19,670

The large numbers of temporary, seasonal jobs in the recreation field typically are filled by high school or college students, generally do not have formal education requirements, and are open to anyone with the desired personal qualities. Employers compete for a share of the vacationing student labor force, and although salaries in recreation often are lower than those in other fields, the nature of the work and the opportunity to work outdoors are attractive to many.

Part-time, seasonal, and volunteer jobs in recreation include summer camp counselors, craft specialists, and afterschool and weekend recreation program leaders. In addition, many teachers and college students accept jobs as recreation workers when school is not in session. The vast majority of volunteers serve as activity leaders at local day camp programs or in youth organizations, camps, nursing homes, hospitals, senior centers, and other settings.

Related Occupations

Other occupations that require leadership skills, as well as a desire to work with and help others, include the following athletes, coaches, umpires, and related workers; counselors; fitness workers; probation officers and correctional treatment specialists; psychologists; recreational therapists; social workers; and teachers—self enrichment education.

Sources of Additional Information

For information on jobs in recreation, contact employers such as local government departments of parks and recreation, nursing

homes and other residential facilities, the Boy Scouts or Girl Scouts, and other local social or religious organizations.

For information on careers, certification, and academic programs in parks and recreation, contact

▸ National Recreation and Park Association, 22377 Belmont Ridge Rd., Ashburn, VA 20148-4501. Internet: www.nrpa.org

For information about a career as a camp counselor, contact

▸ American Camp Association, 5000 State Rd. 67 N., Martinsville, IN 46151-7902. Internet: www.acacamps.org

Registered Nurses

(O*NET 29-1111.00, 29-1111.01, 29-1111.02, and 29-1111.03)

Significant Points

■ Registered nurses (RNs) constitute the largest health-care occupation, with 2.6 million jobs.

■ About 60 percent of RN jobs are in hospitals.

■ The three typical educational paths to registered nursing are a bachelor's degree, an associate degree, and a diploma from an approved nursing program; advanced practice nurses—clinical nurse specialists, nurse anesthetists, nurse-midwives, and nurse practitioners—need a master's degree.

■ Overall job opportunities are expected to be excellent, but may vary by employment and geographic setting; some employers report difficulty in attracting and retaining an adequate number of RNs.

Nature of the Work

Registered nurses (*RNs*), regardless of specialty or work setting, treat patients, educate patients and the public about various medical conditions, and provide advice and emotional support to patients' family members. RNs record patients' medical histories and symptoms, help perform diagnostic tests and analyze results, operate medical machinery, administer treatment and medications, and help with patient follow-up and rehabilitation.

RNs teach patients and their families how to manage their illnesses or injuries, explaining post-treatment home care needs; diet, nutrition, and exercise programs; and self-administration of medication and physical therapy. Some RNs may work to promote general health by educating the public on warning signs and symptoms of disease. RNs also might run general health screening or immunization clinics, blood drives, and public seminars on various conditions.

When caring for patients, RNs establish a care plan or contribute to an existing plan. Plans may include numerous activities, such as administering medication, including careful checking of dosages and avoiding interactions; starting, maintaining, and discontinuing intravenous (IV) lines for fluid, medication, blood, and blood products; administering therapies and treatments; observing the patient and recording those observations; and consulting with physicians and other health-care clinicians. Some RNs provide direction to licensed practical nurses and nursing aides regarding patient care. RNs with advanced educational preparation and training may perform diagnostic and therapeutic procedures and may have prescriptive authority.

Specific work responsibilities will vary from one RN to the next. An RN's duties and title are often determined by their work setting or patient population served. RNs can specialize in one or more areas of patient care. There generally are four ways to specialize. RNs may work a particular setting or type of treatment, such as *perioperative nurses*, who work in operating rooms and assist surgeons. RNs may specialize in specific health conditions, as do *diabetes management nurses*, who assist patients to manage diabetes. Other RNs specialize in working with one or more organs or body system types, such as *dermatology nurses*, who work with patients who have skin disorders. RNs may also specialize with a well-defined population, such as *geriatric nurses*, who work with the elderly. Some RNs may combine specialties. For example, *pediatric oncology nurses* deal with children and adolescents who have cancer. The opportunities for specialization in registered nursing are extensive and are often determined on the job.

There are many options for RNs who specialize in a work setting or type of treatment. *Ambulatory care nurses* provide preventive care and treat patients with a variety of illnesses and injuries in physicians' offices or in clinics. Some ambulatory care nurses are involved in telehealth, providing care and advice through electronic communications media such as videoconferencing, the Internet, or by telephone. *Critical care nurses* provide care to patients with serious, complex, and acute illnesses or injuries that require very close monitoring and extensive medication protocols and therapies. Critical care nurses often work in critical or intensive care hospital units. *Emergency*, or *trauma*, *nurses* work in hospital or stand-alone emergency departments, providing initial assessments and care for patients with life-threatening conditions. Some emergency nurses may become qualified to serve as *transport nurses*, who provide medical care to patients who are transported by helicopter or airplane to the nearest medical facility. *Holistic nurses* provide care such as acupuncture, massage and aroma therapy, and biofeedback, which are meant to treat patients' mental and spiritual health in addition to their physical health. *Home health-care nurses* provide at-home nursing care for patients, often as follow-up care after discharge from a hospital or from a rehabilitation, long-term care, or skilled nursing facility. *Hospice and palliative care nurses* provide care, most often in home or hospice settings, focused on maintaining quality of life for terminally ill patients. *Infusion nurses* administer medications, fluids, and blood to patients through injections into patients' veins. *Long- term care nurses* provide health-care services on a recurring basis to patients with chronic physical or mental disorders, often in long-term care or skilled nursing facilities. *Medical-surgical nurses* provide health promotion and basic medical care to patients with various medical and surgical diagnoses. *Occupational health nurses* seek to prevent job-related injuries and illnesses, provide monitoring and emergency care services, and help employers implement health and safety standards. *Perianesthesia nurses* provide preoperative and postoperative care to patients undergoing anesthesia during surgery or other procedure. *Perioperative nurses* assist surgeons by selecting and handling instruments, controlling bleeding, and suturing incisions. Some of these nurses also can specialize in plastic and reconstructive surgery. *Psychiatric-mental health nurses* treat patients with personality and mood disorders.

Radiology nurses provide care to patients undergoing diagnostic radiation procedures such as ultrasounds, magnetic resonance imaging, and radiation therapy for oncology diagnoses. *Rehabilitation nurses* care for patients with temporary and permanent disabilities. *Transplant nurses* care for both transplant recipients and living donors and monitor signs of organ rejection.

RNs specializing in a particular disease, ailment, or health-care condition are employed in virtually all work settings, including physicians' offices, outpatient treatment facilities, home health-care agencies, and hospitals. *Addictions nurses* care for patients seeking help with alcohol, drug, tobacco, and other addictions. *Intellectual and developmental disabilities nurses* provide care for patients with physical, mental, or behavioral disabilities; care may include help with feeding, controlling bodily functions, sitting or standing independently, and speaking or other communication. *Diabetes management nurses* help diabetics to manage their disease by teaching them proper nutrition and showing them how to test blood sugar levels and administer insulin injections. *Genetics nurses* provide early detection screenings, counseling, and treatment of patients with genetic disorders, including cystic fibrosis and Huntington's disease. *HIV/AIDS nurses* care for patients diagnosed with HIV and AIDS. *Oncology nurses* care for patients with various types of cancer and may assist in the administration of radiation and chemotherapies and follow-up monitoring. *Wound, ostomy, and continence nurses* treat patients with wounds caused by traumatic injury, ulcers, or arterial disease; provide postoperative care for patients with openings that allow for alternative methods of bodily waste elimination; and treat patients with urinary and fecal incontinence.

RNs specializing in treatment of a particular organ or body system usually are employed in hospital specialty or critical care units, specialty clinics, and outpatient care facilities. *Cardiovascular nurses* treat patients with coronary heart disease and those who have had heart surgery, providing services such as postoperative rehabilitation. *Dermatology nurses* treat patients with disorders of the skin, such as skin cancer and psoriasis. *Gastroenterology nurses* treat patients with digestive and intestinal disorders, including ulcers, acid reflux disease, and abdominal bleeding. Some nurses in this field also assist in specialized procedures such as endoscopies, which look inside the gastrointestinal tract using a tube equipped with a light and a camera that can capture images of diseased tissue. *Gynecology nurses* provide care to women with disorders of the reproductive system, including endometriosis, cancer, and sexually transmitted diseases. *Nephrology nurses* care for patients with kidney disease caused by diabetes, hypertension, or substance abuse. *Neuroscience nurses* care for patients with dysfunctions of the nervous system, including brain and spinal cord injuries and seizures. *Ophthalmic nurses* provide care to patients with disorders of the eyes, including blindness and glaucoma, and to patients undergoing eye surgery. *Orthopedic nurses* care for patients with muscular and skeletal problems, including arthritis, bone fractures, and muscular dystrophy. *Otorhinolaryngology nurses* care for patients with ear, nose, and throat disorders, such as cleft palates, allergies, and sinus disorders. *Respiratory nurses* provide care to patients with respiratory disorders such as asthma, tuberculosis, and cystic fibrosis. *Urology nurses* care for patients with disorders of the kidneys, urinary tract, and male reproductive organs, including infections, kidney and bladder stones, and cancers.

RNs who specialize by population provide preventive and acute care in all health-care settings to the segment of the population in which they specialize, including newborns (neonatology), children and adolescents (pediatrics), adults, and the elderly (gerontology or geriatrics). RNs also may provide basic health care to patients outside of health-care settings in such venues as including correctional facilities, schools, summer camps, and the military. Some RNs travel around the United States and throughout the world providing care to patients in areas with shortages of health-care workers.

Most RNs work as staff nurses as members of a team providing critical health care. However, some RNs choose to become advanced practice nurses, who work independently or in collaboration with physicians, and may focus on the provision of primary care services. *Clinical nurse specialists* provide direct patient care and expert consultations in one of many nursing specialties, such as psychiatric-mental health. *Nurse anesthetists* provide anesthesia and related care before and after surgical, therapeutic, diagnostic and obstetrical procedures. They also provide pain management and emergency services, such as airway management. *Nurse-midwives* provide primary care to women, including gynecological exams, family planning advice, prenatal care, assistance in labor and delivery, and neonatal care. *Nurse practitioners* serve as primary and specialty care providers, providing a blend of nursing and health-care services to patients and families. The most common specialty areas for nurse practitioners are family practice, adult practice, women's health, pediatrics, acute care, and geriatrics. However, there are a variety of other specialties that nurse practitioners can choose, including neonatology and mental health. Advanced practice nurses can prescribe medications in all states and in the District of Columbia.

Some nurses have jobs that require little or no direct patient care, but still require an active RN license. *Forensics nurses* participate in the scientific investigation and treatment of abuse victims, violence, criminal activity, and traumatic accident. *Infection control nurses* identify, track, and control infectious outbreaks in health-care facilities and develop programs for outbreak prevention and response to biological terrorism. *Nurse educators* plan, develop, implement, and evaluate educational programs and curricula for the professional development of student nurses and RNs. *Nurse informaticists* manage and communicate nursing data and information to improve decision making by consumers, patients, nurses, and other health-care providers. RNs also may work as health-care consultants, public policy advisors, pharmaceutical and medical supply researchers and salespersons, and medical writers and editors.

Work environment. Most RNs work in well-lit, comfortable health-care facilities. Home health and public health nurses travel to patients' homes, schools, community centers, and other sites. RNs may spend considerable time walking, bending, stretching, and standing. Patients in hospitals and nursing care facilities require 24-hour care; consequently, nurses in these institutions may work nights, weekends, and holidays. RNs also may be on call—available to work on short notice. Nurses who work in offices, schools, and other settings that do not provide 24-hour care are more likely to work regular business hours. About 20 percent of RNs worked part time in 2008.

RNs may be in close contact with individuals who have infectious diseases and with toxic, harmful, or potentially hazardous compounds, solutions, and medications. RNs must observe rigid, standardized guidelines to guard against disease and other dangers, such as those posed by radiation, accidental needle sticks, chemicals used to sterilize instruments, and anesthetics. In addition, they are vulnerable to back injury when moving patients.

Training, Other Qualifications, and Advancement

The three typical educational paths to registered nursing are a bachelor's degree, an associate degree, and a diploma from an approved nursing program. Nurses most commonly enter the occupation by completing an associate degree or bachelor's degree program. Individuals then must complete a national licensing examination in order to obtain a nursing license. Advanced practice nurses—clinical nurse specialists, nurse anesthetists, nurse-midwives, and nurse practitioners—need a master's degree.

Education and training. There are three typical educational paths to registered nursing—a bachelor's of science degree in nursing (BSN), an associate degree in nursing (ADN), and a diploma. BSN programs, offered by colleges and universities, take about 4 years to complete. ADN programs, offered by community and junior colleges, take about 2 to 3 years to complete. Diploma programs, administered in hospitals, last about 3 years. Generally, licensed graduates of any of the three types of educational programs qualify for entry-level positions as a staff nurse. There are hundreds of registered nursing programs that result in ADN or BSN; however, there are relatively few diploma programs.

Individuals considering a career in nursing should carefully weigh the advantages and disadvantages of enrolling each type of education program. Advancement opportunities may be more limited for ADN and diploma holders compared to RNs who obtain a BSN or higher. Individuals who complete a bachelor's degree receive more training in areas such as communication, leadership, and critical thinking, all of which are becoming more important as nursing practice becomes more complex. Additionally, bachelor's degree programs offer more clinical experience in nonhospital settings. A bachelor's or higher degree is often necessary for administrative positions, research, consulting, and teaching.

Many RNs with an ADN or diploma later enter bachelor's degree programs to prepare for a broader scope of nursing practice. Often, they can find an entry-level position and then take advantage of tuition reimbursement benefits to work toward a BSN by completing an RN-to-BSN program. Accelerated master's degree in nursing (MSN) programs also are available. They typically take 3–4 years to complete full time and result in the award of both the BSN and MSN.

There are education programs available for people interested in switching to a career in nursing as well. Individuals who already hold a bachelor's degree in another field may enroll in an accelerated BSN program. Accelerated BSN programs last 12 to 18 months and provide the fastest route to a BSN for individuals who already hold a degree. MSN programs also are available for individuals who hold a bachelor's or higher degree in another field; master's degree programs usually last 2 years.

All nursing education programs include classroom instruction and supervised clinical experience in hospitals and other health-care facilities. Students take courses in anatomy, physiology, microbiology, chemistry, nutrition, psychology and other behavioral sciences, and nursing. Coursework also includes the liberal arts for ADN and BSN students.

Supervised clinical experience is provided in hospital departments such as pediatrics, psychiatry, maternity, and surgery. A number of programs include clinical experience in nursing care facilities, public health departments, home health agencies, and ambulatory clinics.

Licensure and certification. In all states, the District of Columbia, and U.S. territories, students must graduate from an approved nursing program and pass a national licensing examination, known as the National Council Licensure Examination, or NCLEX-RN, in order to obtain a nursing license. Other eligibility requirements for licensure vary by state. Contact your state's board of nursing for details.

Other qualifications. Nurses should be caring, sympathetic, responsible, and detail oriented. They must be able to direct or supervise others, correctly assess patients' conditions, and determine when consultation is required. They need emotional stability to cope with human suffering, emergencies, and other stresses.

RNs should enjoy learning because continuing education credits are required by some states and/or employers at regular intervals. Career-long learning is a distinct reality for RNs.

Some nurses may become credentialed in specialties such as ambulatory care, gerontology, informatics, pediatrics, and many others. Credentialing for RNs is available from the American Nursing Credentialing Center, the National League for Nursing, and many others. Although credentialing is usually voluntary, it demonstrates adherence to a higher standard and some employers may require it.

Advancement. Most RNs begin as staff nurses in hospitals and, with experience and good performance, often move to other settings or are promoted to positions with more responsibility. In management, nurses can advance from assistant unit manager or head nurse to more senior-level administrative roles of assistant director, director, vice president, or chief of nursing. Increasingly, management-level nursing positions require a graduate or an advanced degree in nursing or health services administration. Administrative positions require leadership, communication and negotiation skills, and good judgment.

Some RNs choose to become advanced practice nurses, who work independently or in collaboration with physicians, and may focus on providing primary care services. There are four types of advanced practice nurses: clinical nurse specialists, nurse anesthetists, nurse-midwives, and nurse practitioners. Clinical nurse specialists provide direct patient care and expert consultations in one of many nursing specialties, such as psychiatric-mental health. Nurse anesthetists provide anesthesia and related care before and after surgical, therapeutic, diagnostic, and obstetrical procedures. They also provide pain management and emergency services, such as airway management. Nurse-midwives provide primary care to women, including gynecological exams, family planning advice, prenatal care, assistance in labor and delivery, and neonatal care. Nurse practitioners serve as primary and specialty care providers, providing a blend of nursing and health-care services to patients and families.

All four types of advanced practice nurses require at least a master's degree. In addition, all states specifically define requirements for registered nurses in advanced practice roles. Advanced practice nurses may prescribe medicine, but the authority to prescribe varies by state. Contact your state's board of nursing for specific regulations regarding advanced practice nurses.

Some nurses move into the business side of health care. Their nursing expertise and experience on a health-care team equip them to manage ambulatory, acute, home-based, and chronic care businesses. Employers—including hospitals, insurance companies, pharmaceutical manufacturers, and managed care organizations, among others—need RNs for health planning and development, marketing, consulting, policy development, and quality assurance. Other nurses work as college and university faculty or conduct research.

Employment

As the largest health-care occupation, registered nurses held about 2.6 million jobs in 2008. Hospitals employed the majority of RNs, with 60 percent of such jobs. About 8 percent of jobs were in offices of physicians, 5 percent in home health-care services, 5 percent in nursing care facilities, and 3 percent in employment services. The remainder worked mostly in government agencies, social assistance agencies, and educational services.

Job Outlook

Overall job opportunities for registered nurses are expected to be excellent, but may vary by employment and geographic setting. Some employers report difficulty in attracting and retaining an adequate number of RNs. Employment of RNs is expected to grow much faster than the average and, because the occupation is very large, 581,500 new jobs will result, among the largest number of new jobs for any occupation. Additionally, hundreds of thousands of job openings will result from the need to replace experienced nurses who leave the occupation.

Employment change. Employment of registered nurses is expected to grow by 22 percent from 2008 to 2018, much faster than the average for all occupations. Growth will be driven by technological advances in patient care, which permit a greater number of health problems to be treated, and by an increasing emphasis on preventive care. In addition, the number of older people, who are much more likely than younger people to need nursing care, is projected to grow rapidly.

However, employment of RNs will not grow at the same rate in every industry. The projected growth rates for RNs in the industries with the highest employment of these workers are as follows:

Industry	Percent
Offices of physicians	48
Home health-care services	33
Nursing care facilities	25
Employment services	24
Hospitals, public and private	17

Employment is expected to grow more slowly in hospitals—health care's largest industry—than in most other health-care industries. While the intensity of nursing care is likely to increase, requiring more nurses per patient, the number of inpatients (those who remain in the hospital for more than 24 hours) is not likely to grow by much. Patients are being discharged earlier, and more procedures are being done on an outpatient basis, both inside and outside hospitals. Rapid growth is expected in hospital outpatient facilities, such as those providing same-day surgery, rehabilitation, and chemotherapy.

More and more sophisticated procedures, once performed only in hospitals, are being performed in physicians' offices and in out-patient care centers, such as freestanding ambulatory surgical and emergency centers. Accordingly, employment is expected to grow fast in these places as health care in general expands.

Employment in nursing care facilities is expected to grow because of increases in the number of older persons, many of whom require long-term care. Many elderly patients want to be treated at home or in residential care facilities, which will drive demand for RNs in those settings. The financial pressure on hospitals to discharge patients as soon as possible should produce more admissions to nursing and residential care facilities and referrals to home health care. Job growth also is expected in units that provide specialized long-term rehabilitation for stroke and head injury patients, as well as units that treat Alzheimer's victims.

Employment in home health care is expected to increase in response to the growing number of older persons with functional disabili-ties, consumer preference for care in the home, and technological advances that make it possible to bring increasingly complex treat-ments into the home. The type of care demanded will require nurses who are able to perform complex procedures.

Job prospects. Overall job opportunities are expected to be excellent for registered nurses. Employers in some parts of the country and in certain employment settings report difficulty in attracting and retain-ing an adequate number of RNs, primarily because of an aging RN workforce and a lack of younger workers to fill positions. Qualified applicants to nursing schools are being turned away because of a shortage of nursing faculty. The need for nursing faculty will only increase as many instructors near retirement. Despite the slower employment growth in hospitals, job opportunities should still be excellent because of the relatively high turnover of hospital nurses. To attract and retain qualified nurses, hospitals may offer signing bonuses, family-friendly work schedules, or subsidized training. Although faster employment growth is projected in physicians' offices and outpatient care centers, RNs may face greater competi-tion for these positions because they generally offer regular work-ing hours and more comfortable working environments. Generally, RNs with at least a bachelor's degree will have better job prospects than those without a bachelor's. In addition, all four advanced practice specialties—clinical nurse specialists, nurse practitioners, nurse-midwives, and nurse anesthetists—will be in high demand, particularly in medically underserved areas such as inner cities and rural areas. Relative to physicians, these RNs increasingly serve as lower-cost primary care providers.

Earnings

Median annual wages of registered nurses were $62,450 in May 2008. The middle 50 percent earned between $51,640 and $76,570. The lowest 10 percent earned less than $43,410, and the highest 10 percent earned more than $92,240. Median annual wages in the industries employing the largest numbers of registered nurses in May 2008 were as follows:

Employment services	$68,160
General medical and surgical hospitals	63,880
Offices of physicians	59,210
Home health care services	58,740
Nursing care facilities	57,060

Many employers offer flexible work schedules, child care, educa-tional benefits, and bonuses. About 21 percent of registered nurses are union members or covered by union contract.

Related Occupations

Because of the number of specialties for registered nurses, and the variety of responsibilities and duties, many other health-care occu-pations are similar in some aspects of their job. Some health-care occupations with similar levels of responsibility that work under the direction of physicians or dentists are dental hygienists; diag-nostic medical sonographers; emergency medical technicians and paramedics; licensed practical and licensed vocational nurses; and physician assistants.

Sources of Additional Information

For information on a career as a registered nurse and nursing educa-tion, contact

▸ National League for Nursing, 61 Broadway, 33rd Floor, New York, NY 10006. Internet: www.nln.org

For information on baccalaureate and graduate nursing education, nursing career options, and financial aid, contact

▸ American Association of Colleges of Nursing, 1 Dupont Circle NW, Suite 530, Washington, DC 20036. Internet: www.aacn.nche.edu

For additional information on registered nurses, including creden-tialing, contact

▸ American Nurses Association, 8515 Georgia Ave., Suite 400, Silver Spring, MD 20910. Internet: http://nursingworld.org

For information on the National Council Licensure Examination (NCLEX-RN) and a list of individual state boards of nursing, con-tact

▸ National Council of State Boards of Nursing, 111 E. Wacker Dr., Suite 2900, Chicago, IL 60601. Internet: www.ncsbn.org

Projections Data from the National Employment Matrix

Occupational title	SOC Code	Employment, 2008	Projected employment, 2018	Change, 2008–2018	
				Number	Percent
Registered nurses	29-1111	2,618,700	3,200,200	581,500	22

NOTE: Data in this table are rounded.

For a list of accredited clinical nurse specialist programs, contact

▶ National Association of Clinical Nurse Specialists, 2090 Linglestown Rd., Suite 107, Harrisburg, PA 17110. Internet: www.nacns.org

For information on nurse anesthetists, including a list of accredited programs, contact

▶ American Association of Nurse Anesthetists, 222 S. Prospect Ave., Park Ridge, IL 60068. Internet: www.aana.com/

For information on nurse-midwives, including a list of accredited programs, contact

▶ American College of Nurse-Midwives, 8403 Colesville Rd., Suite 1550, Silver Spring, MD 20910. Internet: www.midwife.org

For information on nurse practitioners, including a list of accredited programs, contact

▶ American Academy of Nurse Practitioners, P.O. Box 12846, Austin, TX 78711. Internet: www.aanp.org

For additional information on registered nurses in all fields and specialties, contact

▶ American Society of Registered Nurses, 1001 Bridgeway, Suite 233, Sausalito, CA 94965. Internet: www.asrn.org

Respiratory Therapists

(O*NET 29-1126.00)

Significant Points

■ Job opportunities should be very good.

■ Hospitals will account for the vast majority of job openings, but a growing number of openings will arise in other settings.

■ An associate degree is the minimum educational requirement, but a bachelor's or master's degree may be important for advancement.

■ All states, except Alaska and Hawaii, require respiratory therapists to be licensed.

Nature of the Work

Respiratory therapists—also known as *respiratory care practitioners*—evaluate, treat, and care for patients with breathing or other cardiopulmonary disorders. Practicing under the direction of a physician, respiratory therapists assume primary responsibility for all respiratory care therapeutic treatments and diagnostic procedures, including the supervision of respiratory therapy technicians. They consult with physicians and other health-care staff to help develop and modify patient care plans. Therapists also provide complex therapy requiring considerable independent judgment, such as caring for patients on life support in intensive-care units of hospitals.

Respiratory therapists evaluate and treat all types of patients, ranging from premature infants whose lungs are not fully developed to elderly people whose lungs are diseased. They provide temporary relief to patients with chronic asthma or emphysema and give emergency care to patients who are victims of a heart attack, stroke, drowning, or shock.

Respiratory therapists interview patients, perform limited physical examinations, and conduct diagnostic tests. For example, respiratory therapists test a patient's breathing capacity and determine the concentration of oxygen and other gases in a patient's blood. They also measure a patient's pH, which indicates the acidity or alkalinity of the blood. To evaluate a patient's lung capacity, respiratory therapists have the patient breathe into an instrument that measures the volume and flow of oxygen during inhalation and exhalation. By comparing the reading with the norm for the patient's age, height, weight, and sex, respiratory therapists can provide information that helps determine whether the patient has any lung deficiencies. To analyze oxygen, carbon dioxide, and blood pH levels, therapists draw an arterial blood sample, place it in a blood gas analyzer, and relay the results to a physician, who then makes treatment decisions.

To treat patients, respiratory therapists use oxygen or oxygen mixtures, chest physiotherapy, and aerosol medications—liquid medications suspended in a gas that forms a mist that is inhaled. They teach patients how to inhale the aerosol properly to ensure its effectiveness. When a patient has difficulty getting enough oxygen into his or her blood, therapists increase the patient's concentration of oxygen by placing an oxygen mask or nasal cannula on the patient and setting the oxygen flow at the level prescribed by a physician. Therapists also connect patients who cannot breathe on their own to ventilators that deliver pressurized oxygen into the lungs. The therapists insert a tube into the patient's trachea, or windpipe; connect the tube to the ventilator; and set the rate, volume, and oxygen concentration of the oxygen mixture entering the patient's lungs.

Therapists perform regular assessments of patients and equipment. If a patient appears to be having difficulty breathing or if the oxygen, carbon dioxide, or pH level of the blood is abnormal, therapists change the ventilator setting according to the doctor's orders or check the equipment for mechanical problems.

Respiratory therapists perform chest physiotherapy on patients to remove mucus from their lungs and make it easier for them to breathe. Therapists place patients in positions that help drain mucus, and then vibrate the patients' rib cages, often by tapping on the chest, and tell the patients to cough. Chest physiotherapy may be needed after surgery, for example, because anesthesia depresses respiration. As a result, physiotherapy may be prescribed to help get the patient's lungs back to normal and to prevent congestion. Chest physiotherapy also helps patients suffering from lung diseases, such as cystic fibrosis, that cause mucus to collect in the lungs.

Therapists who work in home care teach patients and their families to use ventilators and other life-support systems. In addition, these therapists visit patients in their homes to inspect and clean equipment, evaluate the home environment, and ensure that patients have sufficient knowledge of their diseases and the proper use of their medications and equipment. Therapists also make emergency visits if equipment problems arise.

In some hospitals, therapists perform tasks that fall outside their traditional role. Therapists are becoming involved in areas such as pulmonary rehabilitation, smoking-cessation counseling, disease prevention, case management, and polysomnography—the diagnosis of breathing disorders during sleep, such as apnea. Respiratory therapists also increasingly treat critical-care patients, either as part of surface and air transport teams or as part of rapid-response teams in hospitals.

Work environment. Respiratory therapists generally work between 35 and 40 hours a week. Because hospitals operate around the clock, therapists can work evenings, nights, or weekends. They spend long periods standing and walking between patients' rooms. In an emergency, therapists work under the stress of the situation. Respiratory therapists employed in home health care must travel frequently to patients' homes.

Respiratory therapists are trained to work with gases stored under pressure. Adherence to safety precautions and regular maintenance and testing of equipment minimize the risk of injury. As in many other health occupations, respiratory therapists are exposed to infectious diseases, but by carefully following proper procedures, they can minimize these risks.

Training, Other Qualifications, and Advancement

An associate degree is the minimum educational requirement, but a bachelor's or master's degree may be important for advancement. All states, except Alaska and Hawaii, require respiratory therapists to be licensed.

Education and training. An associate degree is required to become a respiratory therapist. Training is offered at the postsecondary level by colleges and universities, medical schools, vocational-technical institutes, and the Armed Forces. Most programs award associate or bachelor's degree and prepare graduates for jobs as advanced respiratory therapists. A limited number of associate degree programs lead to jobs as entry-level respiratory therapists. According to the Commission on Accreditation of Allied Health Education Programs (CAAHEP), 31 entry-level and 346 advanced respiratory therapy programs were accredited in the United States in 2008.

Among the areas of study in respiratory therapy programs are human anatomy and physiology, pathophysiology, chemistry, physics, microbiology, pharmacology, and mathematics. Other courses deal with therapeutic and diagnostic procedures and tests, equipment, patient assessment, cardiopulmonary resuscitation, the application of clinical practice guidelines, patient care outside of hospitals, cardiac and pulmonary rehabilitation, respiratory health promotion and disease prevention, and medical recordkeeping and reimbursement.

High school students interested in applying to respiratory therapy programs should take courses in health, biology, mathematics, chemistry, and physics. Respiratory care involves basic mathematical problem solving and an understanding of chemical and physical principles. For example, respiratory care workers must be able to compute dosages of medication and calculate gas concentrations.

Licensure and certification. A license is required to practice as a respiratory therapist, except in Alaska and Hawaii. Also, most employers require respiratory therapists to maintain a cardiopulmonary resuscitation (CPR) certification.

Licensure is usually based, in large part, on meeting the requirements for certification from the National Board for Respiratory Care (NBRC). The board offers the Certified Respiratory Therapist (CRT) credential to those who graduate from entry-level or advanced programs accredited by CAAHEP or the Committee on Accreditation for Respiratory Care (CoARC) and who also pass an exam.

The board also awards the Registered Respiratory Therapist (RRT) to CRTs who have graduated from advanced programs and pass two separate examinations. Supervisory positions and intensive-care specialties usually require the RRT.

Other qualifications. Therapists should be sensitive to a patient's physical and psychological needs. Respiratory care practitioners must pay attention to detail, follow instructions, and work as part of a team. In addition, operating advanced equipment requires proficiency with computers.

Advancement. Respiratory therapists advance in clinical practice by moving from general care to the care of critically ill patients who have significant problems in other organ systems, such as the heart or kidneys. Respiratory therapists, especially those with a bachelor's or master's degree, also may advance to supervisory or managerial positions in a respiratory therapy department. Respiratory therapists in home health care and equipment rental firms may become branch managers. Some respiratory therapists advance by moving into teaching positions. Some others use the knowledge gained as a respiratory therapist to work in another industry, such as developing, marketing, or selling pharmaceuticals and medical devices.

Employment

Respiratory therapists held about 105,900 jobs in 2008. About 81 percent of jobs were in hospitals, mainly in departments of respiratory care, anesthesiology, or pulmonary medicine. Most of the remaining jobs were in offices of physicians or other health practitioners, consumer-goods rental firms that supply respiratory equipment for home use, nursing care facilities, employment services, and home health-care services.

Job Outlook

Much-faster-than-average growth is projected for respiratory therapists. Job opportunities should be very good.

Employment change. Employment of respiratory therapists is expected to grow by 21 percent from 2008 to 2018, much faster than the average for all occupations. The increasing demand will come from substantial growth in the middle-aged and elderly population—a development that will heighten the incidence of cardiopulmonary disease. Growth in demand also will result from the expanding role of respiratory therapists in case management, disease prevention, emergency care, and the early detection of pulmonary disorders.

Older Americans suffer most from respiratory ailments and cardiopulmonary diseases, such as pneumonia, chronic bronchitis, emphysema, and heart disease. As the number of older persons increases, the need for respiratory therapists is expected to increase as well. In addition, advances in inhalable medications and in the treatment of lung transplant patients, heart attack and accident victims, and premature infants—many of whom depend on a ventilator during part of their treatment—will increase the demand for the services of respiratory care practitioners.

Job prospects. Job opportunities are expected to be very good, especially for those with a bachelor's degree and certification, and those with cardiopulmonary care skills or experience working with infants. The vast majority of job openings will continue to be in hospitals. However, a growing number of openings are expected

Projections Data from the National Employment Matrix

Occupational title	SOC Code	Employment, 2008	Projected employment, 2018	Change, 2008–2018	
				Number	Percent
Respiratory therapists...................................	29-1126	105,900	128,100	22,100	21

NOTE: Data in this table are rounded.

to be outside of hospitals, especially in home health-care services, offices of physicians or other health practitioners, consumer-goods rental firms, or in the employment services industry as a temporary worker in various settings.

Earnings

Median annual wages of wage-and-salary respiratory therapists were $52,200 in May 2008. The middle 50 percent earned between $44,490 and $61,720. The lowest 10 percent earned less than $37,920 and the highest 10 percent earned more than $69,800.

Related Occupations

Under the supervision of a physician, respiratory therapists administer respiratory care and life support to patients with heart and lung difficulties. Other workers who care for, treat, or train people to improve their physical condition include athletic trainers; occupational therapists; physical therapists; radiation therapists; and registered nurses.

Respiratory care practitioners work with advanced medical technology, as do other health-care technicians including cardiovascular technologists and technicians; diagnostic medical sonographers; nuclear medicine technologists; and radiologic technologists and technicians.

Sources of Additional Information

Information concerning a career in respiratory care is available from

▶ American Association for Respiratory Care, 9425 N. MacArthur Blvd., Suite 100, Irving, TX 75063. Internet: www.aarc.org

For a list of accredited educational programs for respiratory care practitioners, contact either of the following organizations:

▶ Commission on Accreditation for Allied Health Education Programs, 1361 Park St., Clearwater, FL 33756. Internet: www.caahep.org

▶ Committee on Accreditation for Respiratory Care, 1248 Harwood Rd., Bedford, TX 76021.

Information on gaining credentials in respiratory care and a list of state licensing agencies can be obtained from

▶ National Board for Respiratory Care, Inc., 18000 W. 105th St., Olathe, KS 66061. Internet: www.nbrc.org

Retail Salespersons

(O*NET 41-2031.00)

Significant Points

■ Good employment opportunities are expected because of the need to replace the large number of workers who leave the occupation each year.

■ Many salespersons work evenings and weekends, particularly during peak retail periods.

■ Employers look for people who enjoy working with others and who have good communication skills, an interest in sales work, a neat appearance, and a courteous demeanor.

■ Although advancement opportunities are limited, having a college degree or a great deal of experience may help retail salespersons move into management positions.

Nature of the Work

Whether selling shoes, computer equipment, or automobiles, *retail salespersons* assist customers in finding what they are looking for. They also try to increase sales by describing a product's features, demonstrating its uses, and promoting its value.

In addition to selling, many retail salespersons—especially those who work in department and apparel stores—conduct financial transactions with their customers. This usually involves receiving payments by cash, check, debit card, or credit card; operating cash registers; and bagging or packaging purchases. Depending on the hours they work, retail salespersons may have to open or close cash registers. This work may include counting the money in the register and separating charge slips, coupons, and exchange vouchers. Retail salespersons also may have to make deposits at a cash office. In addition, retail salespersons may help stock shelves or racks, arrange for mailing or delivery of purchases, mark price tags, take inventory, and prepare displays.

For some sales jobs, particularly those involving expensive and complex items, retail salespersons need special knowledge or skills. For example, salespersons who sell automobiles must be able to explain the features of various models, the manufacturers' specifications, the types of options and financing available, and the details of associated warranties. In addition, all retail salespersons must recognize security risks and thefts and understand their organization's procedure for handling such situations—procedures that may include notifying security guards or calling police.

Work environment. Most retail salespersons work in clean, comfortable, well-lit stores. However, they often stand for long periods and may need supervisory approval to leave the sales floor. They also may work outdoors if they sell items such as cars, plants, or lumber yard materials.

The Monday-through-Friday, 9-to-5 workweek is the exception rather than the rule for retail salespersons. Many salespersons work evenings and weekends, particularly during holidays and other peak sales periods. The end-of-year holiday season often is the busiest time, and as a result, many employers limit the use of vacation time between Thanksgiving and the beginning of January.

This occupation offers opportunities for both full-time and part-time work. About 34 percent of retail salespersons worked part time in 2008. Part-time opportunities may vary by setting, however, as many who sell big-ticket items are required to work full time.

Training, Other Qualifications, and Advancement

Retail salespersons typically learn their skills through on-the-job training. Although advancement opportunities are limited, having a college degree or a great deal of experience may help retail salespersons move into management positions.

Education and training. There usually are no formal education requirements for retail sales positions, but employers often prefer applicants with a high school diploma or its equivalent. This may be especially important for those who sell technical products or "big-ticket" items, such as electronics or automobiles. A college degree may be required for management trainee positions, especially in larger retail establishments.

Most retail salespersons receive on-the-job training, which usually lasts anywhere from a few days to a few months. In small stores, newly hired workers usually are trained by an experienced employee. In large stores, training programs are more formal and generally are conducted over several days. Topics often include customer service, security, the store's policies and procedures, and cash register operation. Depending on the type of product they are selling, employees may be given additional specialized training. For example, those working in cosmetics receive instruction on the types of products the store offers and for whom the cosmetics would be most beneficial. Likewise, those who sell computers may be instructed in the technical differences between computer products. Because providing the best possible service to customers is a high priority for many employers, employees often are given periodic training to update and refine their skills.

Other qualifications. Employers look for people who enjoy working with others and who possess good communication skills. Employers also value workers who have the tact and patience to deal with difficult customers. Among other desirable characteristics are an interest in sales work, a neat appearance, and a courteous demeanor. The ability to speak more than one language may be helpful for employment in communities where people from various cultures live and shop. Before hiring a salesperson, some employers conduct a background check, especially for a job selling high-priced items.

Advancement. Opportunities for advancement vary. In some small establishments, advancement is limited because one person—often the owner—does most of the managerial work. In others, some salespersons can be promoted to assistant manager. Large retail businesses usually prefer to hire college graduates as management trainees, making a college education increasingly important. However, motivated and capable employees without college degrees still may advance to administrative or supervisory positions in large establishments.

As salespersons gain experience and seniority, they often move into positions with greater responsibility and may be given their choice of departments in which to work. This opportunity often means moving to areas with higher potential earnings and commissions. The highest earnings potential usually lies in selling "big-ticket" items—such as cars, jewelry, furniture, and electronic equipment—although doing so often requires extensive knowledge of the product and an excellent talent for persuasion.

Previous sales experience may be an asset when one is applying for positions with larger retailers or in nonretail industries, such as financial services, wholesale trade, or manufacturing.

Employment

Retail salespersons held about 4.5 million jobs in 2008. The largest employers were clothing and clothing accessories stores, department stores, building material and supplies dealers, motor vehicle and parts dealers, and general merchandise stores such as warehouse clubs and supercenters. In addition, about 156,500 retail salespersons were self-employed.

Because retail stores are found in every city and town, employment is distributed geographically in much the same way as the population.

Job Outlook

Employment is expected to grow about as fast as average. Due to the frequency with which people leave this occupation, job opportunities are expected to be good.

Employment change. Employment is expected to grow by 8 percent over the 2008–2018 decade, about as fast as the average for all occupations. In addition, given the size of this occupation, about 374,700 new retail salesperson jobs will arise over the projections decade—more jobs than will be generated in almost any other occupation.

Employment growth among retail salespersons reflects rising retail sales stemming from a growing population. Many retail establishments will continue to expand in size and number, leading to new retail sales positions. Growth will be fastest in general merchandise stores, many of which sell a wide assortment of goods at low prices. As consumers continue to prefer these stores other establishments with higher prices, growth in this industry will be rapid. Employment of retail sales persons is expected to decline in department stores and automobile dealers as these industries see a reduction in store locations.

Despite the growing popularity of electronic commerce, the impact of online shopping on the employment of retail salespersons is expected to be minimal. Internet sales have not decreased the need for retail salespersons. Retail stores commonly use an online presence to complement their in-store sales, and many consumers prefer to buy merchandise in person. Retail salespersons will remain important in assisting customers, providing specialized service, and increasing customer satisfaction.

Projections Data from the National Employment Matrix

Occupational title	SOC Code	Employment, 2008	Projected employment, 2018	Change, 2008–2018	
				Number	Percent
Retail salespersons	41-2031	4,489,200	4,863,900	374,700	8

NOTE: Data in this table are rounded.

Job prospects. Employment opportunities for retail salespersons are expected to be good because of the need to replace the large number of workers who transfer to other occupations or leave the labor force each year. In addition, many new jobs will be created for retail salespersons as businesses seek to expand operations and enhance customer service. A substantial number of these openings should occur in warehouse clubs and supercenters as a result of strong growth among these establishments.

Opportunities for part-time work should be abundant, and demand is expected be strong for temporary workers during peak selling periods, such as the end-of-year holiday season between Thanksgiving and the beginning of January.

During economic downturns, sales volumes and the resulting demand for sales workers usually decline. Consequently, retail sales jobs generally are more susceptible to fluctuations in the economy than are many other occupations.

Earnings

Median hourly wages of wage-and-salary retail salespersons, including commissions, were $9.86 in May 2008. The middle 50 percent earned between $8.26 and $13.35 an hour. The lowest 10 percent earned less than $7.37, and the highest 10 percent earned more than $19.14 an hour. Median hourly wages in the industries employing the largest numbers of retail salespersons in May 2008 were as follows:

Automobile dealers	$18.91
Building material and supplies dealers	11.95
Other general merchandise stores	9.22
Department stores	9.14
Clothing stores	8.94

Many beginning or inexperienced workers earn the federal minimum wage of $7.25 an hour, but many states set minimum wages higher than the federal minimum. In areas where employers have difficulty attracting and retaining workers, wages tend to be higher than the legislated minimum.

Compensation systems can vary by type of establishment and merchandise sold. Salespersons receive hourly wages, commissions, or a combination of the two. Under a commission system, salespersons receive a percentage of the sales they make. This system offers sales workers the opportunity to increase their earnings considerably, but they may find that their earnings depend strongly on their ability to sell their product and on the ups and downs of the economy.

Benefits may be limited in smaller stores, but benefits in large establishments usually are considerable. In addition, nearly all salespersons are able to buy their store's merchandise at a discount, with the savings depending on the type of merchandise. Also, to bolster revenue, employers may use incentive programs such as awards, bonuses, and profit-sharing plans to the sales staff.

Related Occupations

Other occupations that provide customer service, sell items, or operate cash registers include the following cashiers; counter and rental clerks; customer service representatives; gaming cage workers; insurance sales agents; real estate brokers and sales agents; sales engineers; sales representatives, wholesale and manufacturing; and securities, commodities, and financial services sales agents.

Sources of Additional Information

Information on careers in retail sales may be obtained from the personnel offices of local stores or from state merchants' associations.

General information about retailing is available from

▸ National Retail Federation, 325 7th St. NW, Suite 1100, Washington, DC 20004. Internet: www.nrf.com

Information about training for a career in automobile sales is available from

▸ National Automobile Dealers Association, Public Relations Department, 8400 Westpark Dr., McLean, VA 22102-3591. Internet: www.nada.org

Sales Representatives, Wholesale and Manufacturing

(O*NET 41-4011.00, 41-4011.07, and 41-4012.00)

Significant Points

- Job prospects will be best for those with a college degree, the appropriate technical expertise, and the personal traits necessary for successful selling.

- Earnings usually are based on a combination of salary and commission.

- Employment opportunities and earnings may fluctuate from year to year because sales are affected by changing economic conditions.

Nature of the Work

Sales representatives are an important part of manufacturers' and wholesalers' success. Regardless of the type of products they sell, sales representatives' primary duties are to make customers interested in their merchandise and to arrange the sale of that merchandise.

The process of promoting and selling a product can be extensive, at times taking up to several months. Whether in person or over the phone, sales representatives describe their products, conduct demonstrations, explain the benefits that their products convey, and answer any questions that their customers may have.

Sales representatives—sometimes called *manufacturers' representatives* or *manufacturers' agents*—generally work for manufacturers, wholesalers, or technical companies. Some work for a single organization, while others represent several companies and sell a range of products. Rather than selling goods directly to consumers, sales representatives deal with businesses, government agencies, and other organizations.

Some sales representatives specialize in technical and scientific products ranging from agricultural and mechanical equipment to computer and pharmaceutical goods. Other representatives deal with all other types of goods, including food, office supplies, and apparel.

Sales representatives stay abreast of new products and the changing needs of their customers in a variety of ways. They attend trade shows at which new products and technologies are showcased. They also attend conferences and conventions to meet other sales representatives and clients and discuss new product developments. In addition, the entire sales force may participate in company-sponsored meetings to review the firm's sales performance, product development, sales goals, and profitability.

Frequently, sales representatives who lack the necessary expertise about a given product may team with a technical expert. In this arrangement, the technical expert—sometimes a sales engineer—attends the sales presentation to explain the product and answer questions or concerns. The sales representative makes the preliminary contact with customers, introduces the company's product, and closes the sale. Under such an arrangement, the representative is able to spend more time maintaining and soliciting accounts and less time acquiring technical knowledge. After the sale, representatives may make follow up visits to ensure that the equipment is functioning properly and may even help train customers' employees to operate and maintain new equipment. Those selling technical goods also may arrange for the product to be installed. Those selling consumer goods often suggest how and where merchandise should be displayed. When working with retailers, they may help arrange promotional programs, store displays, and advertising.

Sales representatives have several duties beyond selling products. They analyze sales statistics, prepare reports, and handle administrative duties such as filing expense accounts, scheduling appointments, and making travel plans. They also read about new and existing products and monitor the sales, prices, and products of their competitors.

Sales representatives generally work in either inside sales, interacting with customers over the phone from an office location, or outside "field" sales, traveling to meet clients in person.

Inside sales representatives may spend a lot of their time on the phone, selling goods, taking orders, and resolving problems or complaints about the merchandise. These sales representatives typically do not leave the office. Frequently, they are responsible for acquiring new clients by "cold calling" various organizations—calling potential customers to establish an initial contact. They also may be responsible for arranging meetings for outside sales representatives.

Outside sales representatives spend much of their time traveling to, and visiting with, current clients and prospective buyers. During a sales call, they discuss the client's needs and suggest how their merchandise or services can meet those needs. They may show samples or catalogs that describe items their company provides, and they may inform customers about prices, availability, and ways in which their products can save money and boost productivity. Because many sales representatives sell several complementary products made by different manufacturers, they may take a broad approach to their customers' business. For example, sales representatives may help install new equipment and train employees in its use.

Work environment. Some sales representatives have large territories and travel considerably. Because a sales region may cover several states, representatives may be away from home for several days or weeks at a time, often traveling by airplane. Others cover a smaller region and travel mostly by car, spending few nights away from home. Sales representatives frequently are on their feet for long periods and may carry heavy sample products, requiring some physical stamina.

In 2008, about 48 percent of sales representatives worked around 40 hours per week, but about 24 percent worked more than 50 hours per week. Since sales calls take place during regular working hours, much of the planning and paperwork involved with sales must be completed during the evening and on weekends. Although the hours are often irregular, many sales representatives have the freedom to determine their own schedules.

Workers in this occupation can encounter pressure and stress because their income and job security often depend directly on the amount of merchandise they sell and their companies usually set goals or quotas that they are expected to meet. Sales representatives also deal with many different types of people, which can be stimulating but demanding.

Training, Other Qualifications, and Advancement

There generally is no formal educational requirement for sales representative positions, but many jobs require some postsecondary education. Regardless of educational background, factors such as communication skills, the ability to sell, and familiarity with brands are essential to being a successful sales representative.

Education and training. There usually is no formal educational requirement for sales representatives. Some positions, especially those which deal with scientific and technical products, require a bachelor's degree. For other jobs, however, applicants can be fully qualified with a high school diploma or its equivalent. For these positions, previous sales experience may be desirable.

Many sales representatives attend seminars in sales techniques or take courses in marketing, economics, communication, or even a foreign language to provide the extra edge needed to make sales. Often, companies have formal training programs for beginning sales representatives that last up to 2 years. However, most businesses accelerate these programs to much shorter timeframes in order to reduce costs and expedite the returns from training. In some programs, trainees rotate among jobs in plants and offices to learn all phases of production, installation, and distribution of the product. In

Projections Data from the National Employment Matrix

Occupational title	SOC Code	Employment, 2008	Projected employment, 2018	Change, 2008–2018	
				Number	Percent
Sales representatives, wholesale and manufacturing 41-4000		1,973,200	2,116,400	143,200	7
Sales representatives, wholesale and manufacturing, technical and scientific products.............................41-4011		432,900	475,000	42,000	10
Sales representatives, wholesale and manufacturing, except technical and scientific products..................41-4012		1,540,300	1,641,400	101,100	7

NOTE: Data in this table are rounded.

others, trainees take formal classroom instruction at the plant, followed by on-the-job training under the supervision of a field sales manager.

Regardless of where they work, new employees may be trained by accompanying experienced workers on their sales calls. As they gain familiarity with the firm's products and clients, the new workers are given increasing responsibility, until they are eventually assigned their own territory. As businesses experience greater competition, representatives face more pressure to produce sales.

Other qualifications. For sales representative jobs, companies seek individuals who have excellent communication skills and the desire to sell. Those who want to become sales representatives should be goal oriented, persuasive, and able to work well both independently and as part of a team. A pleasant personality and appearance and problem-solving skills are highly valued. Patience and perseverance also are keys to completing a sale, which can take up to several months.

Manufacturers' representatives who operate a sales agency also must manage their business. Doing so requires organizational and general business skills, as well as knowledge of accounting, marketing, and administration.

Certification and advancement. Certifications are available that provide formal recognition of the skills of sales representatives. Many in this profession have either the Certified Professional Manufacturers' Representative (CPMR) certification or the Certified Sales Professional (CSP) certification, offered by the Manufacturers' Representatives Education Research Foundation. Certification typically involves completing formal training and passing an examination.

Frequently, promotion takes the form of an assignment to a larger account or territory, where commissions are likely to be greater. Those who have good sales records and leadership ability may advance to higher level positions such as sales supervisor, district manager, or vice president of sales. Others find opportunities in purchasing, advertising, or marketing research.

Advancement opportunities typically depend on whether the sales representatives are working directly for a manufacturer or wholesaler or whether they are working with an independent sales agency. Experienced sales representatives working directly for a manufacturer or wholesaler may move into jobs as sales trainers and instruct new employees on selling techniques and company policies and procedures. Some leave their organization and start their own independent sales company.

Employment

Manufacturing and wholesale sales representatives held about 2 million jobs in 2008. About 432,900 of these worked with technical and scientific products. Around 61 percent of all representatives worked for wholesale companies. Others were employed in manufacturing establishments, retail organizations, and professional, technical, and scientific firms. Because of the diversity of products and services sold, employment opportunities are available throughout the country. About 73,800 sales representatives were self-employed.

Job Outlook

Job growth is expected to be about as fast as average. Job prospects will be best for those with a college degree, the appropriate technical expertise, and the personal traits necessary for successful selling.

Employment change. Employment of sales representatives, wholesale and manufacturing, is expected to grow by 7 percent between 2008 and 2018, about as fast as the average for all occupations. Given the size of this occupation, a large number of new jobs, about 143,200, will arise over the projection period. Job growth will result from the continued expansion in the variety and number of goods sold throughout the economy. Because they play an important role in the transfer of goods between organizations, sales representatives will be needed to accommodate this expansion. In addition, as technology continues to progress, sales representatives can help ensure that retailers offer the latest products to their customers and that businesses acquire the tools they need to increase their efficiency in operations.

Employment growth will be greatest in independent sales companies as manufacturers continue to outsource sales activities to independent agents rather than using in-house sales workers. Independent sales agents generally are more efficient, reducing the overhead cost to their clients. Also, by using agents who contract their services to more than one company, companies can share costs of the agents with each other.

Job prospects. Job prospects will be best for those with a college degree, the appropriate technical expertise, and the personal traits necessary for successful selling. Opportunities will be better in independent sales companies than with manufacturers, who are expected to continue contracting out field sales duties.

Employment opportunities and earnings may fluctuate from year to year because sales are affected by changing economic conditions and businesses' preferences. In addition, many job openings will result from the need to replace workers who transfer to other occupations or leave the labor force.

Earnings

Median annual wages of sales representatives, wholesale and manufacturing, technical and scientific products, were $70,200, including commissions, in May 2008. The middle 50 percent earned between $48,540 and $99,570 a year. The lowest 10 percent earned less than $34,980, and the highest 10 percent earned more than $133,040 a year. Median annual wages in the industries employing the largest numbers of sales representatives, wholesale and manufacturing, technical and scientific products, were as follows:

Computer systems design and related services	$80,060
Wholesale electronic markets and agents and brokers	77,190
Drugs and druggists' sundries merchant wholesalers	74,840
Professional and commercial equipment and supplies merchant wholesalers	70,140
Electrical and electronic goods merchant wholesalers	63,050

Median annual wages of sales representatives, wholesale and manufacturing, except technical and scientific products, were $51,330, including commission, in May 2008. The middle 50 percent earned between $36,460 and $75,120 a year. The lowest 10 percent earned less than $26,950, and the highest 10 percent earned more than $106,040 a year. Median annual wages in the industries employing the largest numbers of sales representatives, wholesale and manufacturing, except technical and scientific products, were as follows:

Wholesale electronic markets and agents and brokers	$57,100
Machinery equipment and supplies merchant wholesalers	50,310
Professional and commercial equipment and supplies merchant wholesalers	49,750
Grocery and related product merchant wholesalers	47,980
Miscellaneous nondurable goods merchant wholesalers	44,680

Compensation methods for representatives vary significantly by the type of firm and the product sold. Most employers use a combination of salary and commissions or salary plus bonus. Commissions usually are based on the value of sales, whereas bonuses may depend on individual performance, on the performance of all sales workers in the group or district, or on the company's performance. Unlike those working directly for a manufacturer or wholesaler, sales representatives working for an independent sales company usually are not reimbursed for expenses. Depending on the type of product or products they are selling, their experience in the field, and the number of clients they have, they can earn significantly more or less than those working in direct sales for a manufacturer or wholesaler.

In addition to receiving their earnings, sales representatives working directly for a manufacturer or wholesaler usually are reimbursed for expenses such as the costs of transportation, meals, hotels, and entertaining customers. They often receive benefits, including personal use of a company car and frequent flyer mileage. Some companies offer incentives such as free vacation trips or gifts for achieving an outstanding sales performance.

Related Occupations

Sales representatives, wholesale and manufacturing, must have sales ability and knowledge of the products they sell. Other occupations that require similar skills include the following advertising sales agents; insurance sales agents; purchasing managers, buyers, and purchasing agents; real estate brokers and sales agents; retail salespersons; sales engineers; sales worker supervisors; and securities, commodities, and financial services sales agents.

Sources of Additional Information

Information on careers for manufacturers' representatives and sales agents is available from

▸ Manufacturers' Agents National Association, 16 A Journey, Ste. 200, Aliso Viejo, CA 92656-3317. Internet: www.manaonline.org

▸ Manufacturers' Representatives Educational Research Foundation, 8329 Cole St., Arvada, CO 80005. Internet: www.mrerf.org

Science Technicians

(O*NET 19-4011.00, 19-4011.01, 19-4011.02, 19-4021.00, 19-4031.00, 19-4041.00, 19-4041.01, 19-4041.02, 19-4051.00, 19-4051.01, 19-4051.02, 19-4091.00, 19-4092.00, and 19-4093.00)

Significant Points

■ Many science technicians work indoors in laboratory settings, but certain technicians work outdoors, sometimes in remote locations.

■ Most science technicians need some postsecondary training, such as an associate degree or a certificate in applied science or science-related technology; biological and forensic science technicians usually need a bachelor's degree.

■ Overall growth is expected to be about as fast as average, although growth will vary by specialty.

■ Job opportunities are expected to be best for graduates of applied science technology programs who are well trained on equipment used in laboratories or production facilities.

Nature of the Work

Science technicians use the principles and theories of science and mathematics to assist in research and development and to help invent and improve products and processes. However, their jobs are more practically oriented than those of scientists. Technicians set up, operate, and maintain laboratory instruments, monitor experiments, make observations, calculate and record results, and often develop conclusions. They must keep detailed logs of all of their work. Those who perform production work monitor manufacturing processes and may ensure quality by testing products for proper proportions of ingredients, for purity, or for strength and durability.

As laboratory instrumentation and procedures have become more complex, the role of science technicians in research and development has expanded. In addition to performing routine tasks, many technicians, under the direction of scientists, now develop and adapt laboratory procedures to achieve the best results, interpret data, and devise solutions to problems. Technicians must develop expert knowledge of laboratory equipment so that they can adjust settings when necessary and recognize when equipment is malfunctioning.

Most science technicians specialize, learning their skills and working in the same disciplines in which scientists work. Occupational titles, therefore, tend to follow the same structure as those for scientists.

Agricultural and food science technicians work with related scientists to conduct research, development, and testing on food and other agricultural products. Agricultural technicians are involved in food, fiber, and animal research, production, and processing. Some conduct tests and experiments to improve the yield and quality of crops or to increase the resistance of plants and animals to disease, insects, or other hazards. Other agricultural technicians breed animals for the purpose of investigating nutrition. Food science technicians assist food scientists and technologists in research and development, production technology, and quality control. For example, food science technicians may conduct tests on food additives and preservatives to ensure compliance with Food and Drug Administration regulations regarding color, texture, and nutrients. These technicians analyze, record, and compile test results; order supplies to maintain laboratory inventory; and clean and sterilize laboratory equipment.

Biological technicians work with biologists studying living organisms. Many assist scientists who conduct medical research—helping to find a cure for cancer or AIDS, for example. Those who work in pharmaceutical companies help develop and manufacture medicines. Those working in the field of microbiology generally work as laboratory assistants, studying living organisms and infectious agents. Biological technicians also analyze organic substances, such as blood, food, and drugs. Biological technicians working in biotechnology apply knowledge and techniques gained from basic research, including gene splicing and recombinant DNA, and apply them to product development.

Chemical technicians work with chemists and chemical engineers, developing and using chemicals and related products and equipment. Generally, there are two types of chemical technicians: research technicians who work in experimental laboratories and process control technicians who work in manufacturing or other industrial plants. Many chemical technicians working in research and development conduct a variety of laboratory procedures, from routine process control to complex research projects. For example, they may collect and analyze samples of air and water to monitor pollution levels, or they may produce compounds through complex organic synthesis. Most process technicians work in manufacturing, testing packaging for design, integrity of materials, and environmental acceptability. Often, process technicians who work in plants focus on quality assurance, monitoring product quality or production processes and developing new production techniques. A few work in shipping to provide technical support and expertise.

Environmental science and protection technicians perform laboratory and field tests to monitor environmental resources and determine the contaminants and sources of pollution in the environment. They may collect samples for testing or be involved in abating and controlling sources of environmental pollution. Some are responsible for waste management operations, control and management of hazardous materials inventory, or general activities involving

regulatory compliance. Many environmental science technicians employed at private consulting firms work directly under the supervision of an environmental scientist.

Forensic science technicians investigate crimes by collecting and analyzing physical evidence. Often, they specialize in areas such as DNA analysis or firearm examination, performing tests on weapons or on substances such as fiber, glass, hair, tissue, and body fluids to determine their significance to the investigation. Proper collection and storage methods are important to protect the evidence. Forensic science technicians also prepare reports to document their findings and the laboratory techniques used, and they may provide information and expert opinions to investigators. When criminal cases come to trial, forensic science technicians often give testimony as expert witnesses on laboratory findings by identifying and classifying substances, materials, and other evidence collected at the scene of a crime. Some forensic science technicians work closely with other experts or technicians. For example, a forensic science technician may consult either a medical expert about the exact time and cause of a death or another technician who specializes in DNA typing in hopes of matching a DNA type to a suspect.

Forest and conservation technicians compile data on the size, content, and condition of natural lands, such as rangeland and forests. These workers usually work under the supervision of a conservation scientist or forester, doing specific tasks such as measuring timber, tracking wildlife movement, assisting in road building operations, and locating property lines and features. They may gather basic information, such as data on water and soil quality, disease and insect damage to trees and other plants, and conditions that may pose a fire hazard. In addition, forest and conservation technicians train and lead forest and conservation workers in seasonal activities, such as planting tree seedlings and maintaining recreational facilities. Increasing numbers of forest and conservation technicians work in urban forestry—the study of individual trees in cities—and other nontraditional specialties, rather than in forests or rural areas.

Geological and petroleum technicians assist in oil and gas exploration operations, collecting and examining geological data or testing geological samples to determine their petroleum content and their mineral and element composition. Some petroleum technicians, called scouts, collect information about oil well and gas well drilling operations, geological and geophysical prospecting, and land or lease contracts.

Nuclear technicians operate nuclear test and research equipment, monitor radiation, and assist nuclear engineers and physicists in research. Some also operate remote-controlled equipment to manipulate radioactive materials or materials exposed to radioactivity. Workers who control nuclear reactors are classified as nuclear power reactor operators and are not included in this statement.

Other science technicians perform a wide range of activities. Some collect weather information or assist oceanographers; others work as laser technicians or radiographers.

Work environment. Science technicians work under a wide variety of conditions. Most work indoors, usually in laboratories, and have regular hours. Some occasionally work irregular hours to monitor experiments that cannot be completed during regular working hours. Production technicians often work in 8-hour shifts around the clock. Others, such as agricultural, forest and conservation, geological and petroleum, and environmental science and protection technicians, perform much of their work outdoors, sometimes in remote locations.

Advances in automation and information technology require technicians to operate more sophisticated laboratory equipment. Science technicians make extensive use of computers, electronic measuring equipment, and traditional experimental apparatus.

Some science technicians may be exposed to hazards from equipment, chemicals, or toxic materials. Chemical technicians sometimes work with toxic chemicals or radioactive isotopes; nuclear technicians may be exposed to radiation, and biological technicians sometimes work with disease-causing organisms or radioactive agents. Forensic science technicians often are exposed to human body fluids and firearms. However, these working conditions pose little risk if proper safety procedures are followed. For forensic science technicians, collecting evidence from crime scenes can be distressing and unpleasant.

Training, Other Qualifications, and Advancement

Most science technicians need some formal postsecondary training, such as an associate degree or a certificate in applied science or science-related technology. Biological and forensic science technicians usually need a bachelor's degree. Science technicians with a high school diploma and no college degree typically begin work as trainees under the direct supervision of a more experienced technician, and they eventually earn a 2-year degree in science technology.

Education and training. There are many ways to qualify for a job as a science technician. Most employers prefer applicants who have at least two years of specialized postsecondary training or an associate degree in applied science or science-related technology. Some science technicians have a bachelor's degree in the natural sciences, while others have no formal postsecondary education and learn their skills on the job.

Some science technician specialties have higher education requirements. For example, biological technicians often need a bachelor's degree in biology or a closely related field. Forensic science positions also typically require a bachelor's degree, either in forensic science or another natural science. Knowledge and understanding of legal procedures also can be helpful. Chemical technician positions in research and development also often require a bachelor's degree, but most chemical process technicians have a 2-year degree instead, usually an associate degree in process technology.

Many technical and community colleges offer programs in a specific technology or more general education in science and mathematics. A number of associate degree programs are designed to provide easy transfer to bachelor's degree programs at colleges or universities. Technical institutes usually offer technician training, but they provide less theory and general education than community colleges. The length of programs at technical institutes varies, although one-year certificate programs and two-year associate degree programs are common. Some schools offer cooperative-education or internship programs, allowing students the opportunity to work at a local company or some other workplace while attending classes during

alternate terms. Participation in such programs can significantly enhance a student's employment prospects.

Whatever their formal education, science technicians usually need hands-on training, which they can receive either in school or on the job. Job candidates with extensive hands-on experience using a variety of laboratory equipment, including computers and related equipment, usually require only a short period of on-the-job training. Those with a high school diploma and no college degree typically have a more extensive training program where they work as trainees under the direct supervision of a more experienced technician.

People interested in careers as science technicians should take as many high school science and math courses as possible. Science courses taken beyond high school, in an associate or bachelor's degree program, should be laboratory oriented, with an emphasis on bench skills. A solid background in applied chemistry, physics, and math is vital.

Other qualifications. Communication skills are important because technicians are often required to report their findings both orally and in writing. In addition, technicians should be able to work well with others. Because computers often are used in research and development laboratories, technicians should also have strong computer skills, especially in computer modeling. Organizational ability and skill in interpreting scientific results are important as well, as are high mechanical aptitude, attention to detail, and analytical thinking.

Advancement. Technicians usually begin work as trainees in routine positions under the direct supervision of a scientist or a more experienced technician. As they gain experience, technicians take on more responsibility and carry out assignments under only general supervision, and some eventually become supervisors. Technicians who have a bachelor's degree often are able to advance to scientist positions in their field after a few years of experience working as a technician or after earning a graduate degree.

Employment

Science technicians held about 270,800 jobs in 2008. As indicated by the following tabulation, chemical and biological technicians accounted for 54 percent of all jobs:

Biological technicians	79,500
Chemical technicians	66,100
Environmental science and protection technicians, including health	35,000
Forest and conservation technicians	34,000
Agricultural and food science technicians	21,900
Geological and petroleum technicians	15,200
Forensic science technicians	12,800
Nuclear technicians	6,400

About 30 percent of biological technicians worked in professional, scientific, or technical services firms; most other biological technicians worked in educational services, government, or pharmaceutical and medicine manufacturing. Chemical technicians primarily worked in chemical manufacturing and professional, scientific, or technical services firms. Most environmental science and protection technicians worked for professional, scientific, and technical services firms and for state and local governments. About 75 percent

Projections Data from the National Employment Matrix

Occupational title	SOC Code	Employment, 2008	Projected employment, 2018	Change, 2008–2018	
				Number	Percent
Science technicians..................................... —		270,800	302,600	31,800	12
Agricultural and food science technicians.............. 19-4011		21,900	23,800	1,900	9
Biological technicians.. 19-4021		79,500	93,500	14,000	18
Chemical technicians 19-4031		66,100	65,500	–500	–1
Geological and petroleum technicians 19-4041		15,200	15,400	200	2
Nuclear technicians 19-4051		6,400	7,000	600	9
Environmental science and protection technicians, including health 19-4091		35,000	45,200	10,100	29
Forensic science technicians............................... 19-4092		12,800	15,300	2,500	20
Forest and conservation technicians 19-4093		34,000	36,900	2,900	9

NOTE: Data in this table are rounded.

of forest and conservation technicians held jobs in the federal government, mostly in the Forest Service. Around 34 percent of agricultural and food science technicians worked in educational institutions and 25 percent worked for food manufacturing companies. Forensic science technicians worked primarily for state and local governments. Approximately 56 percent of all geological and petroleum technicians worked in the mining and oil and gas industries, while 51 percent of nuclear technicians worked for utilities.

Job Outlook

Employment of science technicians is projected to grow about as fast as the average for all occupations, although employment change will vary by specialty. Job opportunities are expected to be best for graduates of applied science technology programs who are well trained on equipment used in laboratories or production facilities.

Employment change. Overall employment of science technicians is expected to grow by 12 percent during the 2008–2018 decade, about as fast as the average for all occupations. The continued growth of scientific and medical research—particularly research related to biotechnology—will be the primary driver of employment growth, but the development and production of technical products should also stimulate demand for science technicians in many industries.

Employment of biological technicians should increase by 18 percent, faster than average, as the growing number of agricultural and medicinal products developed from the results of biotechnology research boosts demand for these workers. Also, an aging population and continued competition among pharmaceutical companies are expected to contribute to the need for innovative and improved drugs, further spurring demand. Most growth in employment will be in professional, scientific, and technical services and in educational services.

Job growth for chemical technicians is projected to decline by 1 percent, signifying little or no change. The chemical manufacturing industry, except pharmaceutical and medicine manufacturing, is anticipated to experience a decline in overall employment as companies downsize and turn to outside contractors and overseas production. However, there will still be a need for chemical technicians, particularly in pharmaceutical research.

Employment of environmental science and protection technicians is expected to grow much faster than average, at a rate of 29 percent; these workers will be needed to help regulate waste products; to collect air, water, and soil samples for measuring levels of pollutants; to monitor compliance with environmental regulations; and to clean up contaminated sites. Most of this growth is expected to be in firms that assist other companies in environmental monitoring, management, and regulatory compliance.

Employment of forest and conservation technicians is expected to grow by 9 percent, about as fast as average. Opportunities at state and local governments within specialties such as urban forestry may provide some new jobs. In addition, an increased emphasis on specific conservation issues, such as environmental protection, preservation of water resources, and control of exotic and invasive pests, will spur demand.

Employment of agricultural and food science technicians is projected to grow by 9 percent, about as fast as average. Research in biotechnology and other areas of agricultural science will increase as it becomes more important to balance greater agricultural output with protection and preservation of soil, water, and the ecosystem. In addition, there will be increased research into the use of agricultural products as energy sources, also known as biofuels.

Jobs for forensic science technicians are expected to increase by 20 percent, which is much faster than average. Employment growth in state and local government should be driven by the increasing application of forensic science techniques, such as DNA analysis, to examine, solve, and prevent crime.

Employment growth of about 2 percent, representing little or no change, is expected for geological and petroleum technicians as oil companies continue to search for new resource deposits to meet world demand for petroleum products and natural gas. The outlook for these workers is strongly tied to the price of oil; historically, when prices are low, companies limit exploration and curtail hiring of technicians, but when prices are high, they expand exploration activities. In the long run, continued high oil prices will maintain demand for these workers.

Nuclear technicians should grow by 9 percent, about as fast as average, as more are needed to monitor the nation's aging fleet of nuclear reactors and research future advances in nuclear power. Although no new nuclear power plants have been built for decades in the United States, energy demand has recently renewed interest in this form of electricity generation and may lead to future construction. Technicians also will be needed to work in defense-related areas, to develop nuclear medical technology, and to improve and enforce waste management and safety standards.

Job prospects. In addition to job openings created by growth, many openings should arise from the need to replace technicians who retire or leave the labor force for other reasons. Job opportunities are expected to be best for graduates of applied science technology programs who are well trained on equipment used in laboratories or production facilities. As the instrumentation and techniques used in industrial research, development, and production become increasingly more complex, employers will seek individuals with highly developed technical skills.

Earnings

Median hourly wages of science technicians in May 2008 were as follows:

Nuclear technicians	$32.64
Geological and petroleum technicians	25.65
Forensic science technicians	23.97
Chemical technicians	20.25
Environmental science and protection technicians, including health	19.34
Biological technicians	18.46
Agricultural and food science technicians	16.34
Forest and conservation technicians	15.39

In March 2009, the average annual salary in the federal government was $39,538 for biological science technicians, $55,527 for physical science technicians, and $42,733 for forestry technicians.

Related Occupations

Other technicians who apply scientific principles and who usually have some postsecondary education include broadcast and sound engineering technicians and radio operators; clinical laboratory technologists and technicians; diagnostic medical sonographers; drafters; engineering technicians; and radiologic technologists and technicians.

Sources of Additional Information

General information on a variety of technology fields is available from the Pathways to Technology web site: www.pathwaystotechnology.org

For information about a career as a biological technician, contact

▸ Bio-Link, 1855 Folsom St., Suite 643, San Francisco, CA 94103. Internet: www.bio-link.org

For information about a career as a chemical technician, contact

▸ American Chemical Society, Education Division, Career Publications, 1155 16th St. NW, Washington, DC 20036. Internet: www.acs.org

For career information and a list of undergraduate, graduate, and doctoral programs in forensic sciences, contact

▸ American Academy of Forensic Sciences, 410 N. 21st St., Colorado Springs, CO, 80904. Internet: www.aafs.org

For general information on forestry technicians and a list of schools offering education in forestry, contact

▸ Society of American Foresters, 5400 Grosvenor Ln., Bethesda, MD 20814. Internet: www.safnet.org

Secretaries and Administrative Assistants

(O*NET 43-6011.00, 43-6012.00, 43-6013.00, and 43-6014.00)

Significant Points

■ This occupation ranks among those with the largest number of job openings.

■ Opportunities should be best for applicants with extensive knowledge of computer software applications.

■ Secretaries and administrative assistants are increasingly assuming responsibilities once reserved for managerial and professional staff.

Nature of the Work

As the reliance on technology continues to expand in offices, the role of the office professional has greatly evolved. Office automation and organizational restructuring have led *secretaries and administrative assistants* to increasingly assume responsibilities once reserved for managerial and professional staff. In spite of these changes, however, the core responsibilities for secretaries and administrative assistants have remained much the same: performing and coordinating an office's administrative activities and storing, retrieving, and integrating information for dissemination to staff and clients.

Secretaries and administrative assistants perform a variety of administrative and clerical duties necessary to run an organization efficiently. They serve as information and communication managers for an office; plan and schedule meetings and appointments; organize and maintain paper and electronic files; manage projects; conduct research; and disseminate information by using the telephone, mail services, Web sites, and e-mail. They may also handle travel and guest arrangements.

Secretaries and administrative assistants use a variety of office equipment, such as fax machines, photocopiers, scanners, and videoconferencing and telephone systems. In addition, secretaries and administrative assistants often use computers to do tasks previously handled by managers and professionals; they create spreadsheets, compose correspondence, manage databases, and create presentations, reports, and documents using desktop publishing software and digital graphics. They may also negotiate with vendors, maintain and examine leased equipment, purchase supplies, manage areas such as stockrooms or corporate libraries, and retrieve data from various sources. At the same time, managers and professionals have assumed many tasks traditionally assigned to secretaries and administrative assistants, such as keyboarding and answering the telephone. Because secretaries and administrative assistants do less dictation and word processing, they now have time to support more members of the executive staff. In a number of organizations, secretaries and administrative assistants work in teams to work flexibly and share their expertise.

Many secretaries and administrative assistants provide training and orientation for new staff, conduct research on the Internet, and operate and troubleshoot new office technologies.

Specific job duties vary with experience and titles. *Executive secretaries and administrative assistants* provide high-level administrative support for an office and for top executives of an organization. Generally, they perform fewer clerical tasks than do secretaries and more information management. In addition to arranging conference calls and supervising other clerical staff, they may handle more complex responsibilities such as reviewing incoming memos, submissions, and reports in order to determine their significance and to plan for their distribution. They also prepare agendas and make arrangements for meetings of committees and executive boards. They may also conduct research and prepare statistical reports.

Some secretaries and administrative assistants, such as *legal* and *medical secretaries*, perform highly specialized work requiring knowledge of technical terminology and procedures. For instance, legal secretaries prepare correspondence and legal papers such as summonses, complaints, motions, responses, and subpoenas under the supervision of an attorney or a paralegal. They may also review legal journals and assist with legal research—for example, by verifying quotes and citations in legal briefs. Additionally, legal secretaries often teach newly minted lawyers how to prepare documents for submission to the courts. Medical secretaries transcribe dictation, prepare correspondence, and assist physicians or medical scientists with reports, speeches, articles, and conference proceedings. They also record simple medical histories, arrange for patients to be hospitalized, and order supplies. Most medical secretaries need to be familiar with insurance rules, billing practices, and hospital or laboratory procedures. Other technical secretaries who assist engineers or scientists may prepare correspondence, maintain their organization's technical library, and gather and edit materials for scientific papers.

Secretaries employed in elementary schools and high schools perform important administrative functions for the school. They are responsible for handling most of the communications between parents, the community, and teachers and administrators who work at the school. As such, they are required to know details about registering students, immunizations, and bus schedules, for example. They schedule appointments, keep track of students' academic records, and make room assignments for classes. Those who work directly for principals screen inquiries from parents and handle those matters not needing a principal's attention. They may also set a principal's calendar to help set her or his priorities for the day.

Some secretaries and administrative assistants, also known as *virtual assistants*, are freelancers who work at a home office. They use the Internet, e-mail, fax, and the phone to communicate with clients. Other duties include medical or legal transcription, writing and editing reports and business correspondence, answering e-mail, data entry, setting appointments, making travel arrangements, bookkeeping, and desktop publishing.

Work environment. Secretaries and administrative assistants usually work in schools, hospitals, corporate settings, government agencies, or legal and medical offices. Virtual assistants work from a home office. Their jobs often involve sitting for long periods. If they spend a lot of time keyboarding, particularly at a computer monitor, they may encounter problems of eyestrain, stress, and repetitive motion ailments such as carpal tunnel syndrome.

The majority of secretaries and administrative assistants are full-time employees who work a standard 40-hour week. About 18 percent of secretaries work part time and many others work in temporary positions. A few are self-employed, freelance (such as virtual assistants), or participate in job-sharing arrangements, in which two people divide responsibility for a single job.

Training, Other Qualifications, and Advancement

Word processing, writing, and communication skills are essential for all secretaries and administrative assistants. Employers increasingly require extensive knowledge of computer software applications, such as desktop publishing, project management, spreadsheets, and database management.

Education and training. High school graduates who have basic office skills may qualify for entry-level secretarial positions. They can acquire these skills in various ways. Training ranges from high school vocational education programs that teach office skills and typing to 1-year and 2-year programs in office administration offered by business and vocational-technical schools, and community colleges. Many temporary placement agencies also provide formal training in computer and office skills. Most medical and legal secretaries must go through specialized training programs that teach them the language of the industry. Virtual assistant training programs are available at many community colleges in transcription, bookkeeping, website design, project management, and computer technology. There are also online training and coaching programs.

Employers of executive secretaries increasingly are seeking candidates with a college degree, as these secretaries work closely with top executives. A degree related to the business or industry in which a person is seeking employment may provide the jobseeker with an advantage in the application process.

Most secretaries and administrative assistants, once hired, tend to acquire more advanced skills through on-the-job instruction by other employees or by equipment and software vendors. Others may attend classes or participate in online education to learn how to operate new office technologies, such as information storage systems, scanners, or new updated software packages. As office automation continues to evolve, retraining and continuing education will remain integral parts of secretarial jobs.

Other qualifications. Secretaries and administrative assistants should be proficient in typing and good at spelling, punctuation, grammar, and oral communication. Employers also look for good customer service and interpersonal skills because secretaries and administrative assistants must be tactful in their dealings with people. Discretion, good judgment, organizational or management ability, initiative, and the ability to work independently are especially important for higher-level administrative positions. Changes in the office environment have increased the demand for secretaries and administrative assistants who are adaptable and versatile.

Certification and advancement. Testing and certification for proficiency in office skills are available through organizations such as the International Association of Administrative Professionals; National

Association of Legal Secretaries (NALS), Inc.; Legal Secretaries International, Inc; and International Virtual Assistants Association (IVAA). As secretaries and administrative assistants gain experience, they can earn several different designations. Prominent designations include the Certified Professional Secretary (CPS) and the Certified Administrative Professional (CAP), which can be earned by meeting certain experience or educational requirements and passing an examination. Similarly, those with 1 year of experience in the legal field, or who have concluded an approved training course and who want to be certified as a legal support professional, can acquire the Accredited Legal Secretary (ALS) designation through a testing process administered by NALS. NALS offers two additional designations: Professional Legal Secretary (PLS), considered an advanced certification for legal support professionals, and a designation for proficiency as a paralegal. Legal Secretaries International confers the Certified Legal Secretary Specialist (CLSS) designation in areas such as intellectual property, criminal law, civil litigation, probate, and business law to those who have 5 years of legal experience and pass an examination. In some instances, certain requirements may be waived. There is currently no set standard of certification for virtual assistants. A number of certifications exist which involve passing a written test covering areas of core competencies and business ethics. The IVAA has three certifications available: Certified Virtual Assistant, Ethics Checked Virtual Assistant; and the Real Estate Virtual Assistant.

Secretaries and administrative assistants generally advance by being promoted to other administrative positions with more responsibilities. Qualified administrative assistants who broaden their knowledge of a company's operations and enhance their skills may be promoted to senior or executive secretary or administrative assistant, clerical supervisor, or office manager. Secretaries with word processing or data entry experience can advance to jobs as word processing or data entry trainers, supervisors, or managers within their own firms or in a secretarial, word processing, or data entry service bureau. Secretarial and administrative support experience also can lead to jobs such as instructor or sales representative with manufacturers of software or computer equipment. With additional training, many legal secretaries become paralegals.

Employment

Secretaries and administrative assistants held about 4.3 million jobs in 2008, ranking it among the largest occupations in the U.S. economy. The following tabulation shows the distribution of employment by secretarial specialty:

Secretaries, except legal, medical, and
  executive 2,020,000
Executive secretaries and administrative
  assistants... 1,594,400
Medical secretaries 471,100
Legal secretaries 262,600

Secretaries and administrative assistants are employed in organizations of every type. Around 90 percent are employed in service-providing industries, ranging from education and health care to government and retail trade. Most of the rest work for firms engaged in manufacturing or construction.

Job Outlook

Employment is projected to grow about as fast as the average. Secretaries and administrative assistants will have among the largest number of job openings due to growth and the need to replace workers who transfer to other occupations or leave this occupation. Opportunities should be best for applicants with extensive knowledge of computer software applications.

Employment change. Employment of secretaries and administrative assistants is expected to increase by 11 percent, which is about as fast as the average for all occupations, between 2008 and 2018. Projected employment varies by occupational specialty. Above average employment growth in the health-care and social assistance industry should lead to much faster than the average growth for medical secretaries, while moderate growth in legal services is projected to lead to faster than average growth in employment of legal secretaries. Employment of executive secretaries and administrative assistants is projected to grow as fast as the average for all occupations. Growing industries—such as construction; educational services; health care and social assistance; and professional, scientific, and technical services—will continue to generate the most new jobs. Slower than average growth is expected for secretaries, except legal, medical, or executive, who account for about 46 percent of all secretaries and administrative assistants.

Increasing office automation and organizational restructuring will continue to make secretaries and administrative assistants more productive in coming years. Computers, e-mail, scanners, and voice message systems will allow secretaries and administrative assistants to accomplish more in the same amount of time. The use of automated equipment is also changing the distribution of work in many offices. In some cases, traditional secretarial duties as typing, filing, photocopying, and bookkeeping are being done by clerks in other departments or by the professionals themselves. For example, professionals and managers increasingly do their own word processing and data entry, and handle much of their own correspondence. In some law and medical offices, paralegals and medical assistants are assuming some tasks formerly done by secretaries. Also, many small and medium-sized organizations are outsourcing key administrative functions, such as data entry, bookkeeping, and Internet research, to virtual assistants.

Developments in office technology are certain to continue. However, many secretarial and administrative duties are of a personal, interactive nature and, therefore, are not easily automated. Responsibilities such as planning conferences, working with clients, and instructing staff require tact and communication skills. Because technology cannot substitute for these personal skills, secretaries and administrative assistants will continue to play a key role in most organizations.

As paralegals and medical assistants assume more of the duties traditionally assigned to secretaries, offices will continue to replace the traditional arrangement of one secretary per manager with secretaries and administrative assistants who support the work of systems, departments, or units. This approach means that secretaries and administrative assistants will assume added responsibilities and will be seen as valuable members of a team.

Job prospects. In addition to jobs created from growth, numerous job opportunities will arise from the need to replace secretaries and

Projections Data from the National Employment Matrix

Occupational title	SOC Code	Employment, 2008	Projected employment, 2018	Change, 2008–2018	
				Number	Percent
Secretaries and administrative assistants 43-6000	43-6000	4,348,100	4,819,700	471,600	11
Executive secretaries and administrative assistants 43-6011	43-6011	1,594,400	1,798,800	204,400	13
Legal secretaries 43-6012	43-6012	262,600	311,000	48,400	18
Medical secretaries 43-6013	43-6013	471,100	596,600	125,500	27
Secretaries, except legal, medical, and executive.........43-6014	43-6014	2,020,000	2,113,300	93,300	5

NOTE: Data in this table are rounded.

administrative assistants who transfer to other occupations, including exceptionally skilled executive secretaries and administrative assistants who often move into professional occupations. Job opportunities should be best for applicants with extensive knowledge of computer software applications, with experience as a secretary or administrative assistant, or with advanced communication and computer skills. Applicants with a bachelor's degree will be in great demand to act more as managerial assistants and to perform more complex tasks.

Earnings

Median annual wages of secretaries, except legal, medical, and executive, were $29,050 in May 2008. The middle 50 percent earned between $23,160 and $36,020. The lowest 10 percent earned less than $18,440, and the highest 10 percent earned more than $43,240. Median annual wages in the industries employing the largest numbers of secretaries, except legal, medical, and executive in May 2008 were as follows:

Local government	$32,610
Colleges, universities, and professional schools	31,530
General medical and surgical hospitals	30,960
Elementary and secondary schools	29,850
Employment services	28,340

Median annual wages of executive secretaries and administrative assistants were $40,030 in May 2008. The middle 50 percent earned between $32,410 and $50,280. The lowest 10 percent earned less than $27,030, and the highest 10 percent earned more than $62,070. Median annual wages in the industries employing the largest numbers of executive secretaries and administrative assistants in May 2008 were as follows:

Management of companies and enterprises	$45,190
Local government	41,880
Colleges, universities, and professional schools	39,220
State government	35,540
Employment services	33,820

Median annual wages of legal secretaries were $39,860 in May 2008. The middle 50 percent earned between $30,870 and $50,930. The lowest 10 percent earned less than $25,580, and the highest 10 percent earned more than $62,290. Median annual wages of medical secretaries earned median annual wages of $29,680 in May 2008. The middle 50 percent earned between $24,530 and $36,090. The lowest 10 percent earned less than $20,870, and the highest 10 percent earned more than $42,660.

Virtual assistants set their own rate structure and billing terms based on the type of work, skill level, cost of living in their area, experience, and personal financial needs. Those who bill using an hourly rate can range anywhere from $25 to $100 per hour. Some also bill on a per page or project rate.

Related Occupations

Workers in a number of other occupations also type, record information, and process paperwork. Among them are bookkeeping, accounting, and auditing clerks; communications equipment operators; computer operators; court reporters; data entry and information processing workers; human resources assistants, except payroll and timekeeping; medical assistants; medical records and health information technicians; paralegals and legal assistants; and receptionists and information clerks.

A growing number of secretaries and administrative assistants share in managerial and human resource responsibilities. Occupations requiring these skills include administrative services managers; computer and information systems managers; human resources, training, and labor relations managers and specialists; and office and administrative support worker supervisors and managers.

Sources of Additional Information

State employment offices provide information about job openings for secretaries and administrative assistants.

For information on the latest trends in the profession, career development advice, and the CPS or CAP designations, contact

▶ International Association of Administrative Professionals, P.O. Box 20404, Kansas City, MO 64195-0404. Internet: www.iaap-hq.org

▶ Association of Executive and Administrative Professionals, 900 S. Washington St., Suite G-13, Falls Church, VA 22046. Internet: www.theaeap.com

Information on the CLSS designation can be obtained from

▶ Legal Secretaries International Inc., 2302 Fannin St., Suite 500, Houston, TX 77002-9136. Internet: www.legalsecretaries.org

Information on the ALS, PLS, and paralegal certifications is available from

▶ National Association of Legal Secretaries, Inc., 8159 E. 41st. St., Tulsa, OK 74145. Internet: www.nals.org

Information on virtual assistant certification can be obtained from

▶ International Virtual Assistants Association, 561 Keystone Ave., Suite 309, Reno, NV 89503. Internet: www.ivaa.org

Security Guards and Gaming Surveillance Officers

(O*NET 33-9031.00 and 33-9032.00)

Significant Points

- Job opportunities should be favorable, but competition is expected for some higher-paying jobs.
- Because of limited formal training requirements and flexible hours, this occupation attracts many individuals seeking a second or part-time job.
- These jobs can be hazardous.

Nature of the Work

Security guards, also called *security officers*, patrol and inspect property to protect against fire, theft, vandalism, terrorism, and illegal activity. They protect their employer's property, enforce laws on the property, deter criminal activity, and other problems. These workers may be armed. They use various forms of telecommunications to call for assistance from police, fire, or emergency medical services. Security guards write comprehensive reports outlining their observations and activities during their assigned shift. They also may interview witnesses or victims, prepare case reports, and testify in court.

Although all security guards perform essentially the same function, their specific tasks depend on whether they work in a "static," or stationary, security position or on a mobile patrol. Guards assigned to static security positions usually stay at one location for a specified length of time. These guards must become closely acquainted with the property and people associated with their station and must often monitor alarms and closed-circuit TV cameras. In contrast, guards assigned to mobile patrol drive or walk from one location to another and conduct security checks within an assigned area. They may detain or arrest criminal violators, answer service calls concerning criminal activity or other safety concerns, and issue traffic violation warnings.

The security guard's job responsibilities also vary from one employer to another. In department stores, guards protect people, records, merchandise, money, and equipment. They often work with undercover store detectives to prevent theft by customers or employees, and help apprehend shoplifting suspects prior to the arrival of the police. Some shopping centers and theaters have officers who patrol their parking lots to deter assaults, car thefts, and robberies. In office buildings, banks, and hospitals, guards maintain order and protect the institution's customers, staff, and property. At air, sea, and rail terminals and other transportation facilities, guards and *screeners* protect people, freight, property, and equipment. Using metal detectors and other identification equipment, they may screen passengers and visitors for weapons and explosives, ensure that nothing is stolen while a vehicle is being loaded or unloaded, and watch for fires and criminals.

Guards who work in public buildings such as museums or art galleries protect paintings and exhibits by watching people and inspecting packages entering and leaving the building. In factories,

laboratories, government buildings, data processing centers, and military bases, security officers protect information, products, computer codes, and defense secrets and check the credentials of people and vehicles entering and leaving the premises. Guards working at universities, parks, and sports stadiums perform crowd control, supervise parking and seating, and direct traffic. Security guards stationed at the entrance to bars and nightclubs, prevent access by minors, collect cover charges at the door, maintain order among customers, and protect patrons and property.

Armored car guards protect money and valuables during transit. They also protect individuals responsible for making commercial bank deposits from theft or injury. They pick up money or other valuables from businesses and transport them to another location. Carrying money between the truck and the business can be extremely hazardous. As a result, armored car guards usually wear bulletproof vests and often carry firearms.

Gaming surveillance officers, also known as *surveillance agents*, and *gaming investigators* act as security agents for casino employees, managers, and patrons. Using primarily audio and video equipment in an observation room, they observe casino operations for irregular activities, such as cheating or theft, and monitor compliance with rules, regulations and laws. They maintain and organize recordings from security cameras, since these are sometimes used as evidence in police investigations. Some casinos use a catwalk over one-way mirrors located above the casino floor to augment electronic surveillance equipment. Surveillance agents occasionally leave the surveillance room and walk the casino floor.

All security officers must show good judgment and common sense, follow directions, testify accurately in court, and follow company policy and guidelines. In an emergency, they must be able to take charge and direct others to safety. In larger organizations, a security manager might oversee a group of security officers. In smaller organizations, however, a single worker may be responsible for all security.

Work environment. Most security guards and gaming surveillance officers spend considerable time on their feet, either assigned to a specific post or patrolling buildings and grounds. Guards may be stationed at a guard desk inside a building to monitor electronic security and surveillance devices or to check the credentials of people entering or leaving the premises. They also may be stationed at a guardhouse outside the entrance to a gated facility or community and may use a portable radio or cellular telephone to be in constant contact with a central station. Guards who work during the day may have a great deal of contact with other employees and the public. Gaming surveillance officers often work behind a bank of monitors controlling numerous cameras in a casino and thus can develop eyestrain.

Guards usually work shifts of 8 hours or longer and are often on call in case of an emergency. When employers need 24-hour coverage 7 days a week, guards may rotate work schedules for total coverage. In 2008, about 16 percent of security guards and gaming surveillance officers worked part time, and some held a second job as a guard to supplement their primary earnings.

The work usually is routine, but these jobs can be hazardous. Guards must be constantly alert for threats to themselves and the property they are protecting. In 2008, gaming surveillance workers had one of the highest rates of nonfatal on-the-job injuries.

Training, Other Qualifications, and Advancement

Generally, there are no specific education requirements for security guards, but employers usually prefer to fill armed guard positions with people who have at least a high school diploma. Gaming surveillance officers often need some education beyond high school. In most states, guards must be licensed.

Education and training. Many employers of unarmed guards do not have any specific educational requirements. For armed guards, employers usually prefer individuals who are high school graduates or who hold an equivalent certification.

Many employers give newly hired guards instruction before they start the job and provide on-the-job training. The amount of training guards receive varies. Training is more rigorous for armed guards because their employers are legally responsible for any use of force. Armed guards receive formal training in areas such as weapons retention and laws covering the use of force. They may be periodically tested in the use of firearms.

An increasing number of states are making ongoing training a legal requirement for retention of licensure. Guards may receive training in protection, public relations, report writing, crisis deterrence, first aid, and specialized training relevant to their particular assignment.

ASIS International has written voluntary training guidelines that are intended to provide regulating bodies consistent minimum standards for the quality of security services. These guidelines recommend that security guards receive at least 48 hours of training within the first 100 days of employment. The guidelines also suggest that security guards be required to pass a written or performance examination covering topics such as sharing information with law enforcement, crime prevention, handling evidence, the use of force, court testimony, report writing, interpersonal and communication skills, and emergency response procedures. In addition, they recommend annual retraining and additional firearms training for armed officers.

Some employers prefer to hire security guards with some higher education, such as a police science or criminal justice degree. In addition, there are other programs and courses available at some postsecondary schools that focus specifically on security guards.

Guards who are employed at establishments that place a heavy emphasis on security usually receive extensive formal training. For example, guards at nuclear power plants undergo several months of training before going on duty—and even then, they perform their tasks under close supervision for a significant period of time. They are taught to use firearms, administer first aid, operate alarm systems and electronic security equipment, and spot and deal with security problems.

Gaming surveillance officers and investigators usually need some training beyond high school but not usually a bachelor's degree. Several educational institutes offer certification programs. Classroom training usually is conducted in a casino-like atmosphere and includes the use of surveillance camera equipment. Previous security experience is a plus. Employers prefer either individuals with casino experience and significant knowledge of casino operations or those with law enforcement and investigation experience.

Licensure and certification. Most states require that guards be licensed. To be licensed as a guard, individuals must usually be at least 18 years old, pass a background check, and complete classroom training in such subjects as property rights, emergency procedures, and detention of suspected criminals. Drug testing often is required and may be ongoing and random. Guards who carry weapons must be licensed by the appropriate government authority, and some receive further certification as special police officers, allowing them to make limited types of arrests while on duty. Armed guard positions also have more stringent background checks and entry requirements than those of unarmed guards.

In addition to being licensed, some security guards can become certified. Certifications are not mandatory. ASIS International offers the Certified Protection Professional for security people who want a transferrable validation of their knowledge and skills.

Other qualifications. Most jobs require a driver's license. For positions as armed guards, employers often seek people who have had responsible experience in other occupations or former law enforcement officers.

Rigorous hiring and screening programs consisting of background, criminal record, and fingerprint checks are becoming the norm in the occupation. Applicants are expected to have good character references, no serious police record, and good health. They should be mentally alert, emotionally stable, and physically fit to cope with emergencies. Guards who have frequent contact with the public should have good communication skills.

Like security guards, gaming surveillance officers and gaming investigators must have keen observation skills and excellent verbal and writing abilities to document violations or suspicious behavior. They also need to be physically fit and have quick reflexes because they sometimes must detain individuals until local law enforcement officials arrive.

Advancement. Compared with unarmed security guards, armed guards and special police usually enjoy higher earnings and benefits, greater job security, and more potential for advancement. Because many people do not stay long in this occupation, opportunities for advancement are good for those who make a career in security. Most large organizations use a military type of ranking that offers the possibility of advancement in both position and salary. Some guards may advance to supervisor or security manager positions. Guards with postsecondary education often have an advantage in securing supervisory positions. Guards with management skills may open their own contract security guard agencies. Guards can also move to an organization that needs higher levels of security, which may result in more prestige or higher pay.

Employment

Security guards and gaming surveillance officers held 1.1 million jobs in 2008. About 55 percent of all jobs for security guards were in investigation and security services, including guard and armored car services. These organizations provide security on a contract basis, assigning their guards to buildings and other sites as needed. Most other security officers were employed directly by a wide variety of

Projections Data from the National Employment Matrix

Occupational title	SOC Code	Employment, 2008	Projected employment, 2018	Change, 2008–2018	
				Number	Percent
Security guards and gaming surveillance officers................ 33-9030	33-9030	1,086,000	1,239,500	153,600	14
Gaming surveillance officers and gaming investigators ... 33-9031	33-9031	9,300	10,400	1,100	12
Security guards.. 33-9032	33-9032	1,076,600	1,229,100	152,500	14

NOTE: Data in this table are rounded.

businesses and governments. Guard jobs are found throughout the country, most commonly in metropolitan areas.

Gaming surveillance officers work primarily in gambling industries; traveler accommodation, which includes casino hotels; and local government. They are employed only in those states and on those Indian reservations where gambling is legal.

A significant number of law enforcement officers work as security guards when they are off duty, in order to supplement their incomes. Often working in uniform and with the official cars assigned to them, they add a high-profile security presence to the establishment with which they have contracted. At construction sites and apartment complexes, for example, their presence often deters crime.

Job Outlook

Opportunities for security guards and gaming surveillance officers should be favorable, although competition is expected for some higher paying jobs. Numerous job openings will stem from faster than average employment growth—driven by the demand for increased security—and from the need to replace those who leave this large occupation each year.

Employment change. Employment of security guards is expected to grow by 14 percent between 2008 and 2018, which is faster than the average for all occupations. This occupation will have a very large number of new jobs arise, about 152,500 over the projections decade. Concern about crime, vandalism, and terrorism continues to increase the need for security. Demand for guards also will grow as private security firms increasingly perform duties—such as providing security at public events and in residential neighborhoods—that were formerly handled by police officers. Additionally, private security firms are expected to provide more protection to facilities, such as hospitals and nursing homes.

Employment of gaming surveillance officers and gaming investigators is expected to grow by 12 percent between 2008 and 2018, as fast as the average for all occupations. Casinos will hire more surveillance officers if more states legalize gambling or if the number of casinos increases in states where gambling is already legal. In addition, casino security forces will employ more technically trained personnel as technology becomes increasingly important in thwarting casino cheating and theft.

Job prospects. Job opportunities for security guards should be favorable because of growing demand for these workers and the need to replace experienced workers who leave the occupation. In addition to full-time job opportunities, the limited training requirements and flexible hours attract many people seeking part-time or second jobs. However, competition is expected for higher paying positions that require longer periods of training; these positions usually are found at facilities that require a high level of security, such as nuclear power plants or weapons installations. Applicants with prior experience in the gaming industry should enjoy the best prospects for jobs as gaming surveillance officers.

Earnings

Median annual wages of security guards were $23,460 in May 2008. The middle 50 percent earned between $19,150 and $30,100. The lowest 10 percent earned less than $16,680, and the highest 10 percent earned more than $39,360. Median annual wages in the industries employing the largest numbers of security guards were as follows:

General medical and surgical hospitals $29,020
Elementary and secondary schools 27,980
Local government...27,660
Traveler accommodation.....................................25,660
Investigation and security services 22,170

Gaming surveillance officers and gaming investigators had median annual wages of $28,850 in May 2008. The middle 50 percent earned between $23,000 and $37,690. The lowest 10 percent earned less than $19,290, and the highest 10 percent earned more than $48,310.

Related Occupations

Other security and protective service occupations include correctional officers; gaming services occupations; police and detectives; and private detectives and investigators.

Sources of Additional Information

Further information about work opportunities for guards is available from local security and guard firms and state employment service offices. Information about licensing requirements for guards may be obtained from the state licensing commission or the state police department. In states where local jurisdictions establish licensing requirements, contact a local government authority such as the sheriff, county executive, or city manager.

For more information about security careers, about the Certified Protection Professional, and for a list of colleges and universities offering security-related courses and majors, contact

▸ ASIS International, 1625 Prince St., Alexandria, VA 22314-2818. Internet: www.asisonline.org

For more information related to jobs with the Transportation Security Administration, call the TSA Recruitment Center at (800) 887-1895 or (800) 887-5506 (TTY), or visit their website. Internet: www.tsa.gov/join/careers/careers_security_jobs.shtm

Social and Human Service Assistants

(O*NET 21-1093.00)

Significant Points

- A high school diploma is the minimum educational requirement, but employers often seek individuals with relevant work experience or education beyond high school.

- Employment is projected to grow much faster than the average for all occupations.

- Job opportunities should be excellent, particularly for applicants with appropriate postsecondary education, but wages remain low.

Nature of the Work

Social and human service assistants help social workers, healthcare workers, and other professionals to provide services to people. Social and human service assistant is a generic term for workers with a wide array of job titles, including *human service worker, case management aide, social work assistant, community support worker, mental health aide, community outreach worker, life skills counselor, social services aide, youth worker, psychological aide, client advocate,* or *gerontology aide.* They usually work under the direction of workers from a variety of fields, such as nursing, psychiatry, psychology, or social work. The amount of responsibility and supervision they are given varies a great deal. Some have little direct supervision. For example, they may run a group home. Others work under close direction.

Social and human service assistants provide services to clients to help them improve their quality of life. They assess clients' needs, investigate their eligibility for benefits and services such as food stamps, Medicaid and welfare, and help clients obtain them. They also arrange for transportation, if necessary, and provide emotional support. They monitor and keep case records on clients and report progress to supervisors and case managers.

Social and human service assistants play a variety of roles in the community. For example, they may organize and lead group activities, assist clients in need of counseling or crisis intervention, or administer food banks or emergency fuel programs. In halfway houses, group homes, and government-supported housing programs, they assist adults who need supervision with personal hygiene and daily living tasks. They review clients' records, ensure that they take prescribed medication, talk with family members, and confer with medical personnel and other caregivers to provide insight into clients' needs. Assistants also give emotional support and help clients become involved in community recreation programs and other activities.

In psychiatric hospitals, rehabilitation programs, and outpatient clinics, social and human service assistants work with psychiatrists, psychologists, social workers, and others to help clients master everyday living skills, communicate more effectively, and live well with others. They support the client's participation in a treatment plan, such as individual or group counseling or occupational therapy.

The work, while satisfying, can be emotionally draining. Understaffing and relatively low pay can add to the pressure.

Work environment. Working conditions of social and human service assistants vary. Some work in offices, clinics, and hospitals, while others work in group homes, shelters, and day programs. Traveling to see clients is required for some jobs. Sometimes working with clients can be dangerous, even though most agencies do everything they can to ensure their workers' safety. Some work in the evening and on weekends.

Training, Other Qualifications, and Advancement

A high school diploma is the minimum education requirement, but employers often seek individuals with relevant work experience or education beyond high school.

Education and training. Many employers prefer to hire people with some education beyond high school. Certificates or associate degrees in subjects such as human services, gerontology or one of the social or behavioral sciences meet many employers' requirements. Some jobs may require a bachelor's or master's degree in human services or a related field, such as counseling, rehabilitation, or social work.

Human services degree programs have a core curriculum that trains students to observe patients and record information, conduct patient interviews, implement treatment plans, employ problem-solving techniques, handle crisis intervention matters, and use proper case management and referral procedures. Many programs utilize field work to give students hands-on experience. General education courses in liberal arts, sciences, and the humanities also are part of most curriculums. Most programs also offer specialized courses related to addictions, gerontology, child protection, and other areas. Many degree programs require completion of a supervised internship.

Workers level of education often determines the kind of work they are assigned and the degree of responsibility that is given to them. For example, workers with no more than a high school education are likely to work in direct-care services and helping clients to fill out paperwork. They may receive extensive on-the-job training on how to perform these tasks. Workers with a college degree, however, might do supportive counseling, coordinate program activities, or manage a group home. Social and human service assistants with proven leadership ability, especially acquired from paid or volunteer experience in social services, often have greater autonomy in their work. Regardless of the academic or work background of employees, most employers provide some form of in-service training, such as seminars and workshops, to their employees.

Other qualifications. These workers should have a strong desire to help others, effective communication skills, a sense of responsibility, and the ability to manage time effectively. Many human services jobs involve direct contact with people who are vulnerable to exploitation or mistreatment; so patience and understanding are also highly valued characteristics.

It is becoming more common for employers to require a criminal background check, and in some settings, workers may be required to have a valid driver's license.

Projections Data from the National Employment Matrix

Occupational title	SOC Code	Employment, 2008	Projected employment, 2018	Change, 2008–2018	
				Number	Percent
Social and human service assistants.......................... 21-1093		352,000	431,500	374,700	23

NOTE: Data in this table are rounded.

Advancement. Formal education is almost always necessary for advancement. In general, advancement to case management, or social work jobs requires a bachelor's or master's degree in human services, counseling, rehabilitation, social work, or a related field.

Employment

Social and human service assistants held about 352,000 jobs in 2008. More than 65 percent were employed in the health-care and social assistance industries and almost 24 percent were employed by state and local governments.

Job Outlook

Employment of social and human service assistants is expected to grow much faster than the average for all occupations. Job prospects are expected to be excellent, particularly for applicants with relevant postsecondary education.

Employment change. The number of social and human service assistants is expected to grow by nearly 23 percent between 2008 and 2018, which is much faster than the average for all occupations. This is due in large part to the aging population and increased demand for mental health and substance abuse treatment.

As the elderly population continues to grow, the demand for social and human service assistants will expand. This is due in large part to the increased need for social services demanded by this population, such as adult day care, meal delivery programs and support during medical crises. Social and human service assistants, who assist in locating and providing these services, will be needed to meet this increased demand.

Opportunities are expected to be good in private social service agencies. Employment in private agencies will grow, as state and local governments continue to contract out services to the private sector in an effort to cut costs.

The number of jobs for social and human service assistants in state and local governments will grow, but not as fast as employment for social and human service assistants in other industries. Employment in the public sector may fluctuate with the level of funding provided by state and local governments and with the number of services contracted out to private organizations.

Job prospects. Job prospects for social and human service assistants are expected to be excellent, particularly for individuals with appropriate education after high school. Job openings will come from job growth, but also from the need to replace workers, who advance into new positions, retire, or leave the workforce for other reasons. There will be more competition for jobs in urban areas than in rural ones, but qualified applicants should have little difficulty finding employment.

Earnings

Median annual wages of social and human service assistants were $27,280 in May 2008. The middle 50 percent earned between $21,860 and $34,590. The top 10 percent earned more than $43,510, while the lowest 10 percent earned less than $17,900.

Median annual wages in the industries employing the largest numbers of social and human service assistants in May 2008 were the following:

State government...$35,510
Local government... 32,560
Individual and family services............................ 26,250
Vocational rehabilitation services 23,910
Residential mental retardation, mental health
and substance abuse facilities........................... 23,580

Related Occupations

Workers in other occupations that require skills similar to those of social and human service assistants include child care workers; correctional officers; counselors; eligibility interviewers, government programs; health educators; home health aides and personal and home care aides; occupational therapist assistants and aides; probation officers and correctional treatment specialists; psychologists; recreational therapists; and social workers.

Sources of Additional Information

For information on programs and careers in human services, contact

▸ Council for Standards in Human Services Education, 1935 S. Plum Grove Rd., PMB 297, Palatine, IL 60067. Internet: www.cshse.org

▸ National Organization for Human Services, 5341 Old Highway 5, Suite 206, #214, Woodstock, GA 30188. Internet: www.nationalhumanservices.org

Information on job openings may be available from state employment service offices or directly from city, county, or state departments of health, mental health and mental retardation, and human resources.

Social Workers

(O*NET 21-1021.00, 21-1022.00, 21-1023.00, and 21-1029.00)

Significant Points

■ Employment is projected to grow faster than the average for all occupations.

■ About 54 percent of jobs are in health care and social assistance industries, and 31 percent work for government.

- While a bachelor's degree is necessary for entry-level positions, a master's degree in social work or a related field is necessary for some positions.

- Job prospects are expected to be favorable, particularly for social workers who specialize in the aging population or work in rural areas.

Nature of the Work

Social work is a profession for those with a strong desire to help improve people's lives. *Social workers* assist people by helping them cope with and solve issues in their everyday lives, such as family and personal problems and dealing with relationships. Some social workers help clients who face a disability, life-threatening disease, social problem, such as inadequate housing, unemployment, or substance abuse. Social workers also assist families that have serious domestic conflicts, sometimes involving child or spousal abuse. Additionally, they may conduct research, advocate for improved services, or become involved in planning or policy development. Many social workers specialize in serving a particular population or working in a specific setting. In all settings, these workers may also be called *licensed clinical social workers*, if they hold the appropriate state mandated license.

Child, family, and school social workers provide social services and assistance to improve the social and psychological functioning of children and their families. Workers in this field assess their client's needs and offer assistance to improve their situation. This often includes coordinating available services to assist a child or family. They may assist single parents in finding day care, arrange adoptions, or help find foster homes for neglected, abandoned, or abused children. These workers may specialize in working with a particular problem, population or setting, such as child protective services, adoption, homelessness, domestic violence, or foster care.

In schools, social workers often serve as the link between students' families and the school, working with parents, guardians, teachers, and other school officials to ensure that students reach their academic and personal potential. They also assist students in dealing with stress or emotional problems. Many school social workers work directly with children with disabilities and their families. In addition, they address problems such as misbehavior, truancy, teenage pregnancy, and drug and alcohol problems and advise teachers on how to cope with difficult students. School social workers may teach workshops to entire classes on topics like conflict resolution.

Child, family, and school social workers may be known as child welfare social workers, family services social workers, or child protective services social workers. These workers often work for individual and family services agencies, schools, or state or local governments.

Medical and public health social workers provide psychosocial support to individuals, families, or vulnerable populations so they can cope with chronic, acute, or terminal illnesses, such as Alzheimer's disease, cancer, or AIDS. They also advise family caregivers, counsel patients, and help plan for patients' needs after discharge from hospitals. They may arrange for at-home services, such as meals-on-wheels or home care. Some work on interdisciplinary teams that evaluate certain kinds of patients, such as geriatric or organ transplant patients.

Some specialize in services for senior citizens and their families. These social workers may run support groups for the adult children of aging parents. Also, they may assess, coordinate, and monitor services such as housing, transportation, and long-term care. These workers may be known as gerontological social workers.

Medical and public health social workers may work for hospitals, nursing and personal care facilities, individual and family services agencies, or local governments.

Mental health and substance abuse social workers assess and treat individuals with mental illness or substance abuse problems. Such services include individual and group therapy, outreach, crisis intervention, social rehabilitation, and teaching skills needed for everyday living. They also may help plan for supportive services to ease clients' return to the community when leaving in-patient facilities. They may provide services to assist family members of those who suffer from addiction or other mental health issues. These workers may work in outpatient facilities, where clients come in for treatment and then leave, or in inpatient programs, where patients reside at the facility. Some mental health and substance social workers may work in employee-assistance programs. In this setting, they may help people cope with job-related pressures or with personal problems that affect the quality of their work. Other social workers work in private practice, where they are employed directly by the client. These social workers may be known as *clinical social workers*, *occupational social workers*, or *substance abuse social workers*.

Other types of social workers include *social work administrators*, *researchers*, *planners* and *policymakers*, who develop and implement programs to address issues such as child abuse, homelessness, substance abuse, poverty, and violence. These workers research and analyze policies, programs, and regulations. They identify social problems and suggest legislative and other solutions. They may help raise funds or write grants to support these programs.

Work environment. Social workers usually spend most of their time in an office or residential facility, but they also may travel locally to visit clients, meet with service providers, or attend meetings. Some may meet with clients in one of several offices within a local area. Social work, while satisfying, can be challenging. Understaffing and large caseloads add to the pressure in some agencies. Full-time social workers usually work a standard 40-hour week, but some occasionally work evenings and weekends to meet with clients, attend community meetings, and handle emergencies. Some work part time, particularly in voluntary nonprofit agencies.

Training, Other Qualifications, and Advancement

A bachelor's degree is the minimum requirement for entry into the occupation, but some positions require an advanced degree. All states and the District of Columbia have some licensure, certification, or registration requirement; but these regulations vary.

Education and training. A bachelor's degree in social work (BSW) is the most common minimum requirement to qualify for a job as a social worker; however, majors in psychology, sociology, and related fields may qualify for some entry-level jobs, especially in small community agencies. Although a bachelor's degree is sufficient for entry into the field, an advanced degree is required for some positions. A master's degree in social work (MSW) is typically required for positions in health and school settings and is required for clinical work, as well. Some jobs in public and private agencies may require an advanced degree, such as an MSW with a concentration in social services policy or administration. Supervisory, administrative, and staff training positions usually require an advanced degree. College and university teaching positions and most research appointments normally require a doctorate in social work (DSW or Ph.D.).

As of June 2009, the Council on Social Work Education accredited 468 bachelor's programs and 196 master's programs. The Group for the Advancement of Doctoral Education listed 74 doctoral programs in social work (DSW or Ph.D.) in the United States. Bachelor degree programs prepare graduates for direct service positions, such as caseworker, mental health assistant, group home worker and residential counselor. These programs include courses in social work values and ethics, dealing with a culturally diverse clientele and at-risk populations, promotion of social and economic justice, human behavior and the social environment, social welfare policy and services, social work practice, social research methods, and field education. Accredited programs require a minimum of 400 hours of supervised field experience.

Master's degree programs prepare graduates for work in their chosen field of concentration and continue to develop the skills required to perform clinical assessments, manage large caseloads, take on supervisory roles, and explore new ways of drawing upon social services to meet the needs of clients. Master's programs usually last 2 years and include a minimum of 900 hours of supervised field instruction or internship. A part-time program may take 4 years. Entry into a master's program does not require a bachelor's degree in social work, but courses in psychology, biology, sociology, economics, political science, and social work are recommended. In addition, a second language can be very helpful. Most master's programs offer advanced standing for those with a bachelor's degree from an accredited social work program.

Licensure. All states and the District of Columbia have licensing, certification, or registration requirements regarding social work practice and the use of professional titles. Most states require 2 years or 3,000 hours of supervised clinical experience for licensure of clinical social workers. Due to some limitations on what settings unlicensed social workers may work and some variation in the requirements to obtain a license, those interested in becoming a social worker should research requirements in their state.

Other qualifications. Social workers should be emotionally mature, objective, and sensitive to people and their problems. They must be able to handle responsibility, work independently, and maintain good working relationships with clients and coworkers. Volunteer or paid jobs as a social work aide can help people test their interest in this field.

Certification and advancement. Advancement to supervisor, program manager, assistant director, or executive director of a social service agency or department usually requires an advanced degree and related work experience. Other career options for social workers include teaching, research, and consulting. Some of these workers help formulate government policies, by analyzing and advocating policy positions in government agencies, in research institutions, and on legislators' staffs.

Some social workers go into private practice. Most private practitioners are clinical social workers who provide psychotherapy, usually paid for through health insurance or by the client themselves. Private practitioners must have at least a master's degree and a period of supervised work experience. A network of contacts for referrals also is essential.

Employment

Social workers held about 642,000 jobs in 2008. About 54 percent jobs were in health-care and social assistance industries, and 31 percent were employed by government agencies. Although most social workers are employed in cities or suburbs, some work in rural areas. Employment by type of social worker, in 2008, follows:

Child, family and school social workers 292,600
Medical and public health social workers 138,700
Mental health and substance abuse social
   workers 137,300
Social workers, all other 73,400

Job Outlook

Employment for social workers is expected to grow faster than the average for all occupations through 2018. Job prospects are expected to be favorable, particularly for social workers who specialize in the aging population or work in rural areas.

Employment change. Employment of social workers is expected to increase by 16 percent during the 2008–2018 decade, which is faster than the average for all occupations. The growing elderly population and the aging baby boom generation will create greater demand for health and social services, resulting in rapid job growth among gerontological social workers. Employment of social workers in private social service agencies also will increase.

Employment of child, family, and school social workers is expected to grow by about 12 percent, which is as fast as the average for all occupations. Demand for child and family social workers should continue, as these workers are needed to investigate child abuse cases, place children in foster care and with adoptive families. However, growth for these workers may be hampered by the budget constraints of state and local governments, who are amongst the largest employers of these workers. Furthermore, demand for school social workers will continue and lead to more jobs as efforts are expanded to respond to rising student enrollments, as well as the continued emphasis on integrating children with disabilities into the general school population. There could be competition for school social work jobs in some areas because of the limited number of openings. The availability of federal, state, and local funding will be a major factor in determining the actual job growth in schools.

Mental health and substance abuse social workers will grow by almost 20 percent over the 2008–2018 decade, which is much faster than the average. In particular, social workers specializing in substance abuse will experience strong demand. Substance abusers are increasingly being placed into treatment programs instead of being sentenced to prison. Also, growing numbers of the substance abusers sentenced to prison or probation are, increasingly being required by correctional systems to have substance abuse treatment added as a condition to their sentence or probation. As this trend grows, demand will strengthen for treatment programs and social workers to assist abusers on the road to recovery. Opportunities for social workers in private practice will expand, as they are preferred over more costly psychologists. Furthermore, the passage of legislation that requires insurance plans offered by employers to cover mental health treatment in a manner that is equal to treatment of physical health may increase the demand for mental health treatment.

Growth of medical and public health social workers is expected to be about 22 percent, which is much faster than the average for all occupations. One of the major contributing factors is the rise in the elderly population. These social workers will be needed to assist in finding the best care and assistance for the aging, as well as to support their families. Employment opportunities for social workers with backgrounds in gerontology should be excellent, particularly in the growing numbers of assisted-living and senior-living communities. The expanding senior population also will spur demand for social workers in nursing homes, long-term care facilities, home care agencies, and hospices.

Job prospects. Job prospects are expected to be favorable. Many job openings will stem from growth and the need to replace social workers who leave the occupation. However, competition for social worker jobs is expected in cities where training programs for social workers are prevalent. Opportunities should be good in rural areas, which often find it difficult to attract and retain qualified staff. By specialty, job prospects may be best for those social workers with a background in gerontology and substance abuse treatment.

Earnings

Median annual wages of child, family, and school social workers were $39,530 in May 2008. The middle 50 percent earned between $31,040 and $52,080. The lowest 10 percent earned less than $25,870, and the top 10 percent earned more than $66,430. Median annual wages in the industries employing the largest numbers of child, family, and school social workers in May 2008 were the following:

Elementary and secondary schools	$53,860
Local government	46,650
State government	39,600
Individual and family services	34,450
Other residential care facilities	34,270

Median annual wages of medical and public health social workers were $46,650 in May 2008. The middle 50 percent earned between $35,550 and $57,690. The lowest 10 percent earned less than $28,100, and the top 10 percent earned more than $69,090. Median

annual wages in the industries employing the largest numbers of medical and public health social workers in May 2008 were the following:

General medical and surgical hospitals	$51,470
Home health care services	46,930
Local government	44,140
Nursing care facilities	41,080
Individual and family services	38,370

Median annual wages of mental health and substance abuse social workers were $37,210 in May 2008. The middle 50 percent earned between $28,910 and $48,560. The lowest 10 percent earned less than $21,770, and the top 10 percent earned more than $61,430. Median annual wages in the industries employing the largest numbers of mental health and substance abuse social workers in May 2008 were the following:

Outpatient care centers	$36,660
Individual and family services	35,900
Residential mental retardation, mental health and substance abuse facilities	33,950

Median annual wages of social workers, all other were $46,220 in May 2008. The middle 50 percent earned between $34,420 and $60,850. The lowest 10 percent earned less than $27,400, and the top 10 percent earned more than $74,040. Median annual wages in the industries employing the largest numbers of social workers, all other in May 2008 were as follows:

General medical and surgical hospitals	$55,940
Local government	51,700
Individual and family services	36,660
Residential mental retardation, mental health and substance abuse facilities	36,460
Community food and housing, and emergency and other relief services	31,890

About 24 percent of social workers are members of a union or covered by a union contract.

Related Occupations

Through direct counseling or referral to other services, social workers help people solve a range of personal problems. Workers in occupations with similar duties include clergy; counselors; health educators; probation officers and correctional treatment specialists; psychologists; and social and human service assistants.

Projections Data from the National Employment Matrix

Occupational title	SOC Code	Employment, 2008	Projected employment, 2018	Change, 2008–2018	
				Number	Percent
Social workers	21-1020	642,000	745,400	103,400	16
Child, family, and school social workers	21-1021	292,600	328,700	36,100	12
Medical and public health social workers	21-1022	138,700	169,800	31,100	22
Mental health and substance abuse social workers	21-1023	137,300	164,100	26,800	20
Social workers, all other	21-1029	73,400	82,800	9,400	13

NOTE: Data in this table are rounded.

Sources of Additional Information

For information about career opportunities in social work and voluntary credentials for social workers, contact

▸ National Association of Social Workers, 750 First St. NE, Suite 700, Washington, DC 20002-4241. Internet: www.socialworkers.org

▸ Center for Clinical Social Work, 27 Congress St., Suite 501, Salem, MA 01970. Internet: www.centercsw.org

For a listing of accredited social work programs, contact

▸ Council on Social Work Education, 1725 Duke St., Suite 500, Alexandria, VA 22314-3457. Internet: www.cswe.org

Information on licensing requirements and testing procedures for each state may be obtained from state licensing authorities, or from

▸ Association of Social Work Boards, 400 South Ridge Pkwy., Suite B, Culpeper, VA 22701. Internet: www.aswb.org

Stock Clerks and Order Fillers

(O*NET 43-5081.00, 43-5081.01, 43-5081.02, 43-5081.03, and 43-5081.04)

Nature of the Work

Stock clerks receive merchandise in stores, warehouses, stockrooms, and other storage facilities; unpack it; mark items with identifying codes, such as price, stock, or inventory control codes; stock shelves; and help customers with their packages. *Order fillers* complete customers mail, Web, and phone orders by retrieving the ordered merchandise, computing the prices and recording the sale, and preparing it for shipment. Most jobs are physically demanding and may result in minor muscle ailments, scrapes, or other injuries. In retail establishments, evening and weekend hours are common.

Training, Other Qualifications, and Advancement

A high school diploma or GED is usually sufficient for this occupation. Most stock clerks and order fillers learn their jobs through short-term on-the-job training.

Job Outlook

Current and Projected Employment

2008 Employment	1,858,840
2018 Employment	1,993,280
Employment Change	134,400
Growth Rate	7%

Employment change. Average growth in the employment of stock clerks and order fillers is expected. Most stock clerks and order fillers work in retail trade, most notably in grocery and department stores, stocking shelves and retrieving items for customers. These tasks, which usually require handling small quantities of items, are difficult to automate.

Job prospects. Numerous job openings will occur due to the need to replace workers who leave the occupation, a characteristic of very large occupations with minimal training requirements. Job openings in grocery, general merchandise, clothing, and department stores will be greater than in other industries, because much of the work is done manually and is difficult to automate.

Earnings

Median annual wages for stock clerks and order fillers were $20,800 in May 2008.

For current wage data, visit the Occupational Employment Statistics program's Occupational Profile for stock clerks and order fillers.

Related Occupations

Shipping, receiving, and traffic clerks; production, planning, and expediting clerks; order clerks; and procurement clerks.

Surgical Technologists

(O*NET 29-2055.00)

Significant Points

- Employment is expected to grow much faster than average.

- Job opportunities will be best for technologists who are certified and for those who are willing to relocate.

- Training programs last 9 to 24 months and lead to a certificate, diploma, or associate's degree.

- Hospitals will continue to be the primary employer, although much faster employment growth is expected in other health-care industries.

Nature of the Work

Surgical technologists, also called *scrubs* and *surgical* or *operating room technicians*, assist in surgical operations under the supervision of surgeons, registered nurses, or other surgical personnel. Surgical technologists are members of operating room teams, which most commonly include surgeons, anesthesiologists, and circulating nurses.

Before an operation, surgical technologists help prepare the operating room by setting up surgical instruments and equipment, sterile drapes, and sterile solutions. They assemble both sterile and nonsterile equipment, as well as check and adjust it to ensure that it is working properly. Technologists also get patients ready for surgery by washing, shaving, and disinfecting incision sites. They transport patients to the operating room, help position them on the operating table, and cover them with sterile surgical drapes. Technologists also observe patients' vital signs, check charts, and help the surgical team put on sterile gowns and gloves.

During surgery, technologists pass instruments and other sterile supplies to surgeons and surgical assistants. They may hold retractors, cut sutures, and help count sponges, needles, supplies, and instruments. Surgical technologists help prepare, care for, and dispose of specimens taken for laboratory analysis and help apply dressings. Some operate sterilizers, lights, or suction machines and help operate diagnostic equipment.

After an operation, surgical technologists may help transfer patients to the recovery room and clean and restock the operating room.

Certified surgical technologists with additional specialized education or training also may act in the role of the *surgical first assistant* or *circulator*. Under the surgeon's direction, the surgical first assistant, as defined by the American College of Surgeons (ACS), provides aid in exposure, hemostasis (controlling blood flow and stopping or preventing hemorrhage), and other technical functions that help the surgeon carry out a safe operation. A circulating technologist is the "unsterile" member of the surgical team who interviews the patient before surgery, prepares the patient for surgery, helps with anesthesia, obtains and opens packages for the "sterile" people to remove the sterile contents during the procedure, keeps a written account of the surgical procedure, and answers the surgeon's questions about the patient during the surgery.

Work environment. Surgical technologists work in clean, well-lighted, cool environments. They must stand for long periods and remain alert during operations. At times, they may be exposed to communicable diseases and unpleasant sights, odors, and materials.

Most surgical technologists work a regular 40-hour week, although they may be on call or work nights, weekends, and holidays on a rotating basis.

Training, Other Qualifications, and Advancement

Training programs last 9 to 24 months and lead to a certificate, diploma, or associate degree. Professional certification can help in getting jobs and promotions.

Education and training. Surgical technologists receive their training in formal programs offered by community and junior colleges, vocational schools, universities, hospitals, and the military. In 2008, the Commission on Accreditation of Allied Health Education Programs (CAAHEP) recognized more than 450 accredited training programs. Programs last from 9 to 24 months and lead to a certificate, diploma, or associate degree. High school graduation normally is required for admission. Recommended high school courses include health, biology, chemistry, and mathematics.

Programs provide classroom education and supervised clinical experience. Students take courses in anatomy, physiology, microbiology, pharmacology, professional ethics, and medical terminology. Other topics covered include the care and safety of patients during surgery, sterile techniques, and surgical procedures. Students also learn to sterilize instruments; prevent and control infection; and handle special drugs, solutions, supplies, and equipment.

Certification and other qualifications. Most employers prefer to hire certified technologists. Technologists may obtain voluntary professional certification from the Liaison Council on Certification for the Surgical Technologist by graduating from a CAAHEP-accredited program and passing a national certification examination. They may then use the Certified Surgical Technologist (CST) designation. In order to maintain certification, certified surgical technologists must earn 60 hours of approved continuing education over a 4-year period or retake and pass the certifying exam at the end of the 4-year period.

Certification also may be obtained from the National Center for Competency Testing (NCCT). To qualify to take the exam, candidates follow one of three paths: complete an accredited training program, undergo a 2-year hospital on-the-job training program, or acquire 7 years of experience working in the field. After passing the exam, individuals may use the designation Tech in Surgery-Certified, TS-C (NCCT). This certification must be renewed every 5 years through either continuing education or reexamination.

Surgical technologists need manual dexterity to handle instruments quickly. They also must be conscientious, orderly, and emotionally stable to handle the demands of the operating room environment. Technologists must respond quickly and must be familiar with operating procedures in order to have instruments ready for surgeons without having to be told to do so. They are expected to keep abreast of new developments in the field.

Advancement. Technologists advance by specializing in a particular area of surgery, such as neurosurgery or open-heart surgery. They also may work as circulating technologists. With additional training, some technologists advance to first assistant. Some surgical technologists manage central supply departments in hospitals or take positions with insurance companies, sterile supply services, and operating equipment firms.

Employment

Surgical technologists held about 91,500 jobs in 2008. About 71 percent of jobs for surgical technologists were in hospitals, mainly in operating and delivery rooms. Other jobs were in offices of physicians or dentists who perform outpatient surgery and in outpatient care centers, including ambulatory surgical centers. A few technologists, known as private scrubs, are employed directly by surgeons who have special surgical teams, such as those for liver transplants.

Job Outlook

Employment is expected to grow much faster than average. Job opportunities will be best for technologists who are certified and for those who are willing to relocate.

Employment change. Employment of surgical technologists is expected to grow 25 percent between 2008 and 2018, much faster than the average for all occupations, as the volume of surgeries increases. The number of surgical procedures is expected to continue to rise as the population grows and ages. Older people, including the baby-boom generation, which generally requires more surgical procedures, will continue to account for a larger portion of the U.S. population. In addition, technological advances, such as fiber optics and laser technology, have permitted an increasing number of new surgical procedures to be performed and also have allowed surgical technologists to assist with a greater number of procedures.

Hospitals will continue to be the primary employer of surgical technologists, as they try to reduce costs by replacing nurses in the operating room. However, because of better paying opportunities, much faster employment growth is expected in offices of physicians and in outpatient care centers, including ambulatory surgical centers.

Job prospects. Job opportunities will be best for technologists who are certified and for those who are willing to relocate.

Projections Data from the National Employment Matrix

Occupational title	SOC Code	Employment, 2008	Projected employment, 2018	Change, 2008–2018	
				Number	Percent
Surgical technologists 29-2055		91,500	114,700	23,200	25

NOTE: Data in this table are rounded.

Earnings

Median annual wages of wage-and-salary surgical technologists were $38,740 in May 2008. The middle 50 percent earned between $32,490 and $46,910. The lowest 10 percent earned less than $27,510, and the highest 10 percent earned more than $54,300. Median annual wages in the industries employing the largest numbers of surgical technologists were as follows:

Specialty (except psychiatric and substance abuse) hospitals..$40,880	
Outpatient care centers...................................... 39,660	
General medical and surgical hospitals 38,640	
Offices of physicians.. 38,520	
Offices of dentists 36,380	

Wages of surgical technologists vary with their experience and education, the responsibilities of the position, the working hours, and the economy of a given region of the country. Benefits provided by most employers include paid vacation and sick leave; health, medical, vision, dental, and life insurance; and a retirement program. A few employers also provide tuition reimbursement and child care benefits.

Related Occupations

Other health occupations requiring approximately 1 year of training after high school include the following clinical laboratory technologists and technicians; dental assistants; licensed practical and licensed vocational nurses; and medical assistants.

Sources of Additional Information

For additional information on a career as a surgical technologist, and for a list of CAAHEP-accredited programs, contact

▸ Association of Surgical Technologists, 6 W. Dry Creek Circle, Suite 200, Littleton, CO 80120. Internet: www.ast.org

For information on becoming a Certified Surgical Technologist, contact

▸ Liaison Council on Certification for the Surgical Technologist, 6 W. Dry Creek Circle, Suite 100, Littleton, CO 80120. Internet: www.lcc-st.org

For information on becoming a Tech in Surgery-Certified, contact

▸ National Center for Competency Testing, 7007 College Blvd., Suite 705, Overland Park, KS 66211.

Surveyors, Cartographers, Photogrammetrists, and Surveying and Mapping Technicians

(O*NET 17-1021.00, 17-1022.00, 17-1022.01, 17-3031.00, 17-3031.01, and 17-3031.02)

Significant Points

■ About 7 out of 10 jobs are in architectural, engineering, and related services.

■ Employment is expected to grow faster than the average for all occupations.

■ Surveyors, cartographers, and photogrammetrists who have a bachelor's degree and strong technical skills should have favorable job prospects.

Nature of the Work

Surveyors, cartographers, photogrammetrists, and surveying and mapping technicians are responsible for measuring and mapping the Earth's surface. *Surveyors* establish official land, airspace, and water boundaries. They write descriptions of land for deeds, leases, and other legal documents; define airspace for airports; and take measurements of construction and mineral sites. Other surveyors provide data about the shape, contour, location, elevation, or dimension of land or land features. *Cartographers and photogrammetrists* collect, analyze, interpret, and map geographic information using data from surveys and photographs. *Surveying and mapping technicians* assist these professionals by collecting data in the field, making calculations, and helping with computer-aided drafting. Collectively, these occupations play key roles in the field of geospatial information.

Surveyors measure distances, directions, and angles between points on, above, and below the Earth's surface. In the field, they select known survey reference points and determine the precise location of important features in the survey area using specialized equipment. Surveyors also research legal records, look for evidence of previous boundaries, and analyze data to determine the location of boundary lines. They are sometimes called to provide expert testimony in court regarding their work or the work of other surveyors. Surveyors also record their results, verify the accuracy of data, and prepare plots, maps, and reports.

Some surveyors perform specialized functions that support the work of other surveyors, cartographers, and photogrammetrists. For example, *geodetic surveyors* use high-accuracy techniques, including satellite observations, to measure large areas of the earth's surface. *Geophysical prospecting surveyors* mark sites for subsurface exploration, usually to look for petroleum. *Marine or hydrographic surveyors* survey harbors, rivers, and other bodies of water to determine shorelines, the topography of the bottom, water depth, and other features.

Surveyors use the Global Positioning System (GPS) to locate reference points with a high degree of precision. To use this system, a surveyor places a satellite signal receiver—a small instrument mounted on a tripod—on a desired point, and another receiver on a point for which the geographic position is known. The receiver simultaneously collects information from several satellites and the known reference point to establish a precise position. The receiver also can be placed in a vehicle for tracing out road systems. Because receivers now come in different sizes and shapes, and because the cost of receivers has fallen, much more surveying work can be done with GPS. Surveyors then interpret and check the results produced by GPS.

Field measurements are often taken by a survey party that gathers the information needed by the surveyor. A typical survey party consists of a *party chief* and one or more surveying technicians and helpers. The party chief, who may be either a surveyor or a senior surveying technician, leads day-to-day work activities. Surveying technicians assist the party chief by adjusting and operating surveying instruments, such as the total station, which measures and records angles and distances simultaneously. Surveying technicians compile notes, make sketches, and enter the data obtained from surveying instruments into computers either in the field or at the office.

Photogrammetrists and cartographers measure, map, and chart the Earth's surface. Their work involves everything from performing geographical research and compiling data to producing maps. They collect, analyze, and interpret both spatial data—such as latitude, longitude, elevation, and distance—and nonspatial data—such as population density, land-use patterns, annual precipitation levels, and demographic characteristics. Their maps may give both physical and social characteristics of the land. They prepare maps in either digital or graphic form, using information provided by geodetic surveys and remote sensing systems including aerial cameras, satellites, light-imaging detection and ranging (LIDAR), or other technologies.

LIDAR uses lasers attached to planes and other equipment to digitally map the topography of the Earth. It is often more accurate than traditional surveying methods and also can be used to collect other forms of data, such as the location and density of forests. Data developed by LIDAR can be used by surveyors, cartographers, and photogrammetrists to provide spatial information to specialists in geology, seismology, forestry, construction, and other fields.

Geographic Information Systems (GIS) have become an integral tool for surveyors, cartographers, photogrammetrists, and surveying and mapping technicians. Workers use GIS to assemble, integrate, analyze, and display data about location in a digital format. They also use GIS to compile information from a variety of sources. GIS typically are used to make maps which combine information useful for environmental studies, geology, engineering, planning, business marketing, and other disciplines. As more of these systems are developed, many mapping specialists are being called *geographic information specialists*.

Work environment. Surveyors and surveying technicians usually work an 8-hour day, 5 days a week and may spend a lot of time outdoors. Sometimes, they work longer hours during the summer, when weather and light conditions are most suitable for fieldwork. Construction-related work may be limited during times of inclement weather.

Surveyors and technicians engage in active, sometimes strenuous, work. They often stand for long periods, walk considerable distances, and climb hills with heavy packs of instruments and other equipment. They also can be exposed to all types of weather. Traveling is sometimes part of the job, and surveyors and technicians may commute long distances, stay away from home overnight, or temporarily relocate near a survey site. Surveyors also work indoors while planning surveys, searching court records for deed information, analyzing data, and preparing reports and maps.

Cartographers and photogrammetrists spend most of their time in offices using computers. However, certain jobs may require extensive field work to verify results and acquire data.

Training, Other Qualifications, and Advancement

Most surveyors, cartographers, and photogrammetrists have a bachelor's degree in surveying or a related field. Every state requires that surveyors be licensed.

Education and training. In the past, many people with little formal training started as members of survey crews and worked their way up to become licensed surveyors, but this has become increasingly difficult. Now, most surveyors need a bachelor's degree. A number of universities offer bachelor's degree programs in surveying, and many community colleges, technical institutes, and vocational schools offer one-year, two-year, and three-year programs in surveying or surveying technology.

Cartographers and photogrammetrists usually have a bachelor's degree in cartography, geography, surveying, engineering, forestry, computer science, or a physical science, although a few enter these positions after working as technicians. With the development of GIS, cartographers and photogrammetrists need more education and stronger technical skills—including more experience with computers—than in the past.

Most cartographic and photogrammetric technicians also have specialized postsecondary education. High school students interested in surveying and cartography should take courses in algebra, geometry, trigonometry, drafting, mechanical drawing, and computer science.

Licensure. All 50 states and all U.S. territories license surveyors. For licensure, most state licensing boards require that individuals pass a series of written examinations given by the National Council of Examiners for Engineering and Surveying (NCEES). After passing a first exam, the Fundamentals of Surveying, most candidates work under the supervision of an experienced surveyor for four years before taking a second exam, the Principles and Practice of Surveying. Additionally, most states also require surveyors to pass a written examination prepared by the state licensing board.

Specific requirements for training and education vary among the states. An increasing number of states require a bachelor's degree in surveying or in a closely related field, such as civil engineering or forestry, regardless of the number of years of experience. Some states require the degree to be from a school accredited by the Accreditation Board for Engineering and Technology (ABET). Most states also have a continuing education requirement.

Additionally, a number of states require cartographers and photogrammetrists to be licensed as surveyors, and some states have specific licenses for photogrammetrists.

Other qualifications. Surveyors, cartographers, and photogrammetrists should be able to visualize objects, distances, sizes, and abstract forms. They must work with precision and accuracy because mistakes can be costly. Surveying and mapping is a cooperative operation, so good interpersonal skills and the ability to work as part of a team is important.

Certification and advancement. High school graduates with no formal training in surveying usually start as apprentices. Beginners with postsecondary school training in surveying usually can start as technicians or assistants. With on-the-job experience and formal training in surveying—either in an institutional program or from a correspondence school—workers may advance to senior survey technician, then to party chief. Depending on state licensing requirements, they may advance to licensed surveyor in some cases.

The National Society of Professional Surveyors, a member organization of the American Congress on Surveying and Mapping, has a voluntary certification program for surveying technicians. Technicians are certified at four levels requiring progressive amounts of experience and the passing of written examinations. Although not required for state licensure, many employers require certification for promotion to positions with greater responsibilities.

The American Society for Photogrammetry and Remote Sensing (ASPRS) has voluntary certification programs for technicians and professionals in photogrammetry, remote sensing, and GIS. To qualify for these professional distinctions, individuals must meet work experience and training standards and pass a written examination. The professional recognition these certifications bestow can help workers gain promotions.

Employment

Surveyors, cartographers, photogrammetrists, and surveying technicians held about 147,000 jobs in 2008. Employment was distributed by occupational specialty as follows:

Surveying and mapping technicians	77,000
Surveyors	57,600
Cartographers and photogrammetrists	12,300

The architectural, engineering, and related services industry—including firms that provided surveying and mapping services to other industries on a contract basis—provided 7 out of 10 jobs for these workers. Federal, state, and local governmental agencies provided about 15 percent of these jobs. Major federal government employers are the U.S. Geological Survey (USGS), the Bureau of Land Management (BLM), the National Oceanic and Atmospheric Administration, the U.S. Forest Service, and the Army Corps of Engineers. Most surveyors in state and local government work for highway departments or urban planning and redevelopment agencies. Utility companies also employ surveyors, cartographers, photogrammetrists, and surveying technicians.

Job Outlook

These occupations should experience faster-than-average employment growth. Surveyors, cartographers, and photogrammetrists who have a bachelor's degree and strong technical skills should have favorable job prospects.

Employment change. Employment of surveyors, cartographers, photogrammetrists, and surveying and mapping technicians is expected to grow 19 percent from 2008 to 2018, which is faster than the average for all occupations. Increasing demand for fast, accurate, and complete geographic information will be the main source of job growth.

An increasing number of firms are interested in geographic information and its applications. For example, GIS can be used to create maps and information used in emergency planning, security, marketing, urban planning, natural resource exploration, construction, and other applications. Also, the increased popularity of online interactive mapping systems and GPS devices have created a higher demand for and awareness of current and accurate digital geographic information among consumers.

Growth in construction stemming from increases in the population and the related need to upgrade the nation's infrastructure will cause growth for surveyors and surveying technicians who ensure that projects are completed with precision and in line with original plans. These workers are usually the first on the job for any major construction project, and they provide information and recommendations to engineers, architects, contractors, and other professionals during all phases of a construction project.

Job prospects. In addition to openings from growth, job openings will continue to arise from the need to replace workers who transfer to other occupations or who leave the labor force altogether. Many cartographers and surveyors are approaching retirement age. Surveyors, cartographers, and photogrammetrists who have a bachelor's degree and strong technical skills should have favorable job prospects.

Opportunities for surveyors, cartographers, photogrammetrists, and technicians should remain concentrated in engineering, surveying, mapping, building inspection, and drafting services firms. Increasing demand for geographic data, as opposed to traditional surveying services, will mean better opportunities for mapping technicians and professionals who are involved in the development and use of GIS and digital mapmaking.

The demand for traditional surveying services is strongly tied to construction activity and opportunities will vary by year and geographic region, depending on local economic conditions. During a recession, when real estate sales and construction slow down, surveyors and surveying technicians may face greater competition for jobs and sometimes layoffs. However, because these workers can work on many different types of projects, they may have steadier work than other workers when construction slows.

Projections Data from the National Employment Matrix

Occupational title	SOC Code	Employment, 2008	Projected employment, 2018	Change, 2008–2018	
				Number	Percent
Surveyors, cartographers, photogrammetrists, and surveying and mapping technicians.....................................—		147,000	174,500	27,600	19
Surveyors, cartographers, and photogrammetrists 17-1020		70,000	81,800	11,900	17
Cartographers and photogrammetrists....................17-1021		12,300	15,600	3,300	27
Surveyors..17-1022		57,600	66,200	8,600	15
Surveying and mapping technicians..........................17-3031		77,000	92,700	15,700	20

NOTE: Data in this table are rounded.

Earnings

Median annual wages of cartographers and photogrammetrists were $51,180 in May 2008. The middle 50 percent earned between $39,510 and $69,220. The lowest 10 percent earned less than $31,440 and the highest 10 percent earned more than $87,620.

Median annual wages of surveyors were $52,980 in May 2008. The middle 50 percent earned between $38,800 and $70,010. The lowest 10 percent earned less than $29,600 and the highest 10 percent earned more than $85,620. Median annual earnings of surveyors employed in architectural, engineering, and related services were $51,870 in May 2008.

Median annual wages of surveying and mapping technicians were $35,120 in May 2008. The middle 50 percent earned between $27,370 and $45,860. The lowest 10 percent earned less than $21,680, and the highest 10 percent earned more than $58,030. Median annual wages of surveying and mapping technicians employed in architectural, engineering, and related services were $33,220 in May 2008, while those employed by local governments had median annual wages of $40,510.

Related Occupations

Workers who use surveying data in land development and construction include architects, except landscape and naval; engineers; and landscape architects.

Cartography is related to the work of environmental scientists and specialists; social scientists, other; and urban and regional planners.

Sources of Additional Information

For career information on surveyors, cartographers, photogrammetrists, and surveying technicians, contact

▸ American Congress on Surveying and Mapping, 6 Montgomery Village Ave., Suite 403, Gaithersburg, MD 20879. Internet: www.acsm.net

Information about career opportunities, licensure requirements, and the surveying technician certification program is available from

▸ National Society of Professional Surveyors, 6 Montgomery Village Ave., Suite 403, Gaithersburg, MD 20879. Internet: www.nspsmo.org

For information on a career as a geodetic surveyor, contact

▸ American Association of Geodetic Surveying (AAGS), 6 Montgomery Village Ave., Suite 403, Gaithersburg, MD 20879. Internet: www.aagsmo.org

For career information on photogrammetrists, photogrammetric technicians, remote sensing scientists, and image-based cartographers or geographic information system specialists, contact

▸ ASPRS: Imaging and Geospatial Information Society, 5410 Grosvenor Lane, Suite 210, Bethesda, MD 20814-2160. Internet: www.asprs.org

Information on about careers in remote sensing, photogrammetry, surveying, GIS, and other geography-related disciplines also is available from the Spring 2005 *Occupational Outlook Quarterly* article "Geography Jobs", available online at www.bls.gov/opub/ooq/2005/spring/art01.pdf.

Taxi Drivers and Chauffeurs

(O*NET 53-3041.00)

Significant Points

■ Taxi drivers and chauffeurs may work any schedule, including full time, part time, nights, evenings, weekends, and on a seasonal basis.

■ Very few drivers are paid an hourly wage; most rent their vehicles from a cab fleet, although many own their vehicles.

■ Local taxi commissions set licensing standards for driving experience and training.

■ Job opportunities should be plentiful.

Nature of the Work

Taxi and limousine services make it easy for customers to get around when driving their own cars or using public transportation is inconvenient. *Taxi drivers* and *chauffeurs* take passengers to and from their homes, workplaces, and recreational pursuits, such as dining, entertainment, and shopping, and to and from business-related events. These professional drivers help both residents and out-of-town guests get around a city or urban area. In addition to regular point-to-point services, some drivers offer sight-seeing services around their cities.

Drivers must be alert to conditions on the road, especially in heavy and congested traffic or in bad weather. They must take precautions to prevent accidents and avoid sudden stops, turns, and other driving maneuvers that would jar passengers.

The majority of people in this occupation work as taxi drivers. Typically, taxi drivers own their vehicles or rent them from a company called a fleet. Drivers who rent their vehicles usually report to a garage where they are assigned a vehicle, most frequently a large, conventional automobile modified for commercial passenger transport. Drivers check their cabs' fuel and oil levels and make sure that the lights, brakes, and windshield wipers are in good working order. If anything is not working properly, the driver who discovers the problem reports it to a dispatcher or company mechanic. Some drivers own their own cabs. Generally, they park at their homes overnight, so they simply drive to their first pickup when they start working. Like other car owners, they are responsible for their own insurance and maintenance and for making sure that the car is in good working order.

Taxi drivers usually find fares in one of three ways. Most commonly, they work with dispatch services, which allow customers to call in a request for a cab. Dispatchers relay the information to drivers by two-way radio, cellular telephone, or onboard computer. This is the most common method in smaller cities, late at night, or in low-traffic areas. Drivers may also pick up passengers waiting at cabstands or in taxi lines at airports, train stations, hotels, restaurants, and other places where people frequently seek taxis. In major cities, drivers "cruise" the streets looking for fares, although this is not legal in all jurisdictions.

Good drivers are familiar with streets in the areas they serve so they can choose the most efficient route to destinations and avoid traffic. They know the locations of frequently requested destinations, such as airports, bus and railroad terminals, convention centers, hotels, and other points of interest. In case of emergency, drivers should know the location of fire and police stations, as well as hospitals.

Upon arrival at the final destination, the driver determines the fare and announces it to the passenger. Each jurisdiction has its own regulations that set the structure of the fare system covering licensed taxis. In most areas, a taximeter measures the fare based on the distance covered and the amount of time spent in traffic. Drivers start their meters when passengers enter the cab and turn them off when they reach their final destinations. The fare may also include surcharges, such as base fares, dispatcher fees, or fees for additional passengers, tolls, luggage, or other services. Passengers usually add a tip or gratuity to the fare. The amount of the gratuity depends, in part, on the passengers' satisfaction with the quality and efficiency of the ride and the courtesy of the driver. Drivers issue receipts upon request. They may also fill out logs for use by their fleets.

Chauffeurs operate limousines, vans, and private cars. They may work for hire, as taxicabs do; or they may work for private businesses, government agencies, or wealthy individuals. Chauffeur services differ from taxi services in that all trips are prearranged. Many chauffeurs transport customers in large vans between hotels and airports, bus terminals, or train stations. Others drive luxury automobiles, such as private cars or limousines.

At the beginning of each workday, chauffeurs prepare their automobiles or vans for use. They inspect their vehicles for cleanliness and, when needed, clean the interior and wash the exterior body, windows, and mirrors. They check fuel and oil levels and make sure the lights, tires, brakes, and windshield wipers work. Chauffeurs may perform routine maintenance and make minor repairs, such as changing tires or adding oil and other fluids. If a vehicle requires a more complicated repair, they take it to a professional mechanic.

Chauffeurs cater to passengers by providing attentive customer service and paying attention to detail. They help riders into the car by holding open doors, holding umbrellas when it is raining, and loading packages and luggage into the trunk of the car. Chauffeurs may perform errands for their employers such as delivering packages or picking up clients arriving at airports. To ensure a pleasurable ride in their limousines, many chauffeurs offer conveniences and luxuries such as newspapers, magazines, music, drinks, televisions, and telephones. Increasingly, chauffeurs work as full-service executive assistants, simultaneously acting as driver, secretary, and itinerary planner.

Some drivers transport individuals with special needs, such as those with disabilities and the elderly. These drivers, known as *paratransit drivers*, operate specially equipped vehicles designed to accommodate a variety of needs in non-emergency situations. Although special certification is not necessary, some additional training on the equipment and passenger needs may be required.

Work environment. Driving for long periods can be tiring and stressful, especially in densely populated urban areas. Being seated in the same position for most of the day can also be very uncomfortable. Taxi drivers and chauffeurs often have to load and unload heavy luggage and packages. They are also at high risk for robbery, because they work alone and often carry large amounts of cash. Data from the U.S. Bureau of Labor Statistics show that taxi drivers and chauffeurs experienced a work-related injury and illness rate that was much higher than the national average.

Work hours of taxi drivers and chauffeurs vary greatly. Some jobs offer full-time or part-time employment with work hours that can change from day to day or remain the same. It is often necessary for drivers to report to work on short notice. Chauffeurs who work for a single employer may be on call much of the time. Evening and weekend work is common for drivers and chauffeurs employed by limousine and taxicab services.

Whereas the needs of the client or employer dictate the work schedule for chauffeurs, the work of taxi drivers is much less structured. Working free of supervision, they may break for a meal or a rest whenever their vehicle is unoccupied. Many taxi drivers like the independent, unsupervised work of driving.

This occupation is attractive to individuals, such as college and post-graduate students, seeking flexible work schedules and to anyone seeking a second source of income. Other service workers, such as ambulance drivers and police officers, sometimes moonlight as taxi drivers or chauffeurs.

Full-time taxi drivers usually work one shift a day, which may last 8 to 12 hours. Part-time drivers may work half a shift each day, or work a full shift once or twice a week. Drivers may work shifts at all times of the day and night, because most taxi companies offer services 24 hours a day. Early morning and late night shifts are not uncommon. Drivers work long hours during holidays, weekends, and other special times when demand for their services is heavier. Independent drivers set their own hours and schedules.

Training, Other Qualifications, and Advancement

Local governments set licensing standards and requirements for taxi drivers and chauffeurs, which may include minimum amounts of driving experience and training.

Education and training. Little formal education is needed for taxi drivers or chauffeurs, but many have at least a high school diploma, GED, or its equivalent. Drivers need to be able to communicate effectively, read maps, and use basic math. A basic understanding of auto mechanics can also be very useful.

Most taxi and limousine companies give new drivers on-the-job training. This training generally only lasts about a week or two, and is required by law in some jurisdictions. Companies show drivers how to operate the taximeter and communications equipment and how to complete paperwork. Other topics covered include driver safety, customer service, and the best routes to popular sightseeing and entertainment destinations.

Many companies have contracts with social service agencies and transportation services to transport elderly and disabled citizens in non-emergency situations. To support these services, new drivers may get special training in how to handle wheelchair lifts and other mechanical devices.

Licensure. Taxicab or limousine drivers must first have a regular automobile driver's license. In many states, applicants must get a taxi driver or chauffeur's license, commonly called a "hack" license. The Federal Motor Carrier Safety Administration requires a commercial driver's license (CDL) with a passenger (P) endorsement for drivers transporting 16 or more passengers (including the driver). While this is not a concern for taxi drivers, some stretch limousines and other such vehicles may be large enough to require a CDL.

While states set licensing requirements, local regulatory bodies set other terms and conditions. Most cities and urban areas have taxi commissions. These commissions set requirements for drivers, license vehicles to be used as cabs, and even set the rates that drivers are allowed to charge. In many cases, these regulations do not affect chauffeurs.

In most areas, taxis must have medallions that certify them as legally recognized cabs. Passengers generally prefer cars with medallions, as they are guaranteed to be law-abiding by local commissions. Drivers who receive too many complaints can lose their medallions, which discourages unethical behavior.

Regulations can vary greatly among localities. Some areas require new drivers to enroll in up to 80 hours of classroom instruction, to take an exam, or both before they are allowed to work. Some localities require an English proficiency test, usually in the form of listening comprehension; applicants who do not pass the English exam must take an English course, in addition to any formal driving programs.

Other qualifications. Taxi drivers and chauffeurs work almost exclusively with the public, and should be able to get along with many different types of people. They must be patient when waiting for passengers and when dealing with rude customers. It also is helpful for drivers to be tolerant and level-headed when driving in heavy and congested traffic. Drivers should be dependable, since passengers expect to be picked up at a prearranged time and taken to the correct destinations. Drivers must be responsible and self-motivated, because they work with little supervision. Increasingly, companies encourage drivers to develop loyal customers to improve their business.

Many municipalities and taxicab and chauffeur companies require drivers to have a neat appearance. Many chauffeurs wear formal attire, such as tuxedos, suits, dresses, or uniforms.

Advancement. Taxi drivers and chauffeurs have limited advancement opportunities. Experienced drivers may obtain preferred routes or shifts. Some advance to become lead drivers, who help to train new drivers. Others take dispatching and managerial positions. Some drivers become managers at taxi or limousine fleets. Some people start their own taxi or limousine companies.

In many communities, drivers can purchase their own taxis or limousines and go into business for themselves. Independent owner-drivers need an additional permit allowing them to operate as a business. Some big cities limit the number of operating permits, which keeps many owner-drivers out of the market. In these cities, drivers become owner-drivers by buying or renting permits from owner-drivers who leave the business. Although many owner-drivers are successful, some fail to cover expenses and eventually lose their permits and automobiles. Individuals starting their own taxi companies face many obstacles because of the difficulty in running a small fleet. The lack of dispatch and maintenance facilities often is hard for an owner to overcome. Chauffeurs often have a good deal of success as owner-drivers and many companies begin as individually owned and operated businesses.

For both taxi and limousine service owners, good business sense and courses in accounting, business, and business arithmetic can help an owner-driver be successful. Knowledge of mechanics enables owner-drivers to perform their own routine maintenance and minor repairs to cut expenses.

Employment

Taxi drivers and chauffeurs held about 232,300 jobs in 2008. About 26 percent of taxi drivers and chauffeurs were self-employed. Jobs were located throughout the country, but were concentrated in large cities. Metropolitan areas with the largest employment of taxi drivers and chauffeurs in May 2008 were as follows:

New York–Northern New Jersey–Long Island, NY-NJ-PA	16,360
Las Vegas–Paradise, NV	10,160
Los Angeles–Long Beach–Santa Ana, CA	7,510
Chicago-Naperville-Joliet, IL-IN-WI	5,300
Boston-Cambridge-Quincy, MA-NH	5,040

Job Outlook

Employment of taxi drivers and chauffeurs is expected to grow faster than the average for all occupations. Job opportunities should be plentiful. Applicants with good driving records, good customer service instincts, and the ability to work flexible schedules should have the best prospects.

Projections Data from the National Employment Matrix

Occupational title	SOC Code	Employment, 2008	Projected employment, 2018	Change, 2008–2018	
				Number	Percent
Taxi drivers and chauffeurs	53-3041	232,300	268,400	36,100	16

NOTE: Data in this table are rounded.

Employment change. Employment of taxi drivers and chauffeurs is expected to grow 16 percent during the 2008—18 projection period, faster than the average for all occupations. Drivers should see increased business as a result of growth in tourism and business travel. Also, as the number of elderly people increases, taxis will be needed to take them around town. Some growth will stem from federal legislation requiring increased services for people with disabilities.

Because the demand for taxi and limousine services is very sensitive to economic cycles, drivers may see declining demand for their services during economic downturns. This is especially true for chauffeurs, as expensive limousine services are considered a luxury. Chauffeurs who work for private companies or individuals may face layoffs or reduced hours during times of economic distress.

Job prospects. Opportunities for taxi drivers and chauffeurs are expected to be plentiful, because of the need to replace the many people who work in this occupation for short periods and then leave. Also, the occupation has very low barriers to entry. Because most drivers are paid strictly based on fares, companies take on very little risk when they hire a new driver. Applicants who have clean driving records and who are willing to work flexible schedules should have the best prospects. People who are easy going and make their passengers comfortable will be most likely to succeed, as a significant part of drivers' salaries come from the tips they receive.

Opportunities fluctuate significantly with the overall movements of the economy, because the demand for transportation depends on business travel and tourism. Because most drivers own or rent their vehicles, taxi drivers are seldom laid off, but they may have to increase their work hours, and earnings may decline. When the economy is strong, many drivers transfer to other occupations, which often leads to fewer cabs on the road. Extra drivers may be hired during holiday seasons, as well as during peak travel and tourist times.

Rapidly growing metropolitan areas and cities experiencing economic growth should offer the best job opportunities.

Earnings

Earnings of taxi drivers and chauffeurs vary greatly, depending on factors such as the number of hours worked, regulatory conditions, customer tips, and geographic location. Hybrid vehicles, which have improved gas mileage, offer taxi drivers better earnings, because drivers pay for their gas out of pocket. Median annual wages of wage and salary taxi drivers and chauffeurs, including tips, were $21,550 in May 2008. The middle 50 percent earned between $17,770 and $26,800. The lowest 10 percent earned less than $15,620, and the highest 10 percent earned more than $34,210.

Many taxi drivers pay a daily, weekly, or monthly fee to the company allowing them to lease their vehicles and depend on fares for their livelihood. The fee also may include charges for vehicle maintenance, insurance, and a deposit on the vehicle. This occupation includes many self-employed drivers. BLS does not have data on earnings for self-employed taxi and limousine drivers.

Most taxi drivers and chauffeurs do not receive benefits. Drivers may wish to purchase private health insurance.

Related Occupations

Other workers who have similar jobs include bus drivers; and truck drivers and driver/sales workers.

Sources of Additional Information

Information on necessary permits and the registration of taxi drivers and chauffeurs is available from local taxi commissions. Questions regarding licensing should be directed to your state motor vehicle administration. For information about work opportunities as a taxi driver or chauffeur, contact local taxi or limousine companies or state employment service offices in your area.

For general information about the work of taxi drivers, chauffeurs, and paratransit drivers, contact

▶ Taxicab, Limousine and Paratransit Association, 3200 Tower Oaks Blvd., Suite 220, Rockville, MD 20852. Internet: www.tlpa.org

For general information about the work of limousine drivers, contact

▶ National Limousine Association, 49 South Maple Ave., Marlton, NJ 08053. Internet: www.limo.org

Teacher Assistants

(O*NET 25-9041.00)

Significant Points

- Almost 40 percent of teacher assistants work part time.
- Educational requirements range from a high school diploma to some college training.
- Favorable job prospects are expected.
- Opportunities should be best for those with at least two years of formal postsecondary education, those with experience in helping special education students, or those who can speak a foreign language.

Nature of the Work

Teacher assistants provide instructional and clerical support for classroom teachers, allowing teachers more time for lesson planning and teaching. They support and assist children in learning class material using the teacher's lesson plans, providing students with individualized attention. Teacher assistants also supervise students in the cafeteria, schoolyard, and hallways, or on field trips; they record grades, set up equipment, and help prepare materials for instruction. Teacher assistants also are called *teacher aides* or *instructional aides*. Some assistants refer to themselves as *paraprofessionals* or *paraeducators*.

Some teacher assistants perform exclusively non-instructional or clerical tasks, such as monitoring nonacademic settings. Playground and lunchroom attendants are examples of such assistants. Most teacher assistants, however, perform a combination of instructional and clerical duties. They generally provide instructional reinforcement to children, under the direction and guidance of teachers. They work with students individually or in small groups—listening while students read, reviewing or reinforcing class lessons, or helping them find information for reports. At the secondary school level, teacher assistants often specialize in a certain subject, such as math or science. Teacher assistants often take charge of special projects and prepare equipment or exhibits, such as for a science demonstration. Some assistants work in computer laboratories, helping students to use computers and educational software programs.

In addition to instructing, assisting, and supervising students, teacher assistants may grade tests and papers, check homework, keep health and attendance records, do typing and filing, and duplicate materials. They also stock supplies, operate audiovisual equipment, and keep classroom equipment in order.

Many teacher assistants work extensively with special education students. As schools become more inclusive and integrate special education students into general education classrooms, teacher assistants in both general education and special education classrooms increasingly assist students with disabilities. They attend to the physical needs of students with disabilities, including feeding, teaching grooming habits, and assisting students riding the school bus. They also provide personal attention to students with other special needs, such as those who speak English as a second language and those who need remedial education. Some work with young adults to help them obtain a job or to help them apply for community services that will support them after their schooling ends. Teacher assistants help assess a student's progress by observing the student's performance and recording relevant data.

Although the majority of teacher assistants work in primary and secondary educational settings, others work in preschools and other child care centers. Often, one or two assistants will work with a lead teacher in order to better provide the individual attention that young children require. In addition to assisting in educational instruction, teacher assistants supervise the children at play and assist in feeding and other basic care activities.

Teacher assistants also work with infants and toddlers who have developmental delays or other disabilities. Under the guidance of a teacher or therapist, teacher assistants perform exercises or play games to help the child develop physically and behaviorally.

Work environment. Teacher assistants work in a variety of settings—including preschools, child care centers, and religious and community centers, where they work with young adults—but most work in classrooms in elementary, middle, and secondary schools. They also may work outdoors, supervising recess when weather allows, and they may spend time standing, walking, or kneeling. However, many spend much of the day sitting while working with students.

Approximately 40 percent of teacher assistants work part time. Most assistants who provide educational instruction work the traditional 9-month to 10-month school year.

Seeing students develop and learn can be very rewarding. However, working closely with students can be both physically and emotionally tiring. Teacher assistants who work with special education students often perform more strenuous tasks, including lifting, as they help students with their daily routine. Those who perform clerical work may tire of administrative duties, such as copying materials or entering data.

Training, Other Qualifications, and Advancement

Training requirements for teacher assistants vary by state or school district and range from a high school diploma to some college training. Increasingly, employers are preferring applicants with some related college coursework.

Education and training. Many teacher assistants need only a high school diploma and on-the-job training. However, a college degree or related coursework in child development improves job opportunities. In fact, teacher assistants who work in Title 1 schools—those with a large proportion of students from low-income households—must have college training or proven academic skills. They face federal mandates that require assistants to hold a 2-year or higher degree, have a minimum of 2 years of college, or pass a rigorous state or local assessment.

A number of colleges offer associate degrees or certificate programs that either prepare graduates to work as teacher assistants or provide additional training for current teacher assistants.

All teacher assistants receive some on-the-job training. Teacher assistants need to become familiar with the school system and with the operation and rules of the school they work in. Those who tutor and review lessons must learn and understand the class materials and instructional methods used by the teacher. Teacher assistants also must know how to operate audiovisual equipment, keep records, and prepare instructional materials, as well as have adequate computer skills.

Other qualifications. Many schools require previous experience in working with children and a valid driver's license. Most require the applicant to pass a background check. Teacher assistants should enjoy working with children from a wide range of cultural backgrounds and be able to handle classroom situations with fairness and patience. Teacher assistants also must demonstrate initiative and a willingness to follow a teacher's directions. They must have good writing skills and be able to communicate effectively with students and teachers. Teacher assistants who speak a second language, especially Spanish, are in great demand for communicating with growing numbers of students and parents whose primary language is not English.

Advancement. Advancement for teacher assistants—usually in the form of higher earnings or increased responsibility—comes primarily with experience or additional education. Some school districts provide time away from the job or tuition reimbursement so that teacher assistants can earn their bachelor's degrees and pursue licensed teaching positions. In return for tuition reimbursement, assistants are often required to teach for a certain length of time in the school district.

Employment

Teacher assistants held about 1.3 million jobs in 2008. Many worked for public and private educational institutions. Child care centers and religious organizations employed most of the rest.

Job Outlook

Many job openings are expected for teacher assistants due to turnover and about-as-fast-as-the-average employment growth in this large occupation, resulting in favorable job prospects.

Employment change. Employment of teacher assistants is expected to grow by 10 percent between 2008 and 2018, which is about as fast as the average for all occupations. School enrollments are projected to increase slowly over the next decade, but faster growth is expected among special education students and students for whom English is a second language, and those students will increase as a share of the total school-age population. Teacher assistants often are necessary to provide these students with the attention they require.

Legislation that requires both students with disabilities and nonnative English speakers to receive an education equal to that of other students will continue to generate jobs for teacher assistants, who help to accommodate these students' special needs. Children with special needs require more personal attention, and teachers rely heavily on teacher assistants to provide much of that attention. An increasing number of afterschool programs and summer programs also will create new opportunities for teacher assistants.

The greater focus on school quality and accountability that has prevailed in recent years is likely to lead to an increased demand for teacher assistants as well. Growing numbers of teacher assistants may be needed to help teachers prepare students for standardized testing and to provide extra assistance to students who perform poorly on the tests. Job growth of assistants may be moderated, however, if schools are encouraged to hire more teachers for instructional purposes.

Job prospects. Favorable job prospects are expected. Opportunities for teacher assistant jobs should be best for those with at least two years of formal postsecondary education, those with experience in helping special education students, and those who can speak a foreign language. Demand is expected to vary by region of the country. Regions in which the population and school enrollments are expected to grow faster, such as many communities in the South and West, should have rapid growth in the demand for teacher assistants.

In addition to job openings stemming from employment growth, numerous openings will arise as assistants leave their jobs and must be replaced. Many assistant jobs require limited formal education and offer relatively low pay, so many workers transfer to other occupations or leave the labor force to assume family responsibilities, return to school, or for other reasons.

Although opportunities will be favorable, there may be a limited number of full-time positions because many school districts prefer to hire these workers part time.

Earnings

Median annual wages of teacher assistants in May 2008 were $22,200. The middle 50 percent earned between $17,610 and $28,180. The lowest 10 percent earned less than $15,340, and the highest 10 percent earned more than $33,980.

Full-time workers usually receive health coverage and other benefits. Teacher assistants who work part time ordinarily do not receive benefits. In 2008, about 37 percent of teacher assistants belonged to unions or were covered by a union contract—mainly the American Federation of Teachers and the National Education Association—which bargain with school systems over wages, hours, and the terms and conditions of employment.

Related Occupations

Teacher assistants who instruct children have duties similar to those of child care workers; library technicians and library assistants; occupational therapist assistants and aides; teachers—kindergarten, elementary, middle and secondary; teachers—preschool, except special education; teachers—special education; and teachers—vocational.

Sources of Additional Information

For information on teacher assistants, including training and certification, contact

▸ American Federation of Teachers, Paraprofessional and School Related Personnel Division, 555 New Jersey Ave. NW, Washington, DC 20001. Internet: www.aft.org/psrp/index.html

Projections Data from the National Employment Matrix

Occupational title	SOC Code	Employment, 2008	Projected employment, 2018	Change, 2008–2018	
				Number	Percent
Teacher assistants	25-9041	1,312,700	1,447,600	134,900	10

NOTE: Data in this table are rounded.

▸ National Education Association, Educational Support Personnel Division, 1201 16th St. NW, Washington, DC 20036. Internet: www.nea.org/esphome

▸ National Resource Center for Paraprofessionals, 6526 Old Main Hill, Utah State University, Logan, UT 84322. Internet: www.nrcpara.org

Human resource departments in school systems, school administrators, and state departments of education also can provide details about employment opportunities and required qualifications for teacher assistant jobs.

Teachers—Kindergarten, Elementary, Middle, and Secondary

(O*NET 25-2012.00, 25-2021.00, 25-2022.00, and 25-2031.00)

Significant Points

■ Public school teachers must be licensed, which typically requires a bachelor's degree and the completion of an approved teacher education program; private school teachers do not have to be licensed but may still need a bachelor's degree.

■ Many states offer alternative licensing programs to attract people into teaching, especially for hard-to-fill positions.

■ Teachers must have the ability to communicate, inspire trust and confidence, and motivate students, as well as understand students' educational and emotional needs.

■ Job prospects are best for teachers in high-demand fields, such as mathematics, science, and bilingual education, and in less desirable urban or rural school districts.

Nature of the Work

Teachers play an important role in fostering the intellectual and social development of children during their formative years. The education that students acquire is key to determining the future of those students. Whether in elementary or high schools or in private or public schools, teachers provide the tools and the environment for their students to develop into responsible adults.

Teachers act as facilitators or coaches, using classroom presentations or individual instruction to help students learn and apply concepts in subjects such as science, mathematics, and English. They plan, evaluate, and assign lessons; prepare, administer, and grade tests; listen to oral presentations; and maintain classroom discipline. Teachers observe and evaluate a student's performance and potential. They are increasingly asked to use new assessment methods. For example, teachers may examine a portfolio of a student's artwork or writing in order to judge the student's overall progress. They then can provide additional assistance in areas in which the student needs help. Teachers also grade papers, prepare report cards, and meet with parents and school staff to discuss a student's academic progress or personal problems.

Many teachers use a hands-on approach that utilizes props to help children understand abstract concepts, solve problems, and develop critical thinking skills. For example, they may teach the concepts of

numbers or of addition and subtraction by playing board games. As the children get older, teachers use more sophisticated approaches, such as demonstrating science experiments or working with computers. They also encourage collaboration in solving problems by having students work in groups to discuss and solve the problems together. To be prepared for success later in life, students must be able to interact with others, adapt to new technology, and think through problems logically.

Kindergarten and elementary school teachers play a vital role in the development of children. What children learn and experience during their early years can shape their views of themselves and the world and can affect their later success or failure in school, work, and their personal lives. Kindergarten and elementary school teachers introduce children to mathematics, language, science, and social studies. They use games, music, artwork, films, books, computers, and other tools to teach basic skills.

Kindergarten teachers use play and hands-on teaching, but academics begin to take priority in kindergarten classrooms. Letter recognition, phonics, numbers, and awareness of nature and science, introduced at the preschool level, are taught primarily in kindergarten.

Most *elementary school teachers* instruct one class of children in several subjects. In some schools, two or more teachers work as a team and are jointly responsible for a group of students in at least one subject. In other schools, a teacher may teach one special subject—usually music, art, reading, science, arithmetic, or physical education—to a number of classes. A small but growing number of teachers instruct multilevel classrooms, with students at several different learning levels.

Middle school teachers and *secondary school teachers* help students delve more deeply into subjects introduced in elementary school and expose them to more information about the world. Middle and secondary school teachers specialize in a specific subject, such as English, Spanish, mathematics, history, or biology. They also may teach subjects that are career oriented. Additional responsibilities of middle and secondary school teachers may include career guidance and job placement, as well as following up with students after graduation.

In addition to conducting classroom activities, teachers oversee study halls and homerooms, supervise extracurricular activities, and accompany students on field trips. They may identify students who have physical or mental problems and refer the students to the proper authorities. Secondary school teachers occasionally assist students in choosing courses, colleges, and careers. Teachers also participate in education conferences and workshops.

Computers play an integral role in the education teachers provide. Resources such as educational software and the Internet expose students to a vast range of experiences and promote interactive learning. Through the Internet, students can communicate with other students anywhere in the world, allowing them to share experiences and viewpoints. Students also use the Internet for individual research projects and to gather information. Computers play a role in other classroom activities as well, from solving math problems to learning English as a second language. Teachers also may use computers to record grades and perform other administrative and clerical duties. They must continually update their skills so that they can instruct and use the latest technology in the classroom.

Teachers often work with students from varied ethnic, racial, and religious backgrounds. With growing minority populations in most parts of the country, it is important for teachers to work effectively with a diverse student population. Accordingly, some schools offer training to help teachers enhance their awareness and understanding of different cultures. Teachers may include multicultural programming in their lesson plans, to address the needs of all students, regardless of their cultural background.

In recent years, site-based management, which allows teachers and parents to participate actively in management decisions regarding school operations, has gained popularity. In many schools, teachers are increasingly becoming involved in making decisions regarding the budget, personnel, textbooks, curriculum design, and teaching methods.

Work environment. Seeing students develop new skills and gain an appreciation of knowledge and learning can be very rewarding. However, teaching may be frustrating when one is dealing with unmotivated or disrespectful students. Occasionally, teachers must cope with unruly behavior and violence in the schools. Teachers may experience stress in dealing with large classes, heavy workloads, or old schools that are run down and lack modern amenities. Accountability standards also may increase stress levels, with teachers expected to produce students who are able to exhibit a satisfactory performance on standardized tests in core subjects. Many teachers, particularly in public schools, also are frustrated by the lack of control they have over what they are required to teach.

Teachers in private schools generally enjoy smaller class sizes and more control over establishing the curriculum and setting standards for performance and discipline. Their students also tend to be more motivated, since private schools can be selective in their admissions processes.

Teachers are sometimes isolated from their colleagues because they work alone in a classroom of students. However, some schools allow teachers to work in teams and with mentors, to enhance their professional development.

Many teachers work more than 40 hours a week, including school duties performed outside the classroom. Part-time schedules are more common among kindergarten teachers. Although most school districts have gone to all-day kindergartens, some kindergarten teachers still teach two kindergarten classes a day. Most teachers work the traditional 10-month school year, with a 2-month vacation during the summer. During the vacation break, those on the 10-month schedule may teach in summer sessions, take other jobs, travel, or pursue personal interests. Many enroll in college courses or workshops to continue their education. Teachers in districts with a year-round schedule typically work 8 weeks, are on vacation for 1 week, and have a 5-week midwinter break.

Most states have tenure laws that prevent public school teachers from being fired without just cause and due process. Teachers may obtain tenure after they have satisfactorily completed a probationary period of teaching, normally 3 years. Tenure does not absolutely guarantee a job, but it does provide some security.

Training, Other Qualifications, and Advancement

The traditional route to becoming a public school teacher involves completing a bachelor's degree from a teacher education program and then obtaining a license. However, most states now offer alternative routes to licensure for those who have a college degree in other fields. Private school teachers do not have to be licensed but may still need a bachelor's degree.

Education and training. Traditional education programs for kindergarten and elementary school teachers include courses designed specifically for those preparing to teach. Among these courses are mathematics, physical science, social science, music, art, and literature, as well as prescribed professional education courses, such as philosophy of education, psychology of learning, and teaching methods. Aspiring secondary school teachers most often major in the subject they plan to teach, while also taking a program of study in teacher preparation. Many 4-year colleges require students to wait until their sophomore year before applying for admission to teacher education programs. To maintain their accreditation, teacher education programs are now required to include classes in the use of computers and other technologies. Most programs require students to perform a student-teaching internship. Teacher education programs are accredited by the National Council for Accreditation of Teacher Education and the Teacher Education Accreditation Council. Graduation from an accredited program is not necessary to become a teacher, but it may make fulfilling licensure requirements easier.

Many states now offer professional development schools, which are partnerships between universities and elementary or secondary schools. Professional development schools merge theory with practice and allow the student to experience a year of teaching firsthand, under professional guidance. Students enter these 1-year programs after the completion of their bachelor's degree.

Licensure and certification. All 50 states and the District of Columbia require public school teachers to be licensed. Licensure is not required for teachers in most private schools. Usually licensure is granted by the State Board of Education or a licensure advisory committee. Teachers may be licensed to teach the early childhood grades (usually preschool through grade 3); the elementary grades (grades 1 through 6 or 8); the middle grades (grades 5 through 8); a secondary-education subject area (usually grades 7 through 12); or a special subject, such as reading or music (usually grades kindergarten through 12).

Requirements for regular licenses to teach kindergarten through grade 12 vary by state. However, all states require general education teachers to have a bachelor's degree and to have completed an approved teacher training program with a prescribed number of subject and education credits, as well as supervised practice teaching. Some states also require technology training and the attainment of a minimum grade point average. A number of states require that teachers obtain a master's degree in education within a specified period after they begin teaching.

Almost all states require applicants for a teacher's license to be tested for competency in basic skills, such as reading and writing, and in teaching and require teachers to exhibit proficiency in their subject. Many school systems are moving toward implementing performance-based systems for licensure, which usually require teachers to demonstrate satisfactory teaching performance over an extended period in order to obtain a provisional license, in addition to passing an examination in their subject. Most states require teachers to complete a minimum number of hours of continuing education to renew their license. Many states have reciprocity agreements that make it easier for teachers licensed in one state to become licensed in another.

All states now also offer alternative licensure programs for teachers who have a bachelor's degree in the subject they will teach, but who lack the necessary education courses required for a regular license. Many of these alternative licensure programs are designed to ease shortages of teachers of certain subjects, such as mathematics and science. Other programs provide teachers for urban and rural schools that have difficulty filling positions with teachers from traditional licensure programs. Alternative licensure programs are intended to attract people into teaching who do not fulfill traditional licensing standards, including recent college graduates who did not complete education programs and those changing from another career to teaching. In some programs, individuals begin teaching quickly under provisional licensure under the close supervision of experienced educators while taking education courses outside school hours. If they progress satisfactorily, they receive regular licensure after working for 1 or 2 years. In other programs, college graduates who do not meet licensure requirements take only those courses that they lack and then become licensed. This approach may take 1 or 2 semesters of full-time study. The coursework for alternative certification programs may leads to a master's degree. In extreme circumstances, when schools cannot attract enough qualified teachers to fill positions, states may issue emergency licenses that let individuals who do not meet the requirements for a regular license begin teaching immediately.

Private schools are generally exempt from meeting state licensing standards. For secondary school teacher jobs, they prefer candidates who have a bachelor's degree in the subject they intend to teach, or in childhood education for elementary school teachers. They seek candidates from among recent college graduates, as well as from those who have established careers in other fields.

Other qualifications. In addition to being knowledgeable about the subjects they teach, teachers must have the ability to communicate, inspire trust and confidence, and motivate students, as well as understand the students' educational and emotional needs. Teachers must be able to recognize and respond to individual and cultural differences in students and employ different teaching methods that will result in higher student achievement. They should be organized, dependable, patient, and creative. Teachers also must be able to work cooperatively and communicate effectively with other teachers, support staff, parents, and members of the community. Private schools associated with religious institutions desire candidates who share the values that are important to the institution.

Certification and advancement. In some cases, teachers of kindergarten through high school may attain professional certification in order to demonstrate competency beyond that required for a license. The National Board for Professional Teaching Standards offers a voluntary national certification. All states recognize national certification, and many states and school districts provide special benefits to teachers who earn certification. Benefits typically include higher salaries and reimbursement for continuing education and certifica-

tion fees. In addition, many states allow nationally certified teachers to carry a license from one state to another.

With further preparation, teachers may move into such positions as school librarians, reading specialists, instructional coordinators, and guidance counselors. Teachers may become administrators or supervisors. In some systems, highly qualified experienced teachers can become senior or mentor teachers, with higher pay and additional responsibilities. They guide and assist less experienced teachers while keeping most of their own teaching responsibilities.

Employment

Kindergarten, elementary school, middle school, and secondary school teachers, held about 3.5 million jobs in 2008. Of the teachers in those jobs, about 179,500 were kindergarten teachers, 1.5 million were elementary school teachers, 659,500 were middle school teachers, and 1.1 million were secondary school teachers. Employment of teachers is geographically distributed much the same as the population.

Job Outlook

Employment is projected to grow about as fast as the average for all occupations. Job prospects are best for teachers in high-demand fields, such as mathematics, science, and bilingual education, and in less desirable urban or rural school districts.

Employment change. Employment of kindergarten, elementary, middle, and secondary school teachers is expected to grow by 13 percent between 2008 and 2018, which is about as fast as the average for all occupations.

Through 2018, overall student enrollments in elementary, middle, and secondary schools—a key factor in the demand for teachers—are expected to rise more slowly than in the past as children of the baby-boom generation leave the school system. Projected enrollments will vary by region. Rapidly growing states in the South and West will experience the largest enrollment increases. Enrollments in the Midwest are expected to hold relatively steady, while those in the Northeast are expected to decline. Teachers who are geographically mobile and who obtain licensure in more than one subject are likely to have a distinct advantage in finding a job.

The number of teachers employed is dependent on state and local expenditures for education and on the enactment of legislation to increase the quality and scope of public education. At the federal level, there has been a large increase in funding for education, particularly for the hiring of qualified teachers in lower income areas.

Job prospects. Job opportunities for teachers will vary with the locality, grade level, and subject taught. Most job openings will result from the need to replace the large number of teachers who are expected to retire over the 2008–2018 period. Also, many beginning teachers—especially those employed in poor, urban schools—decide to leave teaching for other careers after a year or two, creating additional job openings for teachers.

Job prospects should be better in inner cities and rural areas than in suburban districts. Many inner cities—often characterized by overcrowded, ill-equipped schools and higher-than-average poverty rates—and rural areas—characterized by their remote location and relatively low salaries—have difficulty attracting and retaining

Projections Data from the National Employment Matrix

Occupational title	SOC Code	Employment, 2008	Projected employment, 2018	Change, 2008–2018	
				Number	Percent
Teachers—kindergarten, elementary, middle, and secondary.. —		3,476,200	3,944,900	468,600	13
Kindergarten teachers, except special education............25-2012		179,500	206,500	27,000	15
Elementary school teachers, except special education 25-2021		1,549,500	1,793,700	244,200	16
Middle school teachers, except special and vocational education 25-2022		659,500	760,600	101,200	15
Secondary school teachers, except special and vocational education...25-2031		1,087,700	1,184,100	96,300	9

NOTE: Data in this table are rounded.

enough teachers. Currently, many school districts have difficulty hiring qualified teachers in some subject areas—most often mathematics, science (especially chemistry and physics), bilingual education, and foreign languages. Increasing enrollments of minorities, coupled with a shortage of minority teachers, should cause efforts to recruit minority teachers to intensify. Also, the number of non-English-speaking students will continue to grow, creating demand for bilingual teachers and for those who teach English as a second language. Specialties that have an adequate number of qualified teachers include general elementary education, physical education, and social studies.

The supply of teachers is expected to increase in response to reports of improved job prospects, better pay, more teacher involvement in school policy, and greater public interest in education. In addition, more teachers may be drawn from a reserve pool of career changers, substitute teachers, and teachers completing alternative certification programs. In recent years, the total number of bachelor's and master's degrees granted in education has been increasing slowly. But many states have implemented policies that will encourage even more students to become teachers because of a shortage of teachers in certain locations and in anticipation of the loss of a number of teachers to retirement.

Earnings

Median annual wages of kindergarten, elementary, middle, and secondary school teachers ranged from $47,100 to $51,180 in May 2008; the lowest 10 percent earned $30,970 to $34,280; the top 10 percent earned $75,190 to $80,970.

According to the American Federation of Teachers, beginning teachers with a bachelor's degree earned an average of $33,227 in the 2005–2006 school year.

In 2008, of the majority of all elementary, middle, and secondary school teachers belonged to unions—mainly the American Federation of Teachers and the National Education Association—that bargain with school systems over salaries, hours, and other terms and conditions of employment.

Teachers can boost their earnings in a number of ways. In some schools, teachers receive extra pay for coaching sports and working with students in extracurricular activities. Getting a master's degree or national certification often results in a raise in pay, as does acting as a mentor. Some teachers earn extra income during the summer by teaching summer school or performing other jobs in the school system. Although private school teachers generally earn less than public school teachers, they may be given other benefits, such as free or subsidized housing.

Related Occupations

Kindergarten, elementary school, middle school, and secondary school teaching requires a variety of skills and aptitudes, including a talent for working with children; organizational, administrative, and recordkeeping abilities; research and communication skills; the power to influence, motivate, and train others; patience; and creativity. Workers in other occupations requiring some of these aptitudes include athletes, coaches, umpires, and related workers; child care workers; counselors; education administrators; librarians; social workers; teacher assistants; teachers—postsecondary; teachers—preschool, except special education; teachers—special education; and teachers—vocational.

Sources of Additional Information

Information on licensure or certification requirements and approved teacher training institutions is available from local school systems and state departments of education.

Information on teachers' unions and education-related issues may be obtained from

▸ American Federation of Teachers, 555 New Jersey Ave. NW, Washington, DC 20001. Internet: www.aft.org

▸ National Education Association, 1201 16th St. NW, Washington, DC 20036. Internet: www.nea.org

A list of institutions with accredited teacher education programs can be obtained from

▸ National Council for Accreditation of Teacher Education, 2010 Massachusetts Ave. NW, Suite 500, Washington, DC 20036-1023. Internet: www.ncate.org

▸ Teacher Education Accreditation Council, Suite 300, One Dupont Circle, Suite 320, Washington, DC 20036. Internet: www.teac.org

Information on alternative certification programs can be obtained from

▸ National Center for Alternative Certification, 4401A Connecticut Ave. NW, Suite 212, Washington, DC 20008. Internet: www. teach-now.org

Information on National Board Certification can be obtained from

▸ National Board for Professional Teaching Standards, 1525 Wilson Blvd., Suite 500, Arlington, VA 22209. Internet: www.nbpts.org

Teachers—Postsecondary

(O*NET 25-1011.00, 25-1021.00, 25-1022.00, 25-1031.00, 25-1032.00, 25-1041.00, 25-1042.00, 25-1043.00, 25-1051.00, 25-1052.00, 25-1053.00, 25-1054.00, 25-1061.00, 25-1062.00, 25-1063.00, 25-1064.00, 25-1065.00, 25-1066.00, 25-1067.00, 25-1069.00, 25-1071.00, 25-1072.00, 25-1081.00, 25-1082.00, 25-1111.00, 25-1112.00, 25-1113.00, 25-1121.00, 25-1122.00, 25-1123.00, 25-1124.00, 25-1125.00, 25-1126.00, 25-1191.00, 25-1192.00, 25-1193.00, 25-1194.00, and 25-1199.00)

Significant Points

■ Many postsecondary teachers find the environment intellectually stimulating and rewarding because they are surrounded by others who enjoy the subject.

■ Educational qualifications range from expertise in a particular field to a Ph.D., depending on the subject taught and the type of educational institution.

■ Competition is expected for tenure-track positions; better opportunities are expected for part-time or non-tenure-track positions.

■ Ph.D. recipients should experience the best job prospects.

Nature of the Work

Postsecondary teachers instruct students in a wide variety of academic and vocational subjects beyond the high school level. Most of these students are working toward a degree, but many others are studying for a certificate or certification to improve their knowledge or career skills. Postsecondary teachers include college and university faculty, postsecondary career and technical education teachers, and graduate teaching assistants. Teaching in any venue involves forming a lesson plan, presenting material to students, responding to students learning needs, and evaluating students' progress. In addition to teaching, postsecondary teachers, particularly those at 4-year colleges and universities, perform a significant amount of research in the subject they teach. They also must keep up with new developments in their field and may consult with government, business, nonprofit, and community organizations.

College and university faculty make up the majority of postsecondary teachers. Faculty usually are organized into departments or divisions based on academic subject or field. They typically teach several related courses in their subject—algebra, calculus, and statistics, for example. They may instruct undergraduate or graduate students or both. College and university faculty may give lectures to several hundred students in large halls, lead small seminars, or supervise students in laboratories. They prepare lectures, exercises, and laboratory experiments; grade exams and papers; and advise and work with students individually. In universities, they also supervise graduate students' teaching and research. College faculty work with an increasingly varied student population made up of growing shares of part-time, older, and culturally and racially diverse students.

Faculty keep up with developments in their field by reading current literature, talking with colleagues, and participating in professional conferences. They also are encouraged to do their own research to expand knowledge in their field by performing experiments, collecting and analyzing data, or examining original documents, literature, and other source material. They publish their findings in scholarly journals, books, and electronic media.

Most postsecondary teachers use computer technology extensively, including the Internet, e-mail, and software programs. They may use computers in the classroom as teaching aids and may post course content, class notes, class schedules, and other information on the Internet. The use of e-mail, instant messages, and other computer utilities has improved communications greatly between students and teachers.

Some instructors use the Internet to teach courses to students at remote sites. These distance-learning courses are becoming an increasingly popular option for students who work while attending school. Faculty who teach these courses must be able to adapt existing courses to make them successful online or design a new course that takes advantage of the online format.

Most full-time faculty members serve on academic or administrative committees that deal with the policies of their institution, departmental matters, academic issues, curricula, budgets, purchases of equipment, and hiring. Some work with student and community organizations. Department chairpersons are faculty members who usually teach some courses but have heavier administrative responsibilities.

The proportion of time spent on research, teaching, administrative, and other duties varies by individual circumstance and type of institution. The teaching load often is heavier in 2-year colleges and somewhat lighter at 4-year institutions. At all types of institutions, full professors—those who have reached the highest level in their field—usually spend a larger portion of their time conducting research than do assistant professors, instructors, and lecturers.

An increasing number of postsecondary educators are working in alternative schools or in programs aimed at providing career-related education for working adults. Courses usually are offered online or on nights and weekends. Instructors at these programs generally work part time and are responsible only for teaching, with little to no administrative and research responsibilities.

Graduate teaching assistants, often referred to as *graduate TAs*, assist faculty, department chairs, or other professional staff at colleges and universities by teaching or performing teaching-related duties. In addition, assistants have their own school commitments as students working toward earning a graduate degree, such as a Ph.D. Some teaching assistants have full responsibility for teaching a course, usually one that is introductory. Such teaching can include preparing lectures and exams, as well as assigning final grades to students. Others help faculty members by doing a variety of tasks such as grading papers, monitoring exams, holding office hours or help sessions for students, conducting laboratory sessions, and administering quizzes to the class. Because each faculty member has his or her own needs, teaching assistants generally meet initially with the faculty member whom they are going to assist in order to determine exactly what is expected of them. For example, some faculty members prefer assistants to sit in on classes, whereas others assign them other tasks to do during class time. Graduate teaching assistants may work one-on-one with a faculty member, or, in large classes, they may be one of several assistants.

Work environment. Many postsecondary teachers find the environment intellectually stimulating and rewarding because they are surrounded by others who enjoy the subject. The ability to share their expertise with others also is appealing to many.

Most postsecondary teachers have flexible schedules. They must be present for classes, usually 12 to 16 hours per week, and for faculty and committee meetings. Most establish regular office hours for student consultations, usually 3 to 6 hours per week. Otherwise, teachers are free to decide when and where they will work and how much time to devote to course preparation, grading, study, research, graduate student supervision, and other activities.

Classes typically are scheduled to take place during weekdays, although some occur at night or on the weekend. For teachers at 2-year community colleges or institutions with large enrollments of older students who have full-time jobs or family responsibilities, night and weekend classes are common. Most colleges and universities require teachers to work 9 months of the year, which allows them time to teach additional courses, do research, travel, or pursue nonacademic interests during the summer and on school holidays.

About 29 percent of postsecondary teachers worked part time in 2008. Some part-timers, known as adjunct faculty, have primary jobs outside of academia—in government, private-industry, or non-profit research organizations—and teach on the side. Others have multiple part-time teaching positions at different institutions. Most graduate teaching assistants work part time while pursuing their graduate studies. The number of hours that they work may vary with their assignments.

University faculty may experience a conflict between their responsibility to teach students and the pressure to do research and publish their findings. This may be a particular problem for young faculty seeking advancement in 4-year research universities. Also, recent cutbacks in support workers and the hiring of more part-time faculty have put a greater administrative burden on full-time faculty. In addition, requirements to teach online classes have added greatly to the workloads of postsecondary teachers. Many find that developing the courses to put online is very time consuming, especially when they have to familiarize themselves with the format and answer large amounts of e-mail.

Like college and university faculty, graduate TAs usually have flexibility in their work schedules, but they also must spend a considerable amount of time pursuing their own academic coursework and studies. Work may be stressful, particularly when assistants are given full responsibility for teaching a class. However, these types of positions allow graduate students the opportunity to gain valuable teaching experience, which is especially helpful for those who seek to become college faculty members after completing their degree.

Training, Other Qualifications, and Advancement

The education and training required of postsecondary teachers varies widely, depending on the subject taught and the educational institution employing them. Educational requirements for teachers generally are highest at research universities, where a Ph.D. is the most commonly held degree.

Education and training. Four-year colleges and universities usually require candidates for full-time, tenure-track positions to hold a doctoral degree. However, they may hire master's degree holders or doctoral candidates for certain disciplines, such as the arts, or for part-time and temporary jobs.

Doctoral programs take an average of 6 years of full-time study beyond the bachelor's degree, including time spent completing a master's degree and a dissertation. Some programs, such as those in the humanities, may take longer to complete; others, such as those in engineering, usually are shorter. Candidates specialize in a subfield of a discipline—for example, organic chemistry, counseling psychology, or European history—and also take courses covering the entire discipline. Programs typically include 20 or more increasingly specialized courses and seminars, plus comprehensive examinations in all major areas of the field. Candidates also must complete a dissertation—a paper on original research in the candidate's major field of study. The dissertation sets forth an original hypothesis or proposes a model and tests it. Students in the natural sciences and engineering often do theoretical or laboratory work; in the humanities, they study original documents and other published material. The dissertation is done under the guidance of one or more faculty advisors and usually takes 1 or 2 years of full-time work.

In 2-year colleges, master's degree holders fill most full-time teaching positions. However, in certain fields where there may be more applicants than available jobs, institutions can be more selective in their hiring practices. In these fields, master's degree holders may be passed over in favor of candidates holding Ph.D.s. Many 2-year institutions increasingly prefer job applicants to have some teaching experience or experience with distance learning. Preference also may be given to those holding dual master's degrees, especially at smaller institutions, because those with dual degrees can teach more subjects.

Other qualifications. Postsecondary teachers should communicate and relate well with students, enjoy working with them, and be able to motivate them. They should have inquiring and analytical minds and a strong desire to pursue and disseminate knowledge. In addition, they must be self-motivated and able to work in an environment in which they receive little direct supervision.

Obtaining a position as a graduate teaching assistant is a good way to gain college teaching experience. To qualify, candidates must be enrolled in a graduate school program. In addition, some colleges and universities require teaching assistants to attend classes or take some training prior to being given responsibility for a course.

Although graduate teaching assistants usually work at the institution and in the department where they are earning their degree, teaching or internship positions for graduate students at institutions that do not grant a graduate degree have become more common in recent years. For example, a program called Preparing Future Faculty, administered by the Association of American Colleges and Universities and the Council of Graduate Schools, has led to the creation of many programs that are now independent. These programs offer graduate students at research universities the opportunity to work as teaching assistants at other types of institutions, such as liberal arts or community colleges. Working with a mentor, graduate students teach classes and learn how to improve their teaching techniques. They may attend faculty and committee meetings, develop a curriculum, and learn how to balance the teaching, research, and administrative roles of faculty. These programs provide valuable learning opportunities for graduate students interested in teaching at the postsecondary level and also help to make these students aware of the differences among the various types of institutions at which they may someday work.

Some degree holders, particularly those with degrees in the natural sciences, do postdoctoral research before taking a faculty position. Some Ph.D.s are able to extend postdoctoral appointments or take new ones if they are unable to find a faculty job. Most of these appointments offer a nominal salary.

Advancement. For faculty a major goal in the traditional academic career is attaining tenure, which can take approximately 7 years, with faculty moving up the ranks in tenure-track positions as they meet specific criteria. The ranks are instructor, assistant professor, associate professor, and professor. Colleges and universities usually hire new tenure-track faculty as instructors or assistant professors under term contracts. At the end of the period, their record of teaching, research, and overall contribution to the institution is reviewed, and tenure may be granted if the review is favorable. Those denied tenure usually must leave the institution. Tenured professors cannot be fired without just cause and due process. Tenure protects the faculty member's academic freedom—the ability to advocate controversial or unpopular ideas through teaching and conducting research without fear of being fired. Tenure also gives both faculty and institutions the stability needed for effective research and teaching, and it provides financial security for faculty. Some institutions have adopted post-tenure review policies to encourage ongoing evaluation of tenured faculty.

The number of tenure-track positions is declining as institutions seek flexibility in dealing with financial matters and changing student interests. Institutions are relying more heavily on limited-term contracts and part-time, or adjunct, faculty, thus shrinking the total pool of tenured faculty. Limited-term contracts, typically for 2 to 5 years, may be terminated or extended when they expire and generally do not lead to the granting of tenure. In addition, some institutions have limited the percentage of the faculty that can be tenured.

For tenured postsecondary teachers, further advancement involves a move into an administrative or managerial position, such as departmental chairperson, dean, or president. At 4-year institutions, such advancement requires a doctoral degree. At 2-year colleges, a doctorate is helpful but not usually required for advancement, except for advancement to some top administrative positions, which generally required a doctorate.

Employment

Postsecondary teachers held nearly 1.7 million jobs in 2008. The following tabulation shows postsecondary teaching jobs in specialties having 20,000 or more jobs in 2008:

Graduate teaching assistants 159,700
Health specialties teachers 155,300
Vocational education teachers 120,200
Art, drama, and music teachers 93,800
Business teachers 85,400
English language and literature teachers 74,800
Education teachers 70,200
Biological science teachers 64,700

Nursing instructors and teachers 55,100
Mathematical science teachers 54,800
Engineering teachers 40,600
Psychology teachers... 38,900
Computer science teachers................................. 38,800
Foreign language and literature teachers 32,100
Communications teachers 29,900
History teachers... 26,000
Philosophy and religion teachers 25,100
Chemistry teachers 24,800
Recreation and fitness studies teachers 21,000
Sociology teachers... 20,300
Postsecondary teachers, all other 298,000

Job Outlook

Job openings will stem from faster-than-the-average employment growth and many expected retirements. Competition is expected for tenure-track positions; better opportunities are expected for part-time or non-tenure-track positions. Ph.D. recipients should experience the best job prospects.

Employment change. Postsecondary teachers are expected to grow by 15 percent between 2008 and 2018, which is faster than the average for all occupations. Projected growth in the occupation will be due primarily to increases in college and university enrollment over the next decade. This enrollment growth stems mainly from the expected increase in the population of 18- to 24-year-olds, who constitute the majority of students at postsecondary institutions, and from the increasing number of high school graduates who choose to attend these institutions. Adults returning to college to enhance their career prospects or to update their skills also will continue to create new opportunities for postsecondary teachers, particularly at community colleges and for-profit institutions that cater to working adults. However, many postsecondary educational institutions receive a significant portion of their funding from state and local governments, so expansion of public higher education will be limited by state and local budgets.

Job prospects. Competition is expected for tenure-track positions; better opportunities are expected for part-time or non-tenure-track positions. A significant number of openings in this occupation will be created by growth in enrollments and the need to replace the large numbers of postsecondary teachers who are likely to retire over the next decade. Many postsecondary teachers were hired in the late 1960s and the 1970s to teach members of the baby-boom generation, and they are expected to retire in growing numbers in the years ahead. Ph.D. recipients should experience the best job prospects.

Although competition will remain tight for tenure-track positions at 4-year colleges and universities, there will be available a considerable number of part-time and renewable term appointments at these institutions and at community colleges. Opportunities will be available for master's degree holders because there will be considerable growth at community colleges, career education programs, and other institutions that employ them.

Opportunities for graduate teaching assistants are expected to be good, reflecting expectations of higher undergraduate enrollments. Graduate teaching assistants play an integral role in the postsecond-

Projections Data from the National Employment Matrix

Occupational title	SOC Code	Employment, 2008	Projected employment, 2018	Change, 2008–2018	
				Number	Percent
Postsecondary teachers...	25-1000	1,699,200	1,956,100	256,900	15

NOTE: Data in this table are rounded.

ary education system, and they are expected to continue to do so in the future.

One of the main reasons students attend postsecondary institutions is to prepare themselves for careers, so the best job prospects for postsecondary teachers are likely to be in rapidly growing fields that offer many nonacademic career options, such as business, nursing and other health specialties, and biological sciences.

Earnings

Median annual earnings of all postsecondary teachers in May 2008 were $58,830. The middle 50 percent earned between $41,600 and $83,960. The lowest 10 percent earned less than $28,870, and the highest 10 percent earned more than $121,850.

Earnings for college faculty vary with the rank and type of institution, geographic area, and field. According to a 2008–2009 survey by the American Association of University Professors, salaries for full-time faculty averaged $79,439. By rank, the average was $108,749 for professors, $76,147 for associate professors, $63,827 for assistant professors, $45,977 for instructors, and $52,436 for lecturers. In 2008–2009, full-time faculty salaries averaged $92,257 in private independent institutions, $77,009 in public institutions, and $71,857 in religiously affiliated private colleges and universities. Faculty in 4-year institutions earn higher salaries, on average, than do those in 2-year schools. In fields with high-paying nonacademic alternatives—medicine, law, engineering, and business, among others—earnings exceed these averages. In others fields, such as the humanities and education, earnings are lower. Earnings for postsecondary career and technical education teachers vary widely by subject, academic credentials, experience, and region of the country.

Many faculty members have significant earnings from consulting, teaching additional courses, research, writing for publication, or other employment, in addition to their base salary. Many college and university faculty enjoy unique benefits, including access to campus facilities, tuition waivers for dependents, housing and travel allowances, and paid leave for sabbaticals. Part-time faculty and instructors usually have fewer benefits than full-time faculty have.

Related Occupations

Postsecondary teaching requires the ability to communicate ideas well, motivate students, and be creative. Workers in other occupations that require these skills are authors, writers, and editors; counselors; education administrators; management analysts; librarians; public relations specialists; teachers—kindergarten, elementary, middle, and secondary; and teachers—vocational.

Sources of Additional Information

Professional societies related to a field of study often provide information on academic and nonacademic employment opportunities.

Special publications on higher education, such as *The Chronicle of Higher Education*, list specific employment opportunities for faculty. These publications are available in libraries.

For information on the Preparing Future Faculty program, contact

▸ Council of Graduate Schools, One Dupont Circle NW, Suite 230, Washington, DC 20036-1173. Internet: www.preparing-faculty.org

Teachers—Preschool, Except Special Education

(O*NET 25-2011.00)

Significant Points

■ Training requirements are set by each state and range from a high school diploma to a college degree, although a high school diploma and a little experience is adequate for many preschool teaching jobs.

■ Employment of preschool teachers is projected to grow faster than the average through 2018. Job prospects are expected to be excellent due to high turnover.

Nature of the Work

Preschool teachers nurture, teach, and care for children who have not yet entered kindergarten. They provide early childhood care and education through a variety of teaching strategies. They teach children, usually aged 3 to 5, both in groups and one on one. They do so by planning and implementing a curriculum that covers various areas of a child's development, such as motor skills, social and emotional development, and language development.

Preschool teachers play a vital role in the development of children. They introduce children to reading and writing, expanded vocabulary, creative arts, science, and social studies. They use games, music, artwork, films, books, computers, and other tools to teach concepts and skills.

Preschool children learn mainly through investigation, play, and formal teaching. Preschool teachers capitalize on children's play to further language and vocabulary development (using storytelling, rhyming games, and acting games), improve social skills (having the children work together to build a neighborhood in a sandbox), and introduce scientific and mathematical concepts (showing the children how to balance and count blocks when building a bridge or how to mix colors when painting). Thus, an approach that includes small and large group activities, one-on-one instruction, and learning through creative activities such as art, dance, and music, is adopted to teach preschool children. Letter recognition, phonics, numbers, and awareness of nature and science are introduced at the preschool level to prepare students for kindergarten.

Preschool teachers often work with students from varied ethnic, racial, and religious backgrounds. With growing minority populations in most parts of the country, it is important for teachers to be able to work effectively with a diverse student population. Accordingly, some schools offer training to help teachers enhance their awareness and understanding of different cultures. Teachers may also include multicultural programming in their lesson plans, to address the needs of all students, regardless of their cultural background.

Work environment. Seeing students develop new skills and gain an appreciation of knowledge and learning can be very rewarding. Preschool teachers in private programs and schools generally enjoy smaller class sizes and more control over establishing the curriculum and setting standards for performance and discipline.

Part-time schedules are common among preschool teachers. Many teachers work the traditional 10-month school year with a 2-month vacation during the summer. During the vacation break, those on the 10-month schedule may teach in summer sessions, take other jobs, travel, or pursue personal interests. Many enroll in college courses or workshops to continue their education. Teachers in districts with a year-round schedule typically work 8 weeks, are on vacation for 1 week, and have a 5-week midwinter break. Preschool teachers working in day care settings often work year round.

Training, Other Qualifications, and Advancement

Education requirements vary greatly from state to state and range from a high school diploma to a college degree. The requirements also vary based on employer requirements and the source of the funding of the preschool program.

Education and training. The training and qualifications required of preschool teachers vary widely. Each state has its own licensing requirements that regulate caregiver training. These requirements range from a high school diploma and a national Child Development Associate (CDA) credential to community college courses or a college degree in child development or early childhood education.

Different public funding streams may set other education and professional development requirements. For example, many states have separate funding for prekindergarten programs for 4-year-old children and typically set higher education degree requirements for those teachers, including those providing prekindergarten in a child care center. Head Start programs must meet federal standards for teacher requirements. For example, by 2011 all Head Start teachers must have at least an associate degree.

Some employers may prefer workers who have taken secondary or postsecondary courses in child development and early childhood education or who have work experience in a child care setting. Other employers require their own specialized training. An increasing

number of employers require at least an associate degree in early childhood education

Other qualifications. In addition to being knowledgeable about the subjects they teach, preschool teachers must have the ability to communicate, inspire trust and confidence, and motivate students, as well as an understanding of the students' educational and emotional needs. Preschool teachers must be able to recognize and respond to individual and cultural differences in students and employ different teaching methods that will result in higher student achievement. They should be organized, dependable, patient, and creative. Teachers also must be able to work cooperatively and communicate effectively with other teachers, support staff, parents, and members of the community. Private schools associated with religious institutions also desire candidates who share the values that are important to the institution.

Advancement. Preschool teachers usually work their way up from assistant teacher, to teacher, to lead teacher—who may be responsible for the instruction of several classes—and, finally, to director of the center. Those with a bachelor's degree frequently are qualified to teach kindergarten through grade 3 as well. Teaching at these higher grades often results in higher pay.

Employment

Preschool teachers, except special education, held 457,200 jobs in 2008. They are most often employed in child day care services (65 percent), and public and private educational services (15 percent). Employment of teachers is geographically distributed much the same as the population.

Job Outlook

Employment of preschool teachers is projected to grow faster than the average through 2018. Job prospects are expected to be excellent due to high turnover.

Employment change. Employment of preschool teachers is expected to grow by 19 percent from 2008 to 2018, which is faster than the average for all occupations. Continued emphasis on early childhood education is increasing the demand for preschool teachers. Some states are instituting programs to improve early childhood education, such as offering full day and universal preschool. These programs, along with projected higher enrollment growth for preschool age children, will create new jobs for preschool teachers.

However, this growth will be moderated by slower growth in the number of children aged 3 to 5, the age group most often enrolled in preschool programs. In addition, these workers are often assisted by child care workers and teachers assistants and higher demand for these workers may temper growth for preschool teachers.

Job prospects. High replacement needs should create good job opportunities for preschool teachers. Qualified persons who are interested in this work should have little trouble finding and keeping a job. Many preschool teachers must be replaced each year as they leave the occupation to fulfill family responsibilities, to study, or for other reasons. Others leave because they are interested in pursuing other occupations or because of low wages.

Projections Data from the National Employment Matrix

Occupational title	SOC Code	Employment, 2008	Projected employment, 2018	Change, 2008–2018	
				Number	Percent
Preschool teachers, except special education.............. 25-2011		457,200	543,900	86,700	19

NOTE: Data in this table are rounded.

Earnings

Median annual wages of preschool teachers were $23,870 in May 2008; the middle 50 percent earned $18,840 to $31,430; the bottom 10 percent earned less than $16,030 and the top 10 percent earned more than $41,660.

Related Occupations

Preschool teaching requires a talent for working with young children; related occupations include the following child care workers; teachers assistants; teachers—kindergarten, elementary, middle, secondary; and teachers—special education.

Sources of Additional Information

Information on licensure or certification requirements and approved teacher training institutions is available from local school systems and state departments of education.

For information on careers in educating children and issues affecting preschool teachers, contact either of the following organizations:

▶ National Association for the Education of Young Children, 1313 L St. NW, Suite 500, Washington, DC 20005. Internet: www.naeyc.org

▶ Council for Professional Recognition, 2460 16th St. NW, Washington, DC 20009-3575. Internet: www.cdacouncil.org

Teachers—Self-Enrichment Education

(O*NET 25-3021.00)

Significant Points

■ Many self-enrichment teachers are self-employed or work part time.

■ Teachers should have knowledge and enthusiasm for their subject, but little formal training is required.

■ Employment is projected to grow much faster than the average for all occupations and job prospects should be favorable; opportunities may vary by subject taught.

Nature of the Work

Self-enrichment teachers provide instruction on a wide variety of subjects that students take for fun or self-improvement. Some teach classes that provide students with useful life skills, such as cooking, personal finance, and time management. Others provide group instruction intended solely for recreation, such as photography, pottery, and painting. Many others provide one-on-one instruction in a variety of subjects, including singing, or playing a musical instrument. Some teachers conduct courses on academic subjects, such as literature, foreign languages, and history, in a nonacademic setting. The classes taught by self-enrichment teachers seldom lead to a degree and attendance is voluntary. At the same time, these courses can provide students with useful skills, such as knowledge of computers or foreign languages, which make them more attractive to employers.

Among self-enrichment teachers, their styles and methods of instruction can differ greatly. Most self-enrichment classes are relatively informal. Some classes, such as pottery or sewing, may be largely hands-on, with the instructor demonstrating methods or techniques for the class, observing students as they attempt to do it themselves, and pointing out mistakes to students and offering suggestions for improving their techniques. Other classes, such as those involving financial planning or religion and spirituality, might center on lectures or rely more heavily on group discussions. Self-enrichment teachers may also teach classes offered through religious institutions, such as marriage preparation or classes in religion for children.

Many of the classes that self-enrichment educators teach are shorter in duration than classes taken for academic credit; some finish in 1 or 2 days or several weeks. These brief classes tend to be introductory in nature and generally focus on only one topic—for example, a cooking class that teaches students how to make bread. Some self-enrichment classes introduce children and youth to activities such as piano or drama, and they may be designed to last from 1 week to several months.

Many self-enrichment teachers provide one-on-one lessons to students. The instructor might only work with the student for 1 or 2 hours per week and then provide the student with instructions on what to practice in the interim until the next lesson. Many instructors work with the same students on a weekly basis for years and derive satisfaction from observing them mature and gain expertise.

All self-enrichment teachers must prepare lessons beforehand and stay current in their fields. The amount of time required for preparation can vary greatly, depending on the subject being taught and the length of the course. Many self-enrichment teachers are self-employed and provide instruction as part of a personal business. As such, they must collect any fees or tuition and keep records of their students' accounts. Although not a requirement for most self-enrichment classes, teachers often use computers and other modern technologies in their instruction or to maintain their business records.

Work environment. Few self-enrichment education teachers are full-time salaried workers. Most either work part time or are self-employed. Some have several part-time teaching assignments, but it is most common for teachers to have a full-time job in another occupation, often related to the subject that they teach. Although jobs in this occupation are primarily part time and pay is relatively low, most teachers enjoy their work because it gives them the opportunity to share with others a subject that they enjoy.

Many classes for adults are held in the evenings and on weekends to accommodate students who have a job or family responsibilities. Similarly, self-enrichment classes for children are usually held after school, on weekends, or during school vacations.

Because students in self-enrichment programs attend classes by choice, they tend to be highly motivated and eager to learn. Students bring their own unique experiences to class, and many teachers find this aspect of the work especially rewarding and satisfying. Self-enrichment teachers must have a great deal of patience, however, particularly when working with young children.

Training, Other Qualifications, and Advancement

The main qualification for self-enrichment teachers is expertise in their subject area, but requirements vary greatly with the type of class taught and the place of employment.

Education and training. In general, there are few educational or training requirements for a job as a self-enrichment teacher beyond being an expert in the subject taught. To demonstrate expertise, however, self enrichment teachers may be required to have formal training in disciplines such as art or music, where specific teacher training programs are available. Prospective dance teachers, for example, may complete programs that prepare them to teach many types of dance—from ballroom to ballet. Other employers may require a portfolio of a teacher's work. For example, to secure a job teaching a photography course, an applicant often needs to show examples of previous work. Some self-enrichment teachers are trained educators or other professionals who teach enrichment classes in their spare time. In many self-enrichment fields, however, instructors are simply experienced in the field, and want to share that experience with others.

Other qualifications. Self-enrichment teachers should have good speaking skills and a talent for making the subject interesting. Patience and the ability to explain and instruct students at a basic level are important as well, particularly for teachers who work with children.

Advancement. Opportunities for advancement in this profession are limited. Some part-time teachers are able to move into full-time teaching positions or program administrator positions, such as coordinator or director. Experienced teachers may mentor new instructors.

Employment

Teachers of self-enrichment education held about 253,600 jobs in 2008. The largest numbers of teachers were employed by public and private educational institutions and providers of social assistance.

Job Outlook

Employment of self-enrichment education teachers is expected to grow much faster than the average for all occupations, and job prospects should be favorable. New opportunities arise constantly because many of these kinds of jobs are short term and they are often held as a second job.

Employment change. Employment of self-enrichment education teachers is expected to increase over the 2008–2018 period by 32 percent, which is much faster than the average for all occupations. The need for self-enrichment teachers is expected to grow as more people embrace lifelong learning and course offerings expand. Demand for self-enrichment education will also increase, as more people seek to gain or improve skills that will make them more attractive to prospective employers. Some self-enrichment teachers offer instruction in foreign languages, computer programming or applications, public speaking, and many other subjects that help students gain marketable skills. People increasingly take courses to improve their job skills, which creates more demand for self-enrichment teachers.

Job prospects. Job prospects should be generally favorable in the coming decade, as increasing demand and high turnover create many opportunities. These opportunities may vary, however, because some fields have more prospective teachers than others. Opportunities should be best for teachers of subjects that are not easily researched on the Internet and those that benefit from hands-on experiences, such as cooking, crafts, and the arts. Classes on self-improvement, personal finance, and computer and Internet-related subjects are also expected to be popular.

Earnings

Median hourly wages of self-enrichment teachers were $17.17 in May 2008. The middle 50 percent earned between $12.50 and $24.98. The lowest 10 percent earned less than $9.15, and the highest 10 percent earned more than $32.68. Self-enrichment teachers are generally paid by the hour or for each class that they teach. Earnings may also be tied to the number of students enrolled in the class.

Projections Data from the National Employment Matrix

Occupational title	SOC Code	Employment, 2008	Projected employment, 2018	Change, 2008–2018	
				Number	Percent
Self-enrichment education teachers............................	25-3021	253,600	334,900	81,300	32

NOTE: Data in this table are rounded.

Part-time instructors are usually paid for each class that they teach, and receive few benefits. Full-time teachers are generally paid a salary and may receive health insurance and other benefits.

Related Occupations

The work of self-enrichment teachers is closely related to artists and related workers; athletes, coaches, umpires, and related workers; dancers and choreographers; musicians, singers, and related workers; recreation workers; teachers—kindergarten, elementary, middle, and secondary; and teachers—preschool, except special education.

Sources of Additional Information

For information on employment of self-enrichment teachers, contact local schools, colleges, or companies that offer self-enrichment programs.

Teachers—Special Education

(O*NET 25-2041.00, 25-2042.00, and 25-2043.00)

Significant Points

- Special education teachers must be organized, patient, able to motivate students, understanding of their students' special needs, and accepting of differences in others.

- All states require teachers to be licensed; traditional licensing requires the completion of a special education teacher training program and at least a bachelor's degree, although some states require a master's degree.

- Many states offer alternative licensure programs to attract college graduates who do not have training in education.

- Excellent job prospects are expected due to rising enrollments of special education students and reported shortages of qualified teachers.

Nature of the Work

Special education teachers work with children and youths who have a variety of disabilities. A small number of special education teachers work with students with severe cognitive, emotional, or physical disabilities, primarily teaching them life skills and basic literacy. However, the majority of special education teachers work with children with mild to moderate disabilities, using or modifying the general education curriculum to meet the child's individual needs and providing required remedial instruction. Most special education teachers instruct students at the preschool, elementary, middle, and secondary school level, although some work with infants and toddlers.

The various types of disabilities that may qualify individuals for special education programs are as follows: specific learning disabilities, speech or language impairments, mental retardation, emotional disturbance, multiple disabilities, hearing impairments, orthopedic impairments, visual impairments, autism, combined deafness and blindness, traumatic brain injury, and other health impairments.

Students are identified under one or more of these categories. Early identification of a child with special needs is an important part of a special education teacher's job, because early intervention is essential in educating children with disabilities.

Special education teachers use various techniques to promote learning. Depending on the student, teaching methods can include intensive individualized instruction, problem-solving assignments, and small-group work. When students need special accommodations to learn the general curriculum or to take a test, special education teachers ensure that appropriate accommodations are provided, such as having material read orally or lengthening the time allowed to take the test.

Special education teachers help to develop an Individualized Education Program (IEP) for each student receiving special education. The IEP sets personalized goals for the student and is tailored to that student's individual needs and abilities. When appropriate, the program includes a transition plan outlining specific steps to prepare students for middle school or high school or, in the case of older students, a job or postsecondary study. Teachers review the IEP with the student's parents, school administrators, and the student's general education teachers. Teachers work closely with parents to inform them of their children's progress and suggest techniques to promote learning outside of school.

Special education teachers design and teach appropriate curricula, assign work geared toward each student's needs and abilities, and grade papers and homework assignments. They are involved in the student's behavioral, social, and academic development, helping them develop emotionally and interact effectively in social situations. Preparing special education students for daily life after graduation also is an important aspect of the job. Teachers provide students with career counseling or help them learn life skills, such as balancing a checkbook.

As schools become more inclusive, special education teachers and general education teachers increasingly work together in general education classrooms. Special education teachers help general educators adapt curriculum materials and teaching techniques to meet the needs of students with disabilities. They coordinate the work of teachers, teacher assistants, and related personnel, such as therapists and social workers, to meet the individualized needs of the student within inclusive special education programs. A large part of a special education teacher's job involves communicating and coordinating with others involved in the child's well-being, including parents, social workers, school psychologists, occupational and physical therapists, school administrators, and other teachers.

Special education teachers work in a variety of settings. Some have their own classrooms and teach only special education students; others work as special education resource teachers and offer individualized help to students in general education classrooms; still others teach together with general education teachers in classes including both general and special education students. Some teachers work with special education students for several hours a day in a resource room, separate from their general education classroom. Considerably fewer special education teachers work in residential facilities or tutor students in homebound or hospital environments.

Some special education teachers work with infants and toddlers in the child's home with his or her parents. Many of these infants have challenges that slow or preclude normal development. Special education teachers help parents learn techniques and activities designed to stimulate the infant and encourage the growth and development of the child's skills. Toddlers usually receive their services at a preschool where special education teachers help them develop social, self-help, motor, language, and cognitive skills, often through the use of play.

Technology is becoming increasingly important in special education. Teachers use specialized equipment such as computers with synthesized speech, interactive educational software programs, and audiotapes to assist children.

Work environment. Special education teachers enjoy the challenge of working with students with disabilities and the opportunity to establish meaningful relationships with them. Although helping these students can be highly rewarding, the work also can be emotionally demanding and physically draining. Many special education teachers are under considerable stress due to heavy workloads and administrative tasks. They must produce a substantial amount of paperwork documenting each student's progress and work under the threat of litigation against the school or district by parents if correct procedures are not followed or if the parents feel that their child is not receiving an adequate education. Recently passed legislation, however, is intended to reduce the burden of paperwork and the threat of litigation. The physical and emotional demands of the job cause some special education teachers to leave the occupation.

Some schools offer year-round education for special education students, but most special education teachers work only the traditional 10-month school year.

Training, Other Qualifications, and Advancement

All states require special education teachers to be licensed, which typically requires at least a bachelor's degree and the completion of an approved training program in special education teaching. Some states require a master's degree. Most states have alternative methods for entry for bachelor's degree holders who do not have training in education.

Education and training. Many colleges and universities across the United States offer programs in special education at the undergraduate, master's, and doctoral degree levels. Special education teachers often undergo longer periods of training than do general education teachers. Most bachelor's degree programs last four years and include general and specialized courses in special education. However, an increasing number of institutions are requiring a fifth year or other graduate-level preparation. Some programs require specialization, while others offer generalized special education degrees. The last year of the program usually is spent student teaching in a classroom supervised by a certified special education teacher.

Licensure. All 50 states and the District of Columbia require special education teachers to be licensed. The state board of education or a licensure advisory committee usually grants licenses, and licensure varies by state. In some states, special education teachers receive a general education credential to teach kindergarten through grade 12. These teachers then train in a specialty, such as learning disabilities or behavioral disorders. Many states offer general special education

licenses across a variety of disability categories, while others license several different specialties within special education.

For traditional licensing, all states require a bachelor's degree and the completion of an approved teacher preparation program with a prescribed number of subject and education credits and supervised practice teaching. However, some states also require a master's degree in special education, which involves at least one year of additional coursework, including a specialization, beyond the bachelor's degree. Most states require a prospective teacher to pass a professional assessment test as well. Some states have reciprocity agreements allowing special education teachers to transfer their licenses from one state to another, but many others still require that experienced teachers reapply and pass licensing requirements to work in the state.

Most states also offer alternative routes to licensing that are intended to attract people into teaching who do not fulfill traditional licensing standards. Most alternative licensure programs are open to anyone with a bachelor's degree, although some are designed for recent college graduates or professionals in other education occupations. Programs typically require the completion of a period of supervised preparation and instruction through a partnering college or university and passing an assessment test while teaching under supervision for a period of 1 to 2 years.

Other qualifications. Special education teachers must be organized, patient, able to motivate students, understanding of their students' special needs, and accepting of differences in others. Teachers must be creative and apply different types of teaching methods to reach students who are having difficulty learning. Communication and cooperation are essential skills because special education teachers spend a great deal of time interacting with others, including students, parents, and school faculty and administrators.

Advancement. Special education teachers can advance to become supervisors or administrators. They also may earn advanced degrees and become instructors in colleges that prepare others to teach special education. In some school systems, highly experienced teachers can become mentors to less experienced teachers,.

Employment

Special education teachers held a total of about 473,000 jobs in 2008. Nearly all worked in public and private educational institutions. A few worked for individual and social assistance agencies or residential facilities, or in homebound or hospital environments.

Job Outlook

Employment is expected to increase faster than the average for all occupations. Job prospects should be excellent because many districts report problems finding adequate numbers of licensed special education teachers.

Employment change. The number of special education teachers is expected to increase by 17 percent from 2008 to 2018, which is faster than the average for all occupations. Although student enrollments in general are expected to grow more slowly than in the past, continued increases in the number of special education students needing services will generate a greater need for special education teachers.

Projections Data from the National Employment Matrix

Occupational title	SOC Code	Employment, 2008	Projected employment, 2018	Change, 2008–2018	
				Number	Percent
Special education teachers.................................. 25-2040		473,000	554,900	81,900	17
Special education teachers, preschool, kindergarten, and elementary school.................. 25-2041		226,000	270,300	44,300	20
Special education teachers, middle school.............. 25-2042		100,300	118,400	18,100	18
Special education teachers, secondary school.......... 25-2043		146,700	166,200	19,500	13

NOTE: Data in this table are rounded.

The number of students requiring special education services has grown steadily in recent years because of improvements that have allowed learning disabilities to be diagnosed at earlier ages. In addition, legislation emphasizing training and employment for individuals with disabilities and educational reforms requiring higher standards for graduation have increased demand for special education services. Also, the percentage of foreign-born special education students is expected to grow as teachers become more adept in recognizing disabilities in that population. Finally, more parents are expected to seek special services for children who have difficulty meeting the new, higher standards required of students.

Job prospects. In addition to job openings resulting from growth, a large number of openings will result from the need to replace special education teachers who switch to teaching general education, change careers altogether, or retire. At the same time, many school districts report difficulty finding sufficient numbers of qualified teachers. As a result, special education teachers should have excellent job prospects.

The job outlook does vary by geographic area and specialty. Although most areas of the country report difficulty finding qualified applicants, positions in inner cities and rural areas usually are more plentiful than job openings in suburban or wealthy urban areas. Student populations also are expected to increase more rapidly in certain parts of the country, such as the South and West, resulting in increased demand for special education teachers in those regions. In addition, job opportunities may be better in certain specialties—for example, teachers who work with children with multiple disabilities or those who work with children with severe disabilities such as autism—because of large increases in the enrollment of special education students classified into those categories. Legislation encouraging early intervention and special education for infants, toddlers, and preschoolers has created a need for early childhood special education teachers. Bilingual special education teachers and those with multicultural experience also are needed, to work with an increasingly diverse student population.

Earnings

Median annual wages in May 2008 of special education teachers who worked primarily in preschools, kindergartens, and elementary schools were $50,020. The middle 50 percent earned between $40,480 and $63,500. The lowest 10 percent earned less than $33,770, and the highest 10 percent earned more than $78,980.

Median annual wages of middle school special education teachers were $50,810. The middle 50 percent earned between $41,720 and $63,480. The lowest 10 percent earned less than $35,180, and the highest 10 percent earned more than $78,200.

Median annual wages of special education teachers who worked primarily in secondary schools were $51,340. The middle 50 percent earned between $41,810 and $65,680. The lowest 10 percent earned less than $35,150, and the highest 10 percent earned more than $82,000.

In 2008, about 64 percent of special education teachers belonged to unions or were covered by union contracts.

In most schools, teachers receive extra pay for coaching sports and working with students in extracurricular activities. Some teachers earn extra income during the summer, working in the school system or in other jobs.

Related Occupations

Special education teachers work with students who have disabilities and special needs. Other occupations involved with the identification, evaluation, and development of students with disabilities include audiologists; counselors; occupational therapists; psychologists; recreational therapists; social workers; speech-language pathologists; teacher assistants; teachers—kindergarten, elementary, middle, and secondary; teachers—preschool, except special education; and teachers—vocational.

Sources of Additional Information

For information on professions related to early intervention and education for children with disabilities, listings of schools with special education training programs, information on teacher certification, and general information on related personnel issues, contact

▶ The Council for Exceptional Children, 1110 N. Glebe Rd., Suite 300, Arlington, VA 22201. Internet: www.cec.sped.org

▶ National Center for Special Education Personnel and Related Service Providers, National Association of State Directors of Special Education, 1800 Diagonal Rd., Suite 320, Alexandria, VA 22314. Internet: www.personnelcenter.org

To learn more about the special education teacher certification and licensing requirements in individual states, contact the state's department of education.

Truck Drivers and Driver/Sales Workers

(O*NET 53-3031.00, 53-3032.00, and 53-3033.00)

Significant Points

- Truck drivers and driver/sales workers comprise one of the largest occupations, holding 3.2 million jobs.
- Overall job opportunities should be favorable, especially for long-haul drivers.
- A commercial driver's license is the most important qualification for most jobs.

Nature of the Work

Almost every product sold in the United States spends at least some time in a truck. While planes, trains, and ships are also used to transport goods, no other form of transportation has the same level of flexibility as a truck. As a result, trucks are used to transport everything from canned food to automobiles. *Truck drivers* and *driver/sales workers* operate these vehicles.

Drivers are responsible for picking up and delivering freight from one place to another. This may be from a manufacturer to a distribution center, from a distribution center to a customer, or between distribution centers. In addition, drivers may be responsible for loading and unloading their cargo. They are also responsible for following applicable laws, keeping logs of their activities, and making sure that their equipment is in good working condition.

Heavy truck and tractor-trailer drivers operate trucks or vans with a capacity of at least 26,001 pounds gross vehicle weight (GVW). The vast majority of these are *over-the-road* or *long-haul drivers*, meaning they deliver goods over intercity routes that may span several states. Some drivers have regular routes or regions where they drive the most, while others take on routes throughout the country or even to Canada and Mexico.

Long-haul drivers are often responsible for planning their own routes. In most cases, operators are given a delivery location and deadline, and they must determine how to get the shipment to its destination on time. This can be difficult, as drivers must find routes that allow large trucks, and must work within the rules imposed by the U.S. Department of Transportation. Drivers must fill out logs to show that they have followed these rules, which mandate maximum driving times and rest periods between shifts. Companies sometimes use two drivers on long runs to minimize downtime. On these "sleeper" runs, one driver sleeps in a berth behind the cab while the other operates the truck.

Light or *delivery services truck drivers*, often called *pick-up and delivery* or *P&D drivers*, deliver goods within an urban area or small region. In most cases, they carry shipments from distribution centers to businesses or households. Drivers who work for package delivery services may have a single load and make many stops over the course of the day, while other drivers might have several loads in the course of a day. Depending on the load, drivers may have helpers who load and unload their vehicles. When making deliveries, they

may accept payments for cash-on-delivery shipments, or handle paperwork, such as delivery confirmations and receipts.

Specialized truck drivers work with unusual loads. While most trucks carry freight loads in semi-trailers or vans, some carry liquids, oversized loads, or cars. Others carry hazardous materials, such as dangerous chemicals needed for industrial purposes, or waste from chemical processes that must be stored in approved facilities. Drivers who work with these types of loads must follow strict procedures to make sure their loads are delivered safely.

Some drivers, called *driver/sales workers* or *route drivers*, have sales responsibilities. For example, many driver/sales workers deliver and arrange goods to be sold in grocery stores. They may recommend that a store increase their inventory or encourage store managers to sell new products. Companies that rent linens, towels, or uniforms employ driver/sales workers to visit businesses regularly to replace soiled laundry. Driver/sales workers may also be responsible for soliciting new customers along their routes.

Work environment. Despite new technologies such as power steering, driving a truck is still a physically demanding job. Driving for many hours at a stretch, loading and unloading cargo, and making many deliveries can be tiring. Making the decision to work as a long-haul driver is a major lifestyle choice—drivers may be away from home for days or weeks at a time, and they often spend a great deal of time alone. Local truck drivers usually return home in the evening.

The U.S. Department of Transportation regulates work hours and other working conditions of truck drivers engaged in interstate commerce. A long-distance driver may drive for no more than 11 hours per day, and work a total of no more than 14 hours—including driving and non-driving duties. Between working periods, a driver must have at least 10 hours off duty. Drivers also cannot work more than 60 hours in a week without being off-duty for at least 34 hours straight. Drivers are required to document their time in a log, which shows working hours and mileage by day. Many drivers, particularly on long runs, work close to the maximum time permitted because they are usually compensated according to the number of miles they drive. Drivers on long runs face boredom, loneliness, and fatigue. Drivers often travel nights, holidays, and weekends.

Local truck drivers frequently work 50 or more hours a week. Drivers who handle food for chain grocery stores, produce markets, or bakeries typically work long hours—often late at night or early in the morning. Most drivers have regular routes, although some have different routes each day. Many local truck drivers—particularly driver/sales workers—do a considerable amount of lifting, carrying, and walking.

Training, Other Qualifications, and Advancement

Drivers who operate trucks with a gross vehicle weight of 26,001 pounds, or who operate a vehicle carrying hazardous materials or oversized loads, need a commercial driver's license (CDL). Training for the CDL is offered by many private and public vocational-technical schools. A standard driver's license is required to drive all other trucks. Many jobs driving smaller trucks require only brief on-the-job training.

Education and training. Most prospective truck drivers take driver-training courses at a technical or vocational school to prepare for CDL testing. Driver-training courses teach students how to maneuver large vehicles on crowded streets and in highway traffic. These courses also train drivers how to properly inspect trucks and freight for compliance with regulations.

Some states require prospective drivers to complete a training course in basic truck driving before getting their CDL. Some companies have similar requirements. People interested in attending a driving school should check with local trucking companies to make sure the school's training is acceptable. The Professional Truck Driver Institute (PTDI) certifies driver-training courses at truck driver training schools that meet industry standards and Federal Highway Administration guidelines for training tractor-trailer drivers.

Employers usually have training programs for new drivers who have already earned their CDL. This is often informal and may consist of only a few hours of instruction from an experienced driver. Some companies give 1 to 2 days of classroom instruction covering general duties, the operation and loading of a truck, company policies, and the preparation of delivery forms and company records. New drivers may also ride with and observe experienced drivers before getting their own assignments. Drivers receive additional training to drive special types of trucks or handle hazardous materials. Driver/sales workers receive training on the various types of products their company carries so that they can effectively answer questions about the products and more easily market them to their customers.

Licensure. Federal and state regulations govern the qualifications and standards for truck drivers. Drivers must comply with all federal regulations and any state regulations that are in excess of those federal requirements when under that state's jurisdiction.

Truck drivers must have a driver's license issued by the state in which they live. Drivers of trucks with a GVW of 26,001 pounds or more—including most tractor-trailers, as well as bigger straight trucks—must obtain a CDL. All drivers who operate trucks transporting hazardous materials or oversized loads must obtain a CDL and a special endorsement, regardless of truck capacity. In order to receive the hazardous materials endorsement, a driver must be fingerprinted and submit to a criminal background check by the Transportation Security Administration. In many states, a regular driver's license is sufficient for driving light trucks and vans.

To qualify for a CDL, applicants must have clean driving records, pass written tests on rules and regulations, and demonstrate that they can operate commercial trucks safely. A national database permanently records all driving violations committed by those with a CDL, and issuing authorities reject applicants who have suspended or revoked licenses in other states. Licensed drivers must accompany trainees until they get their own CDLs. A person may not hold more than one driver's license at a time and must surrender any other licenses when issued a CDL. Information on how to apply for a CDL may be obtained from state motor vehicle administrations.

Although many states allow 18-year-olds to drive trucks within their borders, a driver must be at least 21 years of age to cross state lines or get special endorsements. Regulations also require drivers to pass a physical examination every 2 years. Physical qualifications include good hearing, at least 20/40 vision with glasses or corrective lenses, and a 70-degree field of vision in each eye. They must also be able to distinguish between colors on traffic lights. Drivers must also have normal use of arms and legs and normal blood pressure. People with epilepsy or diabetes controlled by insulin are not permitted to be interstate truck drivers.

Other qualifications. Federal regulations require employers to test their drivers for alcohol and drug use as a condition of employment and require periodic random tests of the drivers while they are on duty. Drivers may not use any controlled substances, unless prescribed by a licensed physician. A driver must not have been convicted of a felony involving the use of a motor vehicle or a crime involving drugs, driving under the influence of drugs or alcohol, refusing to submit to an alcohol test required by a state or its implied consent laws or regulations, leaving the scene of a crime, or causing a fatality through negligent operation of a motor vehicle. All drivers must be able to read and speak English well enough to read road signs, prepare reports, and communicate with law enforcement officers and the public.

Many trucking companies have higher standards than those required by federal and state regulations. For example, firms often require that drivers be at least 22 years old, be able to lift heavy objects, and have driven trucks for 3 to 5 years. They may also prefer to hire high school graduates and require annual physical examinations.

Drivers must get along well with people because they often deal directly with customers. Employers seek driver/sales workers who speak well and have self-confidence, initiative, tact, and a neat appearance. Employers also look for responsible, self-motivated individuals who are able to work well with little supervision.

Advancement. Although most new truck drivers are assigned to regular driving jobs immediately, some start as extra drivers—substituting for regular drivers who are ill or on vacation. Extra drivers receive a regular assignment when an opening occurs.

Truck drivers can advance to jobs that provide higher earnings, preferred schedules, or better working conditions. Long-haul truck drivers primarily look for new contracts that offer better pay per mile or higher bonuses. Because companies entrust drivers with millions of dollars worth of equipment and freight, drivers who have a long record of safe driving earn far more than new drivers. Local truck drivers may advance to driving heavy or specialized trucks or transfer to long-distance truck driving. Truck drivers occasionally advance to become dispatchers or managers.

Some long-haul truck drivers—called owner-operators—purchase or lease trucks and go into business for themselves. Although some are successful, others fail to cover expenses and go out of business. Owner-operators should have good business sense as well as truck driving experience. Courses in accounting, business, and business mathematics are helpful. Knowledge of truck mechanics can enable owner-operators to perform their own routine maintenance and minor repairs.

Employment

Truck drivers and driver/sales workers held about 3.2 million jobs in 2008. Of these workers, 56 percent were heavy truck and tractor-trailer drivers; 31 percent were light or delivery services truck drivers; and 13 percent were driver/sales workers. Most truck drivers find employment in large metropolitan areas or along major interstate roadways where trucking, retail, and wholesale companies tend to have their distribution outlets. Some drivers work in rural areas, providing specialized services such as delivering newspapers to customers.

The truck transportation industry employed 27 percent of all truck drivers and driver/sales workers in the United States. Another 26 percent worked for companies engaged in wholesale or retail trade. The remaining truck drivers and driver/sales workers were distributed across many industries, including construction and manufacturing.

Around 8 percent of all truck drivers and driver/sales workers were self-employed. Of these, a significant number were owner-operators who either served a variety of businesses independently or leased their services and trucks to a trucking company.

Job Outlook

Overall job opportunities should be favorable for truck drivers, especially for long-haul drivers. However, opportunities may vary greatly in terms of earnings, weekly work hours, number of nights spent on the road, and quality of equipment. Competition is expected for jobs offering the highest earnings or most favorable work schedules. Average employment growth is expected.

Employment change. Overall employment of truck drivers and driver/sales workers is expected to grow 9 percent over the 2008–2018 decade, which is about as fast as the average for all occupations. As the economy grows, the demand for goods will increase, which will lead to more job opportunities. Because it is such a large occupation, 291,900 new jobs will be created over the 2008–2018 period.

The number of heavy and tractor-trailer truck drivers is expected to grow 13 percent between 2008 and 2018, which is about as fast as average, mainly as a result of increasing demand for goods in the U.S. As the economy continues to grow, companies and households will continue to increase their spending on these products, many of which must be shipped over long distances.

Employment of light or delivery services truck drivers should grow 4 percent over the projections decade, which is more slowly than average. Though experiencing slower growth than heavy trucking, light and delivery trucking will similarly be closely tied to the state of the economy. As economic growth occurs, there will be an increasing need for light trucking services, from the distribution of goods from warehouses to the package delivery to households. The number of driver/sales workers is also expected to grow 4 percent between 2008 and 2018, more slowly than average, for the same basic reasons.

Job prospects. Job opportunities should be favorable for truck drivers, especially for long-haul drivers. In addition to occupational growth, numerous job openings will occur as experienced drivers leave this large occupation to transfer to other fields of work, retire, or leave the labor force. As workers leave these jobs, employers work hard to recruit experienced drivers from other companies. As a result, there may be competition for the jobs with the highest earnings and most favorable work schedules. Jobs with local carriers are often more competitive than those with long-distance carriers because of the more desirable working conditions of local carriers.

Despite projected employment growth, the demand for workers may vary greatly depending on the performance of the American economy. During times of expansion, companies may be forced to pay premiums to attract drivers, while during recessions even experienced drivers may find difficulty keeping steady work. Independent owner-operators will be particularly vulnerable to slowdowns. Industries least likely to be affected by economic fluctuation, such as grocery stores, will be the most stable employers of truck drivers and driver/sales workers.

Earnings

Median hourly wages of heavy truck and tractor-trailer drivers were $17.92 in May 2008. The middle 50 percent earned between $14.21 and $22.56. The lowest 10 percent earned less than $11.63, and the highest 10 percent earned more than $27.07.

Median hourly wages of light or delivery services truck drivers were $13.27 in May 2008. The middle 50 percent earned between $10.07 and $17.74. The lowest 10 percent earned less than $8.10, and the highest 10 percent earned more than $24.15.

Median hourly wages of driver/sales workers, including commissions, were $10.70 in May 2008. The middle 50 percent earned between $7.74 and $15.82. The lowest 10 percent earned less than $7.09, and the highest 10 percent earned more than $21.32.

Employers typically pay long-haul drivers by the mile, with bonus opportunities available for drivers who save the company money. Local truck drivers tend to be paid by the hour, with extra pay for working overtime. The per-mile rate can vary greatly from employer to employer and may even depend on the type of cargo being hauled. Some long-distance drivers—especially owner-operators—are paid a share of the revenue from shipping. Typically, pay increases with experience, seniority, and the size and type of truck driven. Most driver/sales workers receive commissions based on their sales in addition to their wages.

Projections Data from the National Employment Matrix

Occupational title	SOC Code	Employment, 2008	Projected employment, 2018	Change, 2008–2018	
				Number	Percent
Driver/sales workers and truck drivers.........................53-3030		3,189,300	3,481,200	291,900	9
Driver/sales workers 53-3031		406,400	424,100	17,700	4
Truck drivers, heavy and tractor-trailer...................53-3032		1,798,400	2,031,300	232,900	13
Truck drivers, light or delivery services...................53-3033		984,500	1,025,900	41,400	4

NOTE: Data in this table are rounded.

Many truck drivers are members of the International Brotherhood of Teamsters. Some truck drivers employed by companies outside the trucking industry are members of unions representing the plant workers of the companies for which they work. In 2008, about 16 percent of truck drivers and driver/sales workers were union members or covered by union contracts.

Related Occupations

Other driving occupations include bus drivers; postal service mail carriers; and taxi drivers and chauffeurs.

An occupation involving similar sales duties is sales representatives, wholesale and manufacturing.

Sources of Additional Information

Information on truck driver employment opportunities is available from local trucking companies and local offices of the state employment service.

Information on career opportunities in truck driving may be obtained from

▸ American Trucking Associations, Inc., 950 N. Glebe Rd., Suite 210, Arlington, VA 22203. Internet: www.truckline.com

▸ Information on becoming a truck driver may be obtained from the American Trucking Associations, Inc. industry recruiting page: www.gettrucking.com

Information on federal regulations for drivers of commercial vehicles can be obtained from

▸ Federal Motor Carrier Safety Administration, 1200 New Jersey Ave. SE, Washington, DC 20590. Internet: www.fmcsa.dot.gov

A list of certified tractor-trailer driver training courses may be obtained from

▸ Professional Truck Driver Institute, 555 E. Braddock Rd., Alexandria, VA 22314. Internet: www.ptdi.org

Information on union truck driving can be obtained from

▸ The International Brotherhood of Teamsters, 25 Louisiana Ave. NW, Washington, DC 20001. Internet: www.teamster.org

Veterinarians

(O*NET 29-1131.00)

Significant Points

■ Veterinarians should love animals and be able to get along with their owners.

■ Graduation from an accredited college of veterinary medicine and a state license are required; admission to veterinary school is competitive.

■ Job opportunities should be excellent.

■ About 80 percent of veterinarians work in private practice.

Nature of the Work

Veterinarians diagnose and treat diseases and dysfunctions of animals. Specifically, they care for the health of pets, livestock,

and animals in zoos, racetracks, and laboratories. Some veterinarians use their skills to protect humans against diseases carried by animals and conduct clinical research on human and animal health problems. Others work in basic research, broadening our knowledge of animals and medical science, and in applied research, developing new ways to use knowledge.

Most veterinarians diagnose animal health problems, vaccinate against diseases, medicate animals suffering from infections or illnesses, treat and dress wounds, set fractures, perform surgery, and advise owners about animal feeding, behavior, and breeding.

According to the American Medical Veterinary Association, 77 percent of veterinarians who work in private medical practices treat pets. These practitioners usually care for dogs and cats but also treat birds, reptiles, rabbits, ferrets, and other animals that can be kept as pets. About 16 percent of veterinarians work in private mixed and food animal practices, where they see pigs, goats, cattle, sheep, and some wild animals in addition to farm animals. A small proportion of private-practice veterinarians, about 6 percent, work exclusively with horses.

Veterinarians who work with food animals or horses usually drive to farms or ranches to provide veterinary services for herds or individual animals. These veterinarians test for and vaccinate against diseases and consult with farm or ranch owners and managers regarding animal production, feeding, and housing issues. They also treat and dress wounds, set fractures, and perform surgery, including cesarean sections on birthing animals. Other veterinarians care for zoo, aquarium, or laboratory animals. Veterinarians of all types euthanize animals when necessary.

Veterinarians who treat animals use medical equipment such as stethoscopes, surgical instruments, and diagnostic equipment, including radiographic and ultrasound equipment. Veterinarians working in research use a full range of sophisticated laboratory equipment.

Some veterinarians contribute to human as well as animal health. A number of veterinarians work with physicians and scientists as they research ways to prevent and treat various human health problems. For example, veterinarians contributed greatly to conquering malaria and yellow fever, solved the mystery of botulism, produced an anticoagulant used to treat some people with heart disease, and defined and developed surgical techniques for humans, such as hip and knee joint replacements and limb and organ transplants. Today, some determine the effects of drug therapies, antibiotics, or new surgical techniques by testing them on animals.

Some veterinarians are involved in food safety and inspection. Veterinarians who are livestock inspectors, for example, check animals for transmissible diseases such as *E. coli*, advise owners on the treatment of their animals, and may quarantine animals. Veterinarians who are meat, poultry, or egg product inspectors examine slaughtering and processing plants, check live animals and carcasses for disease, and enforce government regulations regarding food purity and sanitation. More veterinarians are finding opportunities in food security as they ensure that the nation has abundant and safe food supplies. Veterinarians involved in food security often work along the country's borders as animal and plant health inspectors, where they examine imports and exports of animal products to prevent disease here and in foreign countries. Many of these workers are employed by the Department of Agriculture's Animal and Plant Health Inspection Service division, or the U.S. Food and Drug Administration's Center for Veterinary Medicine.

Work environment. Veterinarians in private or clinical practice often work long hours in a noisy indoor environment. Sometimes they have to deal with emotional or demanding pet owners. When working with animals that are frightened or in pain, veterinarians risk being bitten, kicked, or scratched.

Veterinarians who work with food animals or horses spend time driving between their offices and farms or ranches. They work outdoors in all kinds of weather and may have to treat animals or perform surgery, often under unsanitary conditions.

Veterinarians working in nonclinical areas, such as public health and research, work in clean, well-lit offices or laboratories and have working conditions similar to those of other professionals who work in these environments. Veterinarians in nonclinical areas spend much of their time dealing with people rather than animals.

Veterinarians often work long hours. Those in group practices may take turns being on call for evening, night, or weekend work; solo practitioners may work extended hours (including weekend hours), responding to emergencies or squeezing in unexpected appointments.

Training, Other Qualifications, and Advancement

Veterinarians must obtain a Doctor of Veterinary Medicine degree and a state license. Admission to veterinary school is competitive.

Education and training. Prospective veterinarians must graduate with a Doctor of Veterinary Medicine (D.V.M. or V.M.D.) degree from a 4-year program at an accredited college of veterinary medicine. There are 28 colleges in 26 states that meet accreditation standards set by the Council on Education of the American Veterinary Medical Association (AVMA).

The prerequisites for admission to veterinary programs vary. Many programs do not require a bachelor's degree for entrance, but all require a significant number of credit hours—ranging from 45 to 90 semester hours—at the undergraduate level. However, most of the students admitted have completed an undergraduate program and earned a bachelor's degree. Applicants without a degree face a difficult task in gaining admittance.

Preveterinary courses should emphasize the sciences. Veterinary medical colleges typically require applicants to have taken classes in organic and inorganic chemistry, physics, biochemistry, general biology, animal biology, animal nutrition, genetics, vertebrate embryology, cellular biology, microbiology, zoology, and systemic physiology. Some programs require calculus; some require only statistics, college algebra and trigonometry, or pre-calculus. Most veterinary medical colleges also require some courses in English or literature, other humanities, and the social sciences. Increasingly, courses in general business management and career development have become a standard part of the curriculum to teach new graduates how to effectively run a practice.

In addition to satisfying preveterinary course requirements, applicants must submit test scores from the Graduate Record Examination (GRE), the Veterinary College Admission Test (VCAT), or the

Medical College Admission Test (MCAT), depending on the preference of the college to which they are applying. Currently, 22 schools require the GRE, 4 require the VCAT, and 2 accept the MCAT.

Admission to veterinary school is competitive. The number of accredited veterinary colleges has remained largely the same since 1983, but the number of applicants has risen significantly. Only about 1 in 3 applicants was accepted in 2007.

New graduates with a Doctor of Veterinary Medicine degree may begin to practice veterinary medicine once they receive their license, but many new graduates choose to enter a 1-year internship. Interns receive a small salary but often find that their internship experience leads to better paying opportunities later, relative to those of other veterinarians. Veterinarians who then seek board certification also must complete a 3-year to 4-year residency program that provides intensive training in one of the 39 AVMA-recognized veterinary specialties including internal medicine, oncology, pathology, dentistry, nutrition, radiology, surgery, dermatology, anesthesiology, neurology, cardiology, ophthalmology, preventive medicine, and exotic-small-animal medicine.

Licensure. All states and the District of Columbia require that veterinarians be licensed before they can practice. The only exemptions are for veterinarians working for some federal agencies and some state governments. Licensing is controlled by the states and is not uniform, although all states require the successful completion of the D.V.M. degree—or equivalent education—and a passing grade on a national board examination, the North American Veterinary Licensing Exam. This 8-hour examination consists of 360 multiple-choice questions covering all aspects of veterinary medicine as well as visual materials designed to test diagnostic skills.

The Educational Commission for Foreign Veterinary Graduates grants certification to individuals trained outside the United States who demonstrate that they meet specified requirements for English language and clinical proficiency. This certification fulfills the educational requirement for licensure in all states.

Most states also require candidates to pass a state jurisprudence examination covering state laws and regulations. Some states do additional testing on clinical competency as well. There are few reciprocal agreements between states, so veterinarians who wish to practice in a different state usually must first pass that state's examinations.

Other qualifications. When deciding whom to admit, some veterinary medical colleges place heavy consideration on candidates' veterinary and animal experience. Formal experience, such as work with veterinarians or scientists in clinics, agribusiness, research, or some area of health science, is particularly advantageous. Less formal experience, such as working with animals on a farm, or at a stable or animal shelter, also can be helpful. Students must demonstrate ambition and an eagerness to work with animals.

Prospective veterinarians should love animals and have the ability to get along with their owners, especially pet owners, who usually have strong bonds with their pets. They need good manual dexterity. Veterinarians who intend to go into private practice should possess excellent communication and business skills, because they will need to successfully manage their practice and employees and promote, market, and sell their services.

Advancement. Most veterinarians begin as employees in established group practices. Despite the substantial financial investment in equipment, office space, and staff, many veterinarians with experience eventually set up their own practice or purchase an established one.

Newly trained veterinarians can become U.S. government meat and poultry inspectors, disease-control workers, animal welfare and safety workers, epidemiologists, research assistants, or commissioned officers in the U.S. Public Health Service or various branches of the U.S. Armed Forces. A state license may be required.

Nearly all states have continuing education requirements for licensed veterinarians. Requirements differ by state and may involve attending a class or otherwise demonstrating knowledge of recent medical and veterinary advances.

Employment

Veterinarians held about 59,700 jobs in 2008. According to the American Veterinary Medical Association, 80 percent of veterinarians were employed in a solo or group practice. Most others were salaried employees of colleges or universities; medical schools; private industry, such as research laboratories and pharmaceutical companies; and federal, state, or local government. Data from the U.S. Bureau of Labor Statistics show that the federal government employed about 1,300 civilian veterinarians, chiefly in the U.S. Department of Agriculture and the U.S. Food and Drug Administration's Center for Veterinary Medicine. A few veterinarians work for zoos, but most veterinarians caring for zoo animals are private practitioners who contract with the zoos to provide services, usually on a part-time basis.

In addition, many veterinarians hold veterinary faculty positions in colleges and universities and are classified as teachers.

Job Outlook

Employment is expected to increase much faster than average. Excellent job opportunities are expected.

Employment change. Employment of veterinarians is expected to increase 33 percent over the 2008–2018 decade, much faster than the average for all occupations. Veterinarians usually practice in animal hospitals or clinics and care primarily for small pets. Recent trends indicate particularly strong interest in cats as pets. Faster growth of the cat population is expected to increase the demand for feline medicine and veterinary services, while demand for veterinary care for dogs should continue to grow at a more modest pace.

Many pet owners consider their pets as members of the family, which serves as evidence that people are placing a higher value on their pets and is an example of the *human-animal bond*. These pet owners are becoming more aware of the availability of advanced care and are more willing to pay for intensive veterinary care than owners in the past. Furthermore, the number of pet owners purchasing pet insurance is rising, increasing the likelihood that considerable money will be spent on veterinary care.

More pet owners also will take advantage of nontraditional veterinary services, such as cancer treatment and preventive dental care. Modern veterinary services have caught up to human medicine; certain procedures, such as hip replacement, kidney transplants, and blood transfusions, which were once only available for humans, are now available for animals.

Continued support for public health and food and animal safety, national disease control programs, and biomedical research on human health problems will contribute to the demand for veterinarians, although the number of positions in these areas is smaller than the number in private practice. Homeland security also may provide opportunities for veterinarians involved in efforts to maintain abundant food supplies and minimize animal diseases in the United States and in foreign countries.

Job prospects. Excellent job opportunities are expected because there are only 28 accredited schools of veterinary medicine in the United States, resulting in a limited number of graduates—about 2,500—each year. However, admission to veterinary school is competitive.

New graduates continue to be attracted to companion-animal medicine because they usually prefer to deal with pets and to live and work near heavily populated areas, where most pet owners live. Employment opportunities are very good in cities and suburbs but even better in rural areas because fewer veterinarians compete to work there.

Beginning veterinarians may take positions requiring evening or weekend work to accommodate the extended hours of operation that many practices are offering. Some veterinarians take salaried positions in retail stores offering veterinary services. Self-employed veterinarians usually have to work hard and long to build a sufficient client base.

The number of jobs for farm-animal veterinarians is likely to grow more slowly than the number of jobs for companion-animal veterinarians. Nevertheless, job prospects should be excellent for farm-animal veterinarians because of their lower earnings and because many veterinarians do not want to work outside or in rural or isolated areas.

Veterinarians with training in food safety and security, animal health and welfare, and public health and epidemiology should have the best opportunities for a career in the federal government.

Projections Data from the National Employment Matrix

Occupational title	SOC Code	Employment, 2008	Projected employment, 2018	Change, 2008–2018	
				Number	Percent
Veterinarians..	29-1131	59,700	79,400	19,700	33

NOTE: Data in this table are rounded.

Earnings

Median annual wages of veterinarians were $79,050 in May 2008. The middle 50 percent earned between $61,370 and $104,110. The lowest 10 percent earned less than $46,610, and the highest 10 percent earned more than $143,660.

The average annual salary for veterinarians in the federal government was $93,398 in March 2009.

According to a survey by the American Veterinary Medical Association, average starting salaries of veterinary medical college graduates in 2008 varied by type of practice as follows:

Small animals, exclusively	$64,744
Large animals, exclusively	62,424
Small animals, predominantly	61,753
Mixed animals	58,522
Large animals, predominantly	57,745
Equine (horses)	41,636

Related Occupations

Animal care and service workers; biological scientists; chiropractors; dentists; medical scientists; optometrists; physicians and surgeons; podiatrists; and veterinary technologists and technicians.

Sources of Additional Information

For additional information on careers in veterinary medicine, a list of U.S. schools and colleges of veterinary medicine, and accreditation policies, send a letter-size, self-addressed, stamped envelope to

▸ American Veterinary Medical Association, 1931 N. Meacham Rd., Suite 100, Schaumburg, IL 60173. Internet: www.avma.org

For information on veterinary education, contact

▸ Association of American Veterinary Medical Colleges, 1101 Vermont Ave. NW, Suite 301, Washington, DC 20005. Internet: www.aavmc.org

For information on scholarships, grants, and loans, contact the financial aid officer at the veterinary schools to which you wish to apply.

For information on veterinarians working in zoos, see the *Occupational Outlook Quarterly* article "Wild jobs with wildlife," online at www.bls.gov/opub/ooq/2001/spring/art01.pdf.

Information on obtaining a veterinary position with the federal government is available from the Office of Personnel Management through USAJOBS, the federal government's official employment information system. This resource for locating and applying for job opportunities can be accessed through the Internet at www.usajobs. opm.gov or through an interactive voice response telephone system at (703) 724-1850 or TDD (978) 461-8404. These numbers are not toll free, so charges may result. For advice on how to find and apply for federal jobs, see the *Occupational Outlook Quarterly* article "How to get a job in the federal government," available online at www.bls.gov/opub/ooq/2004/summer/art01.pdf.

Veterinary Technologists and Technicians

(O*NET 29-2056.00)

Significant Points

■ Animal lovers get satisfaction from this occupation, but aspects of the work can be unpleasant, physically and emotionally demanding, and sometimes dangerous.

■ There are primarily two levels of education and training for entry to this occupation: a two-year program for veterinary technicians and a four-year program for veterinary technologists.

■ Employment is expected to grow much faster than average.

■ Overall job opportunities should be excellent; however, keen competition is expected for jobs in zoos and aquariums.

Nature of the Work

Owners of pets and other animals today expect superior veterinary care. To provide this service, veterinarians use the skills of *veterinary technologists* and *technicians*, who perform many of the same duties for a veterinarian that a nurse would for a physician. Although specific job duties vary by employer, there is often little difference between the tasks carried out by technicians and technologists, despite differences in formal education and training. However, most technicians work in private clinical practice while many technologists have the option to work in more advanced research-related jobs.

Veterinary technologists and technicians typically conduct clinical work in a private practice under the supervision of a licensed veterinarian. Veterinary technologists and technicians often perform various medical tests and treat and diagnose medical conditions and diseases in animals. For example, they may perform laboratory tests such as urinalysis and blood counts, assist with dental care, prepare tissue samples, take blood samples, and assist veterinarians in a variety of other diagnostic tests. While most of these duties are performed in a laboratory setting, many are not. For example, some veterinary technicians record patients' case histories, expose and develop X-rays and radiographs, and provide specialized nursing care. In addition, experienced veterinary technicians may discuss a pet's condition with its owners and train new clinic personnel. Veterinary technologists and technicians assisting small-animal practitioners usually care for small pets, such as cats and dogs, but can perform a variety of duties with mice, rats, sheep, pigs, cattle, monkeys, birds, fish, and frogs. Very few veterinary technologists work in mixed animal practices where they care for both small pets and large, nondomestic animals.

Besides working in private clinics and animal hospitals, some veterinary technologists and technicians work in research facilities under the guidance of veterinarians or physicians. In this role, they may administer medications, prepare samples for laboratory examinations, or record information on an animal's genealogy, diet, weight, medications, food intake, and clinical signs of pain and distress. Some may sterilize laboratory and surgical equipment and provide routine postoperative care. Occasionally, veterinary technologists vaccinate newly admitted animals and may have to euthanize seriously ill, severely injured, or unwanted animals.

While the goal of most veterinary technologists and technicians is to promote animal health, some contribute to human health, as well. Veterinary technologists occasionally assist veterinarians in implementing research projects as they work with other scientists in medical-related fields such as gene therapy and cloning. Some find opportunities in biomedical research, wildlife medicine, livestock management, pharmaceutical sales, and increasingly, in biosecurity and disaster preparedness.

Work environment. While people who love animals get satisfaction from helping them, some of the work may be unpleasant, physically and emotionally demanding, and sometimes dangerous. Data from the U.S. Bureau of Labor Statistics show that full-time veterinary technologists and technicians experienced a work-related injury and illness rate that was much higher than the national average. At times, veterinary technicians must clean cages and lift, hold, or restrain animals, risking exposure to bites or scratches. These workers must take precautions when treating animals with germicides or insecticides. The work setting can be noisy.

Veterinary technologists and technicians who witness abused animals or who euthanize unwanted, aged, or hopelessly injured animals may experience emotional stress. Those working for humane societies and animal shelters often deal with the public, some of whom might react with hostility to any implication that the owners are neglecting or abusing their pets. Such workers must maintain a calm and professional demeanor while they enforce the laws regarding animal care.

In some animal hospitals, research facilities, and animal shelters, a veterinary technician is on duty 24 hours a day, which means that some work night shifts. Most full-time veterinary technologists and technicians work about 40 hours a week, although some work 50 or more hours a week.

Training, Other Qualifications, and Advancement

There are primarily two levels of education and training for entry to this occupation: a 2-year program for veterinary technicians and a 4-year program for veterinary technologists.

Education and training. Most entry-level veterinary technicians have a 2-year associate degree from an American Veterinary Medical Association (AVMA)-accredited community college program in veterinary technology in which courses are taught in clinical and laboratory settings using live animals. Currently, about 20 colleges offer veterinary technology programs that are longer and that culminate in a 4-year bachelor's degree in veterinary technology. These 4-year colleges, in addition to some vocational schools, also offer 2-year programs in laboratory animal science. About 10 schools offer distance learning.

In 2009, about 160 veterinary technology programs in 45 states were accredited by the American Veterinary Medical Association (AVMA). Graduation from an AVMA-accredited veterinary technology program allows students to take the credentialing exam in any state in the country.

Those interested in careers as veterinary technologists and technicians should take as many high school science, biology, and math courses as possible. Science courses taken beyond high school, in an associate or bachelor's degree program, should emphasize practical skills in a clinical or laboratory setting.

Technologists and technicians usually begin work as trainees under the direct supervision of a veterinarian. Entry-level workers whose training or educational background encompasses extensive hands-on experience with diagnostic and medical equipment usually require a shorter period of on-the-job training.

Licensure and certification. Each state regulates veterinary technicians and technologists differently; however, all states require them to pass a credentialing exam following coursework. Passing the state exam assures the public that the technician or technologist has sufficient knowledge to work in a veterinary clinic or hospital. Candidates are tested for competency through an examination that includes oral, written, and practical portions and that is regulated by the State Board of Veterinary Examiners or the appropriate state agency. Depending on the state, candidates may become registered, licensed, or certified. Most states, however, use the National Veterinary Technician (NVT) exam. Prospects usually can have their passing scores transferred from one state to another, so long as both states use the same exam.

Employers recommend American Association for Laboratory Animal Science (AALAS) certification for those seeking employment in a research facility. AALAS offers certification for three levels of technician competence, with a focus on three principal areas— animal husbandry, facility management, and animal health and welfare. Those who wish to become certified must satisfy a combination of education and experience requirements prior to taking the AALAS examination. Work experience must be directly related to the maintenance, health, and well-being of laboratory animals and must be gained in a laboratory animal facility as defined by AALAS. Candidates who meet the necessary criteria can begin pursuing the desired certification on the basis of their qualifications. The lowest level of certification is Assistant Laboratory Animal Technician (ALAT), the second level is Laboratory Animal Technician (LAT), and the highest level of certification is Laboratory Animal Technologist (LATG). The AALAS examination consists of multiple-choice questions and is longer and more difficult for higher levels of certification, ranging from 2 hours and 120 multiple-choice questions for the ALAT to 3 hours and 180 multiple-choice questions for the LATG.

Other qualifications. As veterinary technologists and technicians often deal with pet owners, communication skills are very important. In addition, technologists and technicians should be able to work well with others, because teamwork with veterinarians and other veterinary technicians is common. Organizational ability and the ability to pay attention to detail also are important.

Advancement. As they gain experience, technologists and technicians take on more responsibility and carry out more assignments with little veterinary supervision. Some eventually may become supervisors.

Projections Data from the National Employment Matrix

Occupational title	SOC Code	Employment, 2008	Projected employment, 2018	Change, 2008–2018	
				Number	Percent
Veterinary technologists and technicians 29-2056		79,600	108,100	28,500	36

NOTE: Data in this table are rounded.

Employment

Veterinary technologists and technicians held about 79,600 jobs in 2008. About 91 percent worked in veterinary services. The remainder worked in boarding kennels, animal shelters, rescue leagues, and zoos.

Job Outlook

Excellent job opportunities will stem from the need to replace veterinary technologists and technicians who leave the occupation and from the limited output of qualified veterinary technicians from 2-year programs, which are not expected to meet the demand over the 2008–2018 period. Employment is expected to grow much faster than average.

Employment change. Employment of veterinary technologists and technicians is expected to grow 36 percent over the 2008–2018 projection period, which is much faster than the average for all occupations. Pet owners are becoming more affluent and more willing to pay for advanced veterinary care because many of them consider their pet to be part of the family. This growing affluence and view of pets will continue to increase the demand for veterinary care. The vast majority of veterinary technicians work at private clinical practice under veterinarians. As the number of veterinarians grows to meet the demand for veterinary care, so will the number of veterinary technicians needed to assist them.

The number of pet owners who take advantage of veterinary services for their pets is expected to grow over the projection period, increasing employment opportunities. The availability of advanced veterinary services, such as preventive dental care and surgical procedures, also will provide opportunities for workers specializing in those areas as they will be needed to assist licensed veterinarians. The growing number of cats kept as companion pets is expected to boost the demand for feline medicine and services. Further demand for these workers will stem from the desire to replace veterinary assistants with more highly skilled technicians in animal clinics and hospitals, shelters, boarding kennels, animal control facilities, and humane societies.

Continued support for public health, food and animal safety, and national disease control programs, as well as biomedical research on human health problems, also will contribute to the demand for veterinary technologists, although the number of positions in these areas is fewer than in private practice.

Job prospects. Excellent job opportunities are expected because of the relatively few veterinary technology graduates each year. The number of 2-year programs has recently grown to about 160, but due to small class sizes, fewer than 3,800 graduates are anticipated each year, a number that is not expected to meet demand. Additionally, many veterinary technicians remain in the field less than 10 years,

so the need to replace workers who leave the occupation each year also will produce many job opportunities.

Veterinary technologists also will enjoy excellent job opportunities due to the relatively few graduates from 4-year programs—about 500 annually. However, unlike veterinary technicians who usually work in private clinical practice, veterinary technologists will have better opportunities for research jobs in a variety of settings, including biomedical facilities, diagnostic laboratories, wildlife facilities, drug and food manufacturing companies, and food safety inspection facilities.

Despite the relatively few number of graduates each year, keen competition is expected for veterinary technician jobs in zoos and aquariums, due to expected slow growth in facility capacity, low turnover among workers, the limited number of positions, and the fact that the work in zoos and aquariums attracts many candidates.

Employment of veterinary technicians and technologists is relatively stable during periods of economic recession. Layoffs are less likely to occur among veterinary technologists and technicians than in some other occupations because animals will continue to require medical care.

Earnings

Median annual wages of veterinary technologists and technicians were $28,900 in May 2008. The middle 50 percent earned between $23,580 and $34,960. The bottom 10 percent earned less than $19,770, and the top 10 percent earned more than $41,490. Veterinary technologists in research jobs may earn more than veterinary technicians in other types of jobs.

Related Occupations

Others who work extensively with animals include animal care and service workers; veterinarians; and veterinary assistants and laboratory animal caretakers.

Sources of Additional Information

For information on certification as a laboratory animal technician or technologist, contact

▶ American Association for Laboratory Animal Science, 9190 Crestwyn Hills Dr., Memphis, TN 38125. Internet: www.aalas.org

For information on careers in veterinary medicine and a listing of AVMA-accredited veterinary technology programs, contact

▶ American Veterinary Medical Association, 1931 N. Meacham Rd., Suite 100, Schaumburg, IL 60173-4360. Internet: www.avma.org

Water and Liquid Waste Treatment Plant and System Operators

(O*NET 51-8031.00)

Significant Points

■ Employment is concentrated in local government and water, sewage, and other systems utilities.

■ Because of expected much-faster-than-average employment growth and a large number of upcoming retirements, job opportunities will be excellent.

■ Completion of an associate degree or a one-year certificate program in environmental studies or a related field may help applicants to find jobs and advance more quickly.

Nature of the Work

Water is one of our society's most important resources. While most people take it for granted, it takes a lot of work to get water from natural sources—reservoirs, streams, and groundwater—into our taps. Similarly, it is a complicated process to convert the wastewater in our drains and sewers into a form that is safe to release into the environment. *Water treatment plant and system operators* run the equipment, control the processes, and monitor the plants that treat water so that it is safe to drink. *Liquid waste treatment plant and system operators* do similar work to remove pollutants from domestic and industrial waste.

Fresh water is pumped from wells, rivers, streams, and reservoirs to water treatment plants, where it is treated and distributed to customers. Used water, also known as wastewater, travels through sewage pipes to treatment plants where it is treated and either returned to streams, rivers, and oceans, or reused for irrigation. Operators in both types of plants control equipment and monitor processes that remove or destroy harmful materials, chemicals, and microorganisms from the water. They also run tests to make sure that the processes are working correctly and keep records of water quality and other indicators.

Water and wastewater treatment plant operators operate and maintain the pumps and motors that move water and wastewater through filtration systems. They monitor the indicators at their plants and make adjustments as necessary. They read meters and gauges to make sure that plant equipment is working properly. They take samples and run tests to determine the quality of the water being produced. At times, they may adjust the amount of chemicals, such as chlorine and fluorine, being added to the water.

The specific duties of plant operators depend on the type and size of the plant. In a small plant, one operator may be responsible for maintaining all of the systems. This operator would most likely work during the day and be on call during nights and weekends. In medium-size plants, operators may work in shifts to monitor the plant at all hours of the day. In large plants, multiple operators work the same shifts and are more specialized in their duties, often relying on computerized systems to help monitor plant processes.

Occasionally, operators must work during emergencies. Weather conditions may cause large amounts of storm water and wastewater to flow into sewers, exceeding a plant's capacity. Emergencies also may be caused by malfunctions within a plant, such as chemical leaks or oxygen deficiencies. Operators are trained in emergency management procedures and use safety equipment to protect their health, as well as that of the public.

Both tap water and wastewater are highly regulated by the U.S. Environmental Protection Agency. Plant operators must be familiar with these regulations and ensure that their high standards are met. Operators are also responsible for keeping records that document compliance and for being aware of new regulations that are enacted.

Work environment. Water and wastewater treatment plant and system operators work both indoors and outdoors and may be exposed to noise from machinery and to unpleasant odors. Operators' work is physically demanding and often is performed in locations that are difficult to access or unclean. They must pay close attention to safety procedures because of the presence of hazardous conditions, such as slippery walkways, dangerous gases, and malfunctioning equipment. As a result, operators have a higher-than-average occupational injury rate.

Plants operate 24 hours a day, 7 days a week. In small plants, operators may work during the day and be on call in the evening, at night, and on weekends. Medium-size and large plants that require constant monitoring may employ workers in three 8-hour shifts. Because larger plants require constant monitoring, weekend and holiday work is generally required. Operators may be required to work overtime.

Training, Other Qualifications, and Advancement

Employers usually hire high school graduates who are trained on the job. Completion of a training program may enhance an applicant's competitiveness in the job market.

Education and training. A high school diploma is usually required for an individual to become a water or wastewater treatment plant operator. Some applicants complete certificate or associate degree programs in water-quality and wastewater-treatment technology. Employers prefer to hire such candidates, because completion of a program minimizes the training needed at the plant and also shows a commitment to working in the industry. These programs are offered by community colleges, technical schools, and trade associations, and can be found throughout the country. In some cases, a degree or certificate program can be substituted for experience, allowing a worker to become licensed at a higher level more quickly.

Trainees usually start as attendants or operators-in-training and learn their skills on the job under the direction of an experienced operator. They learn by observing and doing routine tasks such as recording meter readings, taking samples of wastewater and sludge, and performing simple maintenance and repair work on pumps, electric motors, valves, and other plant equipment. Larger treatment plants generally combine this on-the-job training with formal classroom or self-paced study programs.

Licensure and certification. Both water and liquid waste plant and system operators must be certified by their states. Requirements and standards vary widely depending on the state. Most states have four different levels of certification, depending on the operator's experience and training. Although some states will honor licenses from other states, operators who move may have to take a new set of exams to become certified in a different state. The Association of Boards of Certification (ABC) offers a certificate program that may be helpful for operators who plan to move to a different state.

Other qualifications. Water and wastewater treatment plant operators need mechanical aptitude and the ability to solve problems intuitively. They also should be competent in basic mathematics, chemistry, and biology. They must have the ability to apply data to formulas that determine treatment requirements, flow levels, and concentration levels. Some basic familiarity with computers also is necessary, because operators generally use them to record data. Some plants also use computer-controlled equipment and instrumentation.

Advancement. Most states have four levels of certification for water and liquid waste treatment plant and system operators. On the basis of criteria such as the size of the plant and the treatment processes employed, each plant is given a corresponding level. A small system may only require the lowest level of certification. An operator who has that certification would be able to operate the plant without any supervision. In some states, operators in small plants can earn higher certifications through knowledge tests, while in other states, experience in a larger plant is required. Either way, operators in these plants will find it difficult to advance in their careers without moving to a larger plant.

As plants get larger and more complicated, operators need more skills before they are allowed to work without supervision. At the largest plants, operators who have the highest level of certification work as shift supervisors and may be in charge of large teams of operators. Operators in these plants can start as trainees and work through the different levels of certification until they advance to the level of shift supervisor.

Some experienced operators get jobs as technicians with state drinking-water-control or water-pollution-control agencies. In that capacity, they monitor and provide technical assistance to plants throughout the state. Vocational-technical school or community-college training generally is preferred for technician jobs. Experienced operators may transfer to related jobs with industrial liquid-waste treatment plants, water or liquid waste treatment equipment and chemical companies, engineering consulting firms, or vocational-technical schools.

Employment

Water and wastewater treatment plant and system operators held about 113,400 jobs in 2008. About 78 percent of all operators worked for local governments. Others worked primarily for water, sewage, and other systems utilities and for waste treatment and disposal and waste management services. Jobs were located throughout the country.

Job Outlook

Water and wastewater treatment plant and system operator jobs are expected to grow much faster than the average for all occupations. Job opportunities should be excellent for qualified workers.

Employment change. Employment of water and liquid waste treatment plant and system operators is expected to grow by 20 percent between 2008 and 2018, which is much faster than the average for all occupations. A growing population and the increasingly suburban geography of the United States are expected to boost demand for water and wastewater-treatment services. As new plants are constructed to meet this demand, new water and wastewater treatment plant and system operator jobs will arise.

Local governments are the largest employers of water and wastewater treatment plant and system operators. Employment in privately owned facilities will grow faster, because federal certification requirements have increased utilities' reliance on private firms specializing in the operation and management of water- and wastewater-treatment facilities.

Job prospects. Job opportunities should be excellent, both because of the expected much faster than average employment growth and because the retirement of the baby-boomer generation will require that many operators be replaced. Further, the number of applicants for these jobs is normally low, primarily because of the physically demanding and unappealing nature of some of the work. Opportunities should be best for people with mechanical aptitude and problem-solving skills.

Earnings

Median annual wages of water and wastewater treatment plant and system operators were $38,430 in May 2008. The middle 50 percent earned between $30,040 and $48,640. The lowest 10 percent earned less than $23,710, and the highest 10 percent earned more than $59,860. Median annual wages of water and liquid waste treatment plant and systems operators in May 2008 were $38,510 in local government and $37,620 in water, sewage, and other systems.

In addition to their annual salaries, water and wastewater treatment plant and system operators usually receive benefits that may include

Projections Data from the National Employment Matrix

Occupational title	SOC Code	Employment, 2008	Projected employment, 2018	Change, 2008–2018	
				Number	Percent
Water and liquid waste treatment plant and system operators	51-8031	113,400	135,900	22,500	20

NOTE: Data in this table are rounded.

health and life insurance, a retirement plan, and educational reimbursement for job-related courses.

Related Occupations

Other workers whose main activity consists of operating a system of machinery to process or produce materials include chemical plant and system operators; gas plant operators; petroleum pump system operators, refinery operators, and gaugers; power plant operators, distributors, and dispatchers; and stationary engineers and boiler operators.

Sources of Additional Information

For information on employment opportunities, contact state or local water pollution control agencies, state water and liquid waste operator associations, state environmental training centers, or local offices of the state employment service.

For information on certification, contact

▶ Association of Boards of Certification, 208 Fifth St., Suite 201, Ames, IA 50010-6259. Internet: www.abccert.org

For educational information related to a career as a water or liquid waste treatment plant and system operator, contact

▶ American Water Works Association, 6666 W. Quincy Ave., Denver, CO 80235. Internet: www.awwa.org

▶ National Rural Water Association, 2915 S. 13th St., Duncan, OK 73533. Internet: www.nrwa.org

▶ Water Environment Federation, 601 Wythe St., Alexandria, VA 22314-1994. Internet: www.wef.org

QUICK JOB SEARCH

Seven Steps to Getting a Good Job in Less Time

The Complete Text of a Results-Oriented Book by Michael Farr

Millions of job seekers have found better jobs faster using the techniques in the *Quick Job Search*. So can you! The *Quick Job Search* covers the essential steps proven to cut job search time in half and is used widely by job search programs throughout North America. Topics include how to identify your key skills, define your ideal job, write a great resume quickly, use the most effective job search methods, get more interviews, and much more.

If you completed "Using the Job-Match Grid to Choose a Career" earlier in this book, the activities in this section will complement those efforts by helping you to define other skills you possess, focus your resume, and get a job quickly.

While it is a section in this book, the *Quick Job Search* is available from JIST Publishing as a separate booklet.

Quick Job Search Is Short, But It May Be All You Need

While *Quick Job Search* is short, it covers the basics on how to explore career options and conduct an effective job search. While these topics can seem complex, I have found some simple truths about looking for a job:

- If you are going to work, you might as well look for what you really want to do and are good at.

- If you are looking for a job, you might as well use techniques that will reduce the time it takes to find one—and that help you get a better job than you might otherwise.

That's what I emphasize in *Quick Job Search*.

Trust Me—Do the Worksheets. I know you will resist completing the worksheets. But trust me. They are worth your time. Doing them will give you a better sense of what you are good at, what you want to do, and how to go about getting it. You will also most likely get more interviews and present yourself better. Is this worth giving up a night of TV? Yes, I think so.

Once you finish this book and its activities, you will have spent more time planning your career than most people do. And you will know more than the average job seeker about finding a job.

Why Such a Short Book? I've taught job seeking skills for many years, and I've written longer and more-detailed books than this one. Yet I have often been asked to tell someone, in a few minutes or hours, the most important things they should do in their career planning or job search. Instructors and counselors also ask the same question, because they have only a short time to spend with folks they're trying to help. I've given this a lot of thought, and the seven topics in this book are the ones I think are most important to know.

This book is short enough to scan in a morning and conduct a more effective job search that afternoon. Granted, doing all the activities would take more time, but they will prepare you far better than scanning the book. Of course, you can learn more about all the topics it covers, but this book, *Quick Job Search,* may be all you need.

I wish you well.

You can't just read about getting a job. The best way to get a job is to go out and get interviews! And the best way to get interviews is to make a job out of getting a job.

After many years of experience, I have identified just seven basic things you need to do that make a big difference in your job search. Each will be covered and expanded on in this book.

1. Identify your key skills and develop a "skills language" to describe yourself.

2. Define your ideal job.

3. Use the most effective methods to find a job in less time.

4. Write a sample resume now and a better one later.

5. Organize your time to get two interviews a day.

6. Dramatically improve your interviewing skills.

7. Follow up on all leads.

So, without further delay, let's get started!

STEP 1: Identify Your Key Skills and Develop a "Skills Language" to Describe Yourself

One survey of employers found that about 90 percent of the people they interviewed might have the required job skills, but they could not describe those skills and thereby prove that they could do the job they sought. They could not answer the basic question "Why should I hire you?"

Knowing and describing your skills is essential to doing well in interviews. This same knowledge is important to help you decide what type of job you will enjoy and do well. For these reasons, I consider identifying your skills a necessary part of a successful career plan or job search.

The Three Types of Skills

Most people think of their skills as job-related skills, such as using a computer. But we all have other types of skills that are important for success on a job—and that are important to employers. The following triangle arranges skills in three groups, and I think that this is a very useful way to consider skills as you use this book, *Quick Job Search*.

Let's look at these three types of skills—self-management, transferable, and job-related—and identify those that are most important to you.

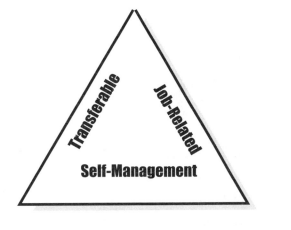

Self-Management Skills

Self-management skills (also known as adaptive skills or personality traits) are the things that make you a good worker. They describe your basic personality and your ability to adapt to new environments, as well as provide the foundation for other skills. They are some of the most important skills to emphasize in interviews, yet most job seekers don't realize their importance—and don't mention them.

Review the Self-Management Skills Checklist that follows and put a check mark beside any skills you have. The key self-management skills listed first cover abilities that employers find particularly important. If one or more of the key self-management skills apply to you, mentioning them in interviews can help you greatly.

SELF-MANAGEMENT SKILLS CHECKLIST

Following are the key self-management skills and characteristics that employers value highly. Place a check mark by those you already have.

- ❑ Honesty
- ❑ Punctuality
- ❑ Ability to follow instructions

- ❑ Ability to get along with coworkers and supervisor
- ❑ Productivity

- ❑ Good attendance
- ❑ Deadline oriented
- ❑ Hardworking

Place a check mark by other self-management skills you have.

- ❑ Ambition
- ❑ Assertiveness
- ❑ Capability
- ❑ Cheerfulness

- ❑ Competency
- ❑ Conscientiousness
- ❑ Coordination
- ❑ Creativity

(continued)

(continued)

- ❏ Dependability
- ❏ Discretion
- ❏ Eagerness
- ❏ Efficiency
- ❏ Energy
- ❏ Enthusiasm
- ❏ Expression
- ❏ Flexibility
- ❏ Formality
- ❏ Friendliness
- ❏ Good nature
- ❏ Helpfulness
- ❏ Humbleness
- ❏ Imagination
- ❏ Independence
- ❏ Industriousness
- ❏ Informality
- ❏ Inquisitiveness

- ❏ Intelligence
- ❏ Intuition
- ❏ Leadership
- ❏ Learning ability
- ❏ Learning oriented
- ❏ Loyalty
- ❏ Maturity
- ❏ Methodicalness
- ❏ Modesty
- ❏ Motivation
- ❏ Open-mindedness
- ❏ Optimism
- ❏ Organization
- ❏ Originality
- ❏ Patience
- ❏ Persistence
- ❏ Physical strength
- ❏ Practice

- ❏ Pride
- ❏ Problem-solving
- ❏ Reliability
- ❏ Responsibility
- ❏ Results orientation
- ❏ Self-confidence
- ❏ Self-motivation
- ❏ Sense of humor
- ❏ Sincerity
- ❏ Spontaneity
- ❏ Steadiness
- ❏ Tact
- ❏ Tenacity
- ❏ Thoroughness
- ❏ Thrift
- ❏ Trustworthiness
- ❏ Versatility

List the other self-management skills you have that are not on the list but you think are important to include.

_____

_____

_____

After you finish checking the list, circle the five skills you feel are most important for the job you want and write them in the box that follows.

YOUR TOP FIVE SELF-MANAGEMENT SKILLS

1. _____

2. _____

3. _____

4. _____

5. _____

Note

When thinking about their skills, some people find it helpful to complete the Essential Job Search Data Worksheet that starts on page 347. It organizes skills and accomplishments from previous jobs and other life experiences. Take a look at it and decide whether to complete it now or later.

Transferable Skills

Transferable skills are skills that can be used on more than one job. Often these skills are things that you naturally do well or that are an essential part of your personality, and are the foundations for other skills. We all have skills that can transfer from one job or career to another. For example, the ability to organize events could be used in a variety of jobs and may be essential for success in certain occupations.

Your mission is to find a job that requires the skills you have and enjoy using. But first, you need to identify your top transferable skills.

> **Quip**
>
> **It's not bragging if it's true.** Using your new skills language might be uncomfortable at first, but employers need to learn about your skills. So practice saying positive things about the skills you have for the job. If you don't, who will?

TRANSFERABLE SKILLS CHECKLIST

Following are the key transferable skills that employers value highly. Place a check mark by those you already have. You may have used them in a previous job or in some non-work setting.

- ❑ Managing money/budgets
- ❑ Speaking in public
- ❑ Managing people
- ❑ Organizing/managing projects

- ❑ Meeting deadlines
- ❑ Solving problems
- ❑ Meeting the public
- ❑ Writing well

- ❑ Negotiating
- ❑ Increasing sales or efficiency

Place a check mark by the skills you have for **working with data.**

- ❑ Analyzing data
- ❑ Auditing/checking for accuracy
- ❑ Budgeting
- ❑ Calculating/computing
- ❑ Classifying data

- ❑ Comparing/evaluating
- ❑ Compiling/recording facts
- ❑ Counting/taking inventory
- ❑ Investigating
- ❑ Keeping financial records

- ❑ Observing/inspecting
- ❑ Paying attention to details
- ❑ Researching/locating information
- ❑ Synthesizing

Place a check mark by the skills you have for **working with people.**

- ❑ Administering
- ❑ Being diplomatic and tactful

- ❑ Being kind
- ❑ Being outgoing

- ❑ Being patient
- ❑ Being sensitive and empathetic

(continued)

(continued)

- ❑ Being sociable
- ❑ Caring for others
- ❑ Coaching
- ❑ Confronting others
- ❑ Counseling people
- ❑ Demonstrating

- ❑ Handling criticism
- ❑ Having insight
- ❑ Helping others
- ❑ Instructing/teaching others
- ❑ Interviewing people
- ❑ Listening

- ❑ Persuading
- ❑ Supervising
- ❑ Tolerating
- ❑ Trusting
- ❑ Understanding

Place a check mark by your skills in **working with words and ideas.**

- ❑ Being articulate
- ❑ Being inventive
- ❑ Being logical
- ❑ Communicating verbally
- ❑ Corresponding with others
- ❑ Creating new ideas
- ❑ Designing

- ❑ Editing
- ❑ Reasoning
- ❑ Remembering information
- ❑ Researching information
- ❑ Speaking publicly
- ❑ Writing clearly

Place a check mark by the **leadership skills** you have.

- ❑ Being competitive
- ❑ Delegating
- ❑ Directing others
- ❑ Explaining concepts
- ❑ Getting results
- ❑ Having self-confidence
- ❑ Influencing others
- ❑ Making decisions

- ❑ Mediating problems
- ❑ Motivating people
- ❑ Motivating yourself
- ❑ Negotiating agreements
- ❑ Planning
- ❑ Running meetings
- ❑ Solving problems
- ❑ Taking risks

Place a check mark by your **creative or artistic skills.**

- ❑ Appreciating music
- ❑ Creating, inventing
- ❑ Dancing
- ❑ Drawing, painting
- ❑ Expressing yourself artistically

- ❑ Performing/acting
- ❑ Playing instruments
- ❑ Presenting artistic ideas
- ❑ Writing creatively

Place a check mark by your skills for **working with things.**

- ❑ Assembling or making things
- ❑ Building, observing, and inspecting things
- ❑ Constructing or repairing things

- ❑ Driving or operating vehicles
- ❑ Operating tools/machines
- ❑ Using your hands

Add the other transferable skills you have that have not been mentioned but you think are important to include.

_____

_____

_____

When you are finished, circle the five transferable skills you feel are most important for you to use in your next job and list them below.

YOUR TOP FIVE TRANSFERABLE SKILLS

1. _____
2. _____
3. _____
4. _____
5. _____

Job-Related Skills

Job-content or job-related skills are those you need to do a particular occupation. A carpenter, for example, needs to know how to use various tools. Before you select job-related skills to emphasize, you must first have a clear idea of the jobs you want. So let's put off developing your job-related skills list until you have defined the job you want—the topic that is covered next.

STEP 2: Define Your Ideal Job

Too many people look for a job without clearly knowing what they are looking for. Before you go out seeking a job, I suggest that you first define exactly what you want—not just _a job_ but _the job_.

Most people think that a job objective is the same as a job title, but it isn't. You need to consider other elements of what makes a job satisfying for you. Then, later, you can decide what that job is called and what industry it might be in. You can compromise on what you consider your ideal job later if you need to.

EIGHT FACTORS TO CONSIDER IN DEFINING YOUR IDEAL JOB

As you try to define your ideal job, consider the following eight important questions. When you know what you want, your task then becomes finding a position that is as close to your ideal job as possible.

1. **What skills do you want to use?** From the skills lists in Step 1, select the top five skills that you enjoy using and most want to use in your next job.

   a. _____

   b. _____

   c. _____

   d. _____

   e. _____

2. **What type of special knowledge do you have?** Perhaps you know how to fix radios, keep accounting records, or cook food. Write down the things you know from schooling, training, hobbies, family experiences, and other sources. One or more of these knowledge areas could make you a very desirable applicant in the right setting.

   _____

   _____

3. **With what types of people do you prefer to work?** Do you like to work with competitive people, or do you prefer hardworking folks, creative personalities, relaxed people, or some other types?

   _____

   _____

4. **What type of work environment do you prefer?** Do you want to work inside, outside, in a quiet place, in a busy place, or in a clean or messy place; or do you want to have a window with a nice view? List the types of environments you prefer.

   _____

   _____

5. **Where do you want your next job to be located—in what city or region?** If you are open to living and working anywhere, what would your ideal community be like? Near a bus line? Close to a childcare center?

   _____

   _____

6. **What benefits or income do you hope to have in your next job?** Many people will take less money or fewer benefits if they like a job in other ways—or if they need a job quickly to survive. Think about the minimum you would take as well as what you would eventually like to earn. Your next job will probably pay somewhere in between.

_____

_____

7. **How much and what types of responsibility are you willing to accept?** Usually, the more money you want to make, the more responsibility you must accept. Do you want to work by yourself, be part of a group, or be in charge? If you want to be in charge, how many people are you willing to supervise?

_____

_____

8. **What values are important or have meaning to you?** Do you have important values you would prefer to include in considering the work you do? For example, some people want to work to help others, clean up the environment, build structures, make machines work, gain power or prestige, or care for animals or plants. Think about what is important to you and how you might include this in your next job.

_____

_____

_____

Is It Possible to Find Your Ideal Job?

Can you find a job that meets all the criteria you just defined? Perhaps. Some people do. The harder you look, the more likely you are to find it. But you will likely need to compromise, so it is useful to know what is _most_ important to include in your next job. Go back over your responses to the eight factors and mark a few of those that you would most like to have in your ideal job.

FACTORS I WANT IN MY IDEAL JOB

Write a brief description of your ideal job. Don't worry about a job title, whether you have the necessary experience, or other practical matters yet.

_____

_____

_____

How Can You Explore Specific Job Titles and Industries?

You might find your ideal job in an occupation you haven't considered yet. And, even if you are sure of the occupation you want, it may be in an industry that is unfamiliar to you. This combination of occupation and industry forms the basis for your job search, and you should consider a variety of options.

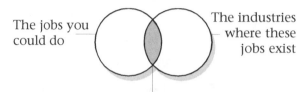

The jobs you could do   The industries where these jobs exist

Your ideal job exists in the overlap of those jobs that interest you most *and* in those industries that best meet your needs and interests!

There are thousands of job titles, and many jobs are highly specialized, employing just a few people. Although one of these more specialized jobs might be just what you want, most work falls within more general job titles that employ large numbers of people.

REVIEW THE TOP JOBS IN THE WORKFORCE

The list of job titles that follows was based on a list developed by the U.S. Department of Labor. It contains 289 major jobs that employ about 88 percent of the U.S. workforce.

The job titles are organized within 16 major groupings called interest areas, presented in all capital letters and bold type. These groupings will help you quickly identify fields most likely to interest you. Job titles are presented in regular type within these groupings.

Begin with the interest areas that appeal to you most, and underline any job title that interests you. (Don't worry for now about whether you have the experience or credentials to do these jobs.) Then quickly review the remaining interest areas, underlining any job titles there that interest you. Note that some job titles are listed more than once because they fit into more than one interest area. When you have gone through all 16 interest areas, go back and circle the 5 to 10 job titles that interest you most. These are the ones you will want to research in more detail.

1. **AGRICULTURE, FOOD, AND NATURAL RESOURCES:** Agricultural and Food Scientists; Agricultural Workers; Animal Care and Service Workers; Conservation Scientists and Foresters; Environmental Scientists and Specialists; Farmers, Ranchers, and Agricultural Managers; Fishers and Fishing Vessel Operators; Floral Designers; Food Processing Occupations; Forest and Conservation Workers; Graders and Sorters, Agricultural Products; Grounds Maintenance Workers; Logging Workers; Pest Control Workers; Recreation Workers; Veterinarians; Water and Liquid Waste Treatment Plant and System Operators.

2. **ARCHITECTURE AND CONSTRUCTION:** Architects, Except Landscape and Naval; Boilermakers; Brickmasons, Blockmasons, and Stonemasons; Carpenters; Carpet, Floor, and Tile Installers and Finishers; Cement Masons, Concrete Finishers, Segmental Pavers, and Terrazzo Workers; Construction and Building Inspectors; Construction Equipment Operators; Construction Laborers; Construction Managers; Cost Estimators; Drafters; Drywall and Ceiling Tile Installers, Tapers, Plasterers, and Stucco Masons; Electricians; Glaziers; Heating, Air-Conditioning, and Refrigeration Mechanics and Installers;

Home Appliance Repairers; Insulation Workers; Interior Designers; Landscape Architects; Line Installers and Repairers; Painters and Paperhangers; Plumbers, Pipelayers, Pipefitters, and Steamfitters; Roofers; Structural and Reinforcing Iron and Metal Workers; Surveyors, Cartographers, Photogrammetrists, and Surveying and Mapping Technicians.

3. **ARTS, AUDIO/VIDEO TECHNOLOGY, AND COMMUNICATIONS:** Actors, Producers, and Directors; Announcers; Archivists, Curators, and Museum Technicians; Artists and Related Workers; Authors, Writers, and Editors; Broadcast and Sound Engineering Technicians and Radio Operators; Commercial and Industrial Designers; Communications Equipment Operators; Dancers and Choreographers; Electronic Home Entertainment Equipment Installers and Repairers; Fashion Designers; Graphic Designers; Interior Designers; Musicians, Singers, and Related Workers; News Analysts, Reporters, and Correspondents; Photographers; Photographic Process Workers and Processing Machine Operators; Prepress Technicians and Workers; Public Relations Specialists; Radio and Telecommunications Equipment Installers and Repairers; Technical Writers; Television, Video, and Motion Picture Camera Operators and Editors.

4. **BUSINESS, MANAGEMENT, AND ADMINISTRATION:** Accountants and Auditors; Administrative Services Managers; Advertising, Marketing, Promotions, Public Relations, and Sales Managers; Advertising Sales Agents; Billing and Posting Clerks and Machine Operators; Bookkeeping, Accounting, and Auditing Clerks; Brokerage Clerks; Budget Analysts; Couriers and Messengers; Customer Service Representatives; Data Entry and Information Processing Workers; Desktop Publishers; Economists; File Clerks; Financial Analysts; Financial Managers; Human Resources Assistants, Except Payroll and Timekeeping; Human Resources, Training, and Labor Relations Managers and Specialists; Interviewers, Except Eligibility and Loan; Management Analysts; Office and Administrative Support Supervisors and Managers; Office Clerks, General; Operations Research Analysts; Order Clerks; Payroll and Timekeeping Clerks; Procurement Clerks; Purchasing Managers, Buyers, and Purchasing Agents; Receptionists and Information Clerks; Secretaries and Administrative Assistants; Shipping, Receiving, and Traffic Clerks; Statisticians; Top Executives; Weighers, Measurers, Checkers, and Samplers, Recordkeeping.

5. **EDUCATION AND TRAINING:** Athletes, Coaches, Umpires, and Related Workers; Counselors; Education Administrators; Fitness Workers; Instructional Coordinators; Interpreters and Translators; Librarians; Library Technicians and Library Assistants; Recreation Workers; Teacher Assistants; Teachers—Adult Literacy and Remedial Education; Teachers—Kindergarten, Elementary, Middle, and Secondary; Teachers—Postsecondary; Teachers—Preschool, Except Special Education; Teachers—Self-Enrichment Education; Teachers—Special Education; Teachers—Vocational.

6. **FINANCE:** Actuaries; Bill and Account Collectors; Budget Analysts; Claims Adjusters, Appraisers, Examiners, and Investigators; Credit Authorizers, Checkers, and Clerks; Financial Analysts; Financial Managers; Insurance Sales Agents; Insurance Underwriters; Loan Interviewers and Clerks; Loan Officers; Personal Financial Advisors; Securities, Commodities, and Financial Services Sales Agents; Tellers.

7. **GOVERNMENT AND PUBLIC ADMINISTRATION:** Accountants and Auditors; Administrative Services Managers; Sociologists and Political Scientists; Tax Examiners, Collectors, and Revenue Agents; Top Executives; Urban and Regional Planners.

8. **HEALTH SCIENCE:** Audiologists; Cardiovascular Technologists and Technicians; Chiropractors; Clinical Laboratory Technologists and Technicians; Counselors; Dental Assistants; Dental Hygienists; Dentists; Diagnostic Medical Sonographers; Dietitians and Nutritionists; Emergency Medical Technicians and Paramedics; Health Educators; Home Health Aides and Personal and Home Care Aides;

(continued)

(continued)

Licensed Practical and Licensed Vocational Nurses; Massage Therapists; Medical and Health Services Managers; Medical Assistants; Medical, Dental, and Ophthalmic Laboratory Technicians; Medical Records and Health Information Technicians; Medical Scientists; Medical Transcriptionists; Nuclear Medicine Technologists; Nursing and Psychiatric Aides; Occupational Therapist Assistants and Aides; Occupational Therapists; Opticians, Dispensing; Optometrists; Pharmacists; Pharmacy Technicians and Aides; Physical Therapist Assistants and Aides; Physical Therapists; Physician Assistants; Physicians and Surgeons; Podiatrists; Psychologists; Radiation Therapists; Radiologic Technologists and Technicians; Recreational Therapists; Registered Nurses; Respiratory Therapists; Respiratory Therapy Technicians; Speech-Language Pathologists; Surgical Technologists.

9. **HOSPITALITY AND TOURISM:** Building Cleaning Workers; Chefs, Head Cooks, and Food Preparation and Serving Supervisors; Cooks and Food Preparation Workers; Food and Beverage Serving and Related Workers; Food Service Managers; Lodging Managers; Reservation and Transportation Ticket Agents and Travel Clerks; Travel Agents.

10. **HUMAN SERVICE:** Barbers, Cosmetologists, and Other Personal Appearance Workers; Child Care Workers; Counselors; Eligibility Interviewers, Government Programs; Epidemiologists; Funeral Directors; Health Educators; Interpreters and Translators; Probation Officers and Correctional Treatment Specialists; Psychologists; Recreation Workers; Social Workers; Sociologists and Political Scientists.

11. **INFORMATION TECHNOLOGY:** Computer and Information Systems Managers; Computer Control Programmers and Operators; Computer Network, Systems, and Database Administrators; Computer Operators; Computer Scientists; Computer Software Engineers and Computer Programmers; Computer Support Specialists; Computer Systems Analysts.

12. **LAW, PUBLIC SAFETY, CORRECTIONS, AND SECURITY:** Correctional Officers; Court Reporters; Fire Fighters; Fire Inspectors and Investigators; Judges, Magistrates, and Other Judicial Workers; Lawyers; Paralegals and Legal Assistants; Police and Detectives; Police, Fire, and Ambulance Dispatchers; Private Detectives and Investigators; Science Technicians; Security Guards and Gaming Surveillance Officers.

13. **MANUFACTURING:** Assemblers and Fabricators; Cost Estimators; Electrical and Electronics Installers and Repairers; Elevator Installers and Repairers; Industrial Machinery Mechanics and Millwrights; Inspectors, Testers, Sorters, Samplers, and Weighers; Jewelers and Precious Stone and Metal Workers; Line Installers and Repairers; Machine Setters, Operators, and Tenders—Metal and Plastic; Machinists; Occupational Health and Safety Specialists; Painting and Coating Workers, Except Construction and Maintenance; Power Plant Operators, Distributors, and Dispatchers; Semiconductor Processors; Sheet Metal Workers; Stationary Engineers and Boiler Operators; Textile, Apparel, and Furnishings Occupations; Tool and Die Makers; Watch Repairers; Welding, Soldering, and Brazing Workers; Woodworkers.

14. **MARKETING, SALES, AND SERVICE:** Advertising, Marketing, Promotions, Public Relations, and Sales Managers; Appraisers and Assessors of Real Estate; Cashiers; Counter and Rental Clerks; Demonstrators and Product Promoters; Market and Survey Researchers; Models; Real Estate Brokers and Sales Agents; Retail Salespersons; Sales Engineers; Sales Representatives, Wholesale and Manufacturing; Sales Worker Supervisors; Stock Clerks and Order Fillers.

15. **SCIENCE, TECHNOLOGY, ENGINEERING, AND MATHEMATICS:** Atmospheric Scientists; Biological Scientists; Chemists and Materials Scientists; Computer Software Engineers and Computer Programmers; Drafters; Engineering and Natural Sciences Managers; Engineering Technicians; Engineers; Epidemiologists; Geoscientists and Hydrologists; Mathematicians; Medical Scientists; Operations Research Analysts; Physicists and Astronomers; Psychologists; Science Technicians; Sociologists and Political Scientists; Statisticians.

16. **TRANSPORTATION, DISTRIBUTION, AND LOGISTICS:** Air Traffic Controllers; Aircraft and Avionics Equipment Mechanics and Service Technicians; Aircraft Pilots and Flight Engineers; Automotive Body and Related Repairers; Automotive Service Technicians and Mechanics; Bus Drivers; Diesel Service Technicians and Mechanics; Material Moving Occupations; Production, Planning, and Expediting Clerks; Rail Transportation Occupations; Shipping, Receiving, and Traffic Clerks; Small Engine Mechanics; Taxi Drivers and Chauffeurs; Truck Drivers and Driver/Sales Workers; Water Transportation Occupations.

N o t e

You can find thorough descriptions for the job titles in the preceding list in the Occupational Outlook Handbook, *published by the U.S. Department of Labor. Its descriptions include information on earnings training and education needed to hold specific jobs, working conditions, advancement opportunities, projected growth, and sources for additional information. Most libraries have this book.*

You also can find descriptions of these jobs on the Internet. Go to www.bls.gov/oco/.

The New Guide for Occupational Exploration *also provides more information on the interest areas and jobs used in this list. This book is published by JIST Publishing and describes more than 900 major jobs, arranged within groupings of related jobs.*

CONSIDER MAJOR INDUSTRIES

What industry you work in is often as important as the career field. For example, some industries pay much better than others, and others may simply be more interesting to you. A book titled *40 Best Fields for Your Career* contains very helpful reviews for each of the major industries mentioned in the following list. Many libraries and bookstores carry this book, as well as the U.S. Department of Labor's *Career Guide to Industries,* or you can find the information on the Internet at www.bls.gov/oco/cg/.

Underline industries that interest you, and then learn more about the opportunities they present. Jobs in most careers are available in a variety of industries, so consider what industries fit you best and focus your job search in these.

Agriculture and natural resources: Agriculture, forestry, and fishing; mining; oil and gas extraction.

Manufacturing, construction, and utilities: Aerospace product and parts manufacturing; chemical manufacturing, except drugs; computer and electronic product manufacturing; food manufacturing; machinery manufacturing; motor vehicle and parts manufacturing; pharmaceutical and medicine manufacturing; printing; steel manufacturing; textile, textile products, and apparel manufacturing; utilities.

(continued)

(continued)

> **Trade:** Automobile dealers; clothing, accessories, and general merchandise stores; grocery stores; wholesale trade.
>
> **Transportation:** Air transportation; truck transportation and warehousing.
>
> **Information:** Broadcasting; Internet service providers, Web search portals, and data-processing services; motion picture and video industries; publishing, except software; software publishing; telecommunications.
>
> **Financial activities:** Banking; insurance; securities, commodities, and other investments.
>
> **Professional and business services:** Advertising and public relations; computer systems design and related services; employment services; management, scientific, and technical consulting services; scientific research and development services.
>
> **Education, health care, and social services:** Child daycare services; educational services; health care; social assistance, except child care.
>
> **Leisure and Hospitality:** Art, entertainment, and recreation; food services and drinking places; hotels and other accommodations.
>
> **Government and advocacy, grantmaking, and civic organizations:** Advocacy, grantmaking, and civic organizations; federal government; state and local government, except education and health care.

THE TOP JOBS AND INDUSTRIES THAT INTEREST YOU

Go back over the lists of job titles and industries. For numbers 1 and 2 below, list the jobs that interest you most. Then select the industries that interest you most, and list them below in number 3. These are the jobs and industries you should research most carefully. Your ideal job is likely to be found in some combination of these jobs and industries, or in more specialized but related jobs and industries. Put a star next to the one you like best.

1. The five job titles that interest you most

     a. _____

     b. _____

     c. _____

     d. _____

     e. _____

2. The five next-most-interesting job titles

     a. _____

     b. _____

     c. _____

     d. _____

     e. _____

3. The industries that interest you most

a. _____

b. _____

c. _____

d. _____

e. _____

Is Self-Employment or Starting a Business an Option?

More than one in 10 workers are self-employed or own their own businesses. If these options interest you, consider them as well. Talk to people in similar roles to gather information, and look for books and Web sites that provide information on options that are similar to those that interest you. Examples of jobs with high percentages of self-employed workers include

❑ Farmers and ranchers

❑ Multimedia artists and animators

❑ Copywriters

❑ Poets, lyricists, and creative writers

❑ Massage therapists

❑ Real estate brokers

The Small Business Administration's Web site at www.sba.gov is a good source of basic information on starting your own business.

SELF-EMPLOYMENT AREAS OF INTEREST

In the following space, write your current interest in self-employment or starting a business in an area related to your general job objective.

Are you interested in working for yourself? _____

What types of businesses are related to the jobs that interest you most?

_____

_____

Who can you talk with to get more information about what it's like to be self-employed in this field?

_____

_____

Identify Your Job-Related Skills for Your Ideal Job

Back on page 307, I suggested that you should first define the job you want and then identify key job-related skills you have that support your ability to do that job. These are the job-related skills to emphasize in interviews.

So, now that you have determined your ideal job (the one you put a star next to on page 314), you can pinpoint the job-related skills it requires. If you haven't done so, complete the Essential Job Search Data Worksheet on pages 347–352. Completing it will give you specific skills and accomplishments to highlight. Look up your ideal job at http://online.onetcenter.org/. See which skills are required for this job. Then see how many of those overlap with the skills you have.

Yes, completing that worksheet requires time, but doing so will help you clearly define key skills to emphasize in interviews—when what you say matters so much. People who complete that worksheet will do better in their interviews than those who don't. After you complete the Essential Job Search Data Worksheet, you are ready to list your top five job-related skills.

YOUR TOP FIVE JOB-RELATED SKILLS

List the five job-related skills you think are most important. Include the job-related skills you have that you would most like to use in your next job.

1. _____

2. _____

3. _____

4. _____

5. _____

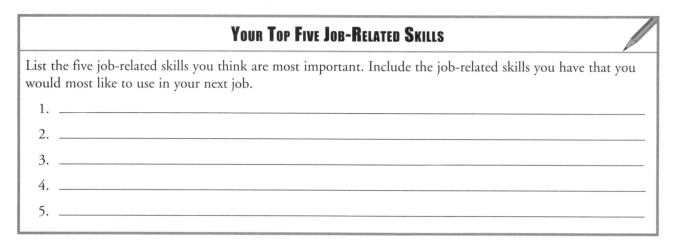

STEP 3: Use the Most Effective Methods to Find a Job in Less Time

Employer surveys have found that most employers don't advertise their job openings. They most often hire people they already know, people who find out about the jobs through word of mouth, or people who happen to be in the right place at the right time. Although luck plays a part in finding job openings, you can use the tips in this step to increase your luck.

Most job seekers don't know how ineffective some traditional job hunting techniques tend to be. For example, the chart below shows that fewer than 15 percent of all job seekers get jobs from the newspaper want ads, most of which also appear online. Other traditional techniques include using public and private employment agencies, filling out paper and electronic applications, and mailing or e-mailing unsolicited resumes.

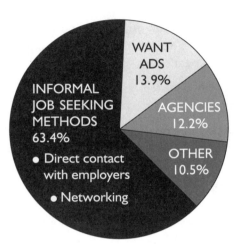

How people find jobs.

Informal, nontraditional job seeking methods have a much larger success rate. These methods are active rather than passive and include making direct contact with employers and networking.

The truth is that every job search method works for someone. But experience and research show that some methods are more effective than others are. Your task in the job search is to spend more of your time using more effective methods—and increase the effectiveness of all the methods you use. Let's start by looking at the most effective job search methods.

Use the Two Job Search Methods That Work Best

The fact is that most jobs are not advertised, so how do *you* find them? The same way that about two-thirds of all job seekers do: networking with people you know (which I call making warm contacts) and directly contacting employers (which I call making cold contacts). Both of these methods are based on the job search rule you should know above all:

> **The Most Important Job Search Rule:** Don't wait until the job opens before contacting the employer!

Employers fill most jobs with people they meet before a job is formally open. The trick is to meet people who can hire you before a job is formally available. Instead of asking whether the employer has any jobs open, I suggest that you say, *"I realize you may not have any openings now, but I would still like to talk to you about the possibility of future openings."*

Most Effective Job Search Method 1: Develop a Network of Contacts in Five Easy Stages

Studies find that 40 percent of all people located their jobs through a lead provided by a friend, a relative, or an acquaintance. That makes the people you know your number one source of job leads—more effective than all the traditional methods combined! Developing and using your contacts is called *networking,* and here's how it works:

1. **Make lists of people you know.** Make a thorough list of anyone you are friendly with. Then make a separate list of all your relatives. These two lists alone often add up to 25 to 100 people or more. Next, think of other groups of people that you have something in common with, such as former coworkers or classmates, members of your social or sports groups, members of your professional association, former

employers, neighbors, and other groups. You might not know many of these people personally or well, but most will help you if you ask them. An easy way to find networking contacts is to join an online networking site such as LinkedIn (www.linkedin.com).

2. **Contact each person in your list in a systematic way.** Obviously, some people will be more helpful than others, but any one of them might help you find a job lead.

3. **Present yourself well.** Begin with your friends and relatives. Call and tell them you are looking for a job and need their help. Be as clear as possible about the type of employment you want and the skills and qualifications you have. Look at the sample JIST Card and phone script later in this step for good presentation ideas.

4. **Ask your contacts for leads.** It is possible that your contacts will know of a job opening that interests you. If so, get the details and get right on it! More likely, however, they will not, so you should ask each person the Three Magic Networking Questions.

The Three Magic Networking Questions

- **Do you know of any openings for a person with my skills?**

  If the answer is "No" (which it usually is), then ask…

- **Do you know of someone else who might know of such an opening?**

  If your contact does, get that name and ask for another one. If he or she doesn't, ask…

- **Do you know of anyone who might know of someone else who might know of a job opening?**

  Another good way to ask this is "Do you know someone who knows lots of people?" If all else fails, this will usually get you a name.

5. **Contact these referrals and ask them the same questions.** From each person you contact, try to get two names of other people you might contact. Doing this consistently can extend your network of acquaintances by hundreds of people. Eventually, one of these people will hire you or refer you to someone who will!

If you are persistent in following these five steps, networking might be the only job search method you need. It works.

Most Effective Job Search Method 2: Contact Employers Directly

It takes more courage, but making direct contact with employers is a very effective job search technique. I call these "cold contacts" because people you don't know in advance will need to warm up to your inquiries. Two basic techniques for making cold contacts follow.

Use the yellow pages to find potential employers. Begin by looking at the index in the front of your phone book's yellow pages. For each entry, ask yourself, "Would an organization of this kind need a person with my skills?" If you answer "Yes," then that organization or business type is a possible target. You can also rate "Yes" entries based on your interest, writing a "1" next to those that seem very interesting, a "2" next to those that you are not sure of, and a "3" next to those that aren't interesting at all.

Next, select a type of organization that got a "Yes" response and turn to that section of the yellow pages. Call each organization listed there and ask to speak to the person who is most likely to hire or supervise you—typically the manager of the business or a department head—not the personnel or human resources manager. A sample telephone script is included later in this section to give you ideas about what to say.

You can easily adapt this approach for use on the Internet by using sites such as www.yellowpages.com to get contacts anywhere in the world, or you can find phone and e-mail contacts on an employer's own Web site.

Drop in without an appointment. Another effective cold contact method is to just walk into a business or organization that interests you and ask to speak to the person in charge. Although dropping in is particularly effective in small businesses, it also works surprisingly well in larger ones. Remember to ask for an interview even if there are no openings now. If your timing is inconvenient, ask for a better time to come back for an interview.

Most Jobs Are with Small Employers

Businesses and organizations with fewer than 250 employees employ half of all workers and create more than 75 percent of all new jobs each year. They are simply too important to overlook in your job search! Many of them don't have personnel departments, which makes direct contacts even easier and more effective.

Create a Powerful Job Search Tool: The JIST Card®

Look at the sample cards that follow. They are JIST Cards, and they get results. They can be computer printed or even neatly written on a 3-by-5–inch card. JIST Cards include the essential information employers want to know.

A JIST Card Is a Mini Resume

JIST Cards have been used by thousands of job search programs and millions of people. Employers like their direct and timesaving format, and they have been proven as an effective tool to get job leads. Attach one to your resume. Give them to friends, relatives, and other contacts and ask them to pass them along to others who might know of an opening. Enclose them in thank-you notes after interviews. Leave one with employers as a business card. However you get them in circulation, you may be surprised at how well they work.

You can easily create JIST Cards on a computer and print them on card stock you can buy at any office-supply store. Or you can have a few hundred printed cheaply by a local quick-print shop. Although they are often done as 3-by-5 cards, they can be printed in any size or format, including standard business card size.

Sandy Nolan

Position: General Office/Clerical

Cell phone: (512) 232-9213

Email: snolan@aol.com

More than two years of work experience plus one year of training in office practices. Type 55 wpm, trained in word processing, post general ledger, have good interpersonal skills, and get along with most people. Can meet deadlines and handle pressure well.

Willing to work any hours.

Organized, honest, reliable, and hardworking.

Richard Straightarrow

Home: (602) 253-9678
Cell: (602) 257-6643
E-mail: RSS@email.com

Objective: **Electronics installation, maintenance, and sales**

Four years of work experience plus a two-year A.S. degree in Electronics Engineering
Technology. Managed a $360K annual business while attending school full time, with
grades in the top 25%. Familiar with all major electronic diagnostic and repair equipment.
Hands-on experience with medical, consumer, communication, and industrial electronics
equipment and applications. Good problem-solving and communication skills.
Customer service oriented.

Willing to do what it takes to get the job done.

A JIST Card Can Lead to an Effective Phone Script

The phone is an essential job search tool that can get you more interviews per hour than any other method. But the technique won't work unless you use it actively throughout your search. After you have created your JIST Card, you can use it as the basis for a phone script to make warm or cold calls. Revise your JIST Card content so that it sounds natural when spoken, and then edit it until you can read it out loud in about 30 seconds. The sample phone script that follows is based on the content of a JIST Card. Use it to help you modify your own JIST Card into a phone script.

> "Hello. My name is Pam Nykanen. I am interested in a position in hotel management. I have four years of experience in sales, catering, and accounting with a 300-room hotel. I also have an associate degree in hotel management, plus one year of experience with the Brady Culinary Institute. During my employment, I helped double revenues from meetings and conferences and increased bar revenues by 46 percent. I have good problem-solving skills and am good with people. I am also well-organized, hardworking, and detail-oriented. When may I come in to talk with you about opportunities in your organization?"

With your script in hand, make some practice calls to warm or cold contacts. If making cold calls, contact the person most likely to supervise you. Then present your script just as you practiced it—without stopping.

Although the sample script assumes that you are calling someone you don't know, you can change it to address warm contacts and referrals. Making cold calls takes courage but works very well for many who are willing to do it.

Use the Internet in Your Job Search

The Internet has limitations as a job search tool. While many have used it to get job leads, it has not worked well for far more. Too many assume they can simply add their resume to resume databases and employers will line up to hire them. Just like the older approach of sending out lots of resumes, good things sometimes happen, but not often.

I recommend two points that apply to all job search methods, including using the Internet:

- It is unwise to rely on just one or two methods in conducting your job search.

- It is essential that you use an active rather than a passive approach in your job search.

Use More Than One Job Search Method

I encourage you to use the Internet in your job search, but I suggest that you use it along with other techniques. Use the same sorts of job search techniques online as you do offline, including contacting employers directly and building up a network of personal contacts that can help you with your search.

Tips to Increase Your Effectiveness in Internet Job Searches

The following tips can increase the effectiveness of using the Internet in your job search:

- **Be as specific as possible in the job you seek.** This is important in using any job search method, and it's even more important in using the Internet in your job search. The Internet is enormous, so it is essential to be as focused as possible in your search. Narrow your job title or titles to be as specific as possible. Limit your search to specific industries or areas of specialization. Locate and use specialized job banks in your area of interest.

- **Have reasonable expectations.** Success on the Internet is more likely if you understand its limitations and strengths. For example, employers trying to find someone with skills in high demand, such as nurses, are more likely to use the Internet to recruit job candidates.

- **Limit your geographic options.** If you don't want to move or would move only to certain areas, state this preference on your resume and restrict your search to those areas. Many Internet sites allow you to view or search for only those jobs that meet your location criteria.

- **Create an electronic resume.** With few exceptions, resumes submitted to Internet resume databases end up as simple text files with no graphic elements. Employers search these databases for resumes that include keywords or meet other searchable criteria. So create a simple text resume for Internet use and include words that are likely to be used by employers searching for someone with your abilities. (See Step 4 for more on creating an electronic resume or online portfolio.)

- **Get your resume into the major resume databases.** Most Internet employment sites let you add your resume for free and then charge employers to advertise openings or to search for candidates. Although adding your resume to these databases is not likely to result in job offers, doing so allows you to use your stored resume to easily apply for positions that are posted at these sites. These easy-to-use sites often provide all sorts of useful information for job seekers.

- **Make direct contacts.** Visit the Web sites of organizations that interest you and learn more about them. Many post openings, allow you to apply online, offer information on benefits and work environment, or even provide access to staff who can answer your questions. Even if they don't, you can always search the site or e-mail a request for the name of the person in charge of the work that interests you and then communicate with that person directly.

- **Network.** You can network online, too, finding names and e-mail addresses of potential employer contacts or of other people who might know someone with job openings. The best place to start your online networking is LinkedIn (www.linkedin.com). Twitter (www.twitter.com) is also a powerful online networking tool, and you can even find some good leads among your Facebook friends. In addition, look at and participate in interest groups, professional association sites, alumni sites, chat rooms, e-mail discussion lists, and employer sites—these are just some of the many creative ways to network and interact with people via the Internet.

Check Out Career-Specific Sites First

Thousands of Internet sites provide lists of job openings and information on careers or education. The best-known general job boards are CareerBuilder (www.careerbuilder.com), Monster (www.monster.com), and Yahoo! Hotjobs (http://hotjobs.yahoo.com/). Perhaps even more helpful are job aggregator sites, which pull jobs from all over the Web into one place. Two of the best-known aggregators are Indeed (www.indeed.com) and Simply Hired (www.simplyhired.com).

Get the Most Out of Less Effective Job Search Methods

Now let's look at some traditional job search methods and how you can increase their effectiveness. Only about one-third of all job seekers get their jobs using one of these methods, but you should still consider using them to some extent in your search.

Newspaper and Internet Help-Wanted Ads

Most jobs are never advertised, and fewer than 15 percent of all people get their jobs through the want ads. Everyone who reads the paper knows about these openings, so competition is fierce for the few advertised jobs.

The Internet also lists many job openings. But, as happens with newspaper ads, enormous numbers of people view these postings. Many job seekers make direct contact with employers via a company's Web site. Some people do get jobs through the bigger sites, so go ahead and apply. Just be sure to spend most of your time using more effective methods.

Filling Out Applications

Most employers require job seekers to complete a paper application form, a kiosk application on a computer at the front of the store, or an online application on the company's Web site. Applications are designed to collect negative information, and employers use applications to screen people out. If, for example, your training or work history is not the best, you will often never get an interview, even if you can do the job.

Completing applications is a more effective approach for young and entry-level job seekers. The reason is that there is usually greater need for workers for the relatively low-paying jobs typically sought by less-experienced job seekers. As a result, when employers try to fill those positions, they are more willing to accept a lack of experience or fewer job skills. Even so, you will get better results by filling out the application, if asked to do so, and then requesting an interview with the person in charge.

When you complete an application, make it neat and error free, and do not include anything that could get you screened out. If necessary, leave a problem section blank. You can always explain situations in an interview.

Public and Private Employment Agencies and Services

There are three types of employment agencies. One is operated by the government and is free. The others, private employment agencies and temp agencies, are run as for-profit businesses and charge a fee to either you or an employer. Following are the advantages and disadvantages to using each.

The government employment service and One-Stop centers. Each state and province has a network of local offices to pay unemployment compensation, provide job leads, and offer other services—at no charge to you or to employers. The service's name varies by region. It may be called Job Service, Department of Labor, Unemployment Office, Workforce Development, WorkOne, or another name. All of these offices are now online. You can find your local office at www.careeronestop.org.

The Employment and Training Administration Web site at www.doleta.gov gives you information on the programs provided by the government employment service, plus links to other useful sites.

Visit your local office early in your job search. Find out whether you qualify for unemployment compensation and learn more about its services. Look into it—the price is right.

Private employment agencies. Private employment agencies are businesses that charge a fee either to you or to the employer that hires you. Fees can be from less than one month's pay to 15 percent or more of your annual salary. You will often see these agencies' ads in the help-wanted section of the newspaper. Most have Web sites.

Be careful about using fee-based employment agencies. Recent research indicates that more people use and benefit from fee-based agencies than in the past. However, relatively few people who register with private agencies get a job through them.

If you use a private employment agency, ask for interviews with the employers who agree to pay the agency's fee. Do not sign an exclusive agreement or be pressured into accepting a job. Also, continue to actively look for your own leads. You can find these agencies in the phone book's yellow pages, and many state- or province-government Web sites offer lists of the private employment agencies in their states.

Temporary agencies. Temporary agencies offer jobs that last from several days to many months. They charge the employer an hourly fee, and then pay you a bit less and keep the difference. You pay no direct fee to the agency. Many private employment agencies now provide temporary jobs as well.

Temp agencies have grown rapidly for good reason. They provide employers with short-term help, and employers often use them to find people they might want to hire later. If the employers are dissatisfied, they can just ask the agency for different temp workers.

Temp agencies can help you survive between jobs and get experience in different work settings. Temp jobs provide a very good option while you look for long-term work, and you might get a job offer while working in a temp job. Holding a temporary job might even lead to a regular job with the same or a similar employer.

School and Other Employment Services

Only a small percentage of job seekers use school and other special employment services, probably because few job seekers have the service available to them. If you are a student or graduate, find out about any employment services at your school. Some schools provide free career counseling, resume writing help, referrals to job openings, career interest tests, reference materials, Web sites listing job openings, and other services. Special career programs work with veterans, people with disabilities, welfare recipients, union members, professional groups, and many others. So check out these services and consider using them.

Mailing Out Lots of Resumes Blindly

Many job search experts used to suggest that sending out lots of resumes was a great technique. That advice probably helped sell their resume books, but mailing resumes to people you do not know was never an effective approach. It very rarely works. A recent survey of 1,500 successful job seekers showed that only 2 percent found their positions through sending an unsolicited resume. The same is true for the Internet.

Although mailing your resume to strangers doesn't make much sense, posting it on the Internet might because

- It doesn't take much time.

- Many employers have the potential to find your resume.

- You can post your resume on niche sites that attract only employers in your field.

- Your Internet resume is easily updated, allowing you to post your current accomplishments.

- You can easily link your resume to projects and Web sites that highlight your accomplishments.

Job searching on the Internet has its limitations, just like other methods. I'll cover resumes in more detail later and provide tips on using the Internet throughout this book.

STEP 4: Write a Simple Resume Now and a Better One Later

Sending out resumes and waiting for responses is not an effective job seeking technique. But many employers *will* ask you for a resume, and it can be a useful tool in your job search. I suggest that you begin with a simple resume you can complete quickly. I've seen too many people spend weeks working on a resume when they could have been out getting interviews instead. If you want a better resume, you can work on it on weekends and evenings. So let's begin with the basics.

The following tips make sense for any resume format:

- **Write it yourself.** It's okay to look at other resumes for ideas, but write yours yourself. Doing so will force you to organize your thoughts and background.

- **Make it error free.** One spelling or grammar error will create a negative impression. Get someone else to review your final draft for any errors. Then review it again because these rascals have a way of slipping in.

- **Make it look good.** Poor copy quality, cheap paper, bad type quality, or anything else that creates a poor appearance will turn off employers to even the best resume content. Get professional help with design and printing if necessary. Many professional resume writers and even print shops offer writing and desktop design services if you need help.

- **Be brief, be relevant.** Many good resumes fit on one page, and few justify more than two. Include only the most important points. Use short sentences and action words. If it doesn't relate to and support the job objective, cut it!

- **Be honest.** Don't overstate your qualifications. If you end up getting a job you can't handle, who does it help? And a lie can result in your being fired later.

- **Be positive.** Emphasize your accomplishments and results. A resume is no place to be too humble or to display your faults.

- **Be specific.** Instead of saying, "I am good with people," say, "I supervised four people in the warehouse and increased productivity by 30 percent." Use numbers whenever possible, such as the number of people served, percentage of sales increase, or amount of dollars saved.

Get Your Resume Online

Employers may ask you to send them your resume online. Pay attention to their instructions, because they will probably specify whether they want you to send your Word file as an attachment, send a PDF, or transmit a plain-text resume via e-mail or their Web site. Louise Kursmark, coauthor of *15-Minute Cover Letter,* provides these steps for converting your resume to plain text:

1. Save your resume with a different name and select "text only," "ASCII," or "Plain Text (*.txt)" in the "Save As Type" option box.

2. Reopen the file. Your word processor has automatically reformatted your resume into Courier font, removed all formatting, and left-justified the text.

3. Reset the margins to 2 inches left and right, so that you have a narrow column of text rather than a full-page width. Adjust line lengths to fit within the narrow margins by adding hard returns.

4. Fix any glitches such as odd characters that may have been inserted to take the place of "curly" quotes, dashes, accents, or other nonstandard symbols.

5. Remove any tabs and adjust spacing as necessary. You might add a few extra blank spaces, move text down to the next line, or add extra blank lines for readability.

6. Consider adding horizontal dividers to break the resume into sections. You can use a row of any standard typewriter symbols, such as *, -, ( ), =, +, ^, or #.

When you close the file, it will be saved with the .txt file extension. When you are ready to use it, just open the file, select and copy the text, and paste it into the online application or e-mail message.

Never delay or slow down your job search because your resume is not good enough. The best approach is to create a simple and acceptable resume as quickly as possible and then use it. As time permits, create a better one if you feel you must.

Writing Chronological Resumes

Most resumes use a chronological format where the most recent experience is listed first, followed by each preceding job. Most employers prefer this format. It works fine for someone with work experience in several similar jobs, but not as well for those with limited experience or for career changers.

Look at the two resumes for Judith Jones that follow. Both use the chronological approach.

The first resume would work fine for most job search needs. It could be completed in about an hour. Notice that the second one includes some improvements. The first resume is good, but most employers would like the additional positive information in the improved resume.

Basic Chronological Resume Example

Everything in this resume supports the candidate's job objective. The emphasis on all related education is important because it helps overcome her lack of extensive work experience.

Judith J. Jones

115 South Hawthorne Avenue
Chicago, Illinois 66204
tel: (312) 653-9217
email: jj@earthlink.com

JOB OBJECTIVE

A position in the office management, accounting, or administrative assistant area that enables me to grow professionally.

EDUCATION AND TRAINING

Acme Business College, Lincoln, IL
Graduate of a one-year business program.

John Adams High School, South Bend, IN
Diploma, business education.

U.S. Army
Financial procedures, accounting functions.

Other: Continuing-education classes and workshops in business communication, spreadsheet and database applications, scheduling systems, and customer relations.

EXPERIENCE

2006–present—Claims Processor, Blue Spear Insurance Co., Wilmette, IL. Process customer medical claims, develop management reports based on created spreadsheets and develop management reports based on those forms, exceed productivity goals.

2005–2006—Returned to school to upgrade business and computer skills. Completed courses in advanced accounting, spreadsheet and database programs, office management, human relations, and new office techniques.

2002–2005—E4, U.S. Army. Assigned to various stations as a specialist in finance operations. Promoted prior to honorable discharge.

2001–2002—Sandy's Boutique, Wilmette, IL. Responsible for counter sales, display design, cash register, and other tasks.

1999–2001—Held part-time and summer jobs throughout high school.

STRENGTHS AND SKILLS

Reliable, hardworking, and good with people. General ledger, accounts payable, and accounts receivable. Proficient in Microsoft Word, WordPerfect, Excel, and Outlook.

Improved Chronological Resume Example

This improved version of the basic resume adds lots of details and specific numbers throughout to reinforce skills.

Judith J. Jones

115 South Hawthorne Avenue
Chicago, IL 66204

jj@earthlink.com
(312) 653-9217 (cell)

JOB OBJECTIVE

A position requiring excellent business management expertise in an office environment. Position should require a variety of skills, including office management, word processing, and spreadsheet and database application use.

EDUCATION AND TRAINING

Acme Business College, Lincoln, IL
Completed one-year program in **Professional Office Management.** Achieved GPA in top 30% of class. Courses included word processing, accounting theory and systems, advanced spreadsheet and database applications, graphics design, time management, and supervision.

John Adams High School, South Bend, IN
Graduated with emphasis on **business courses.** Earned excellent grades in all business topics and won top award for word-processing speed and accuracy.

Other: Continuing-education programs at own expense, including business communications, customer relations, computer applications, and sales techniques.

EXPERIENCE

2006–present—**Claims Processor, Blue Spear Insurance Company,** Wilmette, IL. Process 50 complex medical insurance claims per day, almost 20% above department average. Created a spreadsheet report process that decreased department labor costs by more than $30,000 a year. Received two merit raises for performance.

2005–2006—**Returned to business school to gain advanced office skills.**

2002–2005—**Finance Specialist (E4), U.S. Army.** Systematically processed more than 200 invoices per day from commercial vendors. Trained and supervised eight employees. Devised internal system allowing 15% increase in invoices processed with a decrease in personnel. Managed department with a budget equivalent of more than $350,000 a year. Honorable discharge.

2001–2002—**Sales Associate promoted to Assistant Manager, Sandy's Boutique,** Wilmette, IL. Made direct sales and supervised four employees. Managed daily cash balances and deposits, made purchasing and inventory decisions, and handled all management functions during owner's absence. Sales increased 26% and profits doubled during tenure.

1999–2001—**Held various part-time and summer jobs through high school while maintaining GPA 3.0/4.0.** Earned enough to pay all personal expenses, including car insurance. Learned to deal with customers, meet deadlines, work hard, and handle multiple priorities.

STRENGTHS AND SKILLS

Reliable, with strong work ethic. Excellent interpersonal, written, and oral communication and math skills. Accept supervision well, effectively supervise others, and work well as a team member. General ledger, accounts payable, and accounts receivable expertise. Proficient in Microsoft Word, Excel, PowerPoint, and Outlook; WordPerfect.

Tips for Writing a Simple Chronological Resume

Follow these tips as you write a basic chronological resume:

- **Name:** Use your formal name (not a nickname).

- **Address and contact information:** Avoid abbreviations in your address and include your ZIP code. If you might move, use a friend's address or include a forwarding address. Most employers will not write to you, so provide reliable phone numbers, e-mail addresses, and other contact options. Always include your area code in your phone number because you never know where your resume might travel. Make sure that you have an answering machine or voice mail, and record a professional-sounding message.

- **Job objective/professional summary statement:** You should almost always have one, even if it is general. Notice how Judith Jones keeps her options open with her broad job objective in her basic resume on page 326. Writing "secretary" or "clerical" might limit her from being considered for other jobs. Professional applicants might consider using an impressive summary statement instead, with a heading that states the desired job target.

- **Education and training:** Include any training or education you've had that supports your job objective. If you did not finish a formal degree or program, list what you did complete and emphasize accomplishments. If your experience is not strong, add details here such as related courses and extracurricular activities. In the two examples, Judith Jones puts her business schooling in both the education and experience sections. Doing this fills a job gap and allows her to present her training as equal to work experience.

- **Previous experience:** Include the basics such as employer name, job title, dates employed, and responsibilities—but emphasize specific skills, results, accomplishments, superior performance, and so on.

- **Personal data:** Do not include irrelevant details such as height, weight, and marital status or a photo. Current laws do not allow an employer to base hiring decisions on these points. Providing this information can cause some employers to toss your resume. You can include information about hobbies or leisure activities that directly support your job objective in a special section. The first sample includes a Personal section in which Judith lists some of her strengths, which are often not included in a resume.

- **References:** Make sure that each reference will make nice comments about you and ask each to write a letter of recommendation that you can give to employers. You do not need to list your references on your resume. List them on a separate page and give it to employers who ask.

When you have a simple, errorless, and eye-pleasing resume, get on with your job search. There is no reason to delay! If you want to create a better resume, you can work on improving it in your spare time (evenings or weekends).

Tips for an Improved Chronological Resume

Use these tips to improve your simple resume:

- **Job objective:** A poorly written job objective or summary statement can limit the jobs an employer might consider you for. Think of the skills you have and the types of jobs you want to do; describe them in general terms. Instead of using a narrow job title such as "restaurant manager," you might write "manage a small to mid-sized business."

- **Education and training:** New graduates should emphasize their recent training and education more than those with a few years of related work experience would. A more detailed education and training section might include specific courses you took, and activities or accomplishments that support your job objective or reinforce your key skills. Include other details that reflect how hard you work, such as working your way through school.

The Chronological Resume to Emphasize Results

This resume focuses on accomplishments through the use of numbers. While Jon's resume does not say so, it is obvious that he works hard and that he gets results.

Jon Feder

2140 Beach Road
Pompano Beach, Florida 20000

Phone: (222) 333-4444
E-mail: jfeder@email.com

Objective

Management position in a major hotel

Summary of Experience

Three years of experience in sales, catering banquet services, and guest relations in a 75-room hotel. Doubled sales revenues from conferences and meetings. Increased dining room and bar revenues by 40%. Won prestigious national and local awards for increased productivity and services.

Experience

Beachcomber Hotel, Pompano Beach, Florida
Assistant Manager
20XX to Present
- Oversee a staff of 24, including dining room and bar, housekeeping, and public relations operations.
- Introduced new menus and increased dining room revenues by 40%. Awarded *Saveur* magazine's prestigious first place Hotel Cuisine award as a result of my selection of chefs.
- Attracted 58% more bar patrons by implementing Friday Night Jazz at the Beach.

Tidewater Suites, Hollywood Beach, Florida
Sales and Public Relations
20XX to 20XX
- Doubled revenues per month from weddings, conferences, and meetings.
- Chosen Chamber of Commerce Newcomer of the Year 20XX for the increase in business within the community.

Education

Associate degree in Hotel Management, Sullivan Technical Institute
Certificate in Travel Management, Phoenix University

The Skills Resume for Those with Limited Work Experience

This resume is for a recent high school graduate whose only work experience was at a school office.

Catalina A. Garcia

2340 N. Delaware Street
Denver, Colorado 81613
Cell phone: (413) 123-4567
E-mail: cagarcia@net.net

Position Desired

Office assistant in a fast-paced business

Skills and Abilities

Communication	Excellent written and verbal presentation skills. Use proper grammar and have a good speaking voice.
Interpersonal	Get along well with all types of people. Accept supervision. Helped up to 50 students, visitors, and callers a day in the school office.
Flexible	Willing to try new tasks and am interested in improving efficiency of assigned work.
Attention to Detail	Maintained confidential student records accurately and efficiently.
Hard Working	Worked in the school office during my junior and senior years and maintained above-average grades.
Dependable	Never absent or late in four years.
Award	English Department Student of the Year, May XXXX.

Education

Denver North High School. Graduated in the top 30% of my class. Took advanced English and communication classes. Member of the student newspaper staff for three years.

Girls' basketball team for four years. This activity taught me discipline, teamwork, how to follow instructions, and hard work.

The Combination Resume for Those Changing Careers

This resume emphasizes Grant's relevant education and transferable skills because he has little work experience in the field.

Grant Thomas

717 Carlin Court • Mundelein, IL 60000 • (555) 555-5555 • E-mail: gthomas@aol.com

Profile

- Outstanding student and tutor
- Winner of international computer software design competition three years
- Self-directed and independent, but also a team player
- Effective oral and written communicator
- Creative problem solver

Education and Training

M.S. in Software Engineering, Massachusetts Institute of Technology, Cambridge, MA
B.S. in Computer Engineering, California State University, Fullerton, CA
A rigorous education focusing on topics such as

- Structure and interpretation of computer programs
- Circuits and electronics
- Signals and systems
- Computation structures
- Microelectronic devices and circuits
- Computer system engineering
- Computer language engineering
- Mathematics for computer science
- Analog electronics laboratory
- Digital systems laboratory

Highlights of Experience and Abilities

- Develop, create, and modify general computer applications.
- Analyze user needs and develop software solutions.
- Confer with systems analysts, computer programmers, and others.
- Modify existing software system installation and monitor equipment functioning to ensure specifications are met.
- Supervise work of programmers and technicians.
- Train customers and employees to use new and modified software.

Employment History

Software Specialist, First Rate Computers, Mundelein, IL 20XX to present
- Technician and Customer and Employee Trainer throughout high school
- Promoted to software specialist and worked as a full-time telecommuting employee while completing B.S. and M.S. degrees.

The Electronic Resume

This resume is appropriate for scanning or e-mail submission. It has a plain format that is easily read by scanners. It also has lots of keywords that increase its chances of being selected when an employer searches a database.

```
SAMUEL FEINMAN
489 Smithfield Road
Salem, OR 97301
503.491.3033
samfine@earthlink.net

= = = = = = = = = = = = = = = = = = = = =

SALES PROFESSIONAL

Dynamic, motivated, award-winning sales professional with extensive
experience. Troubleshooter and problem-solver. Team player who can
motivate self and others. Excellent management and training skills.

= = = = = = = = = = = = = = = = = = = = =

RELATED EXPERIENCE

Jackson Chevrolet, Springfield, OR
GENERAL MANAGER, XXXX—Present
* Consistently achieve top-ten volume dealer in the Northwest.
* Manage all dealership operations including computer systems, sales,
parts, service, and administration.
* Profitably operate dealership through difficult economic times.
* Meet or exceed customer service, parts, sales, and car service
objectives.
* Maintain high-profile used-car operation.

Afford-A-Ford, Albany, OR
ASSISTANT GENERAL MANAGER, XXXX—XXXX
* Consistently in top five for sales in district; met or exceeded sales
objectives.
* Supervised and trained staff of 90.
* Helped to convert a consistently money-losing store into a profitable
operation by end of first year.
* Focused on customer satisfaction through employee satisfaction and
training.
* Built strong parts and service business, managing excellent
interaction among parts, service, and sales.
* Instituted fleet-sales department and became top fleet-sales dealer
three years running.
* Built lease portfolio from virtually none to 31% of retail.

WetWater Pool Products, Salem, OR
SALES/CUSTOMER SERVICE, XXXX—XXXX
* Advised customers to purchase products that best met their needs while
focusing attention on products more profitable to company.
* Troubleshot and solved customer problems, identifying rapid solutions
and emphasizing customer satisfaction and retention.
* Oversaw shipping and receiving staff.

= = = = = = = = = = = = = = = = = = = = =

ADDITIONAL EXPERIENCE

State of Oregon, Salem, OR
COMPUTER TECHNICIAN INTERN, XXXX—XXXX
* Built customized computers for state offices.
* Worked with team on installation of computer systems.

= = = = = = = = = = = = = = = = = = = = =

EDUCATION

AS, Oregon Community College, Troy, OR
Major: Business studies

= = = = = = = = = = = = = = = = = = = = =

REFERENCES AVAILABLE ON REQUEST
```

Quick Tips for Writing a Cover Letter in 15 Minutes

Whether you're mailing, faxing, or e-mailing your resume, it is important to provide a letter along with your resume that explains why you are sending it—a cover letter (or cover message, in the case of e-mailing). Even when you post your resume in an online database (also known as a resume bank), the Web site where you're posting often has a place where you can upload or paste a cover letter. A cover letter highlights your key qualifications, explains your situation, and asks the recipient for some specific action, consideration, or response.

No matter to whom you are writing, virtually every good cover letter should follow these guidelines.

1. Write to Someone in Particular

Avoid sending a cover letter "To whom it may concern" or using some other impersonal opening. We all get enough junk mail, and if you don't send your letter to someone by name, it will be treated like junk mail.

2. Make Absolutely No Errors

One way to offend people right away is to misspell their names or use incorrect titles. If you are not 100 percent certain, call and verify the correct spelling of the name and other details before you send the letter. Also, review your letters carefully to be sure that they contain no typographical, grammatical, or other errors.

3. Personalize Your Content

No one is impressed by form letters, and you should not use them. Those computer-generated letters that automatically insert a name (known as merge mailings) never fool anyone, and cover letters done in this way are offensive. Small, targeted mailings to a carefully selected group of prospective employers can be effective if you tailor your cover letter to each recipient, but large mass mailings are a waste of time. If you can't customize your letter in some way, don't send it.

4. Present a Good Appearance

Your contacts with prospective employers should always be professional, so buy good-quality stationery and matching envelopes for times when you'll be mailing or hand-delivering a letter and resume. Use papers and envelopes that match or complement your resume paper. The standard 8 1/2 × 11 paper size is typically used, but you can also use the smaller Monarch-size paper with matching envelopes. For colors, use white, ivory, or light beige—whatever matches your resume paper. Employers expect cover letters to be word processed and produced with excellent print quality.

Use a standard letter format that complements your resume type and format. You might find it easier to use your word-processing software's template functions than to create a format from scratch. Your letters don't have to be fancy; they do have to look professional. And don't forget the envelope! It should be typed and printed carefully, without errors.

> **Note**
> *You will send many of your cover letters as e-mail messages. All the rules for traditional cover letters apply equally to e-mail cover letters. Just because e-mail is a less formal means of communicating doesn't mean you can be careless with writing, spelling, grammar, punctuation, or presentation. But e-mail letters should be shorter and crisper than traditional paper letters.*

5. Begin with a Friendly Opening

Start your letter by sharing the reason you are writing and, if appropriate, a reminder of any prior contacts or the name of the person who referred you. See the examples on pages 337 and 338 for ideas for beginning your letters.

6. Target Your Skills and Experiences

To effectively target your skills and experiences, you must know something about the organization, the job opportunity, or the person with whom you are dealing. Present any relevant background that may be of particular interest to the person to whom you are writing.

7. Close with an Action Statement

Don't close your letter without clearly identifying what you will do next. Don't leave it up to the employer to contact you, because that doesn't guarantee a response. Close on a positive note and let the employer know how and when you will be following up.

Sample Printed Cover Letter

Allan P. Raymond, CPA

29 Brookside Drive, Mystic, CT 06433
860.239.7671 • allanraymond@verizon.net

March 15, 20XX

Carol P. Graves, CPA
President, Graves & Andrews
254 Court Street
New London, CT 06320

Dear Carol:

I enjoyed our conversation at the recent CPA Society meeting and, as you suggested, I am forwarding my resume with this letter of interest in joining your firm.

You and I agreed that your clients deserve the best: the best accountants, the best strategies, and the greatest dedication to customer service. I am confident I can bring "the best" in both attitude and execution to your firm.

With more than ten years of accounting experience—the last five as a CPA and owner of an accounting firm specializing in tax—I have strong and well-proven professional skills. I thrive on the challenges and intricacies of tax accounting and stay up-to-date with tax code changes through both in-person and online training programs.

What satisfies me most in my professional life is the opportunity to help clients better manage, control, and benefit from their money. One of the keys to the good advice I give my clients is my deep understanding of the consequences of investment decisions on their tax situation. I have worked with businesses of all sizes—from one person to complex multimillion-dollar organizations—in diverse industries and have contributed strategies and planning recommendations as well as tax-related accounting services.

Having just concluded the sale of my business, I am eager for new professional challenges. I would like to explore my value as a tax accountant with your firm, and in pursuit of that objective I will call you next week to schedule a meeting. Thank you.

Best regards,

Allan P. Raymond

enclosure: resume

Written by Louise Kursmark

Sample E-mail Cover Letter

Dear Ms. Gold:

My sister, Tracy Oswald, tells me that you are looking for a systems administrator for your growing San Francisco operation.

I am experienced, reliable, loyal, and customer focused and would like to talk with you about joining your team.

The enclosed resume describes nearly 15 years of experience with Anthem Blue Cross/Blue Shield, during which I advanced to increasingly responsible technical positions. Whether independently or with a team, I worked hard to provide the best possible service and support to my "customers." I was recognized for my strong technical skills, ability to guide less experienced support people, and 100% reliability.

A recent downsizing at Anthem caused my position to be eliminated, and I am looking for a new opportunity with a company like yours, where my technical abilities, positive attitude, and dedication will be valued.

I will call you next week in hopes of getting together soon.

Yours truly,

Kevin Oswald

****
Attachment: resume

Written by Louise Kursmark

STEP 5: Organize Your Time to Get Two Interviews a Day

The average job seeker gets about five interviews a month—fewer than two a week. Yet many job seekers use the methods in this *Quick Job Search* to get two interviews a day. Getting two interviews a day equals 10 a week and 40 a month. That's 800 percent more interviews than the average job seeker gets. Who do you think will get a job offer quicker?

You might think that getting two interviews a day sounds impossible. However, getting two interviews a day is quite possible if you redefine what counts as an interview and use the networking techniques from step 3.

> **The New Definition of an Interview:** Any face-to-face contact with someone who has the authority to hire or supervise a person with your skills—even if no opening exists at the time you talk with them.

If you use this new definition, it becomes *much* easier to get interviews. You can now interview with all sorts of potential employers, not just those who have job openings now. While most other job seekers look for advertised or actual openings, you can get interviews before a job opens up or before it is advertised and widely known. You will be considered for jobs that may soon be created but that others will not know about. And, of course, you can also interview for existing openings just as everyone else does.

Spending as much time as possible on your job search and setting a job search schedule are important parts of this step. Researchers at the University of Missouri found in a 2009 study that developing and following a job search plan from the start, as well as having a positive attitude about your search, had a significant impact on job search success (*U.S. News & World Report,* September 24, 2009).

Make Your Search a Full-Time Job

Job seekers average fewer than 15 hours a week looking for work. On average, unemployment lasts three or more months, with some people out of work far longer (for example, older workers and higher earners). My many years of experience researching job seeking indicate that the more time you spend on your job search each week, the less time you will likely remain unemployed.

Of course, using the more effective job search methods presented in this book also helps. Many job search programs that teach job seekers my basic approach of using more effective methods and spending more time looking have proven that these seekers often find a job in half the average time. More importantly, many job seekers also find better jobs using these methods.

So, if you are unemployed and looking for a full-time job, you should plan to look on a full-time basis. It just makes sense to do so, although many do not, or they start out well but quickly get discouraged. Most job seekers simply don't have a structured plan—they have no idea what they are going to do next Thursday. The plan that follows will show you how to structure your job search like a job.

Decide How Much Time You Will Spend Looking for Work Each Week and Day

First and most importantly, decide how many hours you are willing to spend each week on your job search. You should spend a minimum of 25 hours a week on hardcore job search activities with no goofing around. The following worksheet walks you through a simple but effective process to set a job search schedule for each week.

PLAN YOUR JOB SEARCH WEEK

1. How many hours are you willing to spend each week looking for a job?

   _____

   _____

2. Which days of the week will you spend looking for a job?

   _____

   _____

3. How many hours will you look each day? _____

   _____

4. At what times will you begin and end your job search on each of these days?

   _____

   _____

Create a Specific Daily Job Search Schedule

Having a specific daily schedule is essential because most job seekers find it hard to stay productive each day. The sample daily schedule that follows is the result of years of research into what schedule gets the best results. I tested many schedules in job search programs I ran, and this particular schedule worked best.

Consider using a schedule like this sample daily schedule. Why? Because it works.

A Sample Daily Schedule That Works

Time	Activity
7–8 a.m.	Get up, shower, dress, eat breakfast.
8–8:15 a.m.	Organize workspace, review schedule for today's interviews and promised follow-ups, check e-mail, and update schedule as needed.
8:15–9 a.m.	Review old leads for follow-up needed today; develop new leads from want ads, yellow pages, the Internet, warm contact lists, and other sources; complete daily contact list.
9–10 a.m.	Make phone calls and set up interviews.
10–10:15 a.m.	Take a break.
10:15–11 a.m.	Make more phone calls; set up more interviews.
11 a.m.–Noon	Send follow-up notes and do other office activities as needed.
Noon–1 p.m.	Lunch break, relax.
1–3 p.m.	Go on interviews; make cold contacts in the field.
Evening	Read job search books, make calls to warm contacts not reachable during the day, work on a better resume, spend time with friends and family, exercise, relax.

If you are not accustomed to using a daily schedule book or electronic planner, promise yourself to get a good one today. Choose one that allows for each day's plan on an hourly basis, plus daily to-do lists. Record your daily schedule in advance, and then add interviews as they come. Get used to carrying your planner with you and use it!

You can find a variety of computer programs and smartphone apps to help organize your job search. An example of a Web site that offers a free job search planning system online is JibberJobber (www.jibberjobber.com).

STEP 6: Dramatically Improve Your Interviewing Skills

Interviews are where the job search action is. You have to get them; then you have to do well in them. According to surveys of employers, most job seekers do not effectively present the skills they have to do the job. Even worse, most job seekers can't answer one or more problem questions.

This lack of performance in interviews is one reason why employers will often hire a job seeker who does well in the interview over someone with better credentials. The good news is that you can do simple things to dramatically improve your interviewing skills. This section emphasizes interviewing tips and techniques that make the most difference.

Your First Impression May Be the Only One You Make

Some research suggests that if the interviewer forms a negative impression in the first five minutes of an interview, your chances of getting a job offer approach zero. I know from experience that many job seekers can create a lasting negative impression within seconds.

Tips for Interviewing

Because a positive first impression is so important, I share these suggestions to help you get off to a good start:

- **Make a good impression before you arrive.** Your resume, e-mails, applications, and other written correspondence create an impression before the interview, so make them professional and error free.
- **Do some homework on the organization before you go.** You can often get information on a business and on industry trends from the Internet or a library.
- **Dress and groom the same way the interviewer is likely to be dressed—but better!** Employer surveys find that almost half of all people's dress or grooming creates an initial negative impression. So this is a big problem. If necessary, get advice on your interviewing outfits from someone who dresses well. Pay close attention to your grooming, too—little things do count.
- **Be early.** Leave in plenty of time to be a few minutes early to an interview.
- **Be friendly and respectful with the receptionist.** Doing otherwise will often get back to the interviewer and result in a quick rejection.
- **Follow the interviewer's lead in the first few minutes.** The interview often begins with informal small talk, but the interviewer uses this time to see how you interact. This is a good time to make a positive comment on the organization or even something you see in the office.
- **Understand that a traditional interview is not a friendly exchange.** In a traditional interview situation, there is a job opening, and you will be one of several applicants for it. In this setting, the employer's task is to eliminate all applicants but one. The interviewer's questions are designed to elicit information that can be used to screen you out. And your objective is to avoid getting screened out. It's hardly an open and honest interaction, is it?

Setting up interviews before an opening exists eliminates the stress of a traditional interview. In pre-interviews, employers are not trying to screen you out, and you are not trying to keep them from finding out stuff about

(continued)

(continued)

you. Having said that, knowing how to answer questions that might be asked in a traditional interview is good preparation for any interview you face.

- **Be prepared to answer the tough interview questions.** Your answers to a few key problem questions may determine whether you get a job offer. There are simply too many possible interview questions to cover one by one. Instead, 10 basic questions cover variations of most other interview questions. So, if you can learn to answer the Top 10 Problem Interview Questions well, you will know how to answer most others.

- **Be prepared for the most important interview question of all.** "Why should I hire you?" is the most important question of all to answer well. Do you have a convincing argument why someone should hire you over someone else? If you don't, you probably won't get that job you really want. So think carefully about why someone should hire you and practice your response. Then make sure you communicate this in the interview, even if the interviewer never asks the question in a clear way.

Top 10 Problem Interview Questions

1. Why should I hire you?
2. Why don't you tell me about yourself?
3. What are your major strengths?
4. What are your major weaknesses?
5. What sort of pay do you expect to receive?
6. How does your previous experience relate to the jobs we have here?
7. What are your plans for the future?
8. What will your former employer (or references) say about you?
9. Why are you looking for this type of position, and why here?
10. Why don't you tell me about your personal situation?

Follow the Three-Step Process for Answering Interview Questions

I've developed a three-step process for answering interview questions. I know this might seem too simple, but the three-step process is easy to remember and can help you create a good answer to most interview questions. The technique has worked for thousands of people, so consider trying it.

1. **Understand what is really being asked.** Most questions are designed to find out about your self-management skills and personality, but interviewers are rarely this blunt. The employer's *real* question is often one or more of the following:

   - Can I depend on you?

   - Are you easy to get along with?

   - Are you a good worker?

   - Do you have the experience and training to do the job if we hire you?

   - Are you likely to stay on the job for a reasonable period of time and be productive?

   Ultimately, if you don't convince the employer that you will stay and be a good worker, it won't matter if you have the best credentials—he or she won't hire you.

2. **Answer the question briefly in a nondamaging way.** Present the facts of your particular work experience as advantages, not disadvantages. Many interview questions encourage you to provide negative information. One classic question in the list of Top 10 Problem Interview Questions is "What are your major weaknesses?" This is obviously a trick question, and many people are just not prepared for it.

   A good response is to mention something that is not very damaging, such as "I have been told that I am a perfectionist, sometimes not delegating as effectively as I might." But your answer is not complete until you continue with the next step.

3. **Answer the real question by presenting your related skills.** Base your answer on the key skills you have that support the job, and give examples to support these skills. For example, an employer might say to a recent graduate, "We were looking for someone with more experience in this field. Why should we consider you?" Here is one possible answer:

   "I'm sure there are people who have more experience, but I do have more than six years of work experience, including three years of advanced training and hands-on experience using the latest methods and techniques. Because my training is recent, I am open to new ideas and am used to working hard and learning quickly."

   In the previous example (about your need to delegate), a good skills statement might be

   "I've been working on this problem and have learned to let my staff do more, making sure that they have good training and supervision. I've found that their performance improves, and it frees me up to do other things."

Whatever your situation, learn to answer questions in ways that present you well. It's essential to communicate your skills during an interview, and the three-step process can help you answer problem questions and dramatically improve your responses. It works!

How to Earn a Thousand Dollars a Minute

What do you do when the employer asks, "How much money would it take to get you to join our company?"

Tips on Negotiating Pay

Remember these few essential tips when it comes time to negotiate your pay:

- **The #1 Salary Negotiation Rule: The person who names a specific amount first loses.**
- **The only time to negotiate is after you have been offered the job.** Employers want to know how much you want to be paid so that they can eliminate you from consideration. They figure if you want too much, you won't be happy with the job and won't stay. And if you will take too little, they may think you don't have enough experience. So never discuss your salary expectations until an employer offers you the job.
- **If pressed, speak in terms of wide pay ranges.** If you are pushed to reveal your pay expectations early in an interview, ask the interviewer what the normal pay range is for this job. Interviewers will often tell you, and you can say that you would consider offers in this range.

  If you are forced to be more specific, speak in terms of a wide pay range. If you figure that the company will likely pay from $25,000 to $29,000 a year, for example, say that you would consider "any fair offer in the mid-twenties to low thirties." This statement covers the employer's range and goes a bit higher. If all else fails, tell the interviewer that you would consider any reasonable offer.

  For this tip to work, you must know in advance what the job is likely to pay. You can get this information by asking people who do similar work, or from a variety of books and Internet sources of career information, such as the *Occupational Outlook Handbook* (www.bls.gov/oco) or Salary.com.

- **If you want the job, you should say so.** This is no time to be playing games.

(continued)

(continued)

- **Don't say "no" too quickly.** Never, ever turn down a job offer during an interview! Instead, thank the interviewer for the offer and ask to consider the offer overnight. You can turn it down tomorrow, saying how much you appreciate the offer and asking to be considered for other jobs that pay better. And it is okay to ask for additional pay or other concessions. But if you simply can't accept the offer, say why and ask the interviewer to keep you in mind for future opportunities. You just never know.

STEP 7: Follow Up on All Job Leads

It's a fact: People who follow up with potential employers and with others in their network get jobs more quickly than those who do not.

Rules for Effective Follow-Up

Here are four rules to guide you in following up in your job search:

- **Send a thank-you note or e-mail to every person who helps you in your job search.**
- **Send the note within 24 hours after speaking with the person.**
- **Enclose JIST Cards with thank-you notes and all other correspondence.**
- **Develop a system to keep following up with good contacts.**

Thank-You Notes Make a Difference

Although thank-you notes can be e-mailed, most people appreciate and are more impressed by a mailed note. Here are some tips about mailed thank-you notes that you can easily adapt to e-mail use:

- You can handwrite or type thank-you notes on quality paper and matching envelopes.

- Keep the notes simple, neat, and error free.

- Make sure to include a few copies of your JIST Card in the envelope.

Following is an example of a simple thank-you note.

April 5, XXXX

M. Kijek,

Thanks so much for your willingness to see me next Wednesday at 9 a.m. I know that I am one of many who are interested in working with your organization. I appreciate the opportunity to meet you and learn more about the position.

I've enclosed a JIST Card that presents the basics of my skills for this job and will bring my resume to the interview. Please call me if you have any questions at all.

Sincerely,

Bruce Vernon

Use Job Lead Cards to Follow Up

If you use contact management software or an app on your phone, use it to schedule follow-up activities. But the simple paper system I describe here can work very well or can be adapted for setting up your contact management software.

- Use a simple 3-by-5–inch card to record essential information about each person in your network.

- Buy a 3-by-5–inch card file box and tabs for each day of the month.

- File the cards under the date you want to contact the person.

- Follow through by contacting the person on that date.

I've found that staying in touch with a good contact every other week can pay off big. Here's a sample card to give you ideas about creating your own.

ORGANIZATION: _Mutual Health Insurance_

CONTACT PERSON: _Anna Tomey_   PHONE: _317-355-0216_

SOURCE OF LEAD: _Aunt Ruth_

NOTES: _4/10 Called. Anna on vacation. Call back 4/15. 4/15 Interview set 4/20 at 1:30. 4/20 Anna showed me around. They use the same computers we used in school! (Friendly people.) Sent thank-you note and JIST Card, call back 5/1. 5/1 Second interview 5/8 at 9 a.m.!_

In Closing

This is a short book, but it may be all you need to get a better job in less time. I hope this will be true for you, and I wish you well in your search. Remember this: You won't get a job offer because someone knocks on your door and offers one. Job seeking does involve luck, but you are more likely to have good luck if you are out getting interviews.

I'll close this book with a few final tips:

- **Approach your job search as if it were a job itself.** Create and stick to a daily schedule, and spend at least 25 hours a week looking.

- **Follow up on each lead you generate and ask each contact for referrals.**

- **Set out each day to schedule at least two interviews.** Remember the new definition of an interview—an interview can just be talking to a potential employer that doesn't have an opening now but might in the future.

- **Send out lots of thank-you notes and JIST Cards.**

- **When you want the job, tell the employer that you want it and why you should be hired over everyone else.**

Don't get discouraged. There are lots of jobs out there, and someone needs an employee with your skills—your job is to find that someone.

I wish you luck in your job search and in your life.

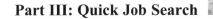

ESSENTIAL JOB SEARCH DATA WORKSHEET

Take some time to complete this worksheet carefully. It will help you write your resume and answer interview questions. You can also photocopy it and take it with you to help complete applications and as a reference throughout your job search. Use an erasable pen or pencil to allow for corrections. Whenever possible, emphasize skills and accomplishments that support your ability to do the job you want. Use extra sheets as needed. You can also find this worksheet online at www.jist.com/pdf/EJSDW.pdf.

Your name _____

Date completed _____

Job objective _____

Key Accomplishments

List three accomplishments that best prove your ability to do the kind of job you want.

1. _____

2. _____

3. _____

Education and Training

Name of high school(s) and specific years attended _____

_____

Subjects related to job objective _____

_____

_____

Related extracurricular activities/hobbies/leisure activities _____

_____

_____

Accomplishments/things you did well _____

_____

_____

Specific things you can do as a result _____

_____

_____

(continued)

(continued)

Schools you attended after high school, specific years attended, and degrees/certificates earned

_____

_____

_____

Courses related to job objective_____

_____

_____

Related extracurricular activities/hobbies/leisure activities_____

_____

_____

Accomplishments/things you did well_____

_____

_____

Specific things you can do as a result_____

_____

_____

Other Training

Include formal or informal learning, workshops, military training, skills you learned on the job or from hobbies—anything that will help support your job objective. Include specific dates, certificates earned, or other details as needed._____

_____

_____

Work and Volunteer History

List your most recent job first, followed by each previous job. Military experience, unpaid or volunteer work, and work in a family business should be included here, too. If needed, use additional sheets to cover *all* significant paid or unpaid work experiences. Emphasize details that will help support your new job objective. Include numbers to support what you did: the number of people served over one or more years, number of transactions processed, percentage of sales increased, total inventory value you were responsible for, payroll of the staff you supervised, total budget responsible for, and so on. Emphasize results you achieved, using numbers to support them whenever possible. Mentioning these things on your resume and in an interview will help you get the job you want.

Job 1

Dates employed _____

Name of organization _____

Supervisor's name and job title _____

Address _____

_____

Phone number/e-mail address/Web site _____

_____

What did you accomplish and do well? _____

_____

_____

Things you learned; skills you developed or used _____

_____

_____

Raises, promotions, positive evaluations, awards _____

_____

_____

Computer software, hardware, and other equipment you used _____

_____

_____

Other details that might support your job objective _____

_____

_____

(continued)

(continued)

Job 2

Dates employed _____

Name of organization _____

Supervisor's name and job title _____

Address _____

_____

Phone number/e-mail address/Web site _____

_____

What did you accomplish and do well? _____

_____

_____

Things you learned; skills you developed or used _____

_____

_____

Raises, promotions, positive evaluations, awards _____

_____

_____

Computer software, hardware, and other equipment you used _____

_____

_____

Other details that might support your job objective _____

_____

Job 3

Dates employed _____

Name of organization _____

Supervisor's name and job title _____

Address _____

_____

Phone number/e-mail address/Web site _____

_____

What did you accomplish and do well? _____

_____

_____

Things you learned; skills you developed or used _____

_____

_____

Raises, promotions, positive evaluations, awards _____

_____

_____

Computer software, hardware, and other equipment you used _____

_____

_____

Other details that might support your job objective _____

_____

_____

References

Think of people who know your work well and will be positive about your work and character. Past supervisors are best. Contact them and tell them what type of job you want and your qualifications, and ask what they will say about you if contacted by a potential employer. Some employers will not provide references by phone, so ask them for a letter of reference in advance. If a past employer may say negative things, negotiate what they will say or get written references from others you worked with there.

Reference name _____

Position or title _____

Relationship to you _____

Contact information (complete address, phone number, e-mail address)

_____

_____

Reference name _____

Position or title _____

Relationship to you _____

Contact information (complete address, phone number, e-mail address)

_____

_____

(continued)

(continued)

Reference name_____

Position or title_____

Relationship to you_____

Contact information (complete address, phone number, e-mail address)

_____

_____

Additional Resources

Thousands of books and countless Internet sites provide information on career subjects. Space limitations do not permit me to describe the many good resources available, so I list here some of the most useful ones. Because this is my list, I've included books I've written or that JIST publishes. You should be able to find these and many other resources at libraries, bookstores, and Web bookselling sites such as Amazon.com.

Resume and Cover Letter Books

My books: *The Quick Resume & Cover Letter Book* is one of the top-selling resume books. It is very simple to follow and has good sample resumes written by professional resume writers. For more in-depth but still quick help, check out my two books in the *Help in a Hurry* series: *Same-Day Resume* (with advice on creating a simple resume in an hour and a better one later) and *15-Minute Cover Letter*, co-authored with Louise Kursmark (offering sample cover letters and tips for writing them fast and effectively).

Other books published by JIST: The following titles include many sample resumes written by professional resume writers, as well as good advice: *Amazing Resumes* by Jim Bright and Joanne Earl; *Cover Letter Magic* by Wendy S. Enelow and Louise M. Kursmark; the entire *Expert Resumes* series by Enelow and Kursmark; *Federal Resume Guidebook* by Kathryn Kraemer Troutman; *Gallery of Best Resumes, Gallery of Best Cover Letters,* and other books by David F. Noble; *Résumé Magic* by Susan Britton Whitcomb; *30-Minute Resume Makeover* by Louise Kursmark; and *Step-by-Step Resumes* by Evelyn Salvador.

Job Search and Interviewing Books

My books: You may want to check out my book in the *Help in a Hurry* series *Next-Day Job Interview* (quick tips for preparing for a job interview at the last minute). *The Very Quick Job Search* is a thorough book with detailed advice and a "quick" section of key tips you can finish in a few hours. *Getting the Job You Really Want* includes many in-the-book activities and good career decision-making and job search advice.

Other books published by JIST: *Job Search Magic, Interview Magic,* and *The Christian's Career Journey* by Susan Britton Whitcomb; *Make Job Loss Work for You* by Richard and Terri Deems; *Military-to-Civilian Career Transition Guide* by Janet Farley; *Your Dream Job Game Plan* by Molly Fletcher; *Ultimate Job Search* by Richard H. Beatty; *The Career Coward's Guide* series by Katy Piotrowski; and *The Twitter Job Search Guide* by Susan Britton Whitcomb, Chandlee Bryan, and Deb Dib.

Books with Information on Jobs

JIST's primary reference books: The *Occupational Outlook Handbook* is the source of job titles listed in this book. Published by the U.S. Department of Labor and updated every other year, the *OOH* covers about 90 percent of the workforce. The *O*NET Dictionary of Occupational Titles* book has descriptions for 950 jobs based on the O*NET (Occupational Information Network) database developed by the Department of Labor. The *Enhanced Occupational Outlook Handbook* includes the *OOH* descriptions plus more than 5,600 additional descriptions of related jobs from the O*NET and other sources. The *New Guide for Occupational Exploration* allows you to explore major jobs based on your interests.

Other books published by JIST: Here are a few good books that include job descriptions and helpful details on career options: *Best Jobs for the 21ˢᵗ Century, 50 Best Jobs for Your Personality, 150 Best Recession-Proof Jobs, 40 Best Fields for Your Career, 200 Best Jobs for College Graduates,* and *300 Best Jobs Without a Four-Year Degree.* These books include selected jobs from the *OOH* and other information: The *Top Careers* series and *Overnight Career Choice.*

Internet Resources

There are too many Web sites to list, but here are a few places you can start. A book by Anne Wolfinger titled *Best Career and Education Web Sites* gives unbiased reviews of the most helpful sites and ideas on how to use them. *Job Seeker's Online Goldmine,* by Janet Wall, lists the extensive free online job search tools from government and other sources. The *Occupational Outlook Handbook's* job descriptions also include Internet addresses for related organizations. Be aware that some Web sites provide poor advice, so ask your librarian, instructor, or counselor for suggestions on those best for your needs.

Other Resources

Libraries: Most libraries have the books mentioned here, as well as many other resources. Many also provide Internet access so that you can research online information. Ask the librarian for help with finding what you need.

People: People who hold the jobs that interest you are among the best career information sources. Ask them what they like and don't like about their work, how they got started, and the education or training needed. Most people are helpful and will give advice you can't get any other way.

Career counseling: A good vocational counselor can help you explore career options. Take advantage of this service if it is available to you! Also consider a career-planning course or program, which will encourage you to be more thorough in your thinking.

Use a Career Portfolio to Support Your Resume

Your resume is impressive, but there is another way that you can show prospective employers evidence of who you are and what you can do: a career portfolio.

What Is a Career Portfolio?

Unlike a resume, a career portfolio is a collection of documents that can include a variety of items. Here are some items you may want to place in your portfolio:

- Resume.

- School transcripts.

- Summary of skills.

- Credentials, such as diplomas and certificates of recognition.

- Reference letters from school officials and instructors, former employers, or coworkers.

- List of accomplishments: Describe hobbies and interests that are not directly related to your job objective and are not included on your resume.

- Examples of your work: Depending on your situation, you can include samples of your art, photographs of a project, audio, video, images of Web pages you developed, and other media that can provide examples of your work.

Place each item on a separate page when you assemble your career portfolio.

Create a Digital Portfolio

A digital portfolio, also known as an electronic portfolio, contains all the information from your career portfolio in an electronic format. This material is then copied onto a CD-ROM or published on a Web site. With a digital portfolio, you can present your skills to a greater number of people than you can your paper career portfolio. VisualCV (www.visualcv.com) one site that helps you build a digital portfolio and post it online.

YOUR CAREER PORTFOLIO

On the following lines, list the items you want to include in your career portfolio. Think specifically of those items that show your skills, education, and personal accomplishments.

_____

_____

_____

_____

_____

_____

_____

_____

_____

_____

_____

_____

_____

_____

_____

_____

_____

_____

_____

_____

_____

_____

_____

_____

_____

_____

_____

_____

_____

Sample Resumes for Some of the Fastest-Growing Careers

If you read the previous information, you know that I believe you should not depend on a resume alone in your job search. Even so, you will most likely need one, and you should have a good one.

Unlike some career authors, I do not preach that there is only one right way to do a resume. I encourage you to be an individual and to do what you think will work well for you. But I also know that some resumes are clearly better than others. The following pages contain some resumes that you can use as examples when preparing your own resume.

Each resume was written by a professional resume writer who is a member of one or more professional associations. These writers are highly qualified and hold various credentials. Most will provide help (for a fee) and welcome your contacting them (although this is not a personal endorsement).

The resumes appear in books published by JIST Publishing, including the following:

- *Expert Resumes for Computer and Web Jobs* by Wendy S. Enelow and Louise M. Kursmark
- *Expert Resumes for Engineers* by Wendy S. Enelow and Louise M. Kursmark
- *Expert Resumes for Teachers and Educators* by Wendy S. Enelow and Louise M. Kursmark
- *Gallery of Best Resumes* by David F. Noble
- *Gallery of Best Resumes for People Without a Four-Year Degree* by David F. Noble

Contact Information for Resume Contributors

The following professional resume writers contributed resumes to this section. Their names are listed in alphabetical order. Each entry indicates which resume(s) that person contributed.

Carol A. Altomare
World Class Resumes
P.O. Box 483
Three Bridges, NJ 08887-0483
Phone: (908) 237-1883
Fax: (908) 237-2069
E-mail: carol@worldclassresumes.com
Web site: www.worldclassresumes.com
Member: PARW/CC
Certification: CPRW
Resume on pages 377–378

Ann Baehr
Best Resumes of New York
East Islip, NY 11730
Phone: (631) 224-9300
Fax: (916) 314-6871
E-mail: resumesbest@earthlink.net
Web site: www.e-bestresumes.com
Member: CMI, NRWA, PARW/CC
Certification: CPRW
Resume on page 374

Karen Bartell
Best-in-Class Resumes
4940 Merrick Rd., Ste. 160
Massapequa Park, NY 11762
Phone: (631) 704-3220
Toll-free: (800) 234-3569
Fax: (516) 799-6300
E-mail: kbartell@bestclassresumes.com
Web site: www.bestclassresumes.com
Certification: CPRW
Resume on pages 367–368

Rosie Bixel
A Personal Scribe, Resume Writing & Design
13039 E. Burnside St.
Portland, OR 97233
Phone: (503) 254-8262
Fax: (503) 608-4065
E-mail: info@apersonalscribe.com
Web site: www.apersonalscribe.com
Member: NRWA
Resume on page 369

Patricia Chapman
Naperville, IL
Phone: (630) 605-2200
Certification: CRW
Resume on page 363

Darlene M. Dassy
Dynamic Resume Solutions
14 Crestview Dr.
Sinking Spring, PA 19608
Phone: (610) 678-0147
Toll free: (866) 202-4818
E-mail:
   info@dynamicresumesolutions.com
Web site: dynamicresumesolutions.com
Certification: CRW
Resume on pages 379–380

MJ Feld
Careers by Choice, Inc.
205 E. Main St., Ste. 2-4
Huntington, NY 11743
Phone: (631) 673-5432
Fax: (631) 673-5824
E-mail: mj@careersbychoice.com
Web site: www.careersbychoice.com
Member: PARW/CC
Certifications: MS, CPRW
Resume on pages 370–371

Susan Guarneri
Guarneri Associates
6670 Crystal Lake Rd.
Three Lakes, WI 54562
Phone: (715) 546-4449
Toll-free: (866) 881-4055
E-mail: Susan@Resume-Magic.com
Web site: www.Resume-Magic.com
Member: ACA, NCDA, CDI, The
  Alliance, PARW/CC, WCDA, NBCC
Certifications: CPRW, MRW, CERW,
  NCC, NCCC, CCMC, CPBS, MBPS,
  COIS, CEIP, IJCTC, DCC
Resume on pages 372–373

Michele Haffner
Advanced Resume Services
Glendale, WI
Phone: (414) 247-1677
Certifications: CPRW, JCTC
Resume on page 362

Myriam-Rose Kohn
JEDA Enterprises
27201 Tourney Rd., Ste. 201
Valencia, CA 91355-1857
Phone: (661) 253-0801
Fax: (661) 253-0744
E-mail: myriam-rose@jedaenterprises.com
Web site: www.jedaenterprises.com
Member: The Alliance, NRWA,
  PARW/CC
Certifications: CPRW, CEIP, IJCTC,
  CCM, CCMC
Resume on pages 364–365

Don Orlando
The McLean Group
640 S. McDonough St.
Montgomery, AL 36104
Phone: (334) 264-2020
Fax: (334) 264-9227
E-mail:
  yourcareercoach@charterinternet.com
Member: CMI, PARW/CC, Phoenix
Career Group
Certifications: MBA, CPRW, JCTC,
  CCM, CCMC
Resume on pages 375–376

Diana Ramirez
Ramirez Career Consulting
Web site:
  www.ramirezcareerconsulting.com
Member: NRWA, NCDA, NAWW
Certifications: NCDA; Registered
  Counselor, Project Management,
  Human Resources Management
Resume on page 366

MeLisa Rogers
Certifications: Ed.D., CPRW, CPBA,
  DDI, Achieve Global, VLST
Resumes on pages 359–360, 381

Jeremy Worthington
Buckeye Resumes
2092 Atterbury Ave.
Columbus, OH 43229
Phone: (614) 861-6606
Fax: (614) 737-6166
E-mail: staff@buckeyeresumes.com
Web site: www.buckeyeresumes.com
Member: CDI
Resume on page 361

Accountants and Auditors

MARY W. Kingston—CPA, MBA

178 Stanton Drive   *Cedar Park, Texas 78795*   *512-785-6857*   *mkingston@aol.com*

PROFFESSIONAL SUMMARY

Degreed Accounting Professional with over 25 years of progressively responsible experience in a detail-oriented, multi-functional setting. Key accomplishments include

Led the audit of a multimillion-dollar construction project.
Developed and implemented multiple *accounting training programs.*
Implemented the concepts and procedures for multiple computerized systems.
Reduced processing time by 70% of raw material contracts, receipts and payments.

Accounts payable	Collections
Payroll	Financial reports
General ledger	System debugging
Financial statement preparation	Legal compliance examination

PROFESSIONAL ACHIEVEMENTS

- Implemented payroll upgrades resulting in *increased payroll processing efficiency and accountability* by allowing department managers to input hours.
- *Corrected $3 million in errors* through identifying and debugging problems with the purchasing and accounts payable invoice matching system.
- *Improved accuracy, efficiency and overall effectiveness* of accounting month-end journals by implementing computerized systems combined with complex Excel workbooks.
- *Enhanced interdepartmental communications* through the development and implementation of training guides and programs in support of non-accounting personnel, including engineers, planning/schedulers, clerks and managers. Topics included sales tax issues, construction in progress, fixed-asset additions and disposals.
- *Strengthened the auditing division* by applying procedures and experience gained in national accounting firms and various small businesses.

PROFESSIONAL EXPERIENCE

University of Texas, Austin, Texas   *2003–Present*
ADJUNCT INSTRUCTOR
- ❖ Teach college-level accounting classes: Intermediate II, Cost and Budget.
- ❖ Research, document and implement strategies for increased learning retention.
- ❖ Draft and present class content outline for College Dean approval.
- ❖ Lead students to master accounting concepts through formal and informal review/grading sessions.
- ❖ Incorporate "hands-on" industry application examples from professional experience.
- ❖ Mentor, counsel and guide students in career options that include the accounting profession.

(continued)

(continued)

MARY W. KINGSTON—CPA, MBA
—Page Two—

Brackenridge Hospital, Austin, Texas   *2000–2002*
DIRECTOR OF ACCOUNTING
- ❖ Managed a staff of seven direct reports, including an accounting supervisor and six administrative personnel.
- ❖ Planned, organized and directed the functions of the accounting department, including accounts payable, payroll, general ledger and financial statement preparation; set goals and objectives for the department at all levels; partnered with the Assistant Administrator of Finance and Administration on special projects; managed outside vendors and auditors.
- ❖ Converted all accounting worksheets from Lotus to Excel and implemented improvements.

Hays County Community Hospital, San Marcos, Texas   *2000–2000*
ACCOUNTANT and CFO
- ❖ Developed procedures to track business office collections, posting and balancing.
- ❖ Trained and coached staff in procedures designed to improve accuracy and efficiency.
- ❖ Prepared financial statements by developing Excel spreadsheets to document work.

TP Chemicals, San Marcos, Texas   *1988–1999*
ACOUNTANT III
- ❖ Maintained financial books, prepared financial reports, mentored and coached accounting department personnel, provided support to Controller and enhanced the effectiveness and efficiency of the department.
- ❖ Supported, mentored, trained and delegated accounting activities to clerical help to expand their skills/abilities and to improve their self worth and value to the company.
- ❖ Developed concepts and procedures; analyzed, debugged and resolved general ledger interfaces with computerized work order/purchasing system and project accounting system.
- ❖ Prepared timely monthly accruals and reversals; posted interfaces, including inventories, work orders, construction in progress, fixed assets; closed timely the financial books, prepared and issued monthly financial reports for efficient and effective operation of the plant.

State of Colorado, Denver, Colorado   *1986–1988*
EXAMINER OF PUBLIC ACCOUNTS
- ❖ Performed financial audits and prepared financial statements for county school boards and county commissioners. Performed legal compliance examination for judges of probate, tax assessors and tax collectors.

EDUCATION and TRAINING

Masters of Business Administration, University of Texas, Austin, Texas, 1993
Bachelor of Science in Accounting, Cum Laude, University of Colorado, Denver, Colorado, 1974

Microsoft Word/Excel * WordPerfect * Lotus Quicken * Quick Books Pro * AS400 Query

AFFILIATES AND MEMBERSHIPS

Professional Association of Certified Public Accountants (PACPA)
CPA—Colorado and Texas
Texas Association of CPAs
Treasurer, Mission of Hope Recovery Outreach, Inc.

Barbers, Cosmetologists, and Other Personal Appearance Workers

EVA RAMIREZ

7704 Greenland Place • Powell, Ohio 43065
Home: 614-237-9671 • Cellular: 614-294-4544
Email: eva@sevilla.com

COSMETIC SUPPLY TERRITORY MANAGEMENT • COSMETIC ARTISTRY

Cosmetology Techniques/Methods • Mask Applications • Facial Spa Equipment • Maneuvers • Manipulations

Customer-oriented cosmetology professional with valuable blend of business ownership and management experience combined with noticeable talent in esthetic skin care leading to customers' enhanced appearance and well-being. Utilize history as licensed **Cosmetologist, Manager and Instructor** to propel all facets of client care, organizational management and strategic planning agendas. Extremely well organized, dedicated and resourceful, with ability to guide operations and associates to **technique improvements, maximized productivity and bottom-line increase.**

AREAS OF STRENGTH

- Relationship Building • Customer Service •
- Time Management • Creative/Strategic Selling •
- Follow-Up • Merchandising/Promotion •
- Relationship Management •
- Product Introduction • Inventory Management •
- Expense Control • Vendor Negotiations •
- Client Needs Analysis •

EDUCATION

TIFFIN ACADEMY OF COSMETOLOGY ... Tiffin, Ohio
• Cosmetology • Manager • Instructor •
Licenses

TIFFIN ACADEMY OF HAIR DESIGN ... Tiffin, Ohio
Graduate in Hair Design

SEMINARS & SPECIALIZED TRAINING

Continuing Education Units
(to meet requirements of 8 credits annually)

Certificate of Achievement for Advanced Basic Esthetics and Spa Therapies, August 2004

Several seminars held by various cosmetic associations

ADDITIONAL BACKGROUND

The Hair Place ... Dublin, Ohio
Manager of Licensed Cosmetologists
(1993–1996)

Beverly Hills Salons ... Worthington, Ohio
Licensed Cosmetologist
(1990–1993)

PROFESSIONAL CAREER

PRINCESS SALONS ... Powell, Ohio (1996 to Present)
Full-service and independent customized hair, nails and tanning boutique positioned in strip mall (suburban locale) setting; operations staffed by 5 employees, contractors and technicians.

Owner/General Manager
Administered entire scope of operations while simultaneously contributing as cosmetologist in one station of four-station salon. As single owner of small business, administered profits and losses, undertook all facets of decision making, strategically guiding salon operations and productivity, and assumed complete responsibility for revenue performance.

Management responsibilities included cosmetic/accessories sales, customer service and client management, accounting and finance, associate development/management, regulation compliance, business/operations legal requisites, retail merchandising and advertising, inventory procurement and control, vendor relationships, contract negotiations, booth rental contracts and leases to licensed cosmetologists and nail technicians.

→ **Successfully conceived and launched full scale of operations** and guided business to strong reputation for quality output of product and services; consistently met challenges of market conditions and business atmosphere to persevere throughout 8 years of ownership.

→ **Maintained operating costs at lowest possible point by reducing inventory and labor hours during seasonal periods.** Also negotiated with vendors to secure better pricing for goods and services.

→ **Facilitated revenue increase by bringing in cosmetic line to enhance product offering to clients.**

→ **Recognized opportunity to supplement revenue** and spearheaded remodel of existing tanning space to provide for salon.

→ **Expanded market visibility by becoming member of Powell Chamber of Commerce.**

→ **Modified policies and procedures to ensure employee compliance with changing licensing regulations.**

→ **Worked in concert with American Cancer Society to provide styling services to cancer patients** with aim of improving appearance, outlook, confidence and self-esteem.

Computer Network, Systems, and Database Administrators

DAVID SUZUKI

Email: davidsuzuki@yahoo.com

145 West Rosecliff Court
Saukville, WI 53080

Office: (414) 629-3676
Res: (262) 344-3449

TECHNICAL PROFILE

A dedicated and loyal systems professional with 20+ years of hands-on experience as a **database administrator and application developer.** Solid understanding of relational databases. Excellent design, coding, and testing skills. Strong oral and written communication abilities.

Databases:	DB2, Oracle, SQL
Languages:	COBOL, IBM/AS, Visual Basic
Operating Systems:	VM, UNIX, DOS, Windows 98 and XP
Third-Party Software:	COGNOS, Impromptu, Informatica, Microsoft Access

PROFESSIONAL EXPERIENCE

Midwest Staffing Inc., Milwaukee, WI   1984 to Present
(A global employment services organization with annual sales in excess of $10 billion.)

LEAD DATABASE ADMINISTRATOR AND DEVELOPER
Lead mainframe and Oracle database administrator with 24/7 responsibility for performance, tuning, recovery, and planning. Use various utilities to transfer data to other platforms and build tables/indexes. Respond to end users' requests for information and resolve discrepancies in data reports. Research and interact with vendors in the purchase of third-party software. Train and supervise assistant DBAs. Write user manuals, operating procedures, and internal documentation.

Selected Database Development Projects and Achievements:

- Administer mission-critical payroll and billing database that bills $5+ million per week.
- Designed, developed, and implemented Oracle databank—a duplicate of the mainframe databank. End users now have greater access to data using desktop tools.
- Developed and maintain franchise fee billing application.
- Developed Central Billing consolidation application that bills $5 million per month.
- Researched and recommended purchase of ETL Informatica PowerMart utility. Data movement to the data repository, the Internet, and databases is now accomplished in one step. Previously, data movement involved large amounts of development time.
- Developed mainframe processes using the ESSCON Channel (high-speed data transfer) to move data from the mainframe to the AIX platform. Compared to the old method using Outbound, this has reduced data transfer time by at least 50%.
- Selected by management to train assistant database administrator. Assistant is now a reliable backup on mainframe-related database issues.

EDUCATION

Oracle and Oracle Tuning, Certificate Courses, University of Wisconsin—Milwaukee, 2003

Construction Laborers

M a r k   A .   B e n t o n

520 E. Ogden Avenue • Naperville, Illinois 06060 • 000–983–8882

PROFILE

Focus: Laborer position in the construction industry

Excel in troubleshooting and problem solving, readily understand instructions of a complicated nature, and respond to challenges with a "get the job done" attitude. Grasp client's requirements and management's needs quickly and apply appropriate actions to complete tasks in a timely manner. Constantly seeking new and more effective methods for performing professional duties. Working knowledge of Microsoft Windows and Word. Focused on personal and professional growth.

EXPERIENCE SUMMARY

- **Tradesman/Warehouseman/Laborer:** Light carpentry, painting, window preparations, frame building, shipping and receiving, loading of building supplies, use of various power tools and forklift operator.
- **Housekeeping Technician:** General housekeeping for one of the largest hotels in Chicago. Responsible for servicing up to 20 floors.
- **Building Services Technician:** General office cleaning, horizontal and vertical dusting, stripping/buffing of floors and restroom maintenance. Provided office security.
- **Security:** Ensured safe, clean and proper order of facility.
- **Administrative Support Technician:** Setup and maintenance of administrative files; answering and routing of phone calls; typing file labels, memos and letters using Microsoft Word. Copying and faxing documents, sorting incoming mail and preparing outgoing mail.

RELATED SKILLS

- Forklift Operator—Certified
- Computer Training and Enhancement
- Building Maintenance Services
- Equipment Maintenance Training

EMPLOYMENT HISTORY

Inventory/Receiving/Laborer, M&P Construction, Chicago, IL (02/01–Present)

Quality Control Coordinator, Teracotta Data Systems, Inc., Chicago, IL (04/99–02/01)

Laborer, Western and Block Construction, Chicago, IL (04/92–04/99)

Laborer, Buillion Construction/Cook County Hospital, Chicago, IL (01/89–04/92)

Housekeeper, Holiday Inn, Chicago, IL (03/86–01/89)

Warehouseman/Mover/Loader/Driver, We Move You, Chicago, IL (05/83–03/86)

Security, Your Answering Service, Bedford Park, IL (08/80–05/83)

EDUCATION

New Cycle Ministries, Inc., Chicago, Illinois. **Computer Training & Enhancement. 2004 Graduate**
Chicago High School, Chicago, Illinois. **1980 Graduate**

Customer Service Representatives

CYD MARSTEN

15722 Arkansas Street
Newhall, California 91321

Residence: 661 253-1908
Cellular: 661 807-1171

CUSTOMER SERVICE / COLLECTIONS

Customer Service

Results-oriented, enthusiastic, creative, client-services professional with extensive experience in client relations **across broad industries** (medical, mortgage, insurance). Excellent problem-solving skills with a strong orientation in customer service/satisfaction. Able to work under pressure in fast-paced, time-sensitive environments. Demonstrated ability in assessing problem areas and offering recommendations resulting in increases in productivity and profitability. Background encompasses **strong leadership** as well as the ability to establish and build positive, solid relationships with clients and all levels of management. Outstanding listening and interpersonal skills. Energetic, with proven stamina. Computer literate.

Collections

- Expertise in reenergizing stagnant customer accounts.
- Superb negotiation skills with the ability to interact with clients, establish equitable payment policies, and resolve billing errors to maintain positive relations.
- Professional and articulate; ability to deal with clients at all levels.
- Conscientious application of policies, procedures, and systems.
- Quick and effective problem solver while dealing with new concepts, systems, and procedures.
- Knowledge of how to deal with difficult people.

SYNOPSIS OF ACHIEVEMENTS

- Captured **$160,000 within one week** by reinstating three loans.
- Collected **$112,000 within a one-month period,** the highest amount ever collected by anyone during entire history of Collection Bureau of Modesto.
- Developed program facilitating processing of **medical claims,** which was implemented company-wide. Still in use today.
- Reorganized high-delinquency, mortgage-accounts unit to lower delinquency ratios to acceptable standards.
- Reactivated key accounts using persuasion/mediation skills.
- **People's Choice Award,** Security Pacific Home Loans

HIGHLIGHTS OF RELATED WORK EXPERIENCE

COLLECTIONS COUNSELOR • Security Pacific Home Loans—Riverside, CA
Communicate regularly and effectively with mortgagees who are delinquent on their mortgage loans. Complete documentation of collection efforts including communications, reason for default, payment plans, updated telephone numbers, and mailing addresses. Explored alternatives to foreclosures, which led to reinstatement of 25 loans in September and 10 in October. Types of loans were various conventional loans and B&C paper loans. **90% performing commitment** for September 2003.

CUSTOMER SERVICE / COLLECTIONS • Archibald Enterprises—Santa Paula, CA
Consistently exceed collection quotas (currently **ranked No. 1** by collecting more than 50%) through diplomatic and sensitive interaction with debtors. Resolve clients' advertising difficulties. Handle all correspondence pertaining to customer service.

CYD MARSTEN Page 2

COLLECTOR / SUPERVISOR ● Collection Bureau of Modesto—San Jose, CA
Resolved most billing problems on behalf of policyholders while maintaining an ongoing professional relationship with most insurance companies. **Ranked No. 1** collector. Created programs that streamlined productivity and increased efficiency.

CLAIMS SUPERVISOR ● Allstate Insurance—River Falls, CA
Proactive planning led to notable increase in morale in all departments and in reestablishing clients' trust and loyalty.

LOAN SERVICE / COLLECTION OFFICER ● Great Western Savings—Northridge, CA
Diplomacy and assertiveness allowed for adherence to payment schedules and resolution of tax problems. Dealt with insurance queries, lawsuits, and culture/communication barriers. Handled FHA, VA, and conventional types of loans.

NON-RELATED EXPERIENCE

OWNER ● L.A. Rottweilers—Modesto, CA
Bred, raised, showed, and sold Rottweilers trained as Pet Therapy Dogs to bring sunshine to patients in Children's Hospital and elderly homes.
Handled all daily administrative affairs, including A/P, A/R, general ledger, and running credit checks.

WORK HISTORY

Collections Counselor	Security Pacific Home Loans	Riverside, CA	2009
Customer Service/Collections	Archibald Enterprises	Santa Paula, CA	2001–2009
Administrative Assistant	Personnel Plus	Santa Clarita, CA	2000–2001
Server/Trainer	Mimi's Café, Birks	Modesto, CA	1995–2000
Business Owner	L.A. Rottweilers	Modesto, CA	1992–1995
Collector/Supervisor	Collection Bureau of Modesto	Modesto, CA	1989–1992
Claims Supervisor	Allstate Insurance	River Falls, CA	1987–1989
Loan Service/Collection Officer	Great Western Savings	Northridge, CA	1985–1986

CONTINUAL TRAINING
B&C 101 New Hire Training Course
B&C 102 New Hire Training Course
B&C 102 On The Job Training Course
Seminar in Customer Service

Dental Assistants

Carol A. Weiss
DENTAL ASSISTANT

62482 110ᵗʰ Avenue S., Federal Way, WA 99999   (000) 000-0000   email: cweiss@resume.com

PROFILE:

More than 25 years of Dental Assistant experience in meeting high infection-control standards, sterilizing and disinfecting instruments and equipment, preparing tray setup for dental procedures, and instructing patients on postoperative and general oral health care.

- ➤ **Supervised** two Dental Assistants.
- ➤ Trained in **product knowledge** (bonding, impression materials, and more).
- ➤ Experienced in working with all ages of people, from small children to senior citizens.
- ➤ **Managed office,** ensuring that it was organized, clean, fully stocked, and prepared daily.
- ➤ Worked in a **lab** within the same facility, making any shade changes or polishing of dentures, crowns, and bridge work.
- ➤ Caring, detailed-oriented, hard worker who has learned different state-of-the-art dentistry styles, **procedures, and techniques.** Always seeks ways to keep skills current.

SUMMARY OF QUALIFICATIONS:

▶ Root canal treatment	▶ Crown and bridge preparation and delivery
▶ Air particle machines	▶ Composite and amalgam fillings
▶ Polishing of all fillings	▶ Denture and partial procedures
▶ Soft and hard relines	▶ Assisted with multiple extractions
▶ Rubber dam replacement	▶ Took full-series radiographs and panolipse radiographs

OFFICE SKILLS:

- ▶ Windows, DOS, MS Office (Word, Excel, PowerPoint), word processing, spreadsheets, databases, Ex-Change+, Internet (Netscape, Explorer), email.
- ▶ Typewriter, word processor, copier, calculator, fax machine, printers, multiline phone systems
- ▶ Records management, medical terminology, healthcare plan knowledge, billing codes

---

PROFESSIONAL EXPERIENCE:

Dr. Ronald McPherson, DDS—Federal Way, WA   2001–Current
Dental Assistant

Dr. D. Maynard Debus, DDS—Federal Way, WA   1999–2001
Dental Assistant

Dr. Larry W. Howard, DDS—Federal Way, WA   1999 (temp)
Dental Assistant

Dr. Abel D. Sanchez, DDS—Federal Way, WA   1979–1989
Dental Assistant

Engineers

JILL KEATING

51 Gibbs Lane • Farmingville, NY 11738
631.555.5555 (H) • 631.555.5555 (C) • jkeating@yahoo.com

ENGINEERING PROFILE

Track record of success in the design and delivery of advanced technology solutions.

Accomplished, technically sophisticated Engineer with extensive experience in the oversight, planning, design, and delivery of diverse mechanical systems and devices. Offer special expertise in the manufacture and design of industrial automation solutions. Possess track record of waste and cost reductions, cycle time and process improvements, and system enhancements arising from effective use of Lean Manufacturing and related techniques. Manage, coordinate, train, and evaluate performance of cross-functional and multidisciplinary teams. Maintain high standards and promote team participation for the attainment of company goals. *Highlights of Expertise:*

- Project/Program Management
- Lean Manufacturing Principles
- Supply Chain Administration
- Customer/Vendor Relationships
- Product Lifecycle Management
- Pneumatic & Electromechanical Devices
- Business Management Systems
- Multidisciplinary Team Management
- Production Planning
- ISO & UL Compliance
- Staff Management
- HR Administration

Technical Proficiencies:

Certifications: ISO Auditor Certification, UL Certification

Tools: Visual Basic, Tour de Force (TDF), Siemens S7 300, Allen Bradley RS Logix 500, PanelBuilder 32, PanelView, Automation Direct (Koyo), Device Net, UltraWare, Festo SPC200, FST4.02, AB 6200, ICOM PLC2/PLC5, Wonderware MMI, SAP R/3, WinTelligent, AutoCAD 2005, RS Logix 500, Device Net/EthernetIP, Uniop Designer, UltraWare, AutoQuoter, Deflection Calculator, Wmermoc, MS Office Suite/MS Project

PROFESSIONAL EXPERIENCE

AUTOMATION CENTRAL, INC., Amherst, MA   2006–Present

Sales Engineer

Sell industrial automation solutions, including pneumatics, machine and motion control devices, sensors, air compressors, vacuum pumps, and associated products. Evaluate and suggest product and service solutions in line with client needs and requirements. Orchestrate conferences to assess and implement product and service enhancements. Utilize MS Outlook-based Tour de Force (TDF) and associated software to manage client relationships and for enterprise-wide reporting. Generate and submit weekly project status and progress reports to senior-level management to support business directives.

Key Contribution:

- Boosted potentiality of securing high-value client account through superior sales and relationship-building skills, greatly advancing organizational objectives.

PETRI CORPORATION, Smithtown, NY   1995–2006

Engineering & Project Supervisor, Automated Systems Division (2002–2006)

Directed 8-member engineering and drafting team in the design and manufacture of industrial automation solutions. Provided full product lifecycle administration, including resource, material, and time management; created and maintained production and engineering Master Schedules to execute directives. Administered department-wide ISO procedural compliance, providing instruction to

…continued…

(continued)

(continued)

JILL KEATING • Page 2

engineering and drafting teams on relevant standards and protocols. Coordinated with clients, vendors, and cross-functional teams to optimize communications in support of project directives. Negotiated and consulted with clients on project design, specifications, pricing, and delivery.

Key Contributions:

- Successfully managed multimillion-dollar projects, regularly exceeding customer expectations through on-time, within-budget project delivery of high-quality products and services.
- Utilized Lean Manufacturing principles to reduce costs and improve on-time delivery by 20%.
- Enhanced design review process by improving interdepartmental communications through the standardization of blueprints and related documentation.
- Improved output by effectively coordinating manufacturing production and documentation processes, as well as enhancing test fixture design.
- Effectively reconciled competing cross-functional team interests to accelerate production time by hundreds of hours.
- Provided full project lifecycle management of one of the company's largest projects in ten years, motivating staff for enhanced efficiency and a 300% increase in output.

Senior Project Engineer, Integrated Systems Unit (1995–2002)

Conceptualized and designed electrical and electro/pneumatic control panels and servo control systems for automation and handling equipment, utilizing in-house and vendor-based PLC controls and programming features. Used ERP, Excel, and related software systems to administer product lifecycle production schedules and operational sequences. Communicated with cross-functional teams to facilitate smooth operations. Produced client instruction manuals providing/describing BOM, schematics, testing procedures, and operational cycles.

Key Contributions:

- Developed and implemented valuable product-line improvements.
- Successfully launched and administered ISO and UL safety compliance standards and procedures, instructing and monitoring cross-functional teams on relevant standards and protocols.

** ** **

Prior Experience as Senior Engineer for Shimada Corporation of Manorville, NY

EDUCATION AND TRAINING

Master of Science Degree in Technological Systems Management
STONY BROOK UNIVERSITY, Stony Brook, NY

Bachelor of Science Degree in Mechanical Engineering
NEW YORK INSTITUTE OF TECHNOLOGY, Old Westbury, NY

Professional Development
Signature Training Program for Supervisors / Certificate of Achievement

Food and Beverage Serving and Related Workers

Valerie W. Butler

333 S.E. Riveredge Drive • Vancouver, Washington 33333

222-222-2222 *cell*   *hom*e 555-555-5555

Server

Professional Profile

Energetic and highly motivated *Food Server* with extensive experience in the food service industry. Expertise lies in working with the fine-dining restaurant, providing top-quality service, and maintaining a professional demeanor. Solid knowledge of the restaurant business, with strengths in excellent customer service and food and wine recommendations.

Get along well with management, coworkers, and customers. Well-developed communication skills. Known as a caring and intuitive "people person," with an upbeat and positive attitude. Highly flexible, honest, and punctual, with the ability to stay calm and focused in stressful situations. Committed to a job well done and a long-term career.

Outstanding Achievements & Recommendations

- Served notable VIP clientele, including clients associated with Murdock Charitable Trust.
  - History of repeat and new customers requesting my service as their waitress.
  - Known for creating an atmosphere of enjoyment and pleasure for the customer.

"...Valerie was warm, friendly, kind, and very efficient.
We didn't feel rushed. She handled our requests, and
we appreciated her genuine 'May I please you' attitude...."

Related Work History

Waitress • Banquets • Heathman Lodge • Vancouver, Washington • *2002–presen*t
Northwest seasonal cuisine.

Banquets • Dolce Skamania Lodge • Stevenson, Washington • *2001–2002*
Casual fine-dining restaurant.

Waitress • Hidden House • Vancouver, Washington • *1993–2001*
Exclusive fine-dining restaurant.

Waitress • Multnomah Falls Lodge Restaurant • Corbett, Oregon • *1992–1993*
Historic Columbia Gorge Falls restaurant serving authentic Northwestern cuisine.

Waitress • The Ahwahnee at Yosemite National Park • California • *1 yea*r
World-renowned, award-winning fine-dining restaurant—sister lodge to Timberline Lodge.

Human Resources, Training, and Labor Relations Managers and Specialists

AARON WALKER

5 Linden Avenue, Roslyn, NY 11576 ▪ aaronwalker00@aol.com
residence 555-555-5555 ▪ *cellular* 555-555-5555

HUMAN RESOURCES PROFESSIONAL

PHR CERTIFICATE

Seeking a Generalist Role

Emphasis on:

Recruitment & Staffing • HRIS • Training & Development

Compensation • Salary Structures • Benefits Administration

Workforce Reengineering & Change Management • Job Task Analysis

Performance Appraisals • Employee Retention • Employee Communications

PROFESSIONAL EXPERIENCE

COMPUTER ASSOCIATES, Islandia, NY   2002–Present
Human Resources Specialist (2003–Present)
Human Resources Generalist[*] (2003)
Human Resources Associate (2002–2003)

[*]*Selected for rotational assignments as a leave replacement for other HR staff members.*

■ ■ ■

HR Generalist Responsibilities and Achievements

Supported and provided HR-related guidance to general-management teams at two newly acquired facilities with a combined staff of approximately 130 employees.

- Contributed to a five-person team charged with establishing and implementing yearly **salary increases.**
- Managed a **job-reclassification project.** Conducted occupational research to determine if job titles were in sync with workplace norms.
- Assisted with **employee-performance** issues. Wrote disciplinary reports and developed a strategy for resolution.
- Reviewed **applicant résumés** and collaborated on **new-hire offers.**
- Tackled the **I-9 recertification** of approximately 2800 employees at 12 locations. Through research, identified all employees whose paperwork was deficient. Trained support staff and line managers in proper documentation, which rectified oversights expediently and improved I-9 administration going forward.
- Articulated **corporate policies and procedures** to employees seeking clarification regarding payroll, disability, terminations, leaves of absence, and COBRA coverage issues.
- Authored a policies and procedures document to address the sometimes-confusing hiring categories of "rehires" and "reinstatements." Created and delivered **PowerPoint presentations** to the HR community, which, together with the written document, served as clarification on this issue.
- Regularly conducted the "benefits" portion of **new-hire orientations.** In one-hour sessions, provided information to 50+ employees.
- Participated in the **campus recruitment** program. Attended college fairs and **interviewed candidates** for internships and entry-level positions.
- Processed **employee data** for new hires and terminations.

Continued…

AARON WALKER

Page Two

HRIS Responsibilities and Achievements

- Identified a significant administrative challenge regarding the inaccuracy of employee time-off accrual plans. Rectified the problem by creating an Access database linked to Lawson HRIS, which accurately provided the needed data.

- Designed, developed, and brought to fruition approximately 30 HRIS audits to ensure the accuracy of employee records. Defined audit parameters for compliance with federal, state, and company policies. Created numerous HRIS ad hoc reports as requested by the HR community and line managers.

- Improved the administration of employee sabbaticals by creating HRIS automation tools. In so doing, decreased processing time by approximately 50%.

- Represented HR Services during a company-wide Lawson system upgrade. As project manager, identified and advocated for the unique needs of the HR Services function. During implementation, served as trainer to the department's staff.

DEVELOPMENTAL DISABILITIES INSTITUTE, Brookville, NY   1999–2002

Residential Manager (2001–2002)
Assistant Residential Manager (2000–2001)
Direct Care Counselor (1999–2000)

- As residential manager, oversaw 20 direct-care counselors and one assistant supervisor.

- Hired approximately 15 direct-care counselors, all of whom became good employees. More than half were rated "exceptional."

- Developed and implemented a staff-training program that provided enhanced quality of care to residents and contributed to a reduction in employee attrition.

- Conducted in-depth analyses of residents' skills and abilities. Set appropriate skill goals based on present functional status. Instilled motivation to reach objectives.

EDUCATIONAL CREDENTIALS

Master of Business Administration, 2005. Hofstra University, Uniondale, NY

Bachelor of Arts, Psychology, 1999. Muhlenberg College, Allentown, PA

Professional in Human Resources (PHR) Certificate, 2003. Pace University, New York, NY
Workforce Planning & Employment, Performance Management, Compensation & Benefits,
Employee & Labor Relations, Occupational Health, Safety & Security,
Organizational Structure, Ethical & Legislative Issues

TECHNICAL SKILLS

Lawson HRIS System, Windows, Word, Excel, PowerPoint, Outlook, and Access

PROFESSIONAL AFFILIATION

Member, Society for Human Resource Management (SHRM)

■ ■ ■

Medical Records and Health Information Technicians

Mary Jane Martha Barclay
135 Killdeer Road, Apt. 721, Ewing, NJ 08628
(609) 771-7665 Residence Phone / Fax ▪ mjmbarclay@yahoo.com

Medical Billing / Medical Records Technician

Dedicated, experienced professional with recent training in medical billing, medical terminology, and ICD-9-CM coding. Strong organizational, communications, and project management skills. Calm demeanor under stress; cooperative team leader. Proven multitasking / operations support skills. Adept in

- ☑ Client Relationship Management
- ☑ Customer Needs Management
- ☑ Medical Records Terminology
- ☑ Administrative Support
- ☑ Budget Controls
- ☑ Project Coordination

KEY SUPPORTING SKILLS

- **Administration:** Diverse administrative expertise includes directing nationwide CHART (California Hospital Association Review Team) Program for American Hospital Association, managing seven-county sales territory in south central California, and maintaining large, upscale apartment complexes.

- **Time Management:** Demonstrate top-notch organizational skills, with ability to prioritize and multi-task. Developed records management systems to expedite back-office operations for sales generation, residential and retail property management, and meeting and event planning.

- **Communications:** Employ proactive problem-solving communications skills to generate "win-win" scenarios. Effectively communicated special situations and potential problem areas to management.

- **Personal Strengths:** Conscientious in following through on commitments and deadlines. Mature, discreet team player with experience interfacing with high-level executives and corporate clients.

EDUCATION
Medical Records Technician Program, The College of New Jersey, Ewing, NJ—2006
Courses: Medical Terminology, Advanced Medical Terminology, Medical Billing, ICD-9-CM Coding
Associate of Arts Degree, San Diego Community College, San Diego, CA

PROFESSIONAL EXPERIENCE

Estate and Health Care Management, Princeton, NJ   2004–2009
✓ **Administrative Management.** Acted as prime interface with 60 physicians, nurses, hospice, attorneys, CPA, stockbroker and insurance companies for elderly parents with progressive, debilitating illnesses. Managed health care appointments and treatment, and daily living arrangements on-site.

✓ **Records Management.** Submitted insurance claims and tracked insurance reimbursements. Oversaw distribution of $1 million estate. Arranged sale of house and distribution of all household goods.

Manufacturer's Representative   2001–2004
Pacific Printing, San Diego, CA, and Elegant Communications, Inc., San Francisco, CA
Independent contractor representing fine gift, paper/stationery, and greeting-card lines for two businesses.

✓ **Account Management.** Grew accounts by 45% (from 175 to 250) and increased sales by 20% in seven-county south central California territory. Generated 25 new key accounts (such as Yellowstone Park gift shops) through thorough market research, competitive market analysis and persuasive prospect interaction. Provided personalized customer service that generated 100% customer retention.

✓ **Customer Relationship Management.** Developed strong client-communications networks, building relationships with 250 buyers for retail stores, museums, hospital gift shops and nurseries. Educated buyers in 60 lines of merchandise, updating them on retail trends and demographics-driven marketing.

Mary Jane Martha Barclay

(609) 771-7665 Residence Phone / Fax ▪ mjmbarclay@yahoo.com   Page 2

PROFESSIONAL EXPERIENCE (continued)

Residential Property Management   1999–2001
Excelsior Properties, San Raphael, CA (2000–2001), and Seaside Views, San Diego, CA (1999–2000)

✓ **Administrative Management.** Managed two upscale apartment communities (up to 516 units), with monthly rent collections of $432,000. Supervised on-site leasing, as well as 18 maintenance and grounds staff. Closely controlled $2,500 per month expense budget, monitoring five vendor services. Oversaw renovation of 35 apartment units, coordinating workflow and scheduling of carpet, flooring, paint, and fixture vendors with tenants.

✓ **Customer Service.** Maintained 92% residency rate and achieved 98% on-time rent collection by developing proactive tenant-relationships programs. Initiated educational newsletter for tenants, as well as open-door policy for tenant complaints. Credited with stabilizing the tenant community through lawful evictions of known drug dealers.

Retail Property Management   1994–1999
Townsend Group Companies, San Diego and San Francisco, CA

✓ **Administrative Management.** Initiated and developed specialty leasing programs for three major developers (12 regional shopping centers) in high-profile metropolitan areas. Maintained high occupancy rates (95%) by actively recruiting retailers for year-round common area, as well as developing long-term, favorable leases for in-line sales operations.

✓ **Program Management.** Conceptualized and supervised design projects for kiosks and store décor, as well as for marketing communications (brochures, print advertising and directories). Developed and met program budgets, generating in excess of $500,000 for each shopping center annually.

Meeting and Event Management   1993–1994
California Hospital Association, San Diego, CA

✓ **Program Management.** Served as Director of CHART (California Hospital Association Review Team) Program. Traveled statewide conducting peer review meetings for 8 to 10 state hospitals. Wrote reports based on participant feedback and critical observations and analysis of policies and procedures. Recommended policy and methodology changes, 90% of which were implemented by the Boards of the state hospitals.

✓ **Customer Service.** Facilitated in-house discussions on-site of hospital personnel and management at all levels to increase quality assurance, strengthen employee relations, improve customer service and streamline processes and procedures. Initiated and encouraged constructive dialogs among groups that had a history of communication breakdowns.

COMPUTER SKILLS

☑ Training in Medical Billing software, Medical Records databases, and ICD-9-CM coding.
☑ Experienced in composing and editing letters, memos, marketing communications and reports.
☑ Use Windows XP, MS Office 2003—Word, Excel, PowerPoint, Access, Internet Explorer, e-mail.

Paralegals and Legal Assistants

PATRICIA JUHASZ

555 Riddle Avenue • Smithtown, NY 55555 • (888) 999-0000 • Pjuhasz@telcomm.net

Legal Assistant/Paralegal Assistant

Experienced Legal Assistant with excellent office management and client-attorney relation skills seeking an entry-level Paralegal Assistant position where a working knowledge of legal terminology, general law, and legal proceedings, and continuing education in Paralegal Studies will be utilized and expanded. Bring experience working within a Legal Department/Collection Agency environment in the following select areas:

Civil Litigation…Collections…Settlements…Affidavits…Skip Tracing…Attorney Sourcing & Selection Bankruptcies…Judgments…Liens…Summons & Complaint…Estate Searches…Statute of Limitations

PROFESSIONAL EXPERIENCE

Legal Assistant, Legal Recoveries, Inc., Lake Grove, NY   1998–present

Joined this Collection Agency's legal department at a time of unit-wide staffing changes. Responsible for managing a high volume of civil litigation case files for major accounts that partially included Century Detection, Credit Union of New York, AB Bank National Association, and St. Mary's Hospital.

- Collaborate extensively with internal departments including collections, medical billing, finance, production, special projects, and clerical to obtain, verify, and process documentation pertaining to the status of more than 50 weekly referred collections cases forwarded to the legal department.
- Carefully source and select nationally based bonded attorneys utilizing the *American Lawyers Quarterly, Commercial Bar Directory, National Directory List,* and *Columbia Directory List;* determine the appropriate choice upon obtainment and review of résumés, copies of insurance policies, and court filing fees.
- Perform estate searches and integrate traditional investigative methods and the DAKCS database system to gather account histories and case-sensitive documentation for attorneys including *debtors and guarantors, credit bureau reports, court affidavits, judgments, skip-tracing records, bankruptcy notices, banking statements, proof of statute of limitations, proof of assets,* and *trial letters.*
- Maintain communications with attorneys and clients from point of referral/discovery to trial phase to facilitate and expedite case settlements that historically award clients a minimum of 80% in recovered funds.

EDUCATION

Bachelor of Science in Paralegal Studies, 1998
ST. JOSEPH'S COLLEGE, Brentwood, NY

COMPUTER SKILLS

DOS/Windows 2000; WordPerfect and Microsoft Word; DAKCS

EARLIER WORK HISTORY

Administrative Assistant, State Insurance, Patchogue, NY   1997–1998
Office Support Assistant, Financial Association of America, Inc., Islip, NY   1995–1997
Appointment Coordinator, Phlebotomy Services, Huntington, NY   1991–1996
Senior Office Support Assistant, AB National Bank, Hicksville, NY   1986–1991

Professional References Provided upon Request

Sales Representatives, Wholesale and Manufacturing

*READY TO RELOCATE TO THE **SEATTLE** AREA*

Charles W. Broadway
4200 Centre Street   Montgomery, Alabama 3 6100   cbroad555@aol.com   ☎ 334.555.5555

WHAT I CAN OFFER **TOPLINE** AS YOUR NEWEST **SALES PROFESSIONAL**

- ○ Penetrating and holding **new markets,**
- ○ Gathering and leveraging **sales intelligence** faster than our competition,
- ○ Mastering our customers' business so well we **anticipate** their **needs,**
- ○ Putting together "win-win" sales deals that yield **enduring profits,**
- ○ Communicating so powerfully that **sales** are **closed**—at every level from shop floor to boardroom, and
- ○ **Managing risk** prudently.

RECENT WORK HISTORY WITH EXAMPLES OF PROBLEMS SOLVED

- ○ *Hired away by the CEO to be* **Sales Development Manager** *and then promoted over four more experienced eligibles to be* **Sales Director,** Arista Corporation, Montgomery, Alabama   Oct 04 to Present
Arista is the world's largest auto transmission manufacturer.

Supervise three regional sales managers directly. Lead a territory that covers all of America east of the Mississippi River and portions of Canada. Build and defend a travel budget of $400K. My district generates $45M in annual sales.

Chosen by the President to **guide us into a new market** dominated by four tough competitors. Found, and really listened to, all potential customers. Identified our market niche. Then made the calls that led to **20 presentations nationwide,** many at presidential levels. *Payoffs:* **From $0 sales to $3.5M** in sales in just 16 months.

Moved faster than our competition to discover an RFP before it hit the street. When none of our products met this customer's needs, **put together a win-win deal** that shared both risks and profits. *Payoffs:* When I showed our customer's CEO how I could **save him $2M** over the life of the contract, I **won a $4M contract for us.**

Used polite persistence to **"steal" a customer from a competitor** who had served them for a decade. Soon uncovered our competitor's weakness. **Carefully timed and executed "cold calls"** on the right people. *Payoffs:* By appealing right to their specific needs, brought in **$8M** in the last two years alone.

Saw opportunity a potential customer missed—even after he awarded his contract to another company. Tracked our competitor's performance right up until contract renewal. *Payoffs:* My presentation, made on the same day as other firms, carried the **sale: $4M** over several years—even though we weren't the lowest bidder.

*More indicators of performance **TopLine** can use ☞*

(continued)

(continued)

CONFIDENTIAL

Charles Broadway	**Sales Professional**	334.555.5555

Uncovered an unmet need in a major market. Worked with the customer and a manufacturer to design a new product. Persuaded our leadership to invest $200K in the prototype I knew we would need for the competition. *Payoffs:* **Won a $14M sale** and **took away our competitor's dominance** in this market.

Picked up the signs that a competitor's customer wasn't happy, and then found out why. Got a 100-percent response to our needs-analysis survey to define the best new product for the market. *Payoffs:* **Profit margin up** four percent—**double the industry average.** My methods became the **corporate standard** for customer analysis.

❍ Plant Manager, Plantar Corporation, Montgomery, Alabama   May 98 to Sep 04

❍ **Sales Manager for Business Products,** Mylar Corporation, Montgomery, Alabama
    Mar 96 to May 98

EDUCATION & PROFESSIONAL DEVELOPMENT

❍ MPA, Auburn University—Montgomery, Montgomery, Alabama   00

❍ BS, Troy State University, Troy, Alabama   96
Earned this degree working 10 hours a week.

❍ Instructed classes in Value Analysis for Product Improvement and Cost of Sales
    96 to 98

Selected from five more experienced professionals to teach these six-week courses, preparing 100 sales professionals to represent up to ten different products.

IT SKILLS

❍ Expert in proprietary **sales, billing, and customer contact software** suite; proficient in Outlook, Word, Excel, PowerPoint, and Internet search methods

Secretaries and Administrative Assistants

CARA WAVERLY

58 Chelsea Way   ◆   Bridgeport, CT 22222   ◆   (333) 333-3333   ◆   cara@aol.com

Executive-level administrative support professional whose accomplishments reflect excellent administrative skills and a demonstrated commitment to providing exemplary service

SUMMARY OF QUALIFICATIONS

- Capable executive assistant with extensive experience in administrative roles.
- Organized and detail-oriented with demonstrated project coordination skills. Practiced in prioritizing and managing tasks. Effective at balancing the competing demands of multiple projects.
- Excellent interpersonal skills. Able to develop easy rapport with others while building trust.
- Versatile and resourceful team player who is willing to do whatever is necessary to complete goals and meet deadlines. Polished and professional, yet warm and accommodating.
- Recognized "go-to" person for a broad range of issues and concerns.
- Committed to providing the highest levels of customer service.

PROFESSIONAL EXPERIENCE

PETPHARMA CORP., Bridgeport, Connecticut   2001 to present
Administrative Assistant

As lead administrative assistant, provide effective support to VP of Global Marketing, VP of International Operations, and three other managers. Handle administrative details such as maintaining calendars, making travel arrangements, scheduling meetings, and coordinating conferences.

Administrative Leadership

- Established strong record in developing best practices for administrative support. Proactively provide support, looking beyond immediate need to maximize effectiveness.
- Hired as first administrative assistant in newly relocated group; developed and documented group processes and procedures. Trained and mentored new administrative assistants.
- Developed administrative checklist for new hires, ensuring smooth transition for more than 20 new employees.
- Implemented filing system for all product-related literature, creating easy-to-use resource for customer inquiries. Also developed individual product binders for each sales rep.
- Effectively support group training efforts by developing manuals and presentations, and scheduling and facilitating training sessions.
- Consistently explore lower-cost options in keeping with company's "Smart Initiatives."

Project Coordination

- Successfully arranged numerous domestic and international conferences, effectively planning and coordinating events for groups of more than 100 people.
- Oversaw all administrative details to ensure flawless events. Booked all facilities, negotiating favorable pricing. Made travel arrangements and scheduled ground transportation for all attendees. Generated handouts and purchased gifts and awards. Shipped materials to site, meeting all project timetables.
- Implemented effective follow-up system to ensure all projects and tasks remain on schedule.
- Effectively supported Transition Team, collecting and collating staff résumés for timely presentation to management.

(continued)

(continued)

CARA WAVERLY   PAGE 2

PETPHARMA CORP., Westport, Connecticut   1998 to 2001

Administrative Assistant

Provided effective administrative support for Customer Development, Sales Training, and Sales Operations groups following relocation. Maintained all personnel and customer files.

- Developed guidelines and procedures for administrative assistants. Documented procedures for new hires.
- Established and managed system to track broker payments.
- Developed process for customer scorecarding, following up with clients to determine satisfaction with products, delivery times, and customer service. Developed spreadsheet to record and track response.
- Maintained divisional "dashboard"—a prominent display that tracked key performance measures and staff awards.
- Successfully planned and coordinated large-scale conferences and sales meetings.

BOYD, INC., Mullica Hill, New Jersey   1992 to 1998

Executive Secretary

Assisted president and controller in managing International Division. Prepared all correspondence and assisted in preparing all confidential salary reviews, business plans, budgets, and presentations.

- Organized office, setting up effective filing systems and archiving old files.
- Developed and implemented more efficient procedures for office operations.
- Effectively organized numerous conferences and sales meetings.
- Served as Board Member for Boyd's Federal Credit Union in addition to regular duties.

Corporate Flight Coordinator

Assisted Manager of Flight Operations and scheduled flights for corporate executives.

- As first full-time coordinator, set up effective scheduling system to accommodate increasing demand for flight services.

UNITED CHEMICALS, Clifton, New Jersey   1985 to 1992

Administrative Assistant

Assisted Region Administrative Manager, providing support in the area of marketing, administration, office services, information systems, and annual planning activities.

- Gathered background information for reports and special projects.
- Coordinated and scheduled system usage, enforcing region guidelines. Mobilized system specialists to handle problems and requests.
- Provided instruction for all software packages.

<u>COMPUTER SKILLS</u>

Word ◆ Excel ◆ PowerPoint ◆ Outlook ◆ Internet ◆ E-mail
DCIS (database for sales reporting)

References Available Upon Request

Teachers—Kindergarten, Elementary, Middle, and Secondary

JUDY CASSIDY

724 West South Street
Philadelphia, PA 19110
215-745-3372 ▪ judyc@aol.com

PROFILE

ELEMENTARY EDUCATOR with more than 20 years of experience fostering academic learning and enhancing critical-thinking abilities. Incorporate effective cooperative learning techniques and unique classroom management style to establish creative and stimulating classroom environment. Dedicated, resourceful teacher skilled in building rapport and respect with students and student teachers.

Honored with **New Teacher Mentor Award** for Outstanding Service (2004).

"Miss Cassidy is an exceptional teacher. She is respectful to and of her students, and that respect is reciprocated. Using a variety of materials and techniques, Miss Cassidy challenges her students to excel. Her classroom is a warm, nurturing atmosphere where children are called to be their best selves."   A.F., School Administrator

---

EDUCATION AND CERTIFICATIONS

Instructional II—Permanent Certification, **State of Pennsylvania** (2002)

Master of Arts—**LaSalle University** (1994)

Bachelor of Science, Elementary Education—**Chestnut Hill College** (1988)

CAREER HIGHLIGHTS

- Developed and executed **Everyday Math Program** at John Smith Elementary School (1999). Program resulted in 180-point improvement in overall math grades in 2002 (versus previous year's scores). Participated in ongoing staff development and district training sessions to ensure utilization of hands-on, cooperative learning approach along with reinforcement and assessment techniques.

- Served as **Middle States Team Evaluator** for Brooklyn Diocese School System (1998). Collaborated with four colleagues in accreditation process that included interviewing teachers/committee, writing evaluation report, and creating recommended action plan. Conducted comprehensive academic assessment in similar capacity as Catholic Elementary School Evaluator for Diocese of Camden (1995).

- Achieved 90% passing rate in students graduating to fifth grade by directing and facilitating promotional requirements for **Multidisciplinary Learning Project** at John Smith Elementary School (1999–2002). Through intensive interaction, students developed research, writing, and computer skills to accomplish long-term school project with City Year members. Initiative strengthened student knowledge, pride, and enthusiasm for learning.

TEACHING EXPERIENCE

Philadelphia Public School District   1999–Present
John Smith Elementary School
Elementary Teacher, Fourth Grade

Plan, implement, and evaluate various curriculum areas. Encourage cooperative learning, peer interaction, and increased achievement levels among disadvantaged and challenged students.

Appointed by principal as **Grade Chairman and Mentor** (2000–2003).

(continued)

(continued)

Judy Cassidy
Page Two

TEACHING EXPERIENCE (continued)

St. Agnes–Sacred Heart School 1995–1998
ELEMENTARY TEACHER, Third Grade

Instructed students in Reading, Integrated Language Arts, Religion, and Social Studies. Coordinated and implemented Language Arts Program for first- to fourth-grade students.

New Jersey Area Parochial School System 1989–1995
ELEMENTARY TEACHER, Third and Fourth Grade

- Saint Joseph Regional School
- Blessed Sacrament School
- Our Lady of Perpetual Help

Philadelphia Parochial School System 1978–1988
ELEMENTARY TEACHER, First and Second Grade

- Immaculate Heart of Mary School
- Our Lady of the Holy Souls School
- Saint Timothy School

TEACHING TESTIMONIALS

"Judith has, from the outset, displayed a level of professional competence and a striving for professional development that has benefited her students, our staff, and the entire school community in concrete ways. She introduced and implemented a variety of innovative classroom management strategies, such as Workshop Way and Integrated Language Arts, having been the first to pilot such a program in our school. She has challenged and motivated students to achievement and activities that have not only developed each child's personal gifts and talents, but also developed cooperative learning strategies to foster collaboration and interaction among her students." G.S., Principal

"Judy's professionalism, enthusiasm, and talent as a teacher are evident on a daily basis. Judy employs a thematic approach, and the varied learning experiences the children have to showcase their talents are not just one-time activities but are related to all curriculum areas. Judy is comfortable with and flexible in following many different styles of administration and has been recommended to assume leadership roles many times during her career." F.B., School Administrator

PROFESSIONAL DEVELOPMENT COURSES

Attended and participated in various courses from 1998–2004, including

- The Middle Years Literacy Framework
- Middle Years Balanced Literacy
- Academy of Reading Program
- Bringing Curriculum to Life
- Accelerated Reading Program

- Professional Education for Central-East AAO
- Rigby Guided Reading and Literature Circles
- Improving Decision-Making/Values Clarification
- Improving Ability to Communicate Mathematically
- Everyday Math Program and PowerPoint for Educators

Truck Drivers and Driver/Sales Workers

Jason A. Zimmerman

2513 West Vista Lane   Miami, FL 33166   (cell) 786.522.9875   (home) 305.779.0036

> *Professional truck driver offers a winning combination to an organization that values stability, dependability, and timely deliveries*

- ❖ *3 Million Miles*
- ❖ *Multiple Safety Awards*
- ❖ *32 Years of Experience*

Single and Team Driver of the following rigs:

Vans	Step Deck	Reefers
Doubles	Flat Deck	Tankers

SAFETY AWARDS

SCHROEDER NATIONAL
6-Year Driver Safety Award
GREENWAY/LOADSTAR
5-Year Driver Safety Award
EAST POINT TRANSIT
800,000-Mile Driver Safety Award
SOUTHEAST EXPRESS
7-Year Driver Safety Award
PULMAN GROUP
2-Year Driver Safety Award

PROFESSIONAL EXPERIENCE

Nov 1996–Present
SCHROEDER NATIONAL
Richmond, Virginia
- Drive vans transporting general freight throughout the United States.
- Supervise the dock management of product: loading, unloading, and accounting.

Oct 1991–Oct 1996
GREENWAY/LOADSTAR
Buffalo, New York
- Drove single and double vans, flatbeds, and step decks transporting general freight throughout the United States.
- Supervised the dock management of product: loading, unloading, accounting, securing freight, and customer interaction.

Jan 1991–Oct 1991
GLOBAL MARINE
Charleston, South Carolina
- Drove specialized boat trailers transporting high-value yachts.
- Supervised the crane work and tie-down of the yachts.
- Coordinated delivery times with the customer.

1970–1991
**GLENDALE SHIPPING / REINOLD TRUCKING CO. / EAST POINT TRANSIT
INTERSTATE TRUCKING CO. / SOUTHEAST EXPRESS / COASTAL TRANSPORT
PULMAN GROUP**

Important Trends in Jobs and Industries

In putting this section together, my objective was to give you a quick review of major labor market trends. To accomplish this, I included an excellent article and other material that originally appeared in U.S. Department of Labor publications.

The article is "Overview of Employment Projections Through 2018." It provides a superb—and short—review of the major trends that will affect your career in the years to come. Read it for ideas on selecting a career path for the long term.

"High-Paying Occupations with Many Openings, Projected 2008–2018" shows median earnings for high-paying occupations that also have a large number of openings.

"Large Metropolitan Areas That Had the Fastest Employment Growth, 2008" lists areas of the U.S. that experienced a high rate of growth.

Overview of Employment Projections Through 2018

Job openings result from the relationship between the population, the labor force, and demand for goods and services. The population restricts the size of the labor force, which consists of working individuals and those looking for work. The size and productivity of the labor force limits the quantity of goods and services that can be produced. In addition, changes in the demand for goods and services influence which industries expand or contract. Industries respond by hiring the workers necessary to produce goods and provide services. However, improvements to technology and productivity, changes in which occupations perform certain tasks, and changes to the supply of workers all affect which occupations will be employed by those industries. Examining past and present changes to these relationships in order to project future shifts is the foundation of the Employment Projections Program. This article presents highlights of population, labor force, and occupational and industry employment projections for 2008–2018. For more information, see the additional information about the projections.

The analysis underlying BLS employment projections uses currently available information to focus on long-term structural changes in the economy. The 2008–2018 projections assume a full-employment economy in 2018. The impact of the recent recession, which began in December of 2007, on long-term structural changes in the economy will not be fully known until some point during or after the recovery. Because the 2008 starting point is a recession year, the projected growth to an assumed full-employment economy in 2018 will generally be stronger than if the starting point were not a recession year.

Population

Shifts in the size and composition of the population can create a number of changes to the U.S. economy. Most importantly, population trends produce corresponding changes in the size and composition of the labor force. The U.S. civilian noninstitutional population, including individuals aged 16 and older, is expected to increase by 25.1 million from 2008 to 2018 (Chart 1). The projected 2008–2018 growth rate of 10.7 percent is less than the 11.2 percent growth rate for the 1988–1998 period and the 13.9 percent rate for the 1998–2008 period. As in the past few decades, population growth will vary by age group, race, and ethnicity.

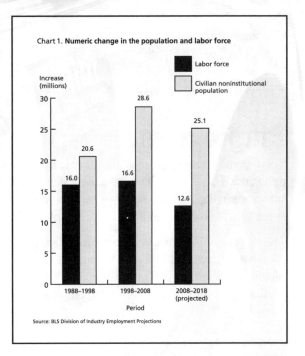

Chart 1. **Numeric change in the population and labor force**

Source: BLS Division of Industry Employment Projections

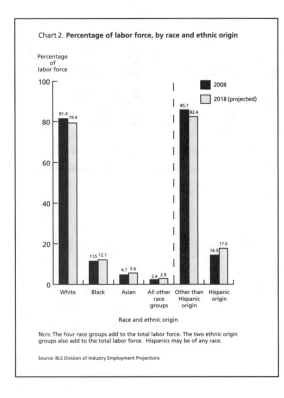

Chart 2. **Percentage of labor force, by race and ethnic origin**

Note: The four race groups add to the total labor force. The two ethnic origin groups also add to the total labor force. Hispanics may be of any race.

Source: BLS Division of Industry Employment Projections

As the baby boomers continue to age, the 55-and-older age group is projected to increase by 29.7 percent, more than any other age group. Meanwhile, the 45-to-54 age group is expected to decrease by 4.4 percent, reflecting the slower birth rate following the baby-boom generation. The 35-to-44 age group is anticipated to experience little change, with a growth rate of 0.2 percent, while the population aged 16 to 24 will grow 3.4 percent over the projection period. Minorities and immigrants are expected to constitute a larger share of the U.S. population in 2018. The numbers of Asians and people of Hispanic origin are projected to continue to grow much faster than those of other racial and ethnic groups.

Labor Force

Population is the single most important factor in determining the size and composition of the labor force. The civilian labor force is projected to reach 166.9 million by 2018, which is an increase of 8.2 percent.

The U.S. workforce is expected to become more diverse by 2018. Among racial groups, Whites are expected to make up a decreasing share of the labor force, while Blacks, Asians, and all other groups will increase their share (Chart 2). Among ethnic groups, persons of Hispanic origin are projected to increase their share of the labor force from 14.3 percent to 17.6 percent, reflecting 33.1 percent growth.

The number of women in the labor force will grow at a slightly faster rate than the number of men. The male labor force is projected to grow by 7.5 percent from 2008 to 2018, compared with 9.0 percent for the female labor force.

The share of the youth labor force, workers aged 16 to 24, is expected to decrease from 14.3 percent in 2008 to 12.7 percent by 2018. The primary working-age group, those between 25 and 54 years old, is projected to decline from 67.6 percent of the labor force in 2008 to 63.5 percent by 2018. Workers aged 55 years and older, by contrast, are anticipated to leap from 18.1 percent to 23.9 percent of the labor force during the same period (Chart 3).

Employment

Total employment is expected to increase by 10 percent from 2008 to 2018. However, the 15.3 million jobs expected to be added by 2018 will not be evenly distributed across major industry and occupational groups. Changes in consumer demand, improvements in technology, and many other factors will contribute to the continually changing employment structure of the U.S. economy.

The next two sections examine projected employment change within industries and occupations. The industry perspective is discussed in terms of wage and salary employment. The exception is employment in agriculture, which includes the self-employed and unpaid family workers in addition to wage and salary workers. The occupational profile is viewed in terms of total employment—including wage and salary, self-employed, and unpaid family workers.

Employment Change by Industry

Goods-producing industries. Employment in goods-producing industries has declined since the 1990s. Although overall employment is expected to change little, projected growth among goods-producing industries varies considerably (Chart 4).

Mining, quarrying, and oil and gas extraction. Employment in mining, quarrying, and oil and gas extraction is expected to decrease by 14 percent by 2018. Employment in support activities for mining will be responsible for most of the job loss in this industry with a decline of 23 percent. Other mining industries, such as nonmetallic mineral mining and quarrying and coal mining, are expected to see little or no change or a small increase in employment. Employment stagnation in these industries is attributable mainly to strict environmental regulations and technology gains that boost worker productivity.

Construction. Employment in construction is expected to rise 19 percent. Demand for commercial construction and an increase in road, bridge, and tunnel construction will account for the bulk of job growth.

Manufacturing. Overall employment in this sector will decline by 9 percent as productivity gains, automation, and international competition adversely affect employment in most manufacturing industries. Employment in household appliance manufacturing is expected to decline by 24 percent over the decade. Similarly, employment in machinery manufacturing, apparel manufacturing, and computer and electronic product manufacturing will decline as well. However, employment in a few manufacturing industries will increase. For example, employment in pharmaceutical and medicine manufacturing is expected to grow by 6 percent by 2018; however, this increase is expected to add only 17,600 new jobs.

Agriculture, forestry, fishing, and hunting. Overall employment in agriculture, forestry, fishing, and hunting is expected to decrease by 1 percent. Employment is projected to continue to decline because of rising costs of production, increasing consolidation, and more imports of food and lumber. Within this sector, the only industry that is expected to add jobs is support activities for agriculture and forestry, which includes farm labor contractors and farm management services. This industry is anticipated to grow by 13 percent, but this corresponds to an increase of only 13,800 new jobs.

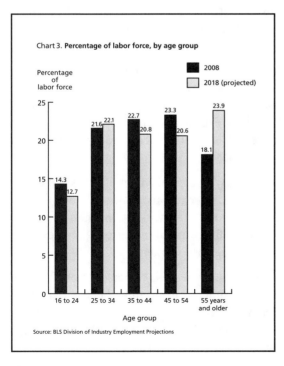

Chart 3. **Percentage of labor force, by age group**

Source: BLS Division of Industry Employment Projections

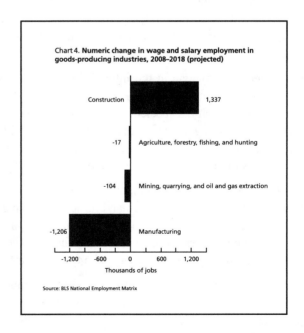

Chart 4. **Numeric change in wage and salary employment in goods-producing industries, 2008–2018 (projected)**

Source: BLS National Employment Matrix

Service-providing industries. The shift in the U.S. economy away from goods-producing in favor of service-providing is expected to continue. Service-providing industries are anticipated to generate approximately 14.5 million new wage and salary jobs. As with goods-producing industries, growth among service-providing industries will vary (Chart 5).

Utilities. Employment in utilities is projected to decrease by 11 percent through 2018. Despite increased output, employment in electric power generation, transmission, and distribution and in natural gas distribution is expected to decline because of improved technology that will increase worker productivity. However, employment in the water, sewage, and other systems industry is anticipated to increase 13 percent by 2018. As the population continues to grow, more water treatment facilities are being built. Further, changing federal and state government water quality regulations may require more workers to ensure that water is safe to drink and to release into the environment.

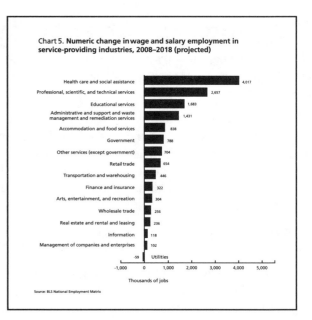

Chart 5. Numeric change in wage and salary employment in service-providing industries, 2008–2018 (projected)

Source: BLS National Employment Matrix

Wholesale trade. The number of workers in wholesale trade is expected to increase by 4 percent, adding about 255,900 jobs. The consolidation of wholesale trade firms into fewer and larger companies will contribute to slower-than-average employment growth in the industry.

Retail trade. Employment in retail trade is expected to increase by 4 percent. Despite slower-than-average growth, this industry is projected to add about 654,000 new jobs over the 2008–2018 period. Slower job growth reflects both continued consolidation and slower growth in personal consumption than in the previous decade.

Transportation and warehousing. Employment in transportation and warehousing is expected to increase by 10 percent, adding about 445,500 jobs to the industry total. Truck transportation is anticipated to grow by 10 percent, and the warehousing and storage sector is projected to grow by 12 percent. Demand for truck transportation and warehousing services will expand as many manufacturers concentrate on their core competencies and contract out their product transportation and storage functions.

Information. Employment in the information sector is expected to increase by 4 percent, adding 118,100 jobs by 2018. The sector contains fast-growing computer-related industries. The data-processing, hosting, and related services industry, which is expected to grow by 53 percent, includes establishments that provide Web and application hosting and streaming services. Internet publishing and broadcasting is expected to grow rapidly as it gains market share from newspapers and other more traditional media. Software publishing is projected to grow by 30 percent as organizations of all types continue to adopt the newest software products.

The information sector also includes the telecommunications industry, whose employment is projected to decline 9 percent. Despite an increase in demand for telecommunications services, more reliable networks along with consolidation among organizations will lead to productivity gains, reducing the need for workers. In addition, employment in the publishing industry is expected to decline by 5 percent, which is the result of increased efficiency in production, declining newspaper revenues, and a trend towards using more freelance workers.

Finance and insurance. The finance and insurance industry is expected to increase by 5 percent from 2008 to 2018. Employment in the securities, commodity contracts, and other financial investments and related activities industry is projected to expand 12 percent by 2018, which reflects the number of baby boomers in their peak savings years, the growth of tax-favorable retirement plans, and the globalization of securities markets. Employment in the credit intermediation and related activities industry, which includes banks, will grow by about 5 percent, adding 42 percent of all new jobs within the finance and insurance sector. Employment in the insurance carriers and related activities industry is expected to grow by 3 percent, translating into 67,600 new jobs by 2018. The number of jobs in the agencies, brokerages, and other insurance-related activities industry is expected to grow by 14 percent. Growth will stem from both the needs of an increasing population and new insurance products on the market.

Real estate and rental and leasing. The real estate and rental and leasing industry is expected to grow by 11 percent through 2018. Growth will be due, in part, to increased demand for housing as the population expands. The fastest-growing industry in the real estate and rental and leasing services sector will be lessors of nonfinancial intangible assets (except copyrighted works), which will increase by 34 percent over the projection period.

Professional, scientific, and technical services. Employment in professional, scientific, and technical services is projected to grow by 34 percent, adding about 2.7 million new jobs by 2018. Employment in computer systems design and related services is expected to increase by 45 percent, accounting for nearly one-fourth of all new jobs in this industry sector. Employment growth will be driven by growing demand for the design and integration of sophisticated networks and Internet and intranet sites. Employment in management, scientific, and technical consulting services is anticipated to expand a staggering 83 percent, making up about 31 percent of job growth in this sector. Demand for these services will be spurred by businesses' continued need for advice on planning and logistics; the implementation of new technologies; and compliance with workplace safety, environmental, and employment regulations.

Management of companies and enterprises. Management of companies and enterprises is projected to grow relatively slowly, by 5 percent, as companies focus on reorganization to increase efficiency.

Administrative and support and waste management and remediation services. Employment in this sector is expected to grow by 18 percent by 2018. The largest growth will occur in employment services, an industry that is anticipated to account for 42 percent of all new jobs in the administrative and support and waste management and remediation services sector. The employment services industry ranks fifth among industries with the most new employment opportunities in the nation over the 2008–2018 period and is expected to grow faster than the average for all industries. Projected growth stems from the strong need for seasonal and temporary workers and for specialized human resources services.

Educational services. Employment in public and private educational services is anticipated to grow by 12 percent, adding about 1.7 million new jobs through 2018. Rising student enrollments at all levels of education will create demand for educational services.

Health care and social assistance. About 26 percent of all new jobs created in the U.S. economy will be in the health-care and social assistance industry. This industry—which includes public and private hospitals, nursing and residential care facilities, and individual and family services—is expected to grow by 24 percent, or 4 million new jobs. Employment growth will be driven by an aging population and longer life expectancies.

Arts, entertainment, and recreation. The arts, entertainment, and recreation industry is expected to grow by 15 percent by 2018. Most of the growth will be in the amusement, gambling, and recreation sector. Job growth will stem from public participation in arts, entertainment, and recreation activities, reflecting increasing incomes, leisure time, and awareness of the health benefits of physical fitness.

Accommodation and food services. Employment in accommodation and food services is expected to grow by 7 percent, adding about 838,200 new jobs through 2018. Job growth will be concentrated in food services and drinking places, reflecting an increase in the population and the convenience of many new food establishments.

Other services (except government and private households). Employment is expected to grow by 13 percent in other services. Personal care services comprise the fastest-growing industry in this sector at 32 percent. This industry includes barbers, salons, and spas, which have experienced growing demand as individuals increasingly are seeking to improve their personal appearance.

Government. Between 2008 and 2018, government employment, excluding employment in public education and hospitals, is expected to increase by 7 percent. Growth in government employment will be fueled by expanding demand for public safety services and assistance provided to the elderly, but dampened by budgetary constraints and the outsourcing of government jobs to the private sector. State and local governments, excluding education and hospitals, are anticipated to grow by 8 percent as a result of the continued shift of responsibilities from the federal government to state and local governments. Federal government employment, including the postal service, is expected to increase by 3 percent.

Employment Change by Occupation

Industry growth or decline will affect demand for occupations. However, job growth is projected to vary among major occupational groups (Chart 6).

Management, business, and financial occupations. Workers in management, business, and financial occupations plan and direct the activities of business, government, and other organizations. Their employment is expected to increase by 11 percent by 2018. These workers will be needed to help organizations navigate the increasingly complex and competitive business environment. A large portion of these jobs will arise in the management, scientific, and technical consulting industry sector. A substantial number, in addition, are expected in several other large or rapidly growing industries, including government, health care and social assistance, finance and insurance, and construction.

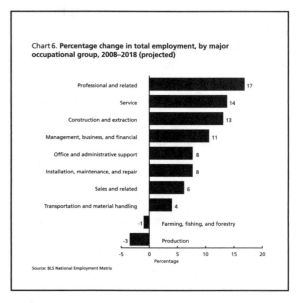

Chart 6. Percentage change in total employment, by major occupational group, 2008–2018 (projected)

Source: BLS National Employment Matrix

Employment in management occupations is projected to grow slowly over the projection period, increasing by 5 percent, an addition of 454,300 new jobs. Growth is being affected by declines in several occupations, including farmers and ranchers. Employment of farmers and ranchers is projected to decline as the agricultural industry produces more output with fewer workers.

Employment in business and financial operations occupations is projected to grow by 18 percent, resulting in 1.2 million new jobs. Increasing financial regulations and the need for greater accountability will drive demand for accountants and auditors, adding roughly 279,400 jobs to this occupation from 2008 to 2018. Further, an increasingly competitive business environment will grow demand for management analysts, an occupation that is expected to add 178,300 jobs. Together, these two occupations are anticipated to account for 38 percent of new business and financial operations jobs.

Professional and related occupations. This occupational group, which includes a wide variety of skilled professions, is expected to be the fastest-growing major occupational group, at 17 percent, and is projected to add the most new jobs—about 5.2 million.

Employment among health-care practitioners and technical occupations, a subgroup of the professional and related category, is expected to increase by 21 percent. This growth, resulting in a projected 1.6 million new jobs, will be driven by increasing demand for health-care services. As the number of older people continues to grow, and as new developments allow for the treatment of more medical conditions, more health-care professionals will be needed.

Education, training, and library occupations are anticipated to add more than 1.3 million jobs, representing a growth rate of more than 14 percent. As the U.S. population increases, and as a larger share of adults seeks educational services, demand for these workers will increase.

Computer and mathematical science occupations are projected to add almost 785,700 new jobs from 2008 to 2018. As a group, these occupations are expected to grow more than twice as fast as the average for all occupations in the economy. Demand for workers in computer and mathematical occupations will be driven by the continuing need for businesses, government agencies, and other organizations to adopt and utilize the latest technologies.

Employment in community and social services occupations is projected to increase by 16 percent, growing by roughly 448,400 jobs. As health insurance providers increasingly cover mental and behavioral health treatment and as a growing number of elderly individuals seek social services, demand for these workers will increase.

Employment in arts, design, entertainment, sports, and media occupations is expected to grow by 12 percent from 2008 to 2018, resulting in almost 332,600 new jobs. Growth will be spread broadly across different occupations within the group. Media and communications occupations will add a substantial number of jobs, led by rapid growth among public relations specialists, who will be needed in greater numbers as firms place a greater emphasis on managing their public image. Employment among entertainers and performers and those in sports and related occupations also will increase, partly as a result of increasing demand for coaches and scouts. Furthermore, art and design occupations will see substantial growth, with demand increasing for graphic and interior designers. As more advertising is conducted over the Internet, a medium that generally includes many graphics, and as businesses and households increasingly seek professional design services, a greater number of these workers will be needed.

Employment in life, physical, and social science occupations is projected to increase by nearly 277,200 jobs over the 2008–2018 projection period. This increase represents a growth rate of 19 percent, almost twice the average for all occupations across the economy. About 116,700 of these jobs are expected to be created among social science and related occupations, led by strong growth among market and survey researchers, as businesses increase their marketing efforts in order to remain competitive and as public policy firms and government agencies utilize more public opinion research. Employment in life science occupations, in addition, will increase rapidly as developments from biotechnology research continue to be used to create new medical technologies, treatments, and pharmaceuticals.

Architecture and engineering occupations are projected to add roughly 270,600 jobs, representing a growth rate of 10 percent. Much of this growth will occur among engineering occupations, especially civil engineers. As greater emphasis is placed on improving the nation's infrastructure, these specialists will be needed to design, implement, or upgrade municipal transportation, water supply, and pollution control systems.

Legal occupations will add the fewest new jobs among all professional and related subgroups, increasing by about 188,400. However, with a growth rate of 15 percent, this group will grow faster than the average for all occupations in the economy. Of the new jobs created, lawyers will account for 98,500 while paralegals and legal assistants will account for 74,100. Paralegals and legal assistants are expected to grow by 28 percent as legal establishments begin to expand the role of these workers and assign them more tasks once performed by lawyers.

Service occupations. The duties of service workers range from fighting fires to cooking meals. Employment in service occupations is projected to increase by 4.1 million, or 14 percent, which is both the second-largest numerical gain and the second-largest growth rate among the major occupational groups.

Among service occupation subgroups, the largest number of new jobs will occur in health-care support occupations. With more than 1.1 million new jobs, employment in this subgroup is expected to increase by 29 percent. Much of the growth will be the result of increased demand for health-care services as the expanding elderly population requires more care.

Employment in personal care and service occupations is anticipated to grow by 20 percent over the projection period, adding more than 1 million jobs. As consumers become more concerned with health, beauty, and fitness, the number of cosmetic and health spas will increase, causing an increase in demand for workers in this group. However, the personal care and service group contains a wide variety of occupations, and two of them—personal and home care aides and child care workers—will account for most of this group's new jobs. Personal and home care aides will experience increased demand as a growing number of elderly individuals require assistance with daily

tasks. Child care workers, in addition, will add jobs as formal preschool programs, which employ child care workers alongside preschool teachers, become more prevalent.

Employment in food preparation and serving and related occupations is projected to increase by roughly 1 million jobs from 2008 to 2018, representing a growth rate of 9 percent. Growth will stem from time-conscious consumers patronizing fast-food establishments and full-service restaurants.

Employment in building and grounds cleaning and maintenance occupations is expected to grow by almost 483,900 jobs over the projection period, representing a growth rate of 8 percent. As businesses place a larger emphasis on grounds aesthetics and as households increasingly rely on contract workers to maintain their yards, grounds maintenance workers will see rapid growth. In addition, more building cleaning workers will be needed to maintain an increasing number of residential and commercial structures.

Protective service occupations are expected to gain the fewest new jobs among all service subgroups: about 400,100, or 12 percent growth. These workers protect businesses and other organizations from crime and vandalism. In addition, there will be increased demand for law enforcement officers to support the growing U.S. population.

Sales and related occupations. Sales and related workers solicit goods and services for businesses and consumers. Sales and related occupations are expected to add 980,400 new jobs by 2018, growing by 6 percent. As organizations offer a wider array of products and devote an increasing share of their resources to customer service, many new retail salesworkers will be needed. Job growth in this group will be spread across a wide variety of industries, but almost half will occur in retail sales establishments.

Office and administrative support occupations. Office and administrative support workers perform the day-to-day activities of the office, such as preparing and filing documents, dealing with the public, and distributing information. Employment in these occupations is expected to grow by 8 percent, adding 1.8 million new jobs by 2018. Customer service representatives are anticipated to add the most new jobs, 399,500, as businesses put an increased emphasis on building customer relationships. Other office and administrative support occupations will experience declines as advanced technology improves productivity, decreasing the number of workers necessary to perform some duties.

Farming, fishing, and forestry occupations. Farming, fishing, and forestry workers cultivate plants, breed and raise livestock, and catch animals. These occupations are projected to decline by about 1 percent, losing 9,100 jobs, by 2018. Productivity increases in agriculture will lead to declining employment among agricultural workers, offsetting small gains among forest, conservation, and logging workers.

Construction and extraction occupations. Construction and extraction workers build new residential and commercial buildings and also work in mines, quarries, and oil and gas fields. Employment of these workers is expected to grow 13 percent, adding about 1 million new jobs. Construction trades and related workers will account for about 808,400 of these jobs. Growth will result from increased construction of homes, office buildings, and infrastructure projects. Declines in extraction occupations will reflect overall employment stagnation in the mining and oil and gas extraction industries.

Installation, maintenance, and repair occupations. Workers in installation, maintenance, and repair occupations install new equipment and maintain and repair older equipment. These occupations are projected to add 440,200 jobs by 2018, growing by 8 percent. More than 1 in 3 new jobs in this group will occur in the construction industry because these workers are integral to the development of buildings, communication structures, transportation systems, and other types of infrastructure. As construction on these types of projects increases over the projection period, installation, maintenance, and repair workers will be needed in greater numbers.

Production occupations. Production workers are employed mainly in manufacturing, where they assemble goods and operate plants. Production occupations are expected to decline by 3 percent, losing 349,200 jobs by 2018. As productivity improvements reduce the need for workers and as a growing number of these jobs are offshored, demand for production workers will decline. Some jobs will be created in production occupations, mostly in food processing and woodworking.

Transportation and material moving occupations. Transportation and material moving workers transport people and materials by land, sea, or air. Employment of these workers is anticipated to increase by 4 percent, accounting for 391,100 new jobs. As the economy grows over the projection period and the demand for goods increases, truck drivers will be needed to transport those goods to businesses, consumers, and other entities. In addition, a substantial number of jobs will arise among bus drivers, as well as taxi drivers and chauffeurs, as a growing number of people utilize public transportation.

Employment Change by Detailed Occupation

Occupational growth can be considered in two ways: by the rate of growth and by the number of new jobs created by growth. Some occupations both have a fast growth rate and create a large number of new jobs. However, an occupation that employs few workers may experience rapid growth, although the resulting number of new jobs may be small. For example, a small occupation that employs just 1,000 workers and is projected to grow 50 percent over a 10-year period will add only 500 jobs. By contrast, a large occupation that employs 1.5 million workers may experience only 10 percent growth, but will add 150,000 jobs. As a result, in order to get a complete picture of employment growth, both measures must be considered.

Occupations with the fastest growth. Of the 20 fastest-growing occupations in the economy (Table 1), half are related to health care. Health care is experiencing rapid growth, due in large part to the aging of the baby-boom generation, which will require more medical care. In addition, some health-care occupations will be in greater demand for other reasons. As health-care costs continue to rise, work is increasingly being delegated to lower-paid workers in order to cut costs. For example, tasks that were previously performed by doctors, nurses, dentists, or other health-care professionals increasingly are being performed by physician assistants, medical assistants, dental hygienists, and physical therapist aides. In addition, patients increasingly are seeking home care as an alternative to costly stays in hospitals or residential care facilities, causing a significant increase in demand for home health aides. Although not classified as health-care workers, personal and home care aides are being affected by this demand for home care as well.

Two of the fastest-growing detailed occupations are in the computer specialist occupational group. Network systems and data communications analysts are projected to be the second-fastest-growing occupation in the economy. Demand for these workers will increase as organizations continue to upgrade their information technology capacity and incorporate the newest technologies. The growing reliance on wireless networks will result in a need for more network systems and data communications analysts as well. Computer applications software engineers also are expected to grow rapidly from 2008 to 2018. Expanding Internet technologies have spurred demand for these workers, who can develop Internet, intranet, and Web applications.

Developments from biotechnology research will continue to be used to create new medical technologies, treatments, and pharmaceuticals. As a result, demand for medical scientists and for biochemists and biophysicists will increase. However, although employment of biochemists and biophysicists is projected to grow rapidly, this corresponds to only 8,700 new jobs over the projection period. Increased medical research and demand for new medical technologies also will affect biomedical engineers. The aging of the population and a growing focus on health issues will drive demand for better medical devices and equipment designed by these workers. In fact, biomedical engineers are projected to be the fastest-growing occupation in the economy. However, because of its small size, the occupation is projected to add only about 11,600 jobs.

Increasing financial regulations will spur employment growth both of financial examiners and of compliance officers, except agriculture, construction, health and safety, and transportation.

Self-enrichment teachers and skin care specialists will experience growth as consumers become more concerned with self-improvement. Self-enrichment teachers are growing rapidly as more individuals seek additional training to

Table 1. Occupations with the fastest growth

Occupations	Percent change	Number of new jobs (in thousands)	Wages (May 2008 median)	Education/ training category
Biomedical engineers 72		11.6	$77,400	Bachelor's degree
Network systems and data communications analysts 53		155.8	71,100	Bachelor's degree
Home health aides 50		460.9	20,460	Short-term on-the-job training
Personal and home care aides 46		375.8	19,180	Short-term on-the-job training
Financial examiners 41		11.1	70,930	Bachelor's degree
Medical scientists, except epidemiologists 40		44.2	72,590	Doctoral degree
Physician assistants 39		29.2	81,230	Master's degree
Skin care specialists 38		14.7	28,730	Postsecondary vocational award
Biochemists and biophysicists 37		8.7	82,840	Doctoral degree
Athletic trainers 37		6.0	39,640	Bachelor's degree
Physical therapist aides 36		16.7	23,760	Short-term on-the-job training
Dental hygienists 36		62.9	66,570	Associate degree
Veterinary technologists and technicians 36		28.5	28,900	Associate degree
Dental assistants 36		105.6	32,380	Moderate-term on-the-job training
Computer software engineers, applications 34		175.1	85,430	Bachelor's degree
Medical assistants 34		163.9	28,300	Moderate-term on-the-job training
Physical therapist assistants 33		21.2	46,140	Associate degree
Veterinarians 33		19.7	79,050	First professional degree
Self-enrichment education teachers 32		81.3	35,720	Work experience in a related occupation
Compliance officers, except agriculture, construction, health and safety, and transportation 31		80.8	48,890	Long-term on-the-job training

SOURCE: BLS Occupational Employment Statistics and Division of Occupational Outlook

make themselves more appealing to prospective employers. Skin care specialists will experience growth as consumers increasingly care about their personal appearance.

Of the 20 fastest-growing occupations, 12 are in the associate degree or higher category. Of the remaining 8, 6 are in an on-the-job training category, 1 is in the work experience in a related occupation category, and 1 is in the postsecondary vocational degree category. Eleven of these occupations earn at least $10,000 more than the national annual median wage, which was $32,390 as of May 2008. In fact, 9 of the occupations earned at least twice the national median in May 2008.

Occupations with the largest numerical growth. The 20 occupations listed in Table 2 are projected to account for more than one-third of all new jobs—5.8 million combined—over the 2008–2018 period. The occupations with the largest numerical increases cover a wider range of occupational categories than do those occupations with the fastest growth rates. Health occupations will account for some of these increases in employment, as will occupations in education, sales, and food service. Office and administrative support services occupations are expected to grow by 1.3 million jobs, accounting for about one-fifth of the job growth among the 20 occupations with the largest growth. Many of the occupations listed in the table are very large and will create more new jobs than occupations with high growth rates. Only 3 out of the 20 fastest-growing occupations—home health aides, personal and home care aides, and computer software application engineers—also are projected to be among the 20 occupations with the largest numerical increases in employment.

Table 2. Occupations with the largest numerical growth

Occupations	Number of new jobs (in thousands)	Percent change	Wages (May 2008 median)	Education/ training category
Registered nurses	581.5	22	$62,450	Associate degree
Home health aides	460.9	50	20,460	Short-term on-the-job training
Customer service representatives	399.5	18	29,860	Moderate-term on-the-job training
Combined food preparation and serving workers, including fast food	394.3	15	16,430	Short-term on-the-job training
Personal and home care aides	375.8	46	19,180	Short-term on-the-job training
Retail salespersons	374.7	8	20,510	Short-term on-the-job training
Office clerks, general	358.7	12	25,320	Short-term on-the-job training
Accountants and auditors	279.4	22	59,430	Bachelor's degree
Nursing aides, orderlies, and attendants	276.0	19	23,850	Postsecondary vocational award
Postsecondary teachers	256.9	15	58,830	Doctoral degree
Construction laborers	255.9	20	28,520	Moderate-term on-the-job training
Elementary school teachers, except special education	244.2	16	49,330	Bachelor's degree
Truck drivers, heavy and tractor-trailer	232.9	13	37,270	Short-term on-the-job training
Landscaping and groundskeeping workers	217.1	18	23,150	Short-term on-the-job training
Bookkeeping, accounting, and auditing clerks	212.4	10	32,510	Moderate-term on-the-job training
Executive secretaries and administrative assistants	204.4	13	40,030	Work experience in a related occupation
Management analysts	178.3	24	73,570	Bachelor's or higher degree, plus work experience
Computer software engineers, applications	175.1	34	85,430	Bachelor's degree
Receptionists and information clerks	172.9	15	24,550	Short-term on-the-job training
Carpenters	165.4	13	38,940	Long-term on-the-job training

SOURCE: BLS Occupational Employment Statistics and Division of Occupational Outlook

The education or training categories and wages of the occupations with the largest numbers of new jobs are significantly different than those of the fastest-growing occupations. Twelve of these occupations are in an on-the-job training category, and just 7 are in a category that indicates any postsecondary education. Ten of the 20 occupations with the largest numbers of new jobs earned less than the national median wage in May 2008.

Occupations with the fastest decline. Declining occupational employment stems from falling industry employment, technological advances, changes in business practices, and other factors. For example, technological developments and the continued movement of textile production abroad are expected to contribute to a decline of 71,500 sewing machine operators over the projection period (Table 3). Fifteen of the 20 occupations with the largest numerical decreases are either production occupations or office and administrative support occupations, both of which are adversely affected by increasing plant and factory automation or the implementation of office technology, reducing the need for workers in those occupations. The difference between the office and administrative support occupations that are expected to experience the largest declines and those that are expected to see the largest increases is the extent to which job functions can be easily automated or performed by other workers. For instance, the duties of executive secretaries and administrative assistants involve a great deal of personal interaction that cannot be automated, whereas the duties of file clerks—adding, locating, and removing business records—can be automated or performed by other workers.

Only two of the occupations with the fastest percent decline are in a category that indicates workers have any postsecondary education, while the rest are in an on-the-job training category. Eleven of these occupations earned less than $30,000 in May 2008, below the national median wage of $32,390.

Table 3. Occupations with the fastest decline

Occupations	Number of new jobs (in thousands)	Percent change	Wages (May 2008 median)	Education/ training category
Textile winding, twisting, and drawing out machine setters, operators, and tenders	−41	−14.2	23,970	Moderate-term on-the-job training
Textile knitting and weaving machine setters, operators, and tenders	−39	−11.5	25,400	Long-term on-the-job training
Shoe machine operators and tenders	−35	−1.7	25,090	Moderate-term on-the-job training
Extruding and forming machine setters, operators, and tenders, synthetic and glass fibers	−34	−4.8	31,160	Moderate-term on-the-job training
Sewing machine operators	−34	−71.5	19,870	Moderate-term on-the-job training
Semiconductor processors	−32	−10.0	32,230	Postsecondary vocational award
Textile cutting machine setters, operators, and tenders	−31	−6.0	22,620	Moderate-term on-the-job training
Postal Service mail sorters, processors, and processing machine operators	−30	−54.5	50,020	Short-term on-the-job training
Fabric menders, except garment	−30	−0.3	28,470	Moderate-term on-the-job training
Wellhead pumpers	−28	−5.3	37,860	Moderate-term on-the-job training
Fabric and apparel patternmakers	−27	−2.2	37,760	Long-term on-the-job training
Drilling and boring machine tool setters, operators, and tenders, metal and plastic	−27	−8.9	30,850	Moderate-term on-the-job training
Lathe and turning machine tool setters, operators, and tenders, metal and plastic	−27	−14.9	32,940	Moderate-term on-the-job training
Order clerks	−26	−64.2	27,990	Short-term on-the-job training
Coil winders, tapers, and finishers	−25	−5.6	27,730	Short-term on-the-job training
Photographic processing machine operators	−24	−12.5	20,360	Short-term on-the-job training
File clerks	−23	−49.6	23,800	Short-term on-the-job training
Derrick operators, oil and gas	−23	−5.8	41,920	Moderate-term on-the-job training
Desktop publishers	−23	−5.9	36,600	Postsecondary vocational award

SOURCE: BLS Occupational Employment Statistics and Division of Occupational Outlook

Employment Change by Education and Training Category

Education and training categories for each occupation are determined by the most significant source of education and training obtained by workers in that occupation. Growth for each education and training category is calculated by adding the growth across all occupations in the category. As a result, there is some variation in the growth rates between categories.

In general, occupations in a category with some postsecondary education are expected to experience higher rates of growth than those in an on-the-job training category. Occupations in the associate degree category are projected to grow the fastest, at about 19 percent. In addition, occupations in the master's and first professional degree categories are anticipated to grow by about 18 percent each, and occupations in the bachelor's and doctoral degree categories are expected to grow by about 17 percent each. However, occupations in the on-the-job training categories are expected to grow by 8 percent each (Chart 7).

Total Job Openings

Job openings stem from both employment growth and replacement needs (Chart 8). Replacement needs arise as workers leave occupations. Some transfer to other occupations, while others retire, return to school, or quit to assume household responsibilities. Replacement needs are projected to account for 67 percent of the approximately 50.9 million job openings between 2008 and 2018. Thus, even occupations that are projected to experience slower-than-average growth or to decline in employment still may offer many job openings.

Professional and related occupations are projected to have the largest number of total job openings, 11.9 million, and 56 percent of those will be due to replacement needs. Replacement needs generally are greatest in the largest occupations and in those with relatively low pay or limited training requirements. As a result, service occupations are projected to have the greatest number of job openings due to replacements, about 7.6 million.

Office automation will significantly affect many individual office and administrative support occupations. Although these occupations are projected to grow about as fast as average, some are projected to decline rapidly. Office and administrative support occupations are expected to create 7.3 million total job openings from 2008 to 2018, ranking third behind professional and related occupations and service occupations.

Farming, fishing, and forestry occupations and production occupations should offer job opportunities despite overall declines in employment. These occupations will lose 9,100 and 349,200 jobs, respectively, but are expected to provide more than 2.4 million total job openings. Job openings will be due solely to the replacement needs of a workforce characterized by high levels of retirement and job turnover.

Additional Information About the 2008–2018 Projections

Readers interested in more information about the projections; about the methods and assumptions that underlie them; or about details on economic growth, the labor force, or industry and occupational employment should consult the November 2009 *Monthly Labor Review* or the Winter 2009–2010 *Occupational Outlook Quarterly* (both of which are available online).

More information about employment change, job openings, earnings, and training requirements by occupation is available on the Bureau's Employment Projections home page at www.bls.gov/emp. The *Career Guide to Industries*, which presents occupational information from an industry perspective, is also accessible.

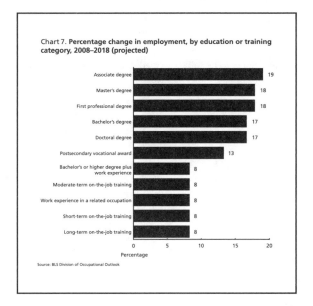

Chart 7. Percentage change in employment, by education or training category, 2008–2018 (projected)

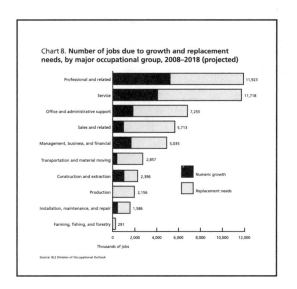

Chart 8. Number of jobs due to growth and replacement needs, by major occupational group, 2008–2018 (projected)

Classification of occupations by most significant source of education or training

Postsecondary awards

First professional degree. Completion of the degree usually requires at least three years of full-time academic study beyond a bachelor's degree. Examples are lawyers and physicians and surgeons.

Doctoral degree. Completion of a Ph.D. or other doctoral degree usually requires at least three years of full-time academic study beyond a bachelor's degree. Examples are postsecondary teachers and medical scientists, except epidemiologists.

Master's degree. Completion of the degree usually requires one or two years of full-time academic study beyond a bachelor's degree. Examples are educational, vocational, and school counselors and clergy.

Bachelor's or higher degree plus work experience. Most occupations in this category are management occupations. All require experience in a related nonmanagement position for which a bachelor's or higher degree is usually required. Examples are general and operations managers and judges, magistrate judges, and magistrates.

Bachelor's degree. Completion of the degree generally requires at least four years, but not more than five years, of full-time academic study. Examples are accountants and auditors and elementary school teachers, except special education.

Associate degree. Completion of the degree usually requires at least two years of full-time academic study. Examples are paralegals and legal assistants and medical records and health information technicians.

Postsecondary vocational award. Some programs last only a few weeks, others more than a year. Programs lead to a certificate or other award, but not a degree. Examples are nursing aides, orderlies, and attendants and hairdressers, hairstylists, and cosmetologists.

Work-related training

Work experience in a related occupation. Most of the occupations in this category are first-line supervisors or managers of service, sales and related, production, or other occupations or are management occupations.

Long-term on-the-job training. Occupations in this category generally require more than 12 months of on-the-job training or combined work experience and formal classroom instruction for workers to develop the skills necessary to be fully qualified in the occupation. These occupations include formal and informal apprenticeships that may last up to five years. Long-term on-the-job training also includes intensive occupation-specific, employer-sponsored programs that workers must complete. Among such programs are those conducted by fire and police academies and by schools for air traffic controllers and flight attendants. In other occupations—insurance sales and securities sales, for example—trainees take formal courses, often provided on the jobsite, to prepare for the required licensing exams. Individuals undergoing training generally are considered to be employed in the occupation. Also included in this category is the development of a natural ability—such as that possessed by musicians, athletes, actors, and other entertainers—that must be cultivated over several years, frequently in a non-work setting.

Moderate-term on-the-job training. In this category of occupations, the skills needed to be fully qualified in the occupation can be acquired during 1 to 12 months of combined on-the-job experience and informal training. Examples are truck drivers, heavy and tractor-trailer and secretaries, except legal, medical, and executive.

Short-term on-the-job training. In occupations in this category, the skills needed to be fully qualified in the occupation can be acquired during a short demonstration of job duties or during one month or less of on-the-job experience or instruction. Examples of these occupations are retail salespersons and waiters and waitresses.

High-Paying Occupations with Many Openings, Projected 2008–2018

Over the 2008–2018 decade, career choices abound for those seeking high earnings and lots of opportunities. High-paying occupations that are projected to have many openings are varied. This diverse group includes teachers, managers, and carpenters.

The job openings shown in the chart on the next page represent the total that are expected each year for workers who are either entering for the first time or moving from job to job within the occupation. The job openings result from each occupation's growth and from the need to replace workers who retire or leave the occupation permanently for some other reason.

Median earnings, such as those listed in the chart, indicate that half of the workers in an occupation made more than that amount, and half made less. The occupations in the chart ranked in the highest or second-highest earnings quartiles for 2008 median earnings. This means that median earnings for workers in these occupations were higher than the earnings for at least 50 percent of all occupations in 2008.

Most of these occupations had another thing going for them in 2008: low or very low unemployment. Workers in occupations that had higher levels of unemployment—carpenters and truck drivers—were more dependent on a strong economy or seasonal employment.

High-Paying Occupations with Many Openings, Projected 2008–2018

Occupation	Average annual job openings due to growth and replacement needs, projected 2008–2018	Median annual earnings 2008
Registered Nurses	103,900	$62,450
Elementary School Teachers, Except Special Education	59,650	$49,330
Truck Drivers, Heavy and Tractor-Trailer	55,460	$37,270
Postsecondary Teachers	55,290	$60,796
General and Operations Managers	50,220	$91,570
Accountants and Auditors	49,750	$59,430
First-Line Supervisors/Managers of Office and Administrative Support Workers	48,900	$45,790
Bookkeeping, Accounting, and Auditing Clerks	46,040	$32,510
Sales Representatives, Wholesale and Manufacturing, Except Technical and Scientific Products	45,790	$51,330
First-Line Supervisors/Managers of Retail Sales Workers	45,010	$35,310
Executive Secretaries and Administrative Assistants	41,920	$40,030
Secondary School Teachers, Except Special and Vocational Education	41,240	$51,180
Licensed Practical and Licensed Vocational Nurses	39,130	$39,030
Business Operations Specialists, All Other	36,830	$59,920
Maintenance and Repair Workers, General	35,750	$33,710
Carpenters	32,540	$38,940
Management Analysts	30,650	$73,570
Managers, All Other	29,750	$90,230
Physicians and Surgeons	26,050	$148,134
Middle School Teachers, Except Special and Vocational Education	25,110	$49,700

Source: U.S. Department of Labor, Office of Occupational Statistics and Employment Projections.

Large Metropolitan Areas That Had the Fastest Employment Growth, 2008

The Sun Belt and the Rockies showed the most impressive employment growth from 2007 to 2008, according to data from the Bureau of Labor Statistics. Between May 2007 and May 2008, these two regions were home to all the large metropolitan areas in the United States in which employment growth was highest. Total U.S. nonfarm payroll employment increased only 0.6 percent over this period as the nation's economic growth slowed just before going into recession. As the chart on the next page shows, employment in 10 of the metropolitan areas with at least 300,000 workers in May 2007 grew by at least seven times the national rate over the same period—and one of them increased at more than 29 times the national rate.

But before packing your bags for one of these metropolitan areas, remember that these data do not show the variation in the kinds of jobs added.

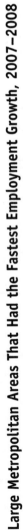

Large Metropolitan Areas That Had the Fastest Employment Growth, 2007–2008

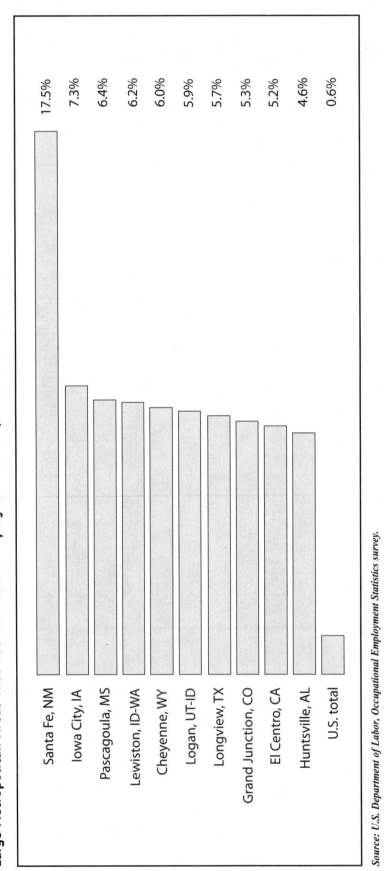

Santa Fe, NM	17.5%
Iowa City, IA	7.3%
Pascagoula, MS	6.4%
Lewiston, ID-WA	6.2%
Cheyenne, WY	6.0%
Logan, UT-ID	5.9%
Longview, TX	5.7%
Grand Junction, CO	5.3%
El Centro, CA	5.2%
Huntsville, AL	4.6%
U.S. total	0.6%

Source: U.S. Department of Labor, Occupational Employment Statistics survey.

Index